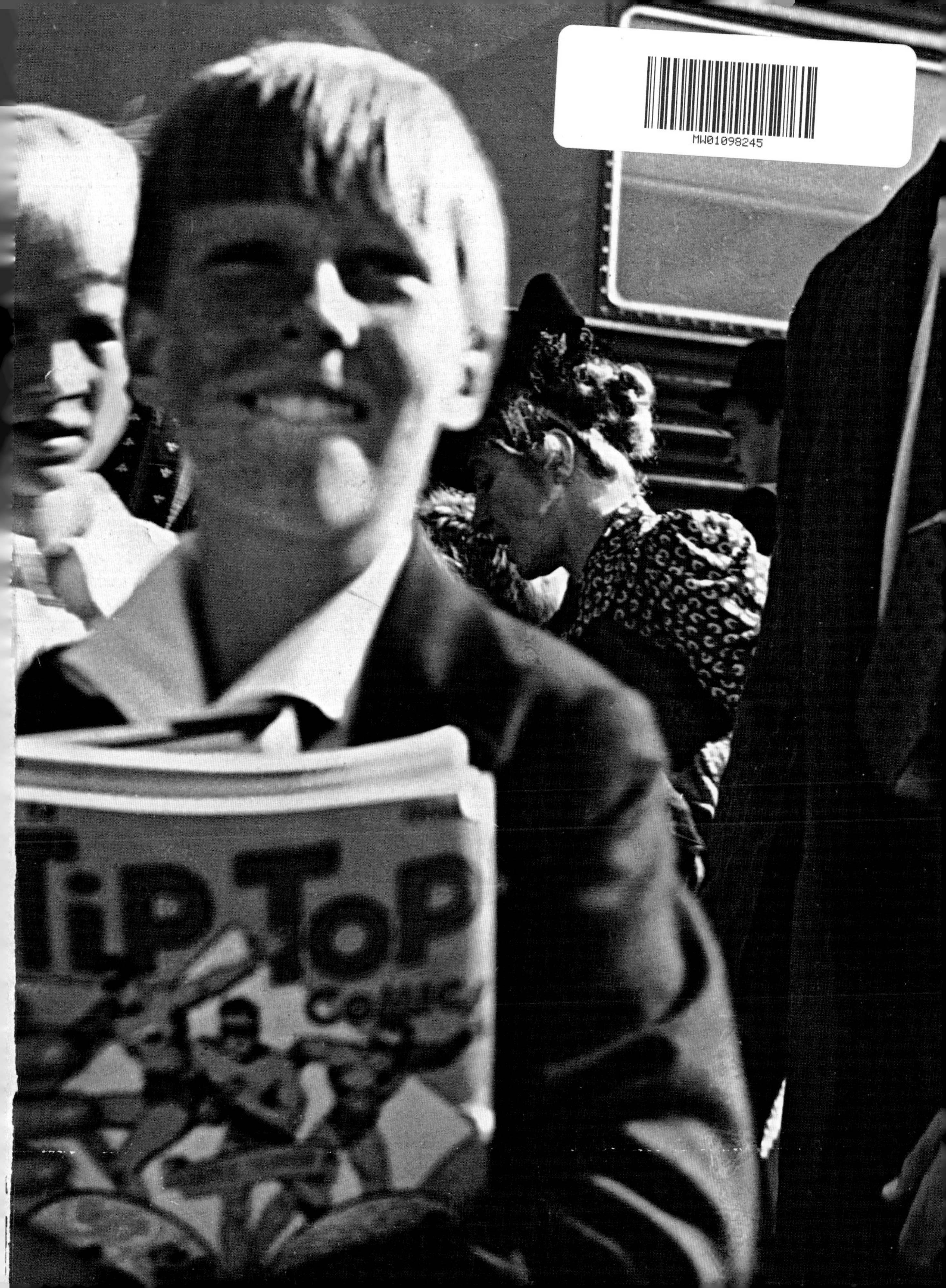
Tip Top

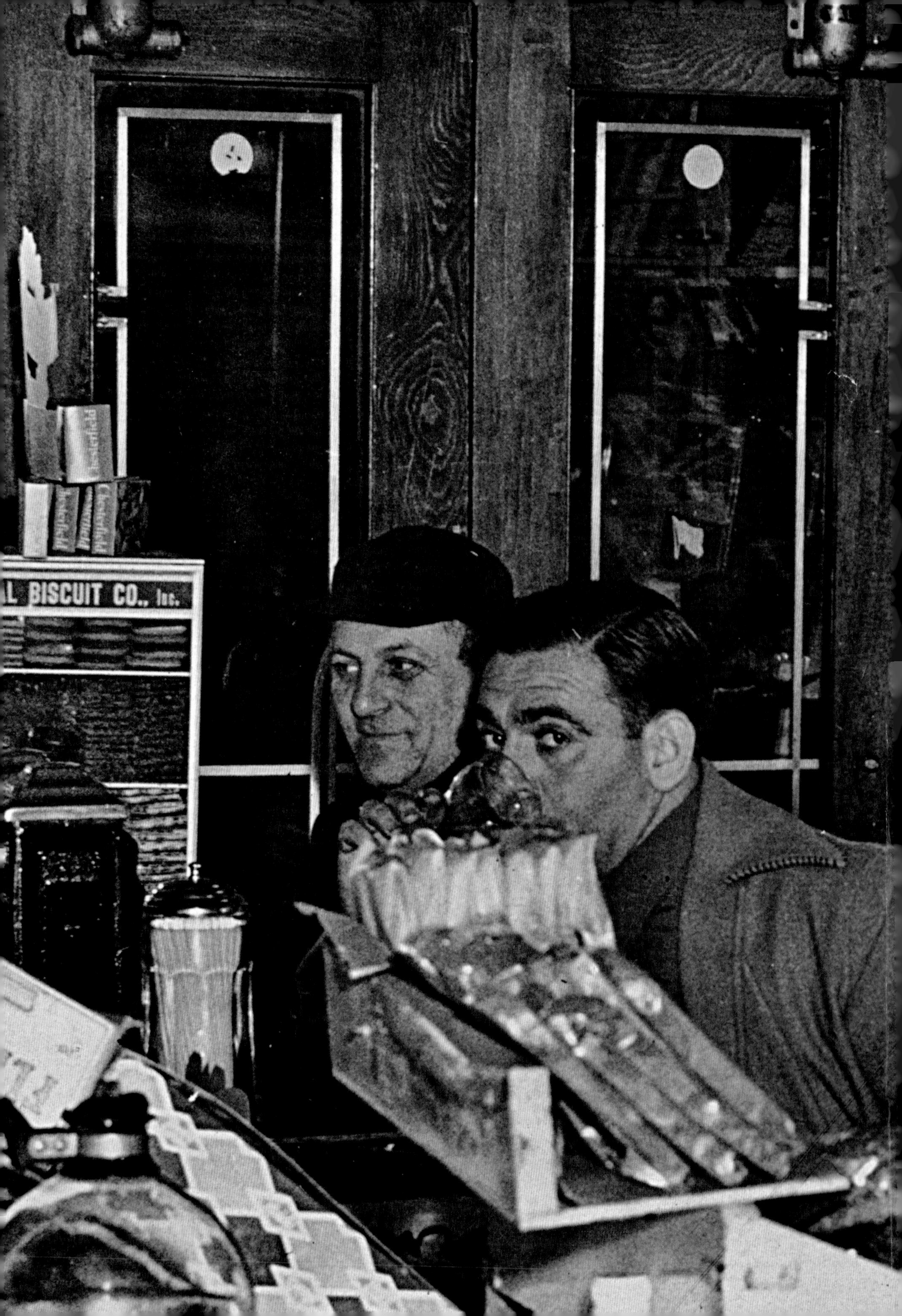
L BISCUIT CO., Inc.

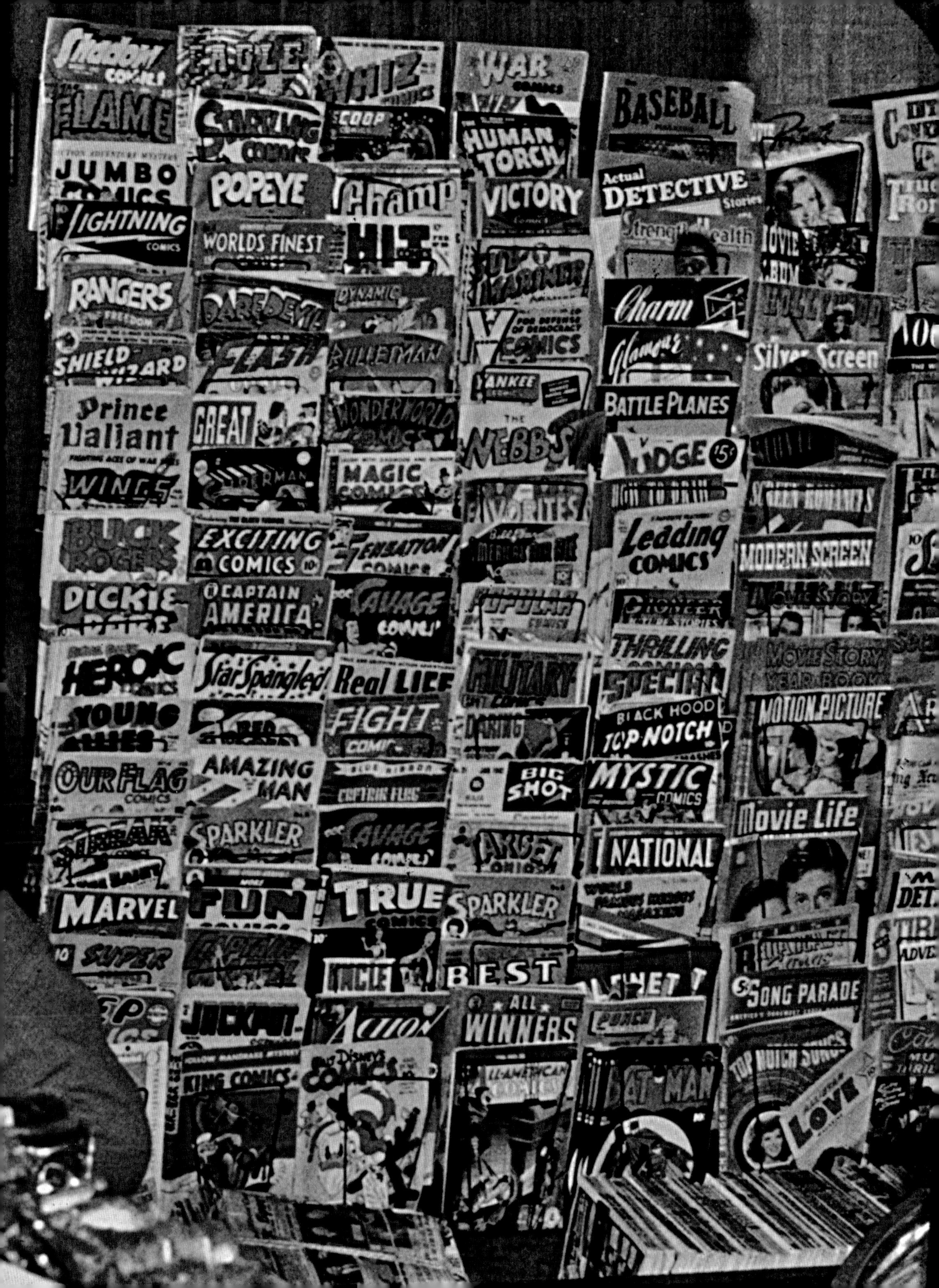
Shadow Comics
Eagle
Whiz
War Comics
Baseball
Flame
Startling Comics
Scoop Comics
Human Torch
Jumbo Comics
Popeye
Champ
Victory
Actual Detective Stories
Lightning Comics
Worlds Finest
Hit
Strength & Health
Rangers of Freedom
Daredevil
Dynamic Comics
Charm
Shield Wizard
Flash
Bulletman
V for Defense of Democracy Comics
Glamour
Silver Screen
Yankee Comics
Prince Valiant
Great
Wonderworld Comics
Battle Planes
The Nebbs
Judge 15¢
Fighting Aces of War Birds Wings
Magic Comics
Favorites
Buck Rogers
Exciting Comics 10¢
Sensation Comics
Leading Comics
Modern Screen
Dickie Dare
Captain America
Savage Comics
Popular Comics
Heroic Comics
Star Spangled
Real Life
Military Comics
Thrilling Comics
Movie Story Year Book
Young Allies
Fight Comics
Special
Black Hood Top-Notch
Motion Picture
Our Flag Comics
Amazing Man
Captain Flag
Big Shot
Mystic Comics
Sparkler
Savage Comics
National
Movie Life
Marvel
Fun
True Comics
Sparkler
Super
Best
Song Parade
Jackpot
Action
All Winners
Punch
King Comics
Walt Disney's Comics
All-American Comics
Batman
Top Notch Songs
Love

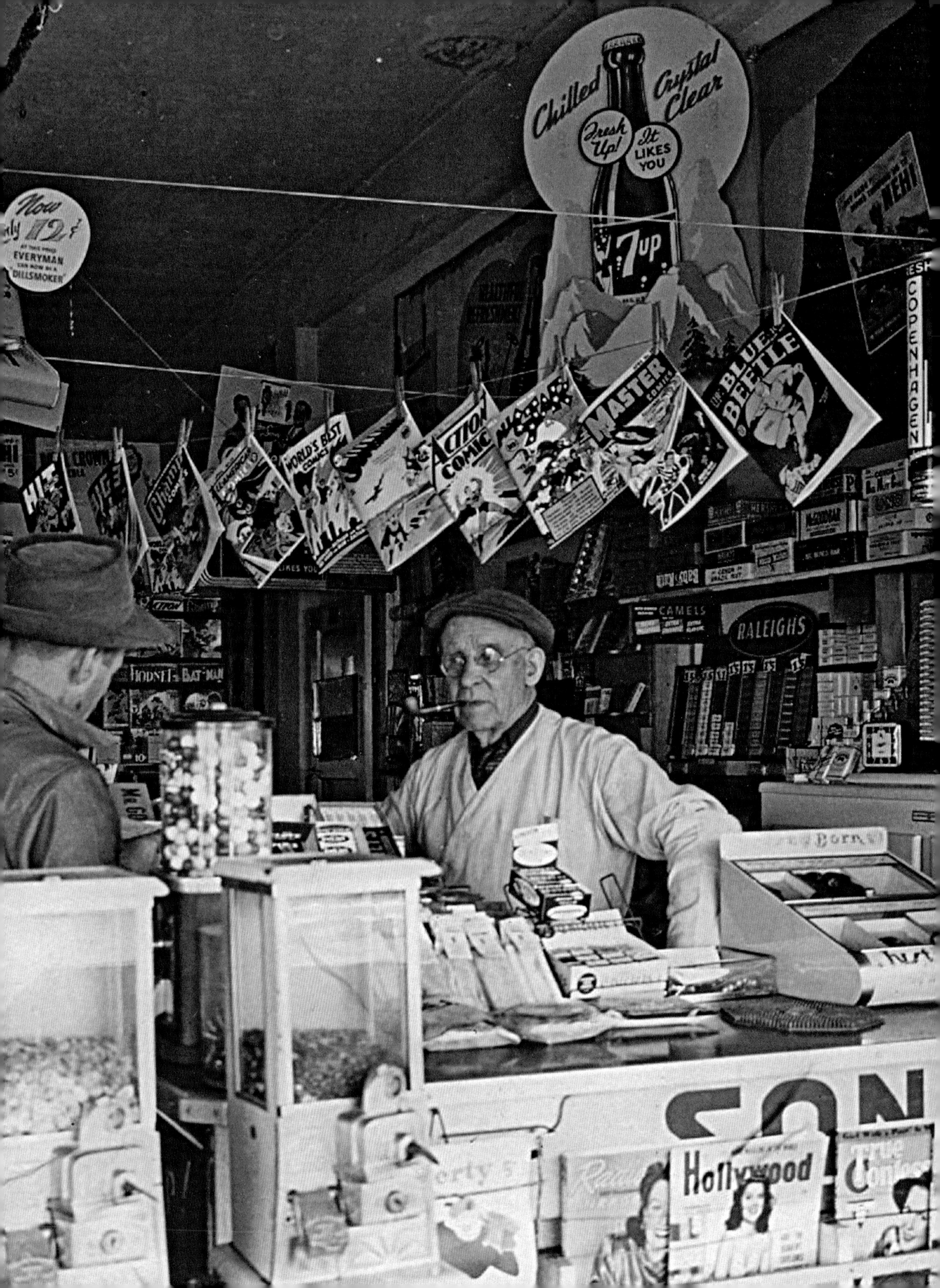

Chilled Crystal Clear
Fresh Up!
It LIKES YOU
7up
EVERYMAN
DILLSMOKER
NEHI
COPENHAGEN
BLUE BEETLE
MASTER COMICS
ACTION COMICS
WORLD'S BEST COMICS
CAMELS
RALEIGHS
BAT-MAN
Hollywood

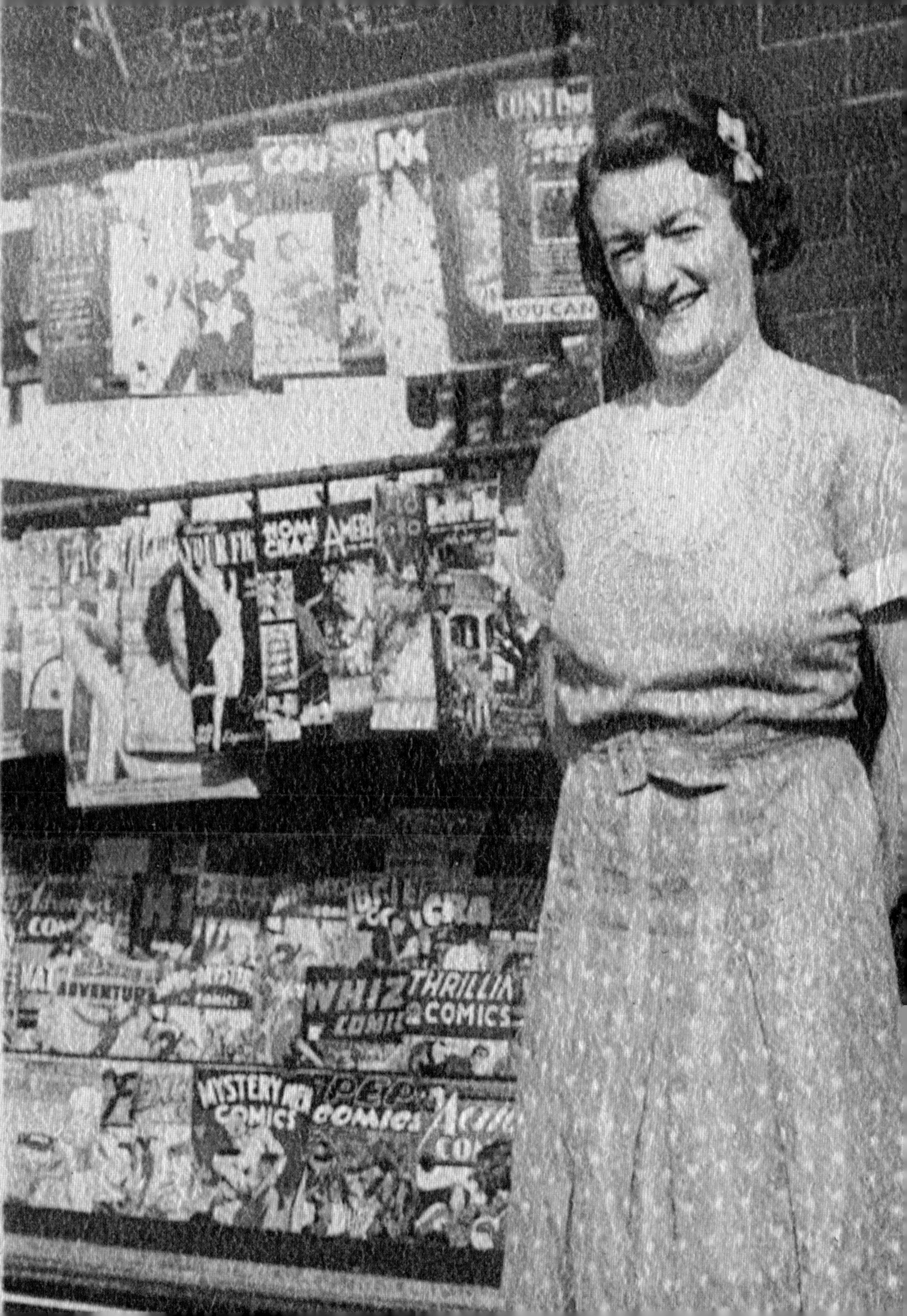
WHIZ COMICS
THRILLING COMICS
MYSTERY MEN COMICS
PEP COMICS

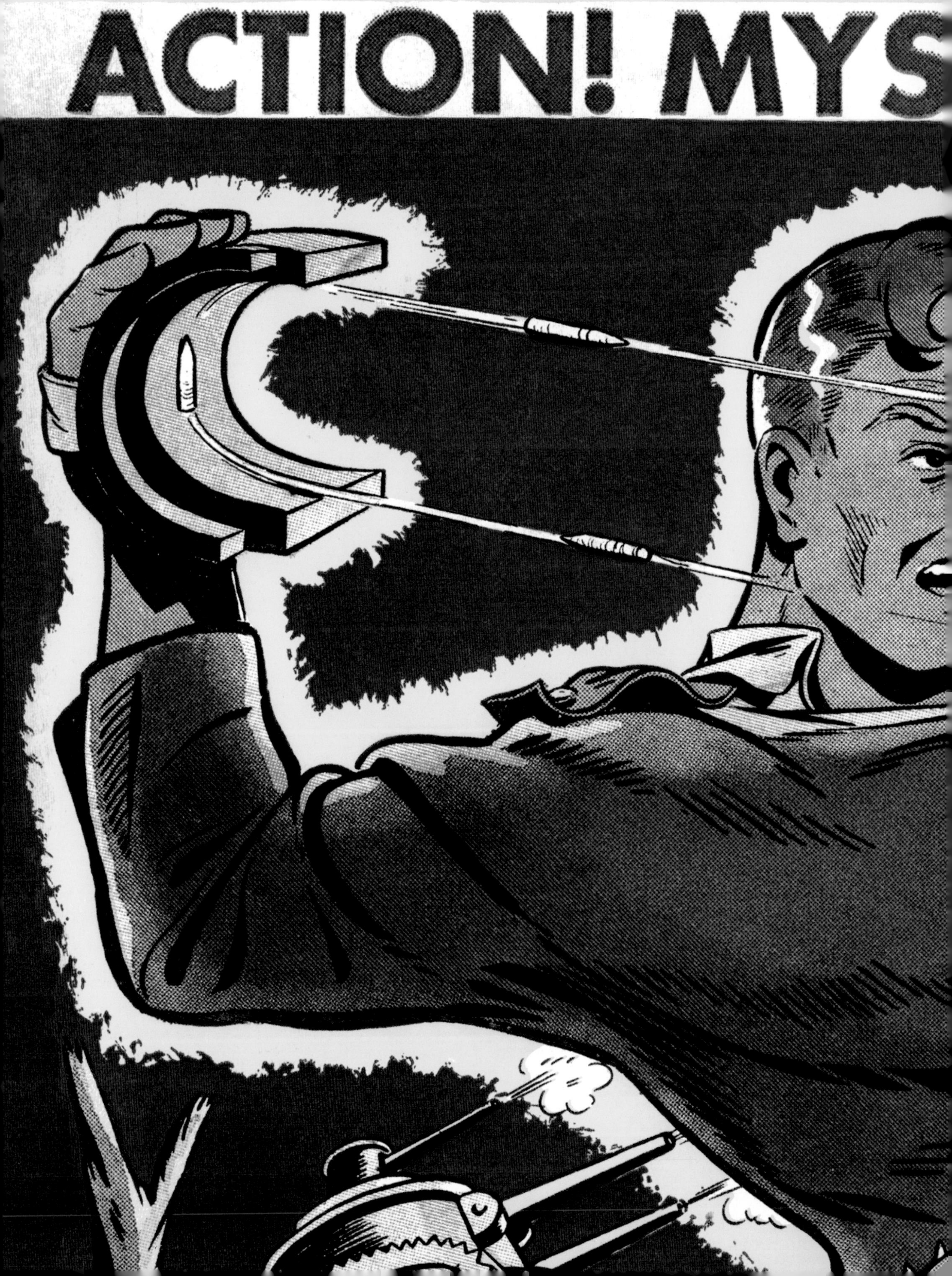
ACTION! MYS

TERY! THRILLS!

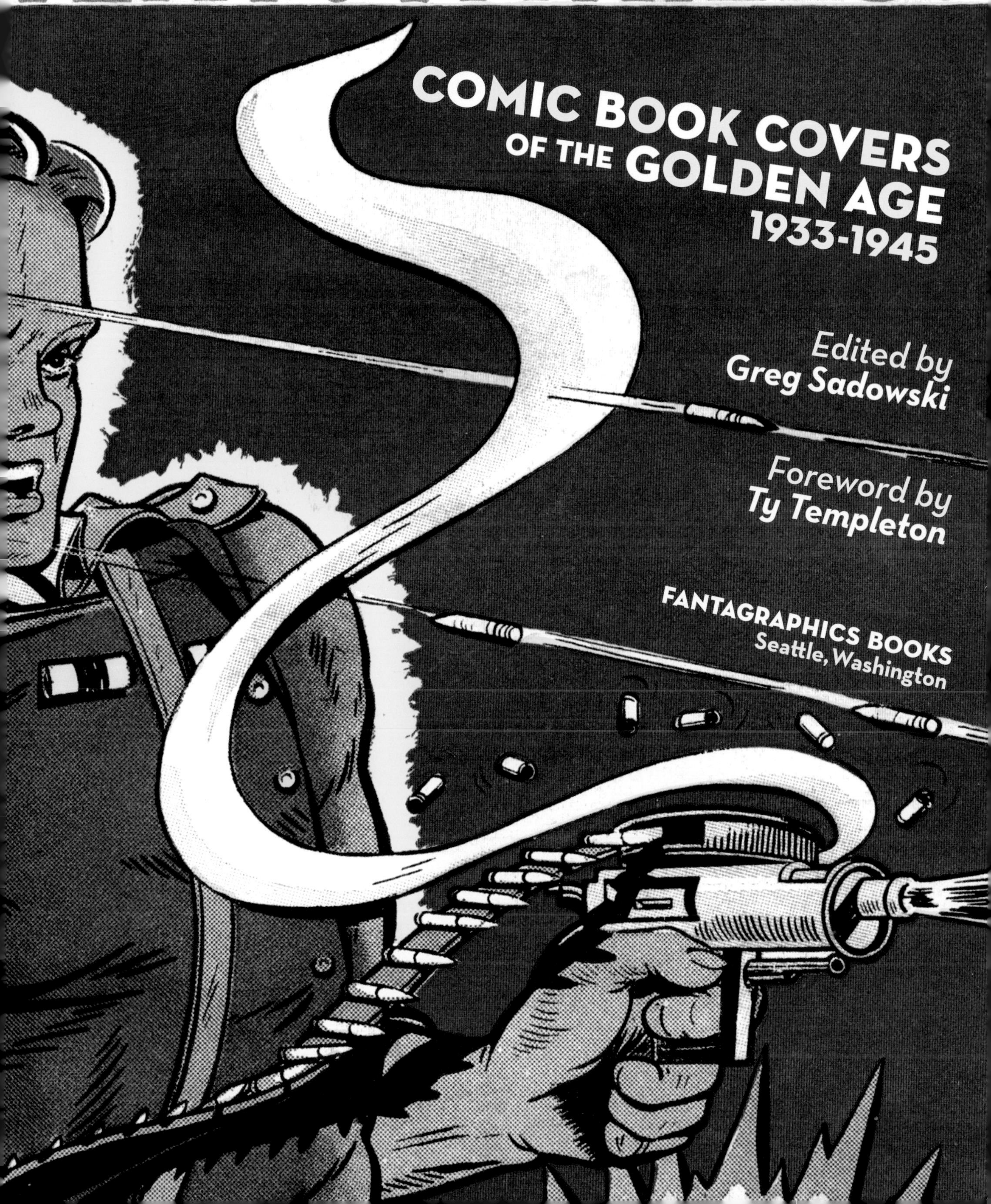

COMIC BOOK COVERS OF THE GOLDEN AGE 1933-1945

Edited by
Greg Sadowski

Foreword by
Ty Templeton

FANTAGRAPHICS BOOKS
Seattle, Washington

Foreword

IN THE PAST I distrusted the phrase "the Golden Age of Comics" as a shorthand for comic books produced during the 1930s and 1940s. It suggested master craftsmen at the top of their game, and I was never convinced of that. To me, the shine painted over the calendar was applied by those who had lived then as children, making the term "Golden Age" more of a generation bias than an official seal. Apart from nostalgia, how much evidence do we have that the age earned its gold?

Okay. Superman, Batman, Wonder Woman, Hawkman, Captain Marvel, Captain America, and the Human Torch were all very cool, but their stories were unevenly written and drawn. Creators such as Jack Cole, Will Eisner, Joe Simon, and Jack Kirby showed more promise than payoff, and they were the era's exception, not the rule.

Weren't the majority of comic books published in the '30s and '40s just a crude pulpy mash of quack science fiction, fistfights, jodhpurs, capes, cowboys, racism, talking animals, private eyes, and badly drawn dames in barely drawn outfits? Wasn't the industry too young and too hack to pronounce it all "Golden" without the misty overlay of idyllic youth to cloud the issue? And wasn't the Golden Age of Comics really in the 1970s, when I lived *my* cloudy, idyllic youth?

In 1957, writer Peter Graham said that the "golden age of science fiction is twelve." He was correct, and not just about sf — but everything. Adolescence is the moment in our existence where the world shows itself to us without first going through our parents. It's the age we discover the best comics, the best music, the best films, the best food, the best of all things — and these discoveries and experiences are what measure out the chains, weights, and gears that will run our unique mental mechanism for the rest of our adult lives. We *all* grow up into our adult selves in a remembered golden age, not because of the time it was, but because of biology. We can't help it.

Now, while it's not quite biology, the case can be made that the very time covered in this handsome volume was the period in which comic books were measuring out their own mechanism and maturing into adulthood.

The mid-1930s to mid-1940s didn't see the birth of the art (*that* happened decades earlier with the Yellow Kid and the original Sunday funnies). It instead represents the industry's adolescence, and what a time that was. After a childhood nestled in the center of the family newspaper, the comics section looked to stand on its own, alongside the pulps and the movie magazines, discovering what it wanted to be from the world of its era.

Witness it in the pages of this book: the Art Deco stylings of Alex Schomburg, Jack Cole, and Reed Crandall battling it out with the more intuitive Modernism of Joe Simon, Jack Kirby, and Charles Biro. The external realities of war and depression, counterbalanced by magic and fantasy, each vying for the public's hearts, minds, and dimes. The layouts, the logos, the limits of the printing technology, and the size of the product are tested and refined, with genres and audience coalescing at the same time. And we find that this period was so much more than superheroes, and all being done by master craftsmen at the top of their game after all.

This is a fresh and new collection. Though I was already familiar with the magnificent Will Eisner, Mac Raboy and Walt Kelly, I hadn't seen most of the beautiful covers chosen herein. And amidst the previously unseen work by well-known cartoonists Sheldon Mayer, Bob Kane, Joe Shuster, Bill Everett, and Lou Fine, I've been introduced to the stunning L. B. Cole, Edd Ashe, and Jimmy Thompson. I've been forever scrubbed of my own generation bias after swimming around these pages. You will be too.

It was an unparalleled time of creativity, skill, and daring, this decade when comic books grew up. Though there was plenty of high craft and brilliance to come, never again did the medium advance on so grand a scale, and never has it been this much fun to discover that those who grew up with these comics were actually right.

It turns out it *was* the Golden Age.

Ty the Guy Templeton

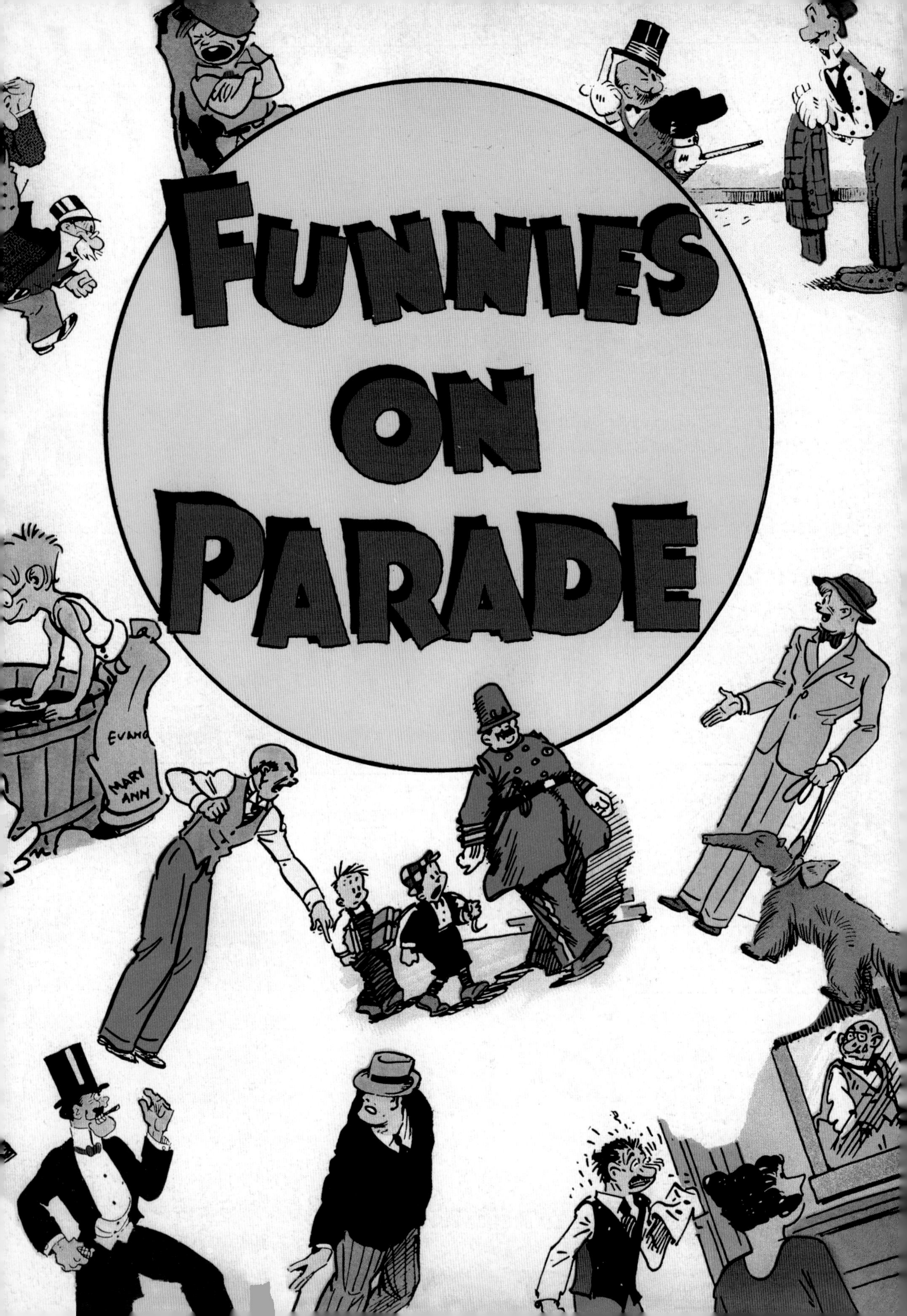
FUNNIES ON PARADE
EVANS
MARY ANN

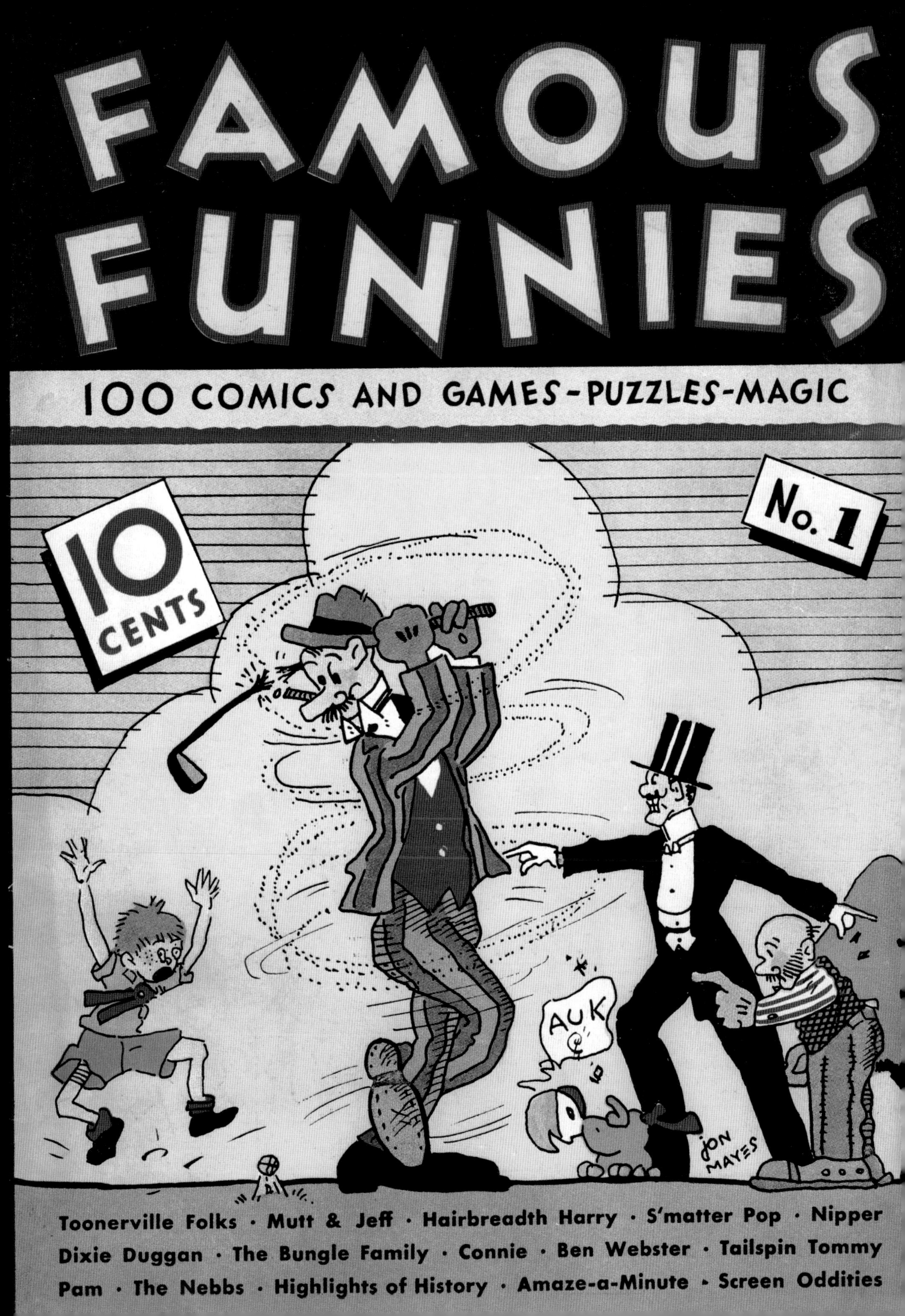
FAMOUS FUNNIES
100 COMICS AND GAMES-PUZZLES-MAGIC
10 CENTS
No. 1
AUK
JON MAYES
Toonerville Folks · Mutt & Jeff · Hairbreadth Harry · S'matter Pop · Nipper
Dixie Duggan · The Bungle Family · Connie · Ben Webster · Tailspin Tommy
Pam · The Nebbs · Highlights of History · Amaze-a-Minute · Screen Oddities

ALL ORIGINAL

NEW

APRIL 1935

FUN

THE BIG COMIC MAGAZINE

10 CENTS

DON DRAKE
ON THE PLANET SARO
THE GONDOLA CONTAINING DON AND BETTY AND THE MIDGET MEN FALLS OFF THE CLIFF INTO THE WATER
BUT A GIANT SENTINEL AT THE BASE OF THE CLIFF SPIES THE STRANGE OBJECT
THE ANT-PEOPLE ARE NOT DANGEROUS – IT'S THEIR MASTERS, THE MANY ARMED BEASTS WHOM WE HAVE TO FEAR!!
WHAT THEY SAW –
LOOK !! ALL THE GREAT ANTS ARE FLEEING! AND WHAT IS THAT HORRIBLE THING?
WEE-O-W WE ARE LOST!
AT THE MERCY OF A FOUL AND PITILESS CREATURE
CONTINUED
NATIONAL ALLIED PUBLICATIONS, INC.

NOW IN COLORS • ADVENTURE - FLYING - MYSTERY
COMIC STRIPS • STORIES - MOVIES - SCIENCE • PRIZES

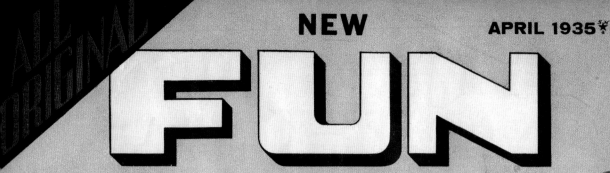

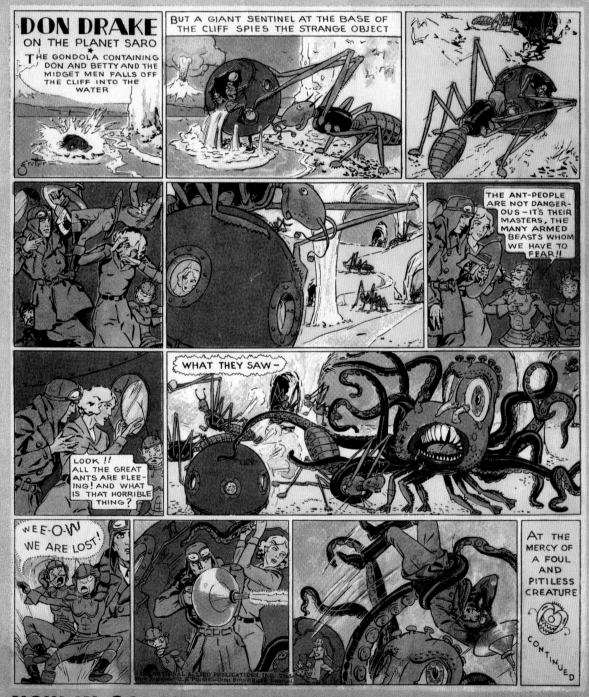

NOVEMBER 1935

10¢ 15 Cents in Canada (Including Tax)

Mickey Mouse Magazine

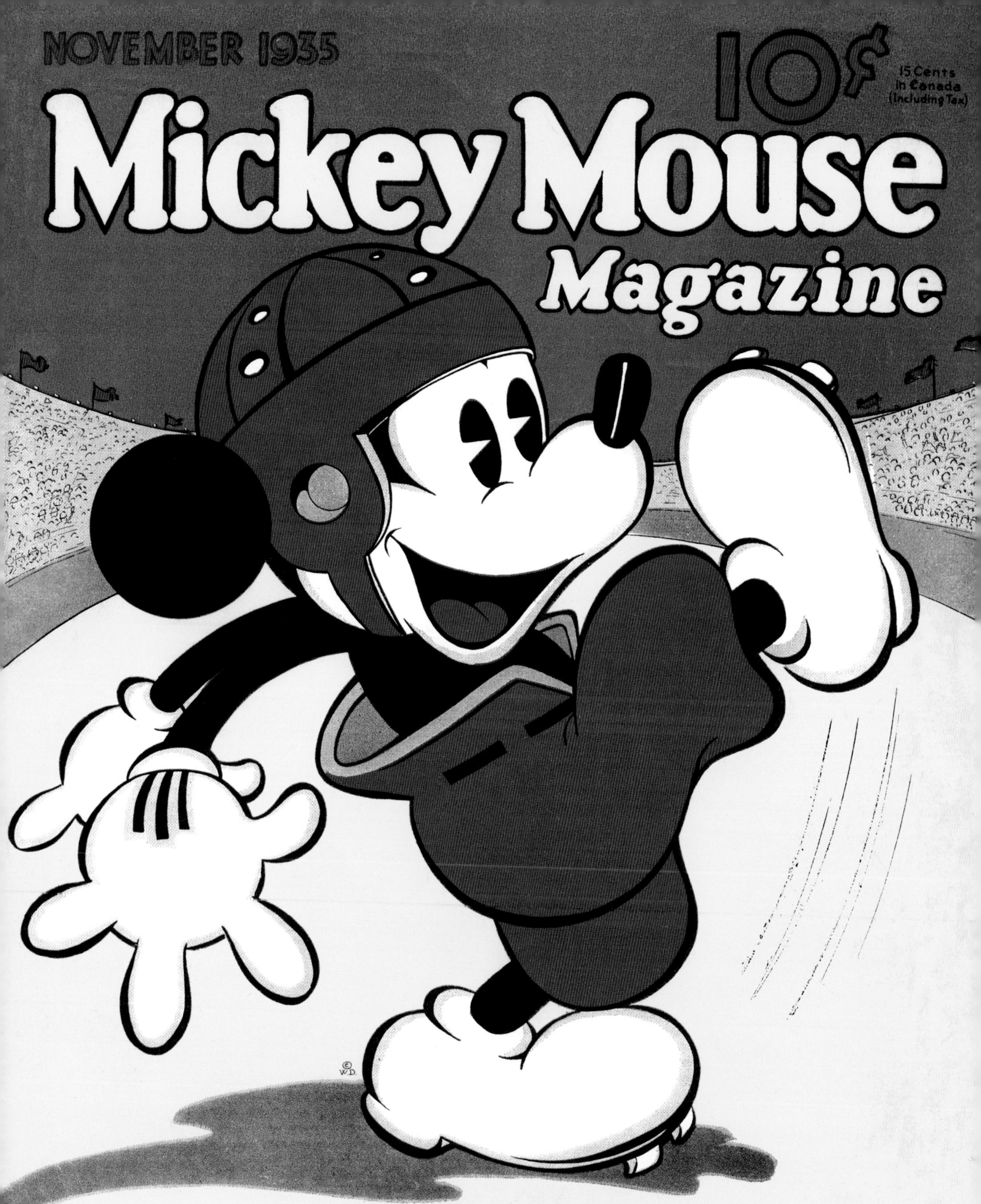

© W.D.

IN THIS ISSUE: ANOTHER BIG

$5,000.00 CONTEST

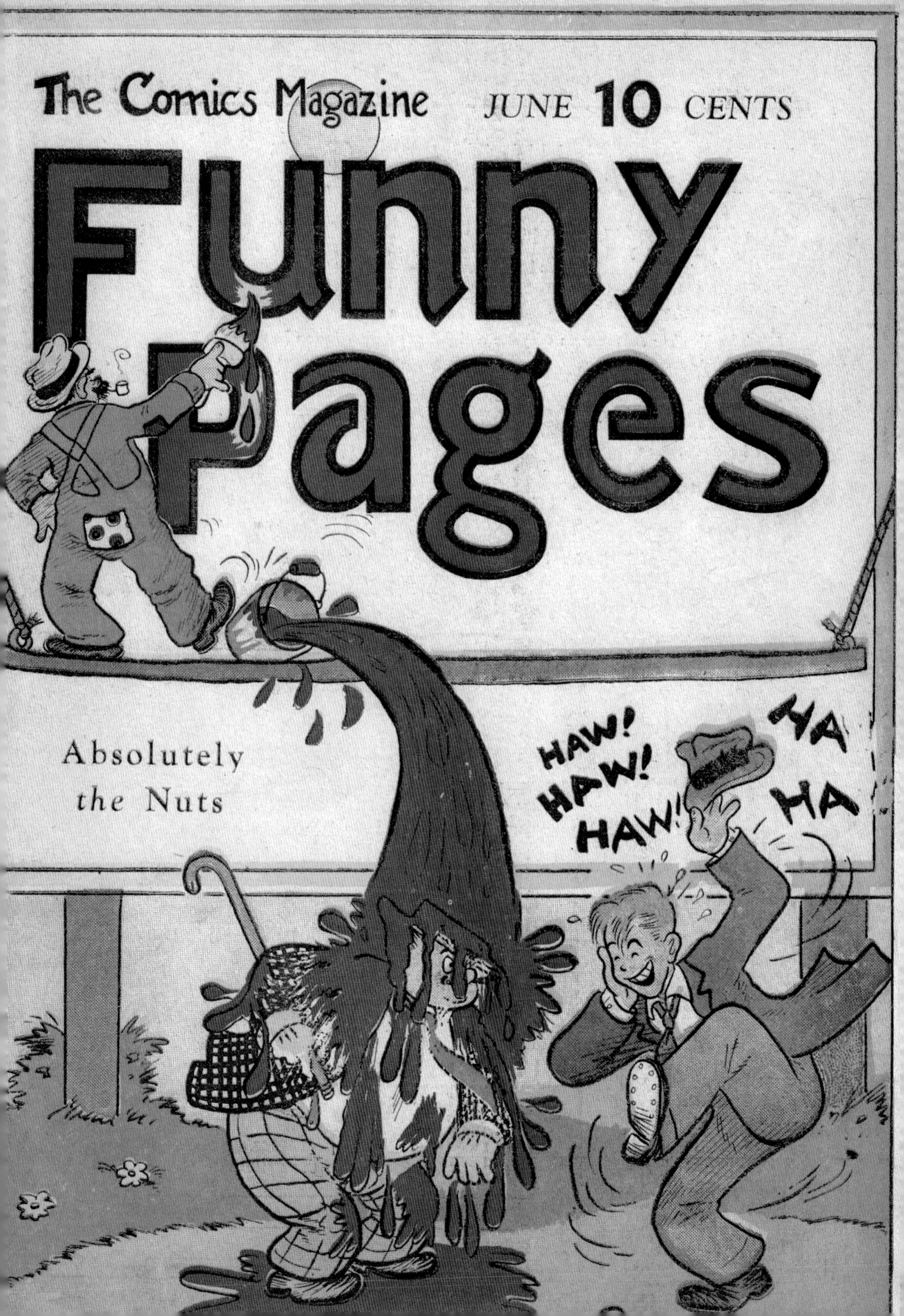
The Comics Magazine
JUNE 10 CENTS
Funny Pages
Absolutely the Nuts
HAW! HAW! HAW!
HA HA

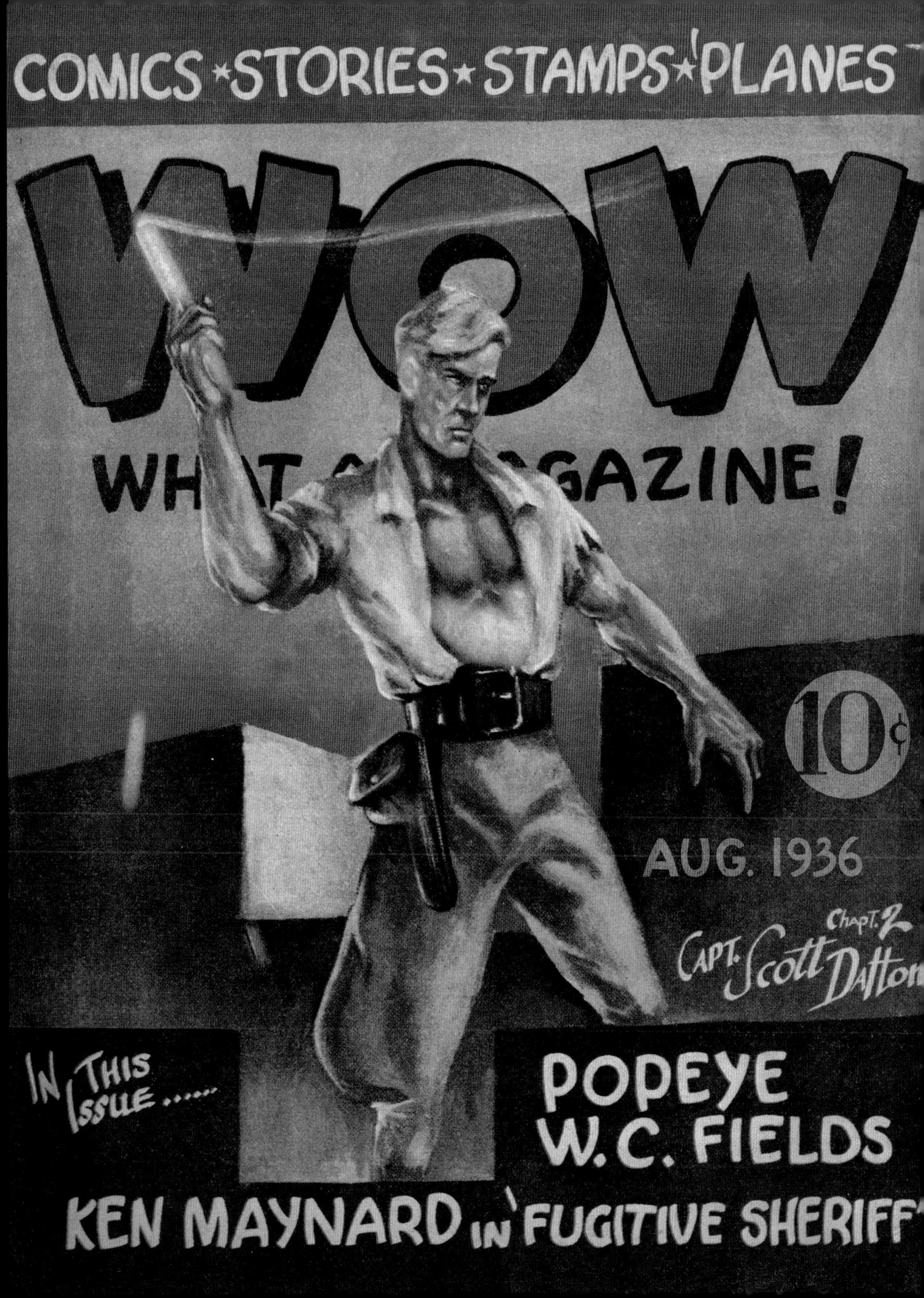
COMICS ★ STORIES ★ STAMPS ★ PLANES
WOW
WH
GAZINE!
10¢
AUG. 1936
Chapt. 2
Capt. Scott Dalton
IN THIS ISSUE......
POPEYE
W.C. FIELDS
KEN MAYNARD IN 'FUGITIVE SHERIFF'

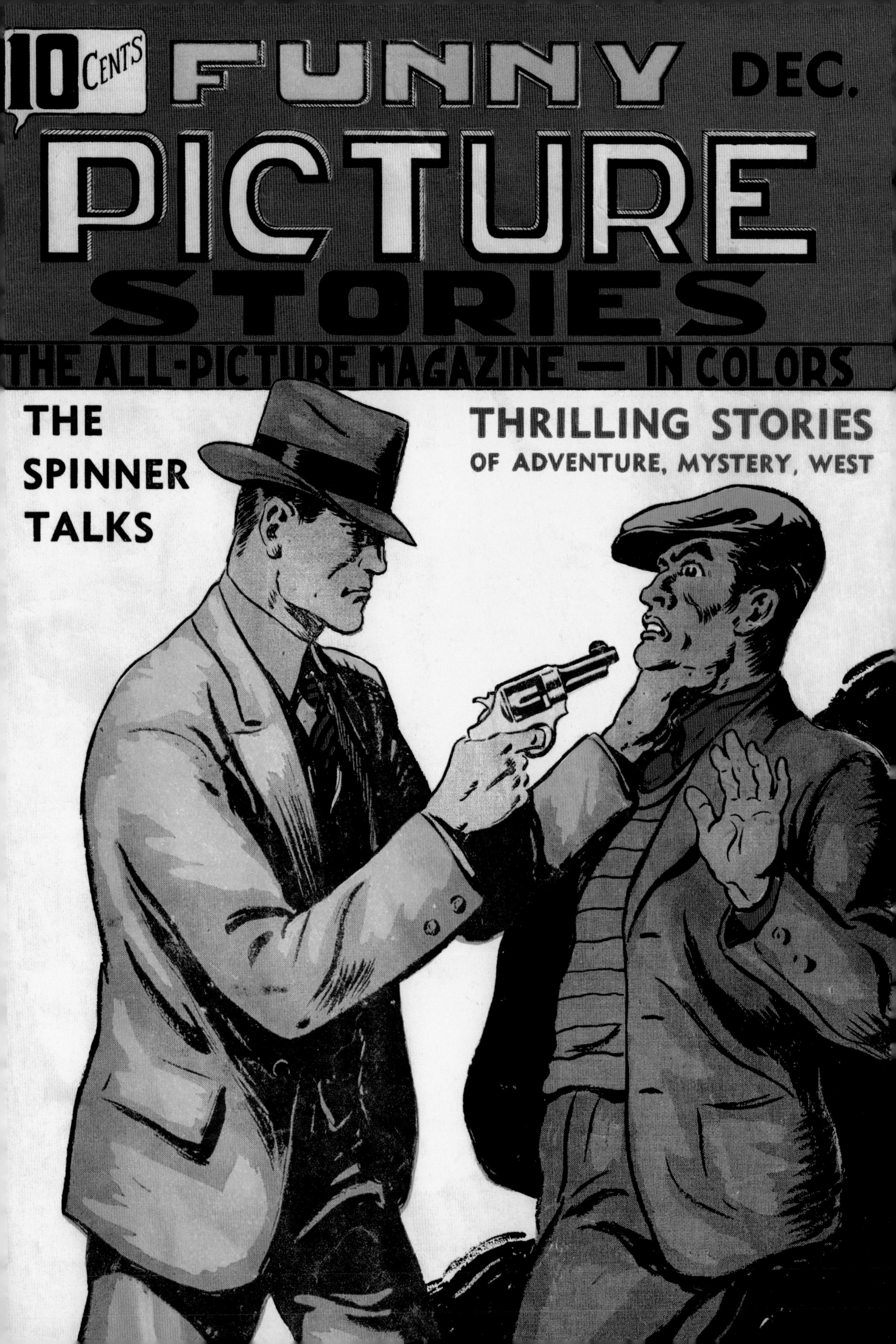
10 CENTS
FUNNY
DEC.
PICTURE
STORIES
THE ALL-PICTURE MAGAZINE — IN COLORS
THE
SPINNER
TALKS
THRILLING STORIES
OF ADVENTURE, MYSTERY, WEST

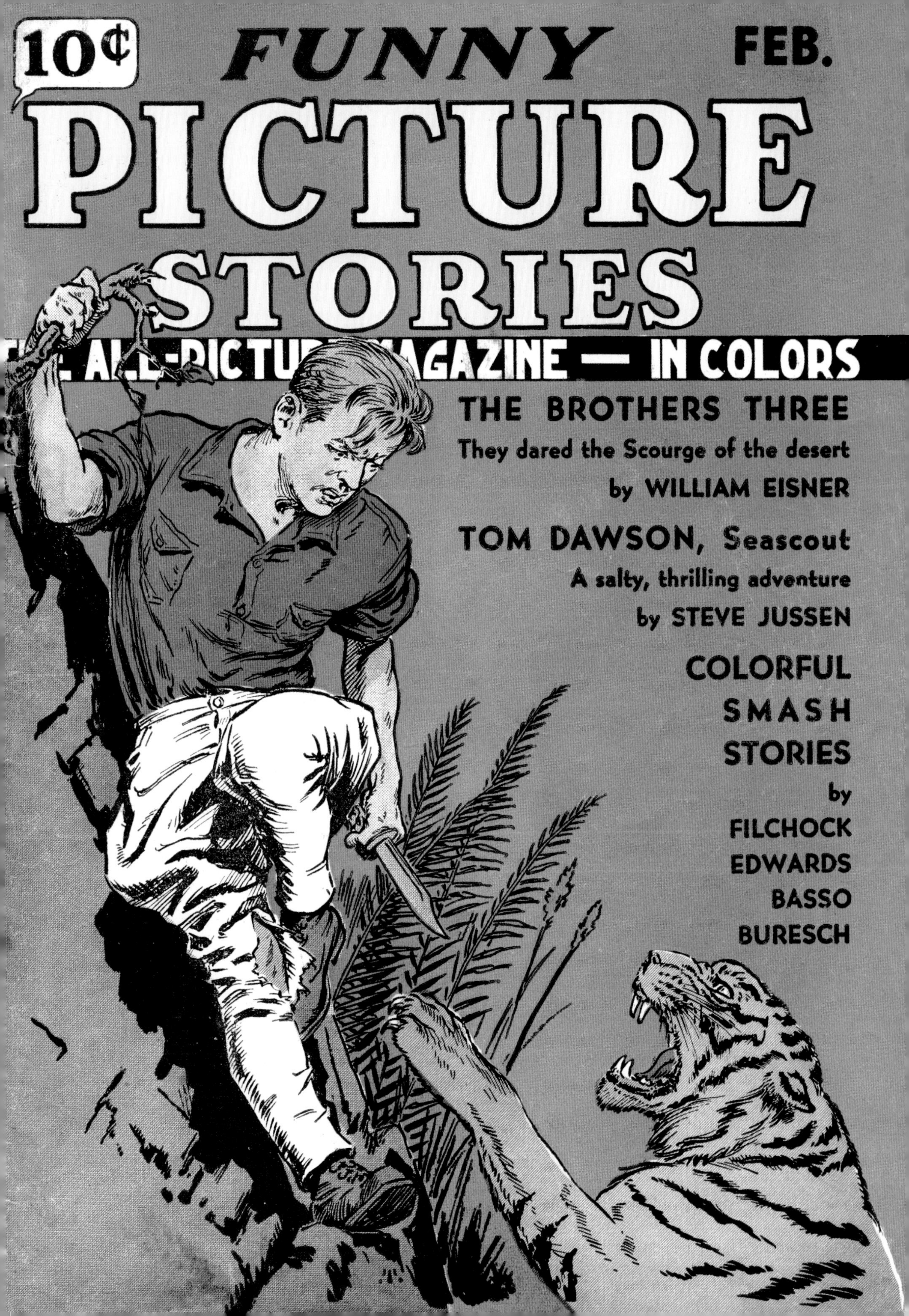
10¢
FUNNY
FEB.
PICTURE
STORIES
MAGAZINE — IN COLORS
THE BROTHERS THREE
They dared the Scourge of the desert
by WILLIAM EISNER
TOM DAWSON, Seascout
A salty, thrilling adventure
by STEVE JUSSEN
COLORFUL
SMASH
STORIES
by
FILCHOCK
EDWARDS
BASSO
BURESCH

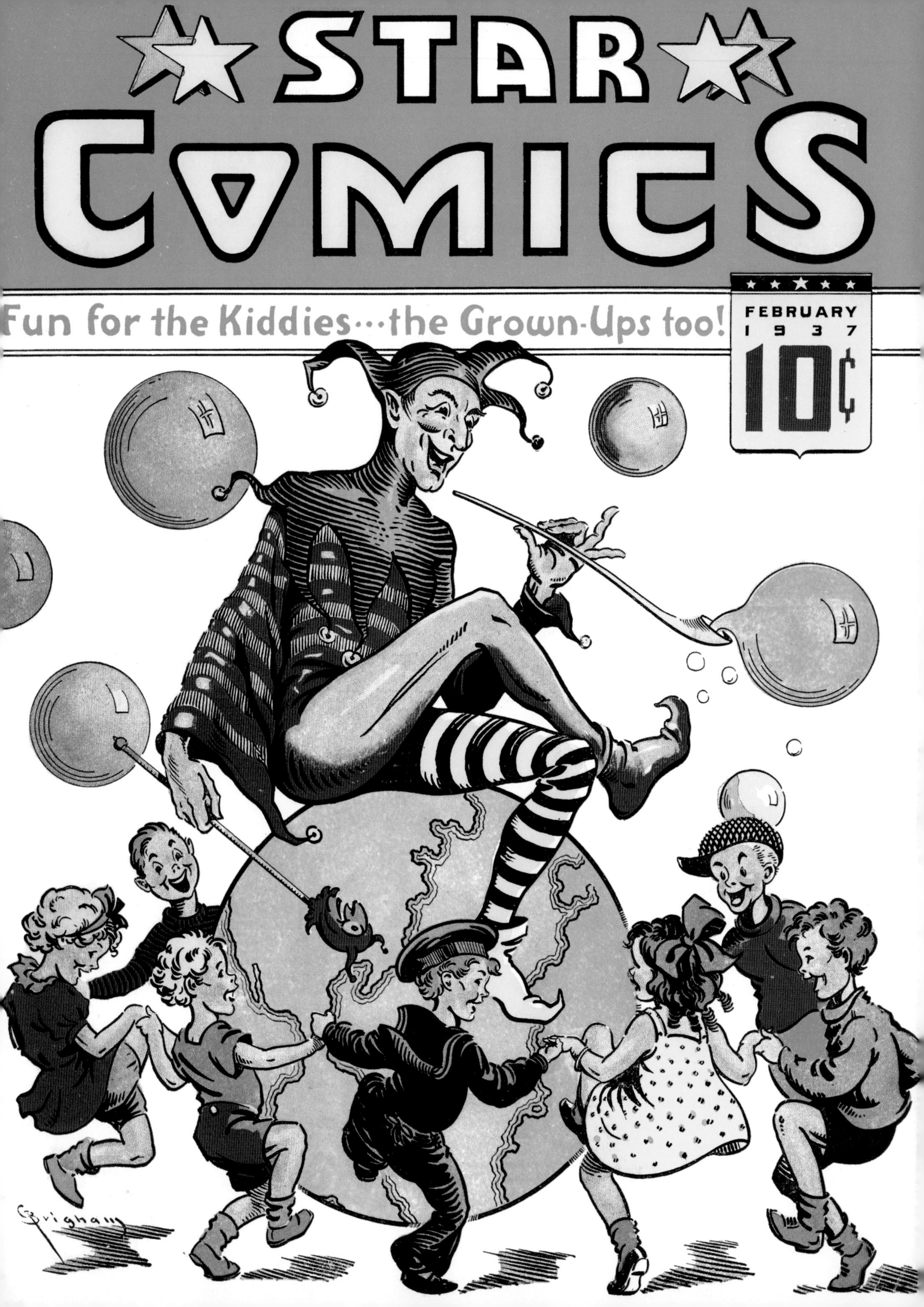
STAR COMICS
Fun for the Kiddies···the Grown-Ups too!
FEBRUARY 1937
10¢
Brigham

STAR RANGER

ACTION---SPEED---EXCITEMENT

FEBRUARY 1937

10¢

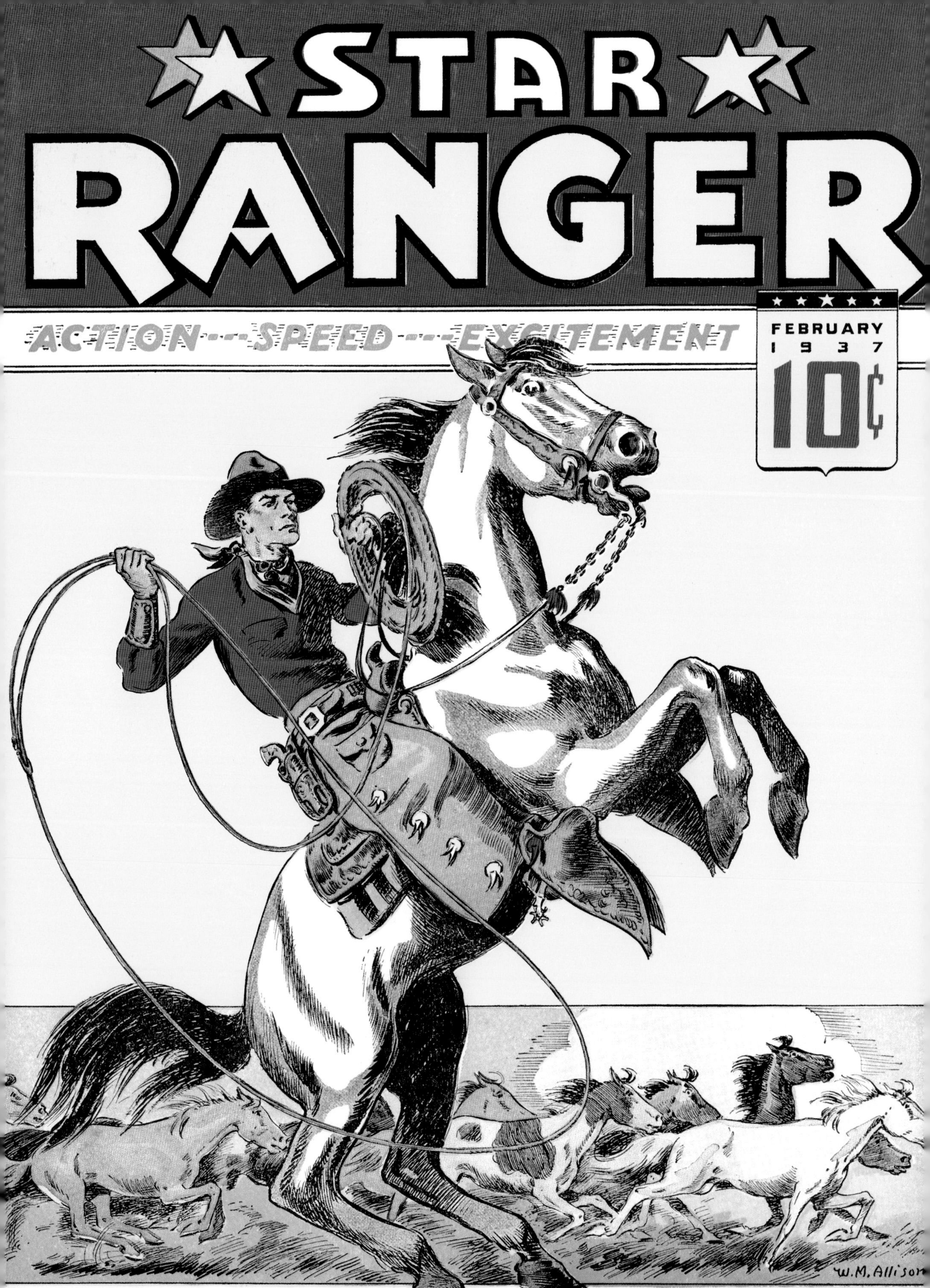
W.M. Allison

PICTORIAL STORIES OF THE GOLDEN WEST

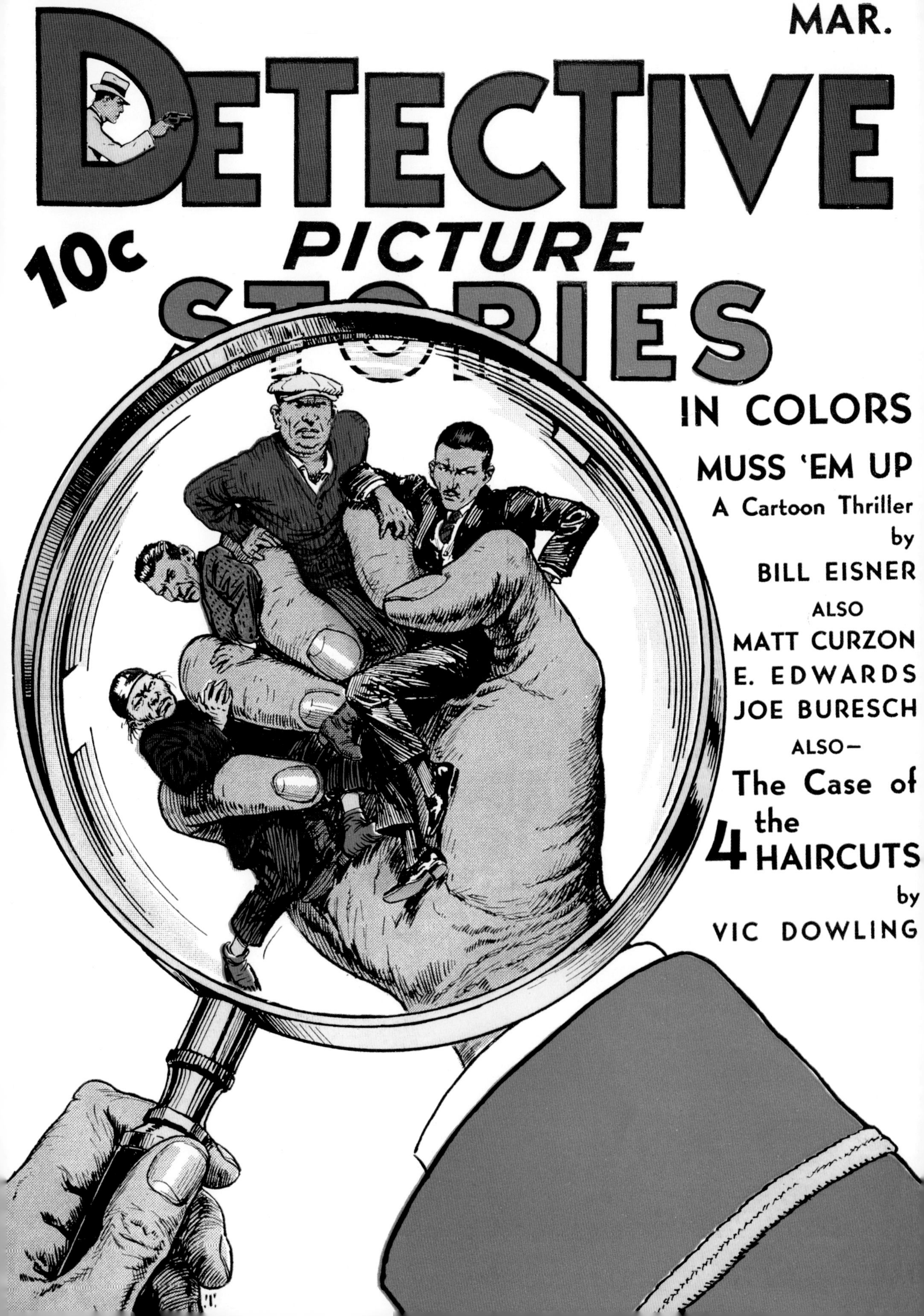
MAR.
DETECTIVE
10c
PICTURE
STORIES
IN COLORS
MUSS 'EM UP
A Cartoon Thriller
by
BILL EISNER
ALSO
MATT CURZON
E. EDWARDS
JOE BURESCH
ALSO—
The Case of
the
4 HAIRCUTS
by
VIC DOWLING

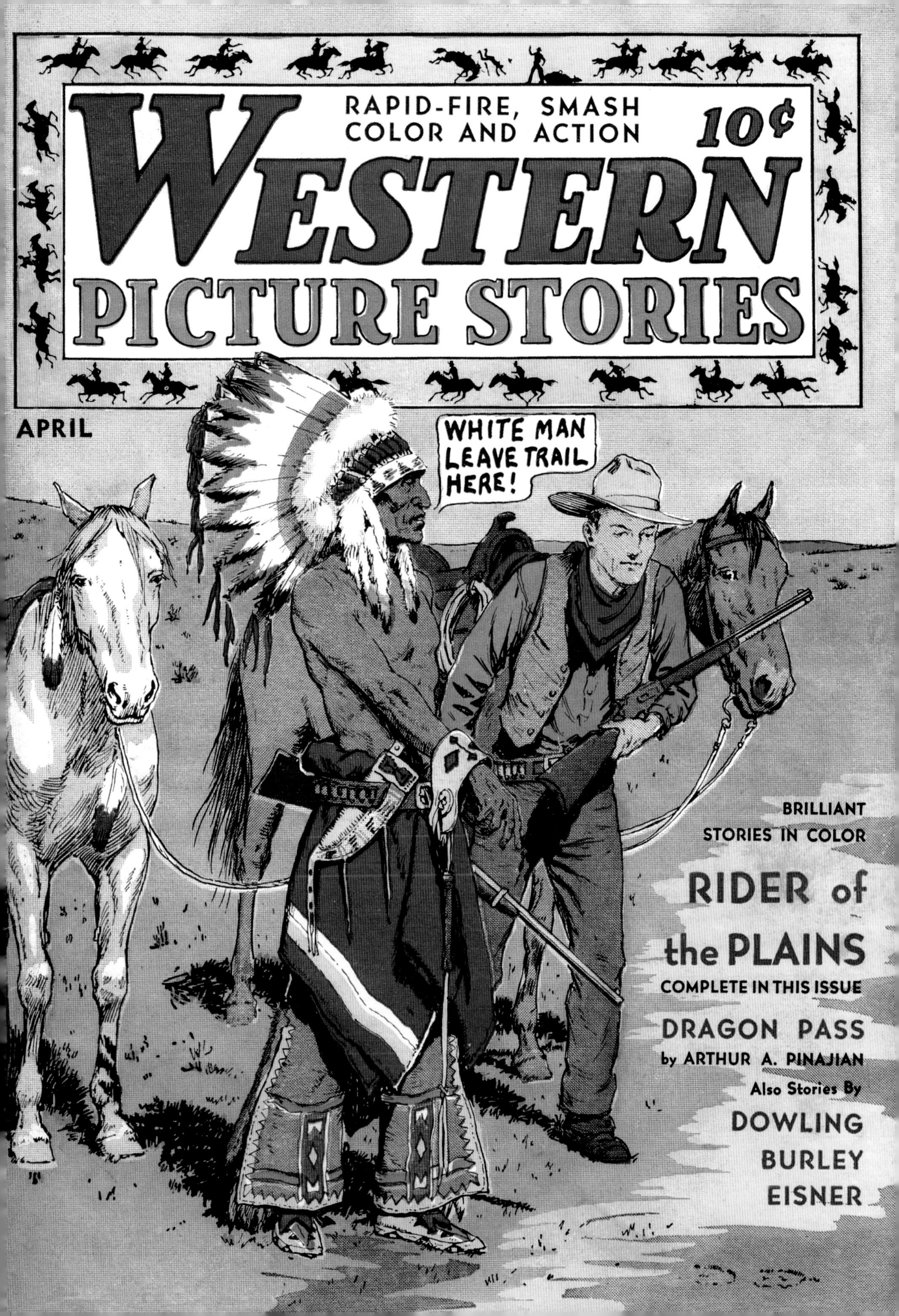
RAPID-FIRE, SMASH COLOR AND ACTION
10¢
WESTERN PICTURE STORIES
APRIL
WHITE MAN LEAVE TRAIL HERE!
BRILLIANT STORIES IN COLOR
RIDER of the PLAINS
COMPLETE IN THIS ISSUE
DRAGON PASS
by ARTHUR A. PINAJIAN
Also Stories By
DOWLING
BURLEY
EISNER

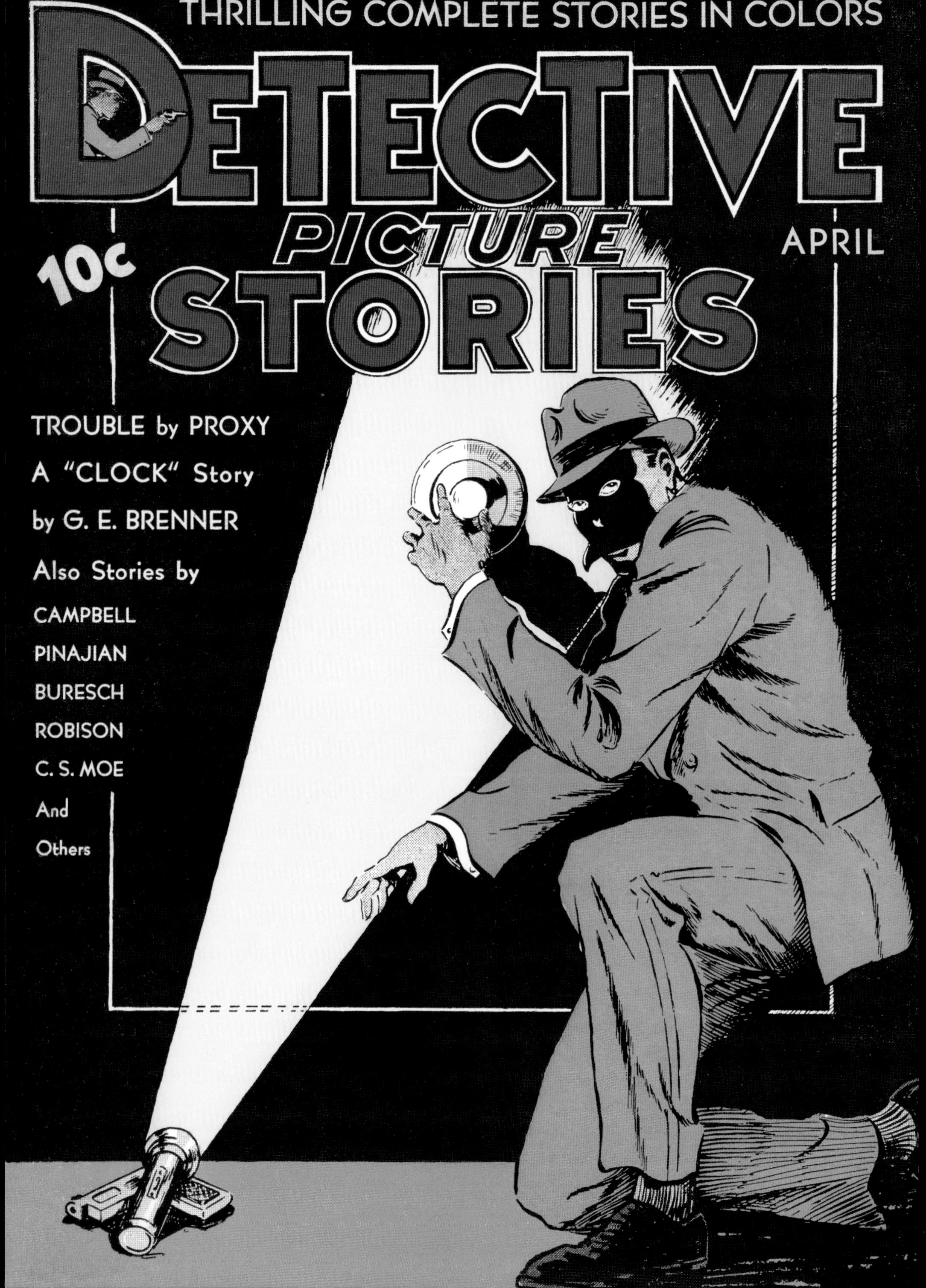
THRILLING COMPLETE STORIES IN COLORS
DETECTIVE
PICTURE
STORIES
10c
APRIL
TROUBLE by PROXY
A "CLOCK" Story
by G. E. BRENNER
Also Stories by
CAMPBELL
PINAJIAN
BURESCH
ROBISON
C. S. MOE
And
Others

No. 6 AUGUST, 1937

Detective COMICS

10¢

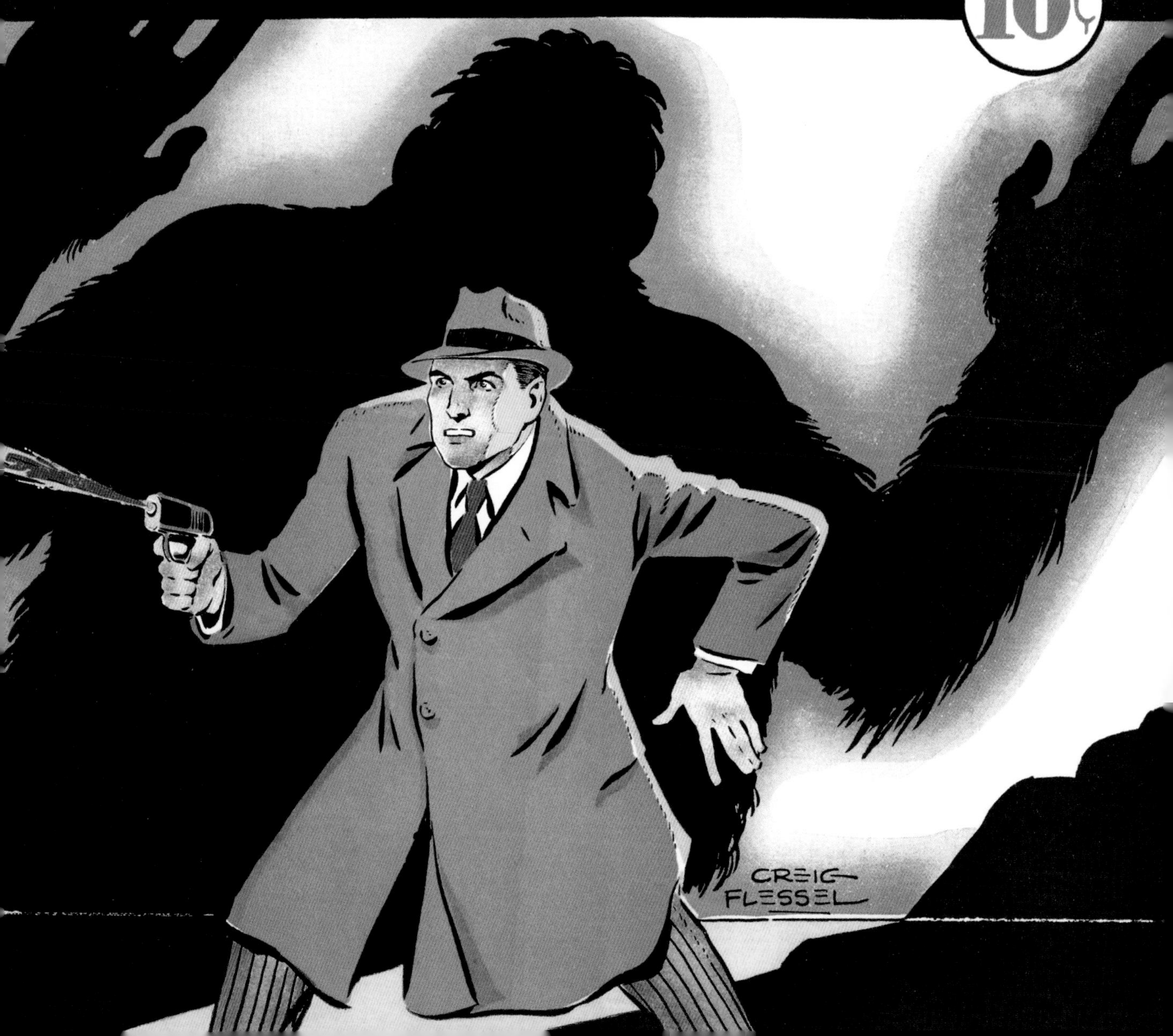
CREIG FLESSEL

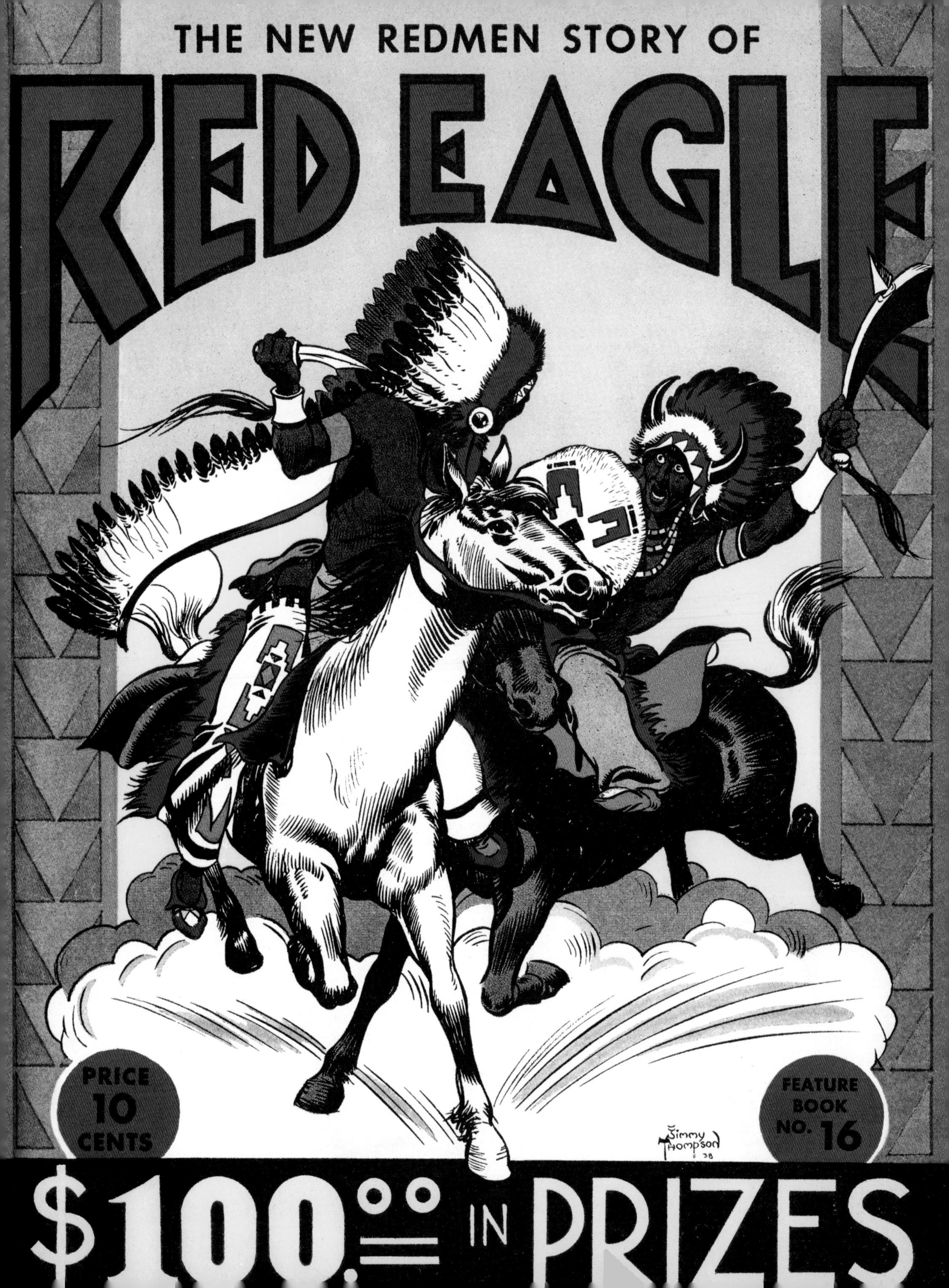
THE NEW REDMEN STORY OF
RED EAGLE
PRICE 10 CENTS
FEATURE BOOK NO. 16
Jimmy Thompson
$100.00 IN PRIZES

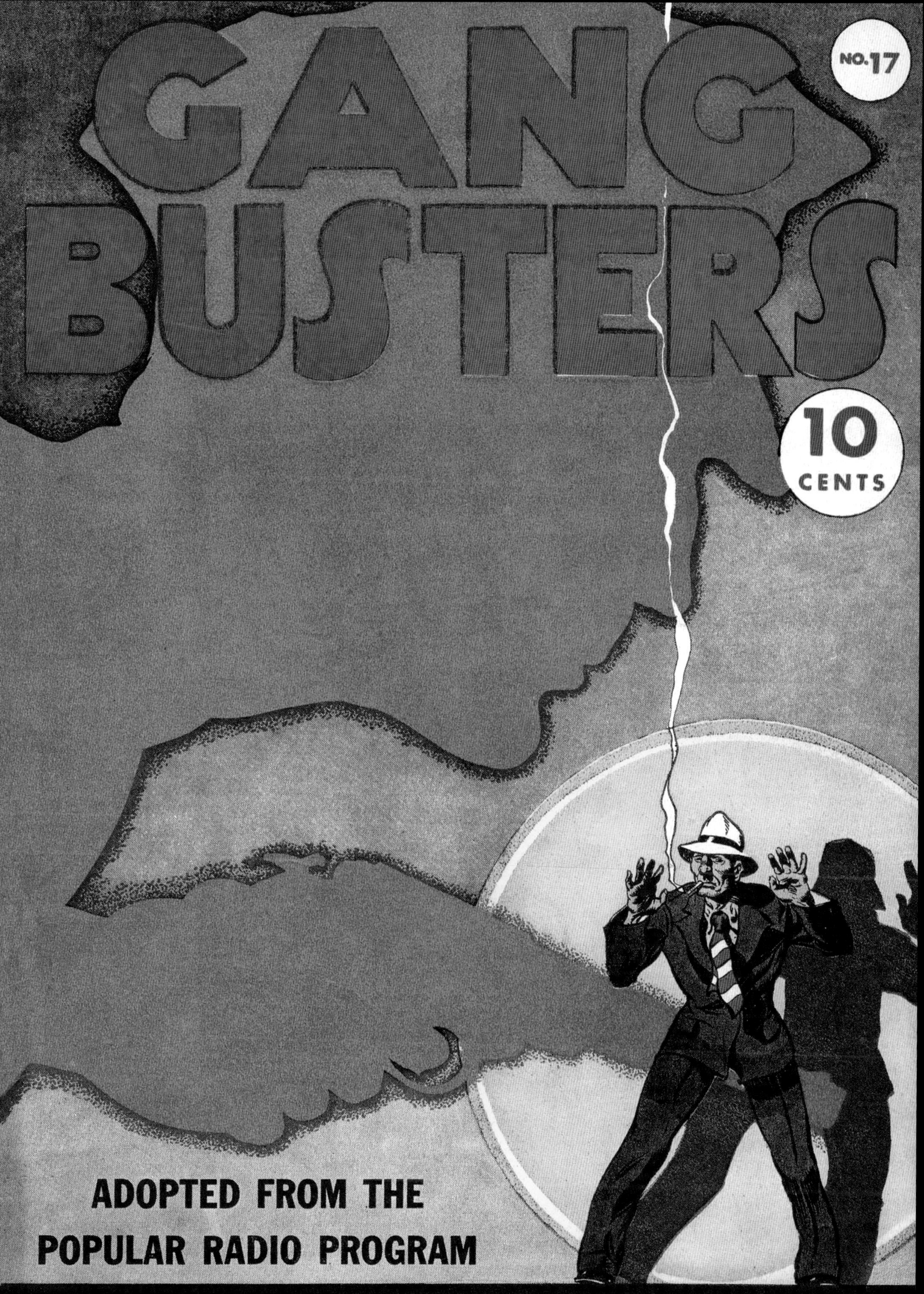

GANG BUSTERS
NO. 17
10 CENTS
ADOPTED FROM THE POPULAR RADIO PROGRAM

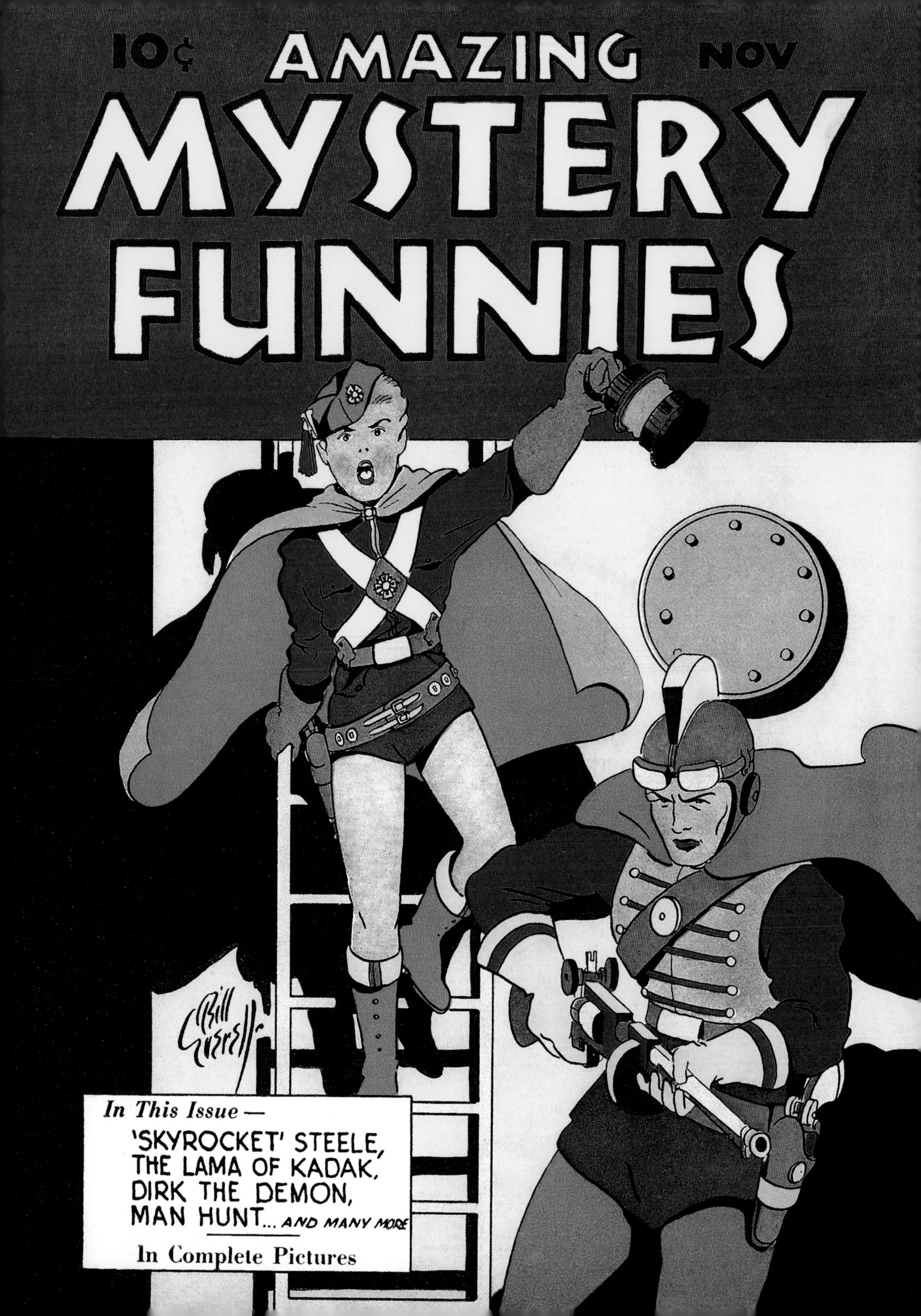
10¢
AMAZING
NOV
MYSTERY FUNNIES
Bill Everett
In This Issue —
'SKYROCKET' STEELE,
THE LAMA OF KADAK,
DIRK THE DEMON,
MAN HUNT... AND MANY MORE
In Complete Pictures

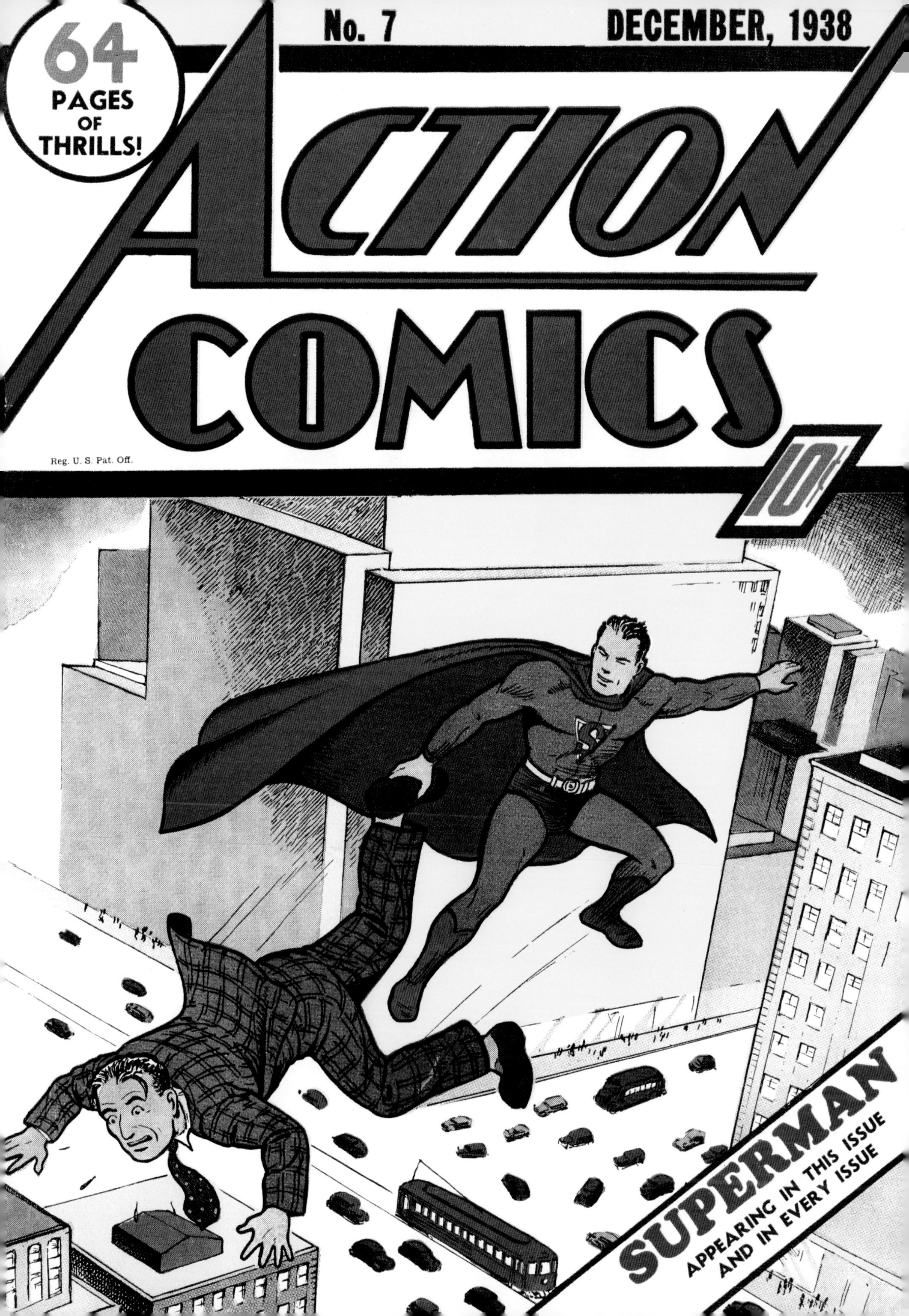
64 PAGES OF THRILLS!
No. 7
DECEMBER, 1938
ACTION COMICS
Reg. U. S. Pat. Off.
10¢
SUPERMAN
APPEARING IN THIS ISSUE AND IN EVERY ISSUE

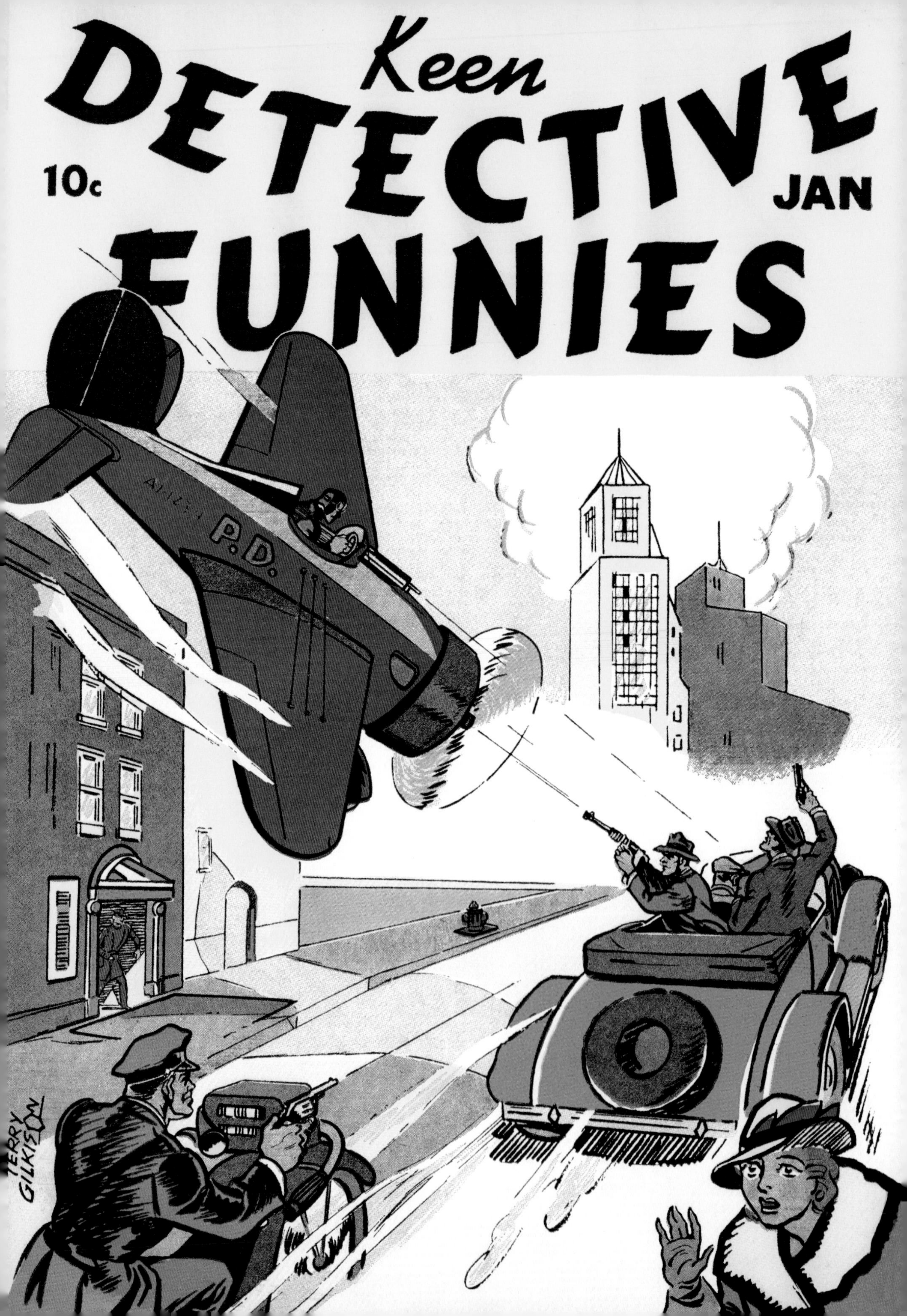
Keen
DETECTIVE
FUNNIES
10c
JAN
P.D.
TERRY GILKISON

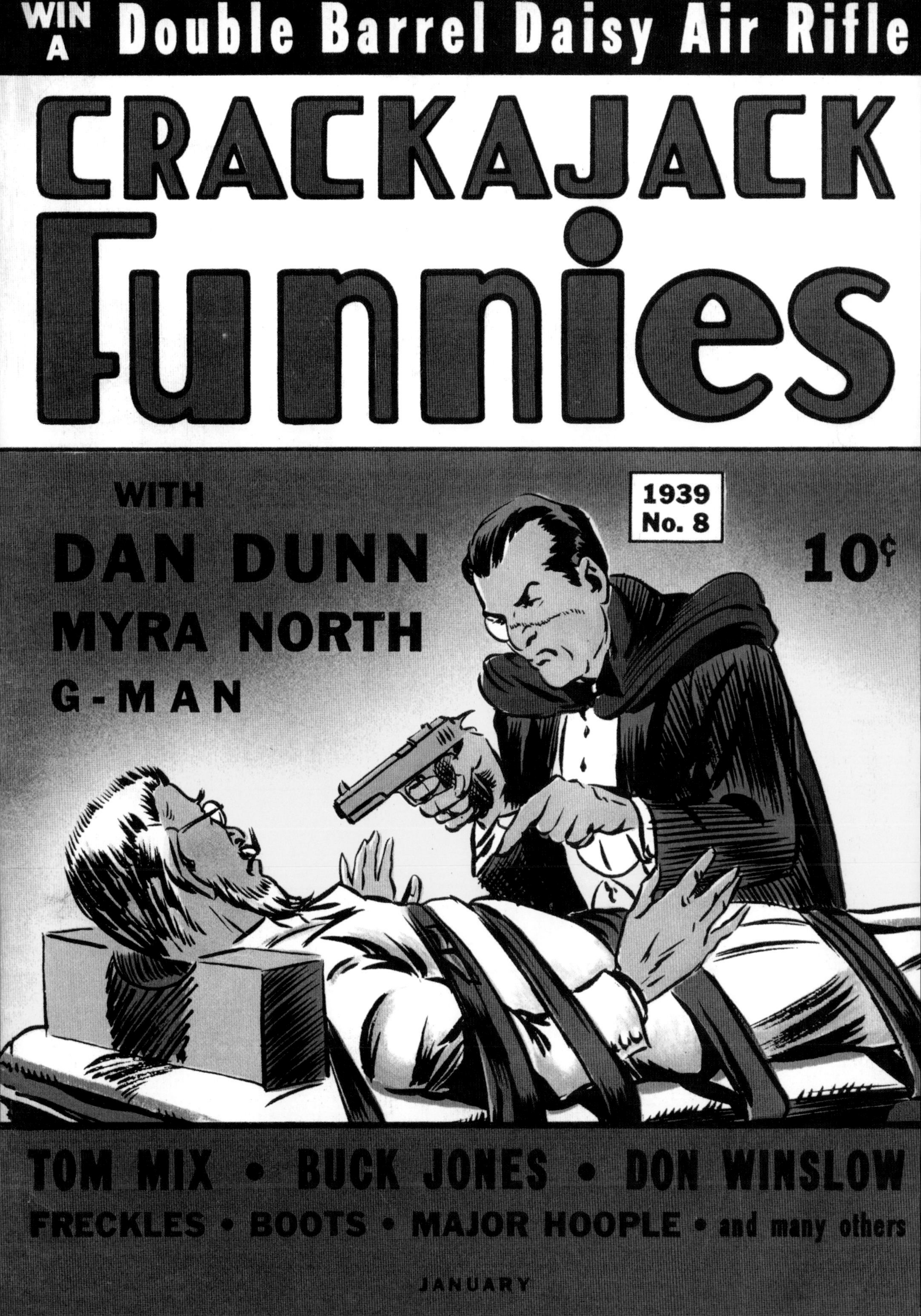
WIN A Double Barrel Daisy Air Rifle
CRACKAJACK Funnies
1939 No. 8
10¢
WITH
DAN DUNN
MYRA NORTH
G-MAN
TOM MIX • BUCK JONES • DON WINSLOW
FRECKLES • BOOTS • MAJOR HOOPLE • and many others
JANUARY

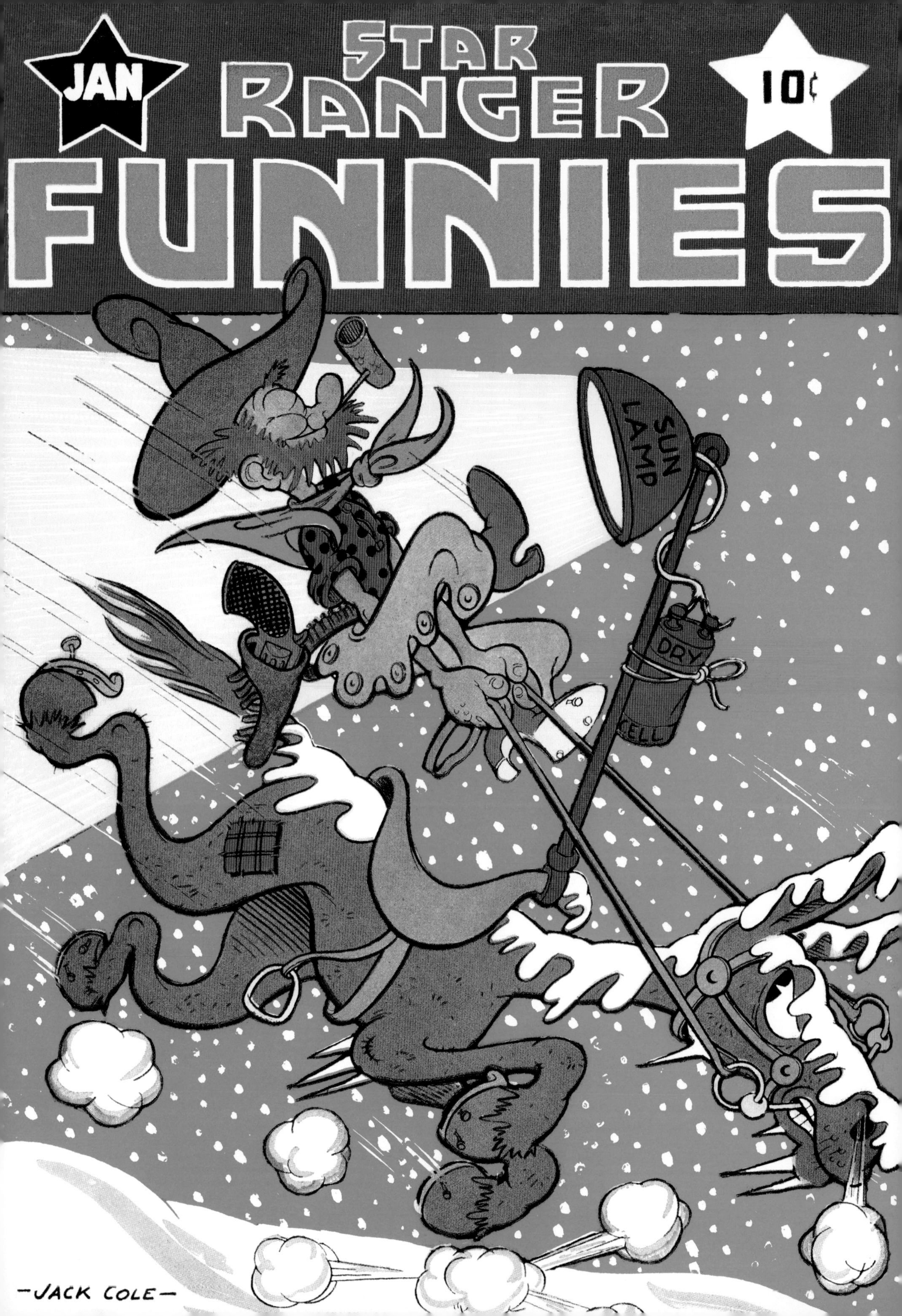
JAN
STAR RANGER
10¢
FUNNIES
SUN LAMP
DRY
CELL
-JACK COLE-

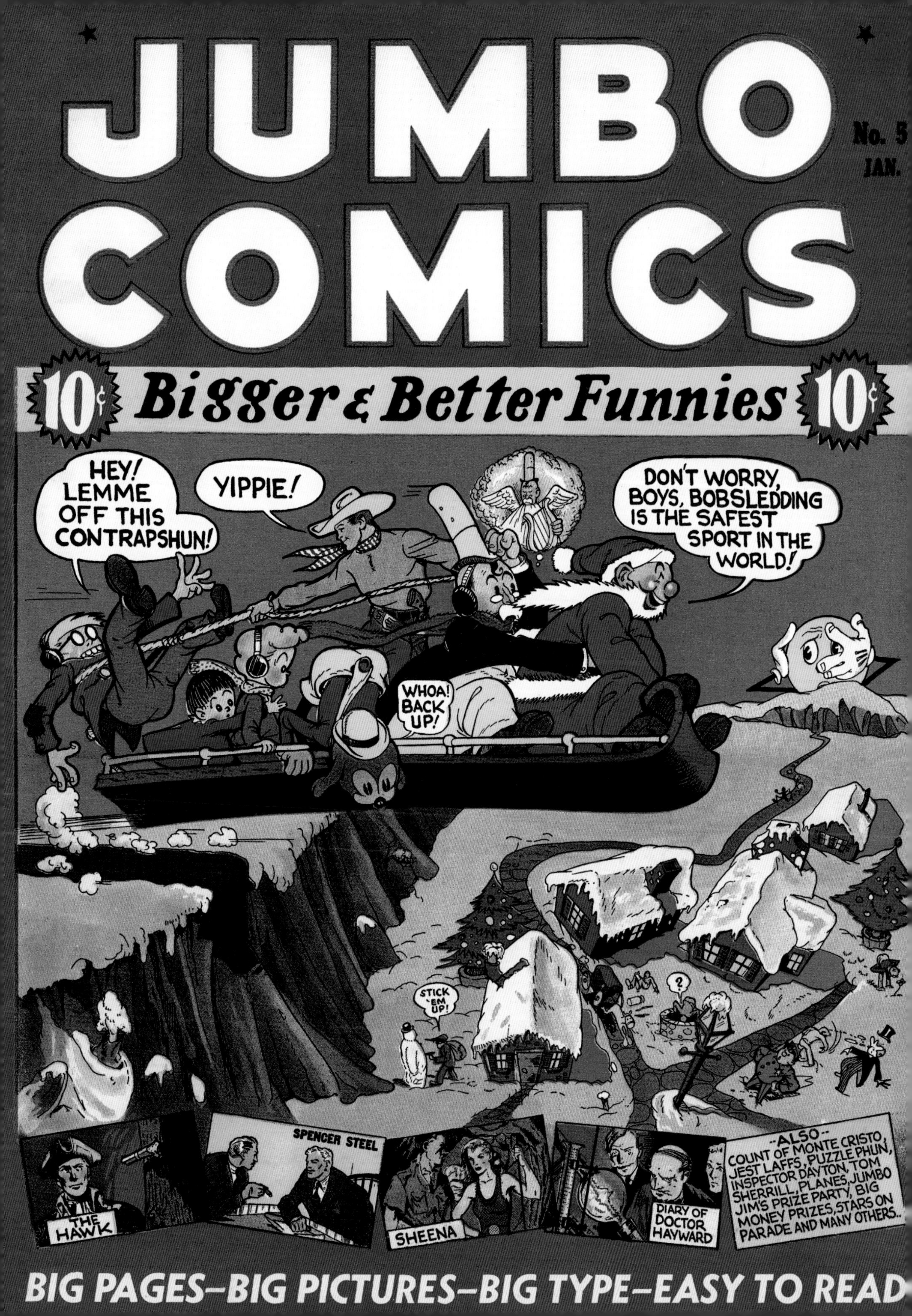
JUMBO COMICS
No. 5
JAN.
10¢
Bigger & Better Funnies
10¢
HEY! LEMME OFF THIS CONTRAPSHUN!
YIPPIE!
DON'T WORRY, BOYS, BOBSLEDDING IS THE SAFEST SPORT IN THE WORLD!
WHOA! BACK UP!
STICK 'EM UP!
?
THE HAWK
SPENCER STEEL
SHEENA
DIARY OF DOCTOR HAYWARD
--ALSO-- COUNT OF MONTE CRISTO, JEST LAFFS, PUZZLE PHUN, INSPECTOR DAYTON, TOM SHERRILL, PLANES, JUMBO JIM'S PRIZE PARTY, BIG MONEY PRIZES, STARS ON PARADE AND MANY OTHERS.
BIG PAGES—BIG PICTURES—BIG TYPE—EASY TO READ

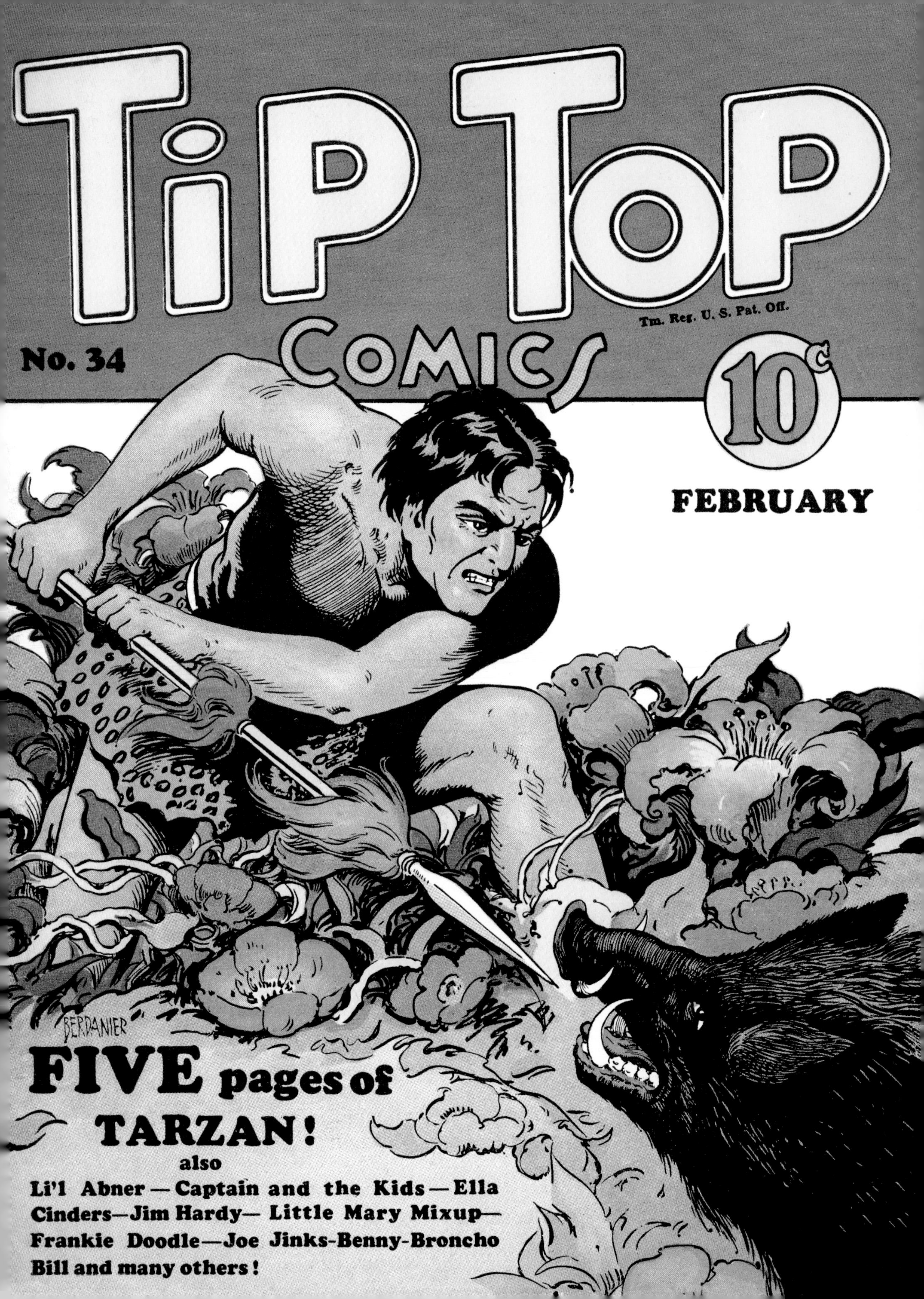

Tip Top
Comics
Tm. Reg. U. S. Pat. Off.
No. 34
10c
FEBRUARY
BERDANIER
FIVE pages of
TARZAN!
also
Li'l Abner — Captain and the Kids — Ella Cinders—Jim Hardy— Little Mary Mixup— Frankie Doodle—Joe Jinks-Benny-Broncho Bill and many others!

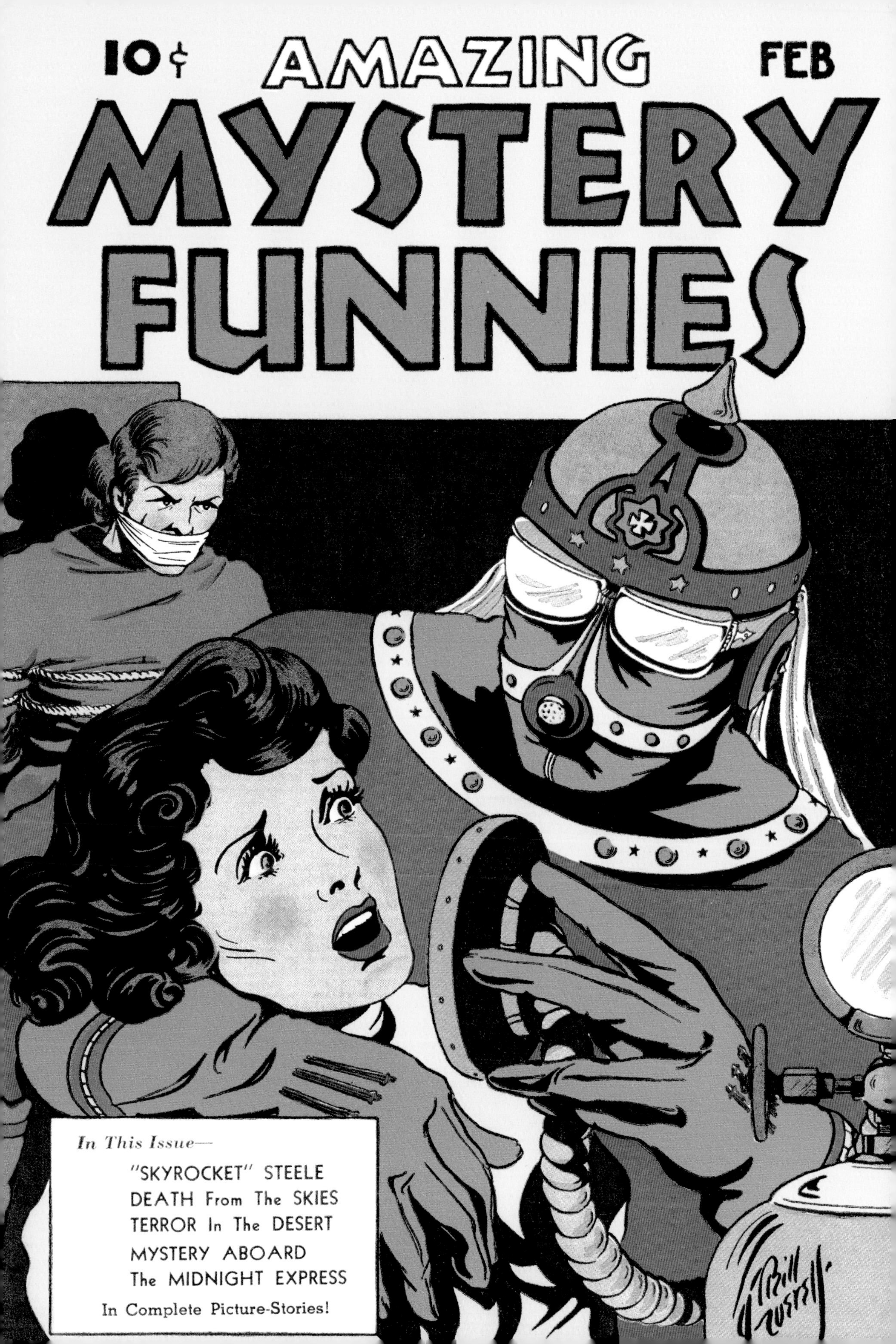
10¢
AMAZING
FEB
MYSTERY
FUNNIES
In This Issue—
"SKYROCKET" STEELE
DEATH From The SKIES
TERROR In The DESERT
MYSTERY ABOARD
The MIDNIGHT EXPRESS
In Complete Picture-Stories!

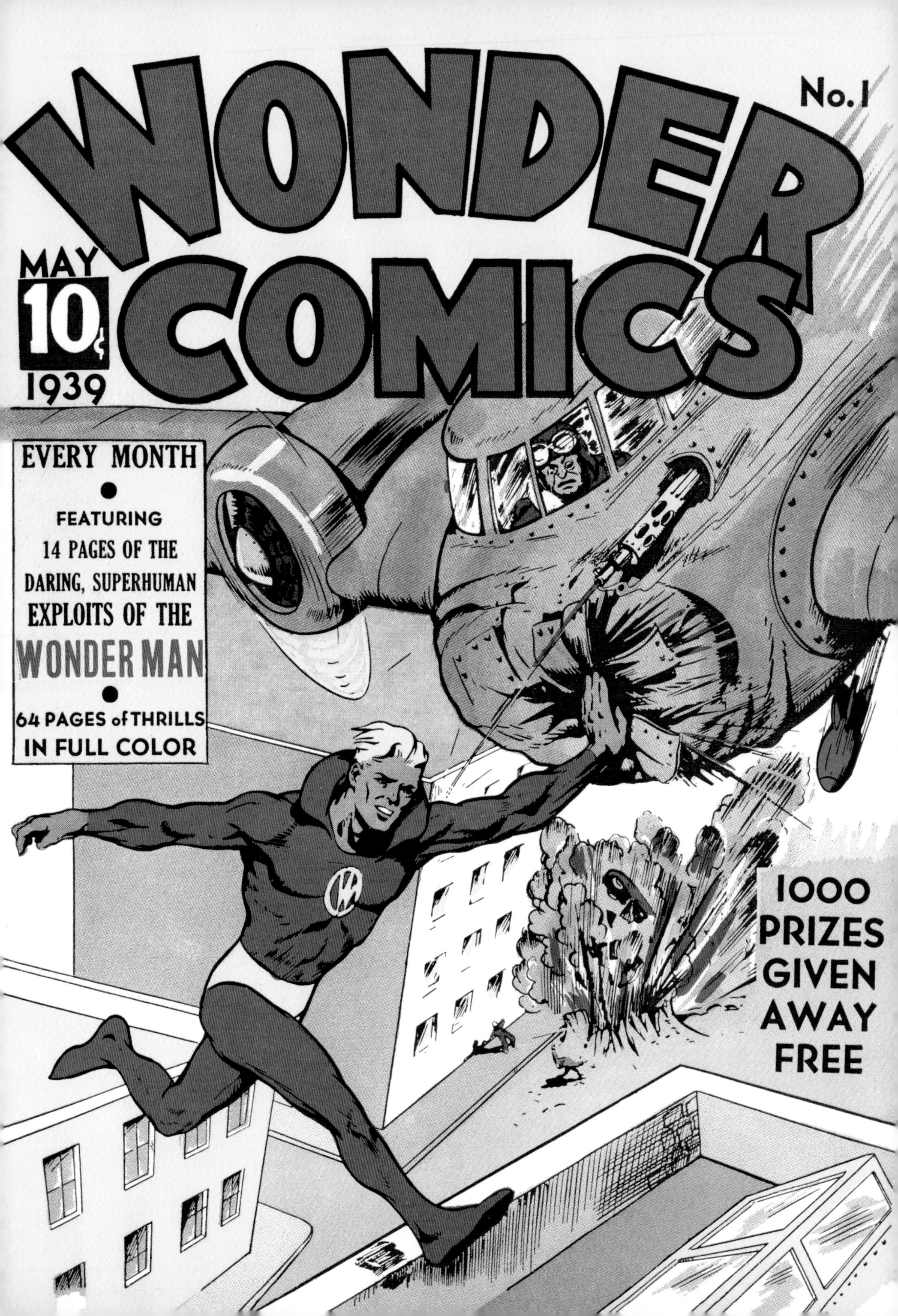
WONDER COMICS
No. 1
MAY
10¢
1939
EVERY MONTH
FEATURING
14 PAGES OF THE
DARING, SUPERHUMAN
EXPLOITS OF THE
WONDER MAN
64 PAGES of THRILLS
IN FULL COLOR
1000
PRIZES
GIVEN
AWAY
FREE

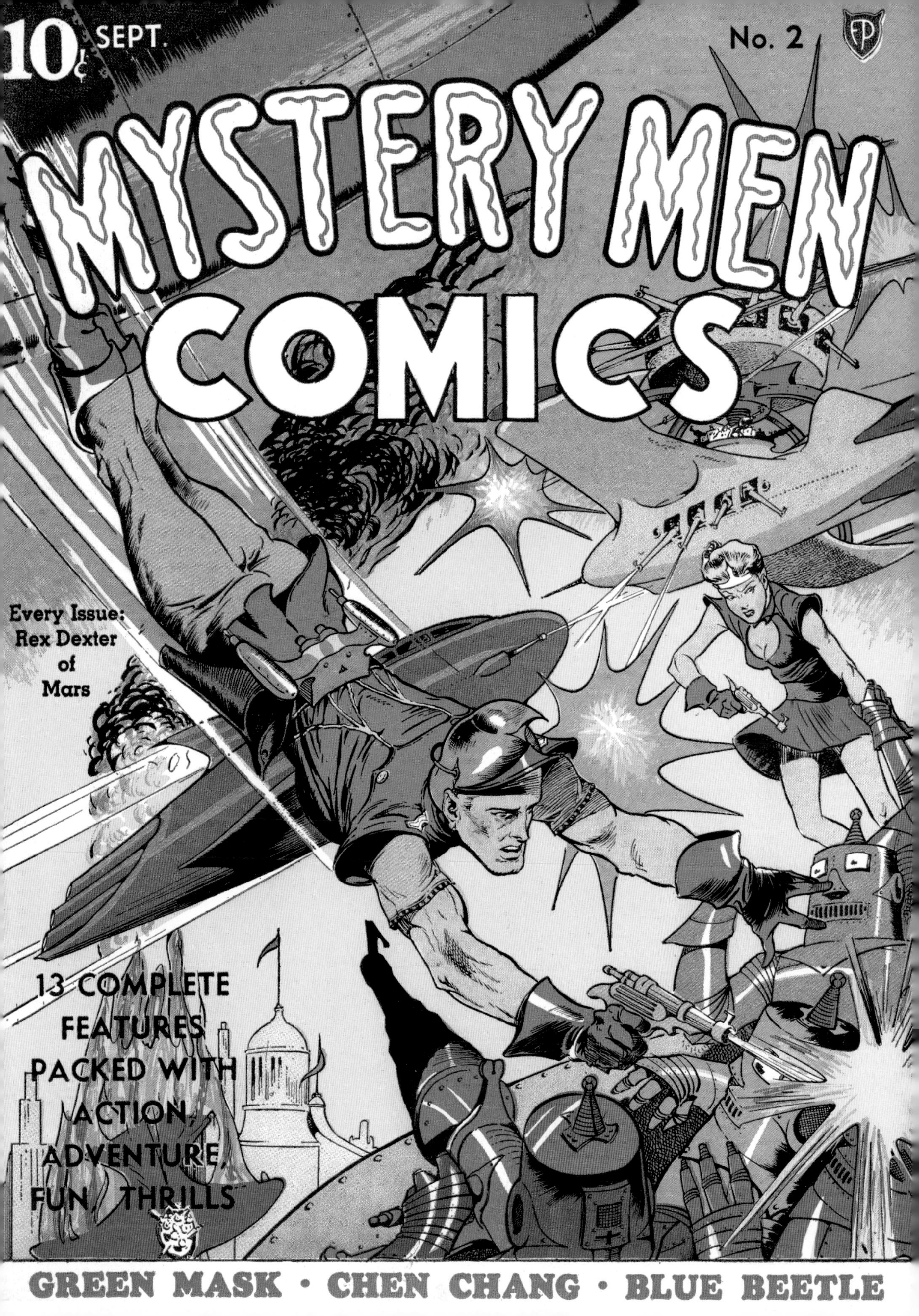

10¢
SEPT.
No. 2
FP
MYSTERY MEN
COMICS
Every Issue:
Rex Dexter
of
Mars
13 COMPLETE
FEATURES
PACKED WITH
ACTION
ADVENTURE
FUN THRILLS
GREEN MASK · CHEN CHANG · BLUE BEETLE

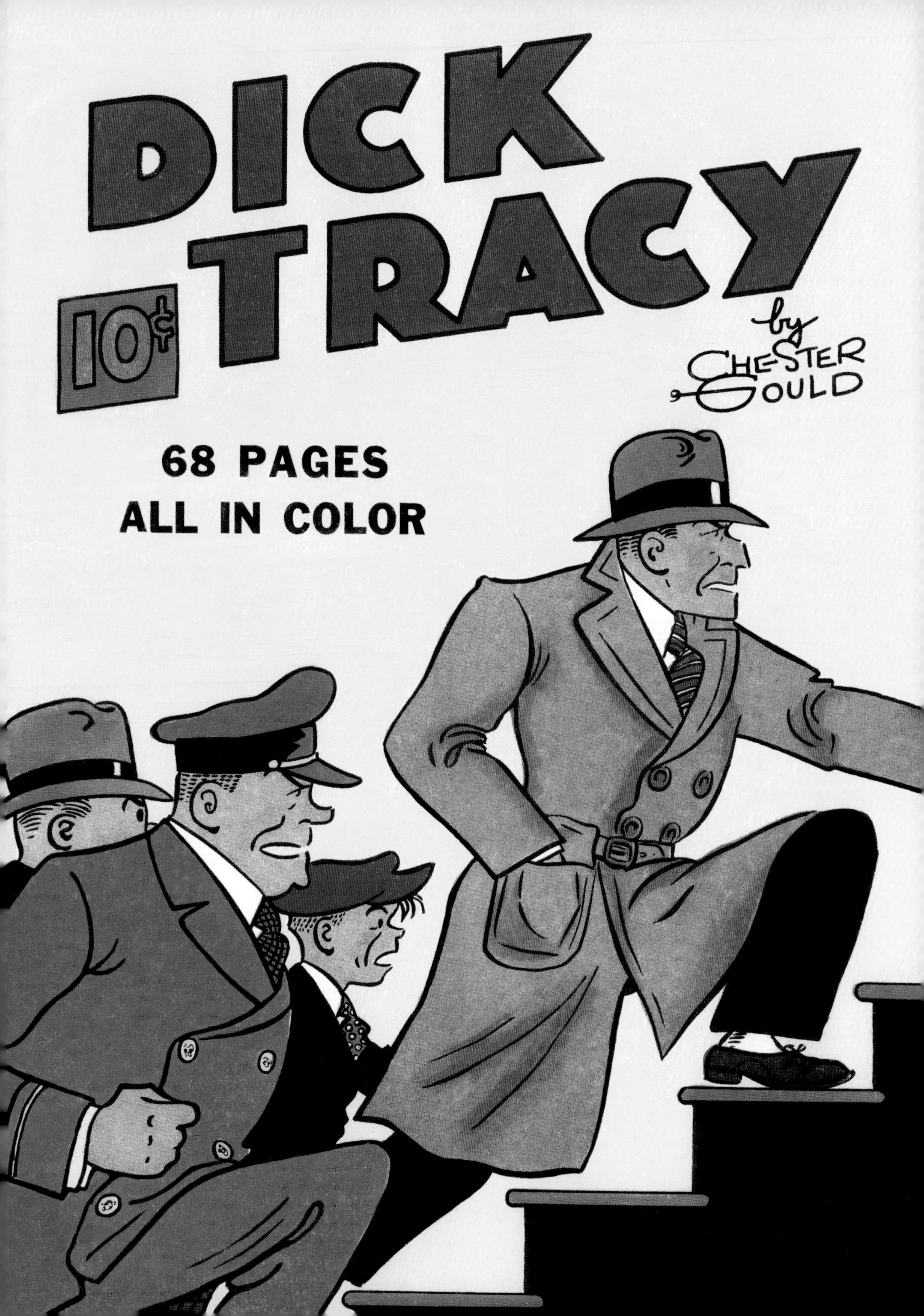
DICK TRACY
10¢
by CHESTER GOULD
68 PAGES
ALL IN COLOR

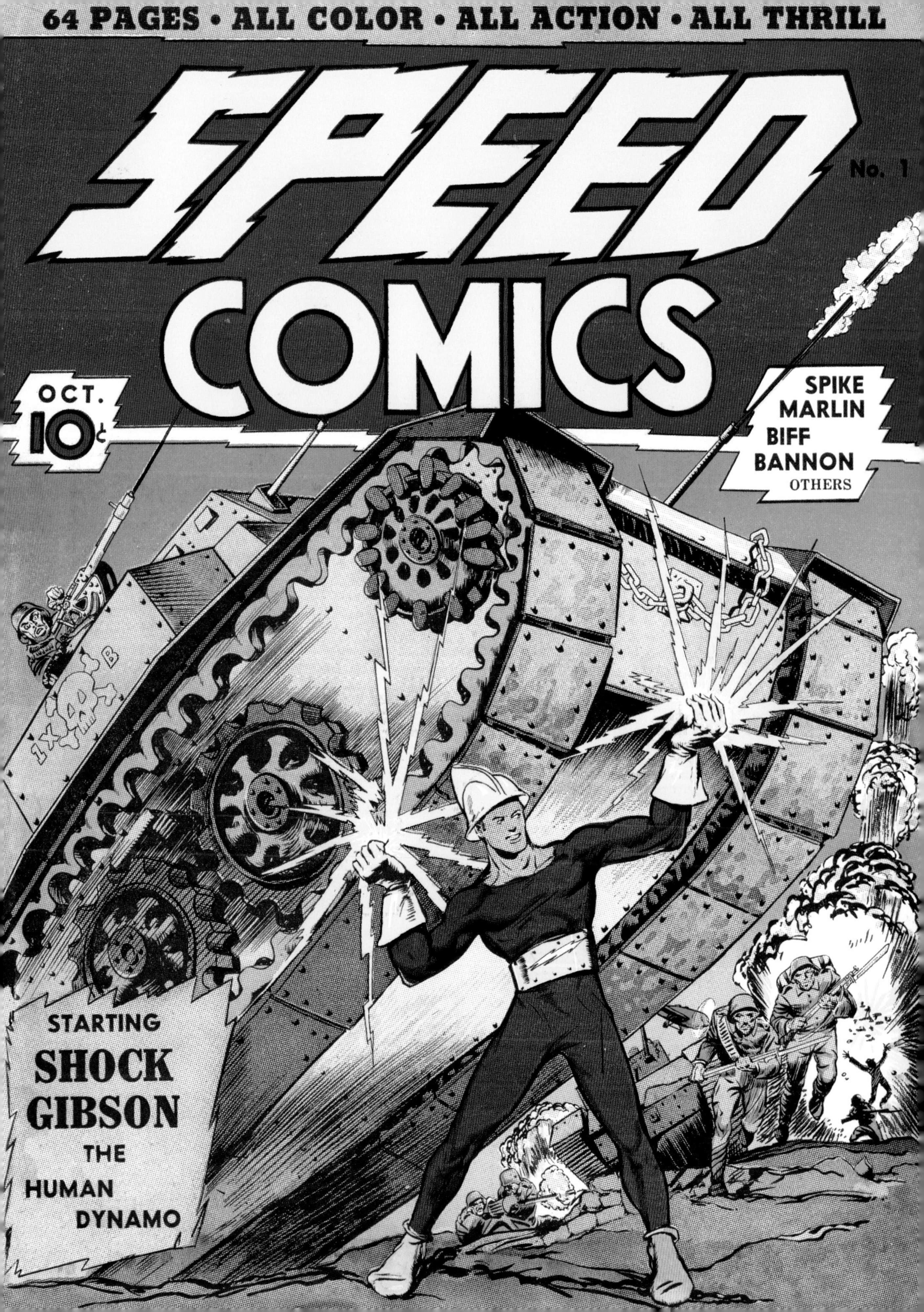
64 PAGES • ALL COLOR • ALL ACTION • ALL THRILL
SPEED COMICS
No. 1
OCT.
10¢
SPIKE MARLIN
BIFF BANNON
OTHERS
STARTING
SHOCK GIBSON
THE HUMAN DYNAMO

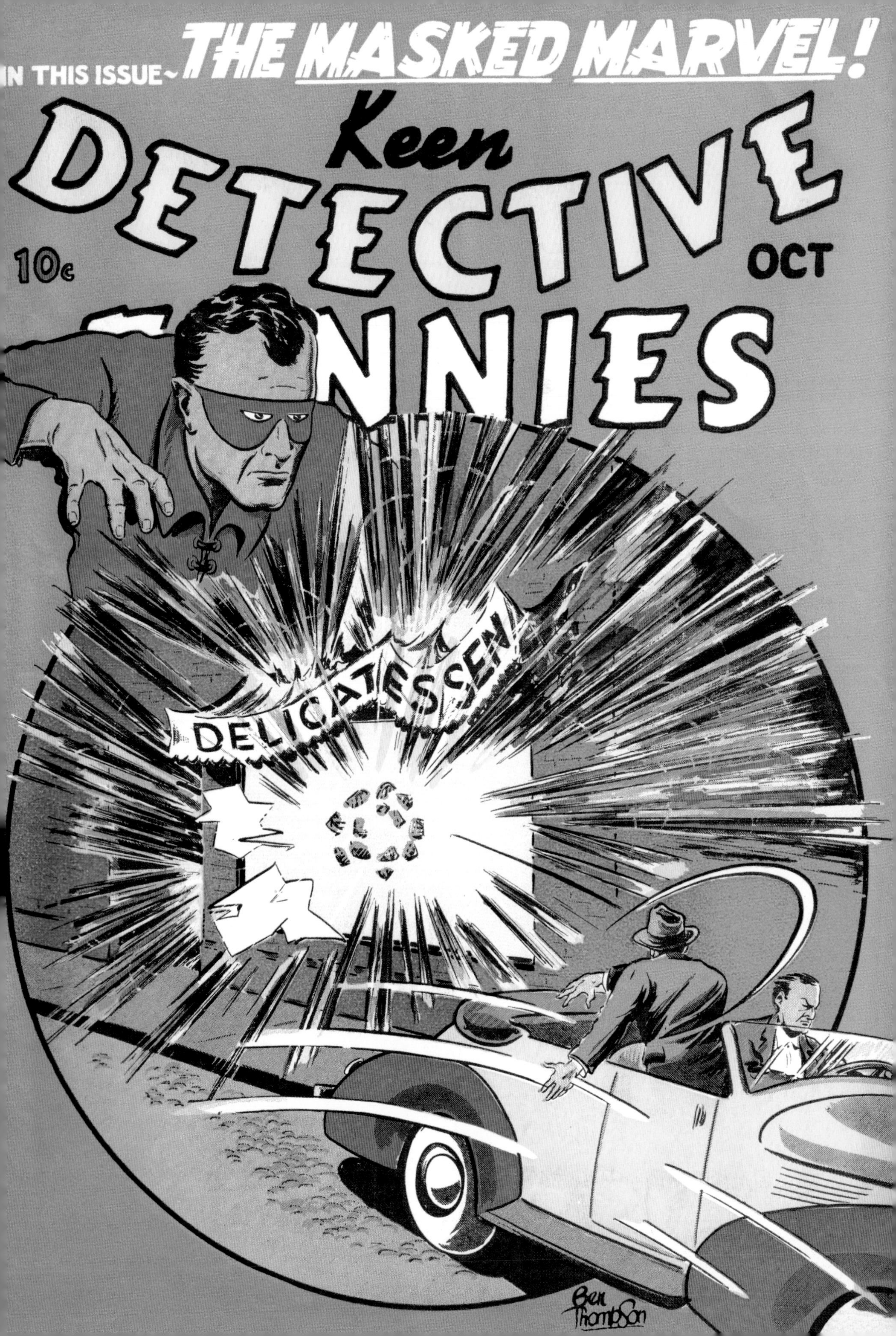

IN THIS ISSUE~ THE MASKED MARVEL!
Keen
DETECTIVE
10¢
OCT
NNIES
DELICATESSEN
Ben Thompson

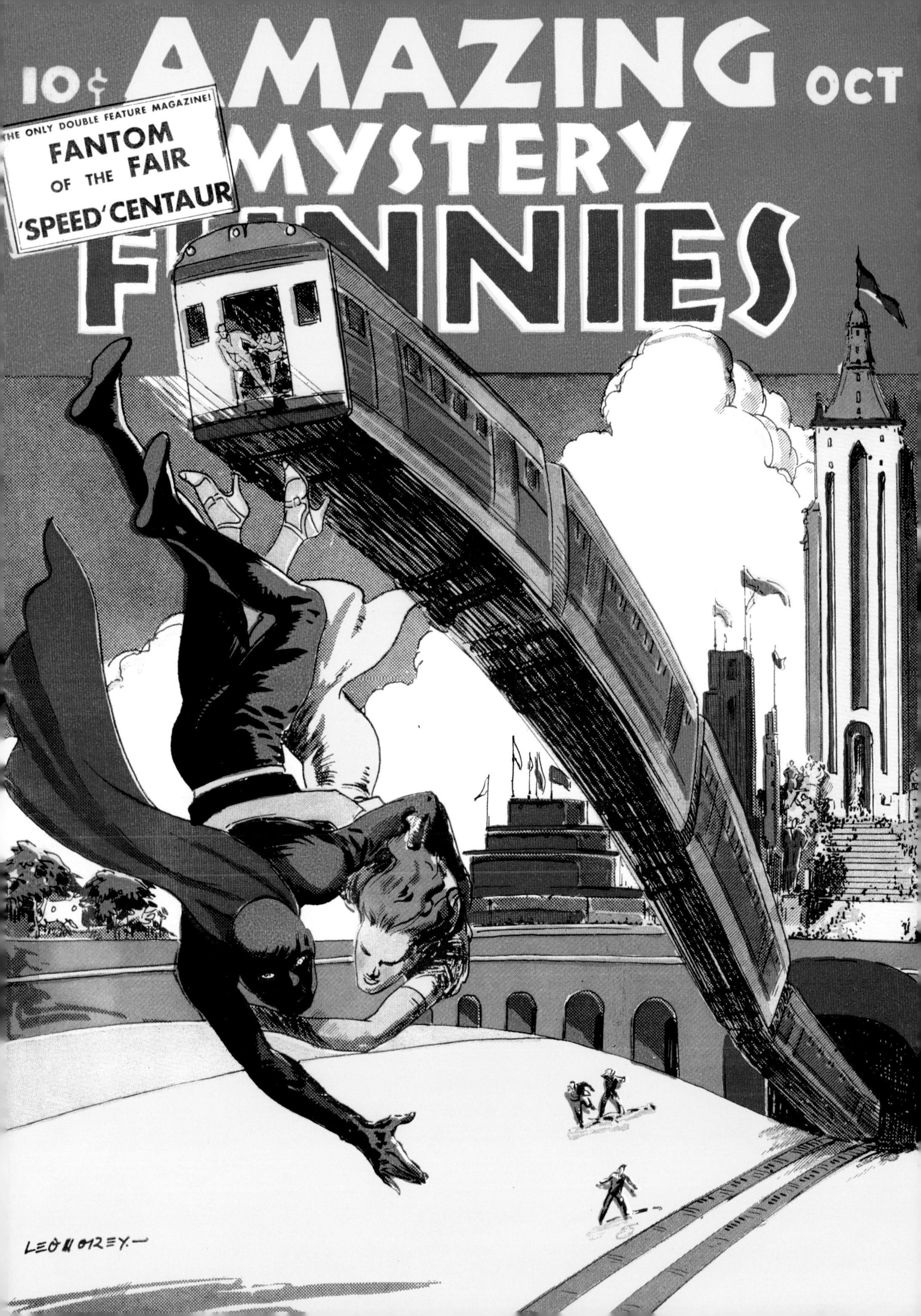

10¢
AMAZING
OCT
MYSTERY
FUNNIES
THE ONLY DOUBLE FEATURE MAGAZINE!
FANTOM OF THE FAIR
'SPEED' CENTAUR
LEON MOREY

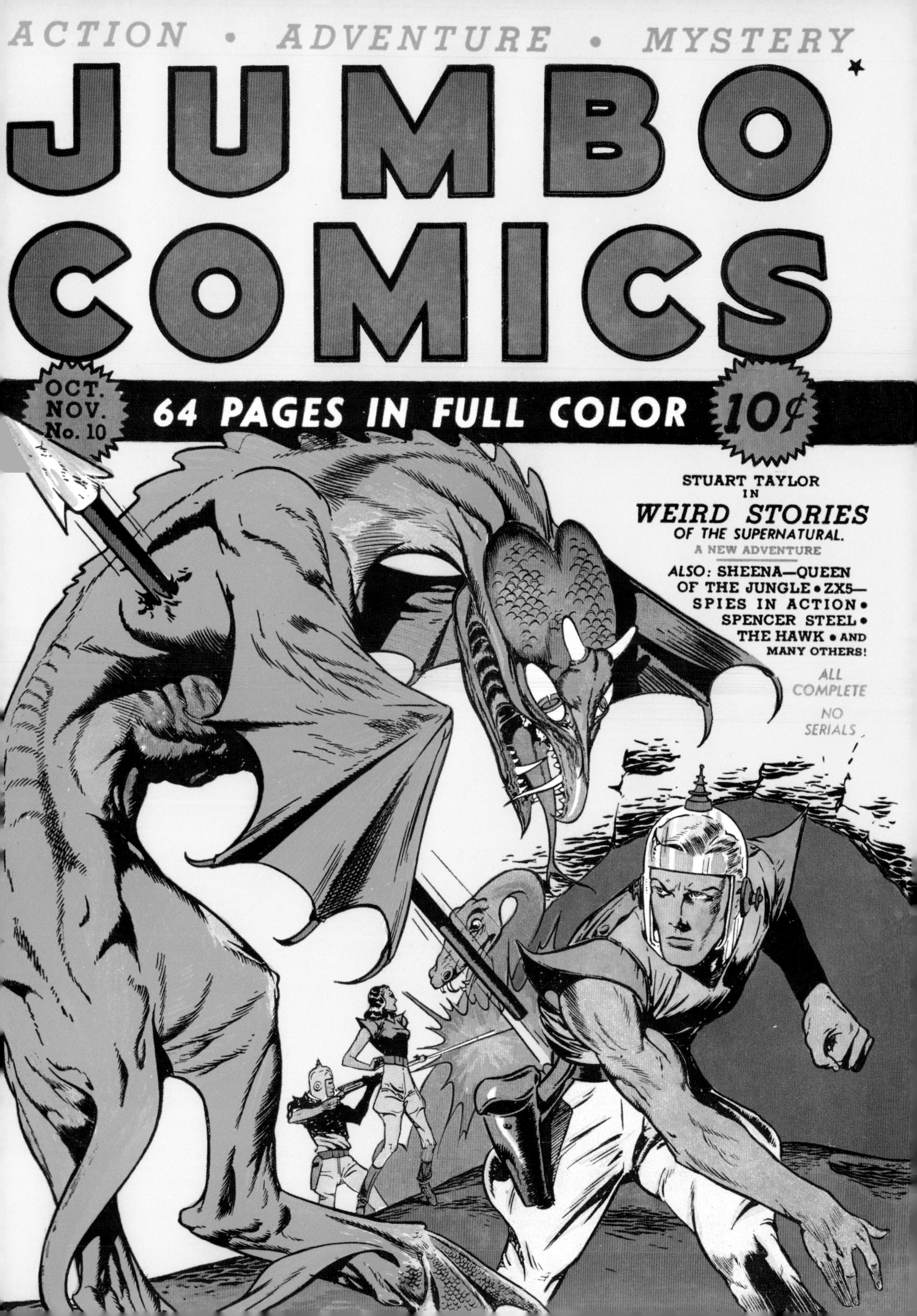
ACTION • ADVENTURE • MYSTERY
JUMBO COMICS
OCT. NOV. No. 10
64 PAGES IN FULL COLOR
10¢
STUART TAYLOR IN
WEIRD STORIES
OF THE SUPERNATURAL.
A NEW ADVENTURE
ALSO: SHEENA—QUEEN OF THE JUNGLE • ZX5—SPIES IN ACTION • SPENCER STEEL • THE HAWK • AND MANY OTHERS!
ALL COMPLETE
NO SERIALS

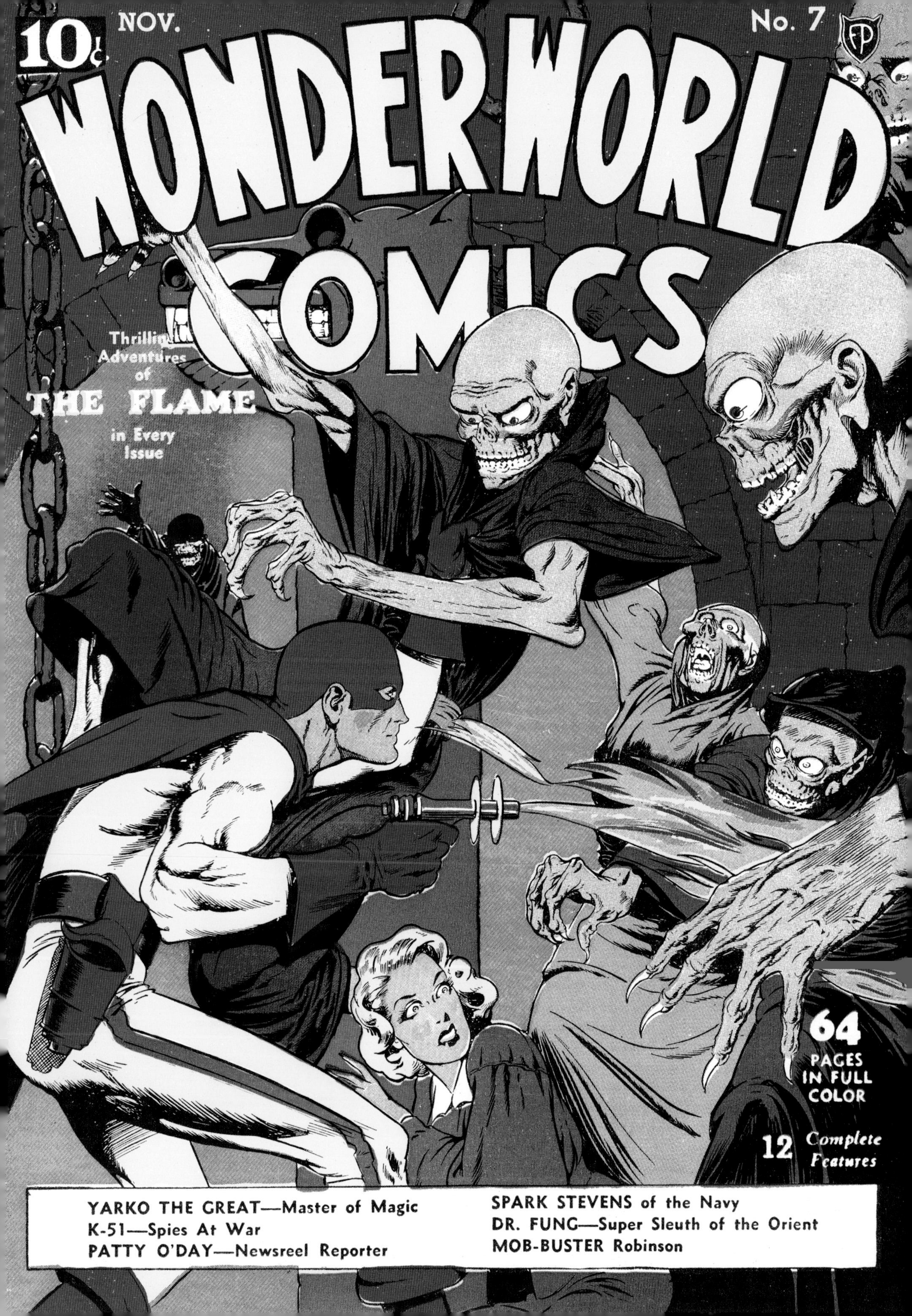

10¢
NOV.
No. 7
FP
WONDER WORLD COMICS
Thrilling Adventures of THE FLAME in Every Issue
64 PAGES IN FULL COLOR
12 Complete Features
YARKO THE GREAT—Master of Magic
K-51—Spies At War
PATTY O'DAY—Newsreel Reporter
SPARK STEVENS of the Navy
DR. FUNG—Super Sleuth of the Orient
MOB-BUSTER Robinson

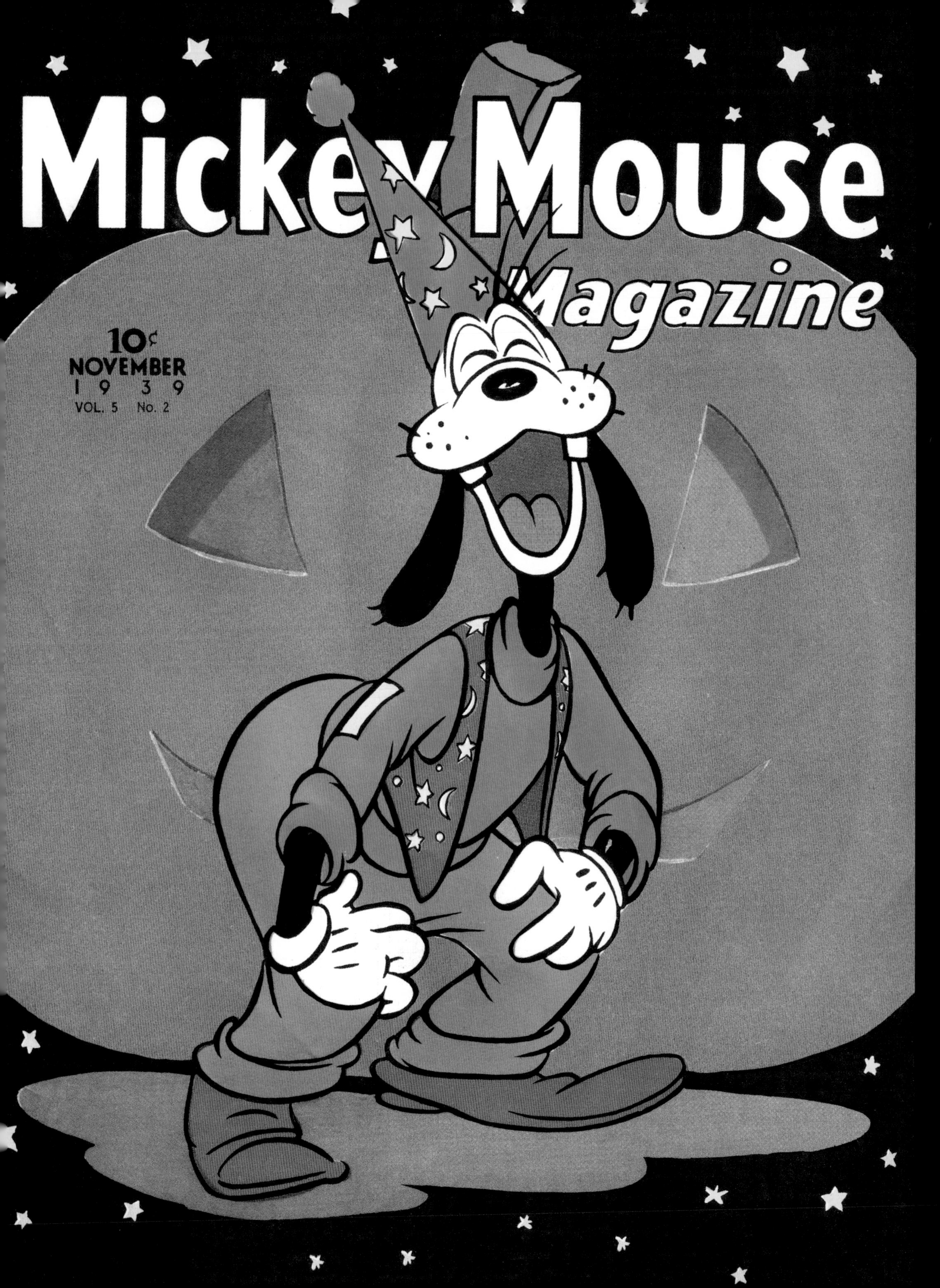
Mickey Mouse
Magazine
10¢
NOVEMBER
1 9 3 9
VOL. 5 No. 2

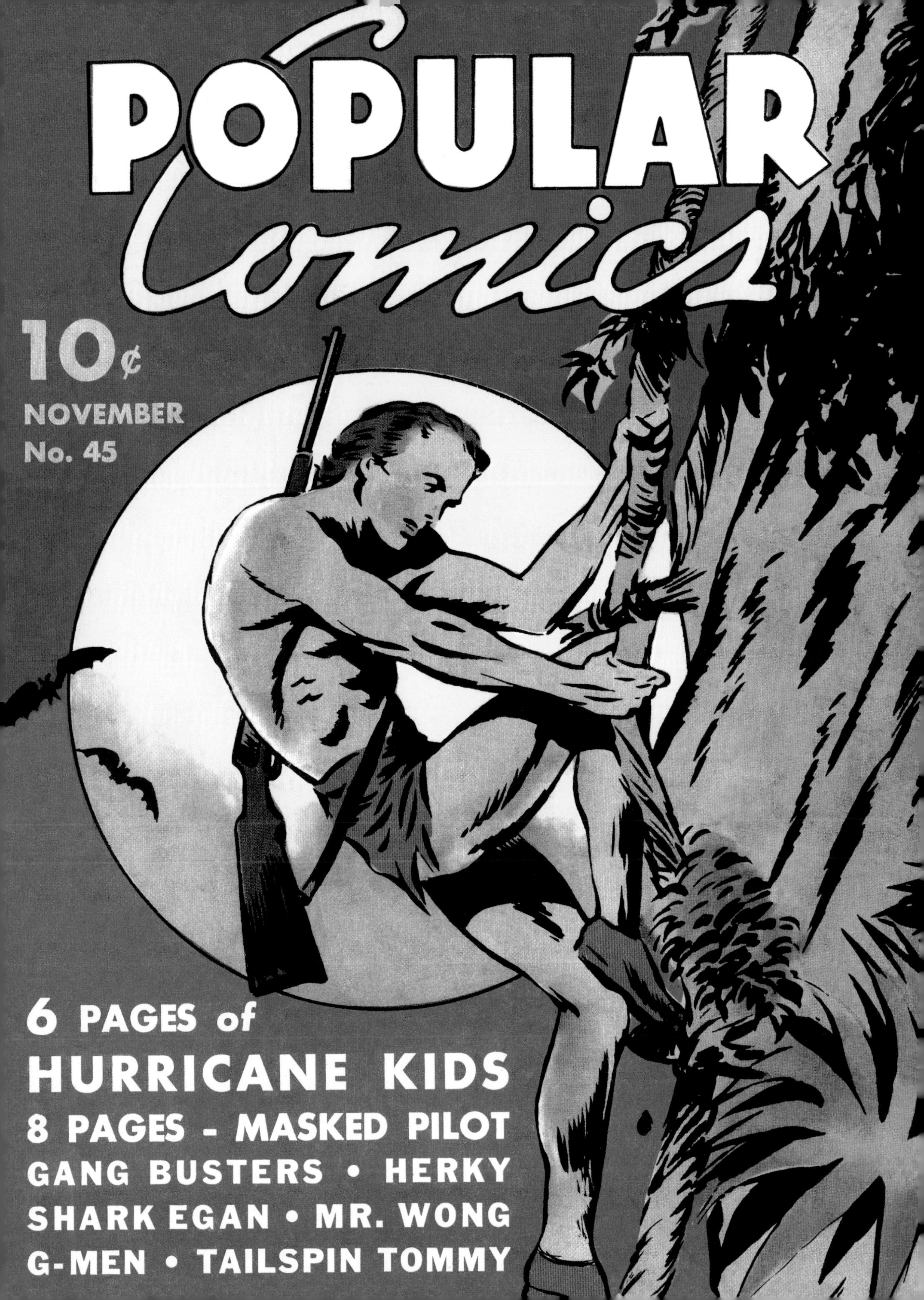
POPULAR
Comics
10¢
NOVEMBER
No. 45
6 PAGES of
HURRICANE KIDS
8 PAGES - MASKED PILOT
GANG BUSTERS • HERKY
SHARK EGAN • MR. WONG
G-MEN • TAILSPIN TOMMY

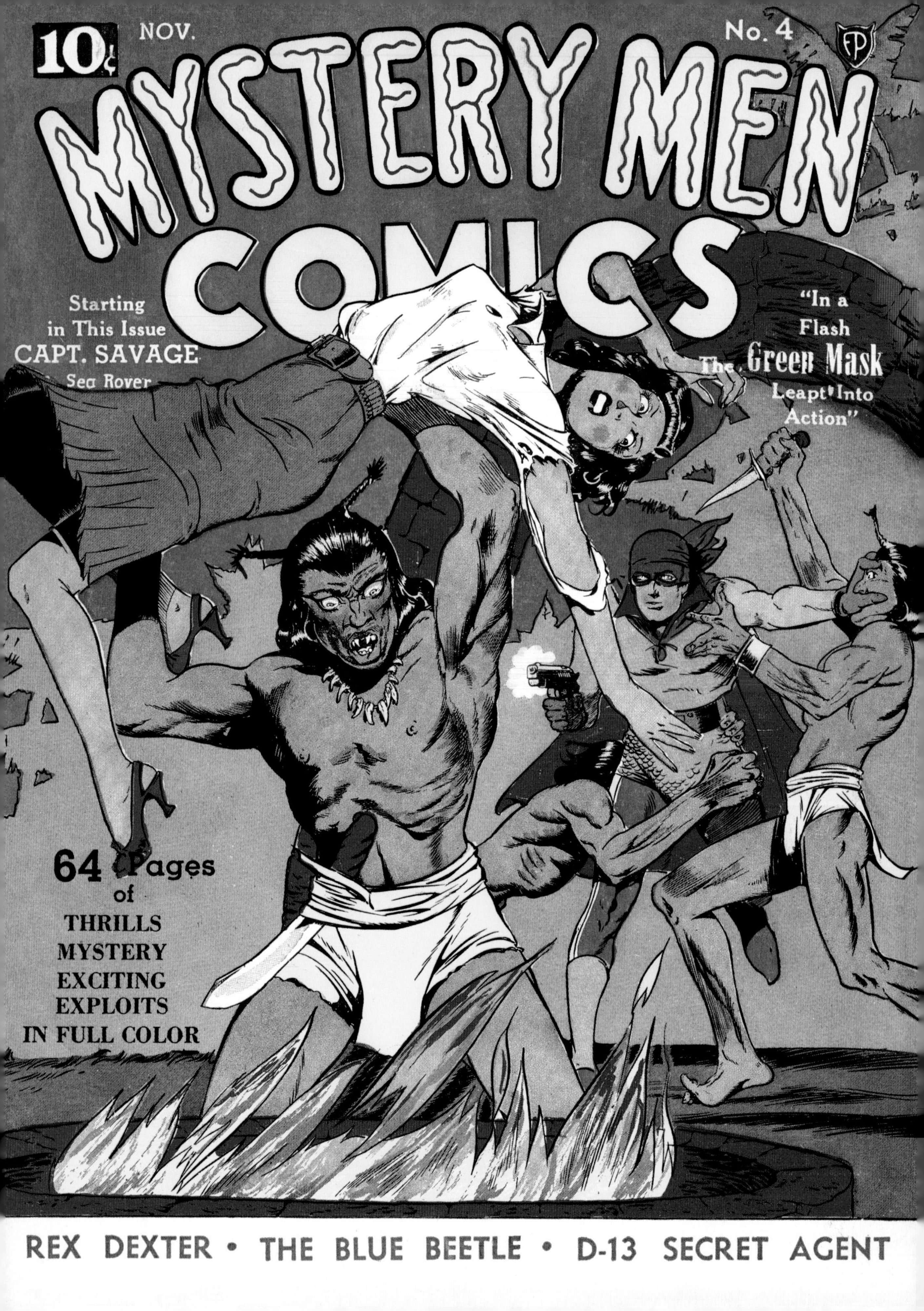
10¢
NOV.
No. 4
MYSTERY MEN
COMICS
Starting in This Issue
CAPT. SAVAGE
Sea Rover
"In a Flash The Green Mask Leapt Into Action"
64 Pages of
THRILLS
MYSTERY
EXCITING
EXPLOITS
IN FULL COLOR
REX DEXTER • THE BLUE BEETLE • D-13 SECRET AGENT

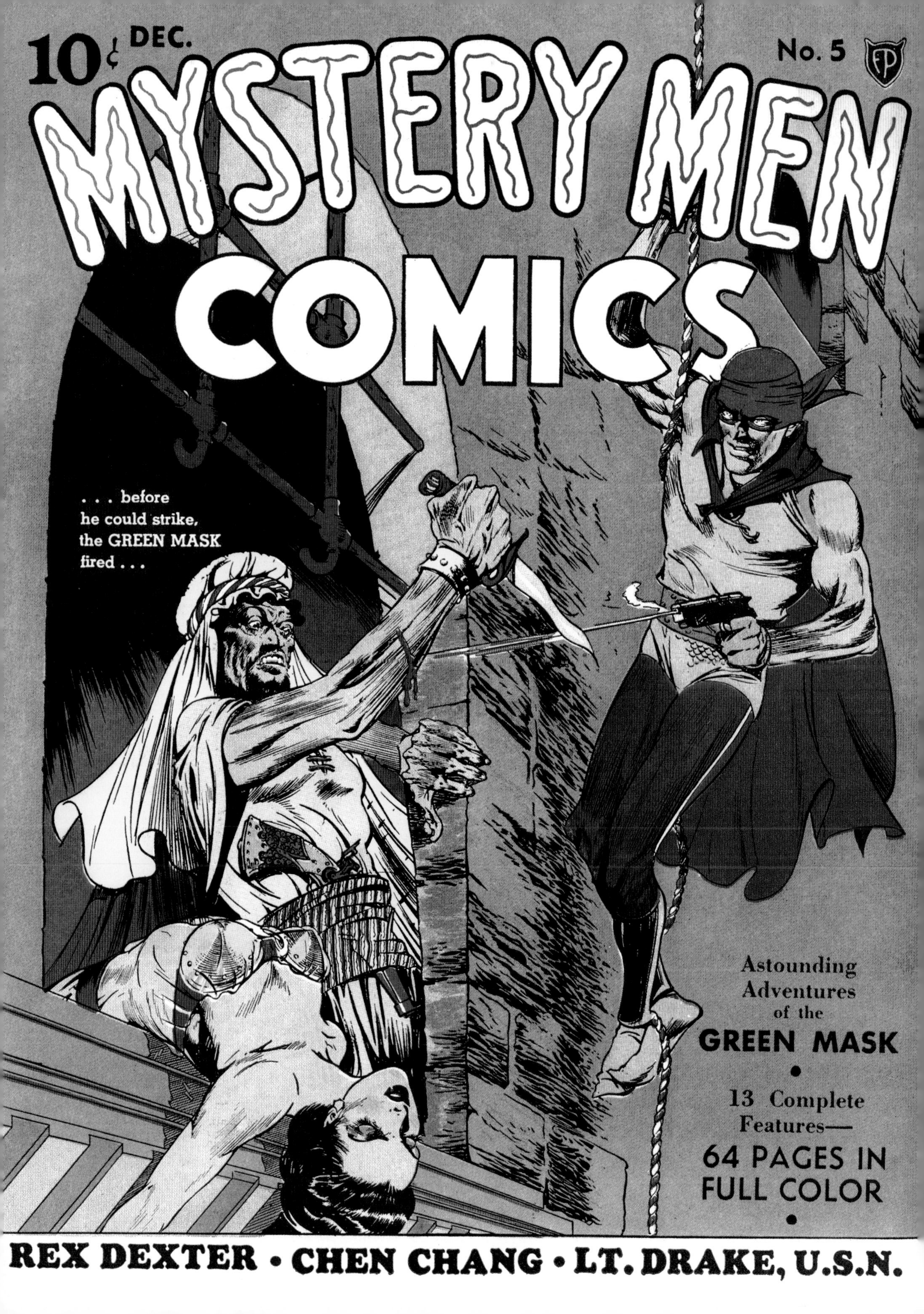
10¢ DEC.
No. 5
FP
MYSTERY MEN COMICS
. . . before he could strike, the GREEN MASK fired . . .
Astounding Adventures of the GREEN MASK
13 Complete Features—
64 PAGES IN FULL COLOR
REX DEXTER • CHEN CHANG • LT. DRAKE, U.S.N.

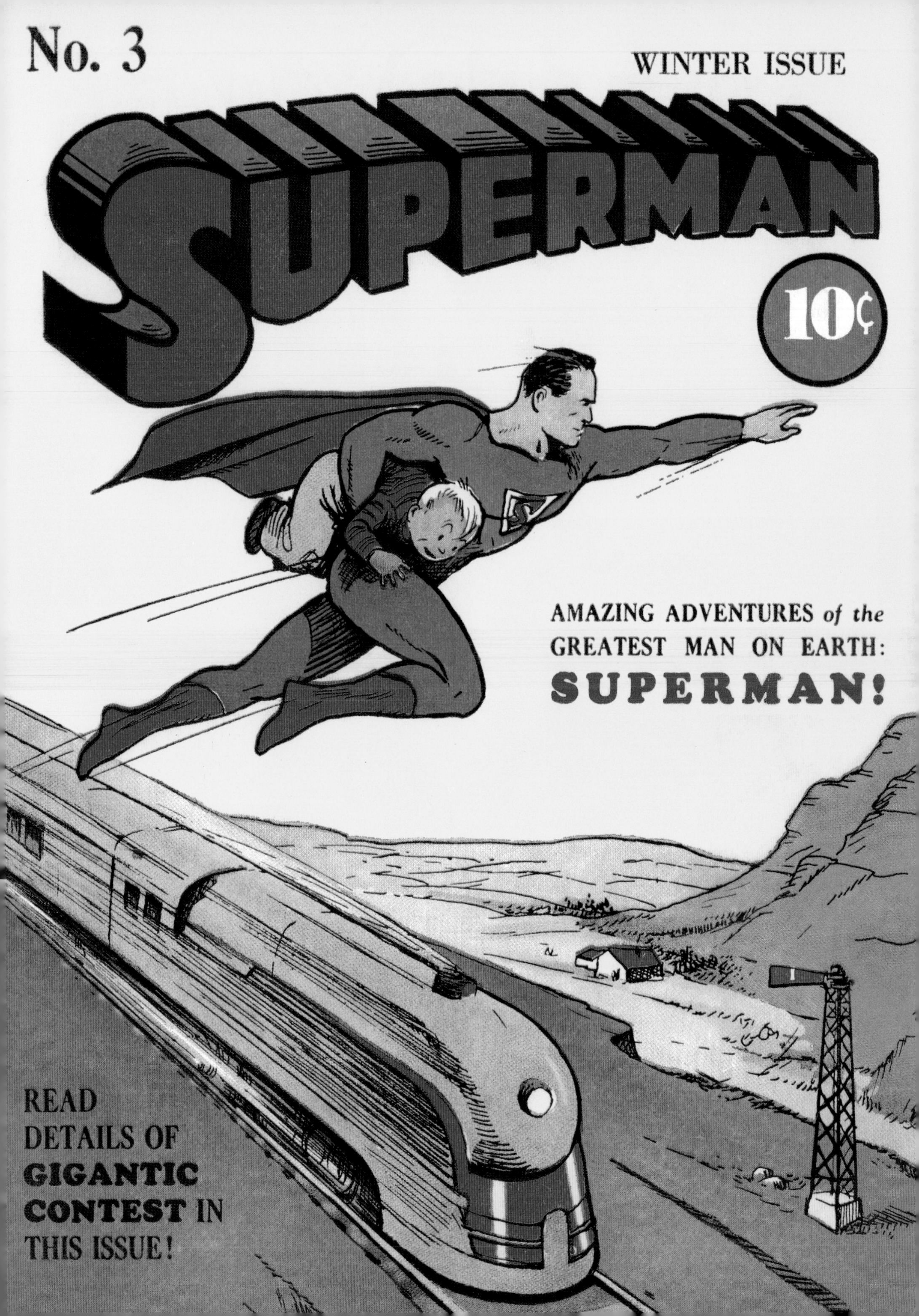
No. 3
WINTER ISSUE
SUPERMAN
10¢
AMAZING ADVENTURES of the GREATEST MAN ON EARTH: SUPERMAN!
READ DETAILS OF GIGANTIC CONTEST IN THIS ISSUE!

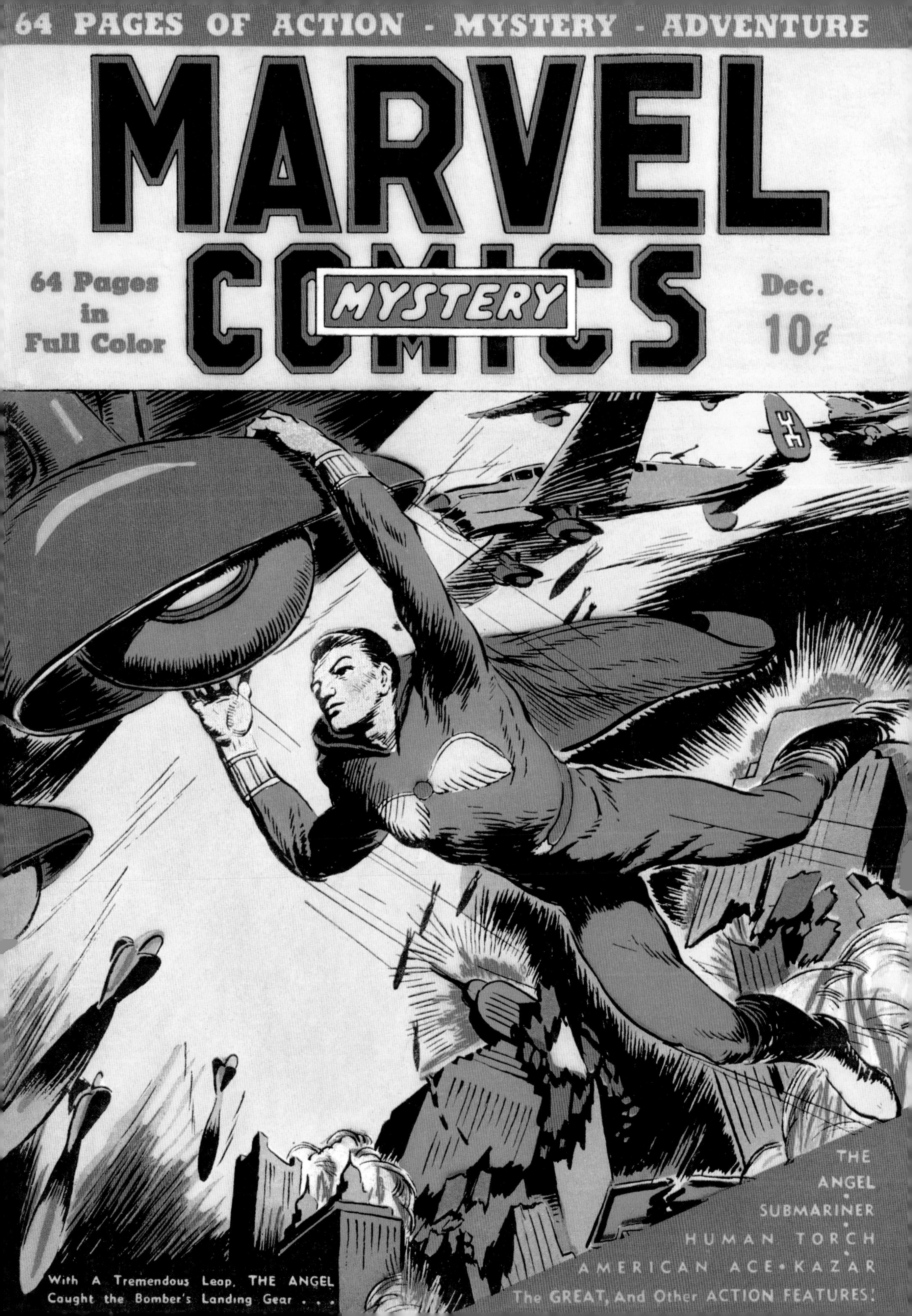
64 PAGES OF ACTION - MYSTERY - ADVENTURE
MARVEL MYSTERY COMICS
64 Pages in Full Color
Dec.
10¢
With A Tremendous Leap, THE ANGEL Caught the Bomber's Landing Gear . . .
THE ANGEL • SUBMARINER • HUMAN TORCH • AMERICAN ACE • KAZAR The GREAT, And Other ACTION FEATURES!

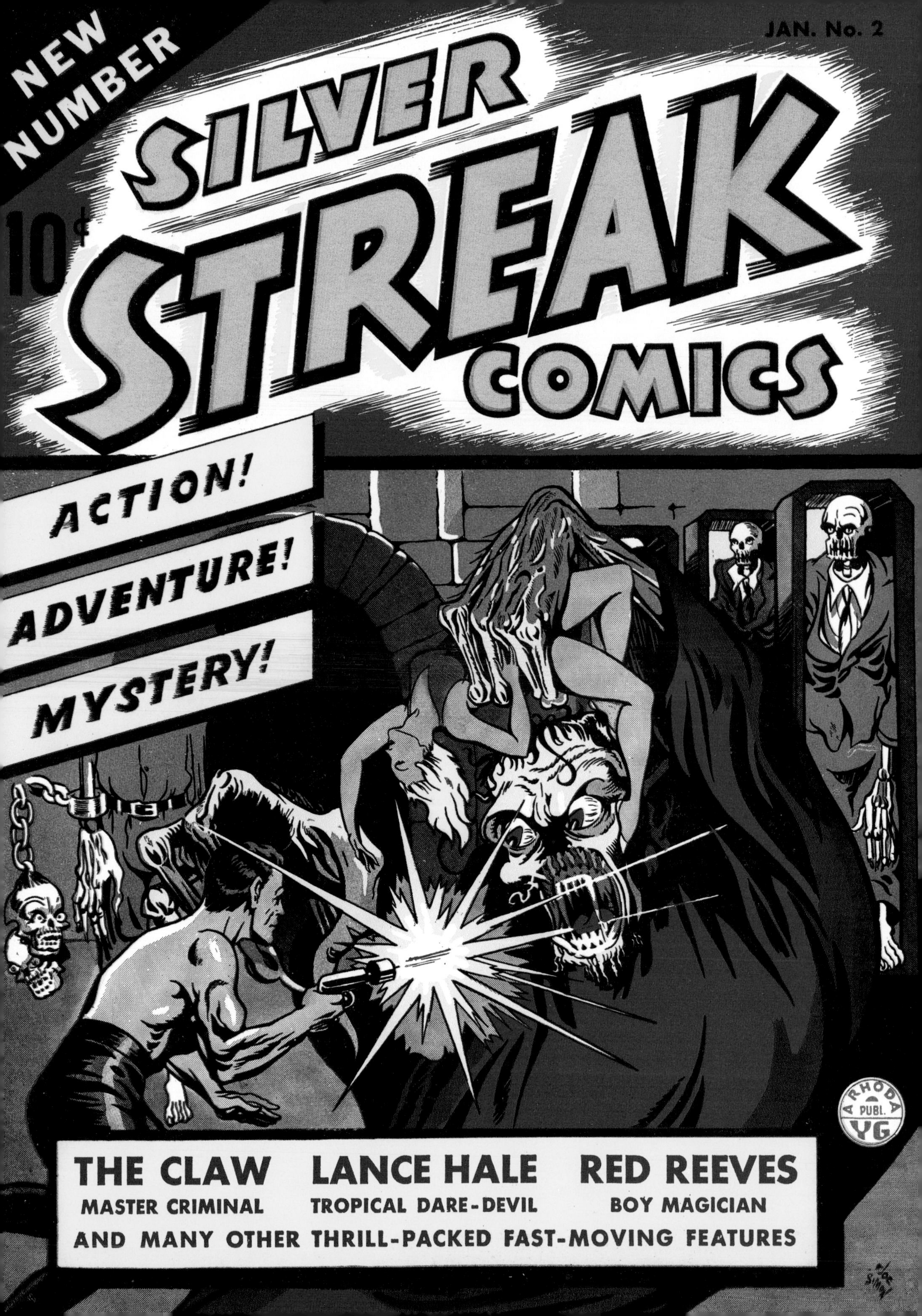
NEW NUMBER
JAN. No. 2
10¢
SILVER STREAK COMICS
ACTION!
ADVENTURE!
MYSTERY!
ARHODA PUBL. YG
THE CLAW
MASTER CRIMINAL
LANCE HALE
TROPICAL DARE-DEVIL
RED REEVES
BOY MAGICIAN
AND MANY OTHER THRILL-PACKED FAST-MOVING FEATURES

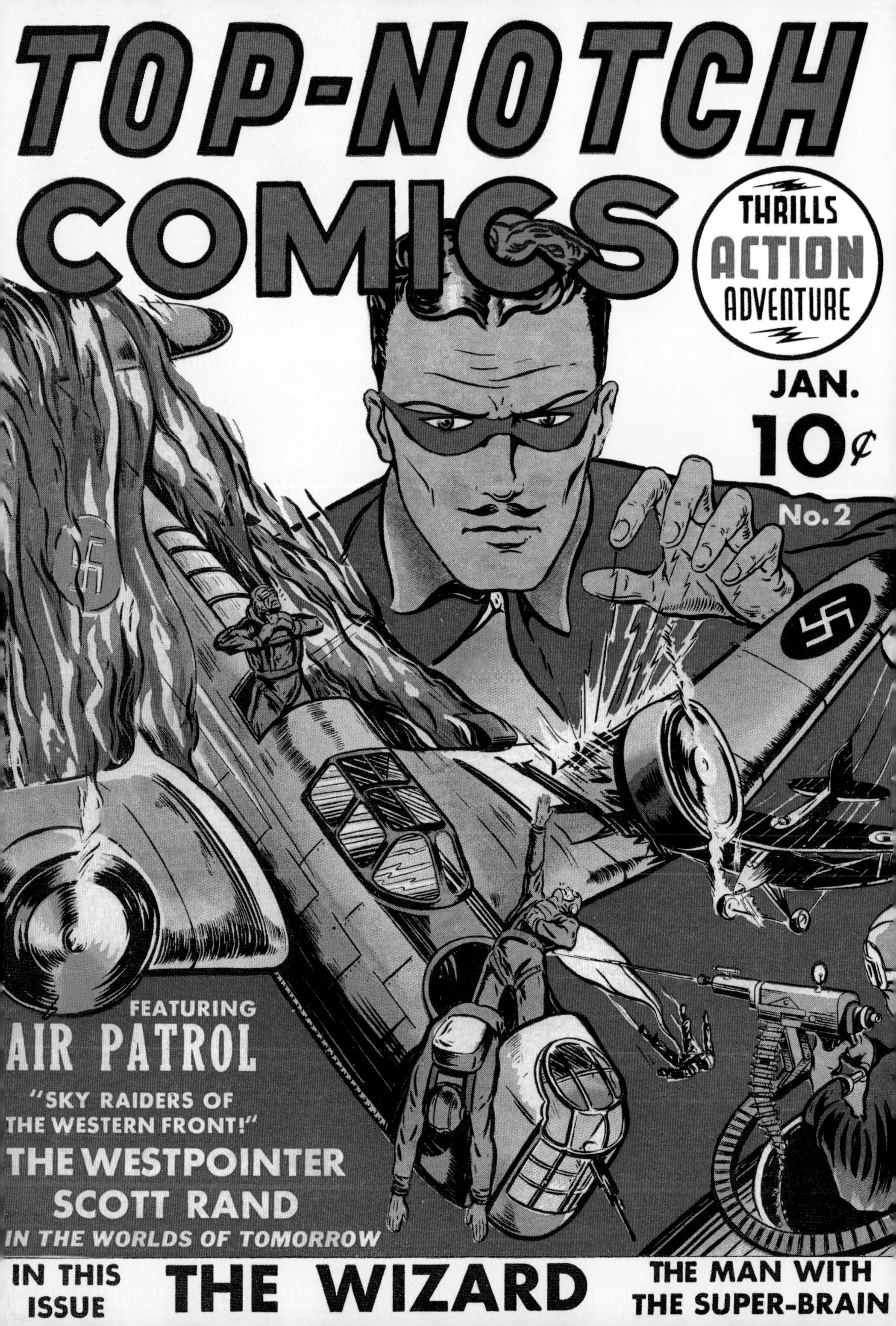
TOP-NOTCH COMICS
THRILLS ACTION ADVENTURE
JAN.
10¢
No. 2
FEATURING
AIR PATROL
"SKY RAIDERS OF THE WESTERN FRONT!"
THE WESTPOINTER
SCOTT RAND
IN THE WORLDS OF TOMORROW
IN THIS ISSUE
THE WIZARD
THE MAN WITH THE SUPER-BRAIN

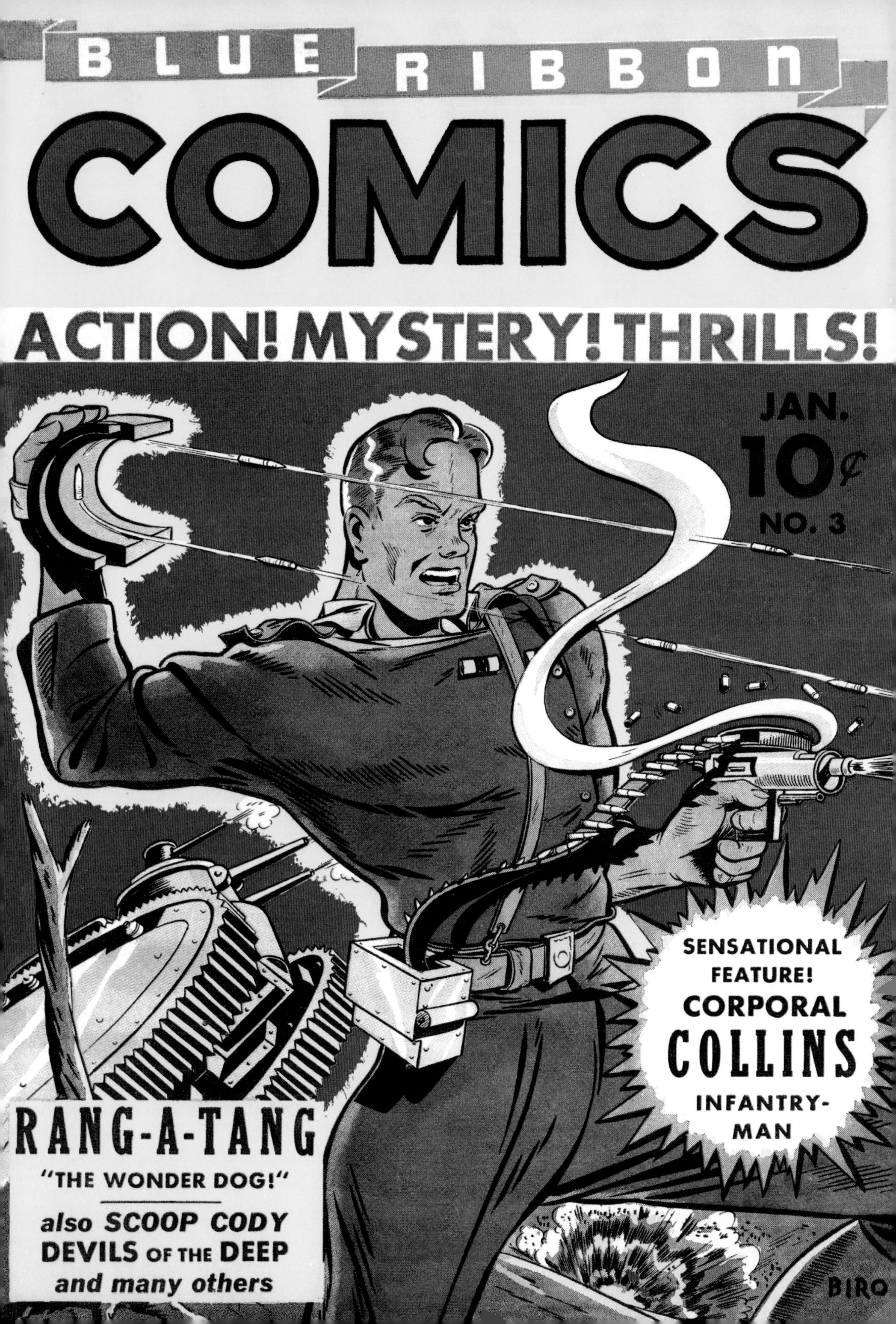

BLUE RIBBON
COMICS
ACTION! MYSTERY! THRILLS!
JAN.
10¢
NO. 3
SENSATIONAL FEATURE!
CORPORAL COLLINS
INFANTRY-MAN
RANG-A-TANG
"THE WONDER DOG!"
also SCOOP CODY
DEVILS OF THE DEEP
and many others
BIRO

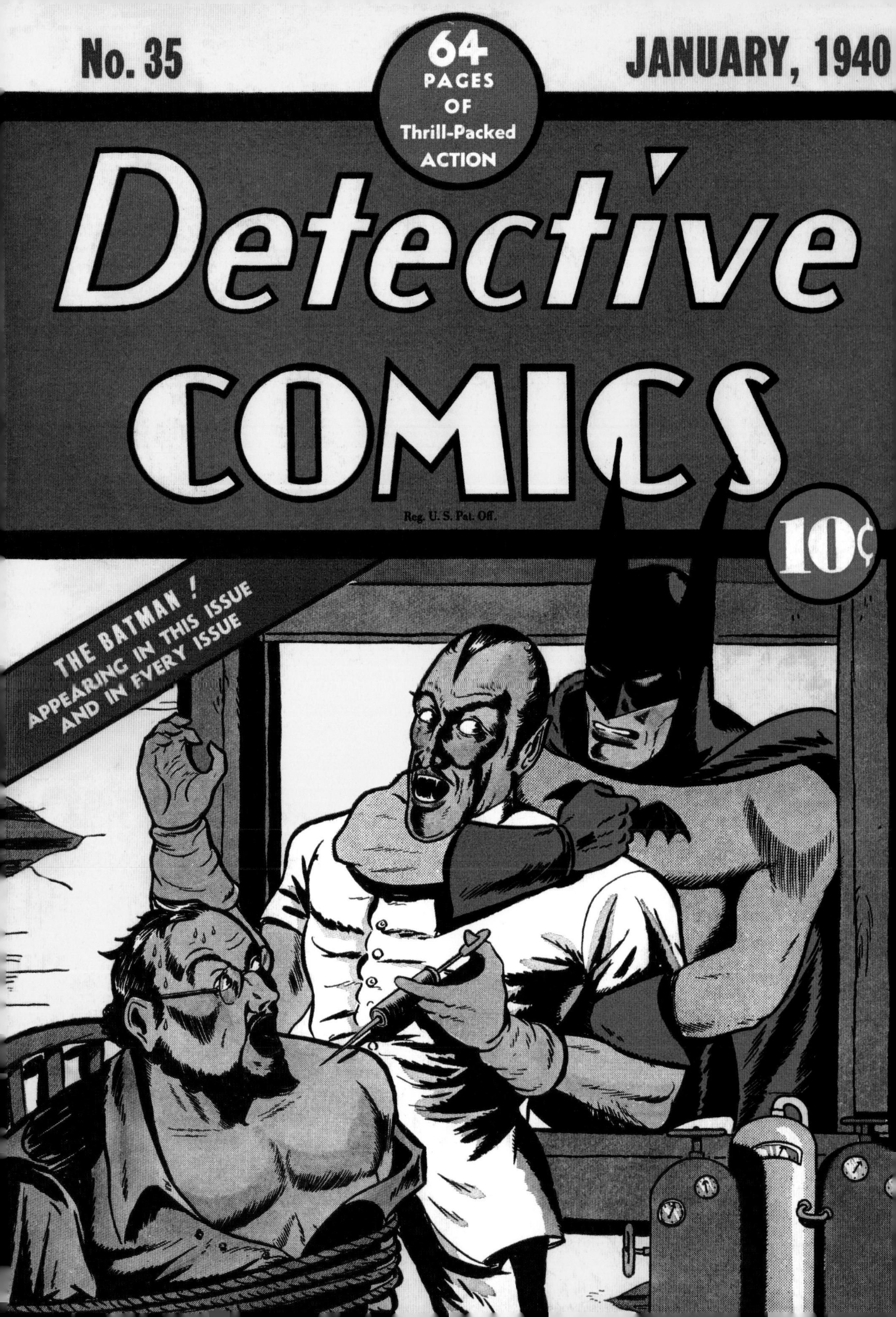
No. 35
64 PAGES OF Thrill-Packed ACTION
JANUARY, 1940
Detective COMICS
Reg. U. S. Pat. Off.
10¢
THE BATMAN !
APPEARING IN THIS ISSUE
AND IN EVERY ISSUE

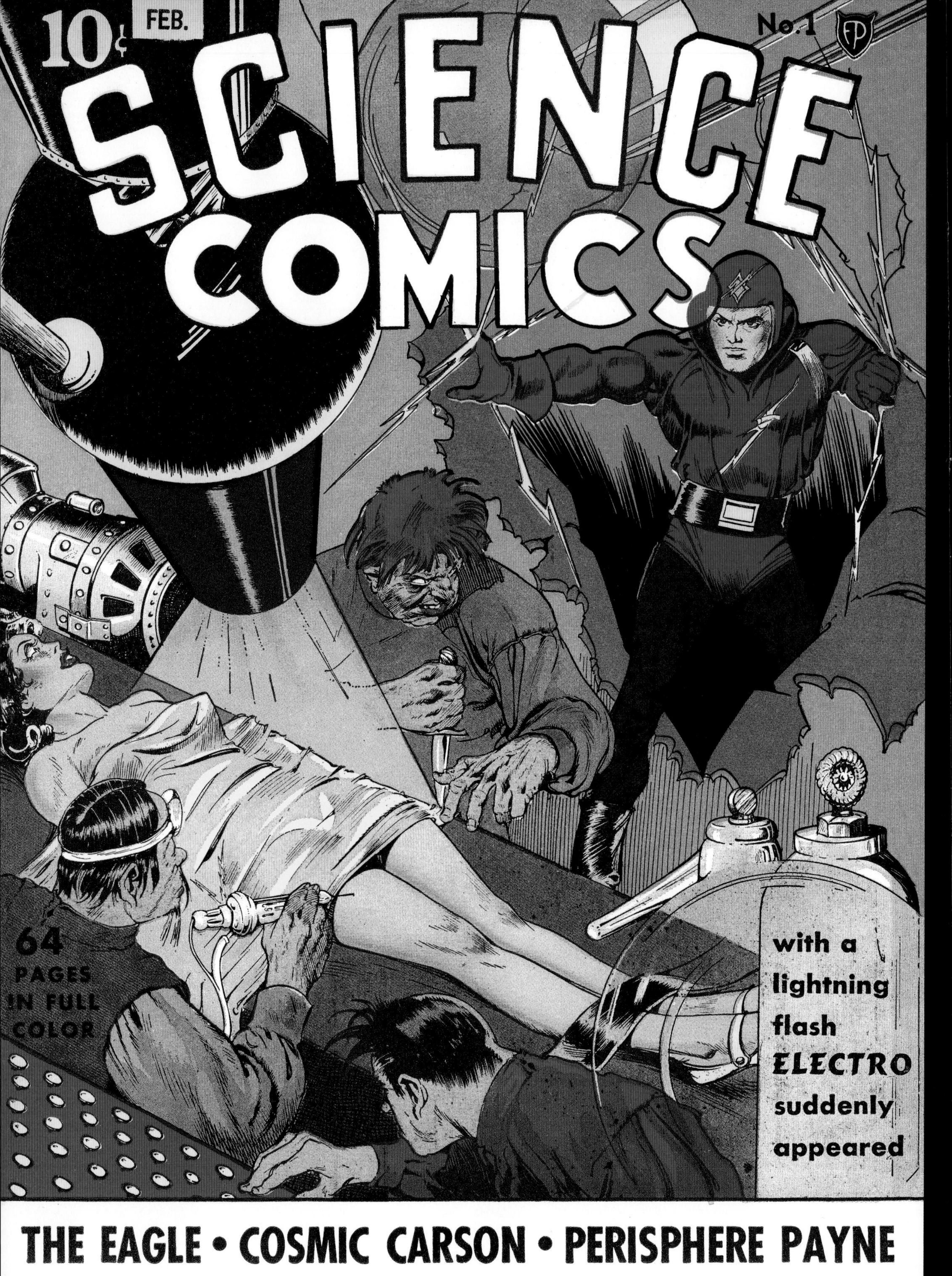
10¢
FEB.
No.1
FP
SCIENCE
COMICS
64
PAGES
IN FULL
COLOR
with a
lightning
flash
ELECTRO
suddenly
appeared
THE EAGLE • COSMIC CARSON • PERISPHERE PAYNE

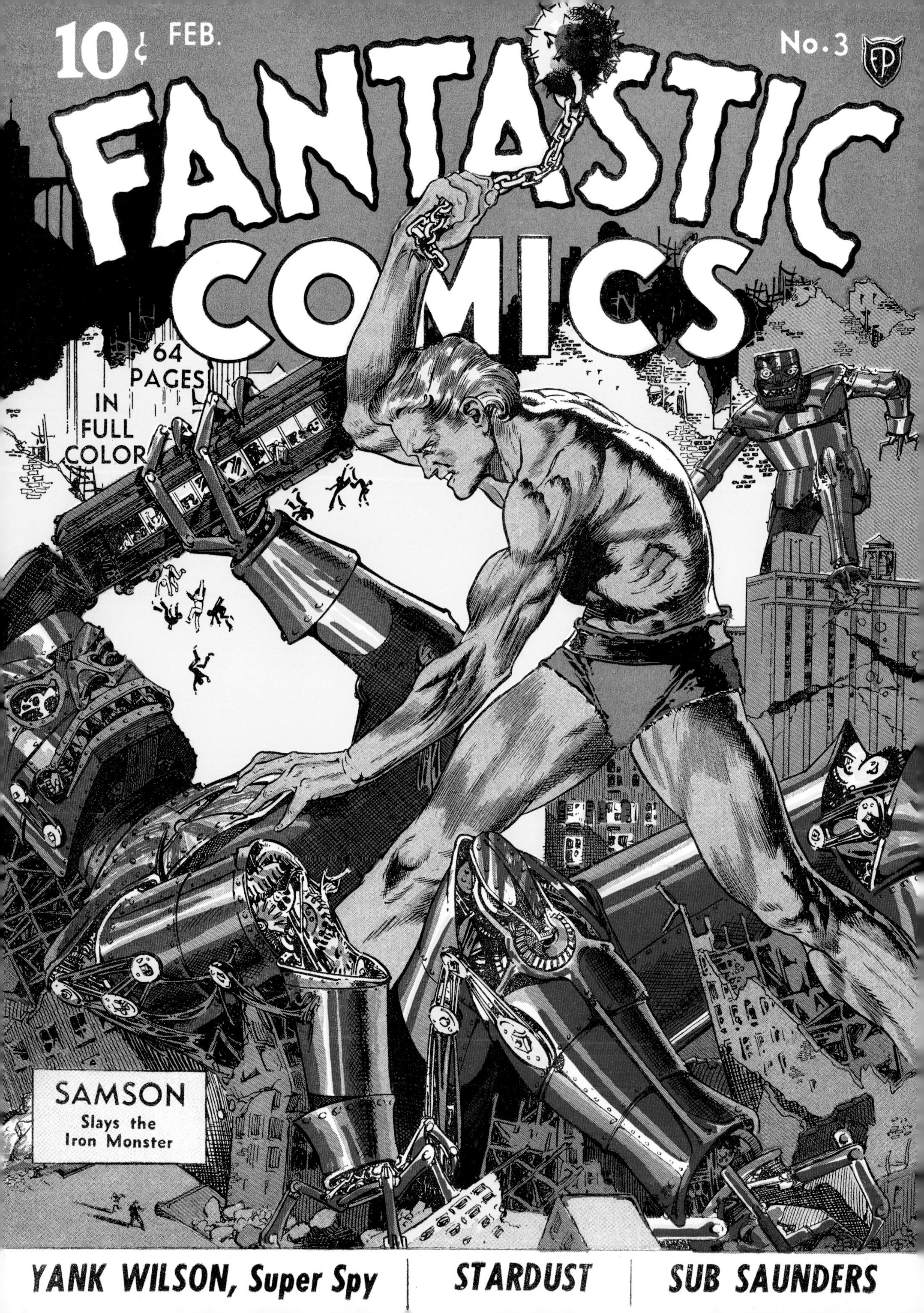

10¢ FEB.
No. 3
FP
FANTASTIC COMICS
64 PAGES IN FULL COLOR
SAMSON
Slays the Iron Monster
YANK WILSON, Super Spy
STARDUST
SUB SAUNDERS

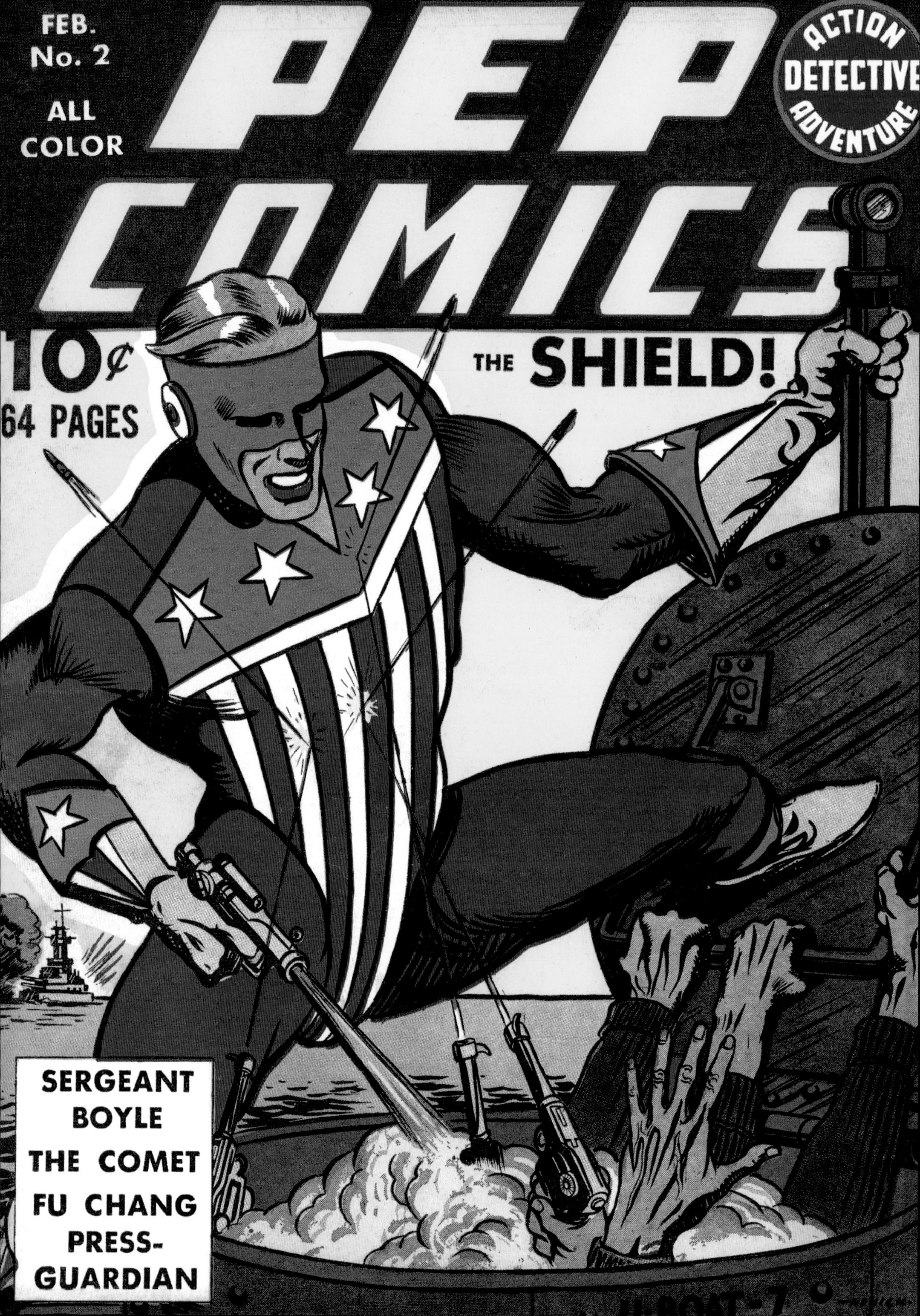
FEB.
No. 2
ALL COLOR
PEP COMICS
ACTION DETECTIVE ADVENTURE
10¢
64 PAGES
THE SHIELD!
SERGEANT BOYLE
THE COMET
FU CHANG
PRESS-GUARDIAN

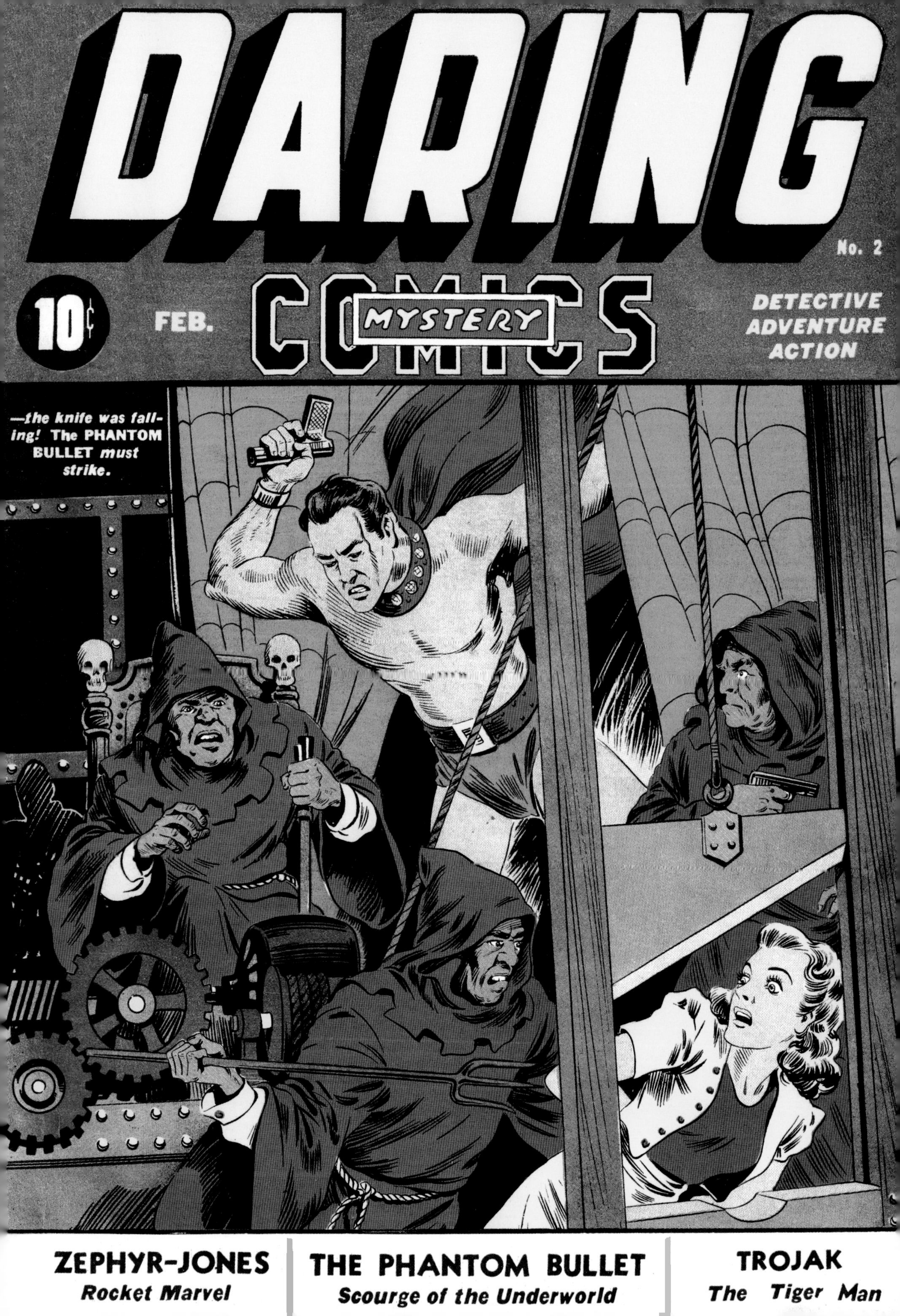
DARING
No. 2
10¢
FEB.
MYSTERY
COMICS
DETECTIVE
ADVENTURE
ACTION
—the knife was falling! The PHANTOM BULLET must strike.
ZEPHYR-JONES
Rocket Marvel
THE PHANTOM BULLET
Scourge of the Underworld
TROJAK
The Tiger Man

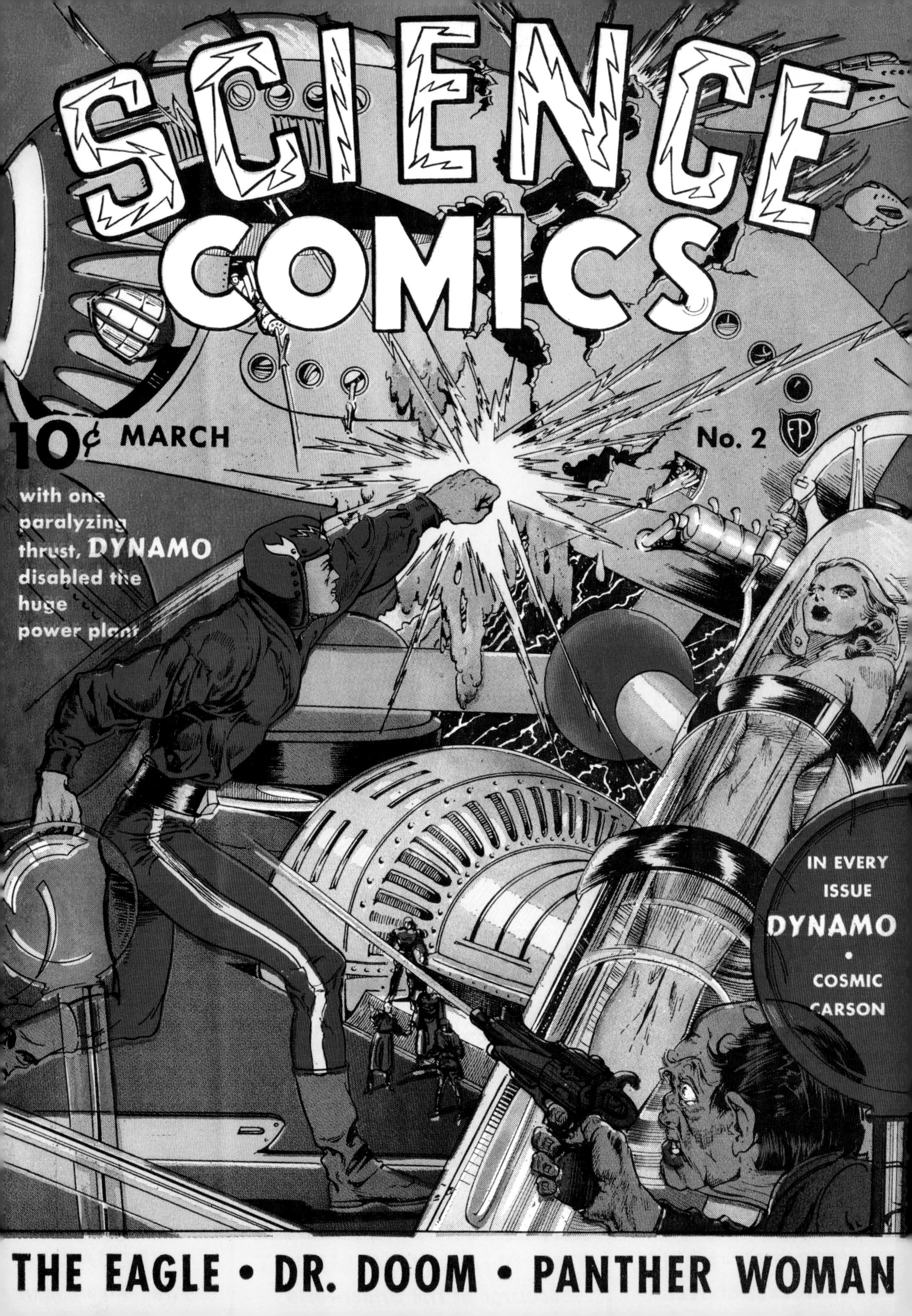
SCIENCE COMICS
10¢ MARCH
No. 2
with one paralyzing thrust, DYNAMO disabled the huge power plant
IN EVERY ISSUE DYNAMO • COSMIC CARSON
THE EAGLE • DR. DOOM • PANTHER WOMAN

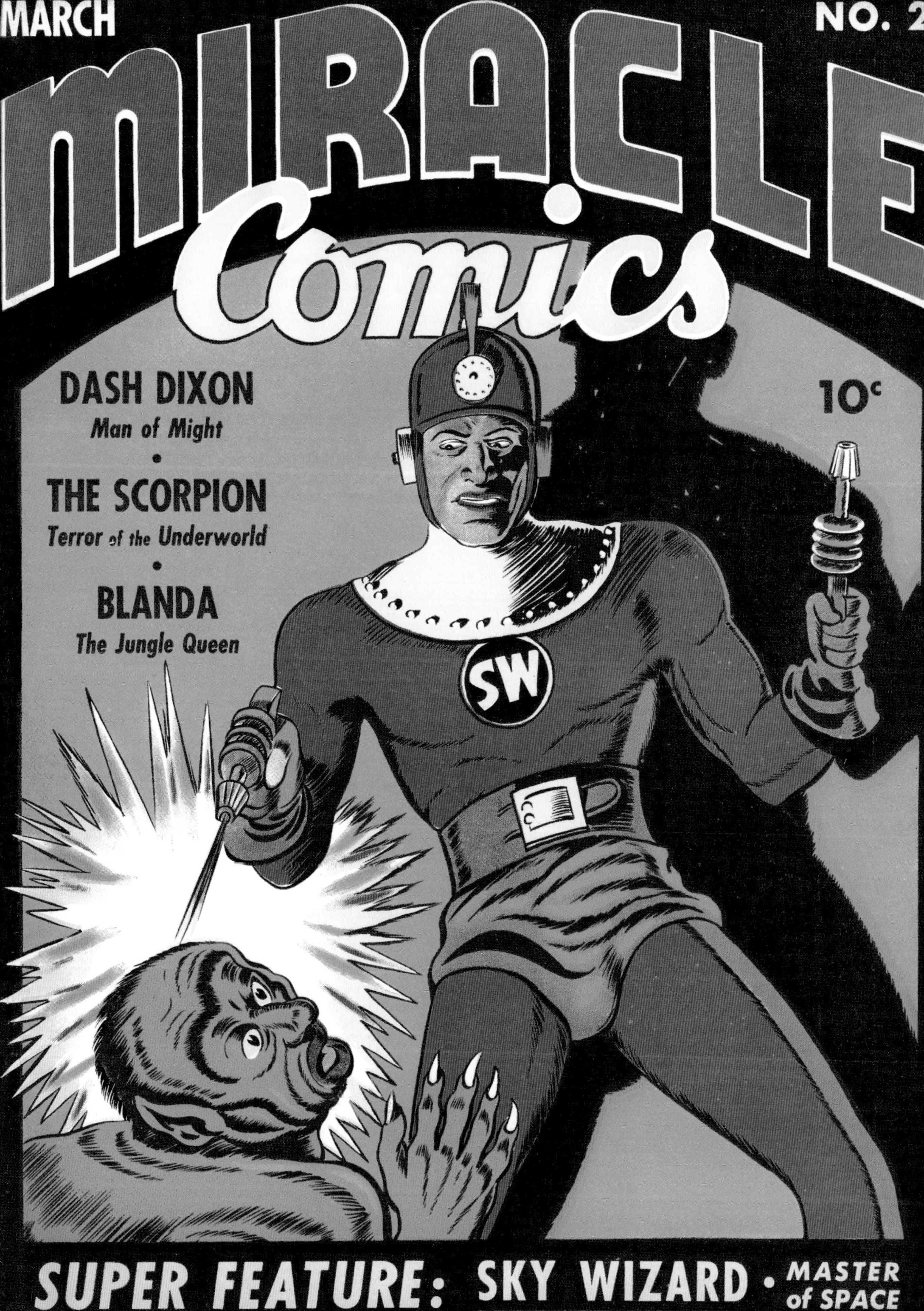
MARCH
NO. 2
MIRACLE Comics
10¢
DASH DIXON
Man of Might
THE SCORPION
Terror of the Underworld
BLANDA
The Jungle Queen
SW
SUPER FEATURE: SKY WIZARD · MASTER of SPACE

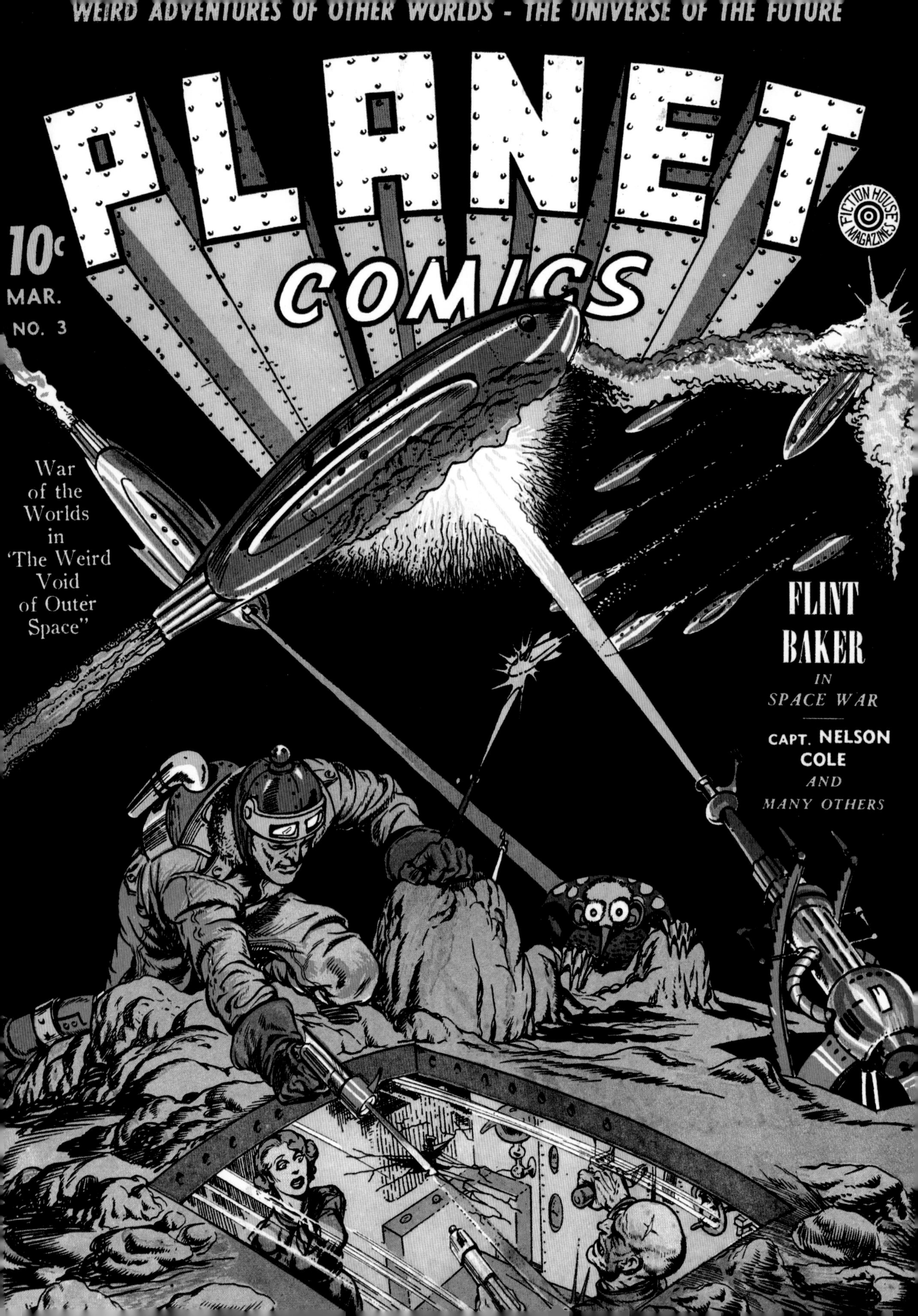
WEIRD ADVENTURES OF OTHER WORLDS - THE UNIVERSE OF THE FUTURE
PLANET COMICS
10¢
MAR.
NO. 3
FICTION HOUSE MAGAZINES
War of the Worlds in 'The Weird Void of Outer Space"
FLINT BAKER IN SPACE WAR
CAPT. NELSON COLE AND MANY OTHERS

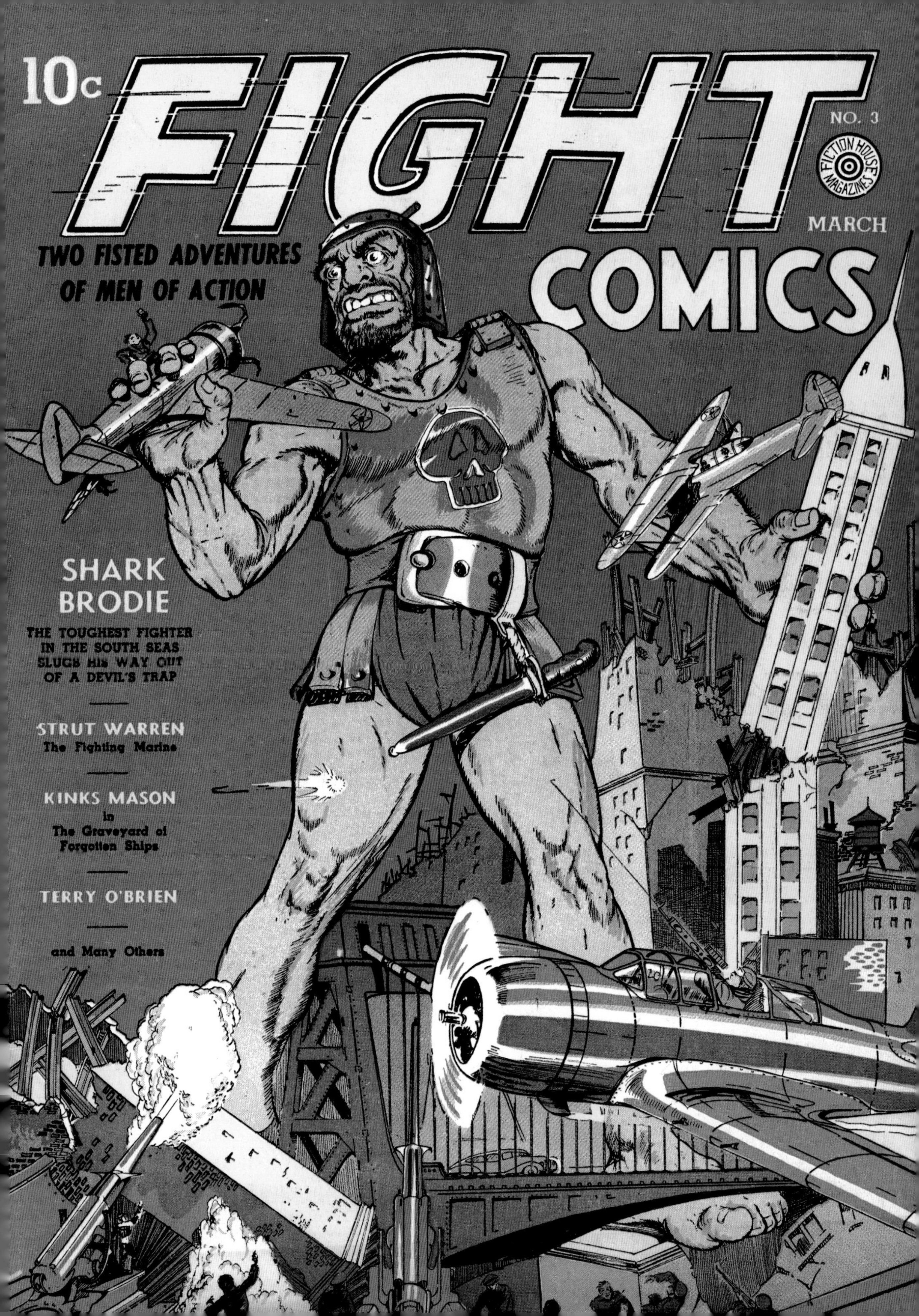

10c
FIGHT
NO. 3
FICTION HOUSE MAGAZINES
MARCH
COMICS
TWO FISTED ADVENTURES OF MEN OF ACTION
SHARK BRODIE
THE TOUGHEST FIGHTER IN THE SOUTH SEAS SLUGS HIS WAY OUT OF A DEVIL'S TRAP
STRUT WARREN
The Fighting Marine
KINKS MASON
in
The Graveyard of Forgotten Ships
TERRY O'BRIEN
and Many Others

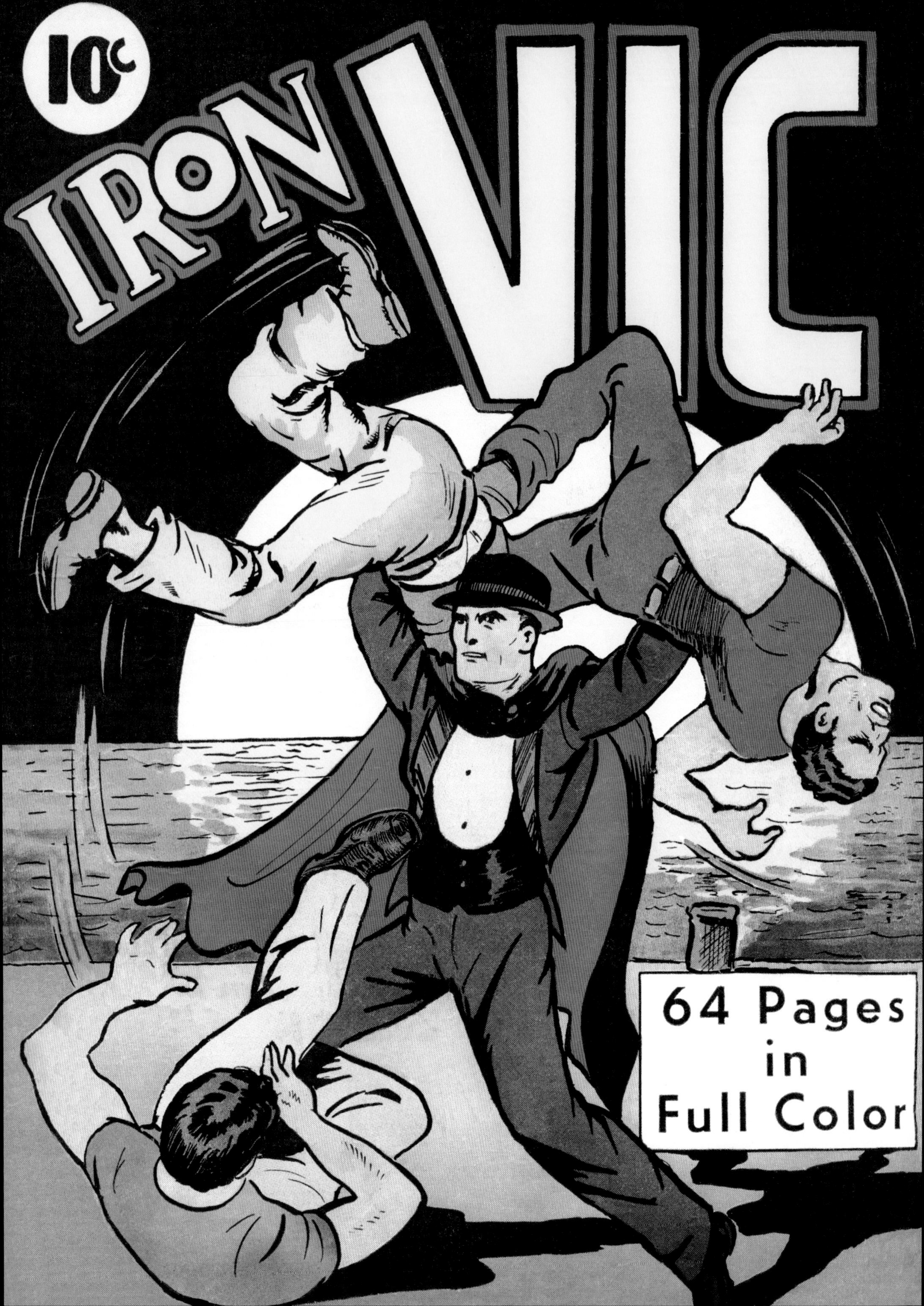
10c
IRON VIC
64 Pages in Full Color

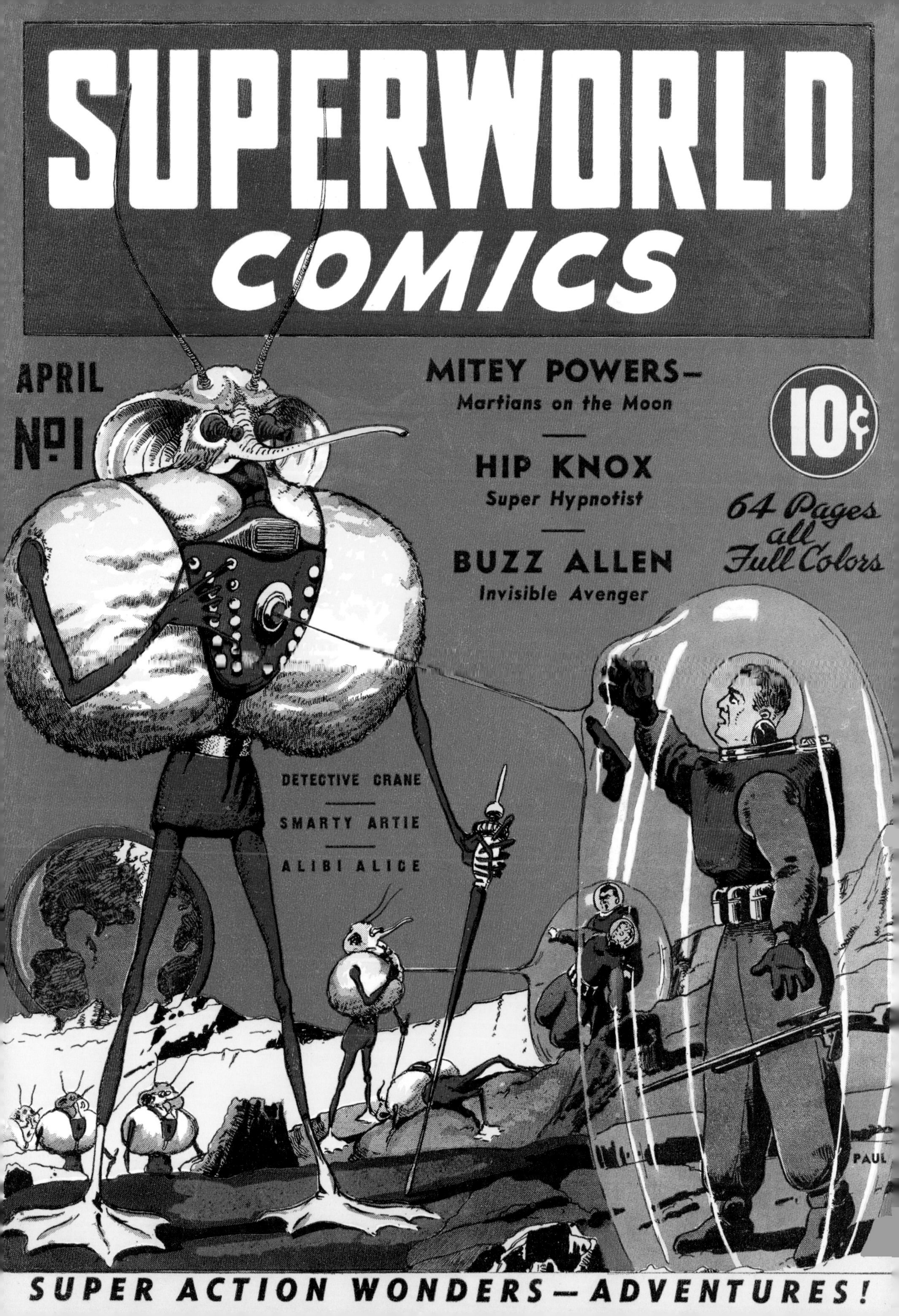
SUPERWORLD COMICS
APRIL
No. 1
10¢
MITEY POWERS—
Martians on the Moon
HIP KNOX
Super Hypnotist
BUZZ ALLEN
Invisible Avenger
64 Pages all Full Colors
DETECTIVE CRANE
SMARTY ARTIE
ALIBI ALICE
PAUL
SUPER ACTION WONDERS—ADVENTURES!

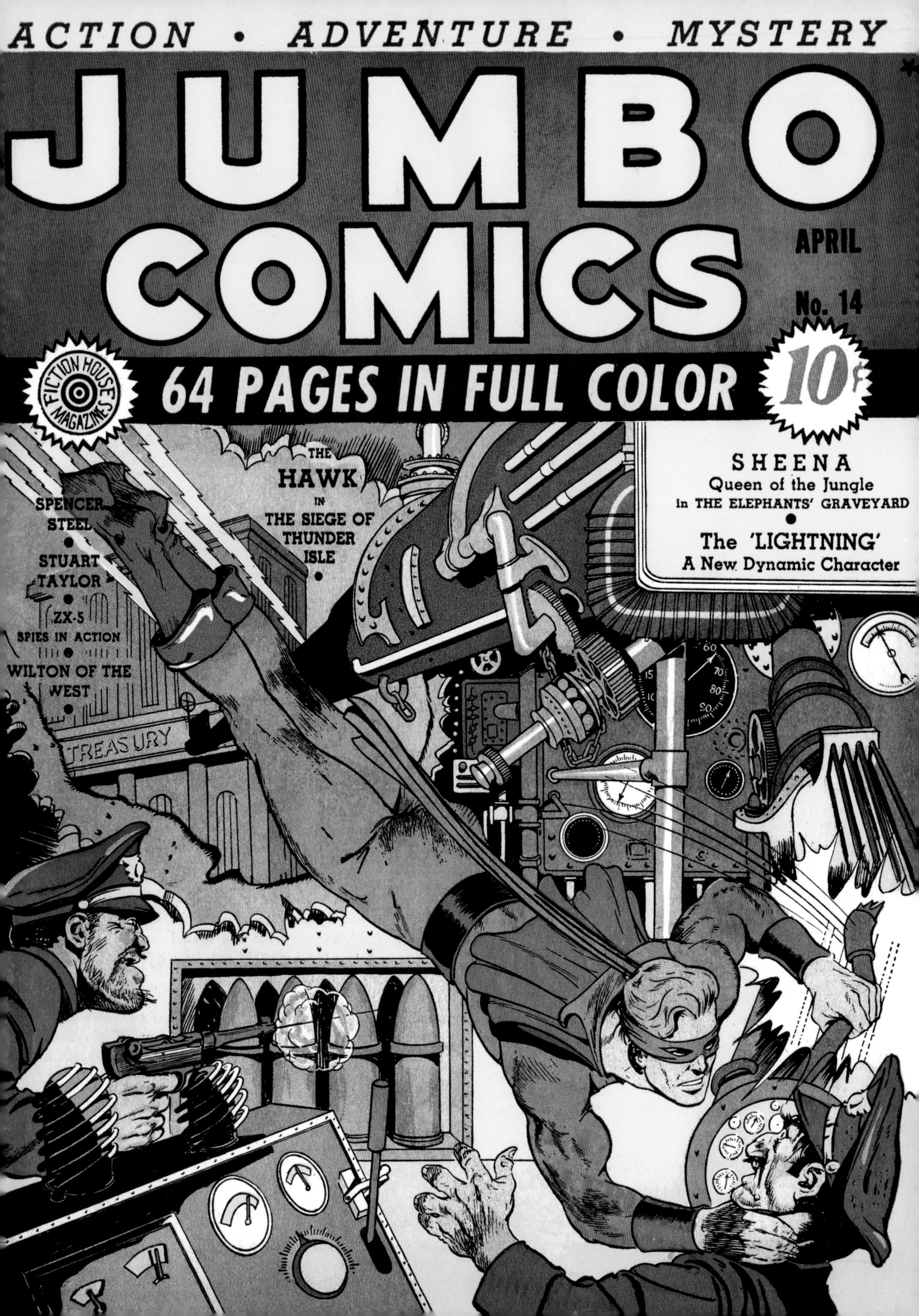
ACTION • ADVENTURE • MYSTERY
JUMBO COMICS
APRIL
No. 14
FICTION HOUSE MAGAZINES
64 PAGES IN FULL COLOR
10¢
SHEENA
Queen of the Jungle
in THE ELEPHANTS' GRAVEYARD
The 'LIGHTNING'
A New Dynamic Character
THE HAWK IN THE SIEGE OF THUNDER ISLE
SPENCER STEEL
STUART TAYLOR
ZX-5 SPIES IN ACTION
WILTON OF THE WEST
TREASURY

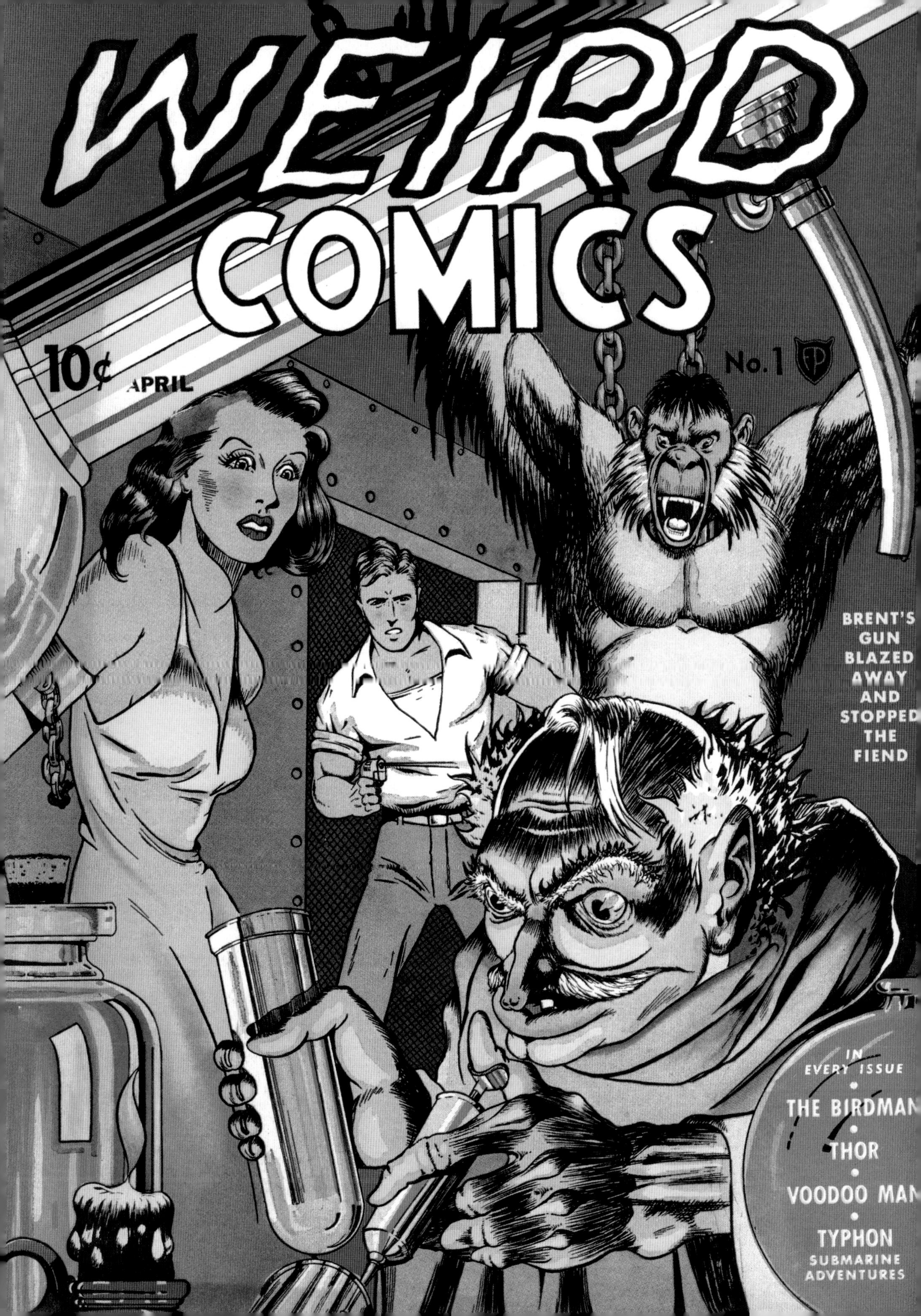

WEIRD COMICS
10¢
APRIL
No. 1
BRENT'S GUN BLAZED AWAY AND STOPPED THE FIEND
IN EVERY ISSUE
THE BIRDMAN
THOR
VOODOO MAN
TYPHON
SUBMARINE ADVENTURES

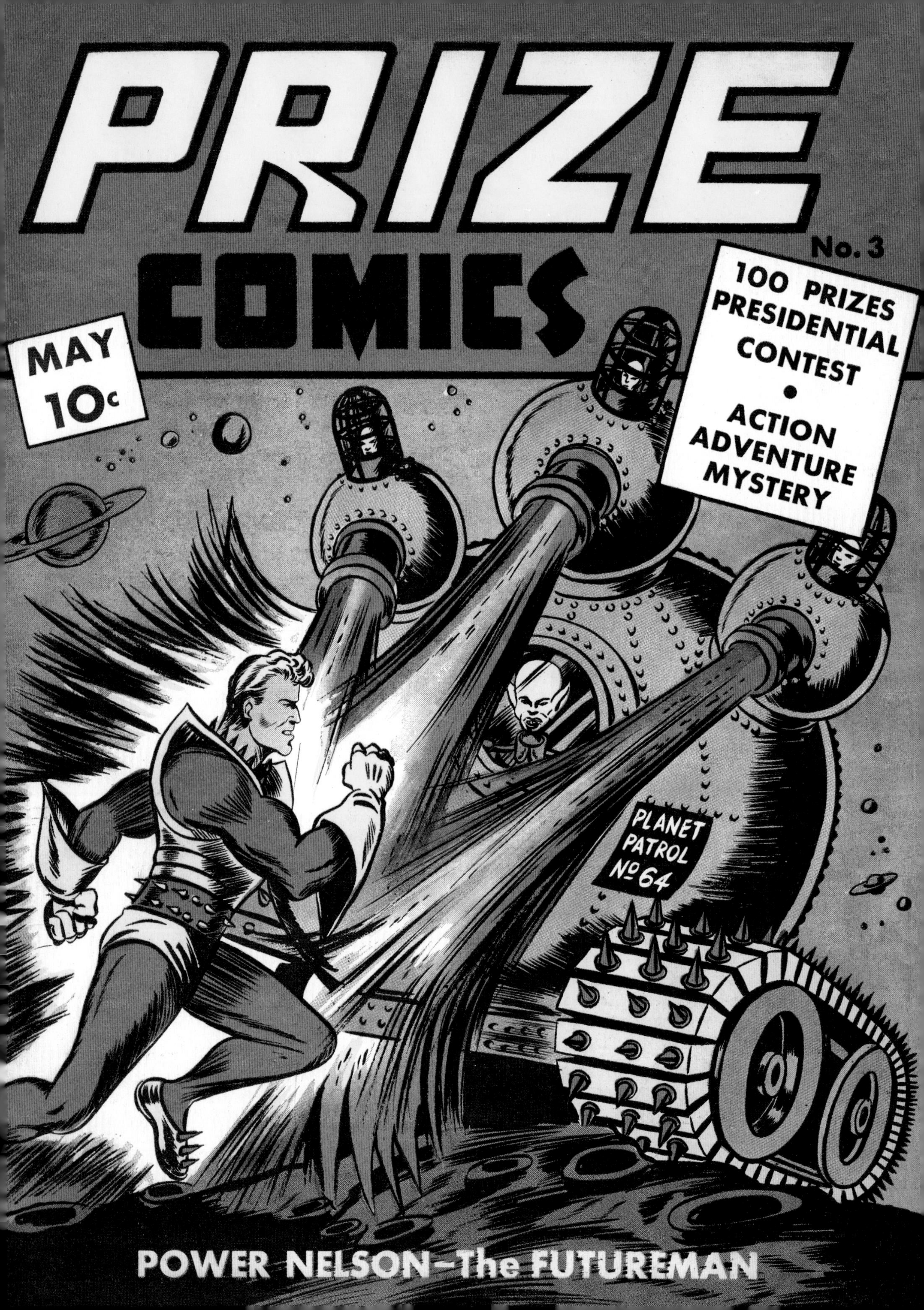
PRIZE
COMICS
No. 3
MAY
10c
100 PRIZES
PRESIDENTIAL
CONTEST
•
ACTION
ADVENTURE
MYSTERY
PLANET
PATROL
No 64
POWER NELSON—The FUTUREMAN

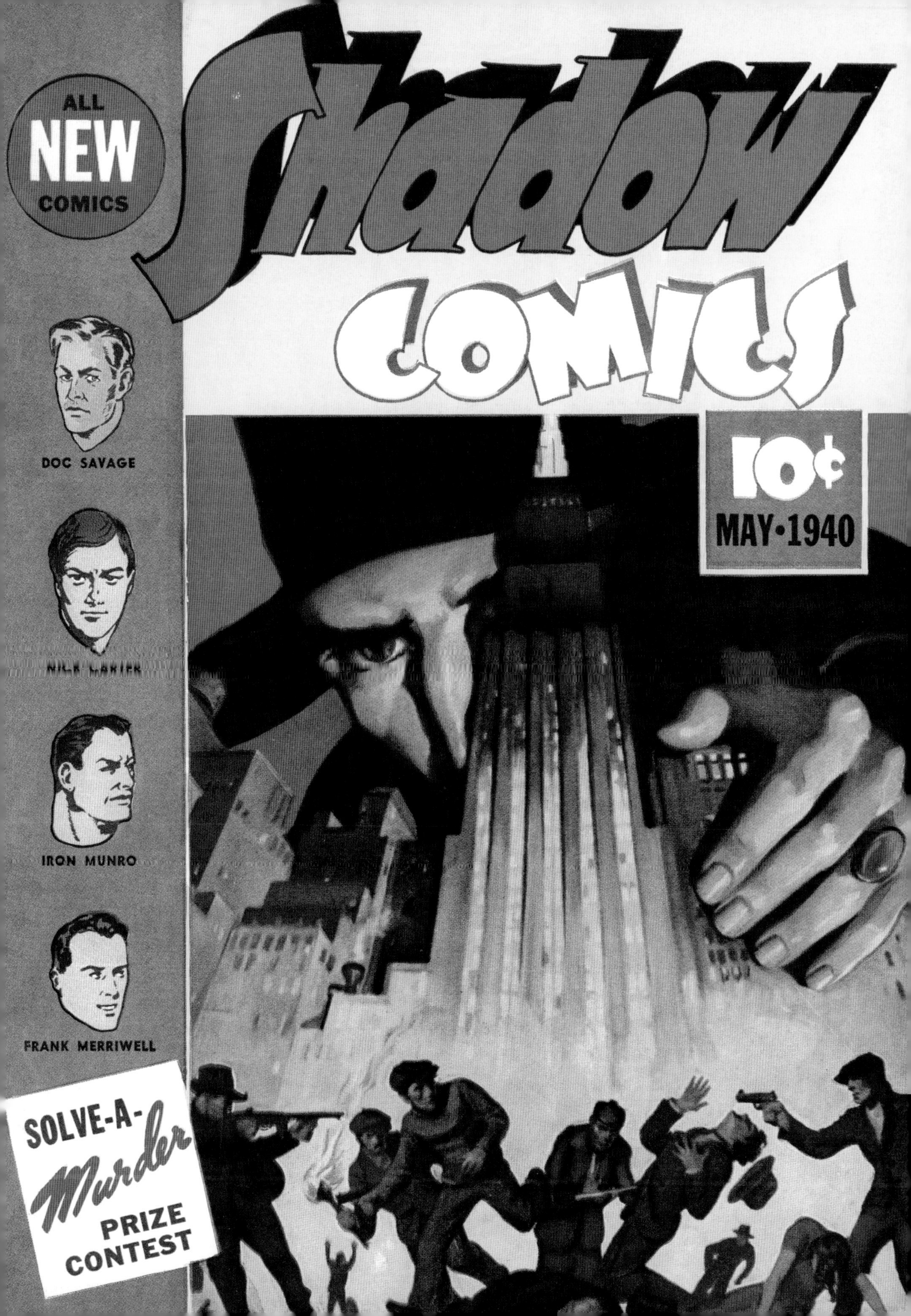
ALL NEW COMICS
Shadow COMICS
10¢
MAY • 1940
DOC SAVAGE
NICK CARTER
IRON MUNRO
FRANK MERRIWELL
SOLVE-A-Murder PRIZE CONTEST

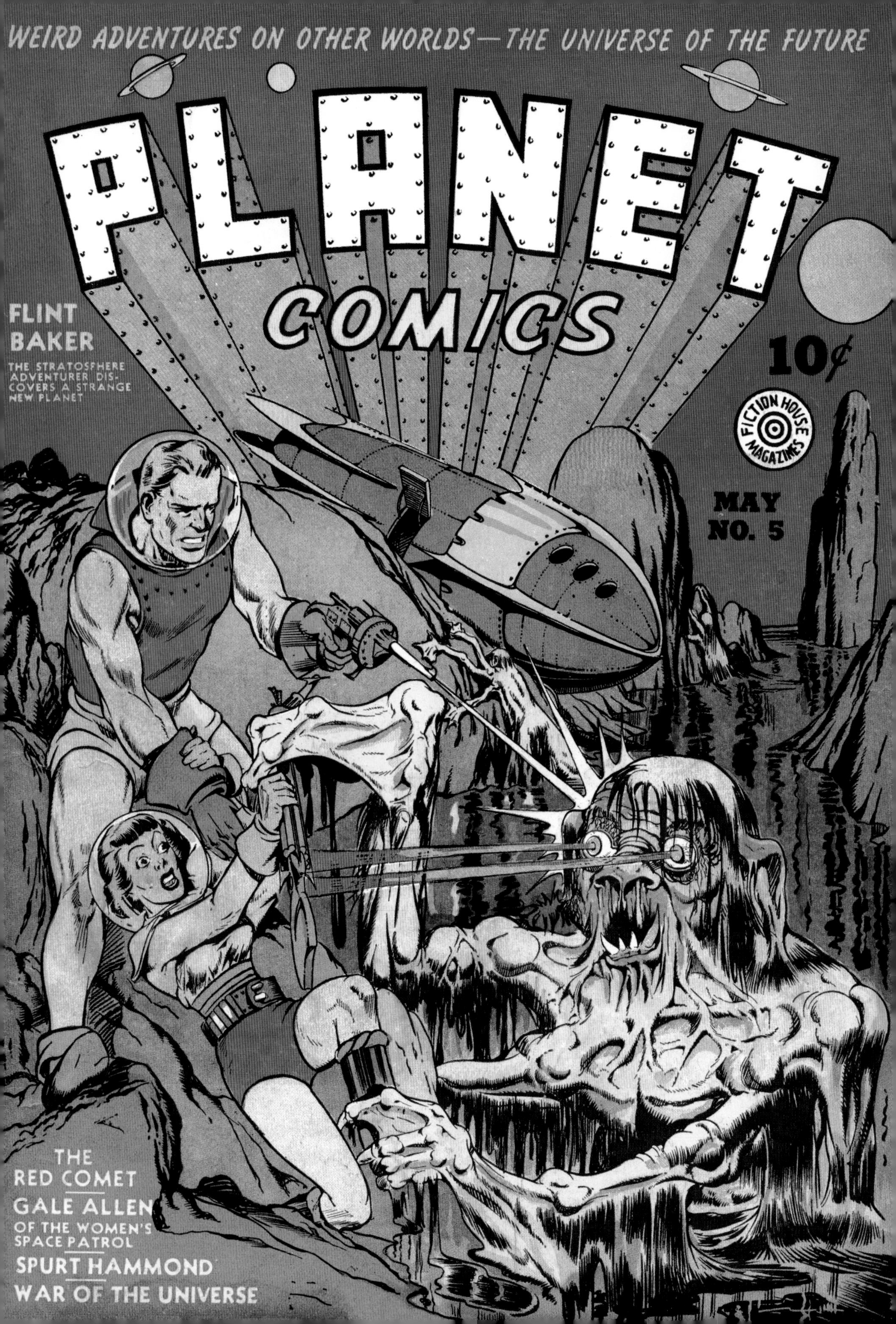
WEIRD ADVENTURES ON OTHER WORLDS—THE UNIVERSE OF THE FUTURE
PLANET COMICS
FLINT BAKER
THE STRATOSPHERE ADVENTURER DISCOVERS A STRANGE NEW PLANET
10¢
FICTION HOUSE MAGAZINES
MAY NO. 5
THE RED COMET
GALE ALLEN OF THE WOMEN'S SPACE PATROL
SPURT HAMMOND
WAR OF THE UNIVERSE

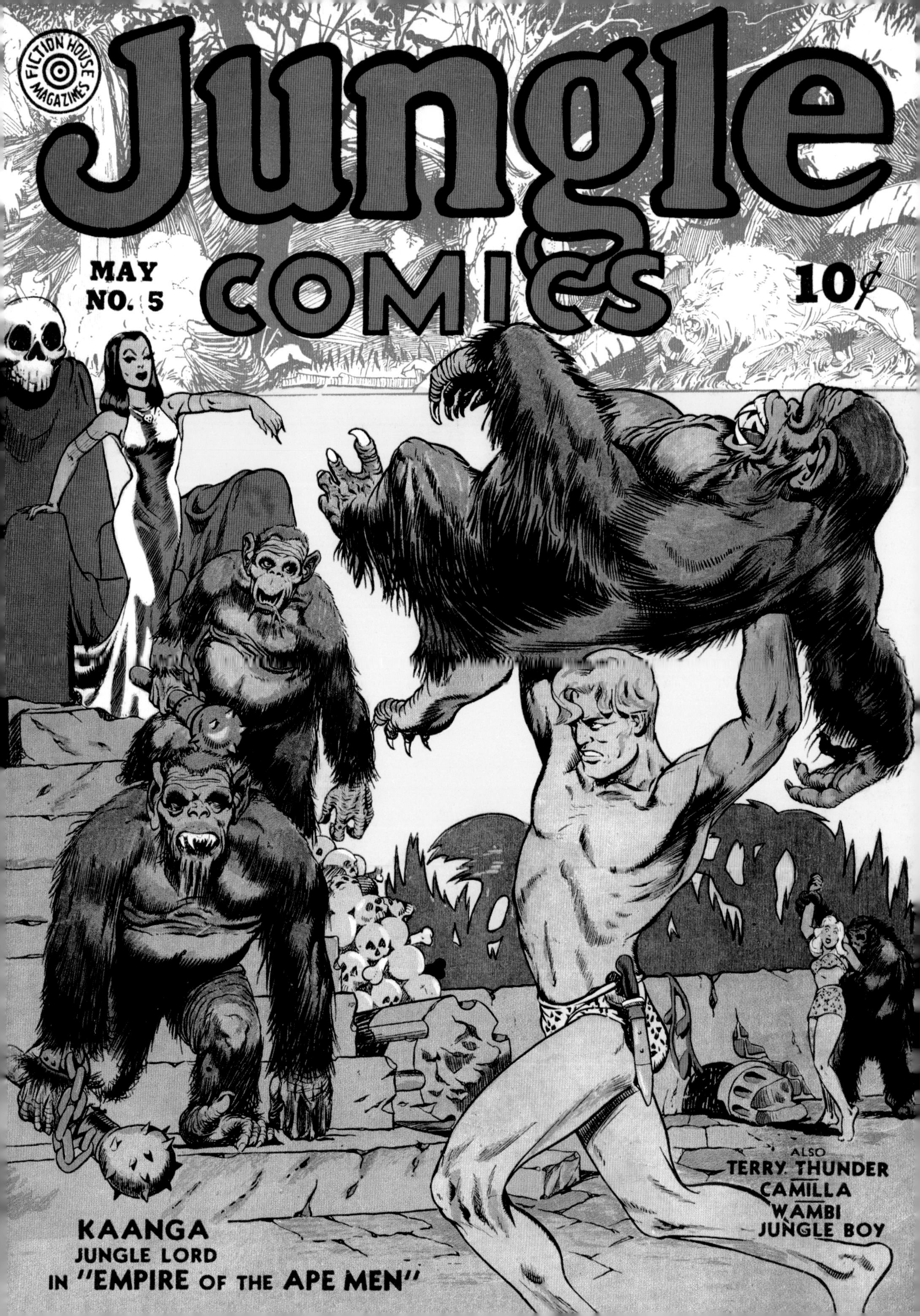
FICTION HOUSE MAGAZINES
Jungle COMICS
MAY
NO. 5
10¢
ALSO
TERRY THUNDER
CAMILLA
WAMBI
JUNGLE BOY
KAANGA
JUNGLE LORD
IN "EMPIRE OF THE APE MEN"

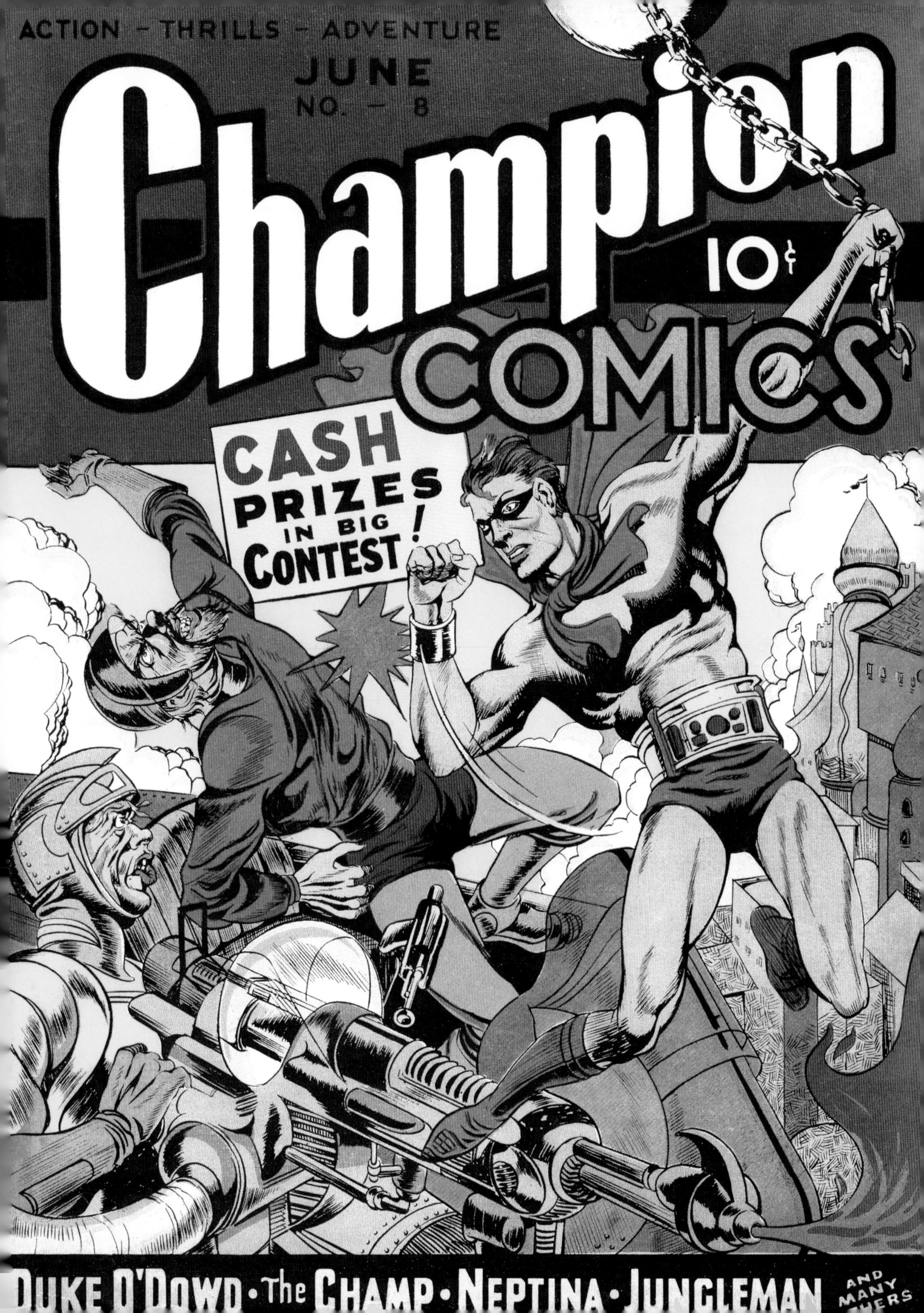
ACTION - THRILLS - ADVENTURE
JUNE
NO. - 8
Champion
10¢
COMICS
CASH PRIZES IN BIG CONTEST!
DUKE O'DOWD · The CHAMP · NEPTINA · JUNGLEMAN
AND MANY

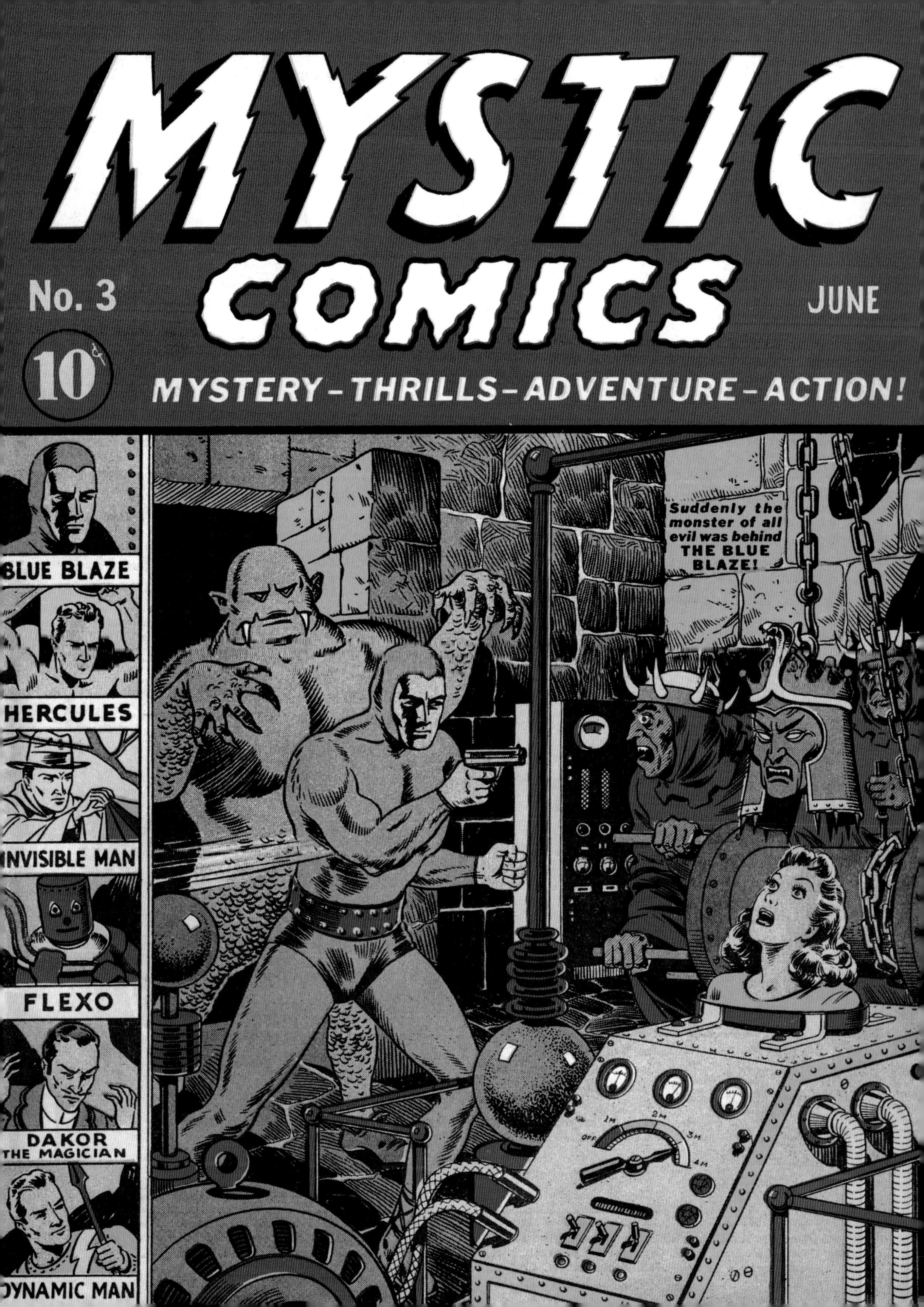

MYSTIC COMICS
No. 3
JUNE
10¢
MYSTERY-THRILLS-ADVENTURE-ACTION!
Suddenly the monster of all evil was behind THE BLUE BLAZE!
BLUE BLAZE
HERCULES
INVISIBLE MAN
FLEXO
DAKOR THE MAGICIAN
DYNAMIC MAN

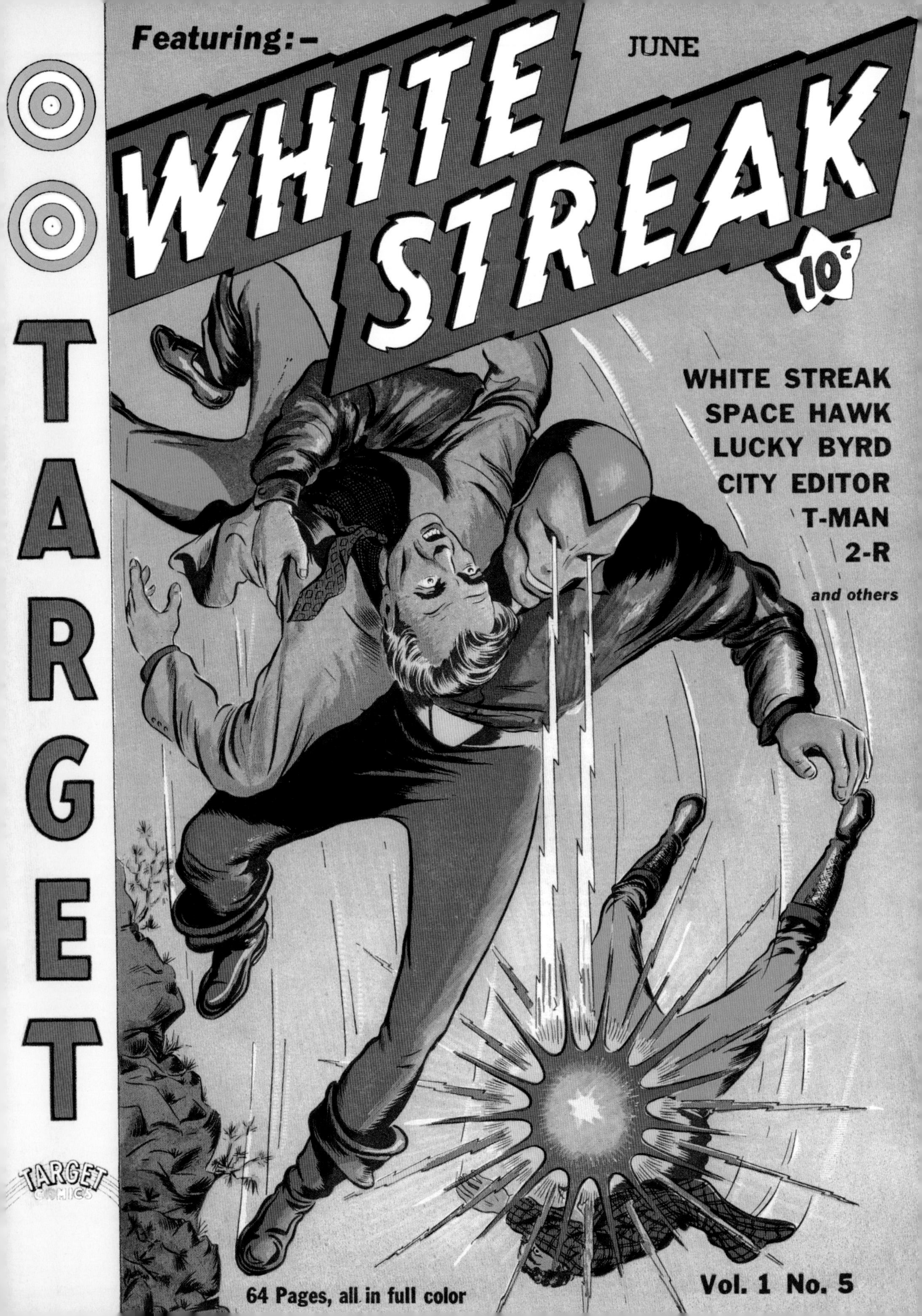
Featuring:-
JUNE
WHITE STREAK
10¢
WHITE STREAK
SPACE HAWK
LUCKY BYRD
CITY EDITOR
T-MAN
2-R
and others
TARGET
TARGET COMICS
64 Pages, all in full color
Vol. 1 No. 5

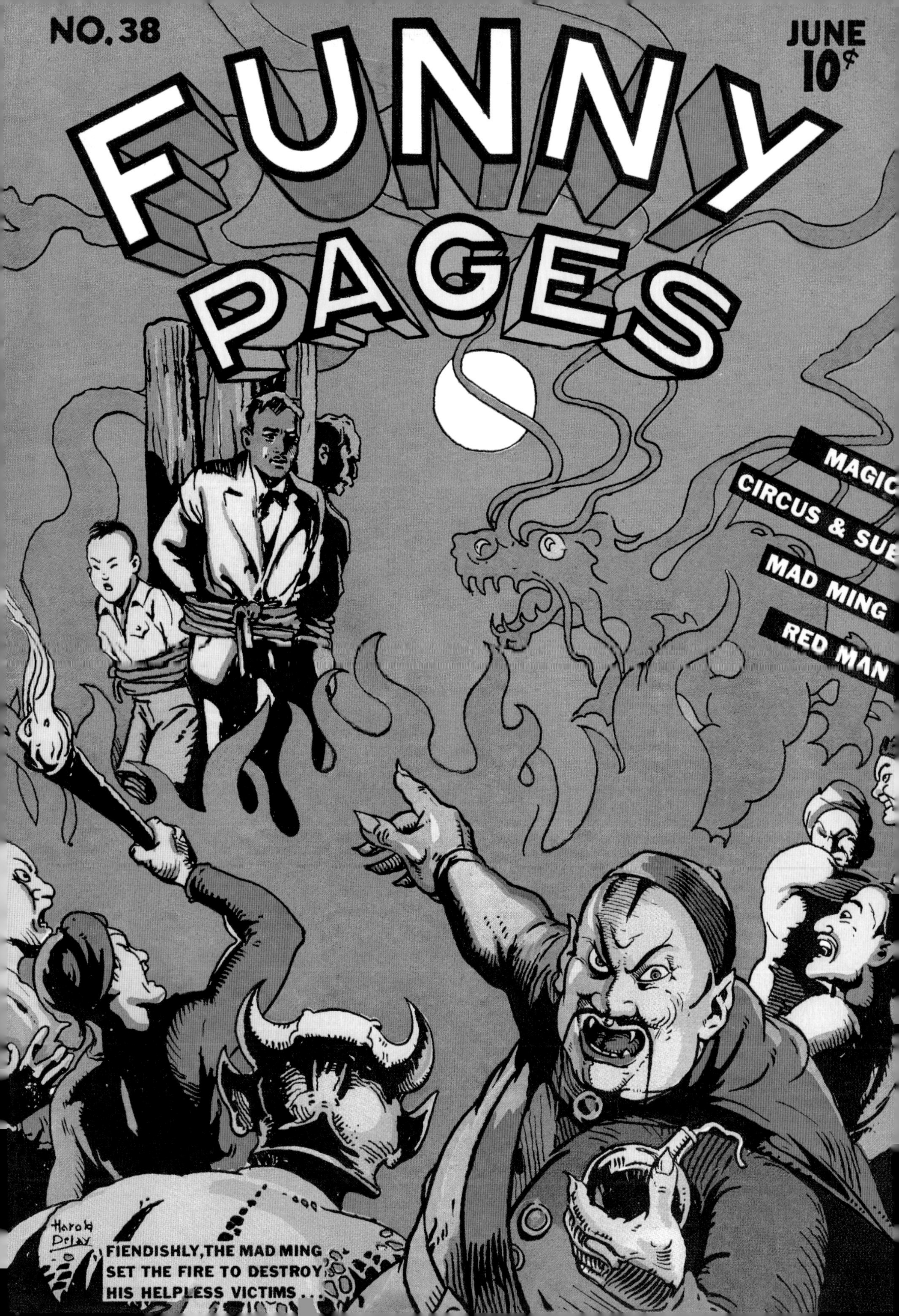

NO. 38
JUNE
10¢
FUNNY PAGES
MAGIC
CIRCUS & SUE
MAD MING
RED MAN
Harold Delay
FIENDISHLY, THE MAD MING SET THE FIRE TO DESTROY HIS HELPLESS VICTIMS . . .

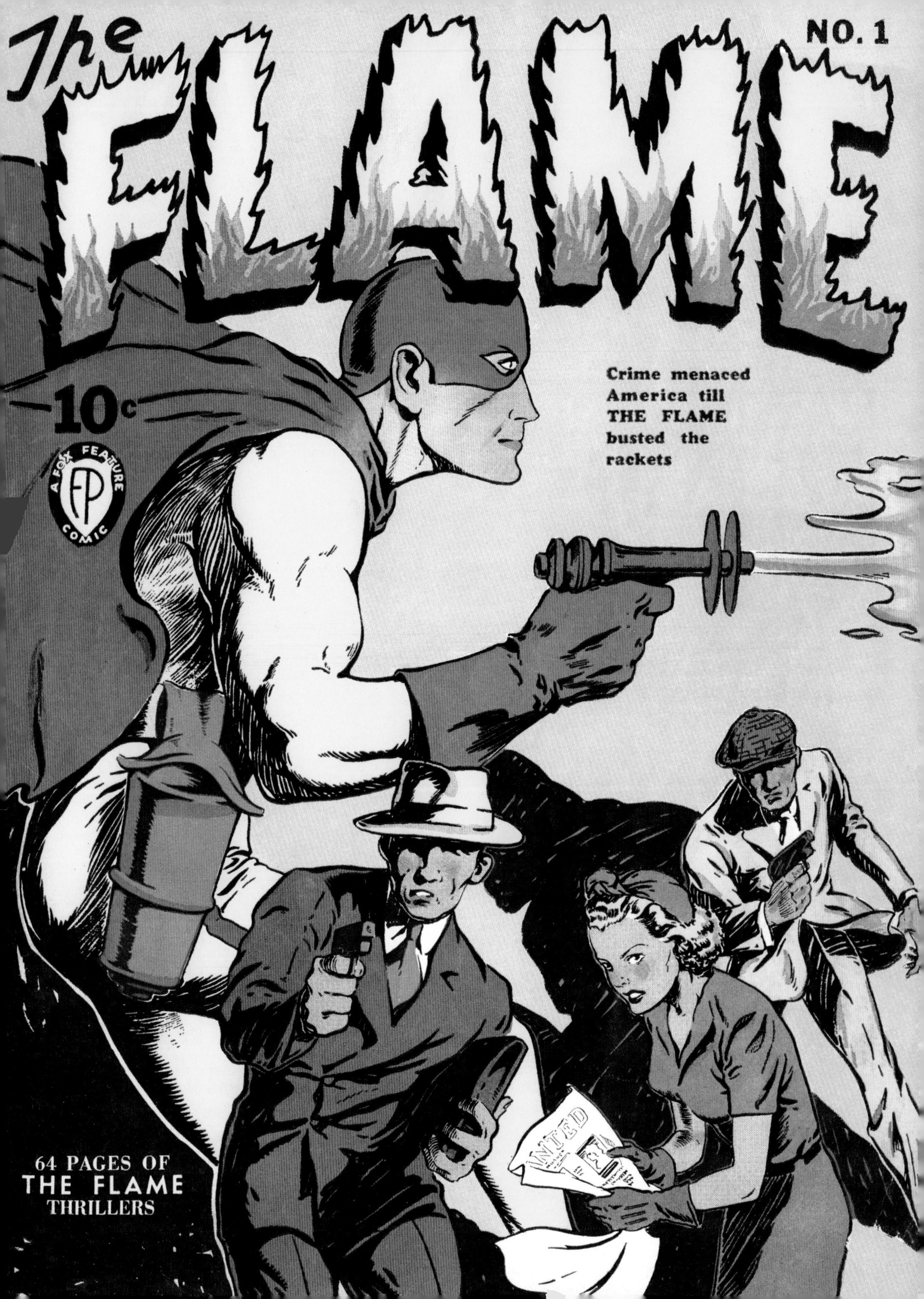
The FLAME
NO. 1
10c
A FOX FEATURE COMIC
FP
Crime menaced America till THE FLAME busted the rackets
64 PAGES OF THE FLAME THRILLERS

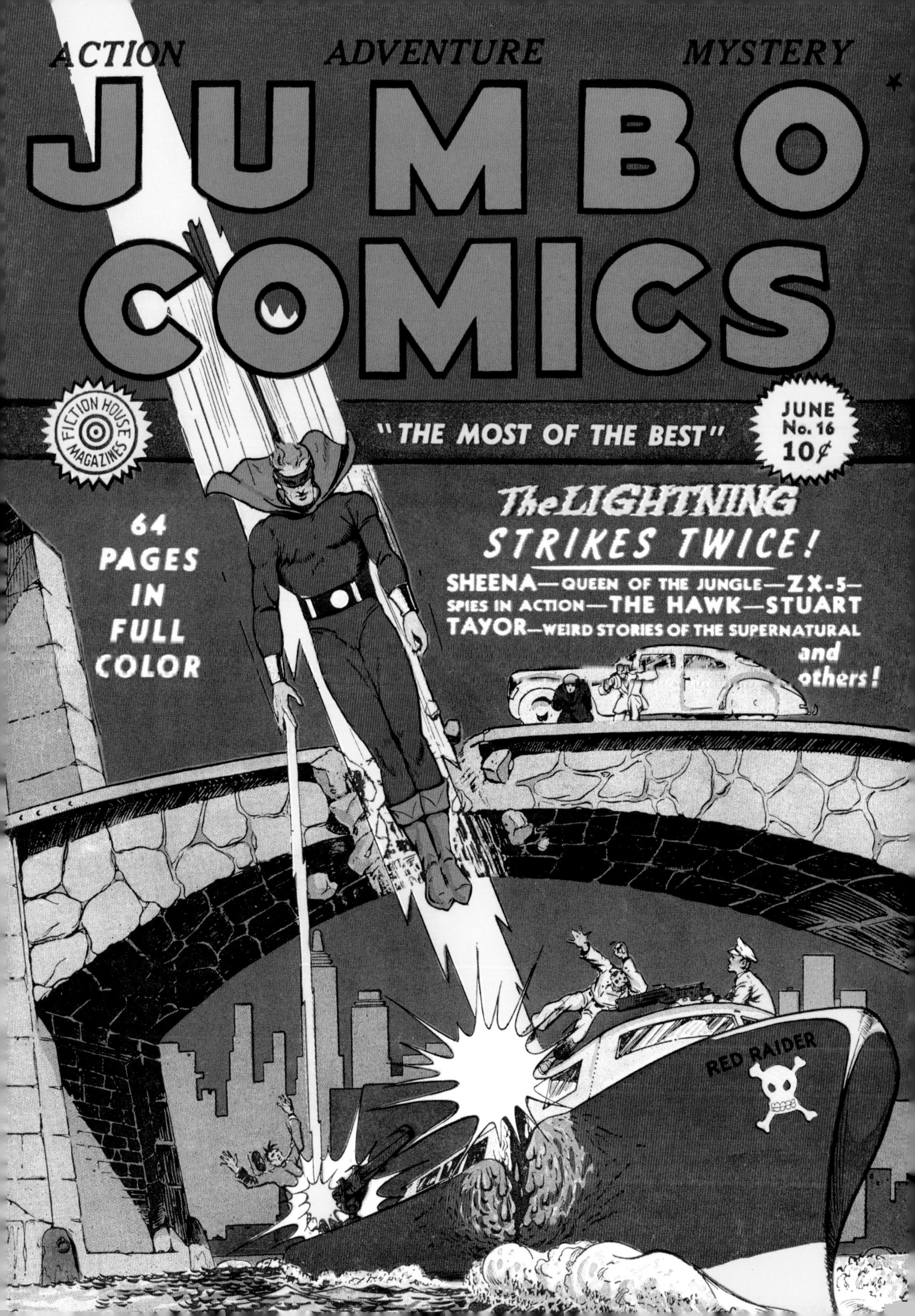
ACTION ADVENTURE MYSTERY
JUMBO COMICS
FICTION HOUSE MAGAZINES
"THE MOST OF THE BEST"
JUNE No. 16 10¢
64 PAGES IN FULL COLOR
The LIGHTNING STRIKES TWICE!
SHEENA—QUEEN OF THE JUNGLE—ZX-5—SPIES IN ACTION—THE HAWK—STUART TAYOR—WEIRD STORIES OF THE SUPERNATURAL and others!
RED RAIDER

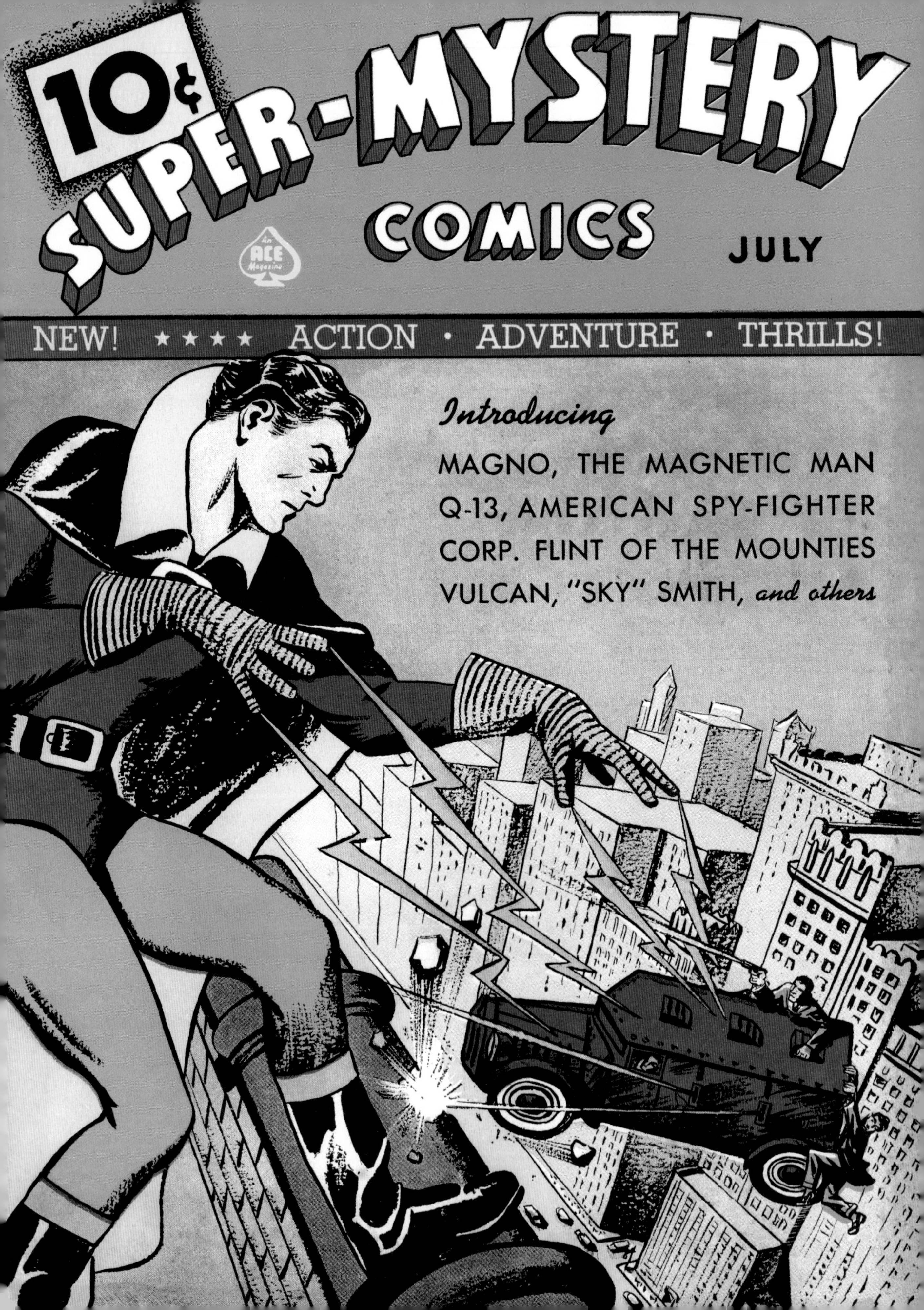

10¢
SUPER-MYSTERY
COMICS
An ACE Magazine
JULY
NEW! ★★★★ ACTION · ADVENTURE · THRILLS!
Introducing
MAGNO, THE MAGNETIC MAN
Q-13, AMERICAN SPY-FIGHTER
CORP. FLINT OF THE MOUNTIES
VULCAN, "SKY" SMITH, and others

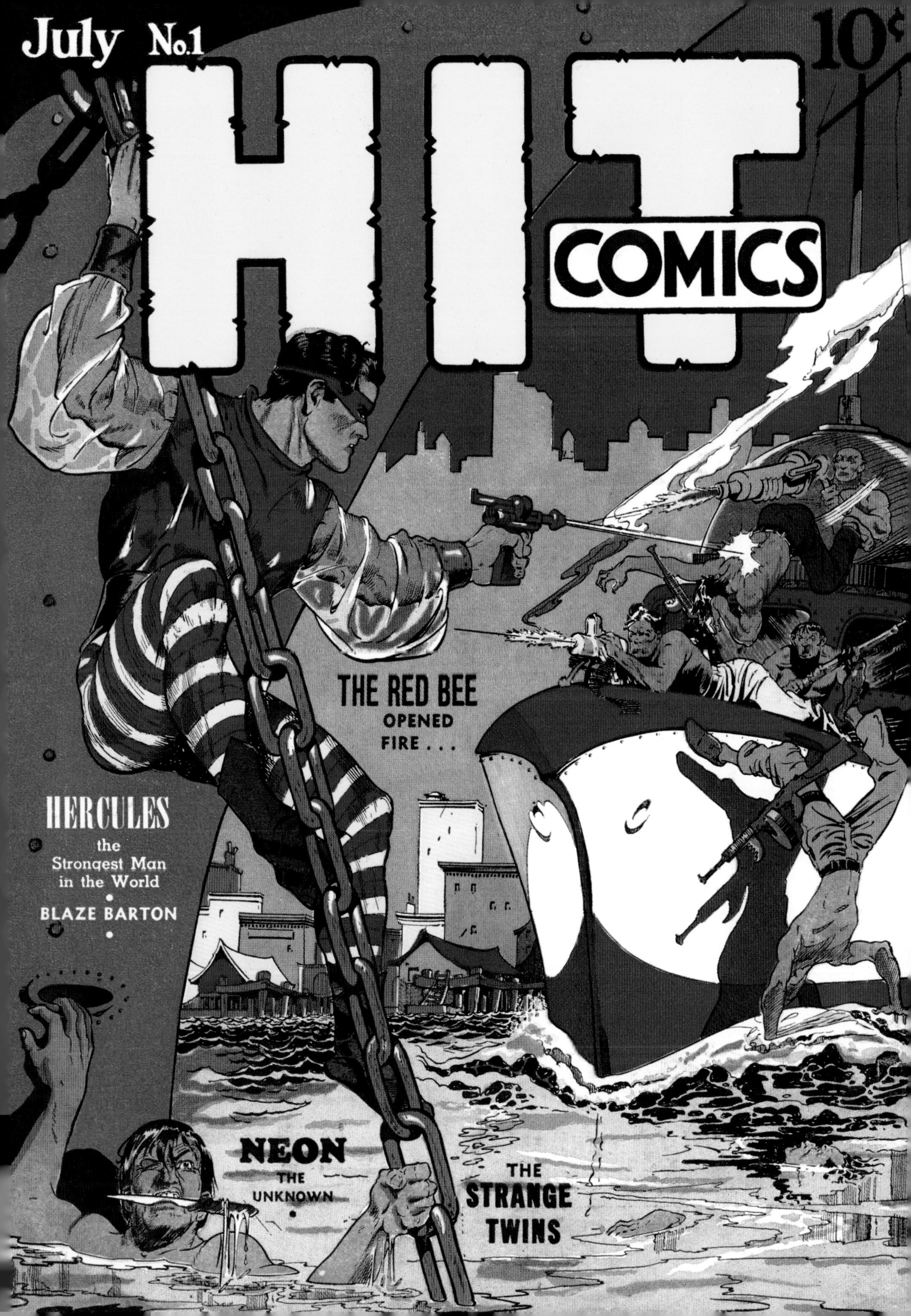

July No.1
10¢
HIT
COMICS
THE RED BEE OPENED FIRE . . .
HERCULES the Strongest Man in the World
BLAZE BARTON
NEON THE UNKNOWN
THE STRANGE TWINS

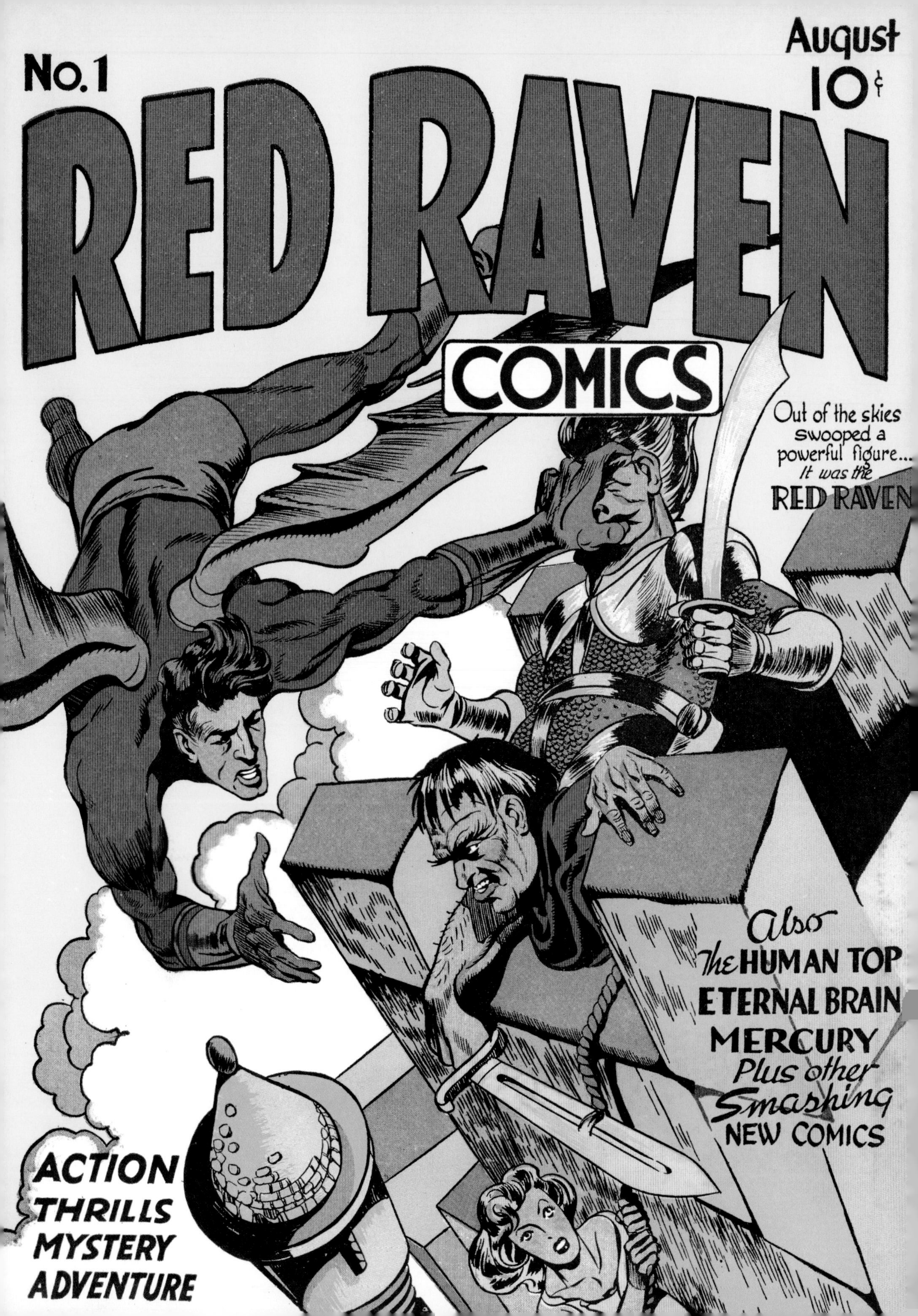

No. 1
August
10¢
RED RAVEN
COMICS
Out of the skies swooped a powerful figure... It was the RED RAVEN
Also The HUMAN TOP
ETERNAL BRAIN
MERCURY
Plus other Smashing NEW COMICS
ACTION
THRILLS
MYSTERY
ADVENTURE

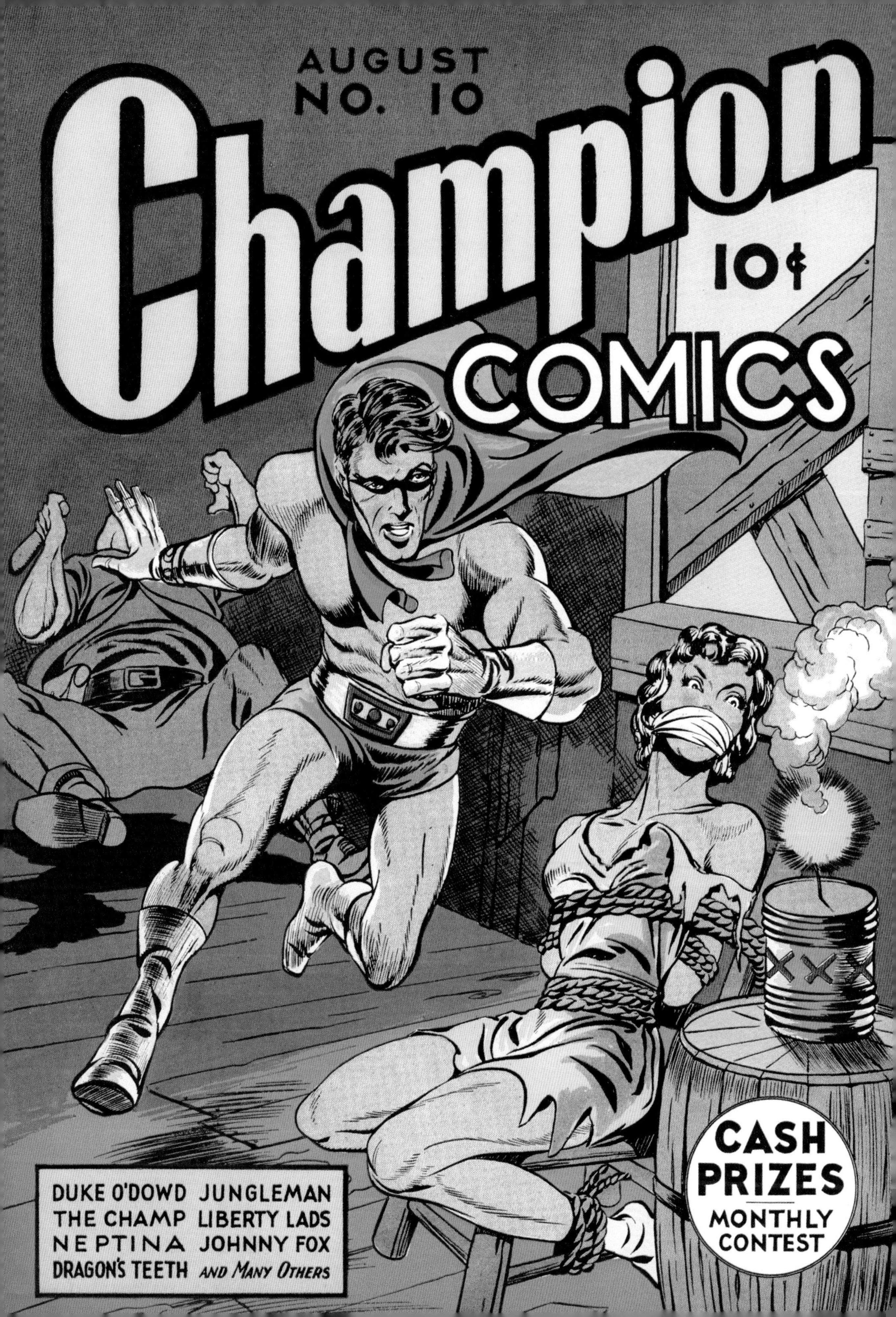
AUGUST
NO. 10
Champion
10¢
COMICS
CASH PRIZES MONTHLY CONTEST
DUKE O'DOWD JUNGLEMAN
THE CHAMP LIBERTY LADS
NEPTINA JOHNNY FOX
DRAGON'S TEETH AND MANY OTHERS

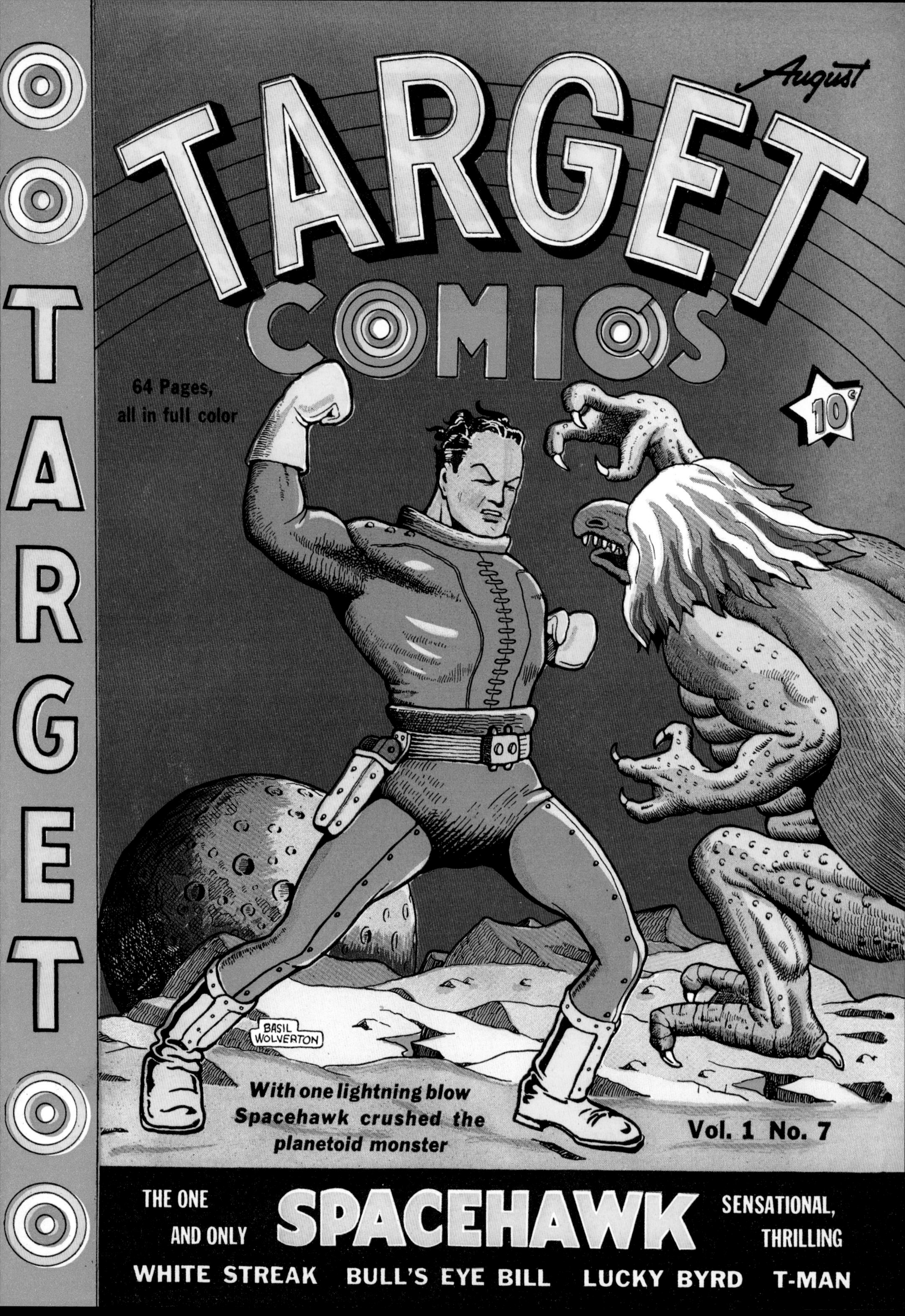
August
TARGET
COMICS
TARGET
64 Pages,
all in full color
10¢
BASIL WOLVERTON
With one lightning blow
Spacehawk crushed the
planetoid monster
Vol. 1 No. 7
THE ONE
AND ONLY
SPACEHAWK
SENSATIONAL,
THRILLING
WHITE STREAK BULL'S EYE BILL LUCKY BYRD T-MAN

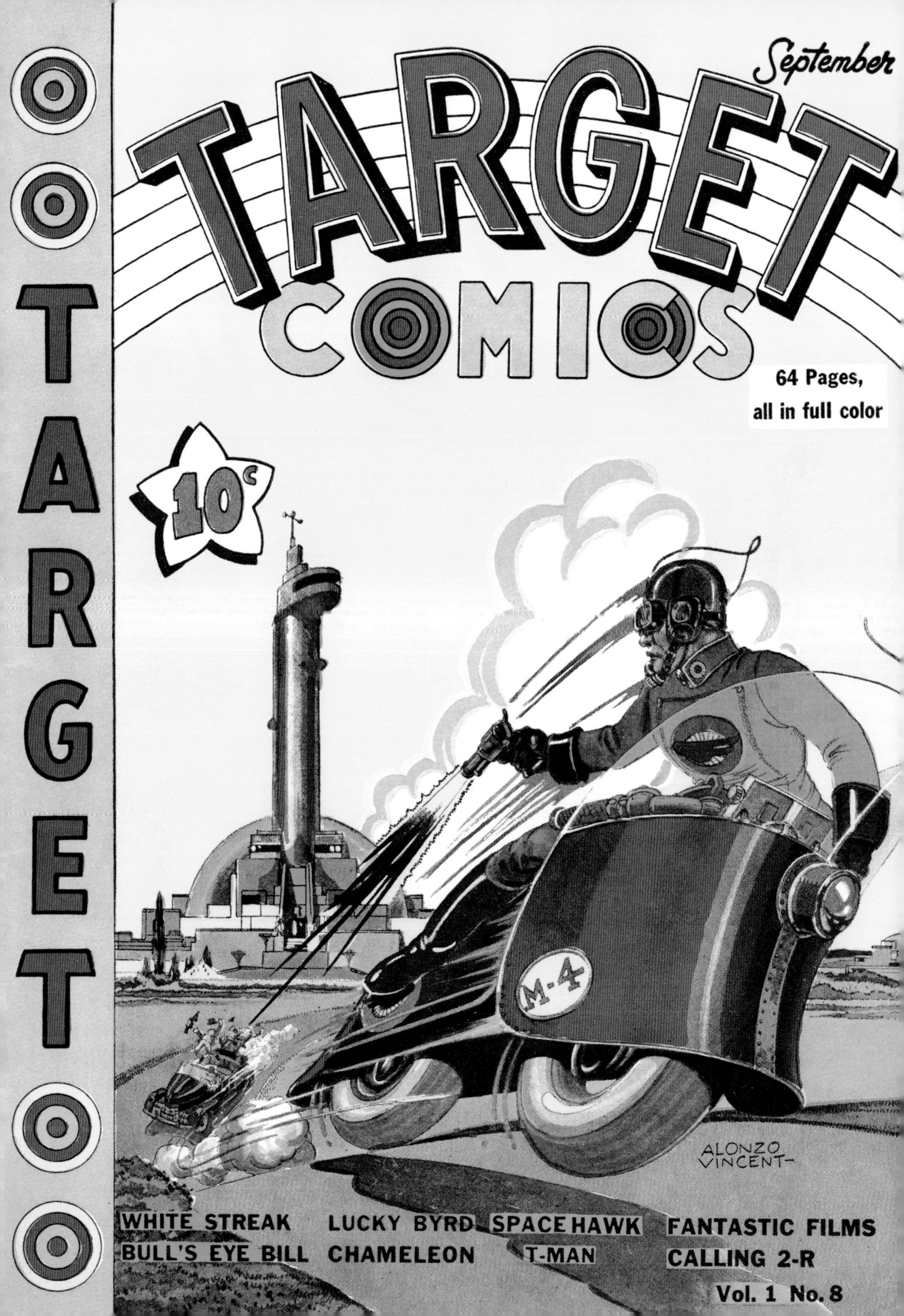
September
TARGET
COMICS
64 Pages,
all in full color
10c
M-4
ALONZO VINCENT
WHITE STREAK
LUCKY BYRD
SPACEHAWK
FANTASTIC FILMS
BULL'S EYE BILL
CHAMELEON
T-MAN
CALLING 2-R
Vol. 1 No. 8
TARGET

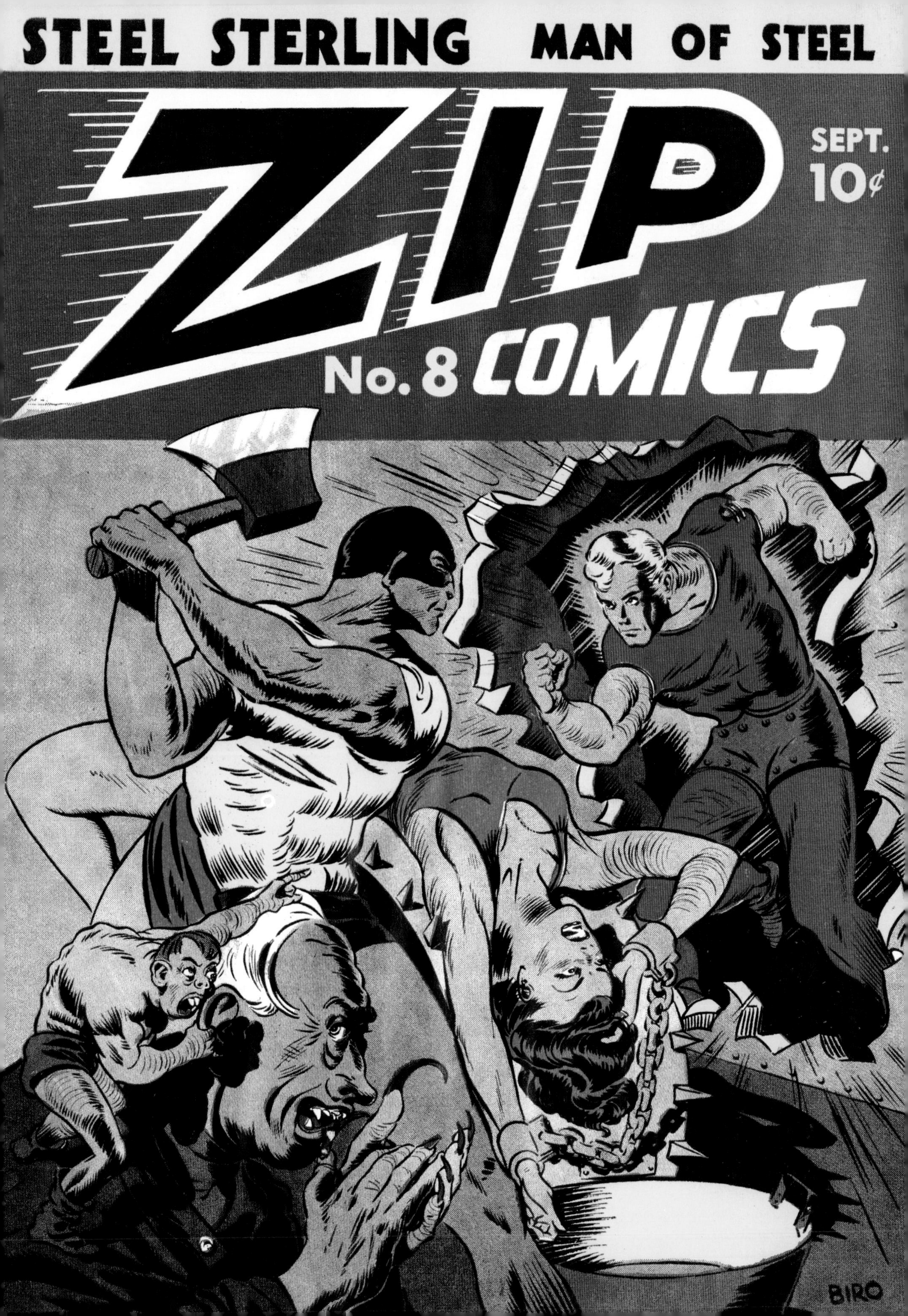

STEEL STERLING MAN OF STEEL
ZIP
SEPT.
10¢
No. 8 COMICS
BIRO

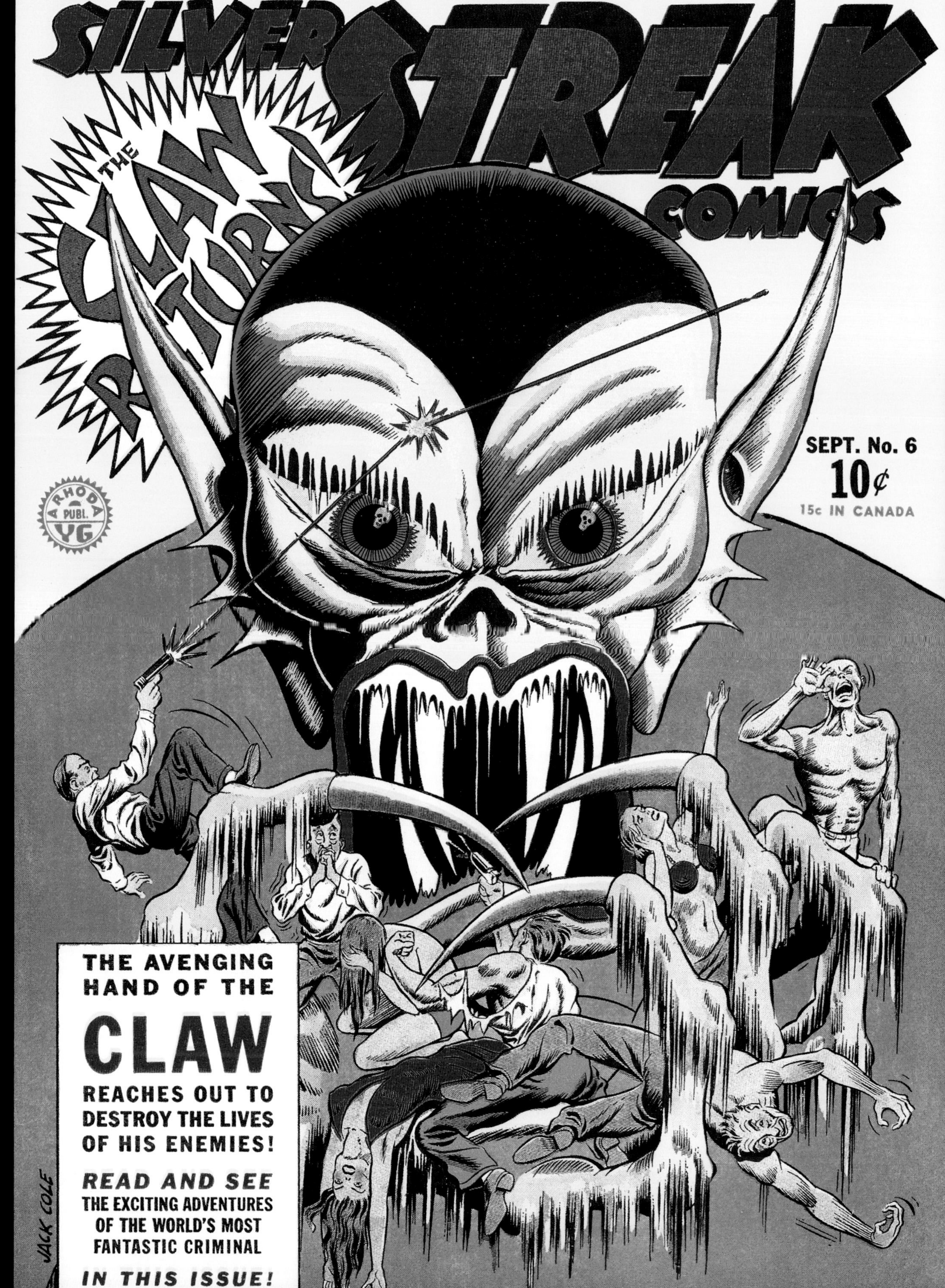

SILVER STREAK COMICS
THE CLAW RETURNS!
ARHODA PUBL. YG
SEPT. No. 6
10¢
15c IN CANADA
THE AVENGING HAND OF THE
CLAW
REACHES OUT TO DESTROY THE LIVES OF HIS ENEMIES!
READ AND SEE
THE EXCITING ADVENTURES OF THE WORLD'S MOST FANTASTIC CRIMINAL
IN THIS ISSUE!
JACK COLE

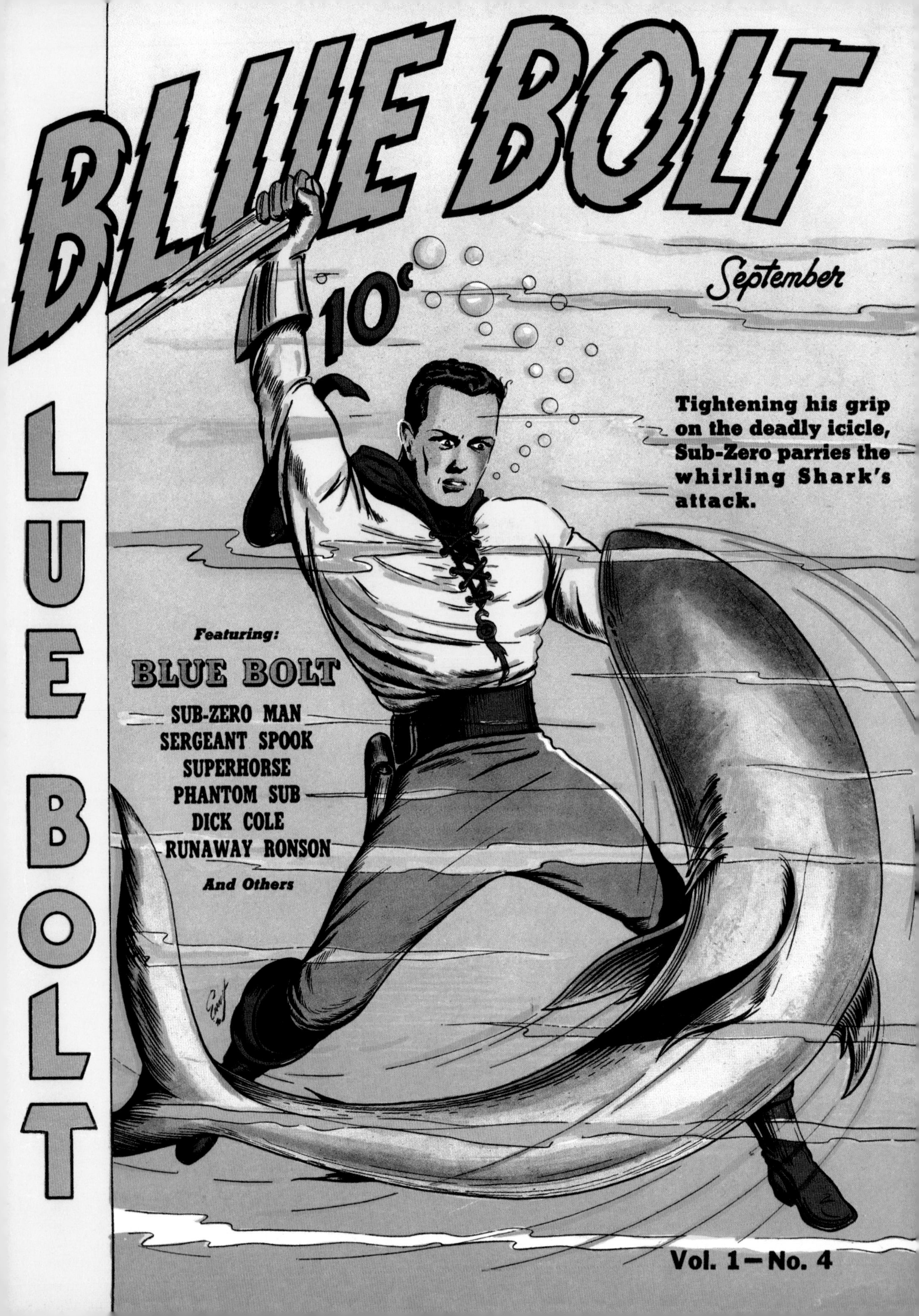

BLUE BOLT
10¢
September
Tightening his grip on the deadly icicle, Sub-Zero parries the whirling Shark's attack.
Featuring:
BLUE BOLT
SUB-ZERO MAN
SERGEANT SPOOK
SUPERHORSE
PHANTOM SUB
DICK COLE
RUNAWAY RONSON
And Others
Vol. 1—No. 4
BLUE BOLT

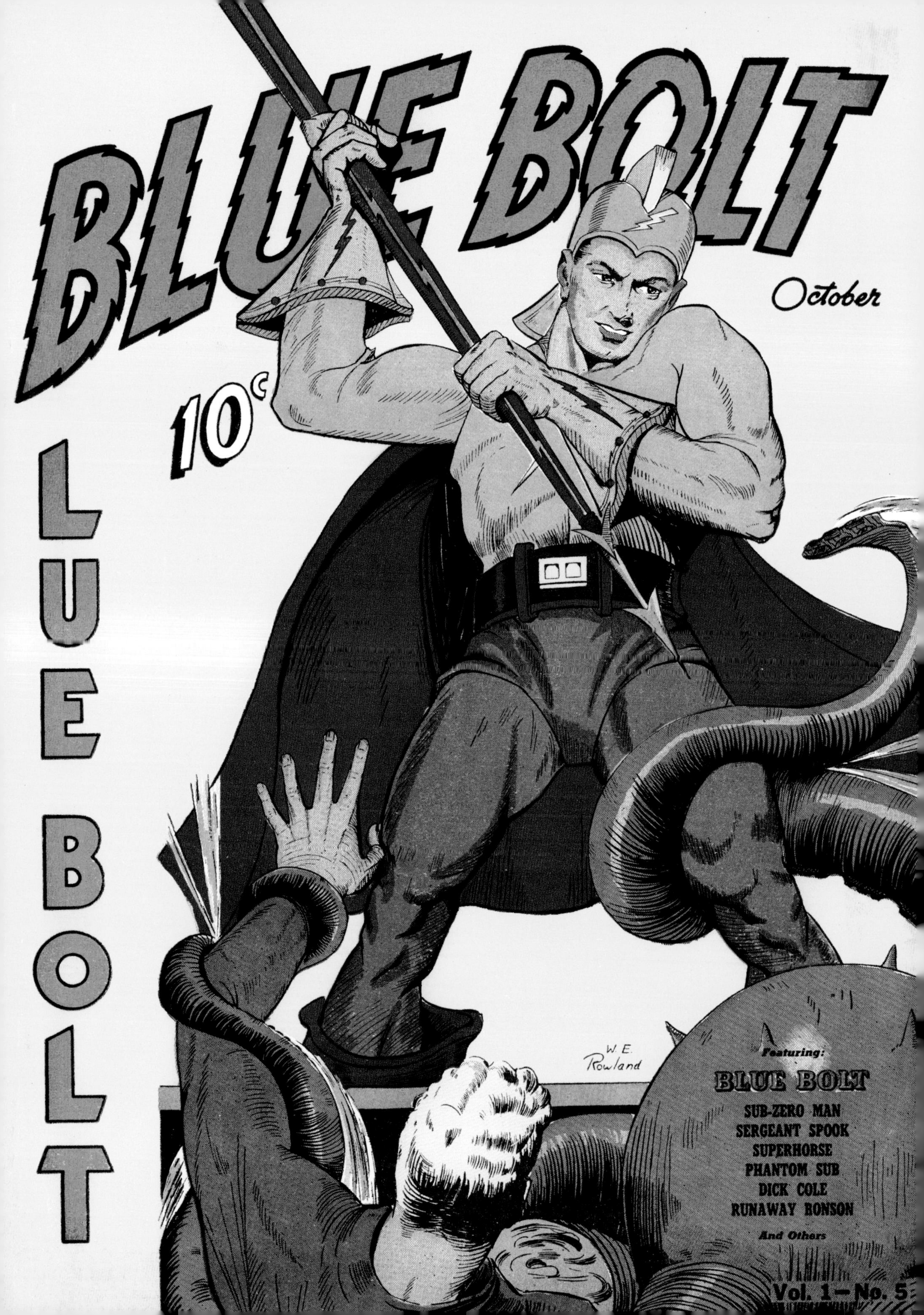
BLUE BOLT
October
10c
BLUE BOLT
W. E. Rowland
Featuring:
BLUE BOLT
SUB-ZERO MAN
SERGEANT SPOOK
SUPERHORSE
PHANTOM SUB
DICK COLE
RUNAWAY BONSON
And Others
Vol. 1—No. 5

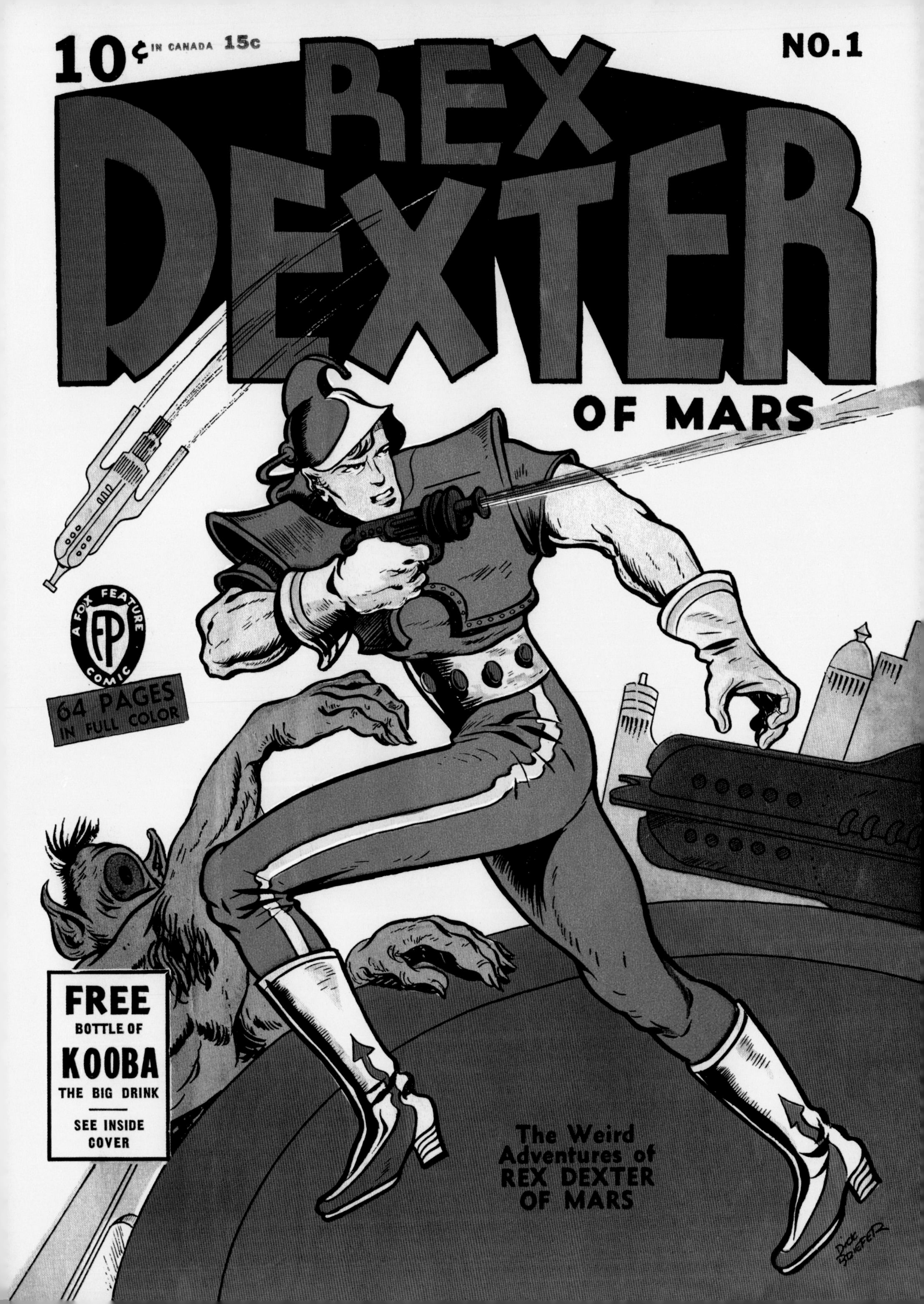
10¢ IN CANADA 15c
NO.1
REX DEXTER
OF MARS
A FOX FEATURE COMIC
FP
64 PAGES IN FULL COLOR
FREE
BOTTLE OF
KOOBA
THE BIG DRINK
SEE INSIDE COVER
The Weird Adventures of REX DEXTER OF MARS

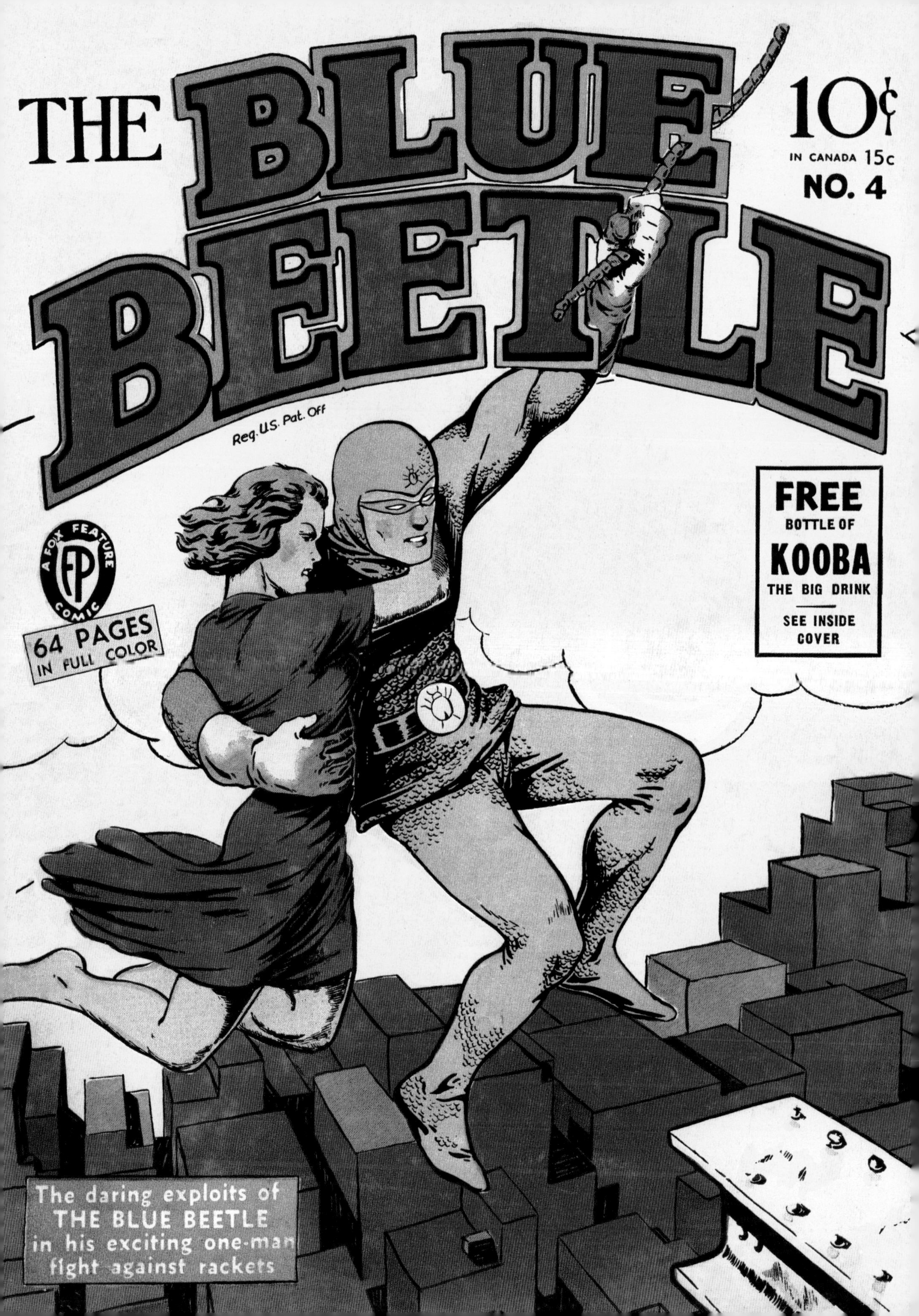
THE BLUE BEETLE
10¢
IN CANADA 15c
NO. 4
Reg. U.S. Pat. Off
FREE
BOTTLE OF
KOOBA
THE BIG DRINK
SEE INSIDE
COVER
A FOX FEATURE
FP
COMIC
64 PAGES
IN FULL COLOR
The daring exploits of
THE BLUE BEETLE
in his exciting one-man
fight against rackets

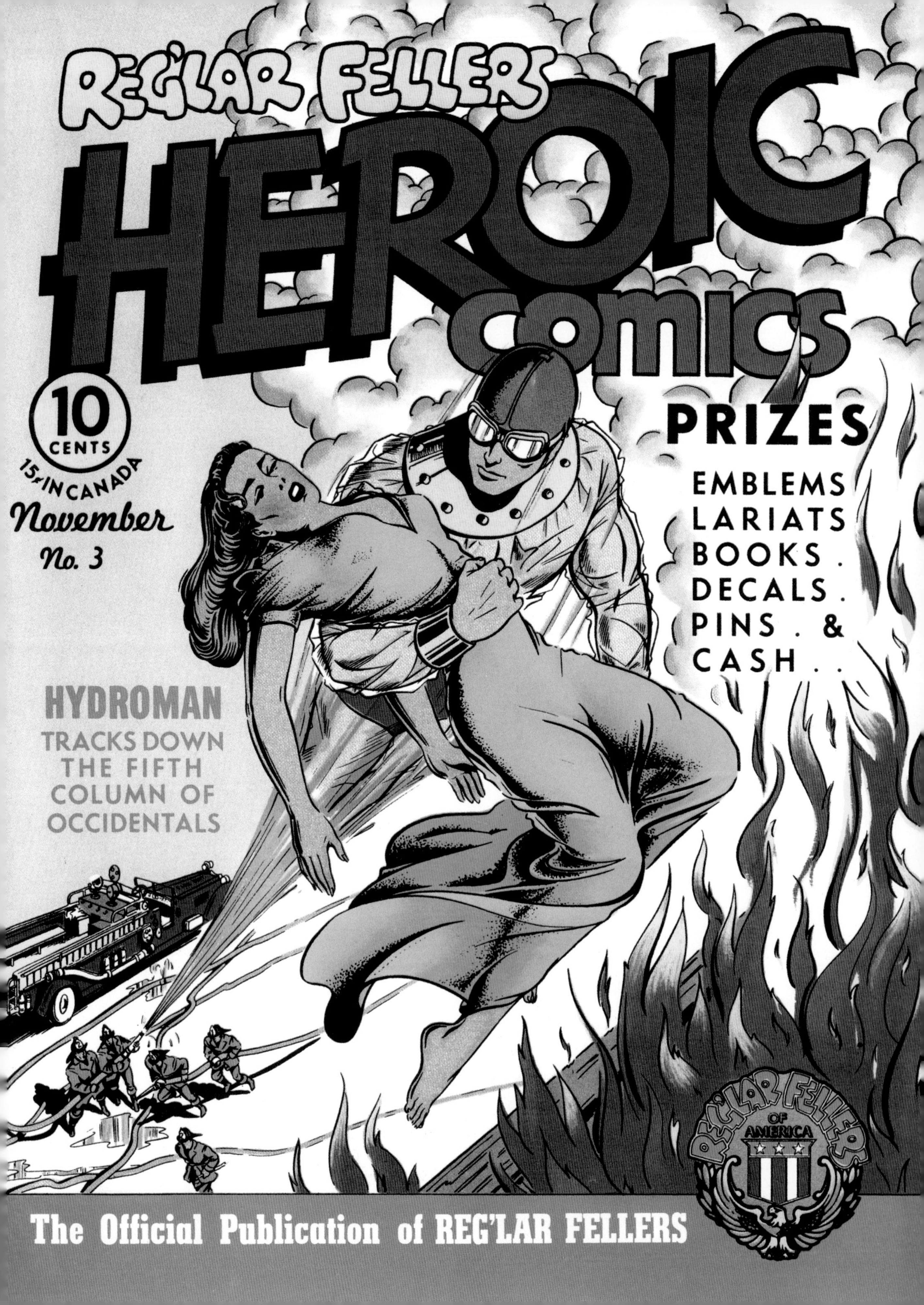

REG'LAR FELLERS
HEROIC
COMICS
10 CENTS
15¢ IN CANADA
November
No. 3
PRIZES
EMBLEMS
LARIATS
BOOKS.
DECALS.
PINS. &
CASH..
HYDROMAN
TRACKS DOWN
THE FIFTH
COLUMN OF
OCCIDENTALS
REG'LAR FELLERS OF AMERICA
The Official Publication of REG'LAR FELLERS

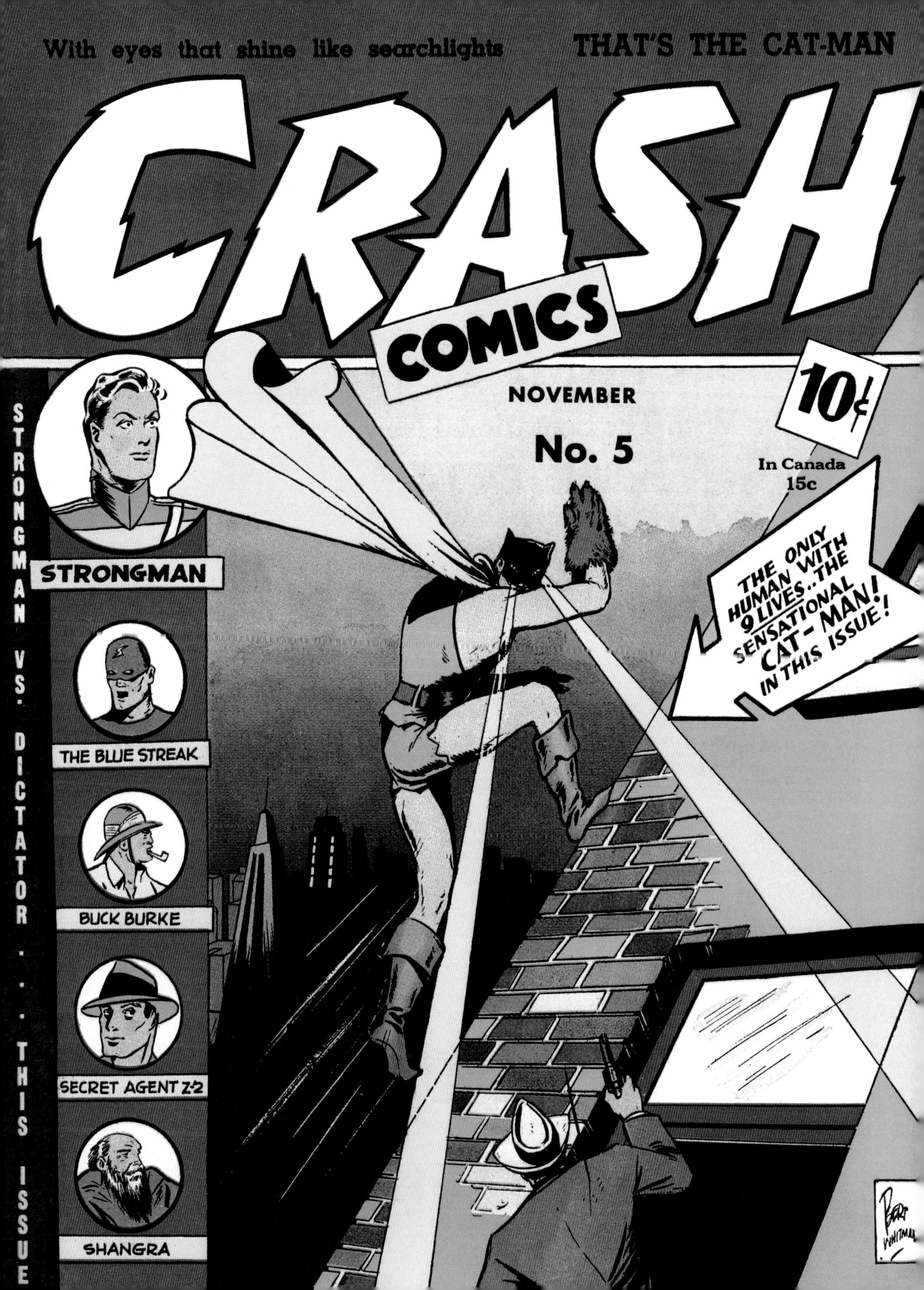
With eyes that shine like searchlights
THAT'S THE CAT-MAN
CRASH
COMICS
NOVEMBER
No. 5
10¢
In Canada 15c
THE ONLY HUMAN WITH 9 LIVES..THE SENSATIONAL CAT-MAN! IN THIS ISSUE!
STRONGMAN
THE BLUE STREAK
BUCK BURKE
SECRET AGENT Z-2
SHANGRA
STRONGMAN VS. DICTATOR .. THIS ISSUE
BERT WHITMAN

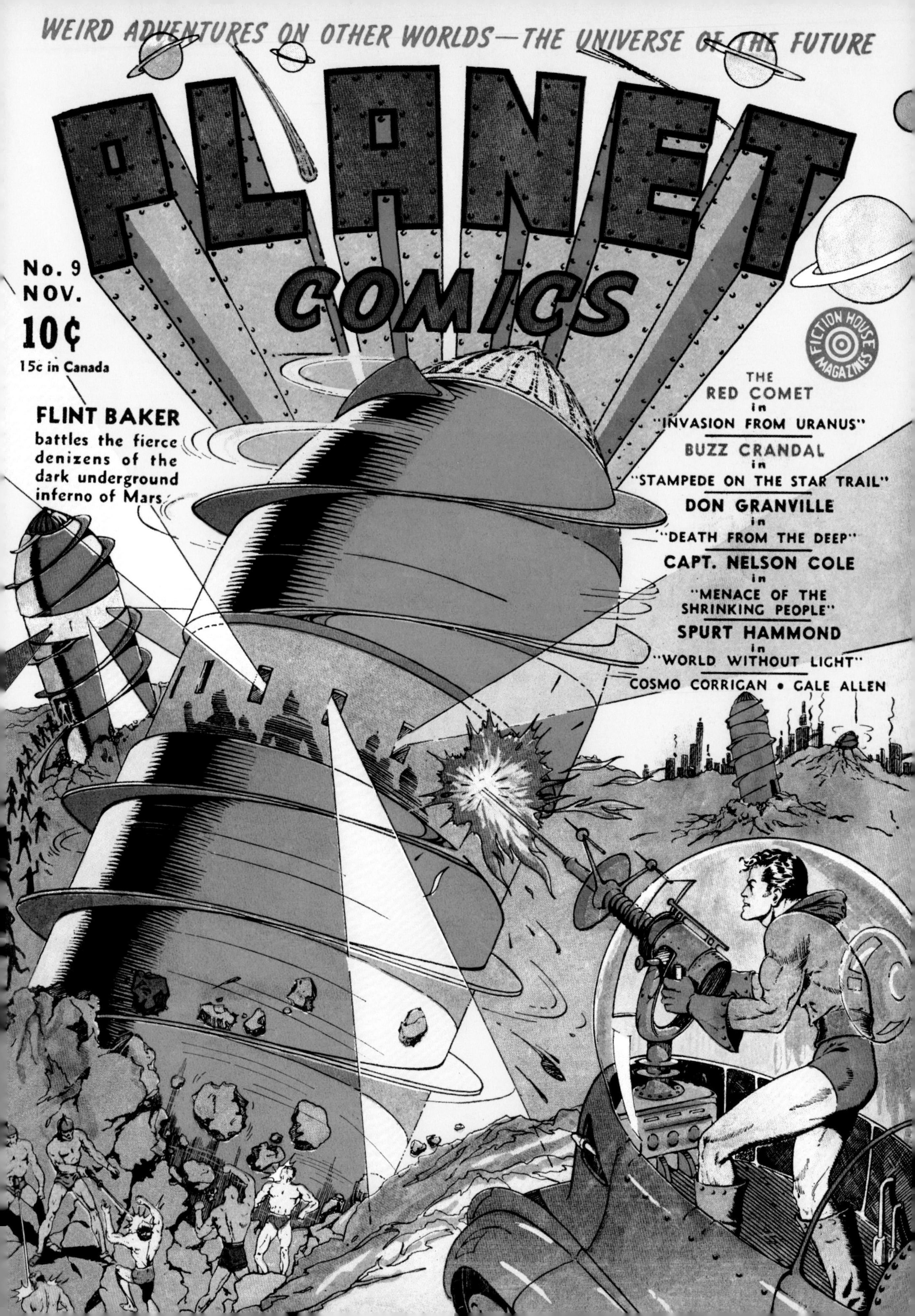

WEIRD ADVENTURES ON OTHER WORLDS—THE UNIVERSE OF THE FUTURE
PLANET COMICS
No. 9
NOV.
10¢
15c in Canada
FICTION HOUSE MAGAZINES
FLINT BAKER battles the fierce denizens of the dark underground inferno of Mars
THE RED COMET in "INVASION FROM URANUS"
BUZZ CRANDAL in "STAMPEDE ON THE STAR TRAIL"
DON GRANVILLE in "DEATH FROM THE DEEP"
CAPT. NELSON COLE in "MENACE OF THE SHRINKING PEOPLE"
SPURT HAMMOND in "WORLD WITHOUT LIGHT"
COSMO CORRIGAN • GALE ALLEN

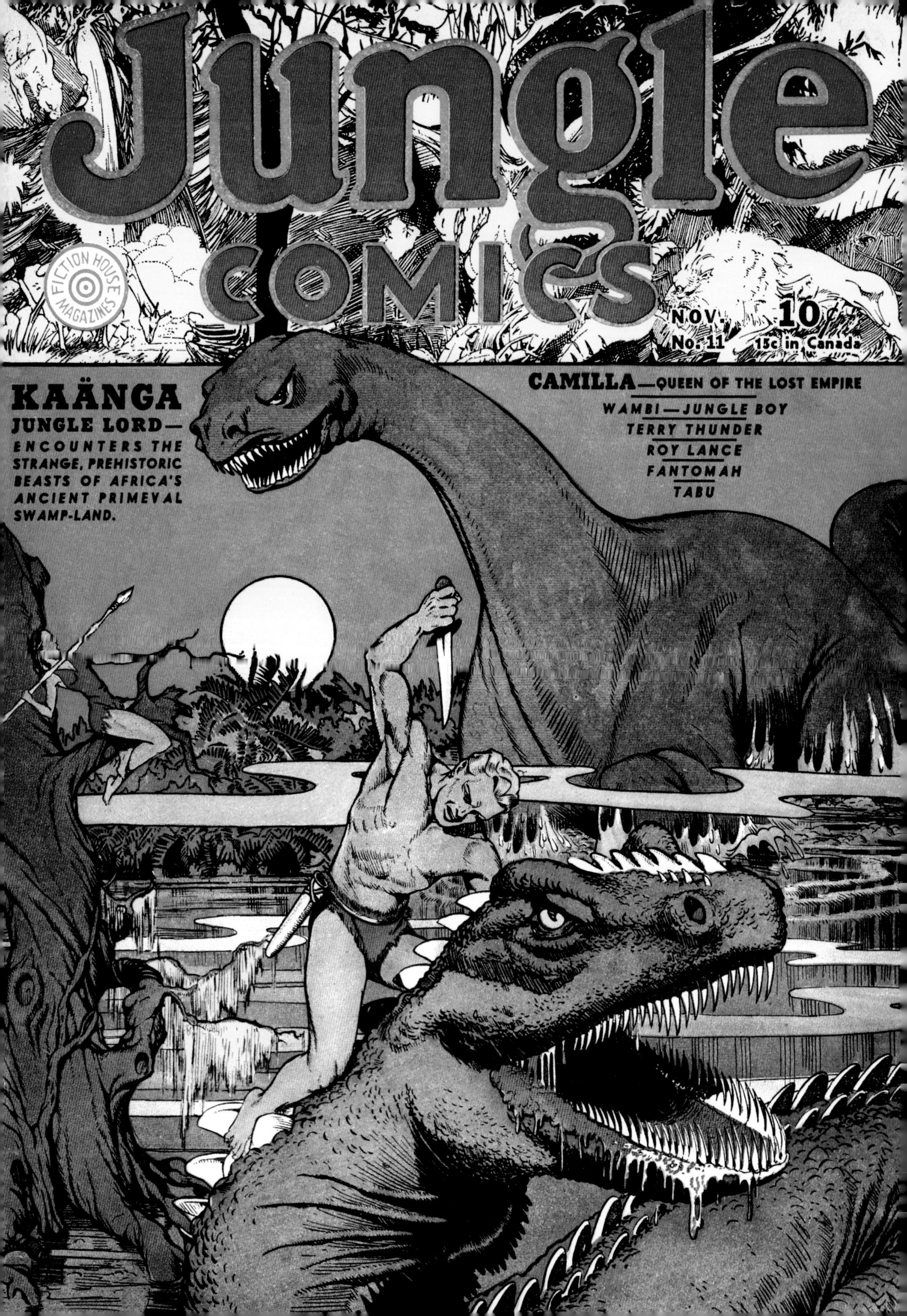

Jungle Comics
FICTION HOUSE MAGAZINES
NOV. No. 11
10¢ 15c in Canada
KAÄNGA JUNGLE LORD— ENCOUNTERS THE STRANGE, PREHISTORIC BEASTS OF AFRICA'S ANCIENT PRIMEVAL SWAMP-LAND.
CAMILLA—QUEEN OF THE LOST EMPIRE
WAMBI—JUNGLE BOY
TERRY THUNDER
ROY LANCE
FANTOMAH
TABU

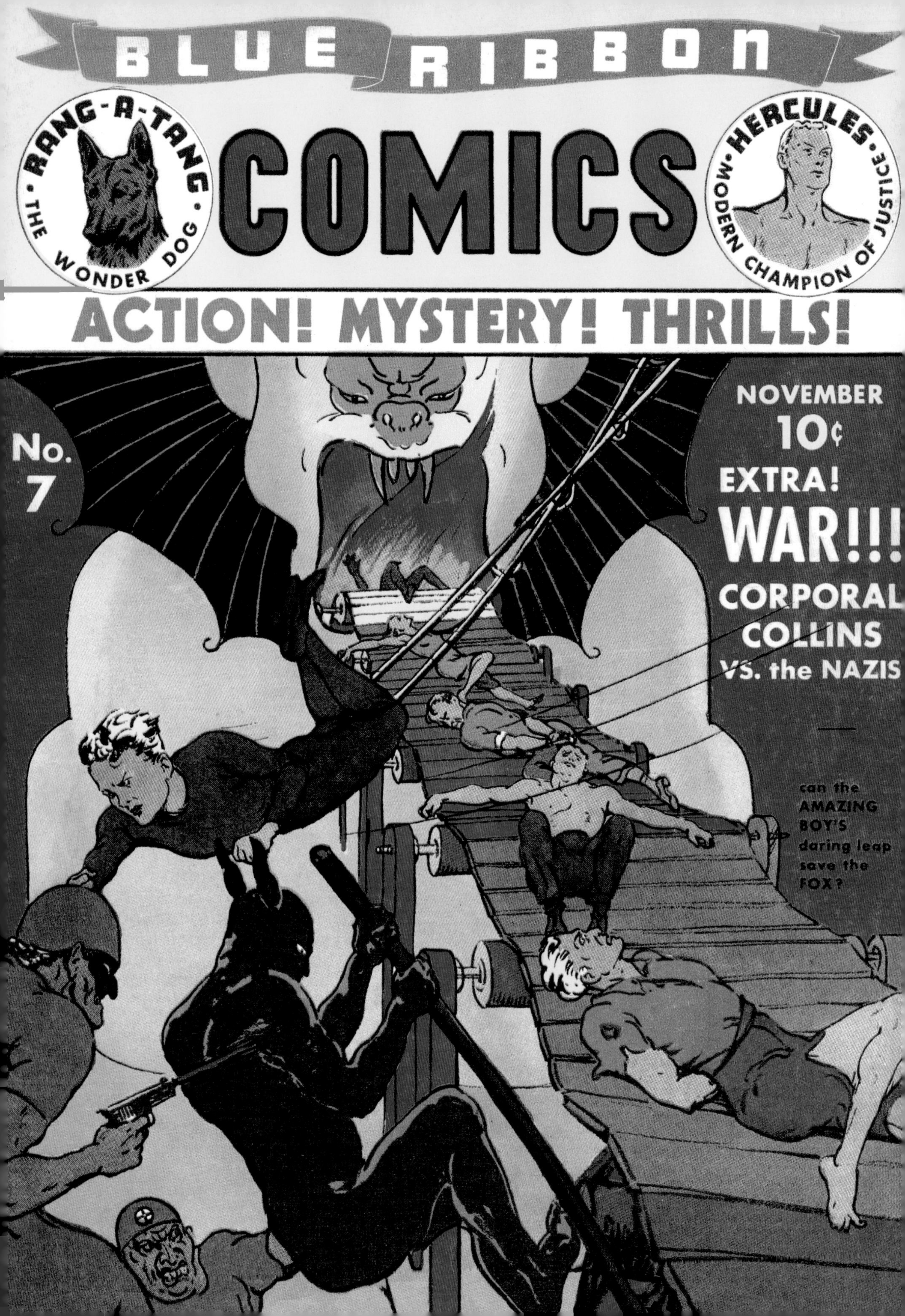
BLUE RIBBON
RANG-A-TANG · THE WONDER DOG ·
COMICS
HERCULES · MODERN CHAMPION OF JUSTICE
ACTION! MYSTERY! THRILLS!
No. 7
NOVEMBER
10¢
EXTRA!
WAR!!!
CORPORAL COLLINS VS. the NAZIS
can the AMAZING BOY'S daring leap save the FOX?

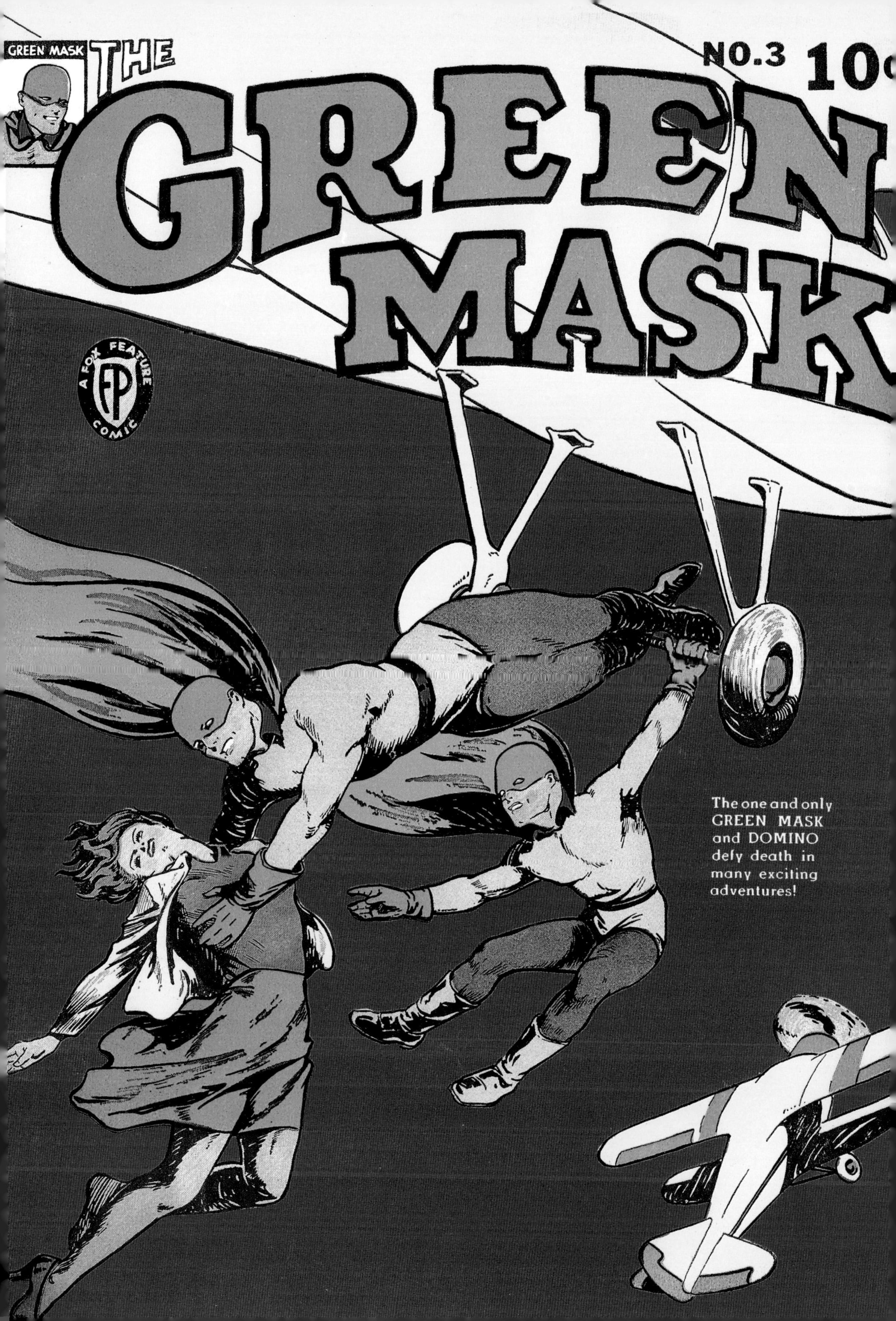
GREEN MASK
THE GREEN MASK
NO.3
10¢
A FOX FEATURE COMIC
FP
The one and only GREEN MASK and DOMINO defy death in many exciting adventures!

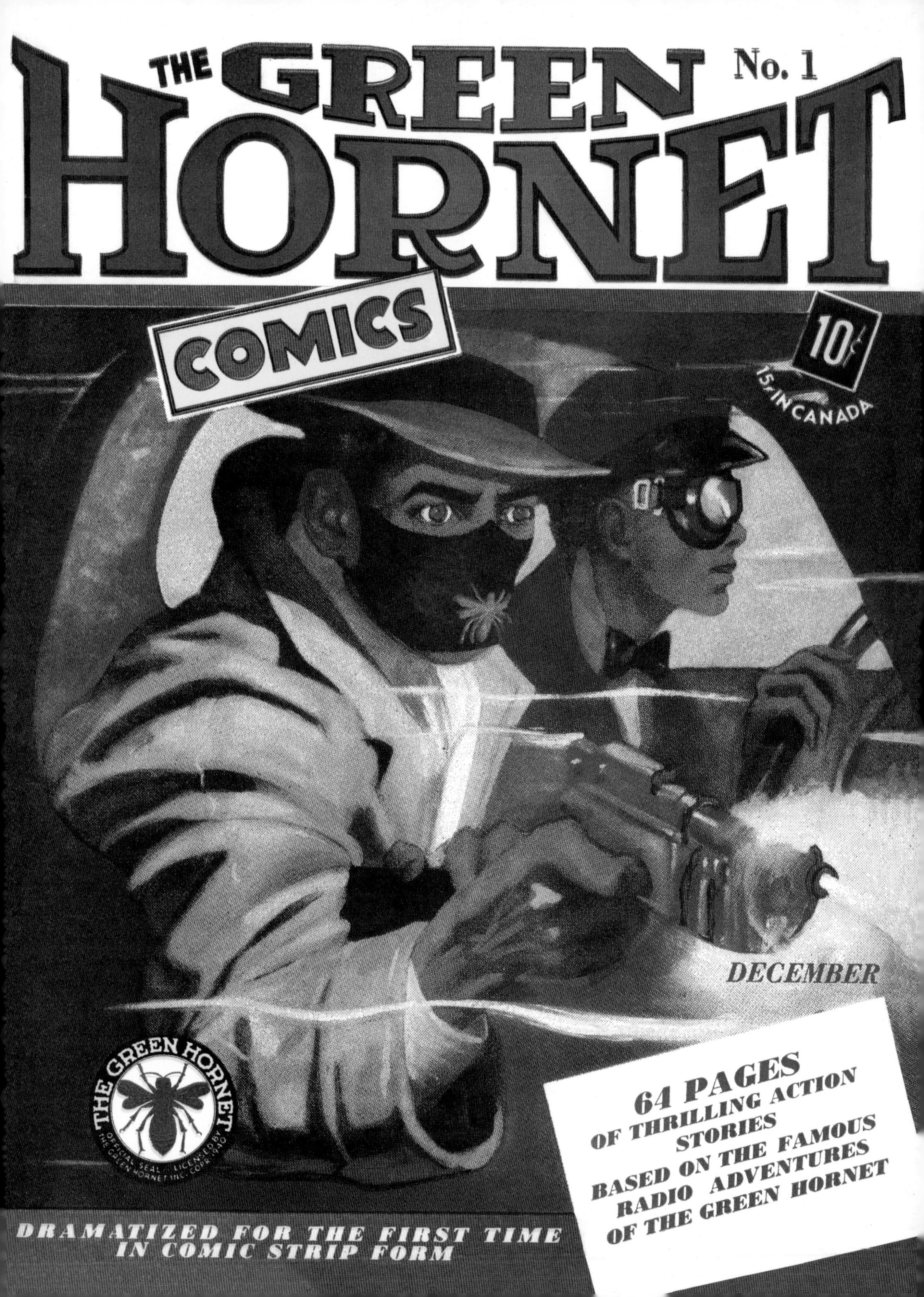

THE GREEN HORNET
No. 1
COMICS
10¢
15¢ IN CANADA
DECEMBER
THE GREEN HORNET
OFFICIAL SEAL LICENSED BY THE GREEN HORNET INC. COPR. 1940
64 PAGES
OF THRILLING ACTION
STORIES
BASED ON THE FAMOUS
RADIO ADVENTURES
OF THE GREEN HORNET
DRAMATIZED FOR THE FIRST TIME
IN COMIC STRIP FORM

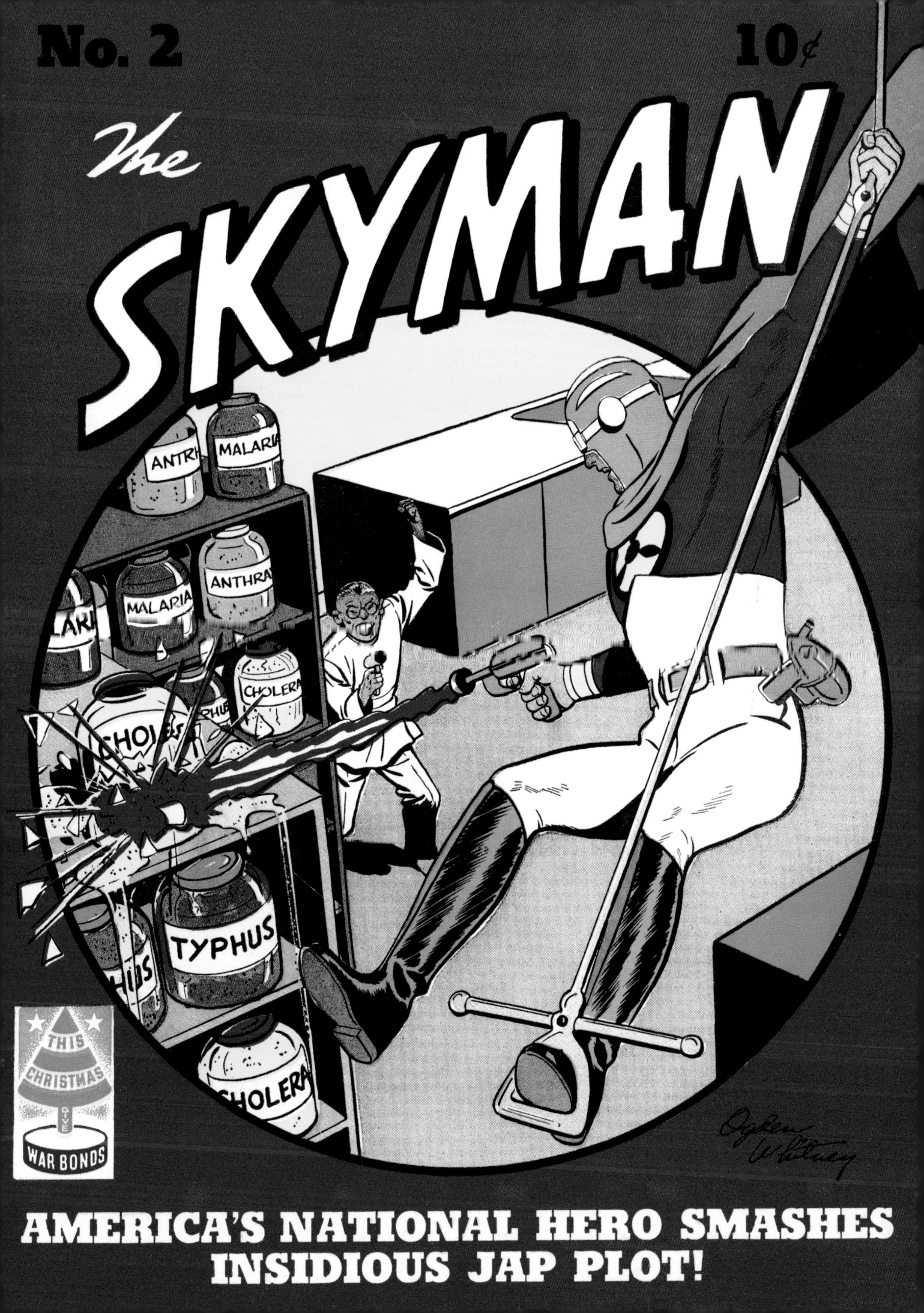
No. 2
10¢
The SKYMAN
MALARIA
CHOLERA
TYPHUS
THIS CHRISTMAS GIVE WAR BONDS
Ogden Whitney
AMERICA'S NATIONAL HERO SMASHES INSIDIOUS JAP PLOT!

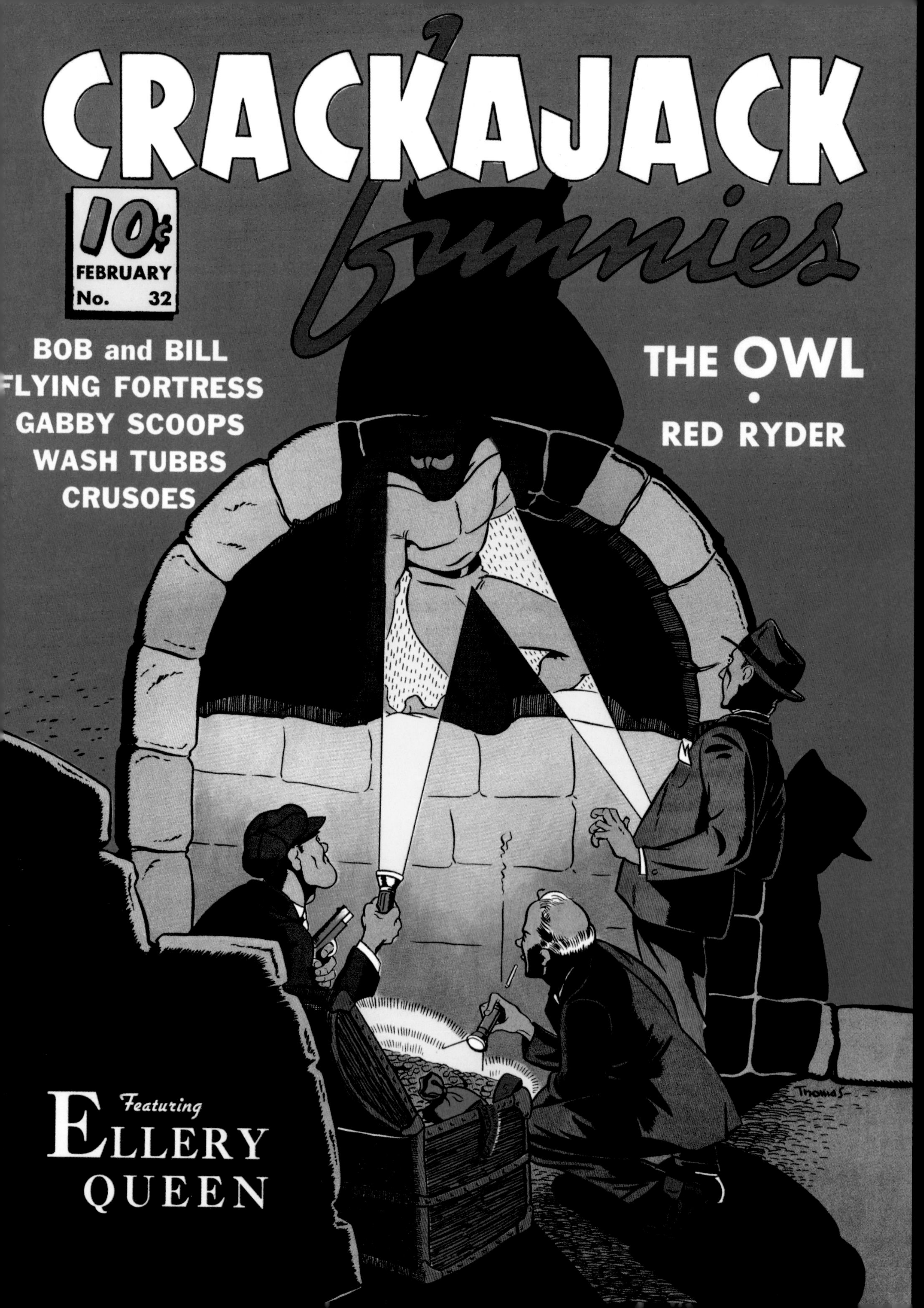
CRACKAJACK funnies
10¢
FEBRUARY
No. 32
BOB and BILL
FLYING FORTRESS
GABBY SCOOPS
WASH TUBBS
CRUSOES
THE OWL
RED RYDER
Featuring
ELLERY QUEEN
THOMAS

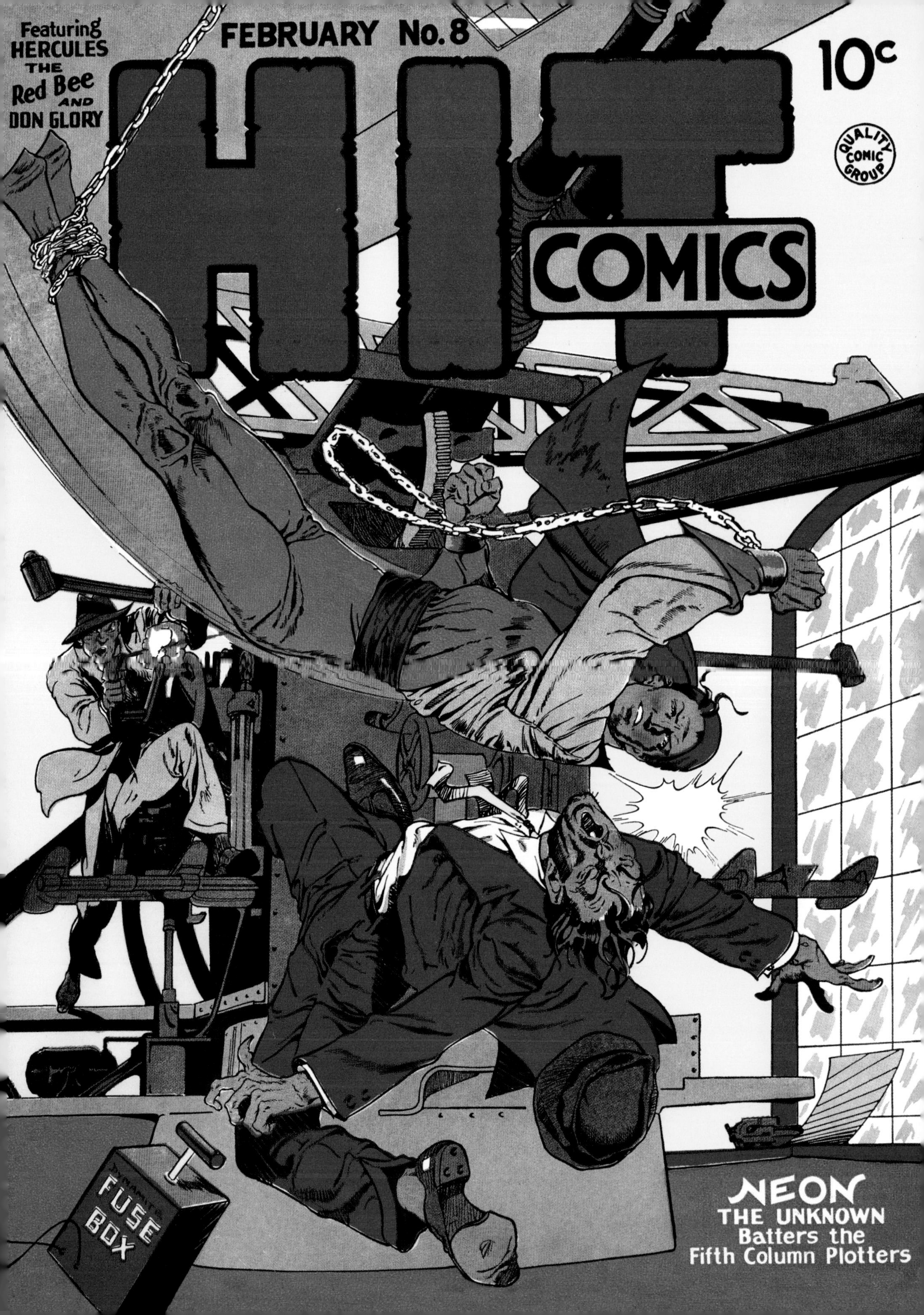
Featuring HERCULES THE Red Bee AND DON GLORY
FEBRUARY No. 8
HIT COMICS
10c
QUALITY COMIC GROUP
DYNAMITE FUSE BOX
NEON THE UNKNOWN Batters the Fifth Column Plotters

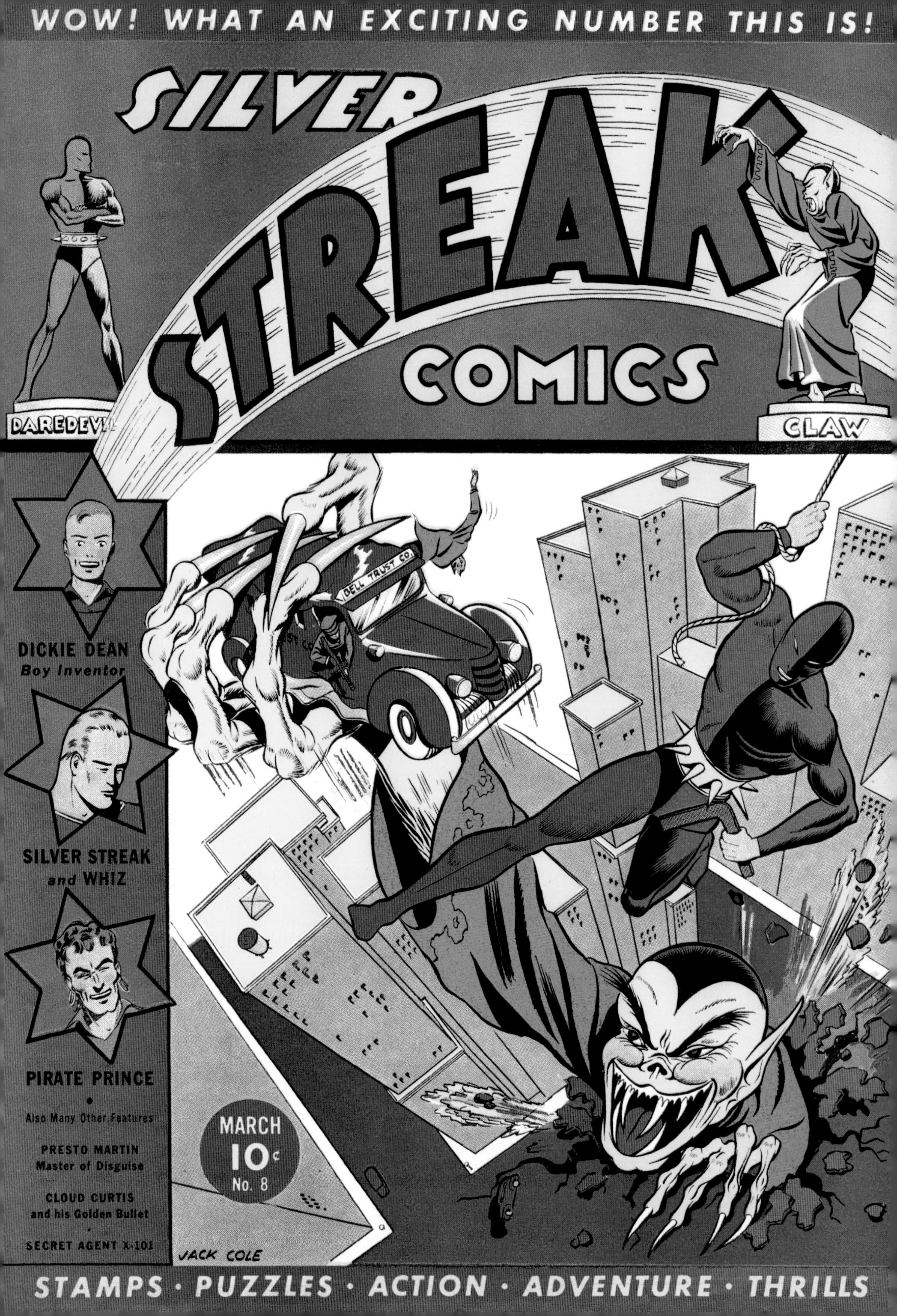
WOW! WHAT AN EXCITING NUMBER THIS IS!
SILVER STREAK COMICS
DAREDEVIL
CLAW
DICKIE DEAN
Boy Inventor
SILVER STREAK
and WHIZ
PIRATE PRINCE
Also Many Other Features
PRESTO MARTIN
Master of Disguise
CLOUD CURTIS
and his Golden Bullet
SECRET AGENT X-101
BELL TRUST CO.
MARCH
10¢
No. 8
JACK COLE
STAMPS · PUZZLES · ACTION · ADVENTURE · THRILLS

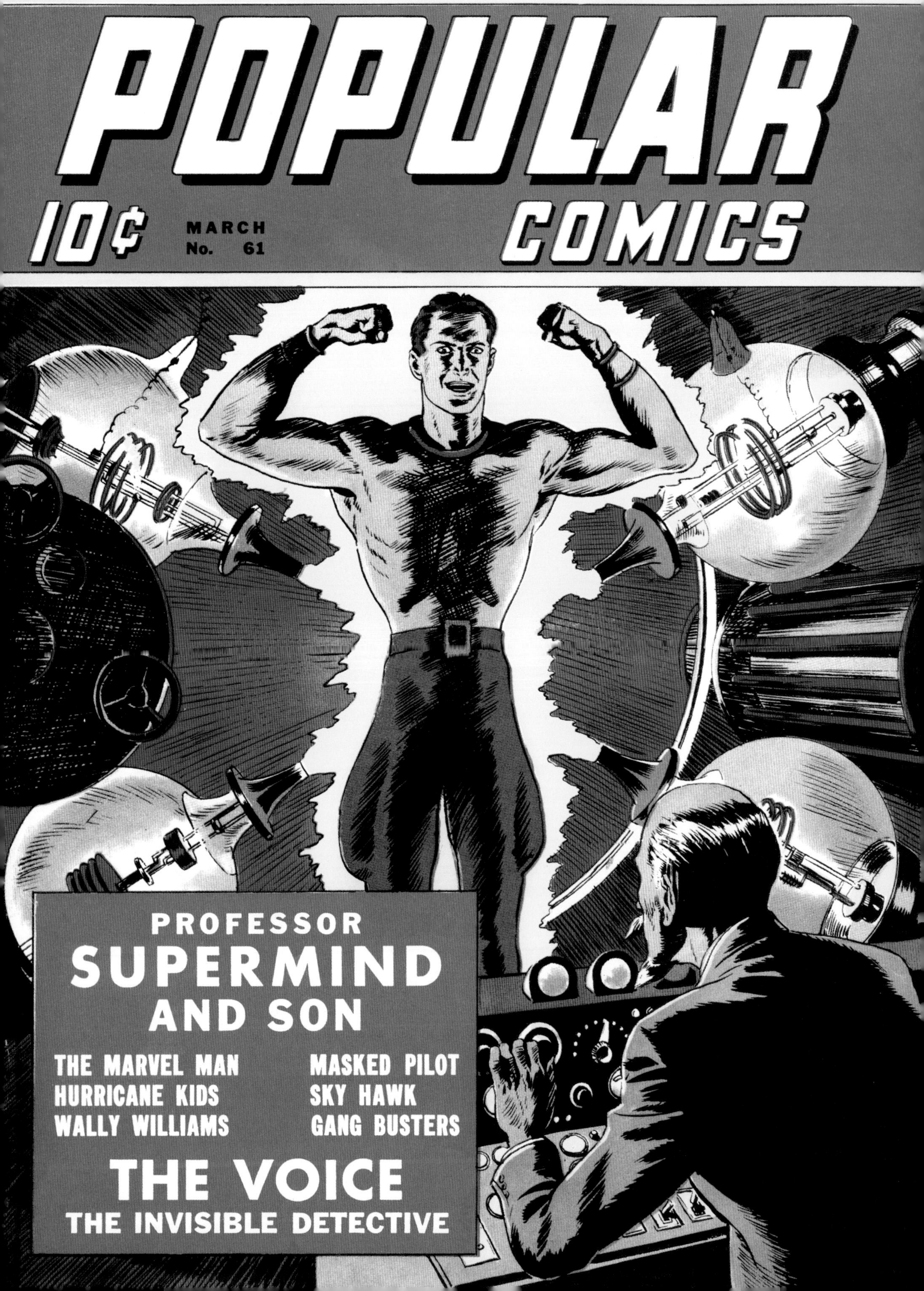
POPULAR COMICS
10¢
MARCH
No. 61
PROFESSOR
SUPERMIND
AND SON
THE MARVEL MAN
HURRICANE KIDS
WALLY WILLIAMS
MASKED PILOT
SKY HAWK
GANG BUSTERS
THE VOICE
THE INVISIBLE DETECTIVE

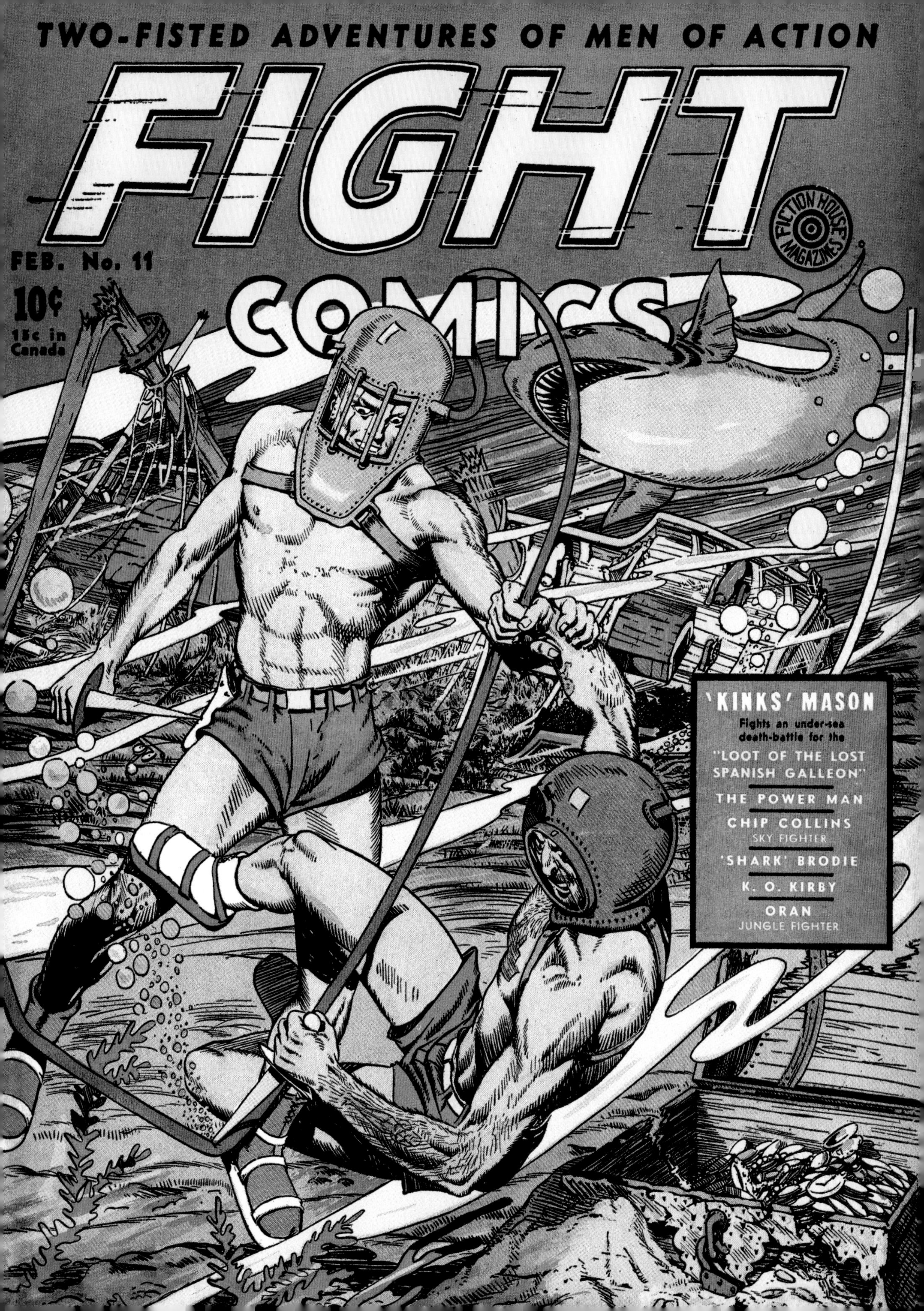

TWO-FISTED ADVENTURES OF MEN OF ACTION
FIGHT
COMICS
FEB. No. 11
10¢
15¢ in Canada
FICTION HOUSE MAGAZINES
'KINKS' MASON
Fights an under-sea death-battle for the
"LOOT OF THE LOST SPANISH GALLEON"
THE POWER MAN
CHIP COLLINS
SKY FIGHTER
'SHARK' BRODIE
K. O. KIRBY
ORAN
JUNGLE FIGHTER

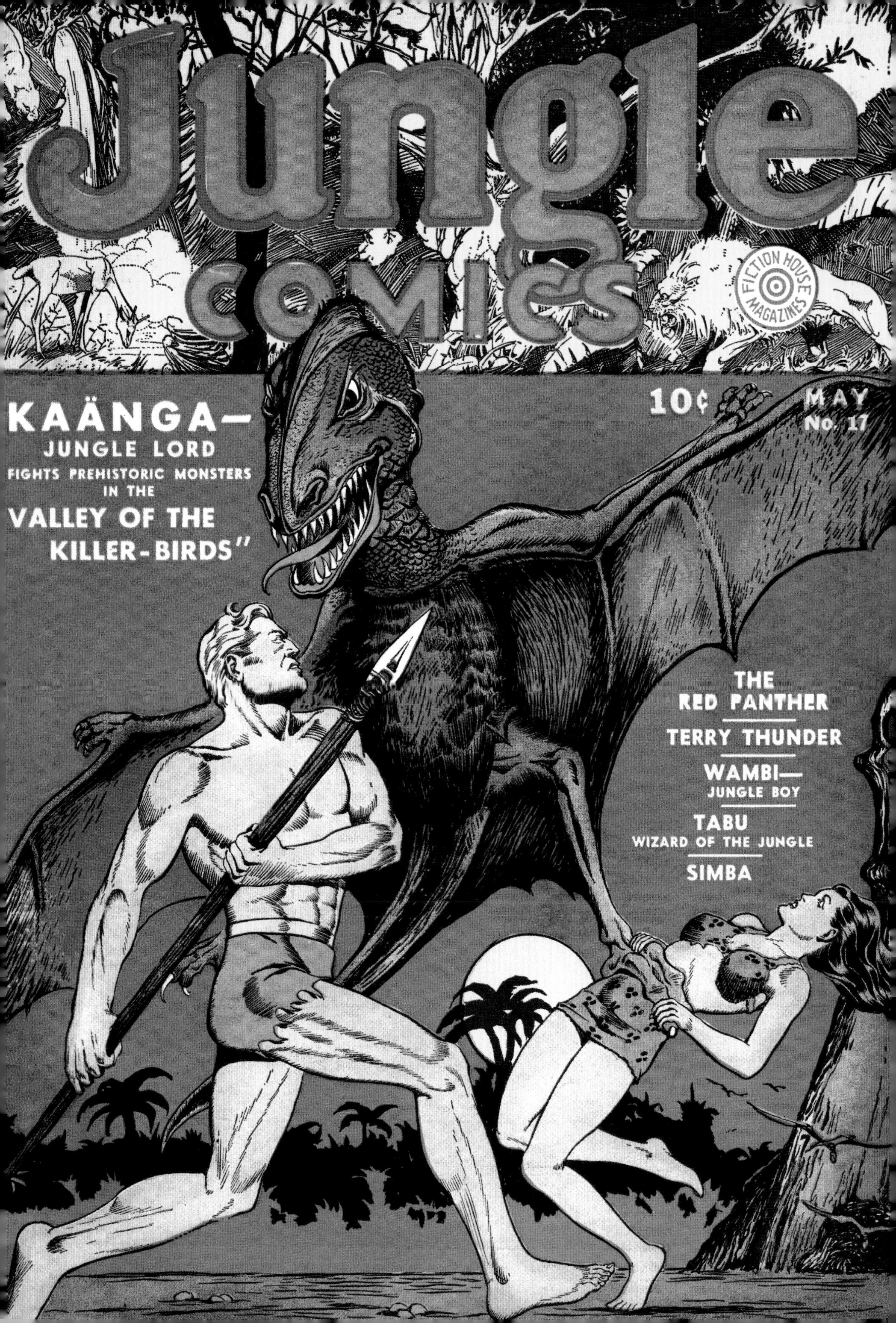

Jungle Comics
Fiction House Magazines
10¢
MAY
No. 17
KAÄNGA—
JUNGLE LORD
FIGHTS PREHISTORIC MONSTERS
IN THE
VALLEY OF THE
KILLER-BIRDS"
THE
RED PANTHER
TERRY THUNDER
WAMBI—
JUNGLE BOY
TABU
WIZARD OF THE JUNGLE
SIMBA

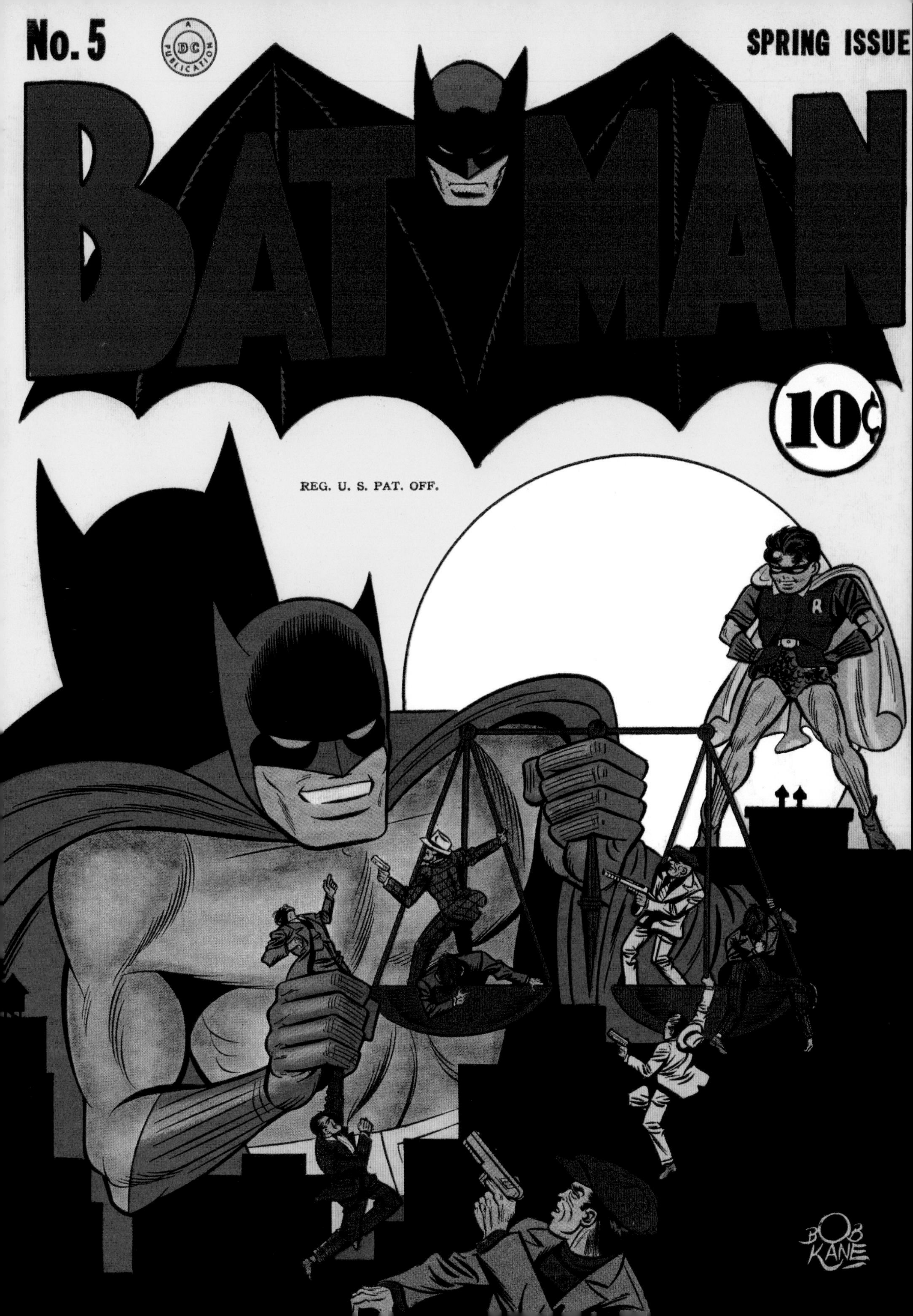
No. 5
A DC PUBLICATION
SPRING ISSUE
BATMAN
10¢
REG. U. S. PAT. OFF.
BOB KANE

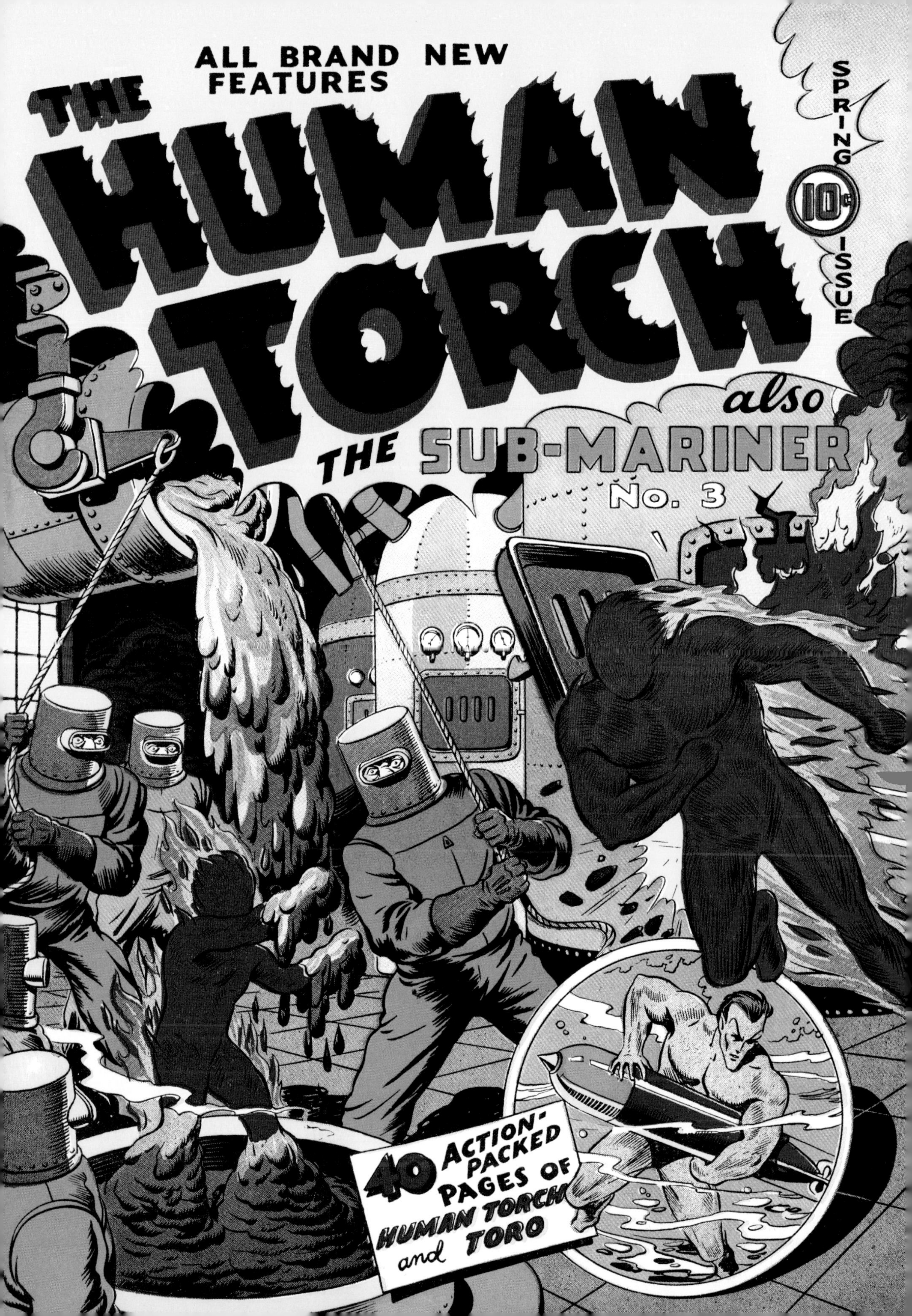

ALL BRAND NEW FEATURES
THE HUMAN TORCH
SPRING ISSUE
10¢
also
THE SUB-MARINER
No. 3
40 ACTION-PACKED PAGES OF HUMAN TORCH and TORO

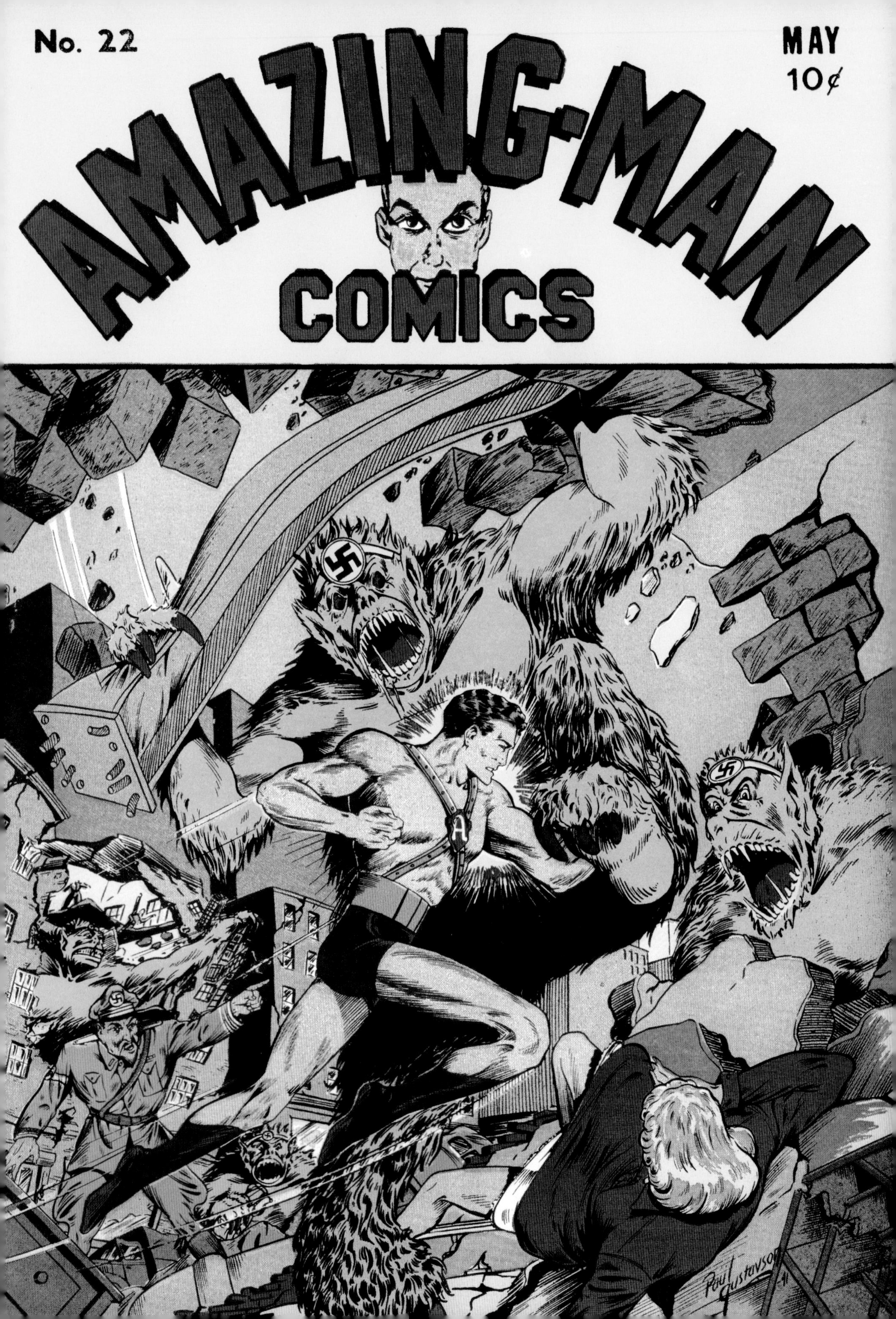
No. 22
MAY
10¢
AMAZING-MAN
COMICS
Paul Gustavson '41

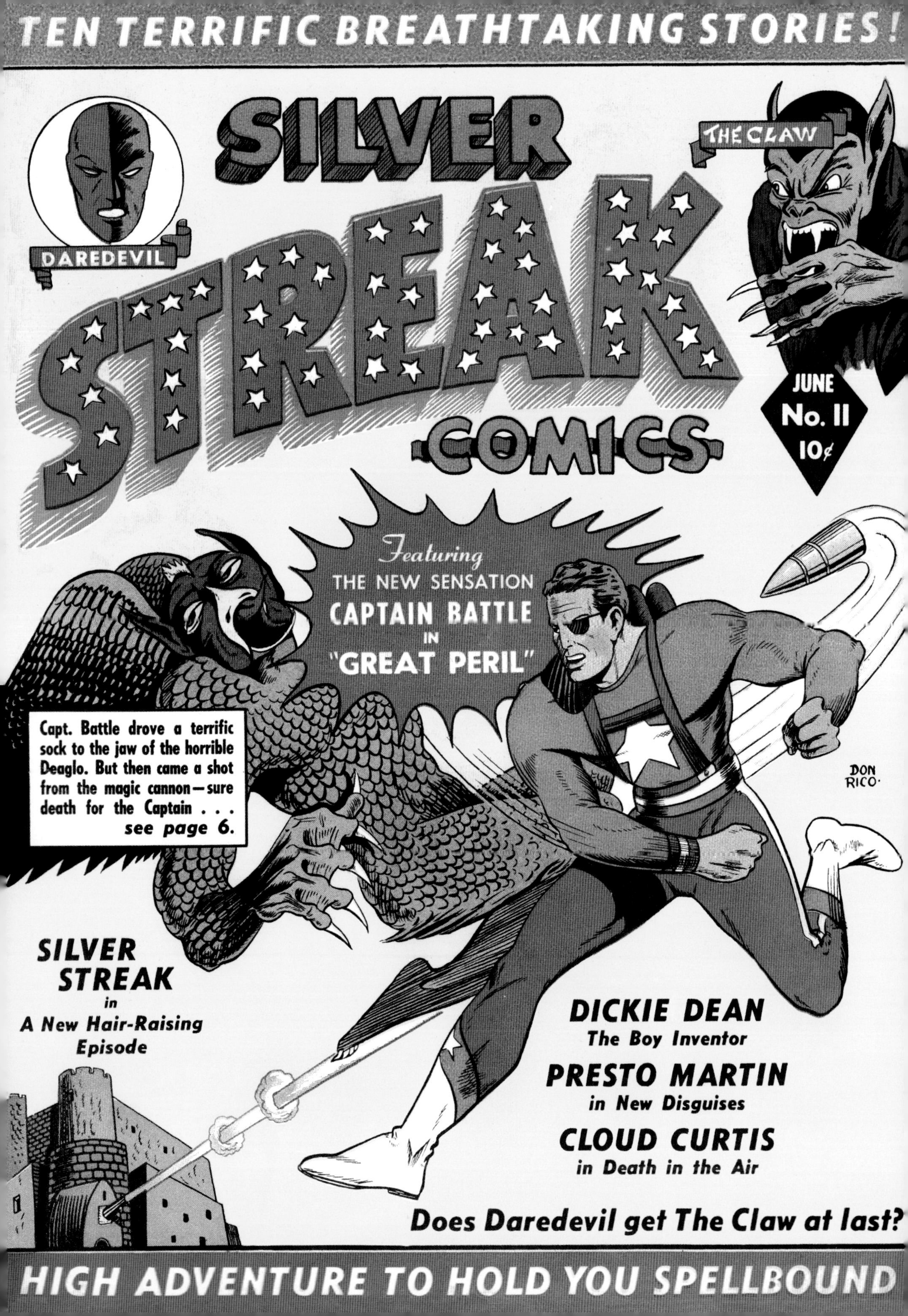
TEN TERRIFIC BREATHTAKING STORIES!
DAREDEVIL
SILVER STREAK COMICS
THE CLAW
JUNE
No. 11
10¢
Featuring
THE NEW SENSATION
CAPTAIN BATTLE
IN
"GREAT PERIL"
Capt. Battle drove a terrific sock to the jaw of the horrible Deaglo. But then came a shot from the magic cannon—sure death for the Captain . . .
see page 6.
DON RICO
SILVER STREAK
in
A New Hair-Raising Episode
DICKIE DEAN
The Boy Inventor
PRESTO MARTIN
in New Disguises
CLOUD CURTIS
in Death in the Air
Does Daredevil get The Claw at last?
HIGH ADVENTURE TO HOLD YOU SPELLBOUND

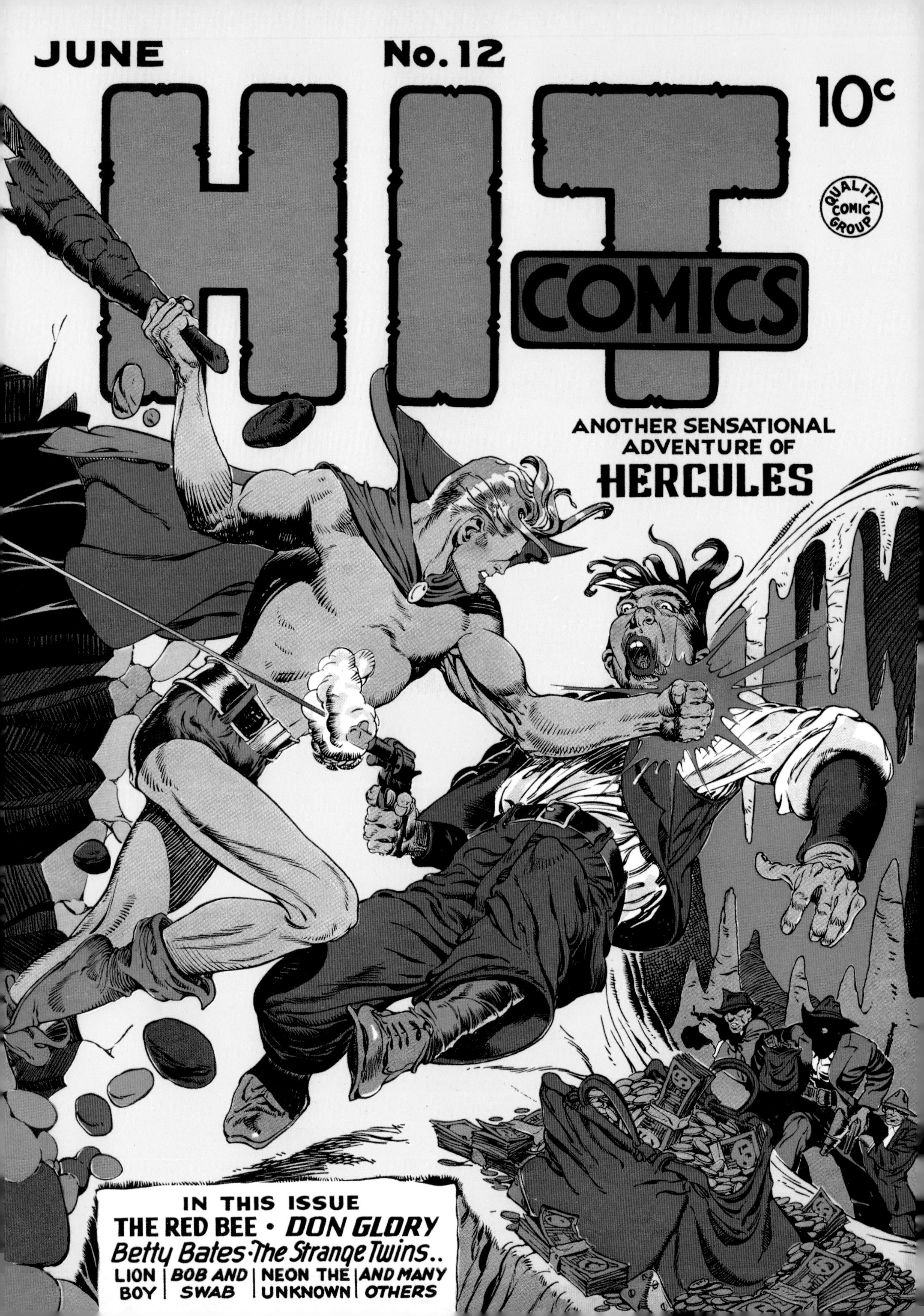
JUNE
No. 12
10c
HIT
COMICS
QUALITY COMIC GROUP
ANOTHER SENSATIONAL ADVENTURE OF
HERCULES
IN THIS ISSUE
THE RED BEE • DON GLORY
Betty Bates · The Strange Twins..
LION BOY | BOB AND SWAB | NEON THE UNKNOWN | AND MANY OTHERS

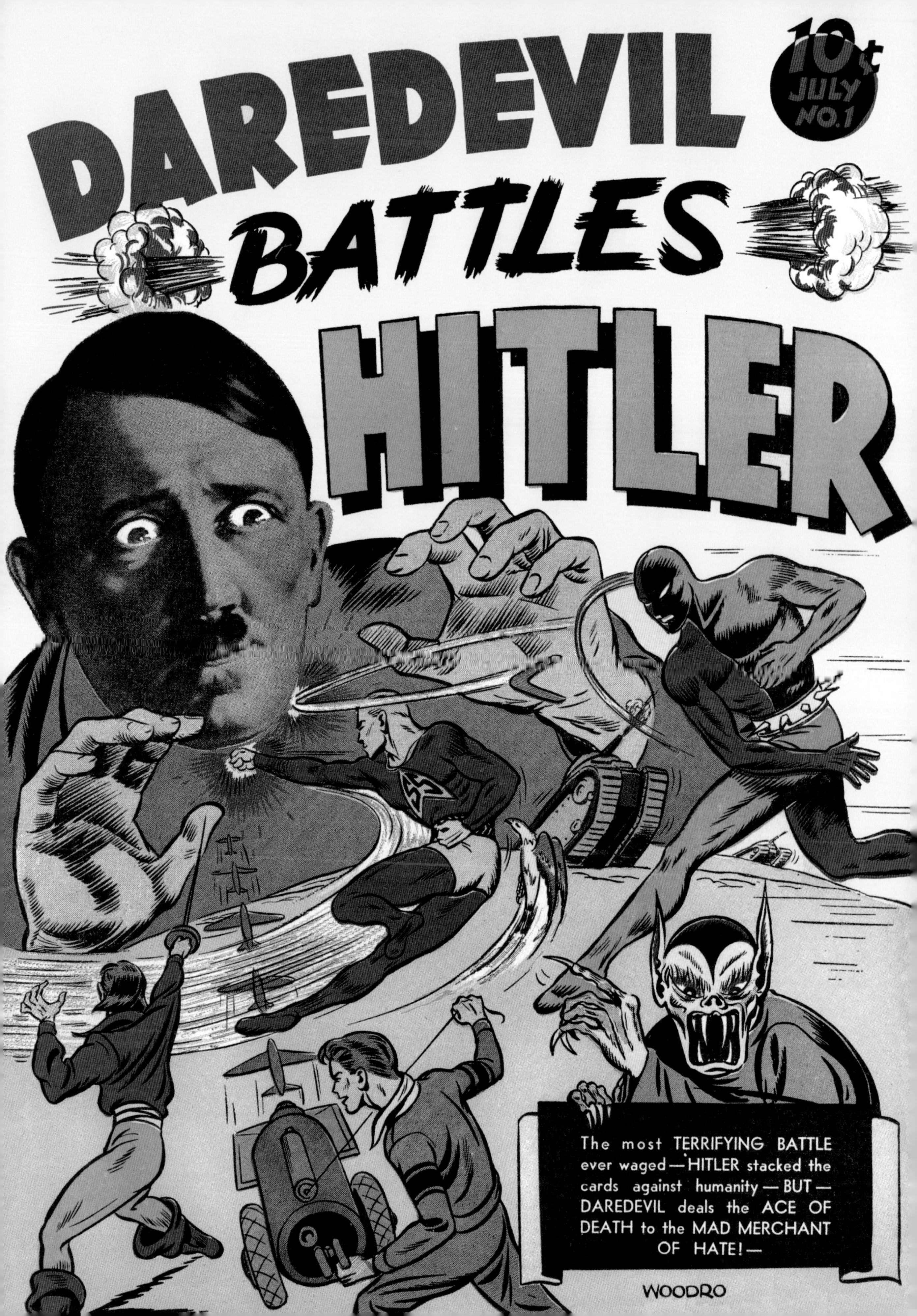
10¢
JULY
NO.1
DAREDEVIL
BATTLES
HITLER
The most TERRIFYING BATTLE ever waged — HITLER stacked the cards against humanity — BUT — DAREDEVIL deals the ACE OF DEATH to the MAD MERCHANT OF HATE! —
WOODRO

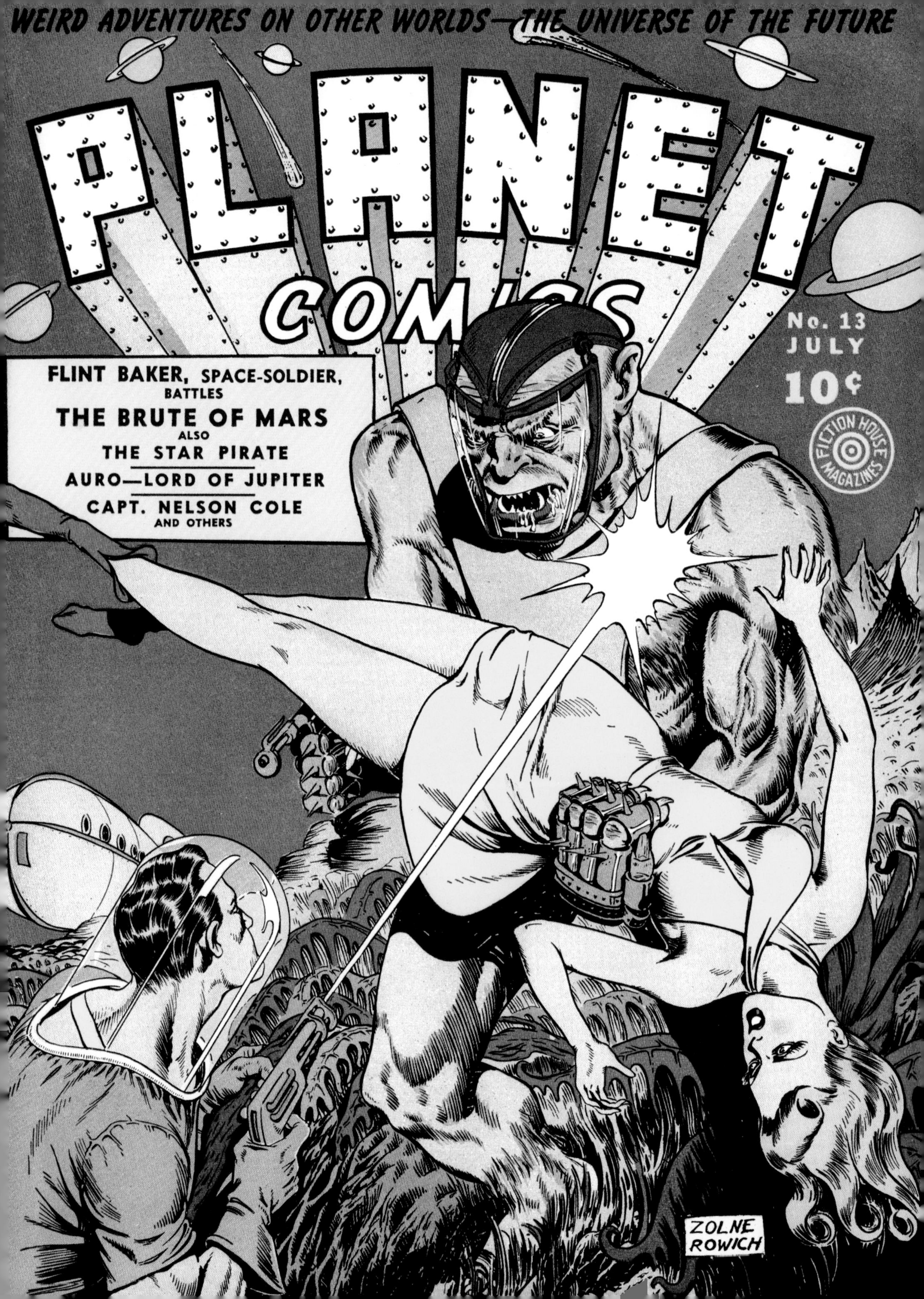
WEIRD ADVENTURES ON OTHER WORLDS—THE UNIVERSE OF THE FUTURE
PLANET COMICS
No. 13
JULY
10¢
FICTION HOUSE MAGAZINES
FLINT BAKER, SPACE-SOLDIER, BATTLES
THE BRUTE OF MARS
ALSO
THE STAR PIRATE
AURO—LORD OF JUPITER
CAPT. NELSON COLE
AND OTHERS
ZOLNE ROWICH

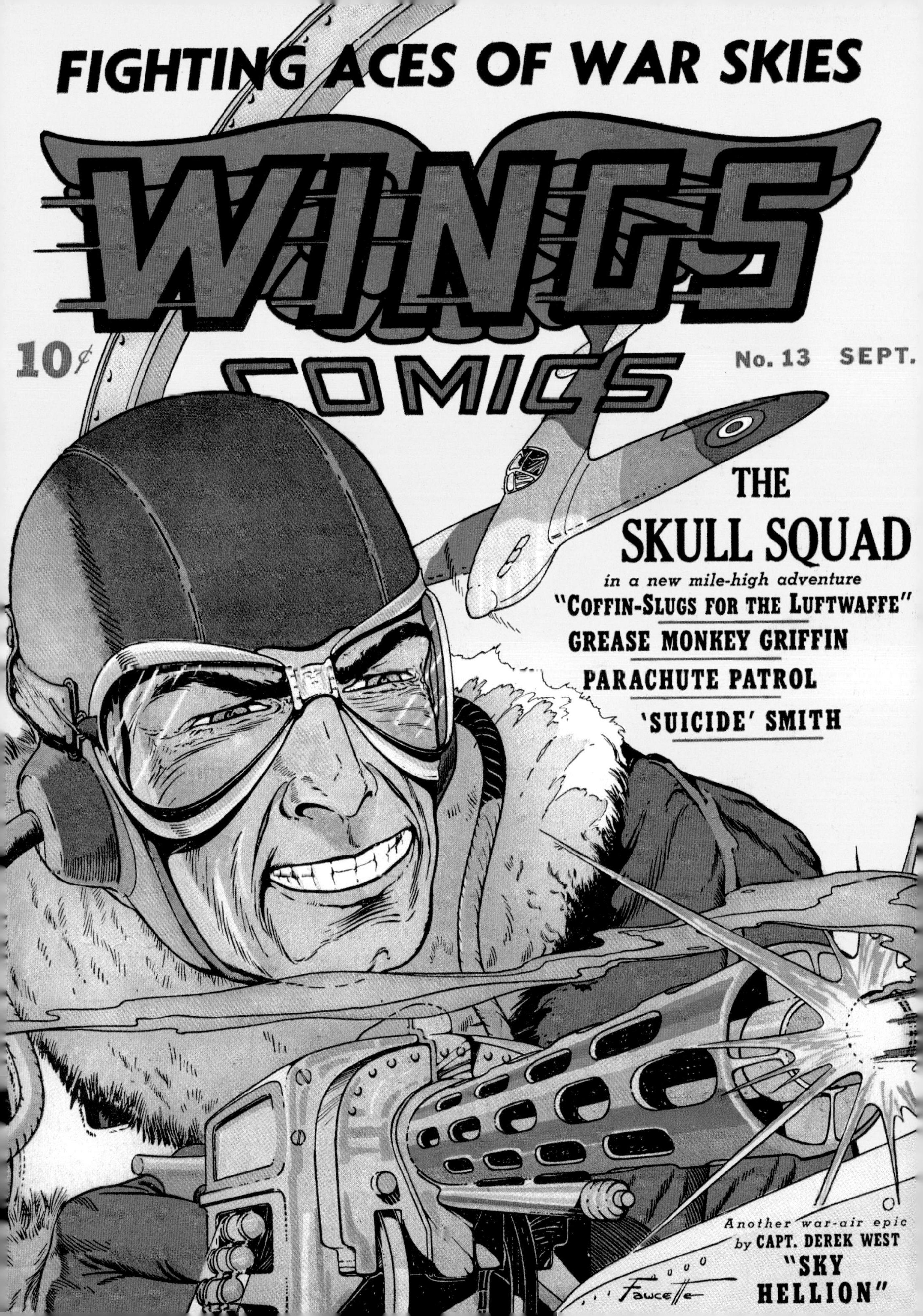
FIGHTING ACES OF WAR SKIES
WINGS
COMICS
10¢
No. 13 SEPT.
THE
SKULL SQUAD
in a new mile-high adventure
"COFFIN-SLUGS FOR THE LUFTWAFFE"
GREASE MONKEY GRIFFIN
PARACHUTE PATROL
'SUICIDE' SMITH
Another war-air epic
by CAPT. DEREK WEST
"SKY
HELLION"
Fawcette

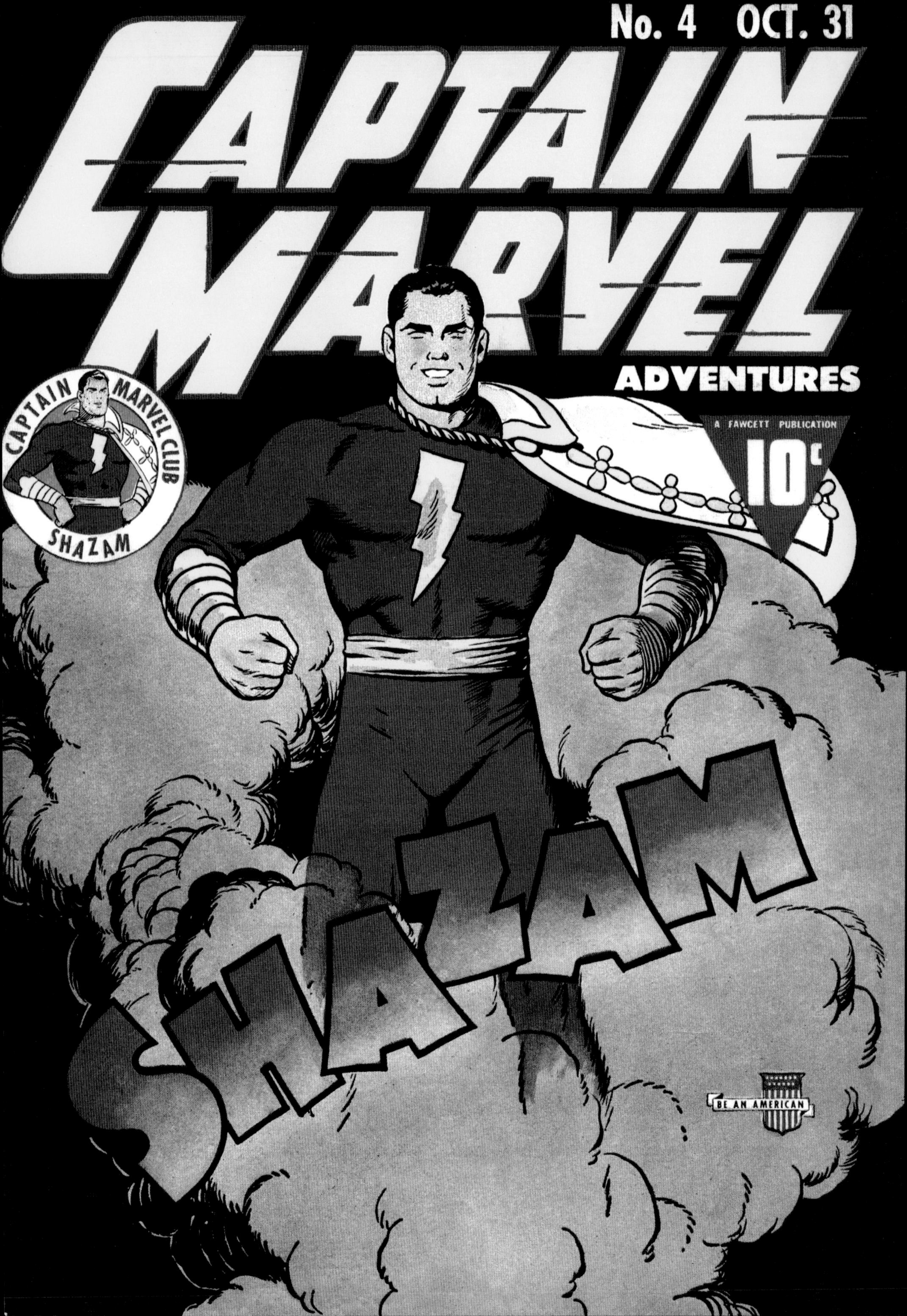

No. 4 OCT. 31
CAPTAIN MARVEL
ADVENTURES
A FAWCETT PUBLICATION
10¢
CAPTAIN MARVEL CLUB
SHAZAM
SHAZAM
BE AN AMERICAN

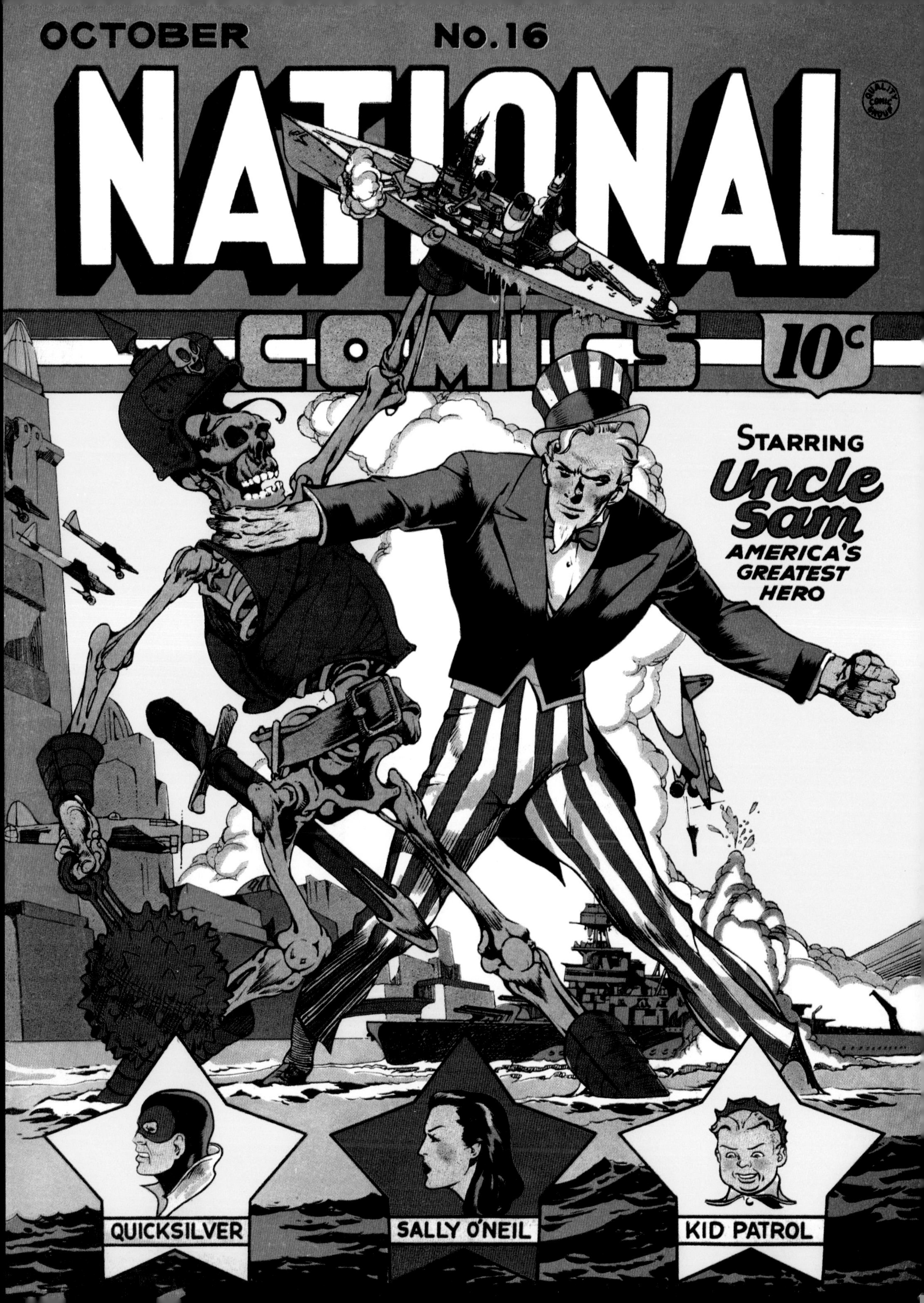

OCTOBER
No. 16
NATIONAL
COMICS
10¢
QUALITY COMIC GROUP
STARRING
Uncle Sam
AMERICA'S GREATEST HERO
QUICKSILVER
SALLY O'NEIL
KID PATROL

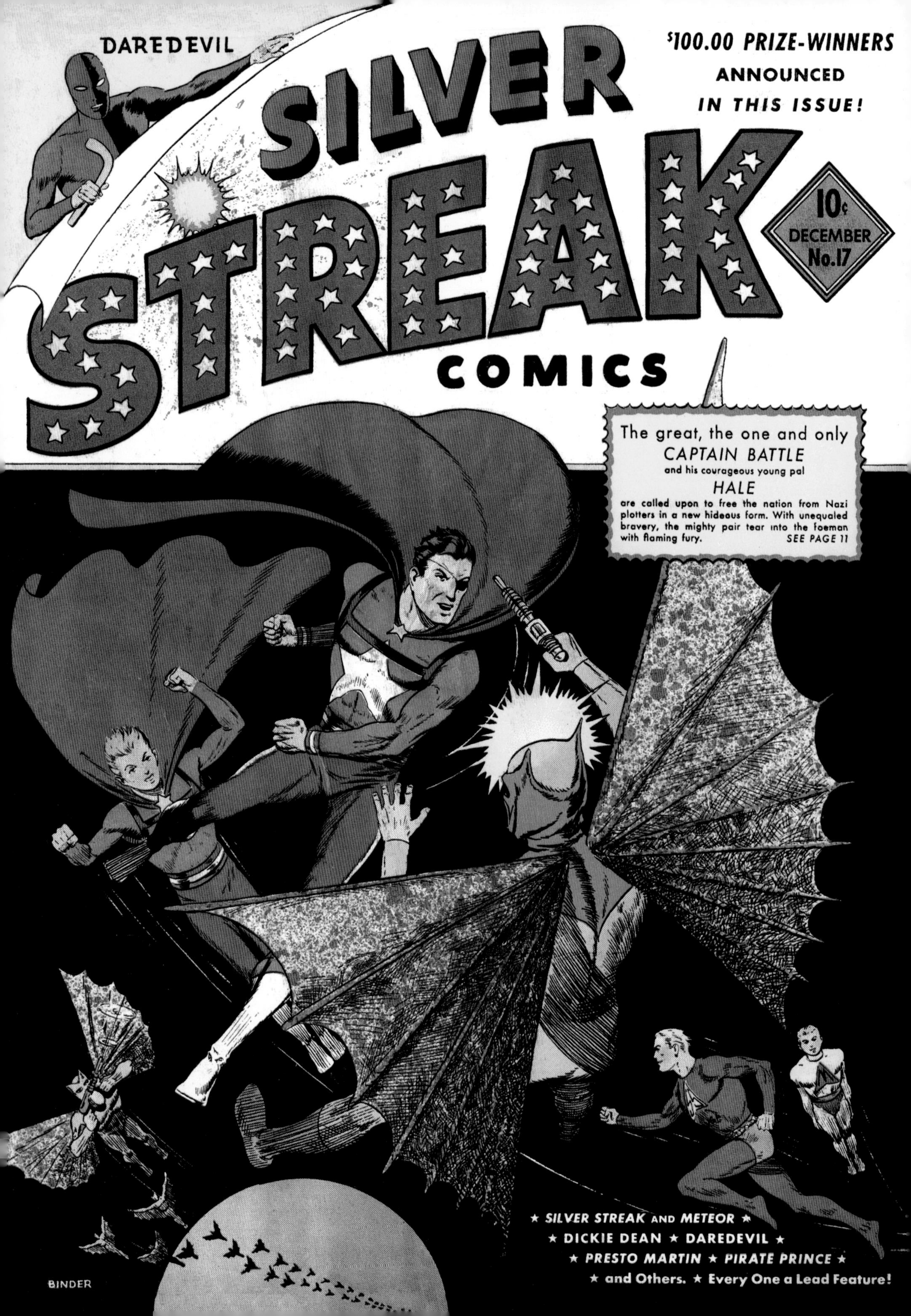

DAREDEVIL
SILVER STREAK COMICS
$100.00 PRIZE-WINNERS ANNOUNCED IN THIS ISSUE!
10¢
DECEMBER
No.17
The great, the one and only
CAPTAIN BATTLE
and his courageous young pal
HALE
are called upon to free the nation from Nazi plotters in a new hideous form. With unequaled bravery, the mighty pair tear into the foeman with flaming fury. SEE PAGE 11
★ SILVER STREAK AND METEOR ★
★ DICKIE DEAN ★ DAREDEVIL ★
★ PRESTO MARTIN ★ PIRATE PRINCE ★
★ and Others. ★ Every One a Lead Feature!
BINDER

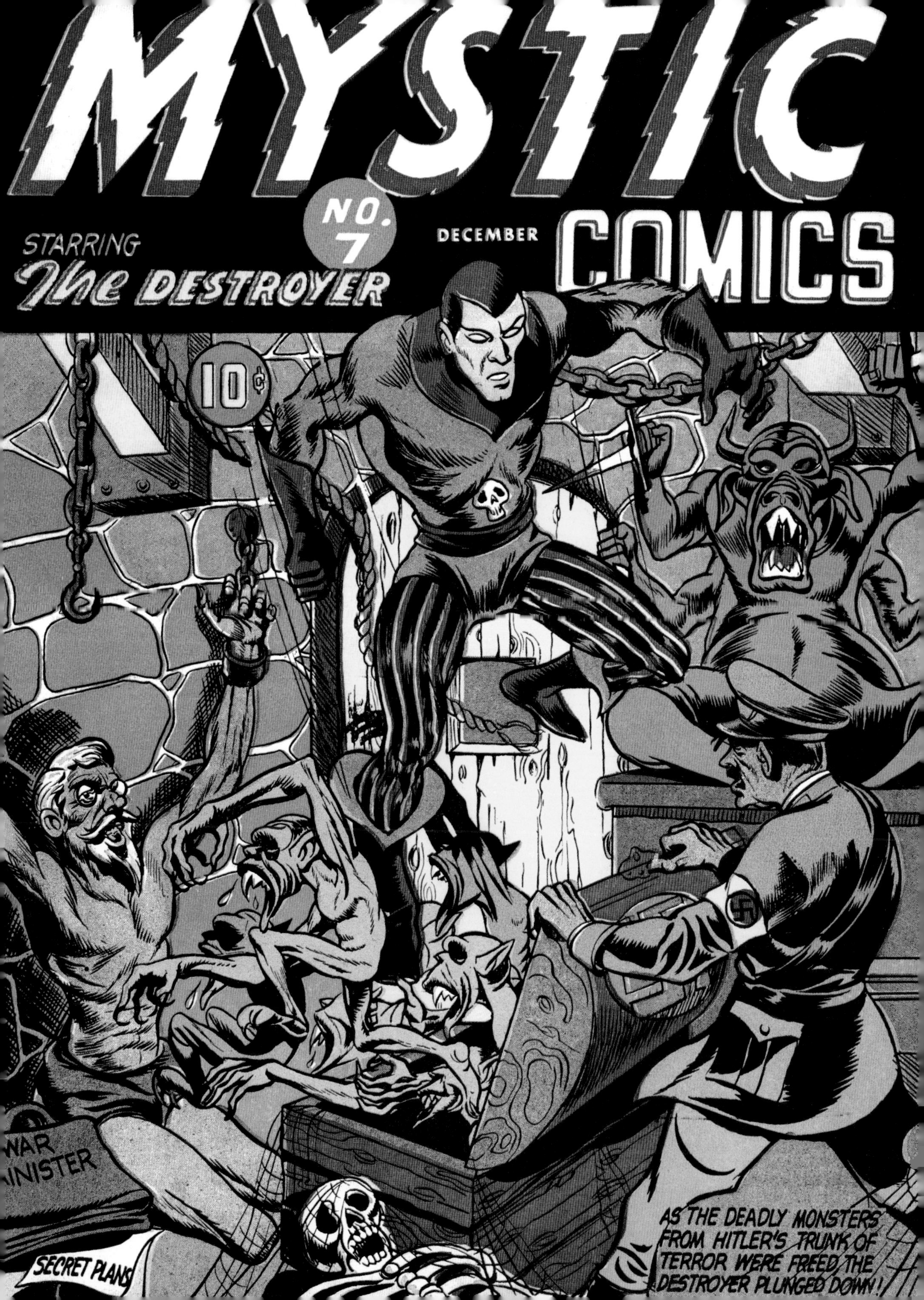
MYSTIC
NO. 7
DECEMBER
COMICS
STARRING
The DESTROYER
10¢
WAR
MINISTER
SECRET PLANS
AS THE DEADLY MONSTERS FROM HITLER'S TRUNK OF TERROR WERE FREED THE DESTROYER PLUNGED DOWN!

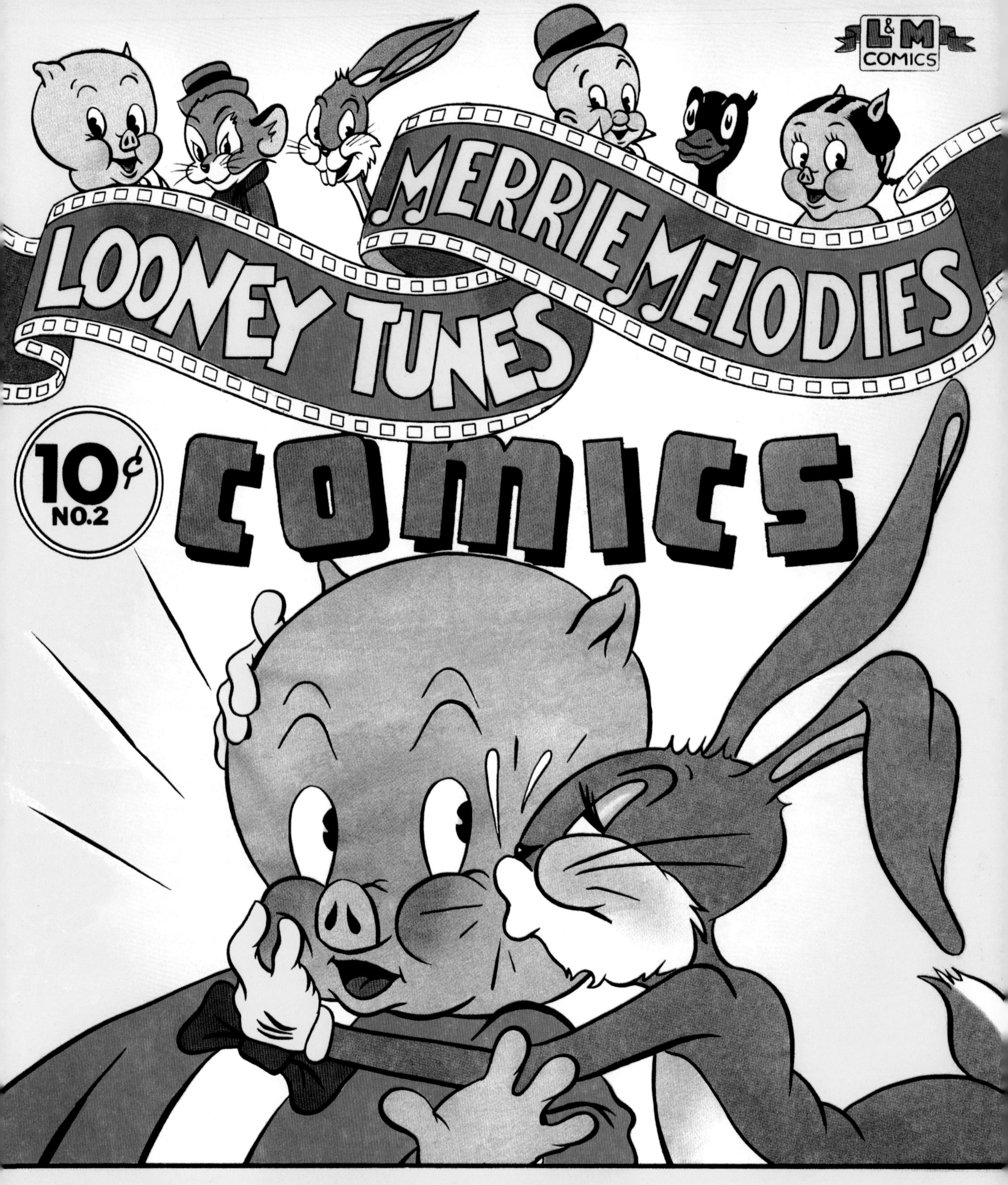
L&M COMICS
MERRIE MELODIES
LOONEY TUNES
10¢
NO.2
COMICS

LEON SCHLESINGER'S FAMOUS CHARACTERS

PORKY PIG • BUGS BUNNY

PETUNIA, ELMER, SNIFFLES AND MANY OTHERS

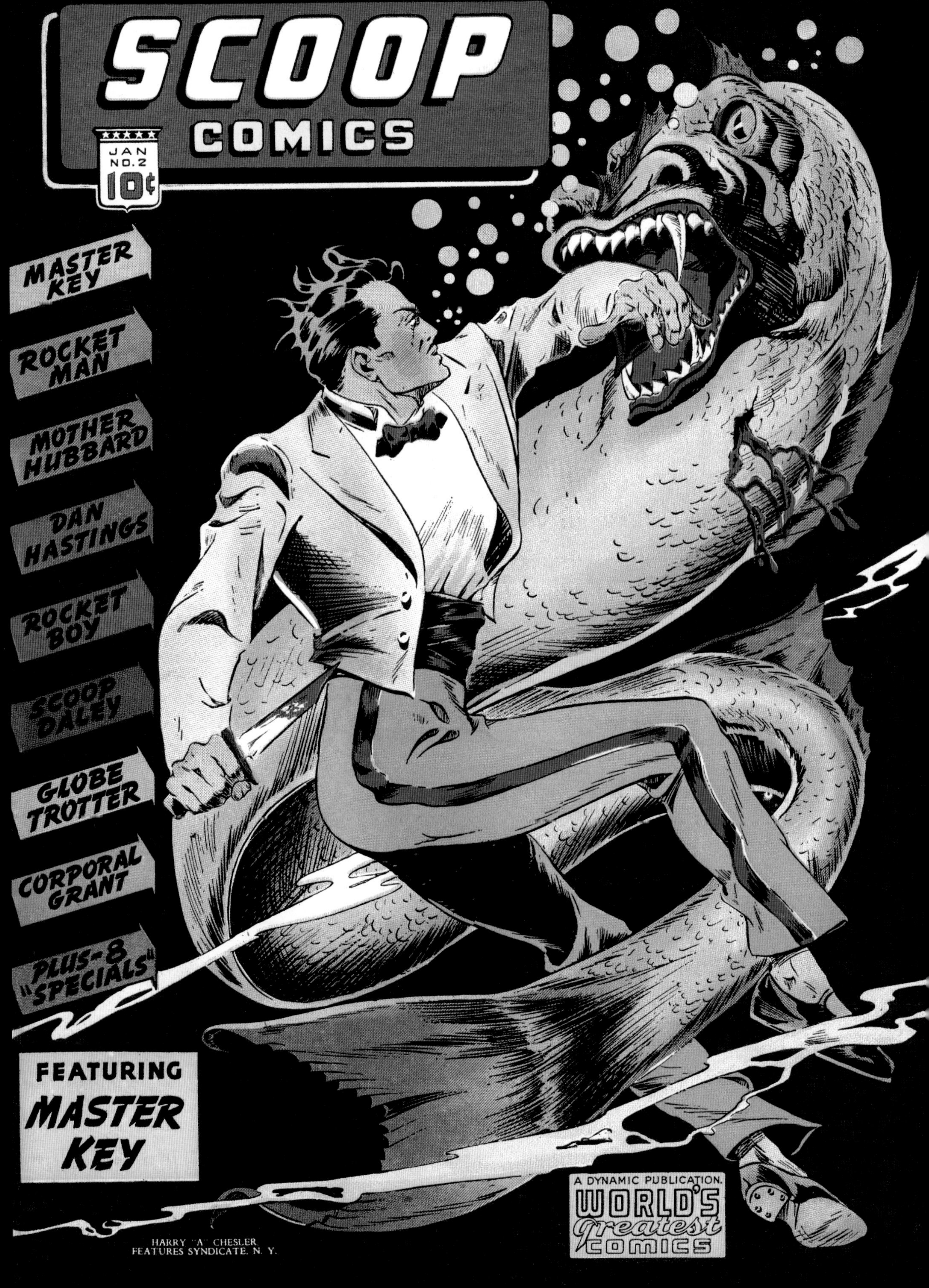

SCOOP COMICS
JAN NO. 2 10¢
MASTER KEY
ROCKET MAN
MOTHER HUBBARD
DAN HASTINGS
ROCKET BOY
SCOOP DALEY
GLOBE TROTTER
CORPORAL GRANT
PLUS-8 "SPECIALS"
FEATURING MASTER KEY
HARRY "A" CHESLER FEATURES SYNDICATE, N. Y.
A DYNAMIC PUBLICATION
WORLD'S Greatest COMICS

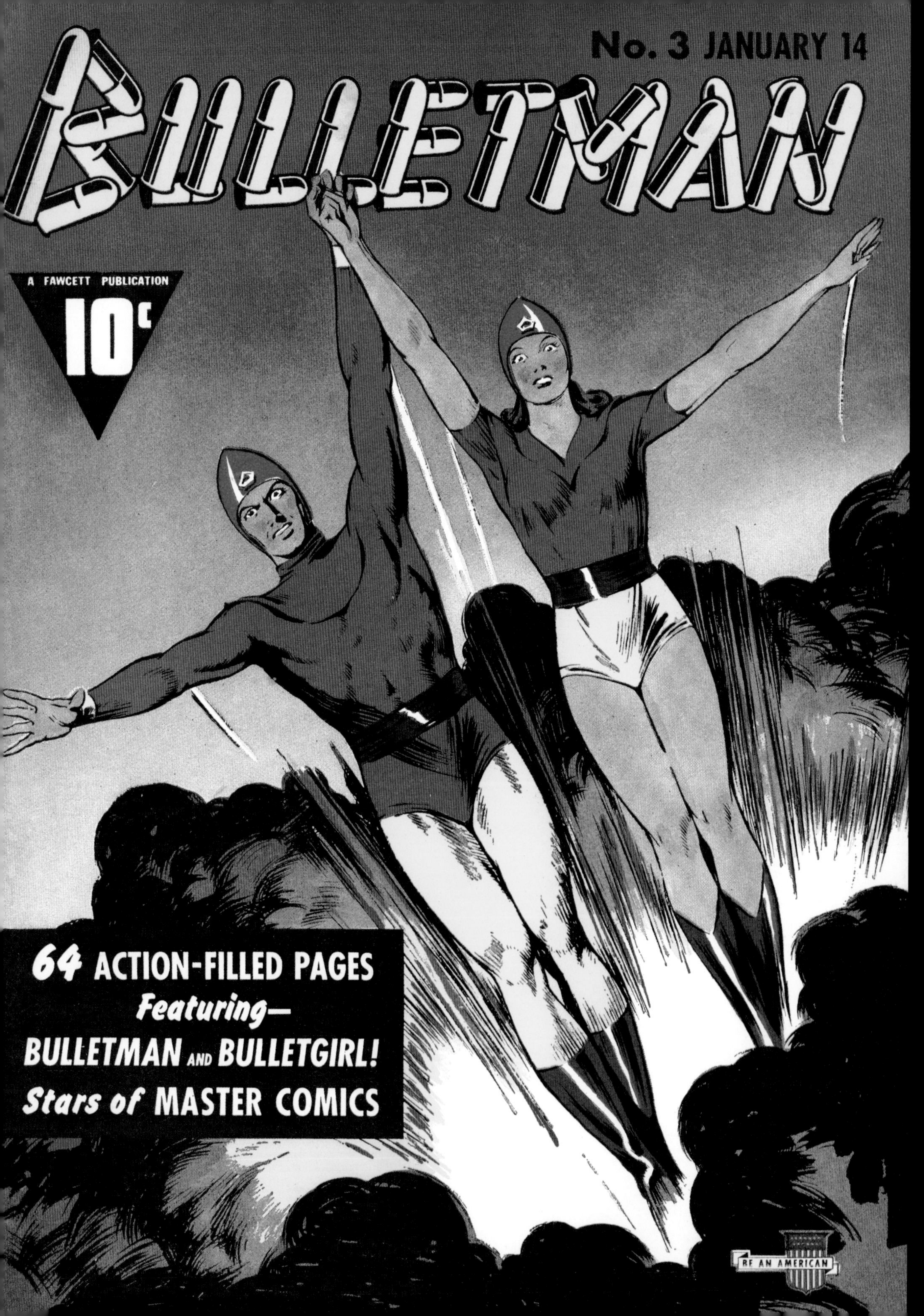
No. 3 JANUARY 14
BULLETMAN
A FAWCETT PUBLICATION
10¢
64 ACTION-FILLED PAGES
Featuring—
BULLETMAN AND BULLETGIRL!
Stars of MASTER COMICS
BE AN AMERICAN

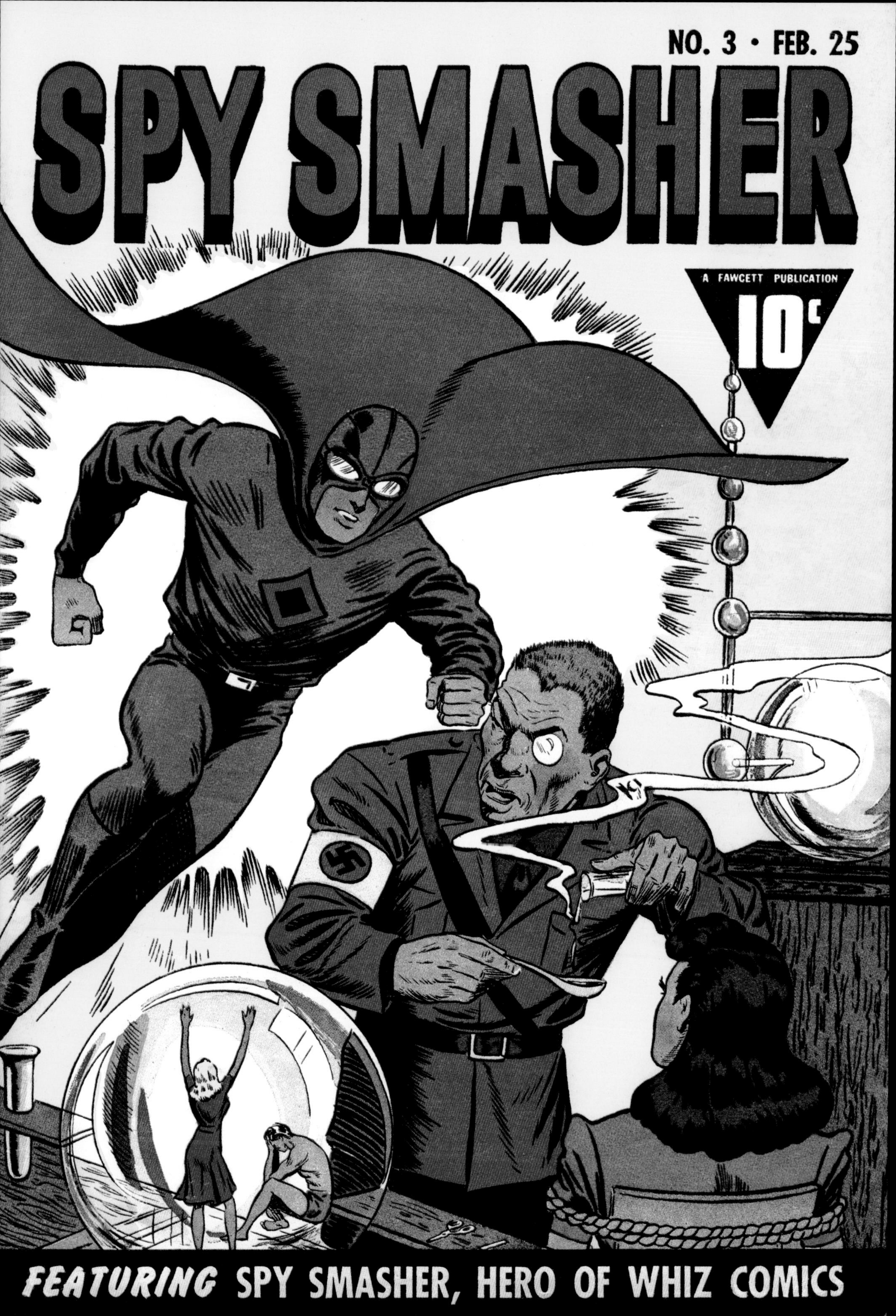
NO. 3 • FEB. 25
SPY SMASHER
A FAWCETT PUBLICATION
10¢
FEATURING SPY SMASHER, HERO OF WHIZ COMICS

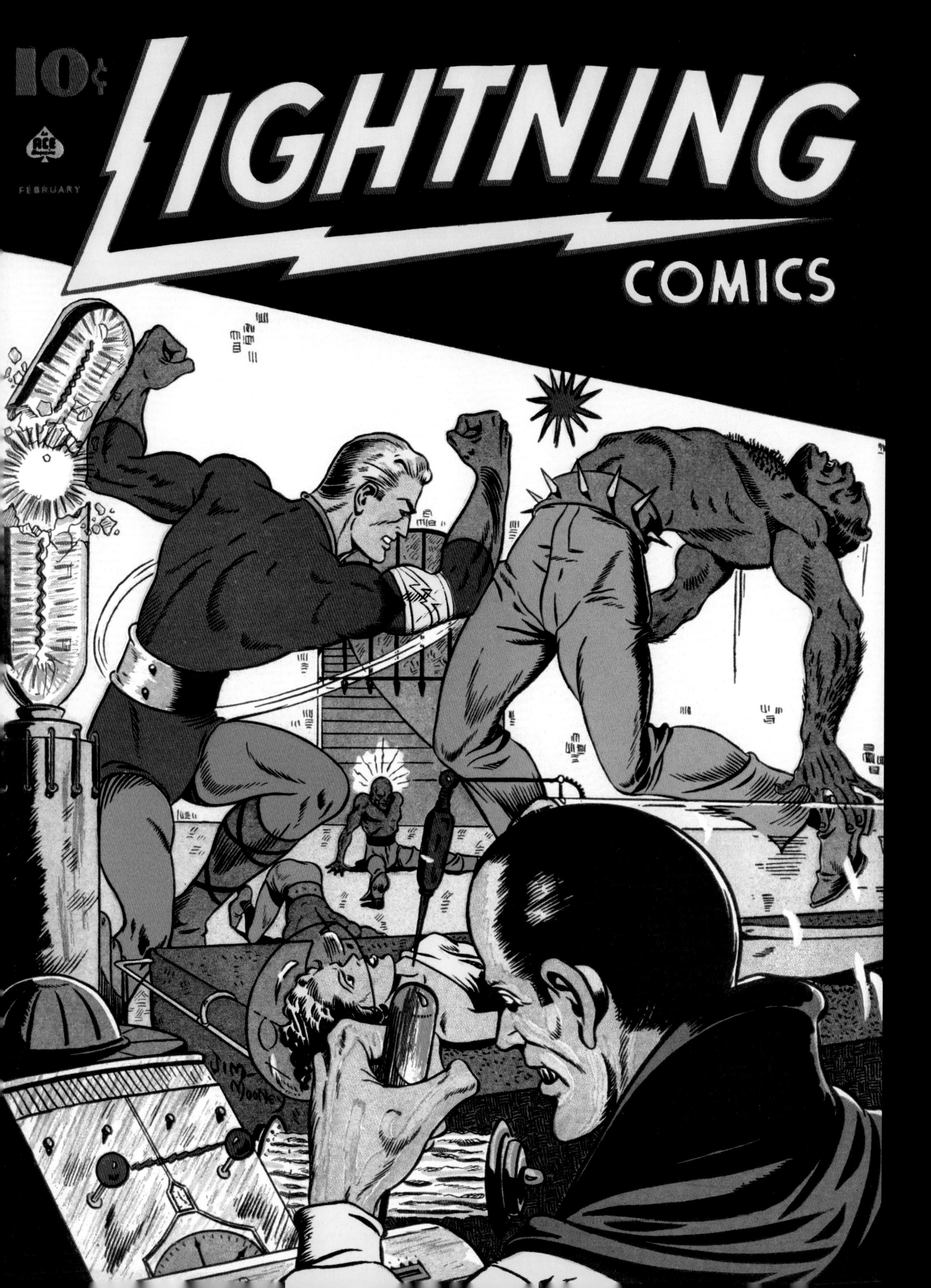
10¢
ACE
FEBRUARY
LIGHTNING
COMICS
JIM MOONEY

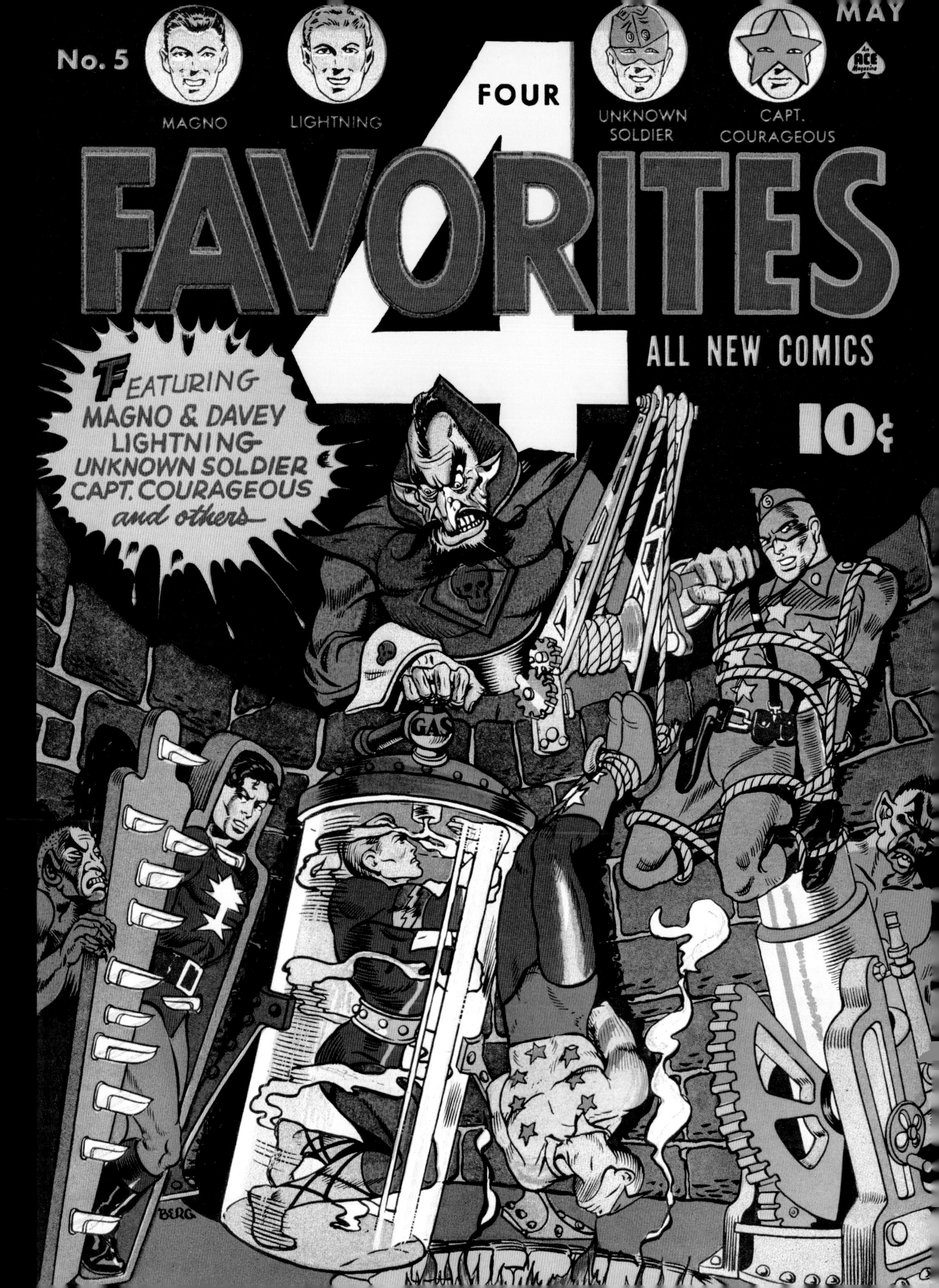

MAY
No. 5
An ACE Magazine
MAGNO
LIGHTNING
UNKNOWN SOLDIER
CAPT. COURAGEOUS
FOUR
FAVORITES
4
ALL NEW COMICS
10¢
FEATURING
MAGNO & DAVEY
LIGHTNING
UNKNOWN SOLDIER
CAPT. COURAGEOUS
and others
GAS
BERG

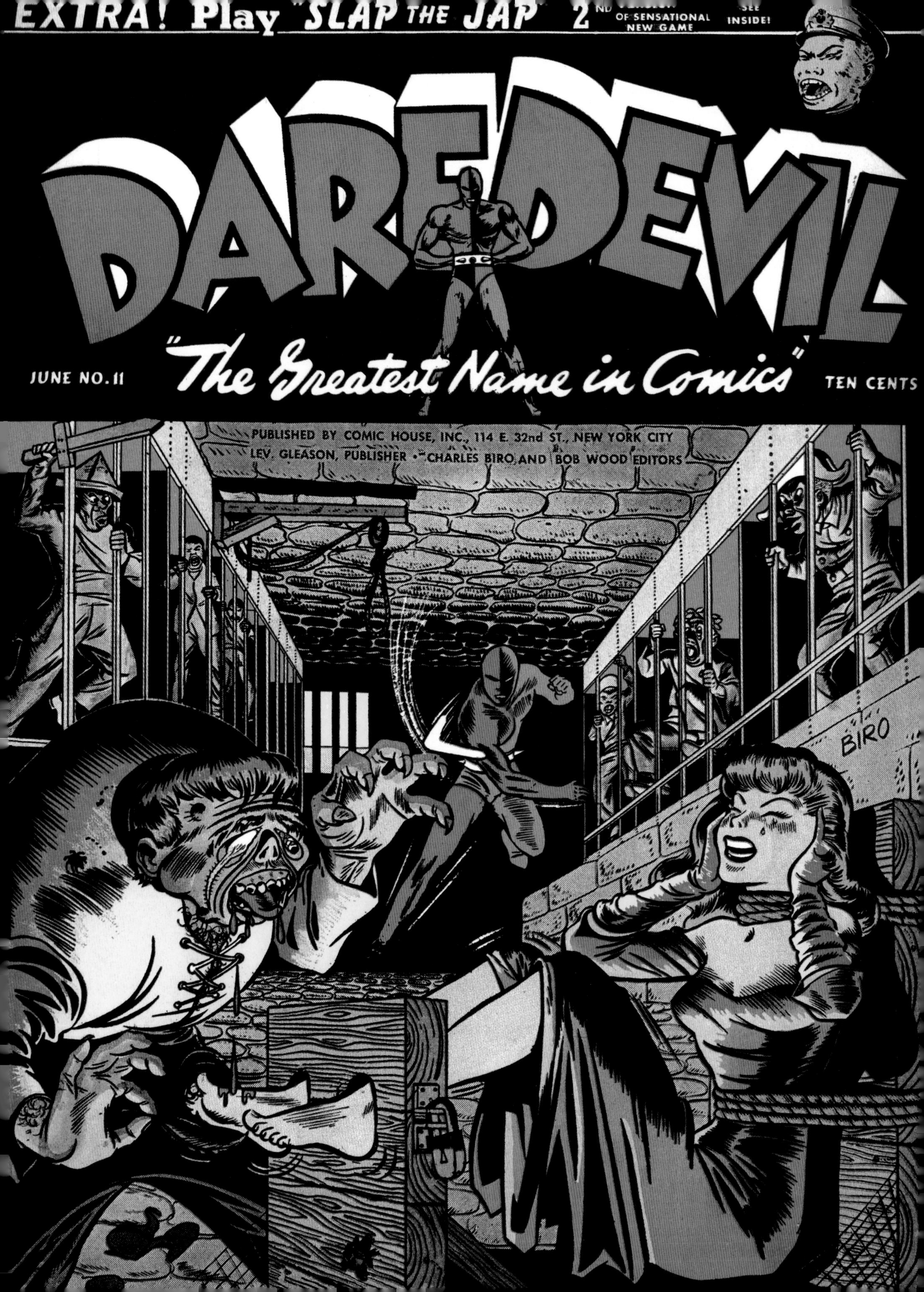

EXTRA! Play "SLAP THE JAP"
2ND
OF SENSATIONAL NEW GAME
SEE INSIDE!
DAREDEVIL
JUNE NO. 11
"The Greatest Name in Comics"
TEN CENTS
PUBLISHED BY COMIC HOUSE, INC., 114 E. 32nd ST., NEW YORK CITY
LEV. GLEASON, PUBLISHER • CHARLES BIRO AND BOB WOOD EDITORS
BIRO

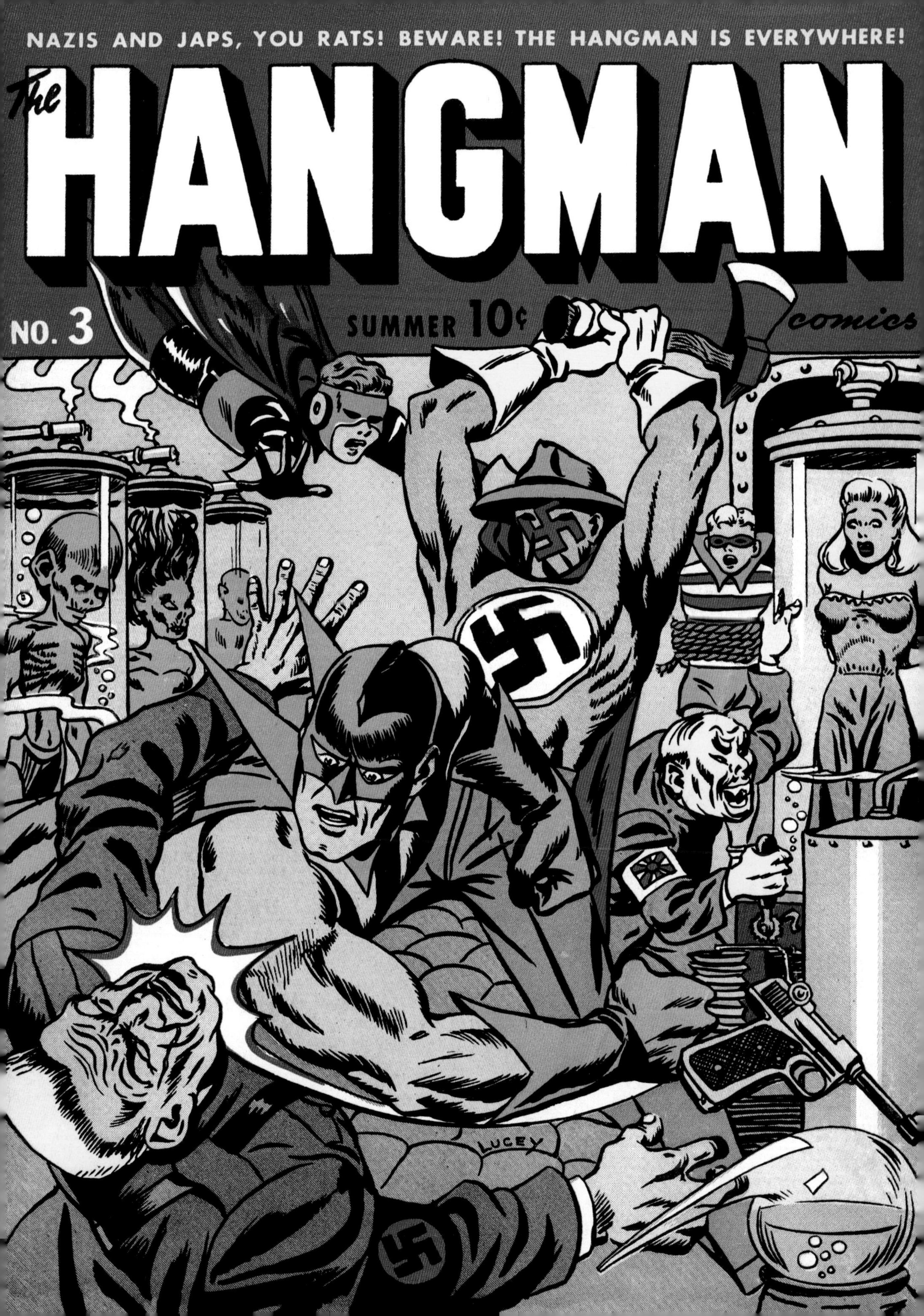
NAZIS AND JAPS, YOU RATS! BEWARE! THE HANGMAN IS EVERYWHERE!
The HANGMAN
NO. 3
SUMMER 10¢
comics
LUCEY

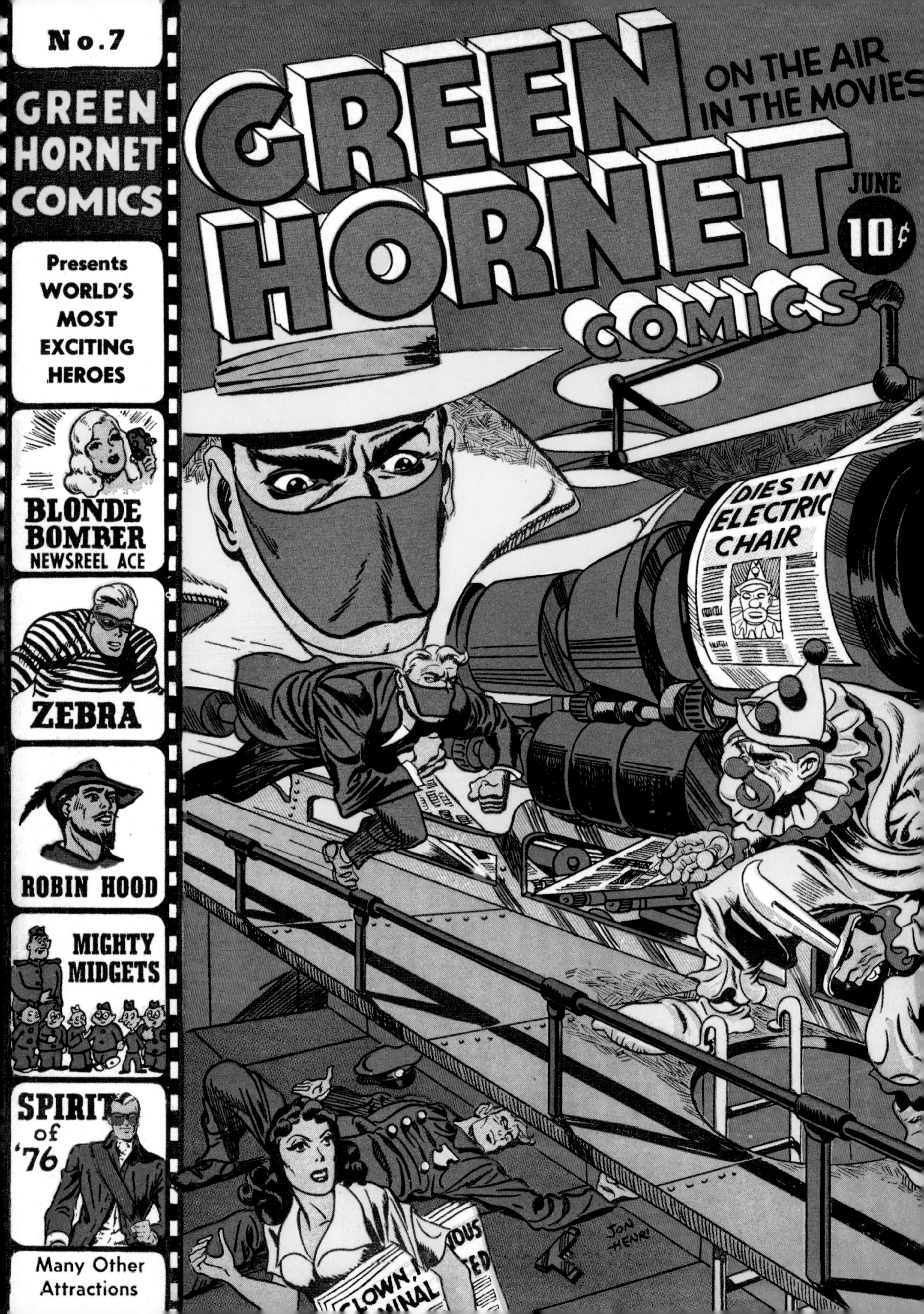
No.7
GREEN HORNET COMICS
Presents WORLD'S MOST EXCITING HEROES
BLONDE BOMBER
NEWSREEL ACE
ZEBRA
ROBIN HOOD
MIGHTY MIDGETS
SPIRIT of '76
Many Other Attractions
GREEN HORNET
ON THE AIR
IN THE MOVIES
JUNE
10¢
COMICS
DIES IN ELECTRIC CHAIR
JON HENRI

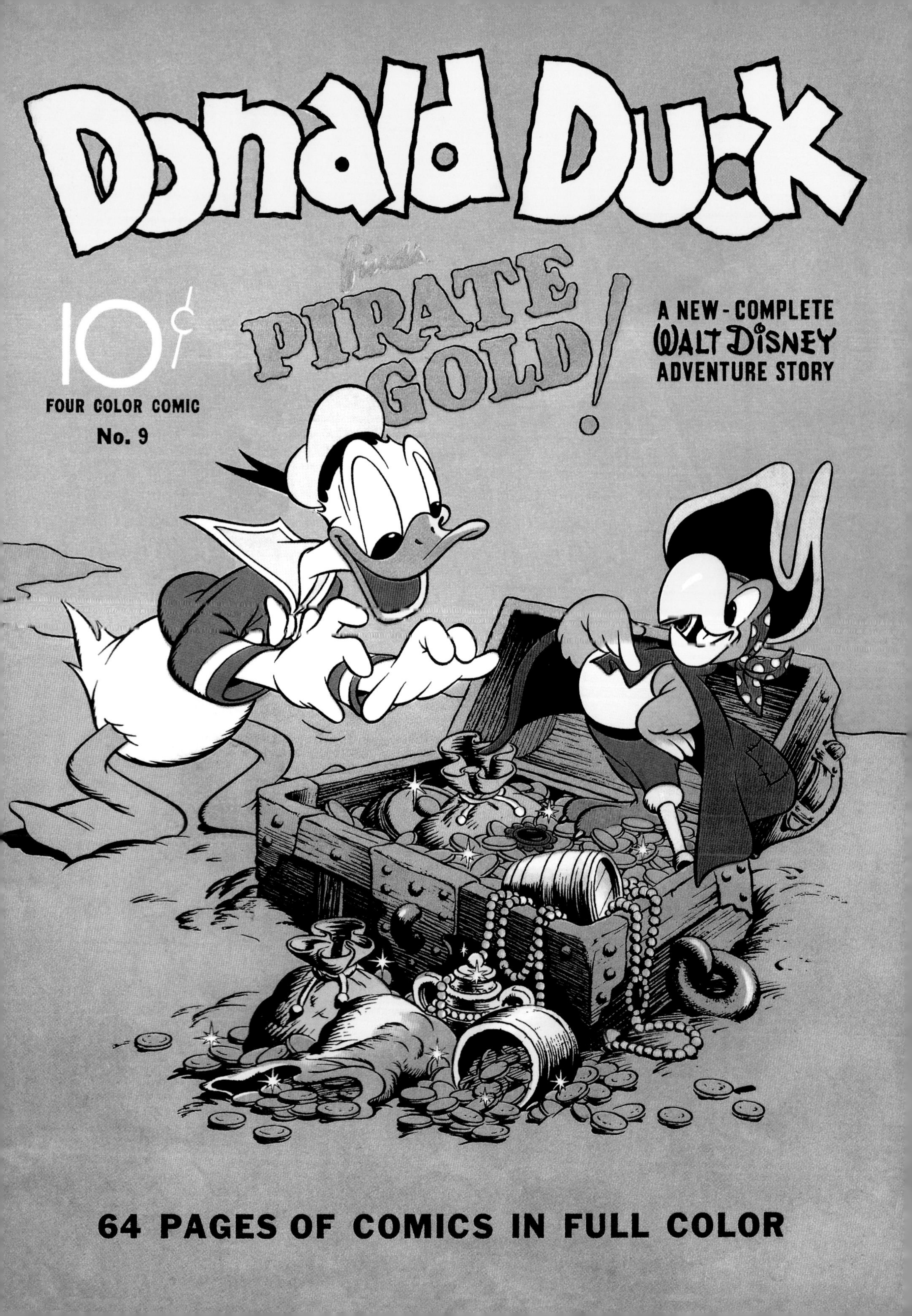
Donald Duck
finds
PIRATE GOLD!
10¢
FOUR COLOR COMIC
No. 9
A NEW-COMPLETE
WALT DISNEY
ADVENTURE STORY
64 PAGES OF COMICS IN FULL COLOR

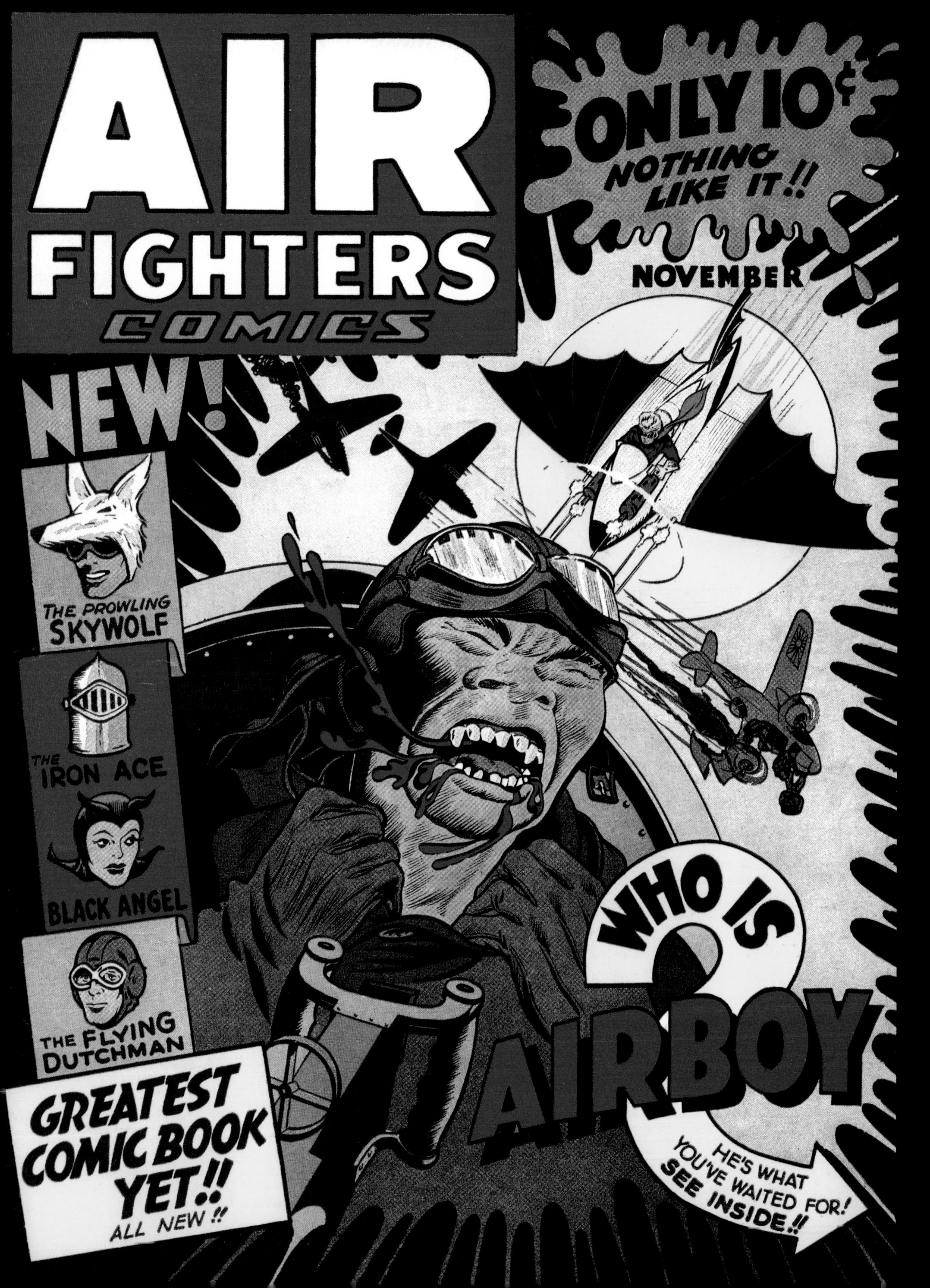
AIR FIGHTERS COMICS
ONLY 10¢
NOTHING LIKE IT!!
NOVEMBER
NEW!
THE PROWLING SKYWOLF
THE IRON ACE
BLACK ANGEL
THE FLYING DUTCHMAN
GREATEST COMIC BOOK YET!!
ALL NEW!!
WHO IS AIRBOY?
HE'S WHAT YOU'VE WAITED FOR!
SEE INSIDE!!

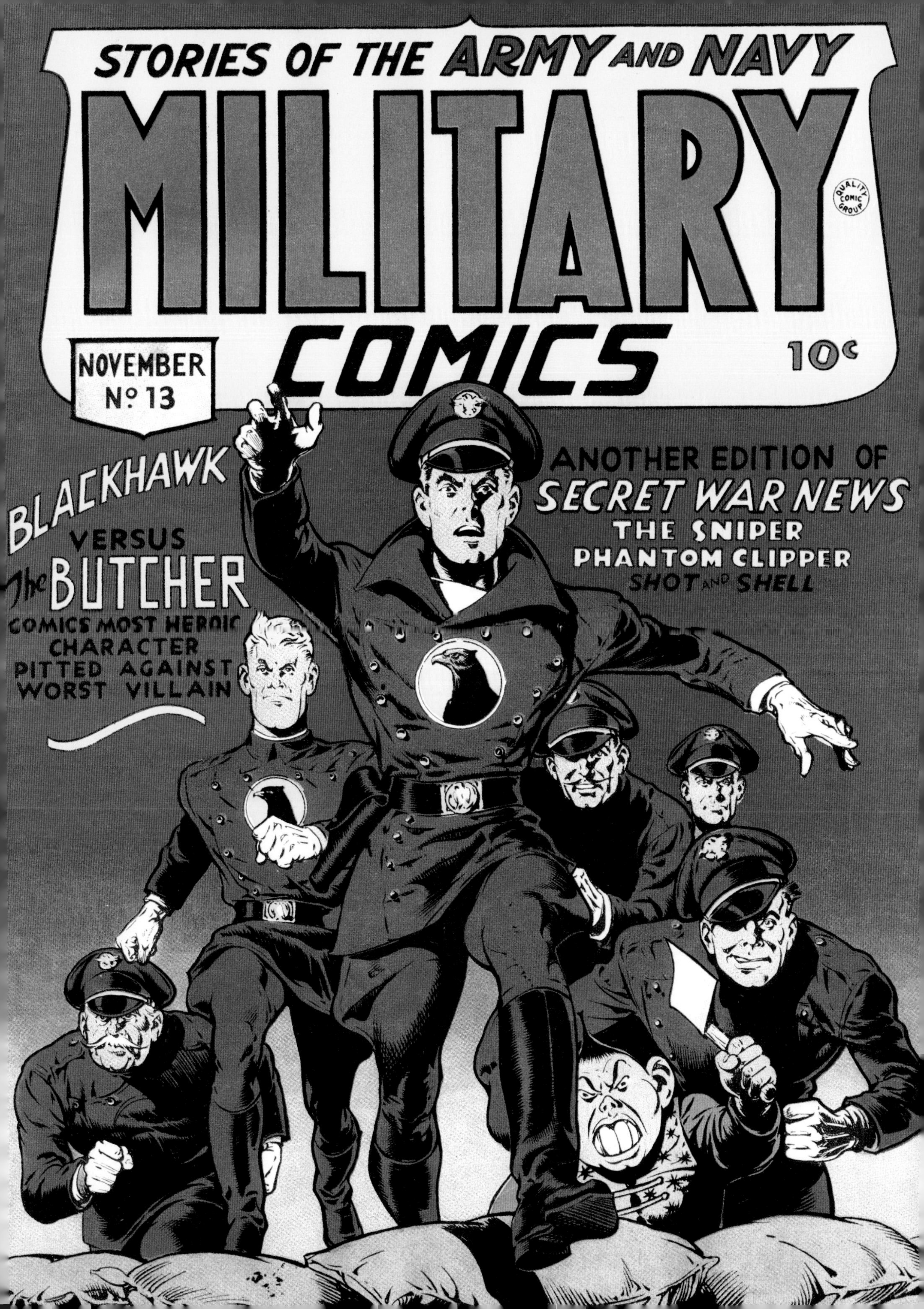

STORIES OF THE ARMY AND NAVY
MILITARY COMICS
QUALITY COMIC GROUP
NOVEMBER
Nº 13
10¢
BLACKHAWK
VERSUS
The BUTCHER
COMICS MOST HEROIC
CHARACTER
PITTED AGAINST
WORST VILLAIN
ANOTHER EDITION OF
SECRET WAR NEWS
THE SNIPER
PHANTOM CLIPPER
SHOT AND SHELL

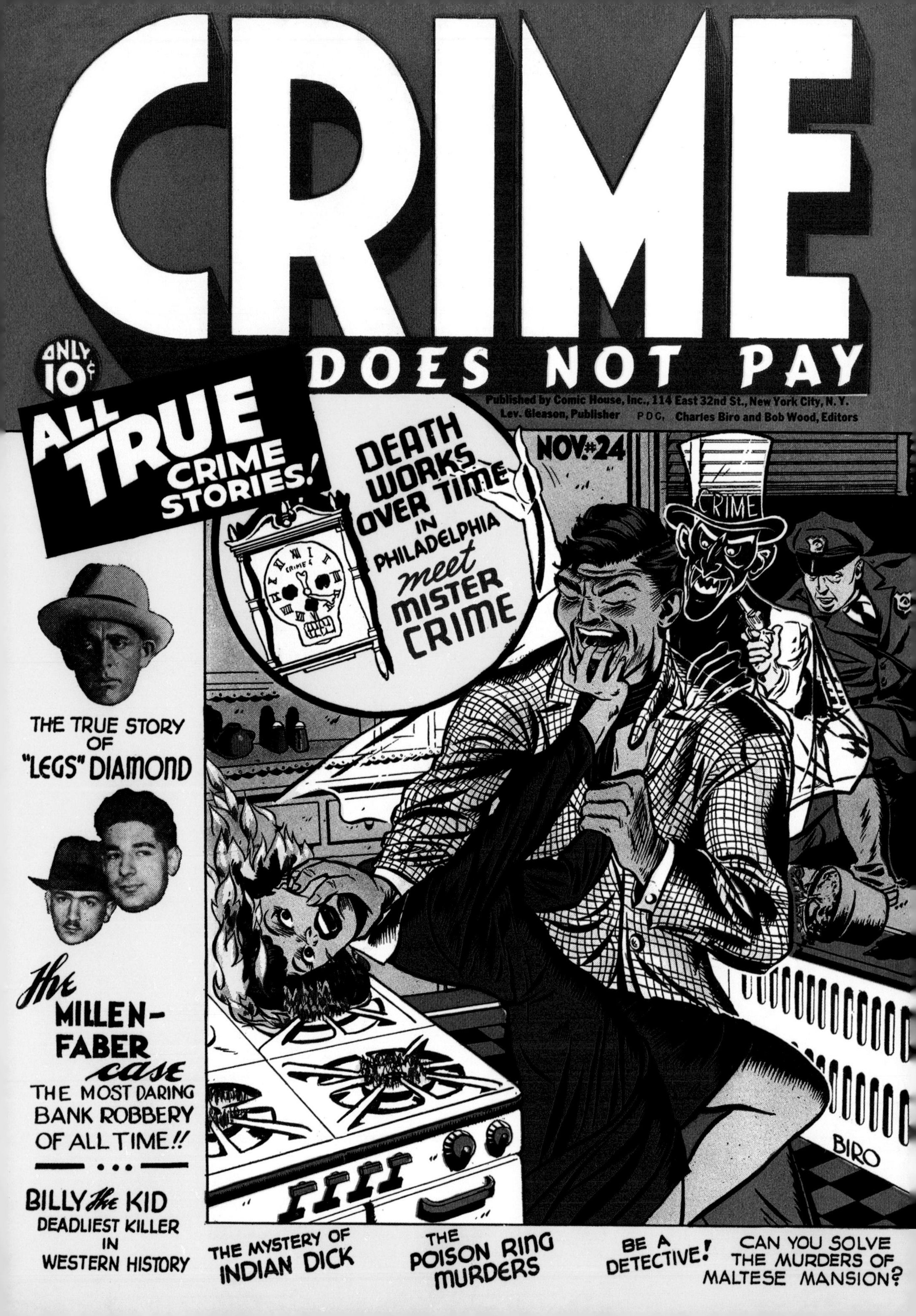
CRIME
DOES NOT PAY
ONLY 10¢
Published by Comic House, Inc., 114 East 32nd St., New York City, N. Y.
Lev. Gleason, Publisher P D C, Charles Biro and Bob Wood, Editors
ALL TRUE CRIME STORIES!
NOV. #24
DEATH WORKS OVER TIME IN PHILADELPHIA
meet MISTER CRIME
CRIME
THE TRUE STORY OF "LEGS" DIAMOND
The MILLEN-FABER case
THE MOST DARING BANK ROBBERY OF ALL TIME!!
BILLY the KID
DEADLIEST KILLER IN WESTERN HISTORY
THE MYSTERY OF INDIAN DICK
THE POISON RING MURDERS
BE A DETECTIVE!
CAN YOU SOLVE THE MURDERS OF MALTESE MANSION?
BIRO

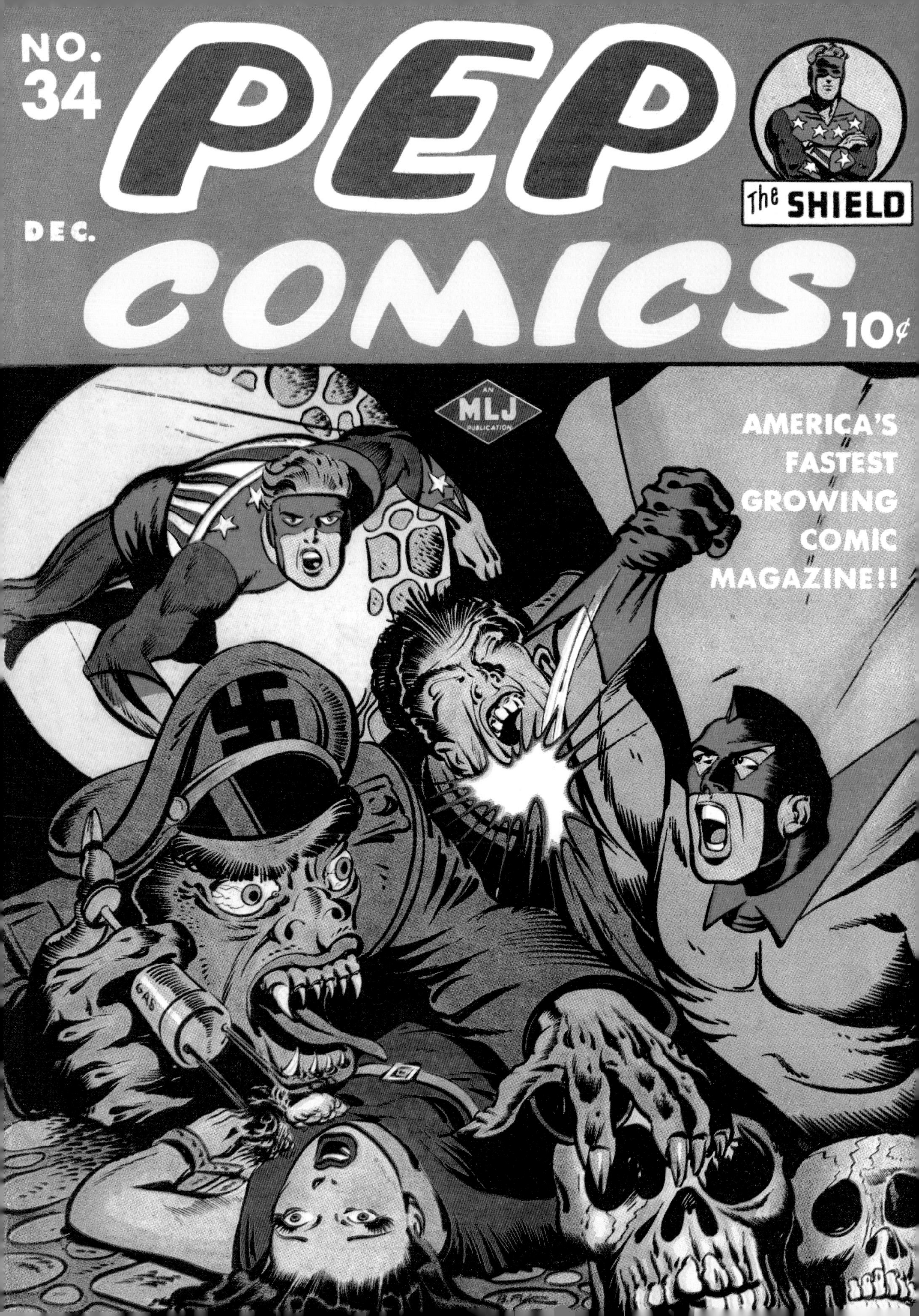

NO. 34
PEP
COMICS
DEC.
The SHIELD
10¢
AN MLJ PUBLICATION
AMERICA'S FASTEST GROWING COMIC MAGAZINE!!
GAS

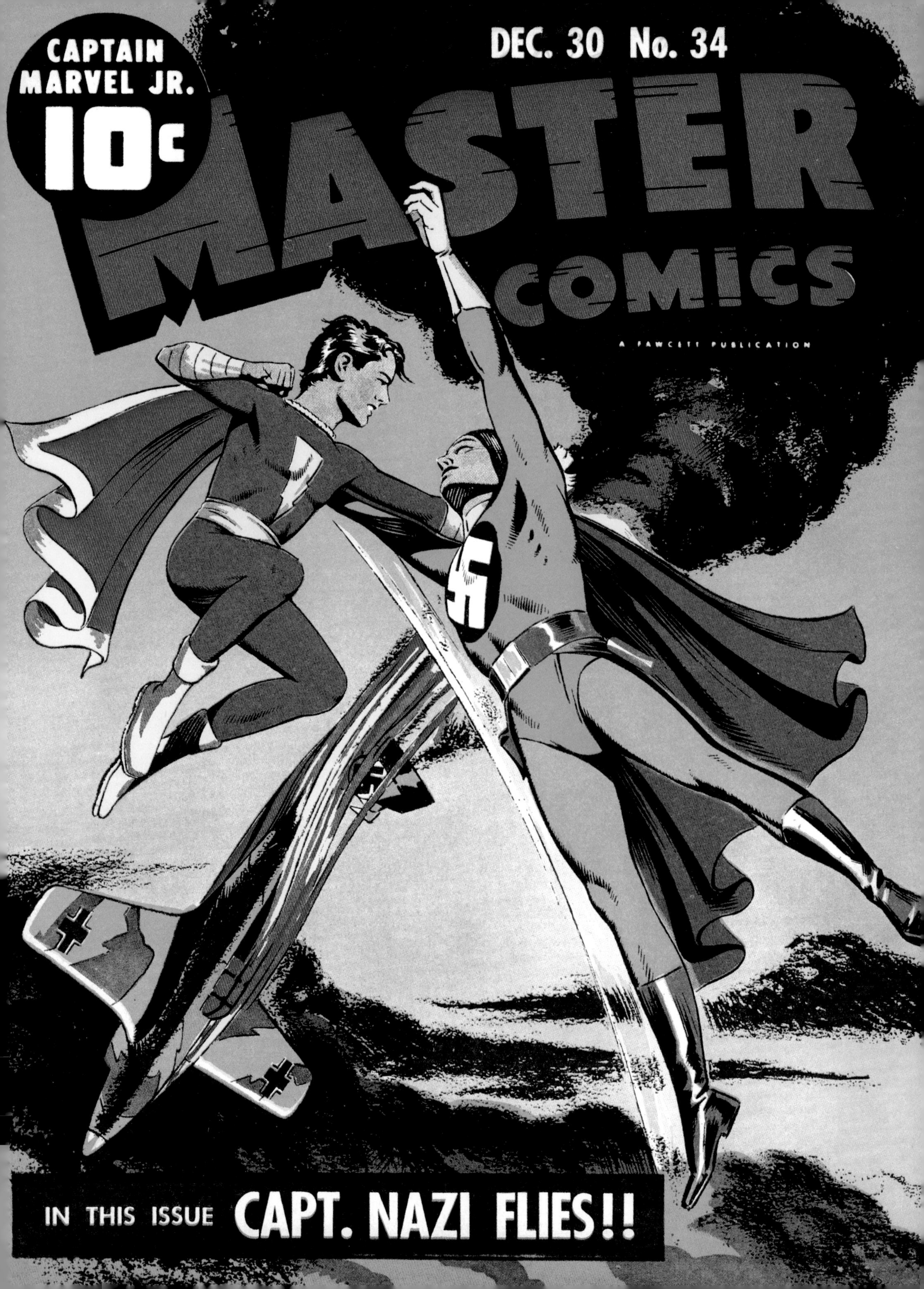

CAPTAIN MARVEL JR.
10¢
DEC. 30 No. 34
MASTER COMICS
A FAWCETT PUBLICATION
IN THIS ISSUE CAPT. NAZI FLIES!!

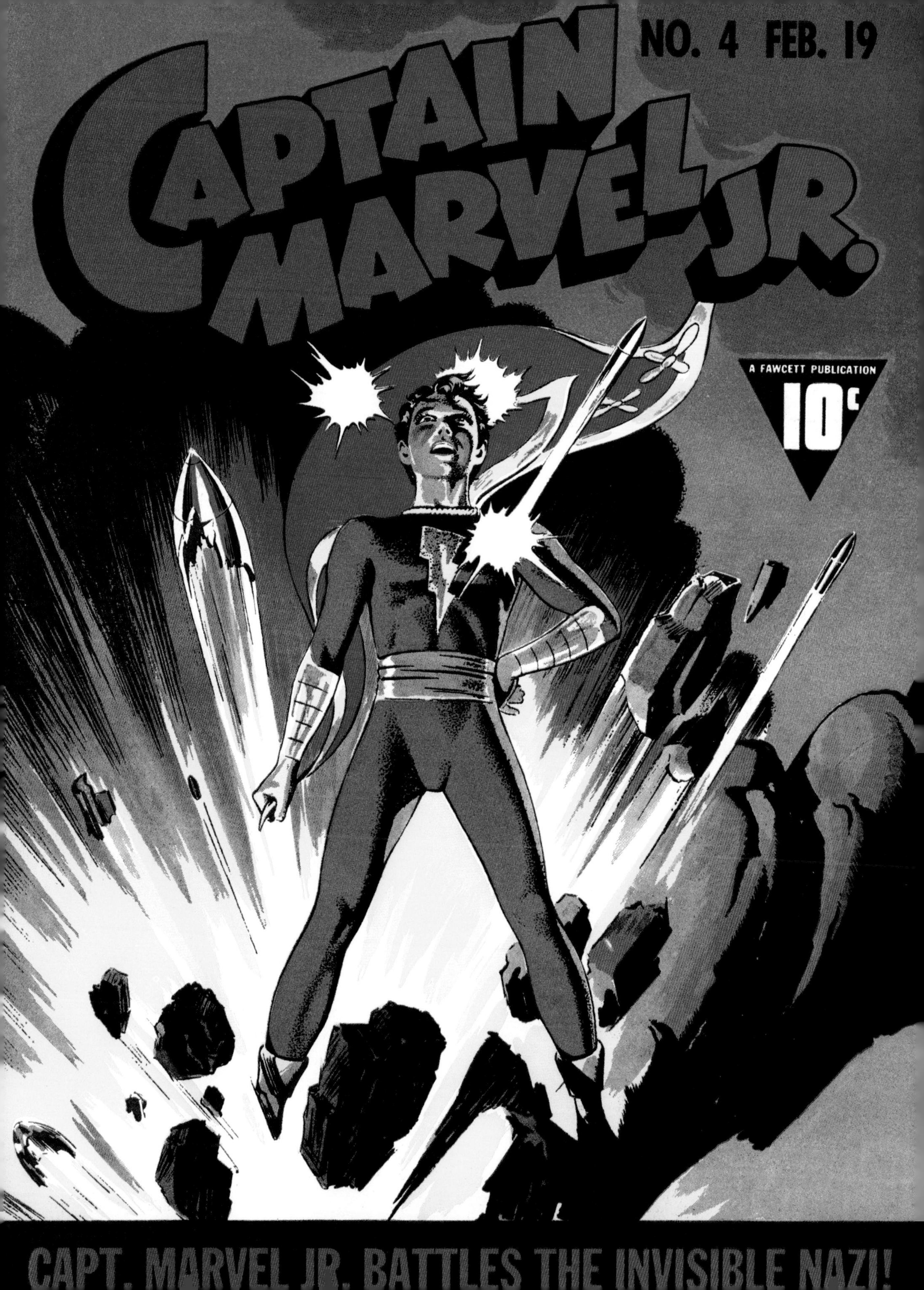
NO. 4 FEB. 19
CAPTAIN MARVEL JR.
A FAWCETT PUBLICATION
10¢
CAPT. MARVEL JR. BATTLES THE INVISIBLE NAZI!

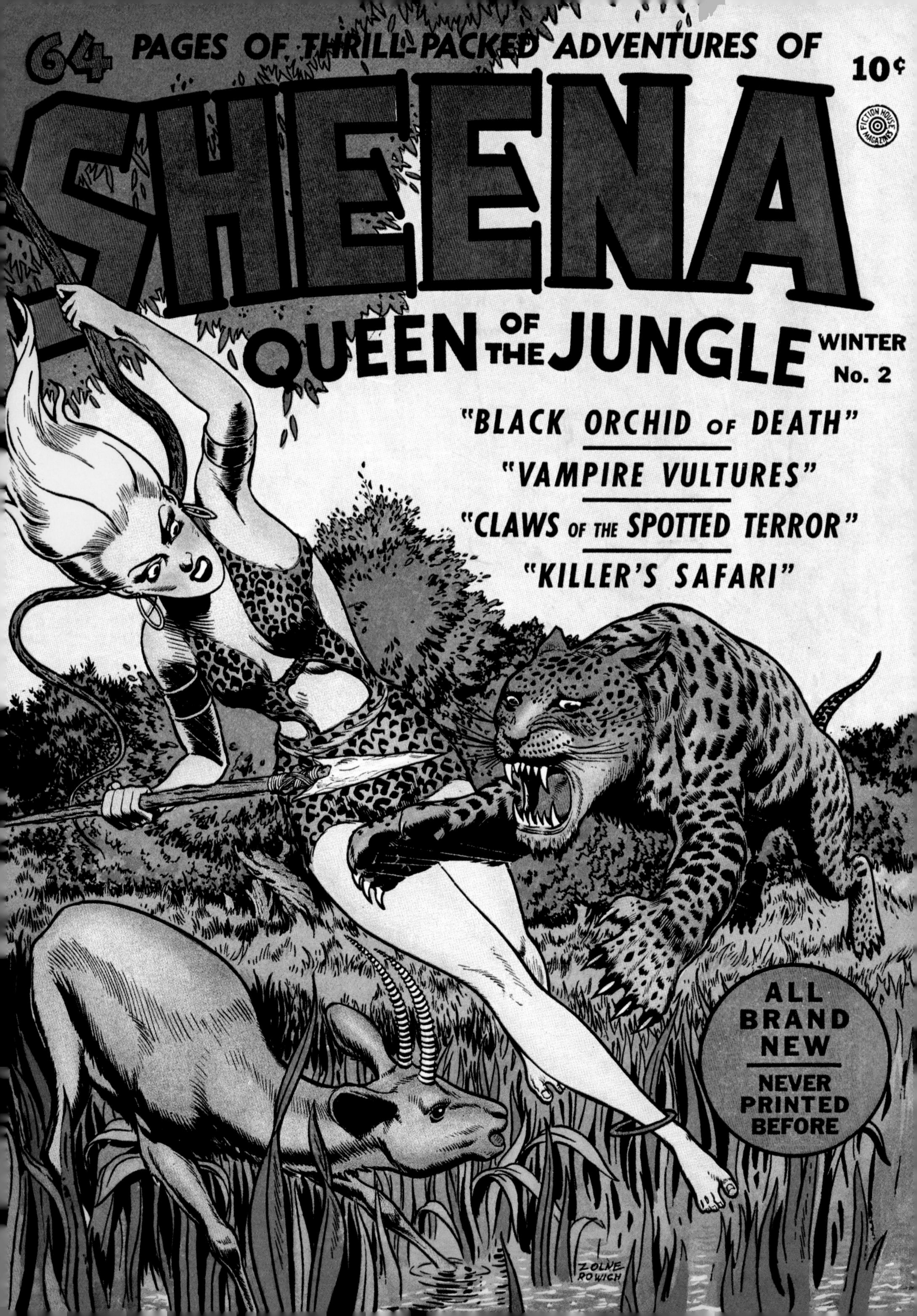

64 PAGES OF THRILL-PACKED ADVENTURES OF
10¢
FICTION HOUSE MAGAZINES
SHEENA
QUEEN OF THE JUNGLE
WINTER
No. 2
"BLACK ORCHID OF DEATH"
"VAMPIRE VULTURES"
"CLAWS OF THE SPOTTED TERROR"
"KILLER'S SAFARI"
ALL BRAND NEW
NEVER PRINTED BEFORE
ZOLNE ROWICH

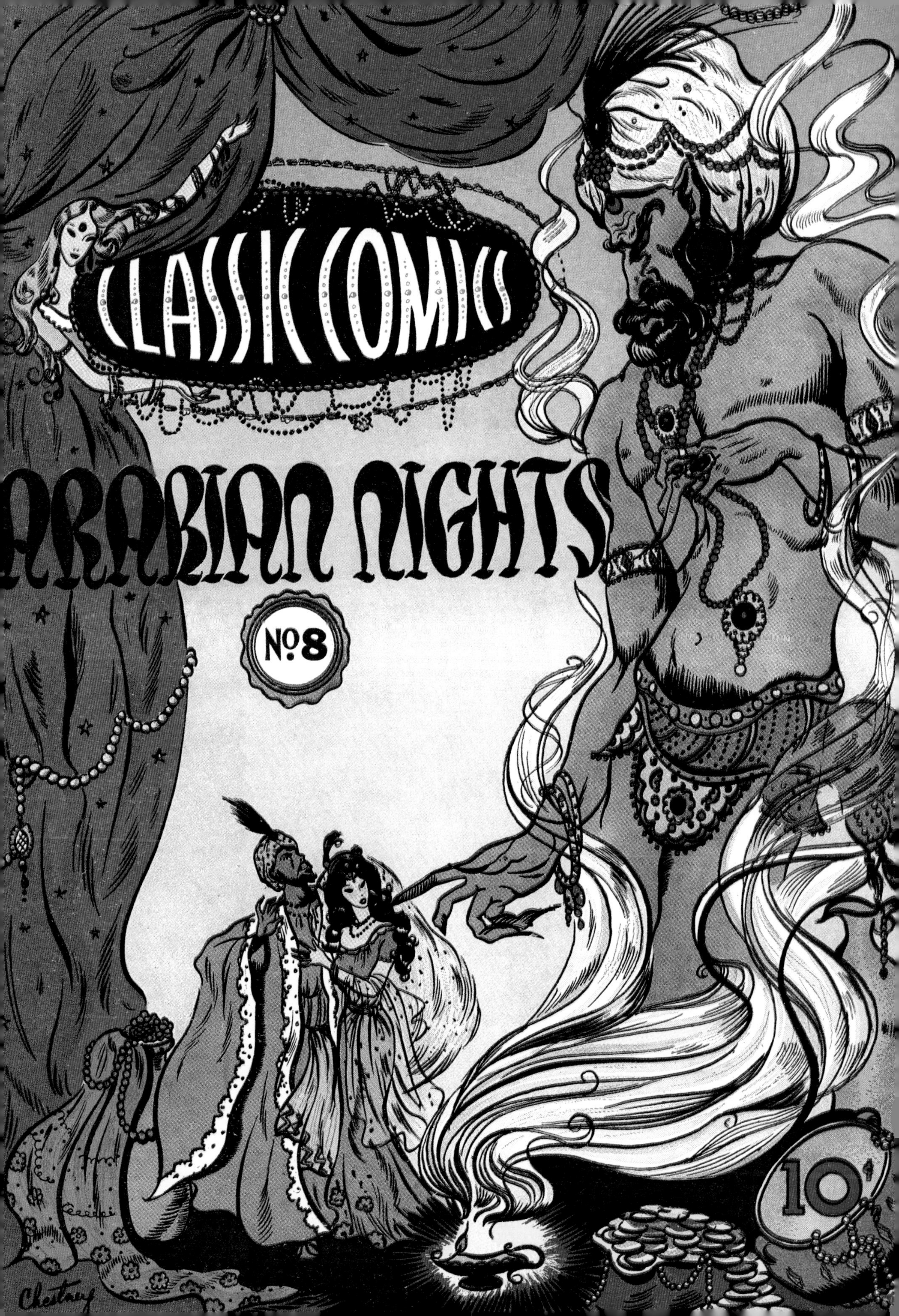
CLASSIC COMICS
ARABIAN NIGHTS
No. 8
10¢
Chesler

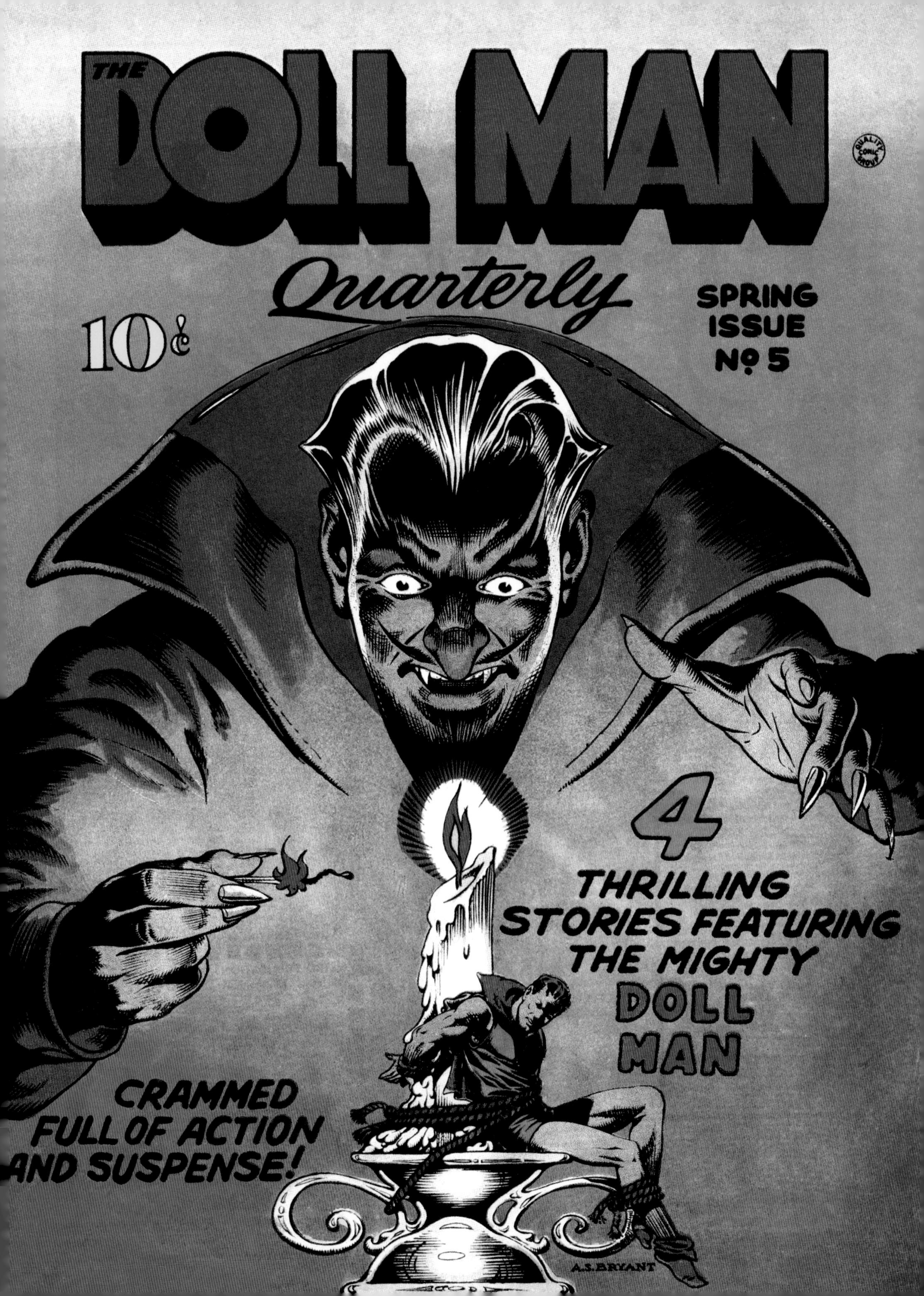
THE
DOLL MAN
Quarterly
10¢
SPRING
ISSUE
Nº 5
QUALITY COMIC GROUP
4
THRILLING
STORIES FEATURING
THE MIGHTY
DOLL
MAN
CRAMMED
FULL OF ACTION
AND SUSPENSE!
A.S. BRYANT

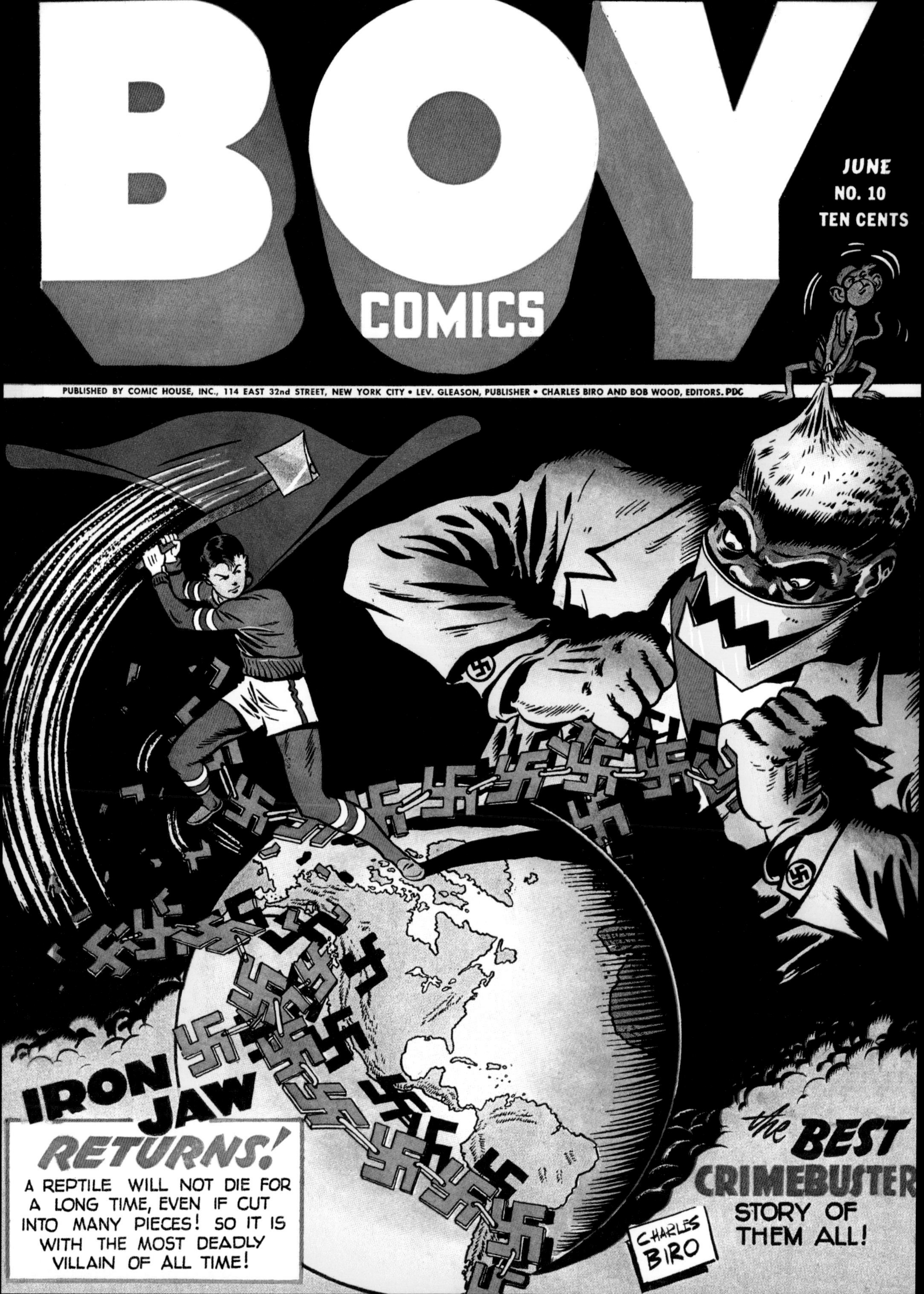
BOY
COMICS
JUNE
NO. 10
TEN CENTS
PUBLISHED BY COMIC HOUSE, INC., 114 EAST 32nd STREET, NEW YORK CITY • LEV. GLEASON, PUBLISHER • CHARLES BIRO AND BOB WOOD, EDITORS. PDC
IRON JAW RETURNS!
A REPTILE WILL NOT DIE FOR A LONG TIME, EVEN IF CUT INTO MANY PIECES! SO IT IS WITH THE MOST DEADLY VILLAIN OF ALL TIME!
CHARLES BIRO
the BEST CRIMEBUSTER STORY OF THEM ALL!

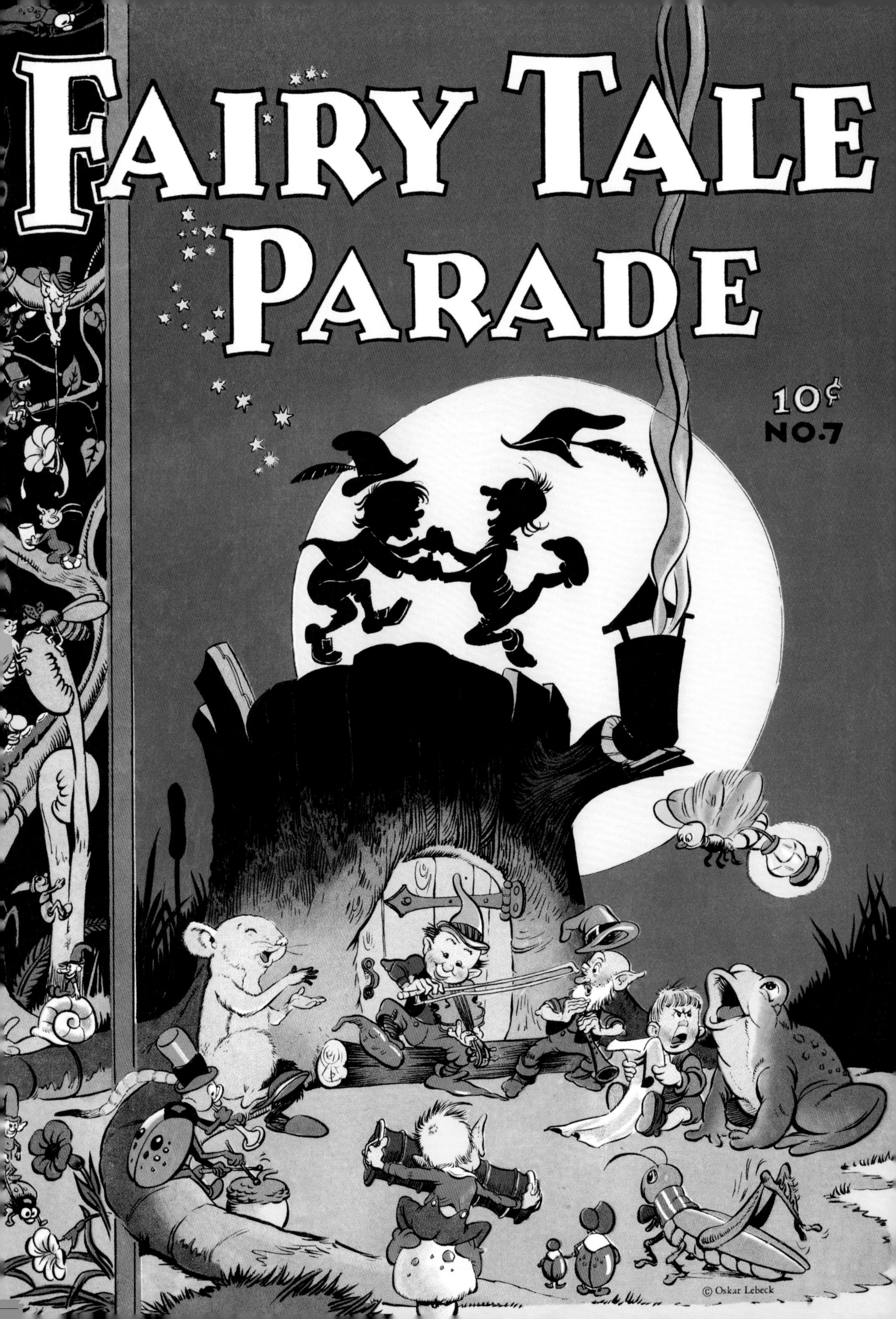
FAIRY TALE PARADE
10¢
NO.7
© Oskar Lebeck

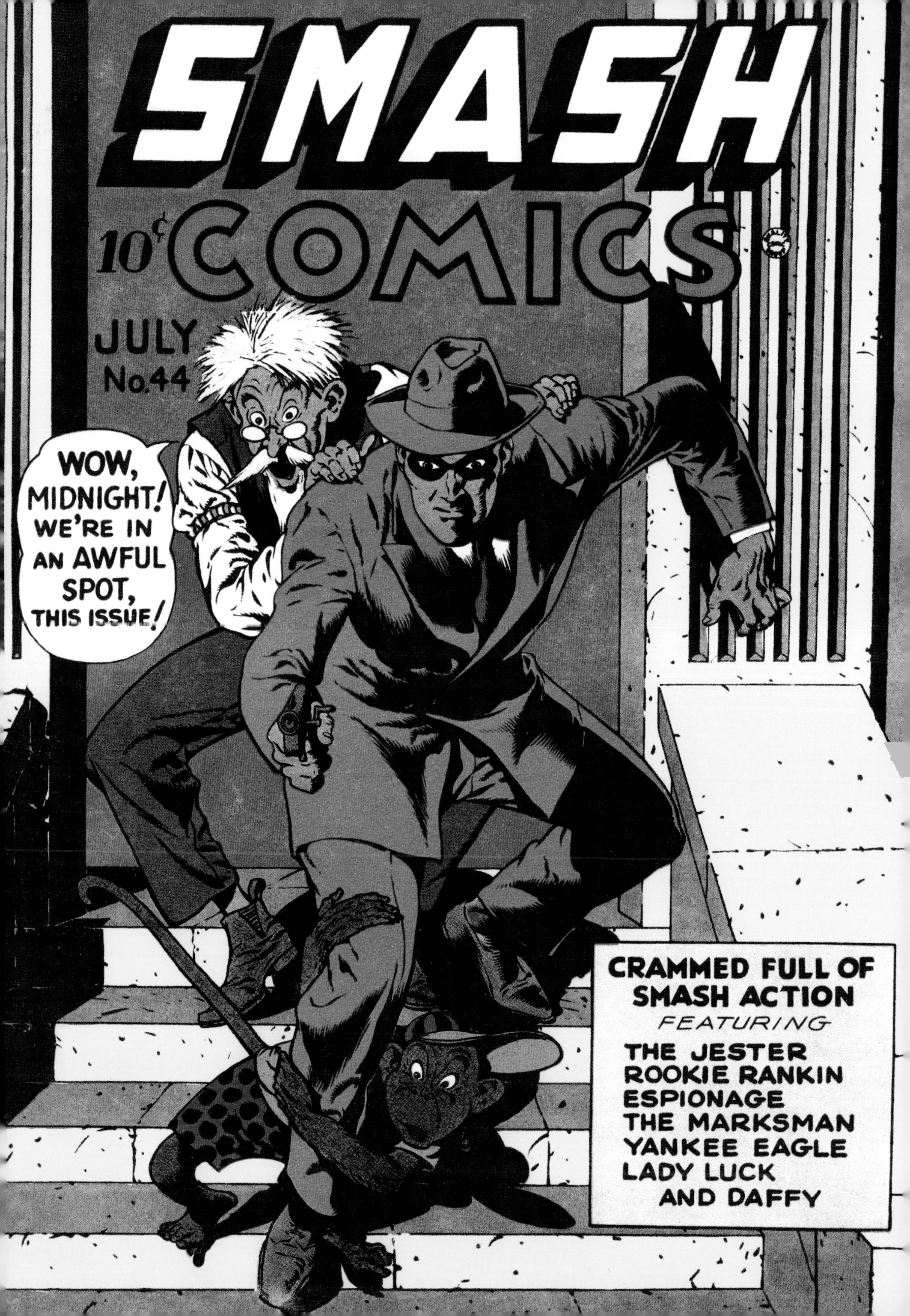
SMASH COMICS
10¢
JULY
No.44
WOW, MIDNIGHT! WE'RE IN AN AWFUL SPOT, THIS ISSUE!
CRAMMED FULL OF SMASH ACTION
FEATURING
THE JESTER
ROOKIE RANKIN
ESPIONAGE
THE MARKSMAN
YANKEE EAGLE
LADY LUCK
AND DAFFY

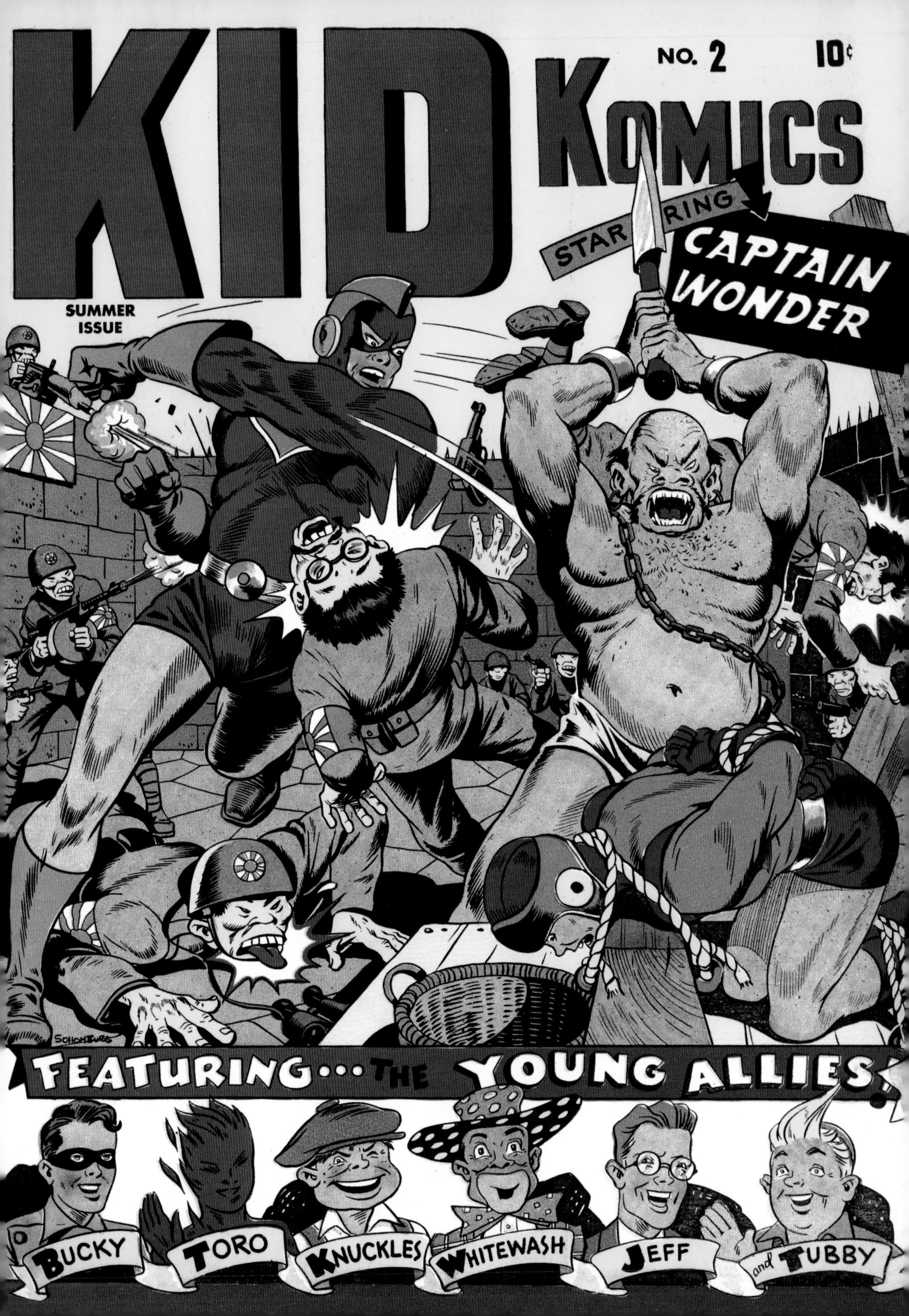

KID KOMICS
NO. 2
10¢
STARRING
CAPTAIN WONDER
SUMMER ISSUE
SCHOMBURG
FEATURING... THE YOUNG ALLIES!
BUCKY
TORO
KNUCKLES
WHITEWASH
JEFF
and TUBBY

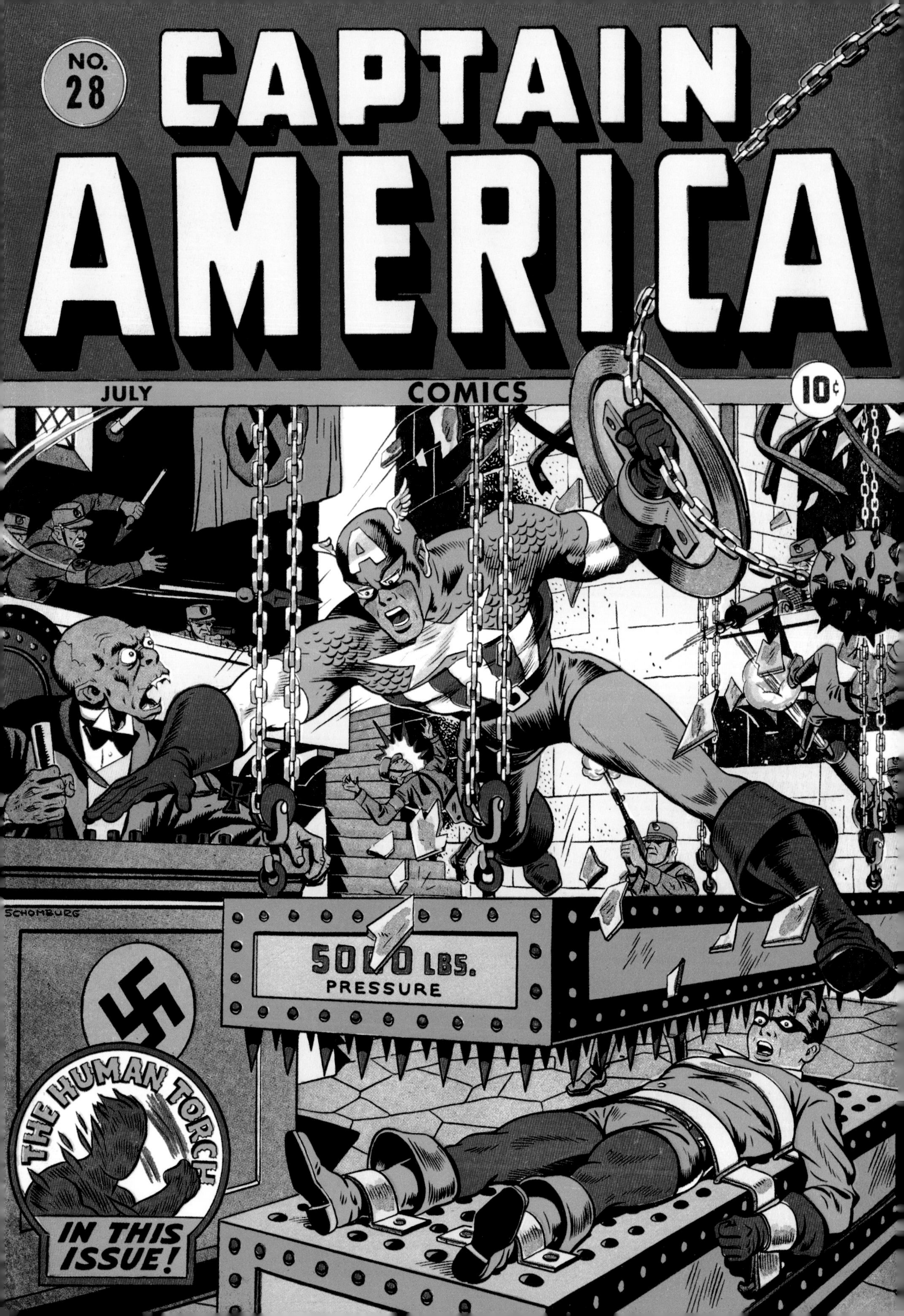
NO. 28
CAPTAIN AMERICA
JULY
COMICS
10¢
SCHOMBURG
5000 LBS.
PRESSURE
THE HUMAN TORCH
IN THIS ISSUE!

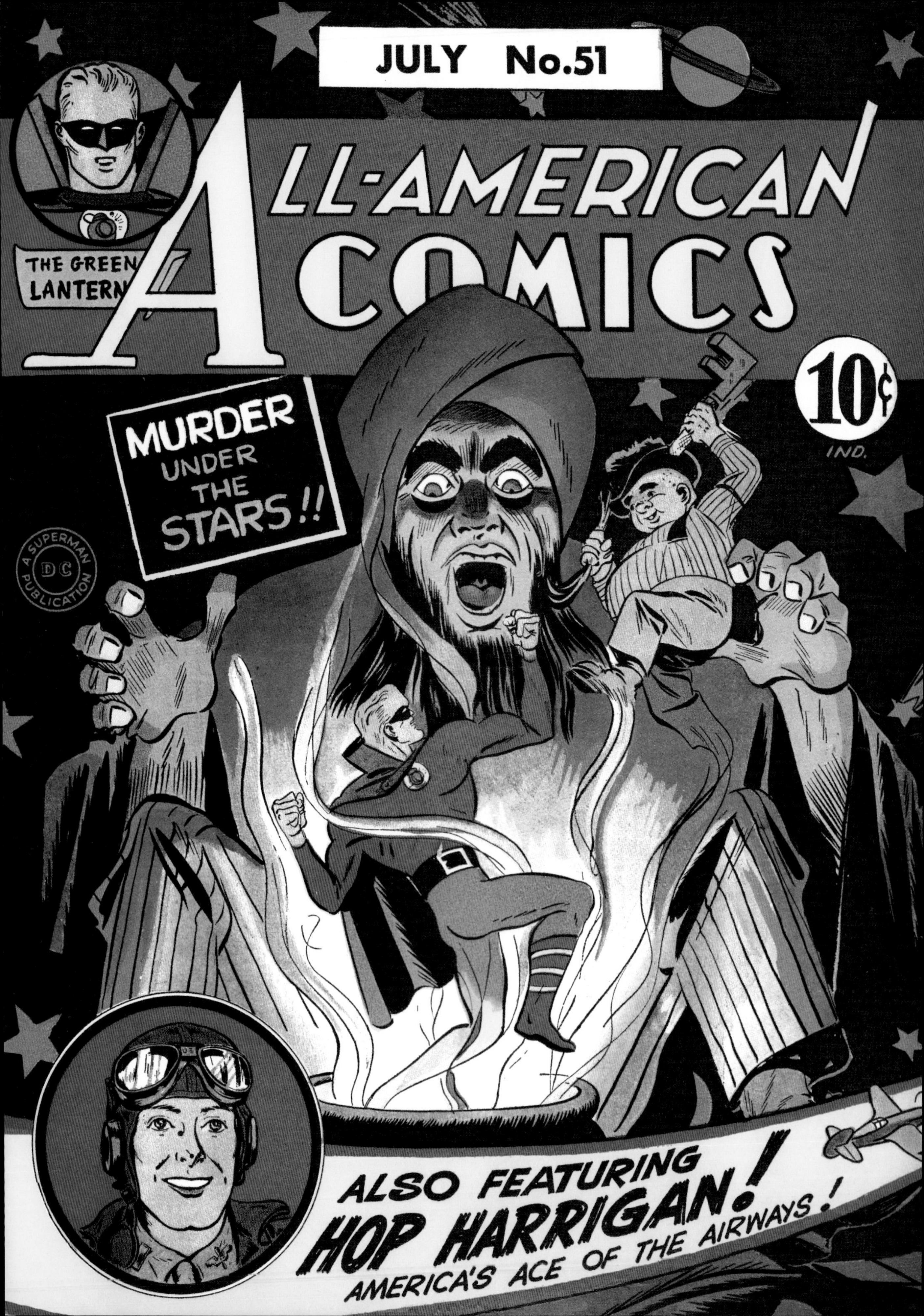
JULY No.51
ALL-AMERICAN COMICS
THE GREEN LANTERN
10¢
IND.
MURDER UNDER THE STARS!!
A SUPERMAN DC PUBLICATION
ALSO FEATURING
HOP HARRIGAN!
AMERICA'S ACE OF THE AIRWAYS!

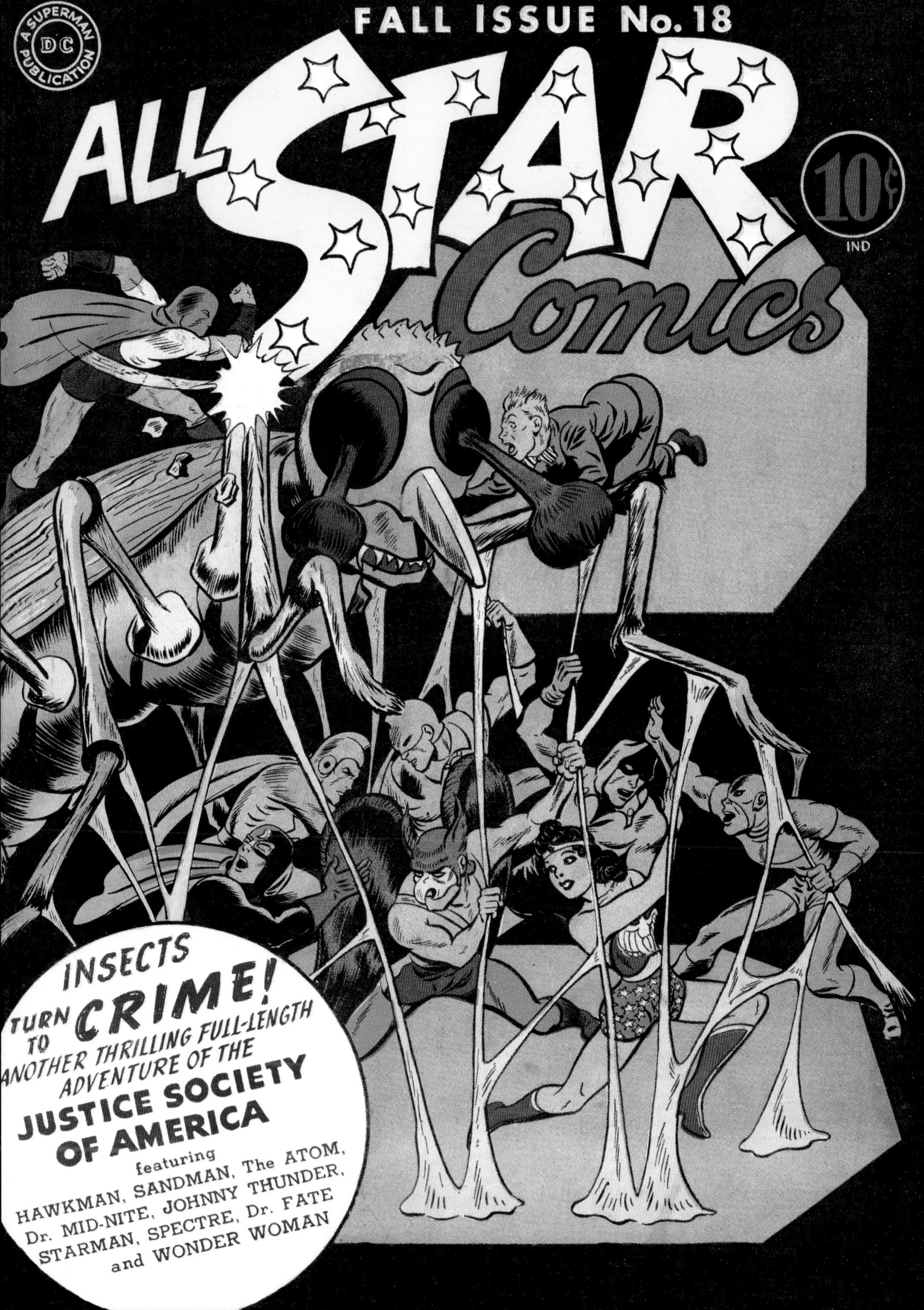
A SUPERMAN DC PUBLICATION
FALL ISSUE No. 18
ALL STAR Comics
10¢
IND
INSECTS TURN TO CRIME!
ANOTHER THRILLING FULL-LENGTH ADVENTURE OF THE
JUSTICE SOCIETY OF AMERICA
featuring
HAWKMAN, SANDMAN, The ATOM, Dr. MID-NITE, JOHNNY THUNDER, STARMAN, SPECTRE, Dr. FATE and WONDER WOMAN

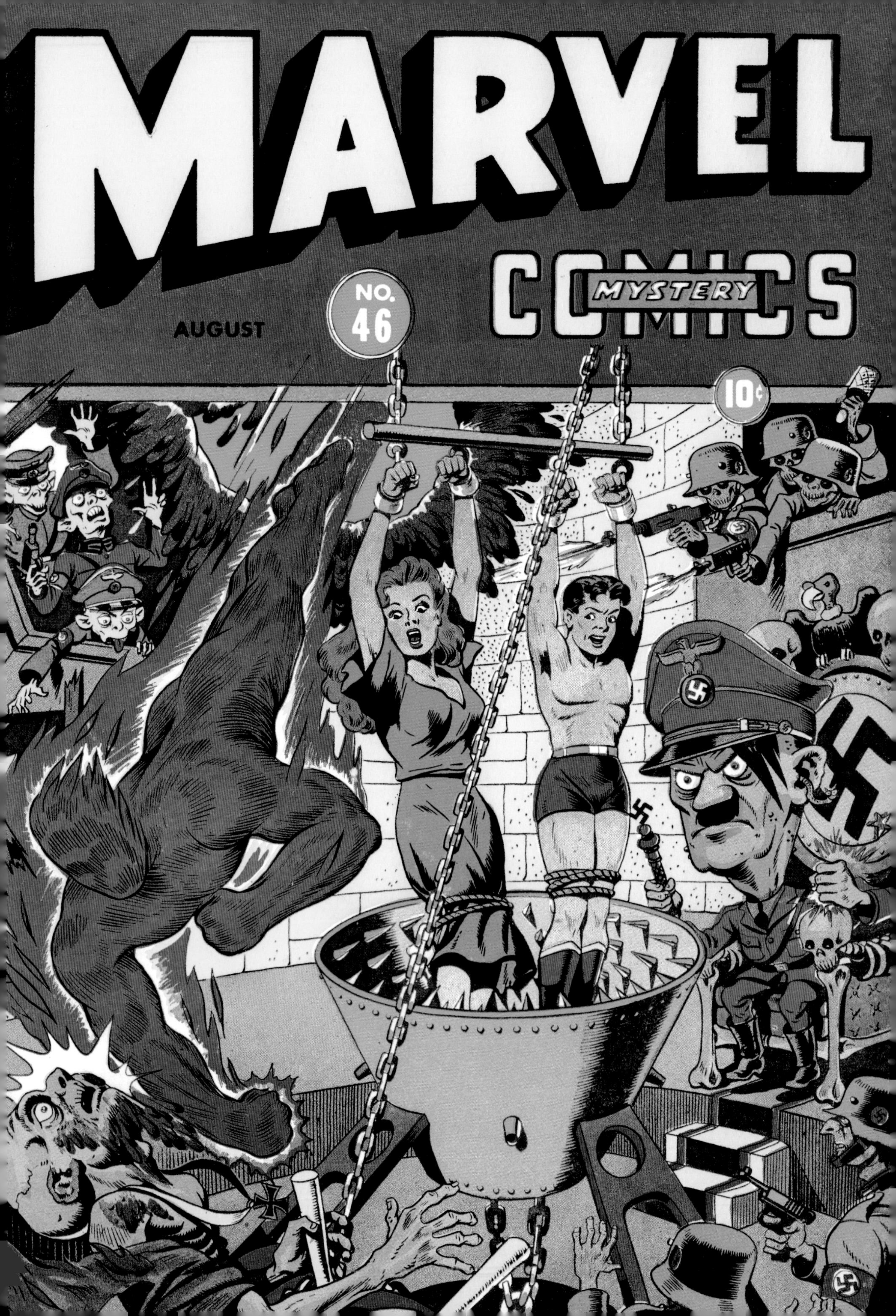

MARVEL
MYSTERY
COMICS
AUGUST
NO. 46
10¢

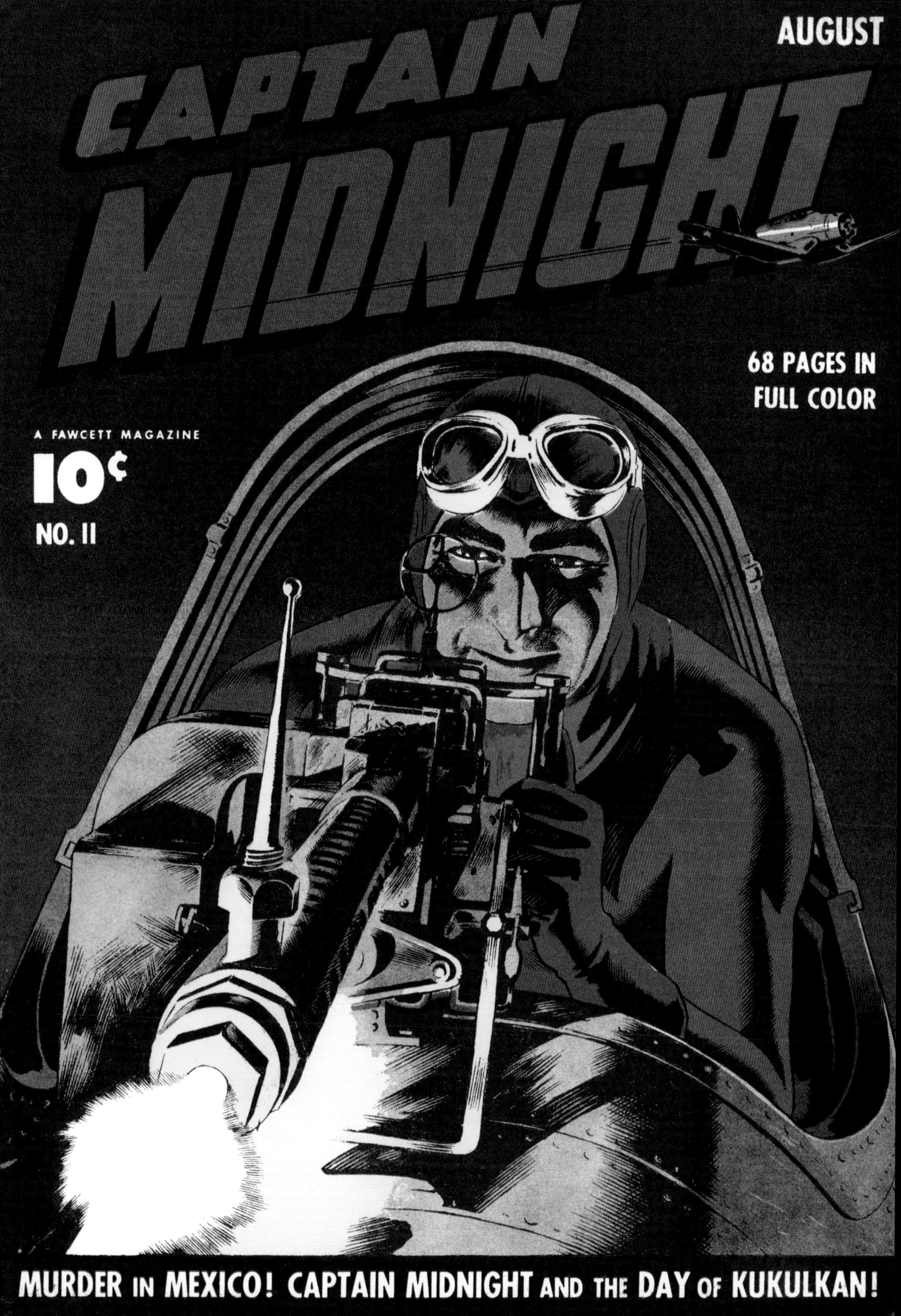

AUGUST
CAPTAIN MIDNIGHT
68 PAGES IN FULL COLOR
A FAWCETT MAGAZINE
10¢
NO. 11
MURDER IN MEXICO! CAPTAIN MIDNIGHT AND THE DAY OF KUKULKAN!

YANK & DOODLE — BLACK OWL — UNITED!! IN THIS ISSUE DON'T MISS IT!

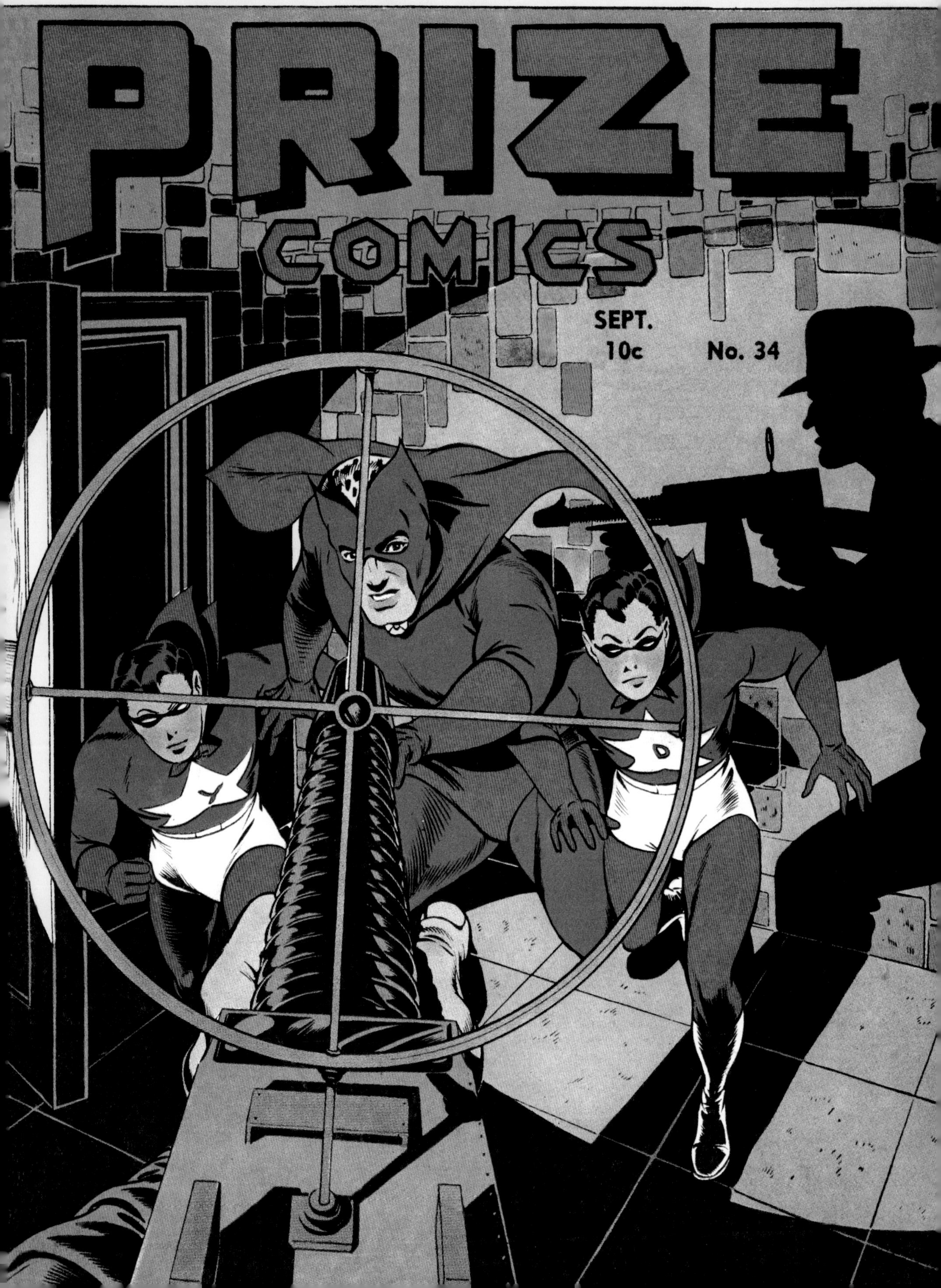
PRIZE
COMICS
SEPT.
10c
No. 34

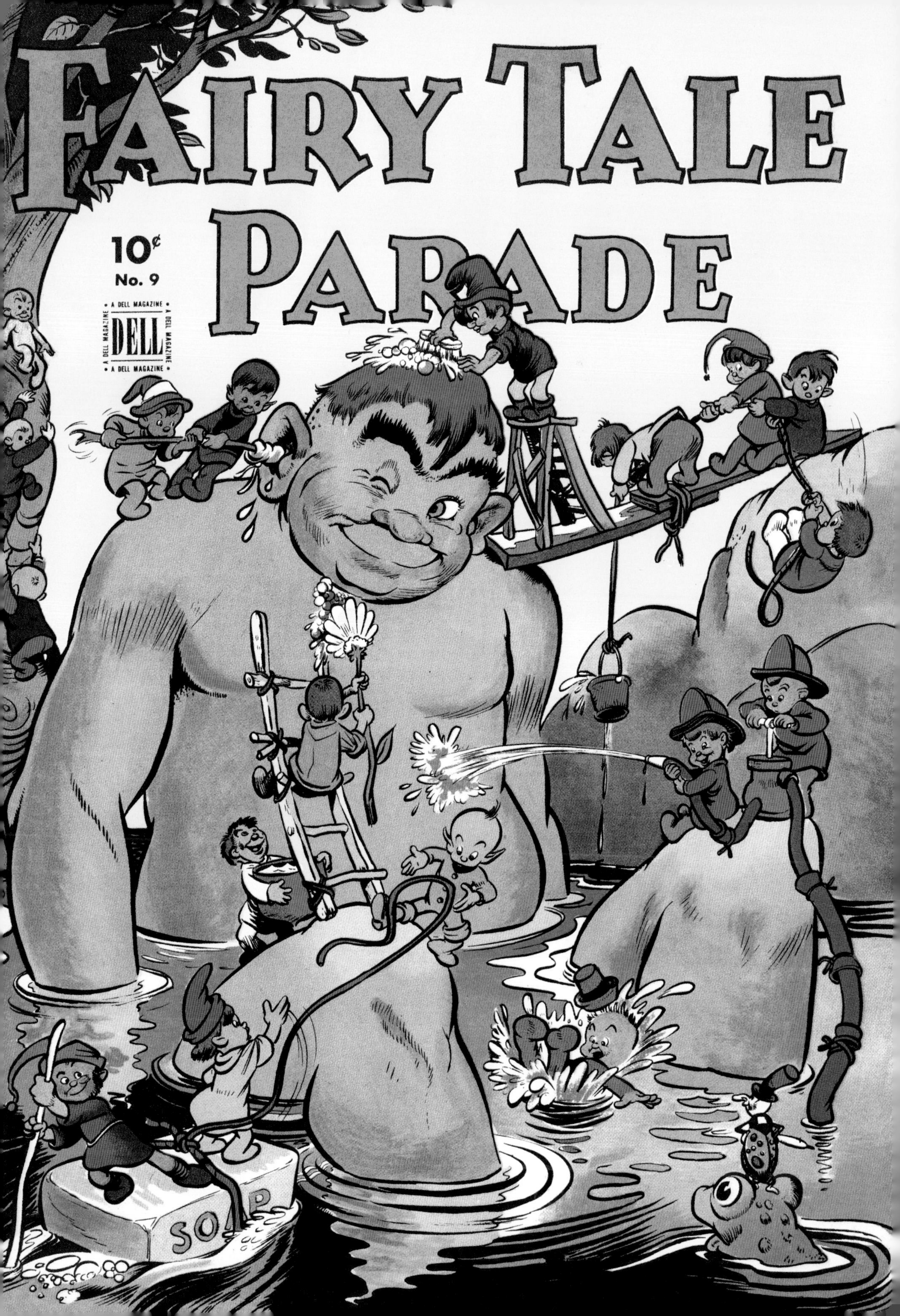
FAIRY TALE PARADE
10¢
No. 9
A DELL MAGAZINE
DELL
SOAP

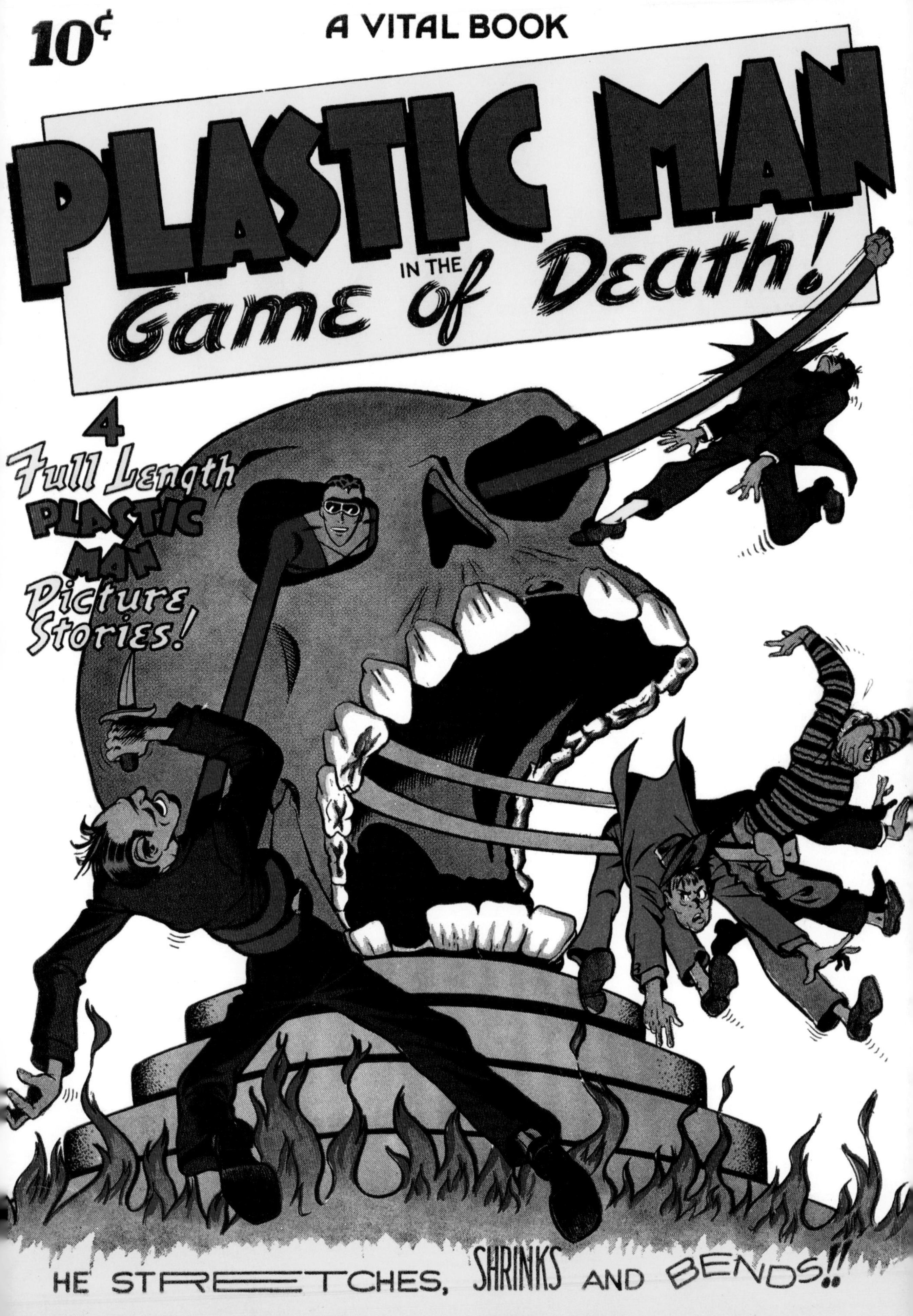

10¢
A VITAL BOOK
PLASTIC MAN
IN THE
Game of Death!
4
Full Length
PLASTIC
MAN
Picture
Stories!
HE STREETCHES, SHRINKS AND BENDS!!

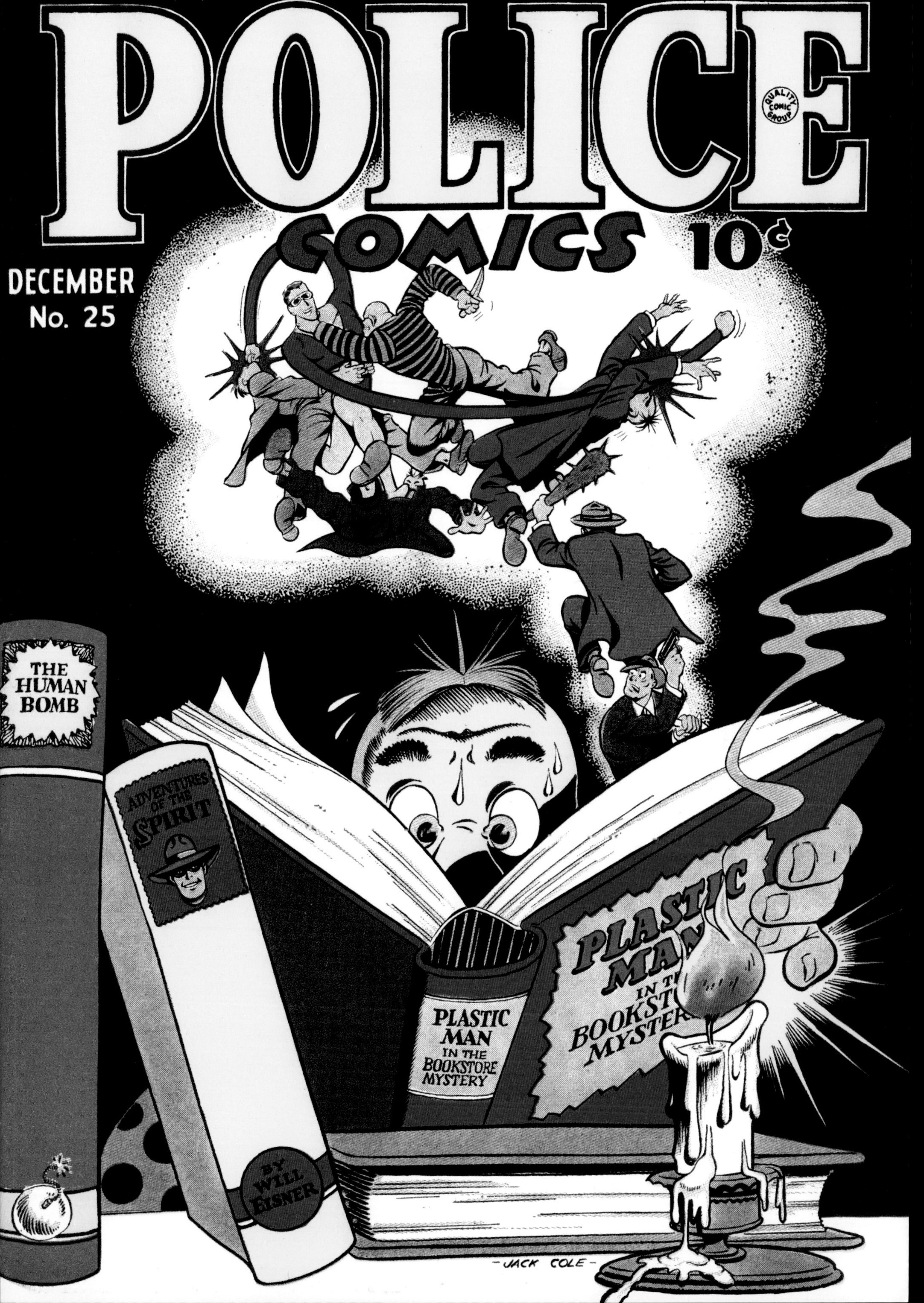
POLICE COMICS
QUALITY COMIC GROUP
10¢
DECEMBER No. 25
THE HUMAN BOMB
ADVENTURES OF THE SPIRIT
BY WILL EISNER
PLASTIC MAN IN THE BOOKSTORE MYSTERY
PLASTIC MAN IN THE BOOKSTORE MYSTERY
-JACK COLE-

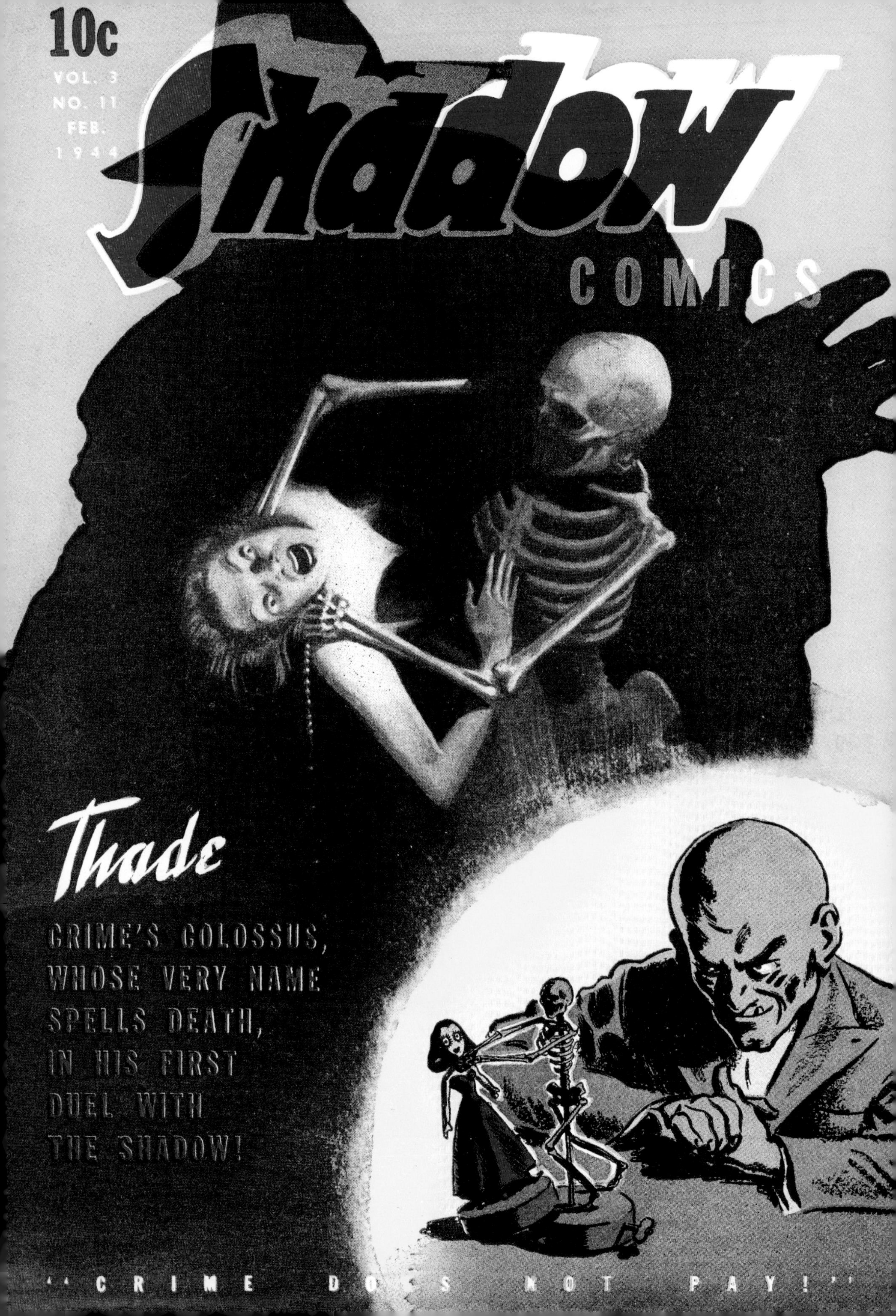
10c
VOL. 3
NO. 11
FEB.
1944
Shadow
COMICS
Thade
GRIME'S COLOSSUS,
WHOSE VERY NAME
SPELLS DEATH,
IN HIS FIRST
DUEL WITH
THE SHADOW!
"CRIME DOES NOT PAY!"

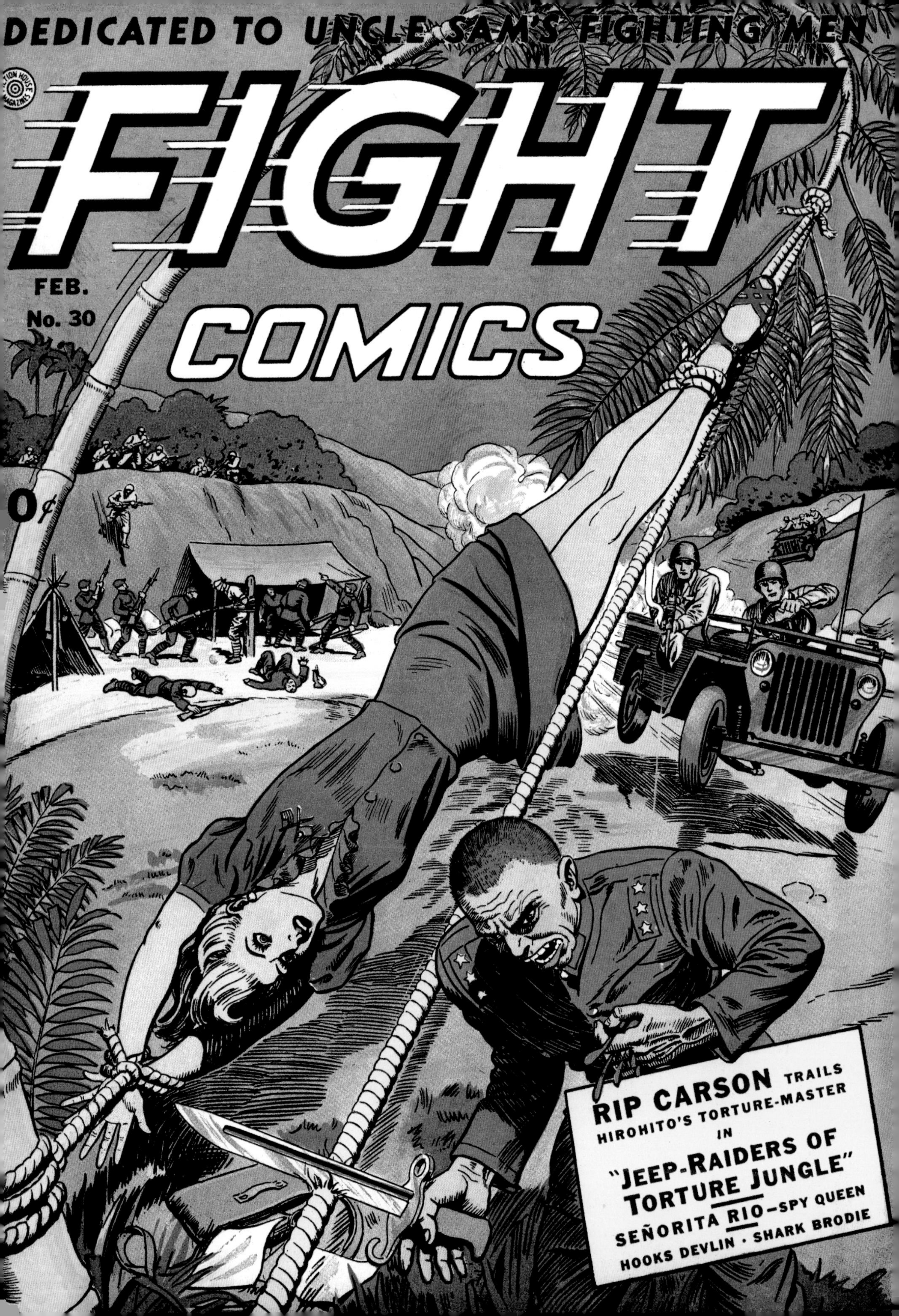
DEDICATED TO UNCLE SAM'S FIGHTING MEN
FIGHT COMICS
FEB.
No. 30
RIP CARSON TRAILS HIROHITO'S TORTURE-MASTER IN "JEEP-RAIDERS OF TORTURE JUNGLE"
SEÑORITA RIO-SPY QUEEN
HOOKS DEVLIN · SHARK BRODIE

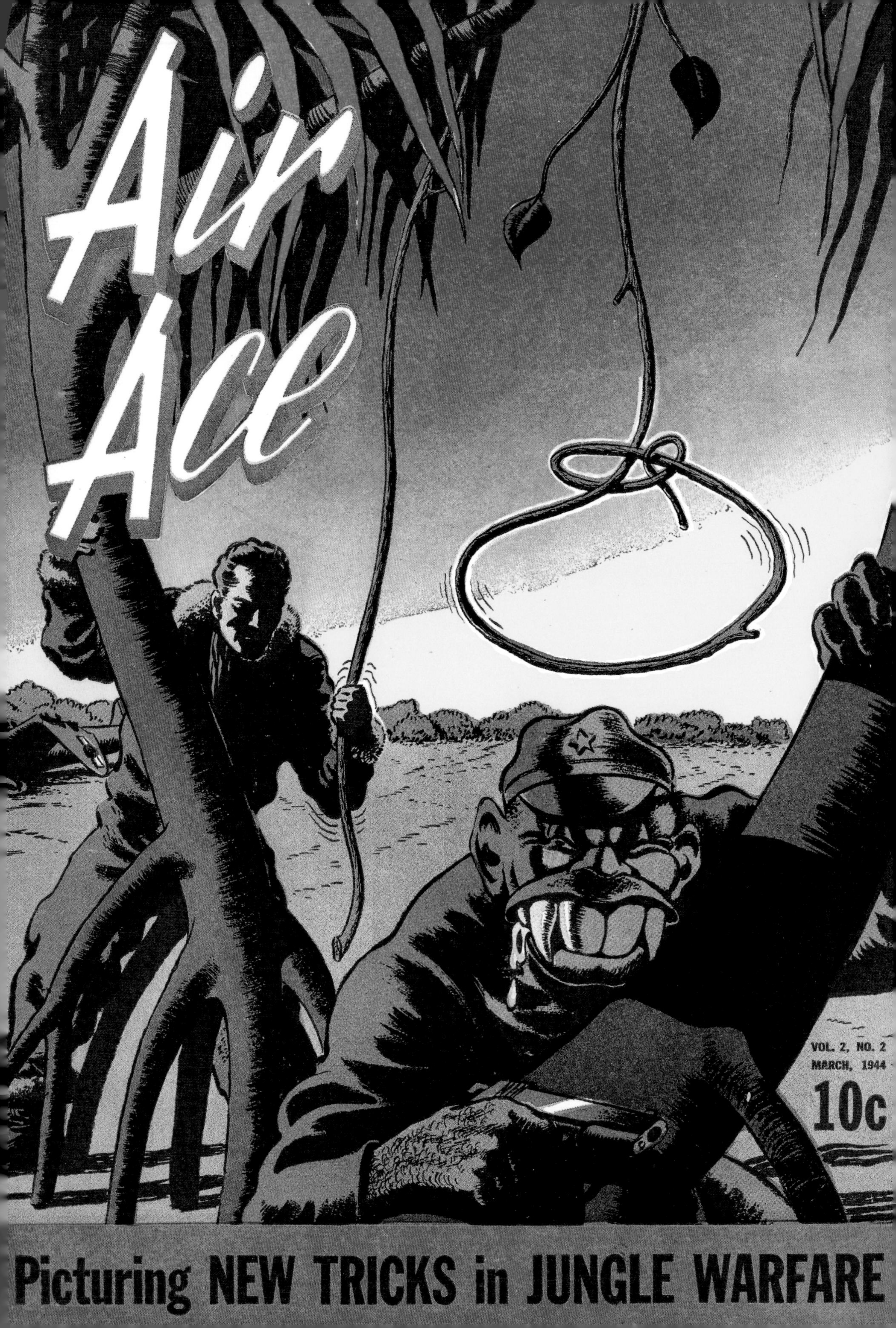
Air Ace
VOL. 2, NO. 2
MARCH, 1944
10c
Picturing NEW TRICKS in JUNGLE WARFARE

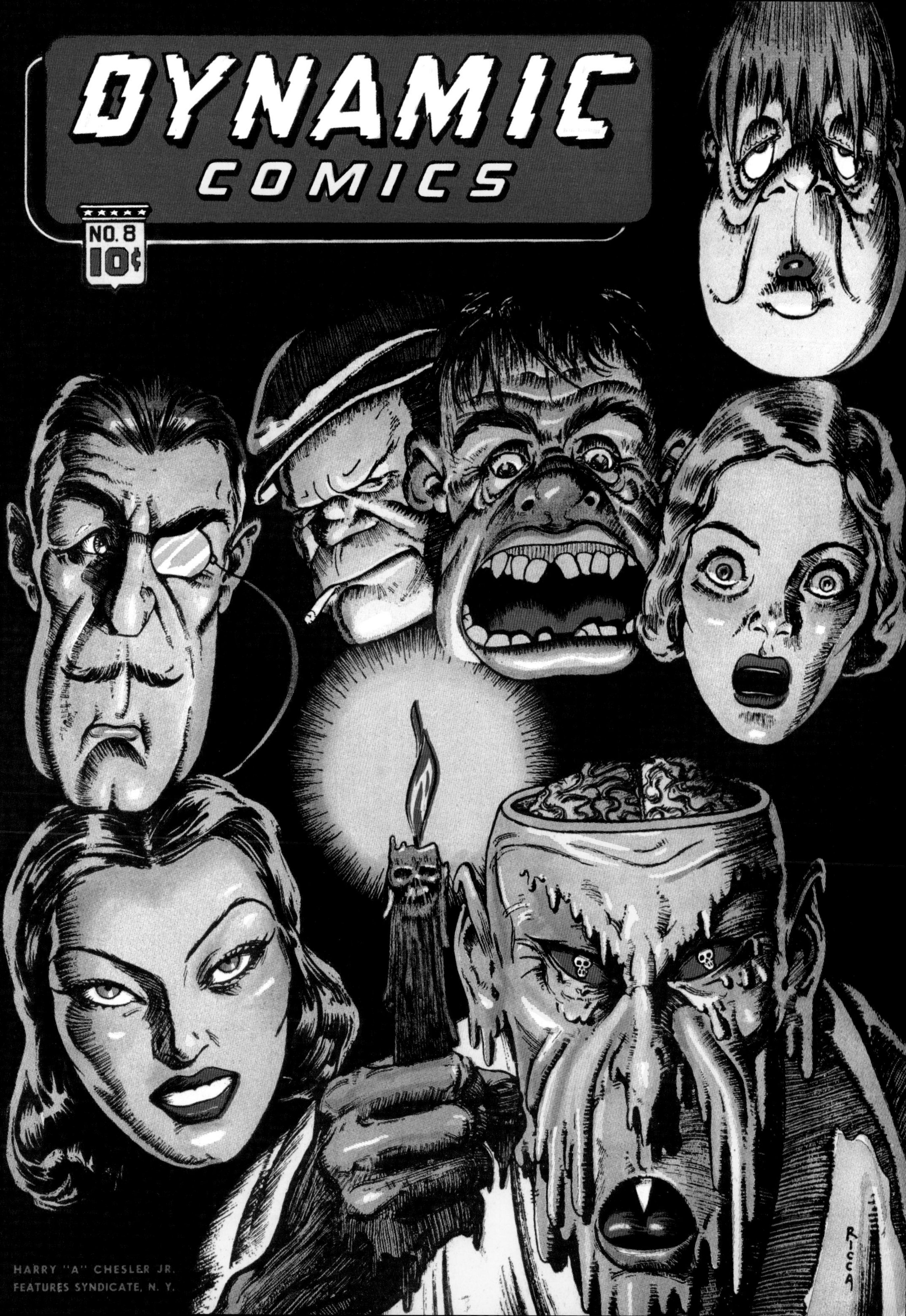

DYNAMIC COMICS
NO. 8
10¢
RICCA
HARRY "A" CHESLER JR.
FEATURES SYNDICATE, N. Y.

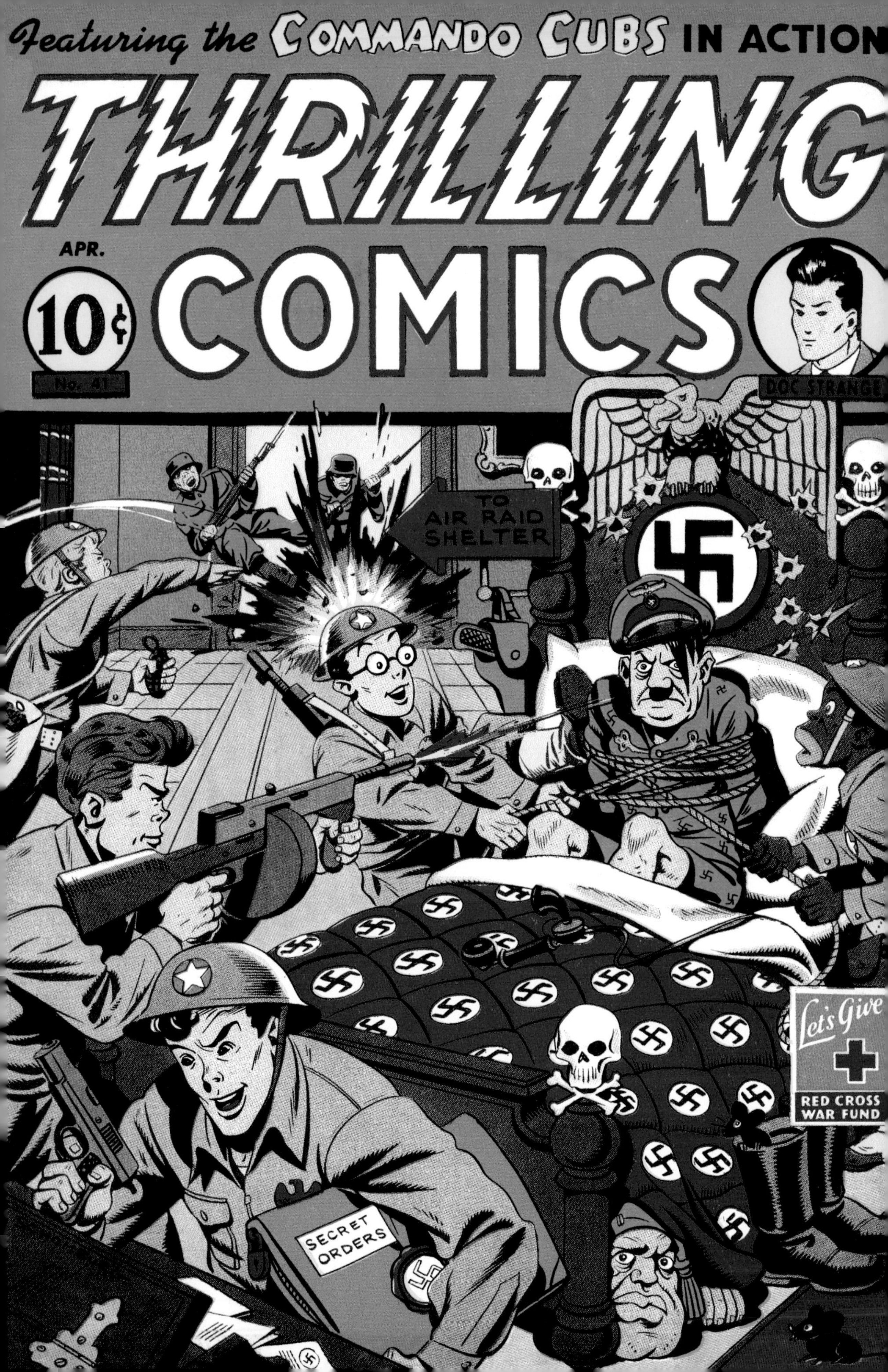
Featuring the COMMANDO CUBS IN ACTION
THRILLING COMICS
APR.
10¢
No. 41
DOC STRANGE
TO AIR RAID SHELTER
SECRET ORDERS
Let's Give
RED CROSS WAR FUND

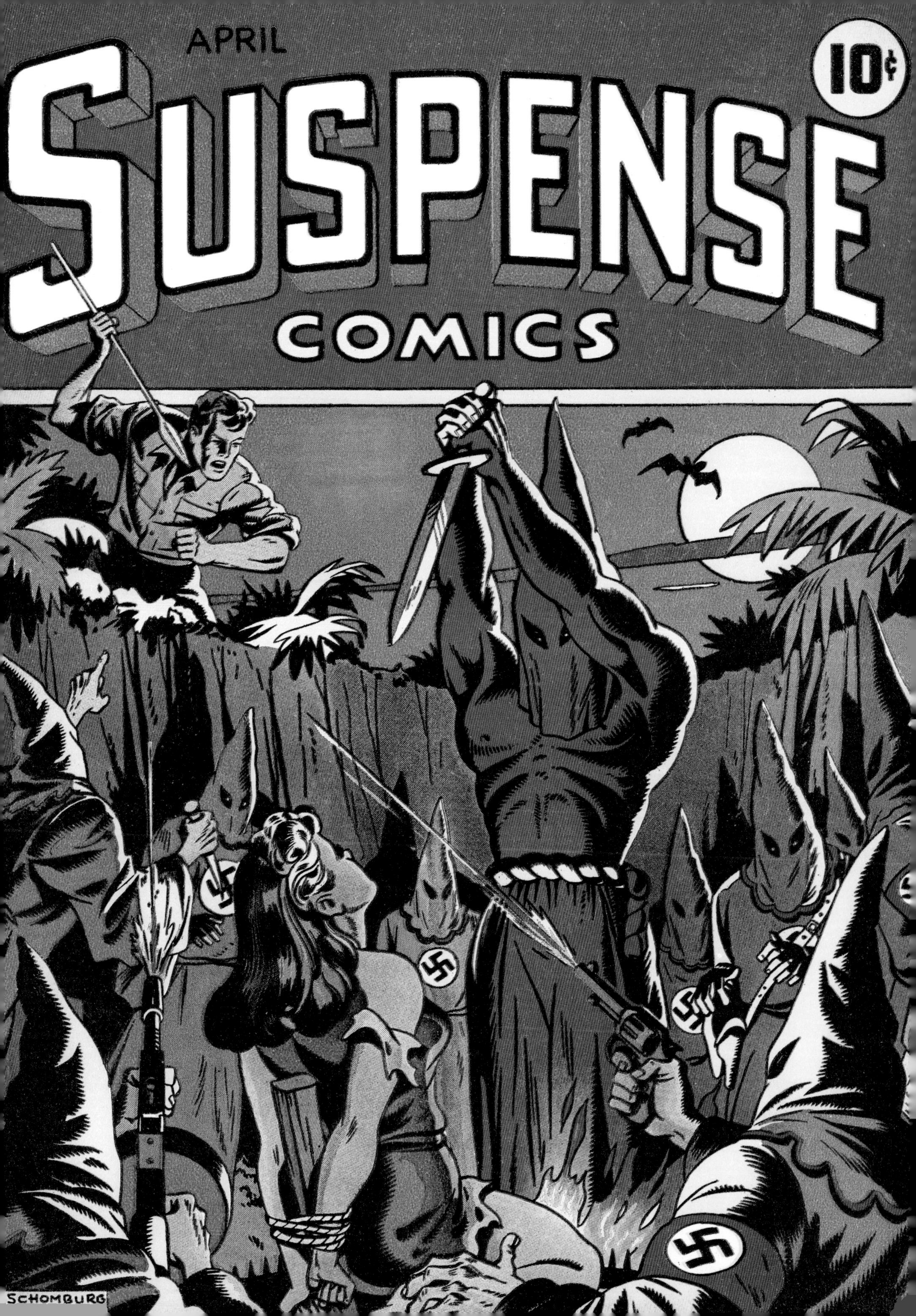
APRIL
10¢
SUSPENSE
COMICS
SCHOMBURG

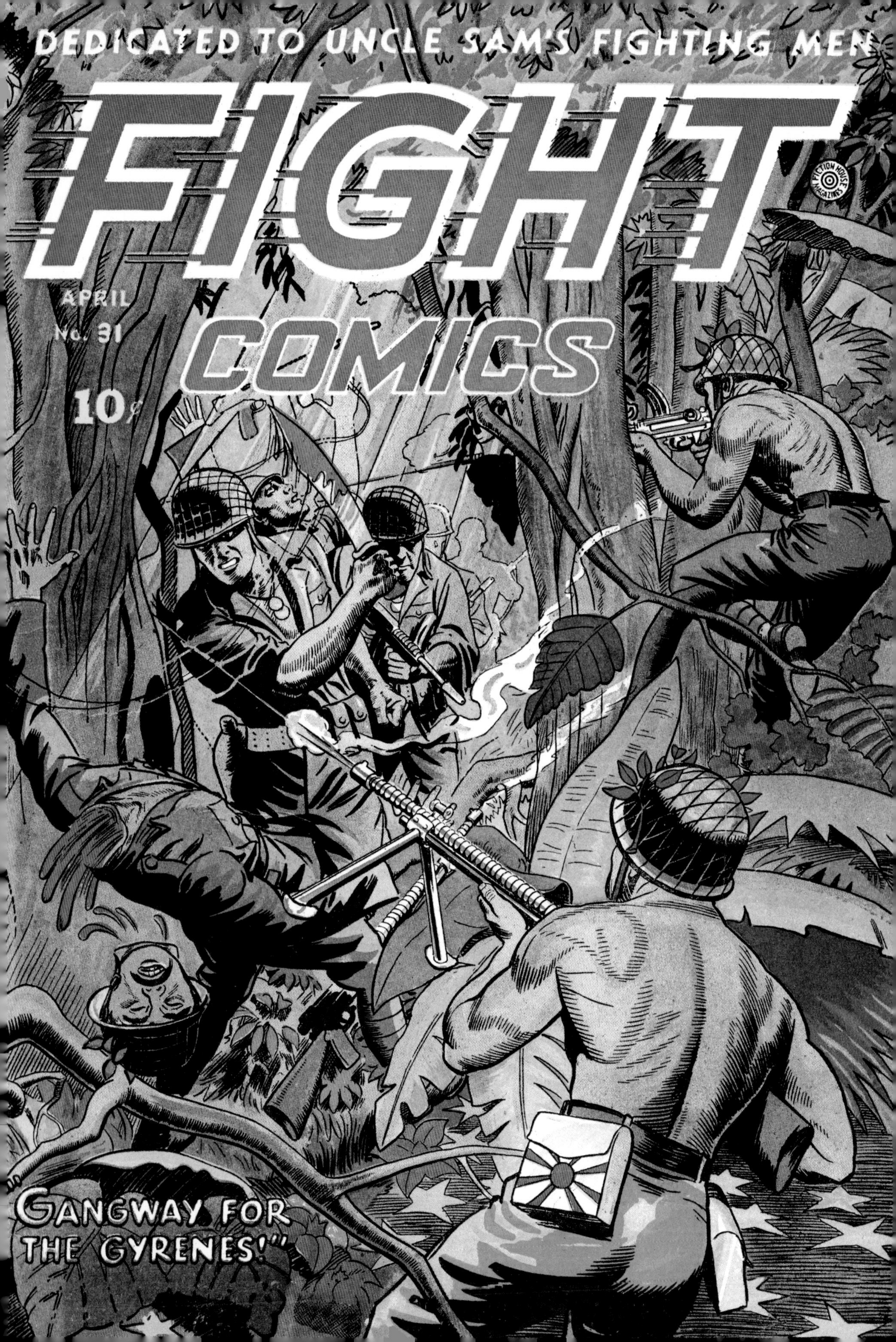

DEDICATED TO UNCLE SAM'S FIGHTING MEN
FIGHT
COMICS
APRIL
No. 31
10¢
FICTION HOUSE MAGAZINES
"GANGWAY FOR THE GYRENES!"

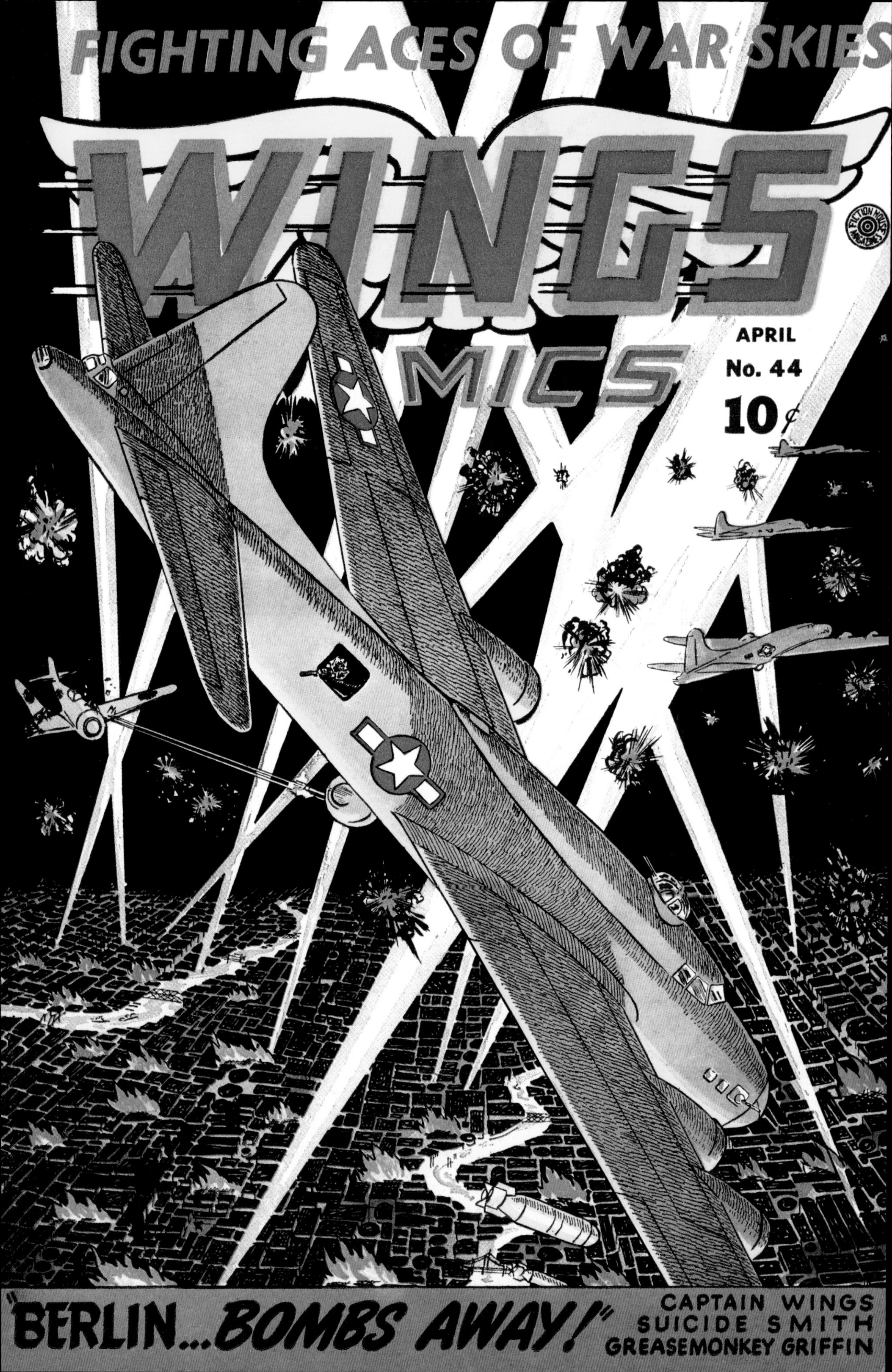

FIGHTING ACES OF WAR SKIES
WINGS
COMICS
FICTION HOUSE MAGAZINES
APRIL
No. 44
10¢
"BERLIN...BOMBS AWAY!"
CAPTAIN WINGS
SUICIDE SMITH
GREASEMONKEY GRIFFIN

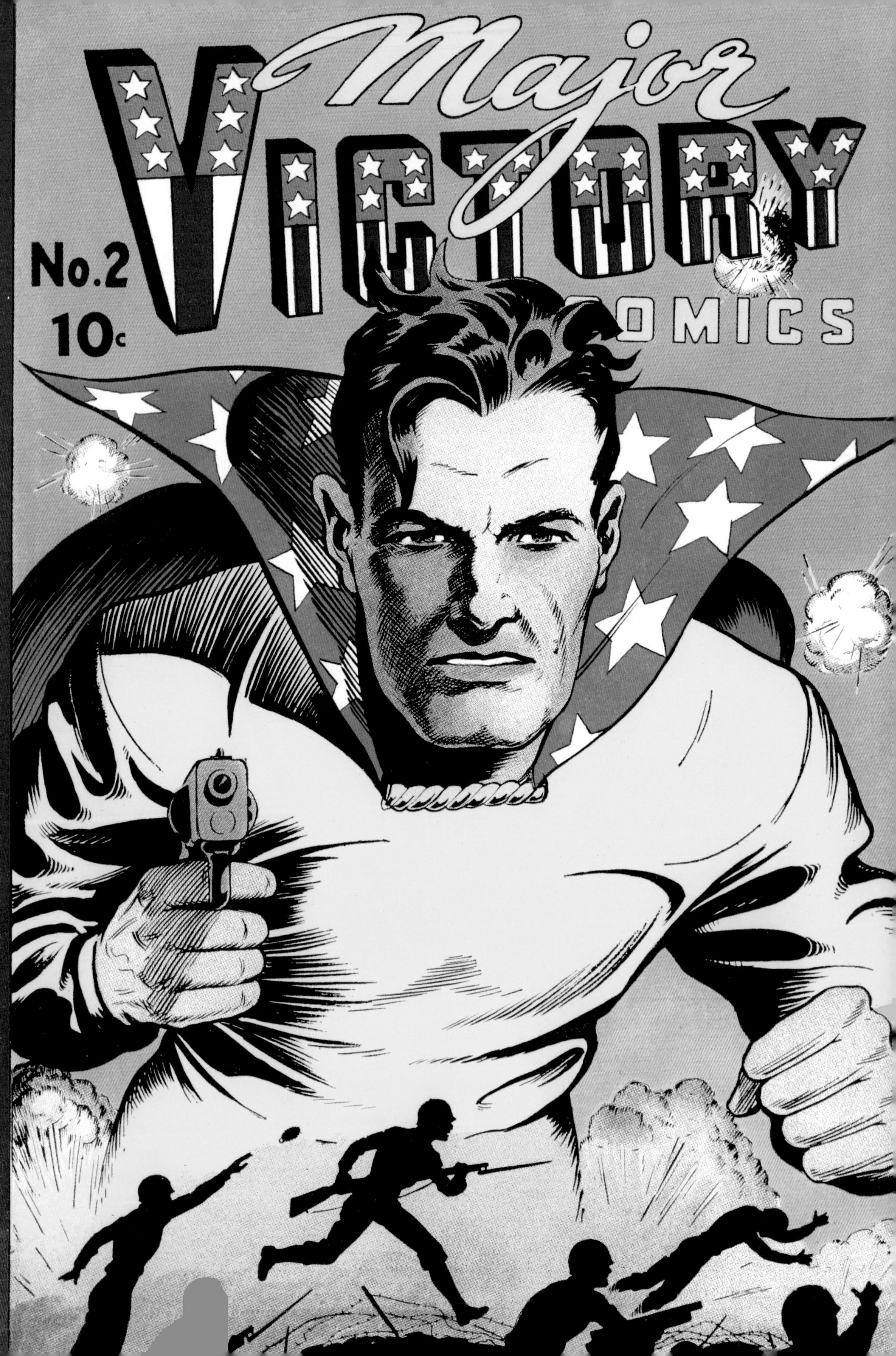
Major
VICTORY
COMICS
No. 2
10c

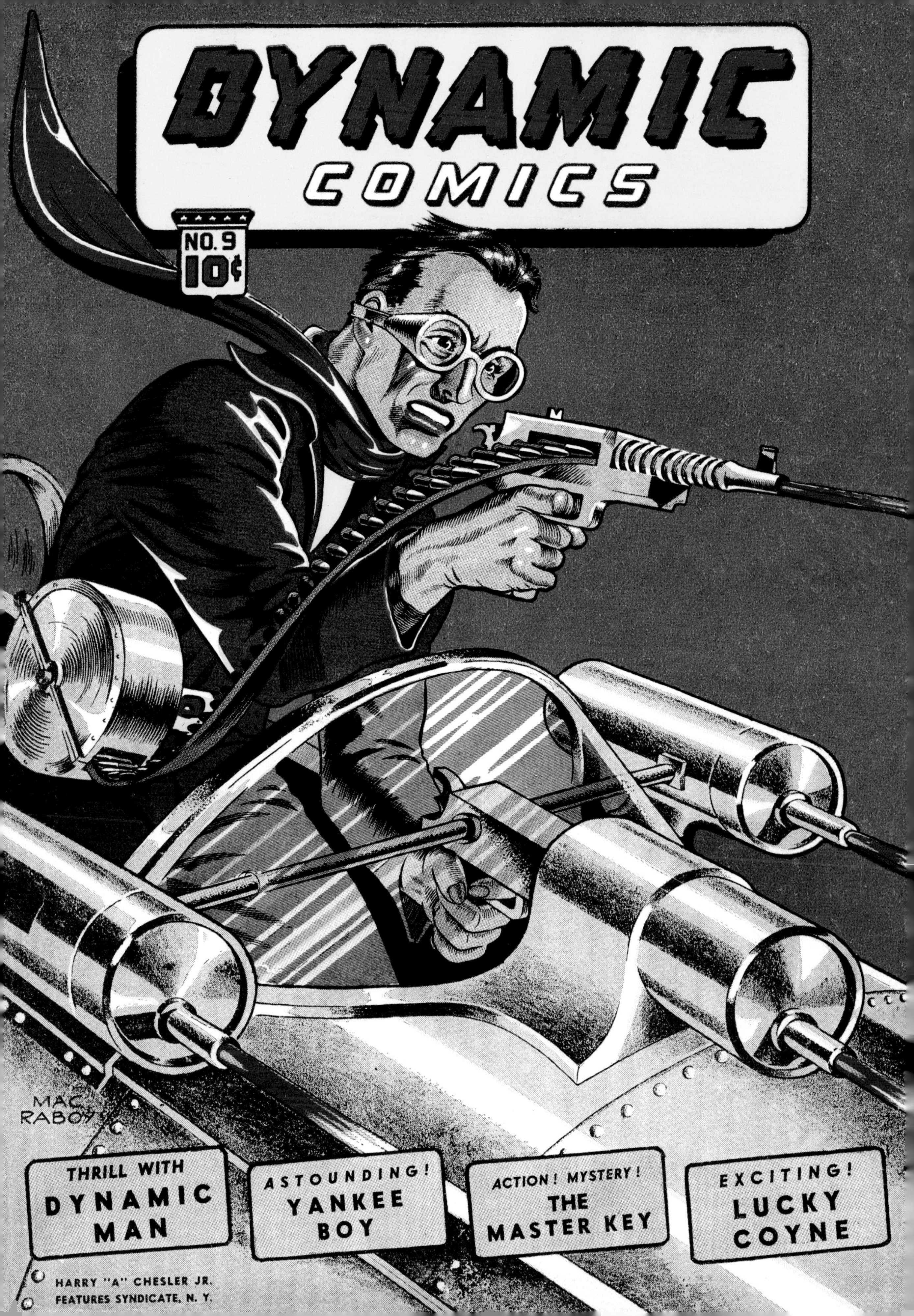
DYNAMIC COMICS
NO. 9
10¢
MAC RABOY
THRILL WITH DYNAMIC MAN
ASTOUNDING! YANKEE BOY
ACTION! MYSTERY! THE MASTER KEY
EXCITING! LUCKY COYNE
HARRY "A" CHESLER JR. FEATURES SYNDICATE, N. Y.

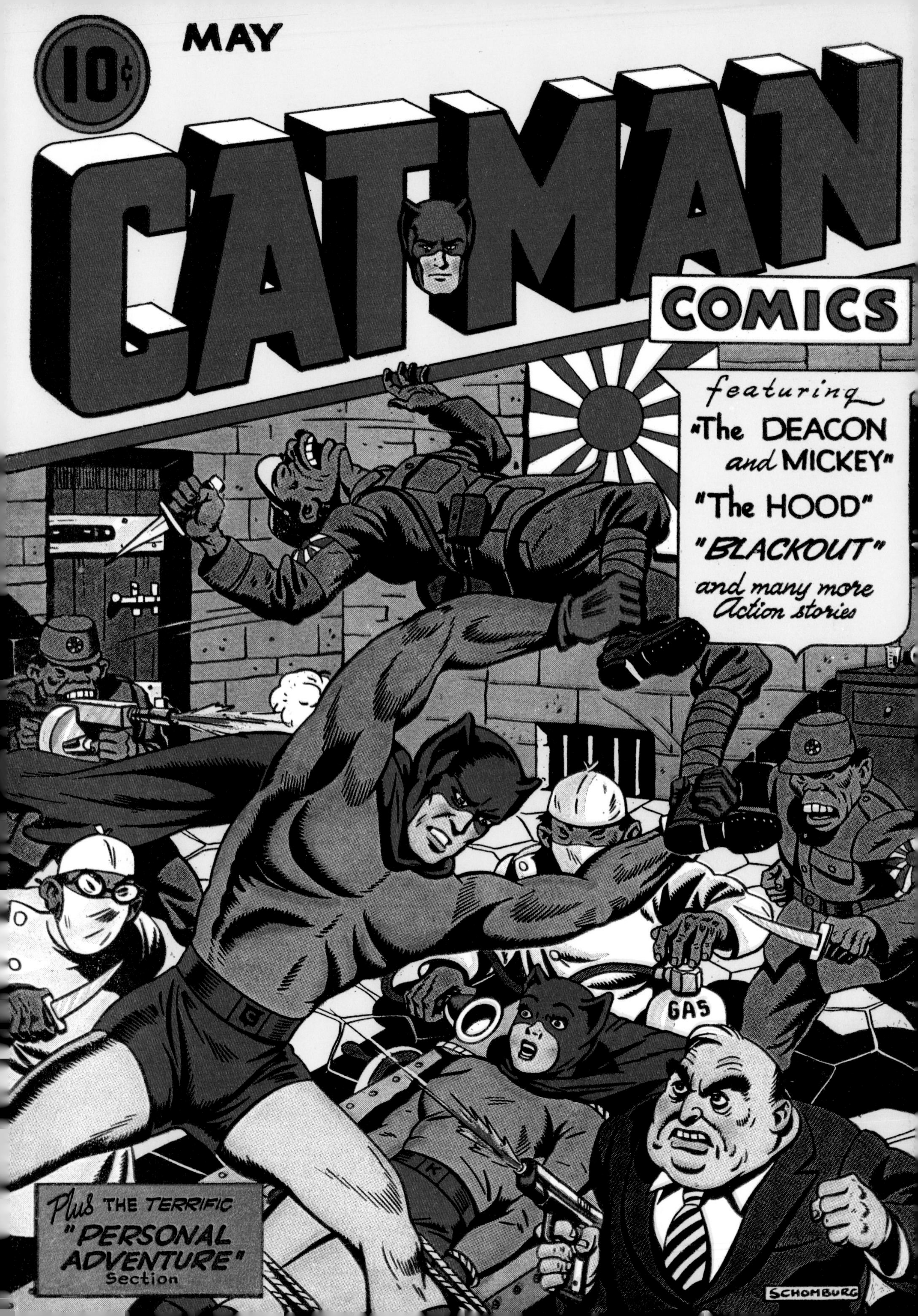
MAY
10¢
CAT-MAN
COMICS
featuring
"The DEACON and MICKEY"
"The HOOD"
"BLACKOUT"
and many more Action stories
GAS
Plus THE TERRIFIC "PERSONAL ADVENTURE" Section
SCHOMBURG

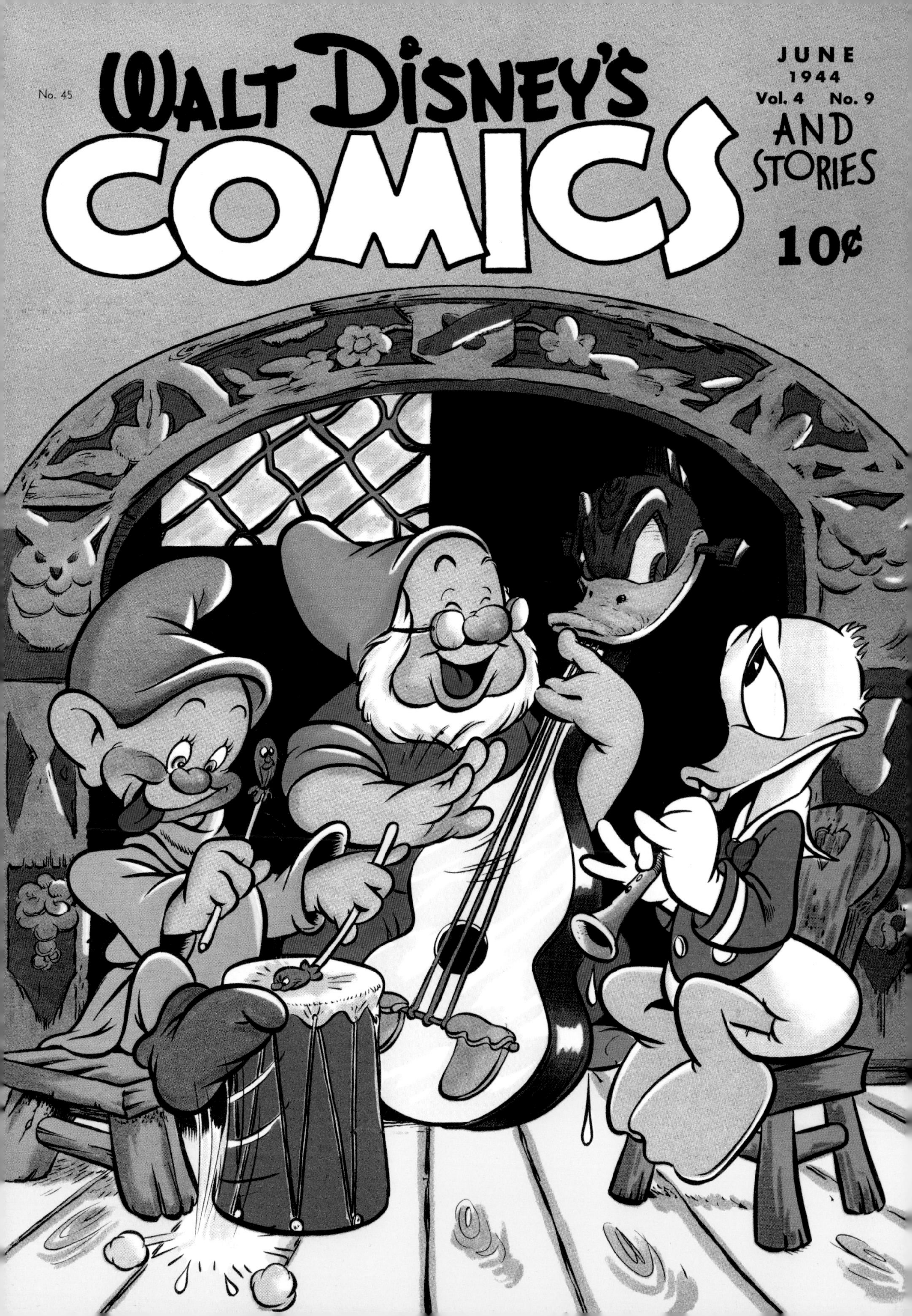
No. 45
WALT DISNEY'S
COMICS
AND STORIES
JUNE
1944
Vol. 4 No. 9
10¢

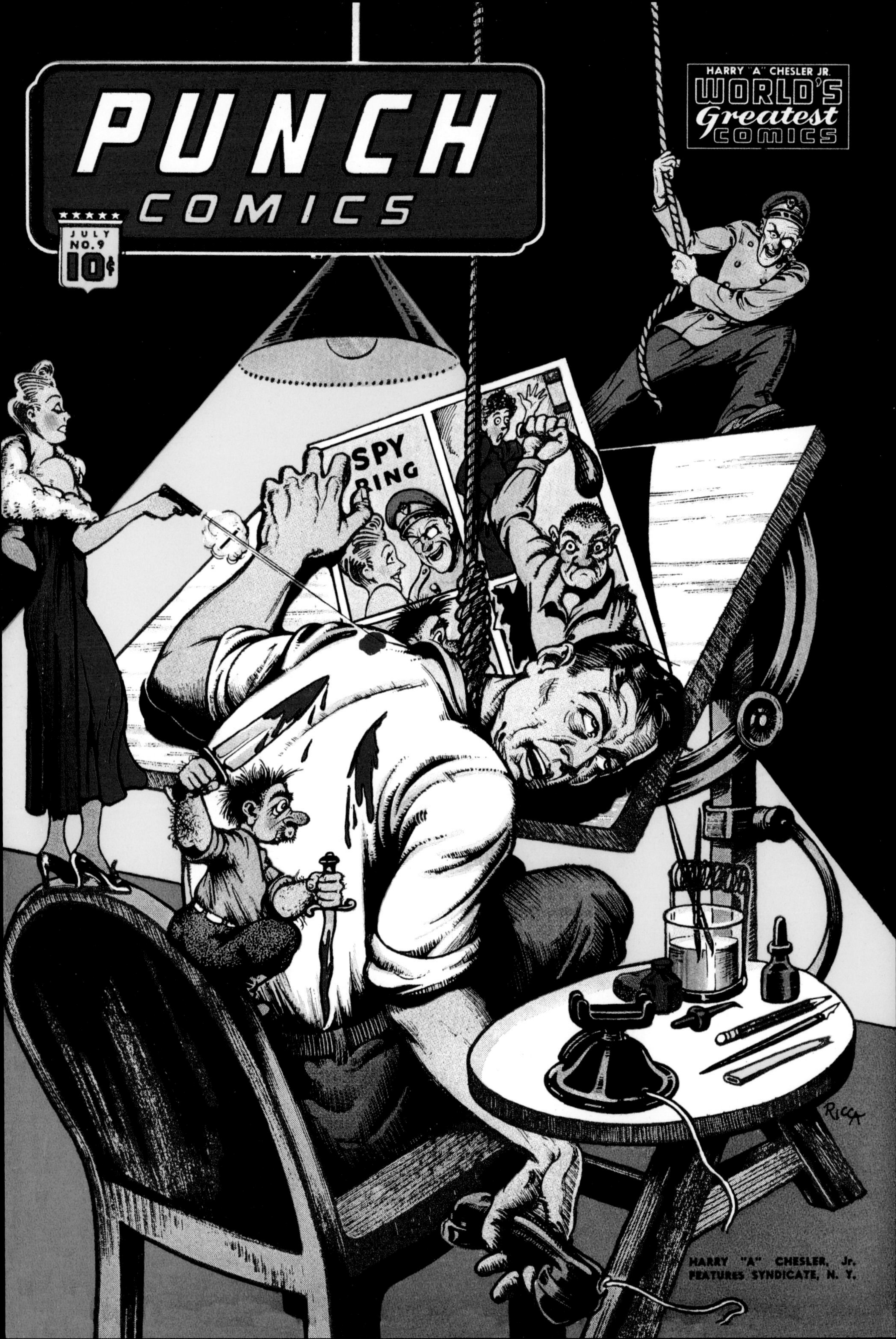
PUNCH COMICS
JULY NO. 9
10¢
HARRY "A" CHESLER JR.
WORLD'S Greatest COMICS
SPY RING
RICCA
HARRY "A" CHESLER, Jr.
FEATURES SYNDICATE, N. Y.

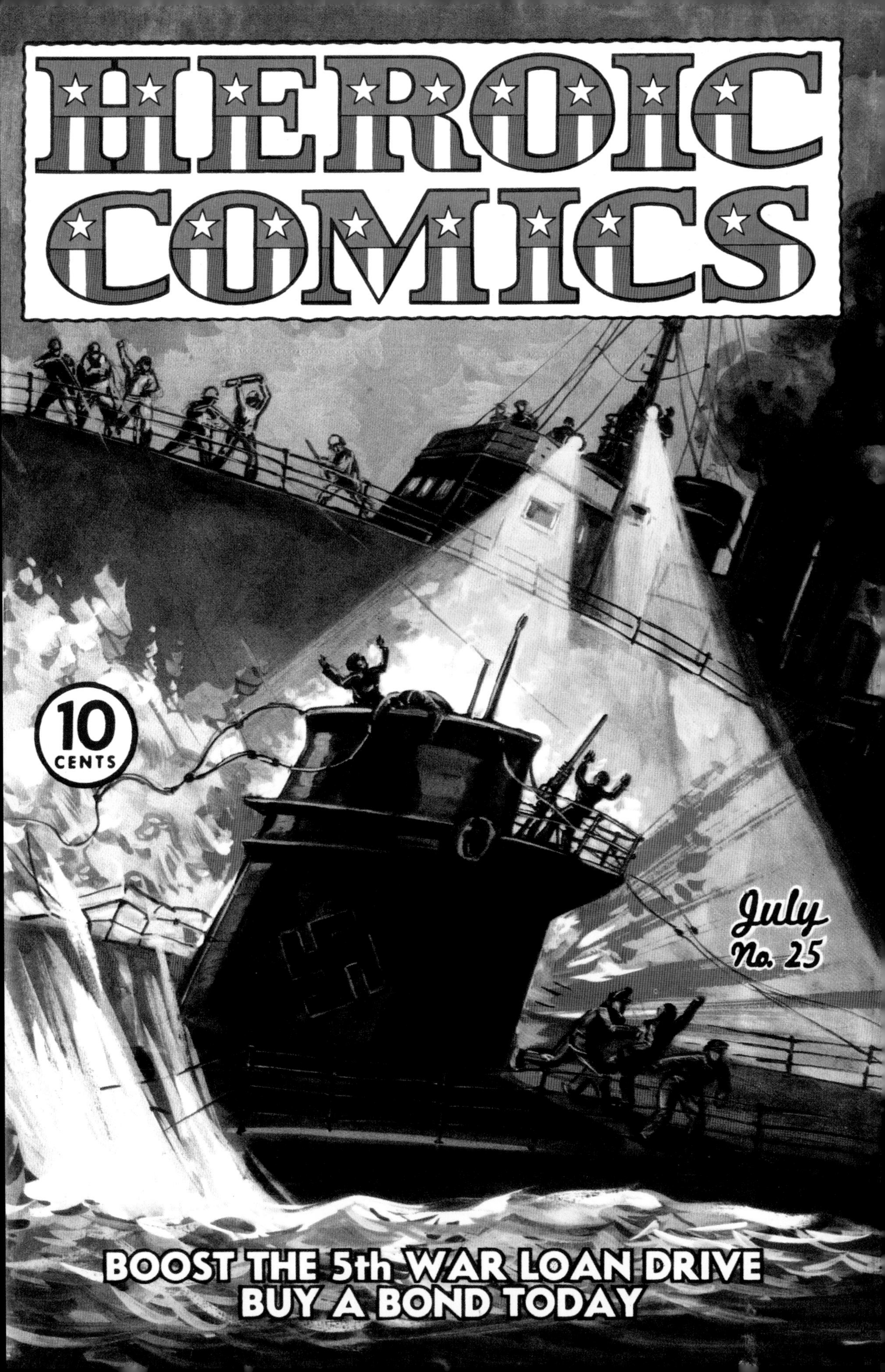
HEROIC COMICS
10 CENTS
July
No. 25
BOOST THE 5th WAR LOAN DRIVE
BUY A BOND TODAY

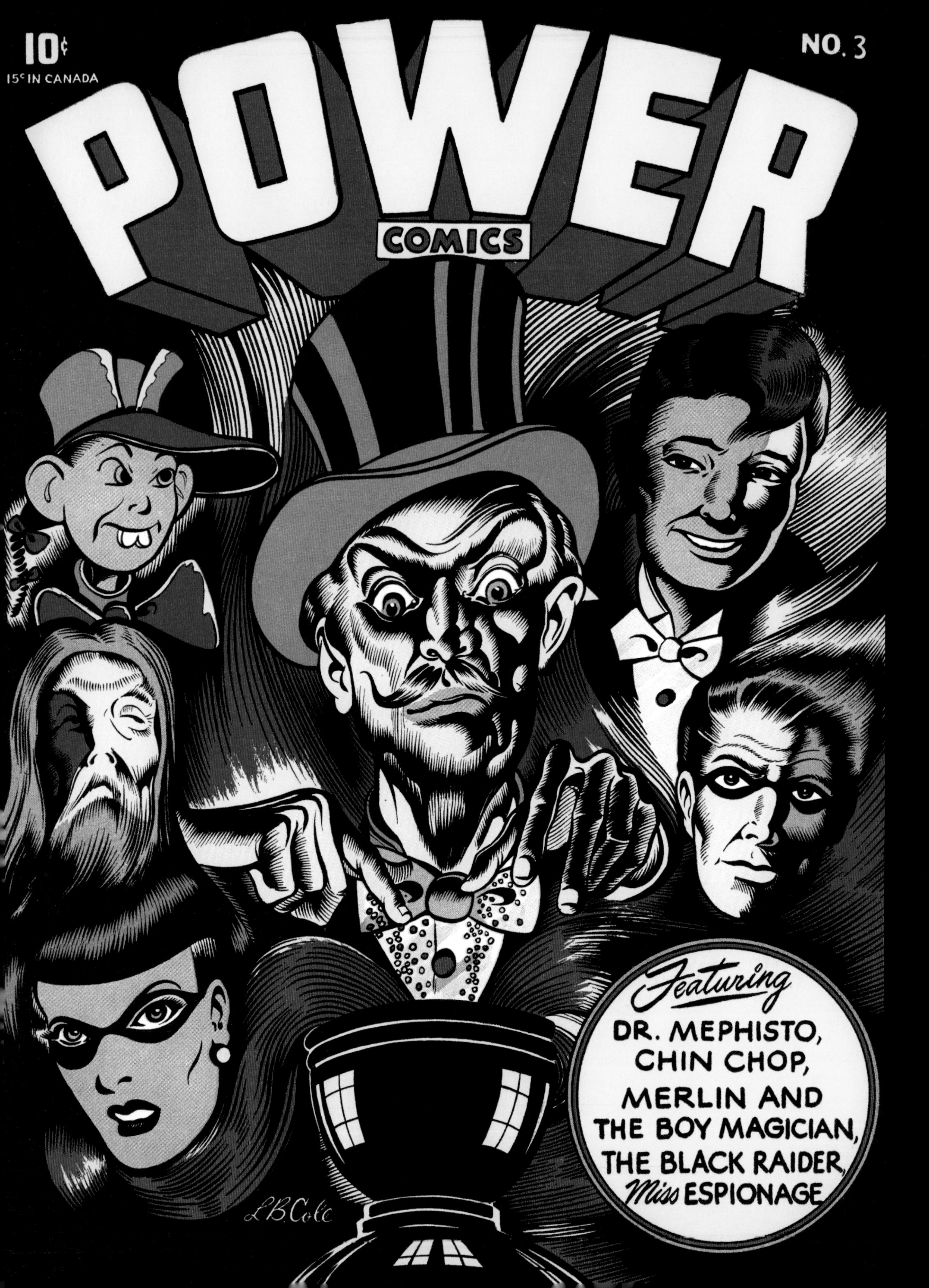
10¢
15¢ IN CANADA
NO. 3
POWER
COMICS
Featuring
DR. MEPHISTO,
CHIN CHOP,
MERLIN AND
THE BOY MAGICIAN,
THE BLACK RAIDER,
Miss ESPIONAGE
L.B. Cole

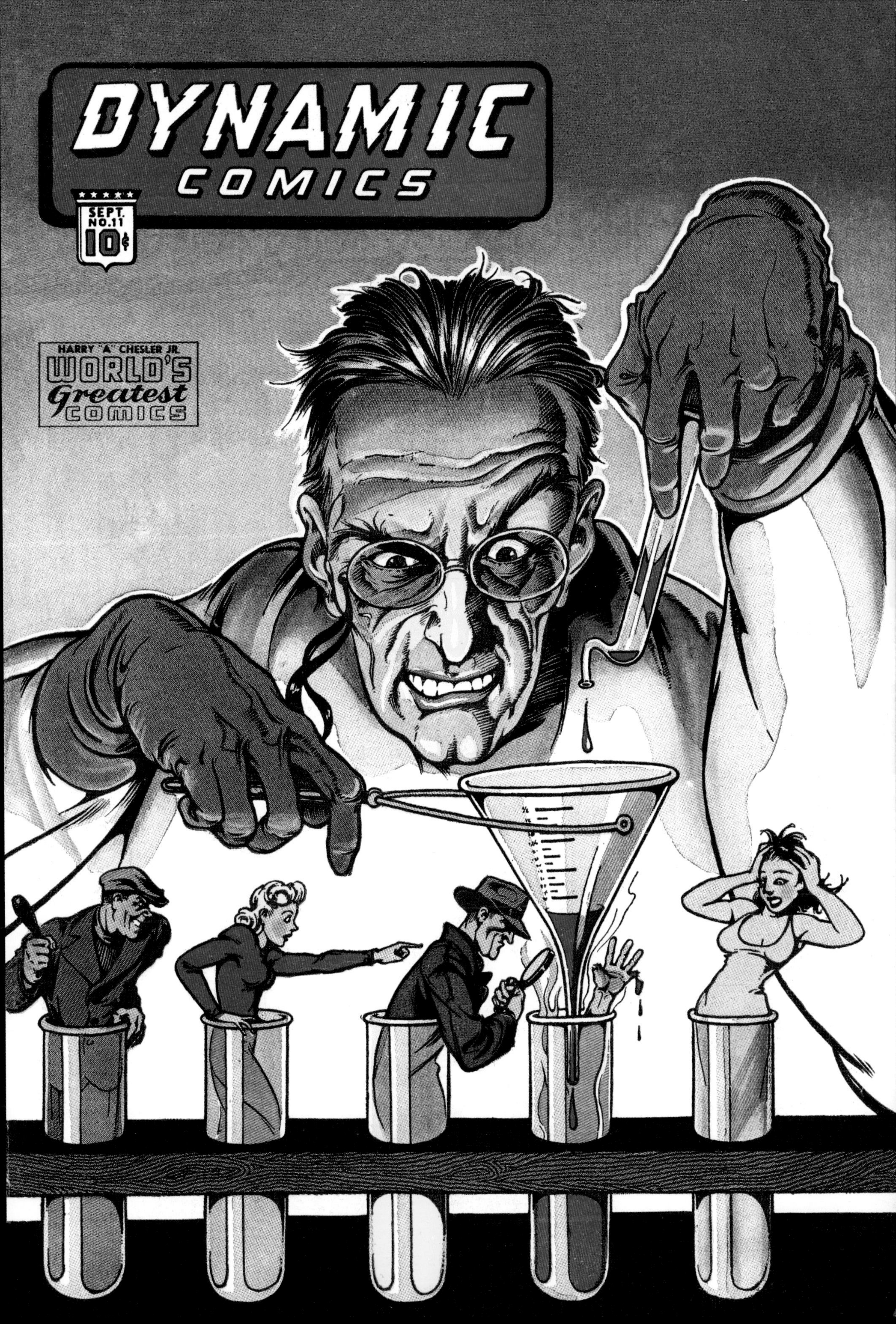

DYNAMIC COMICS
SEPT. NO.11
10¢
HARRY "A" CHESLER JR.
WORLD'S Greatest COMICS

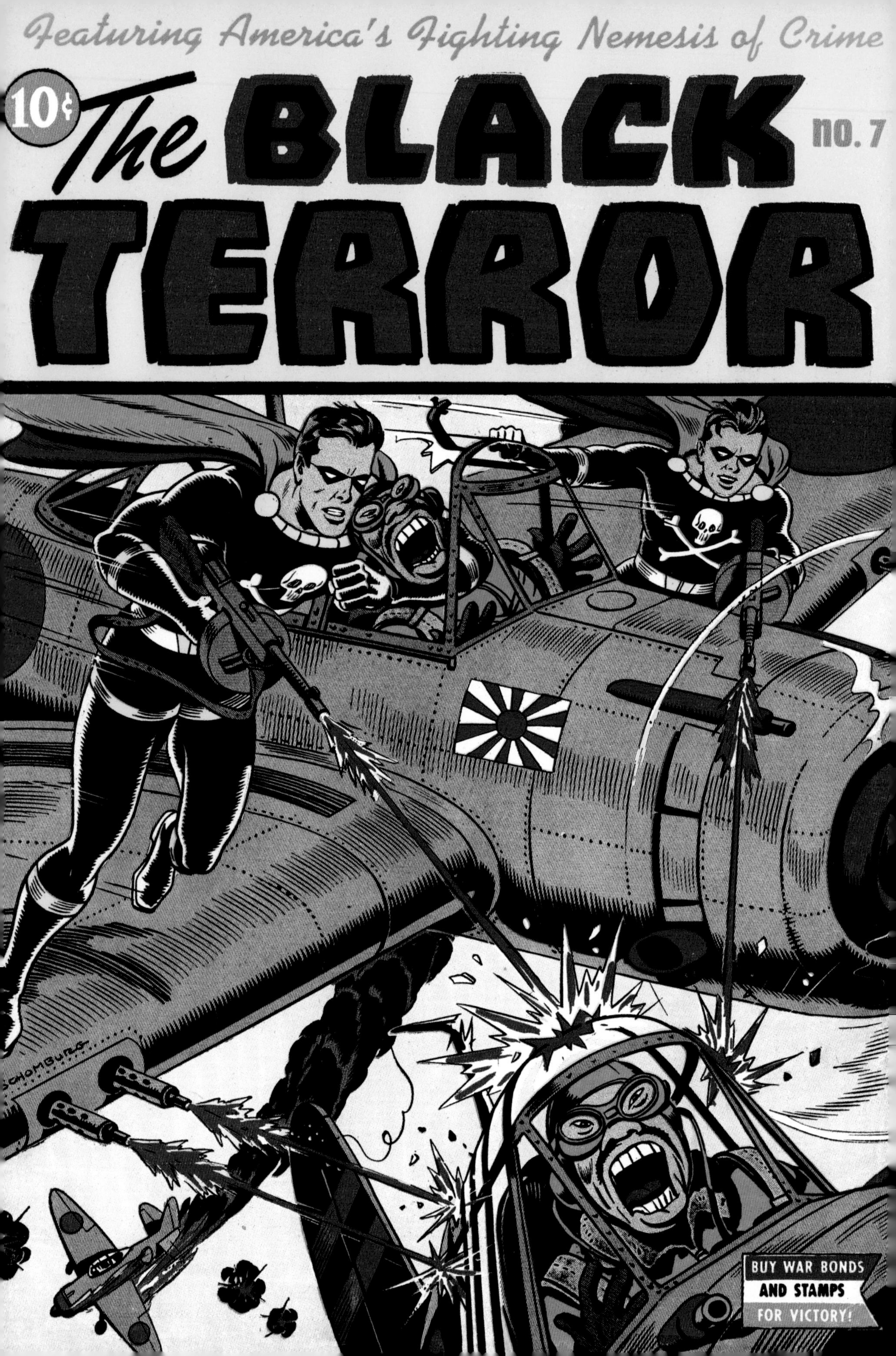
Featuring America's Fighting Nemesis of Crime
10¢
The BLACK TERROR
no. 7
SCHOMBURG
BUY WAR BONDS
AND STAMPS
FOR VICTORY!

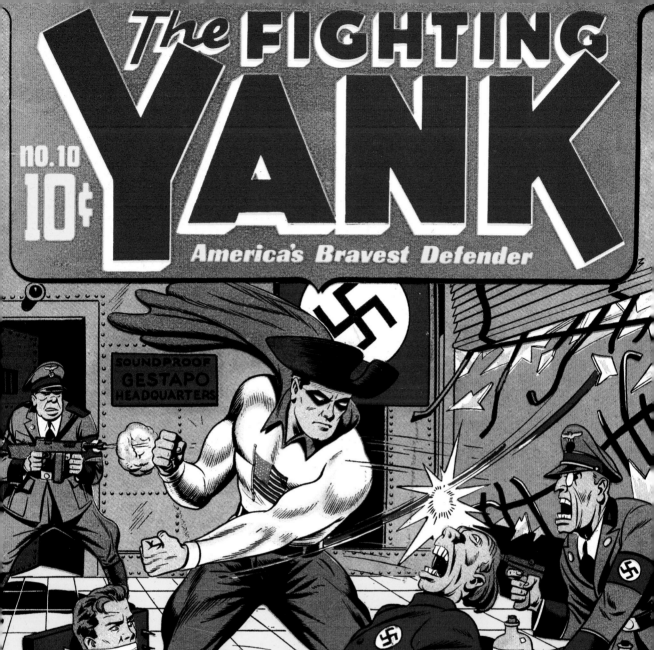

The FIGHTING YANK

NO. 10
10¢

America's Bravest Defender

SOUNDPROOF GESTAPO HEADQUARTERS

POISON

POISON

BUY WAR BONDS AND STAMPS FOR VICTORY!

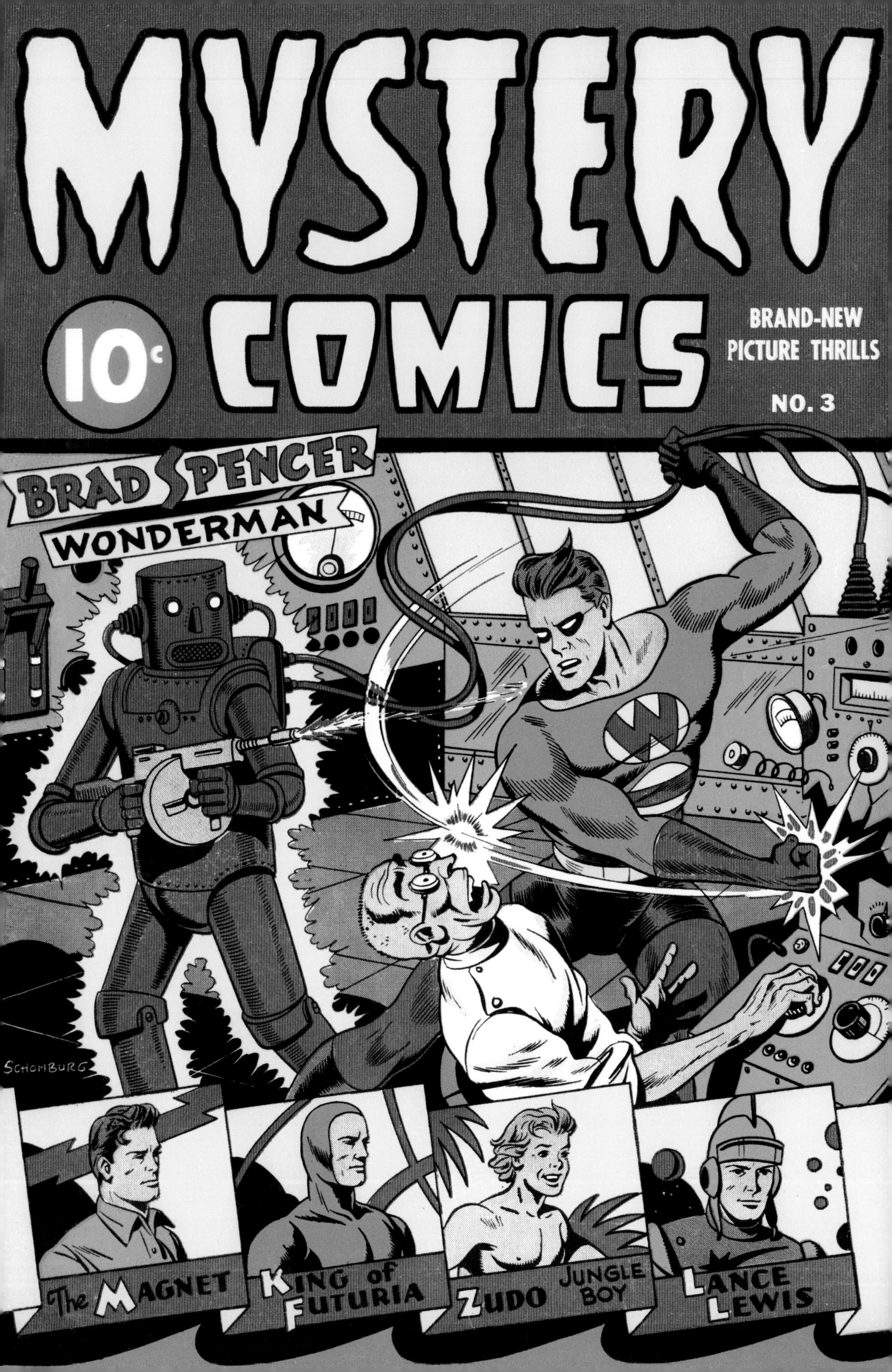
MYSTERY COMICS
10¢
BRAND-NEW PICTURE THRILLS
NO. 3
BRAD SPENCER
WONDERMAN
SCHOMBURG
The MAGNET
KING of FUTURIA
ZUDO JUNGLE BOY
LANCE LEWIS

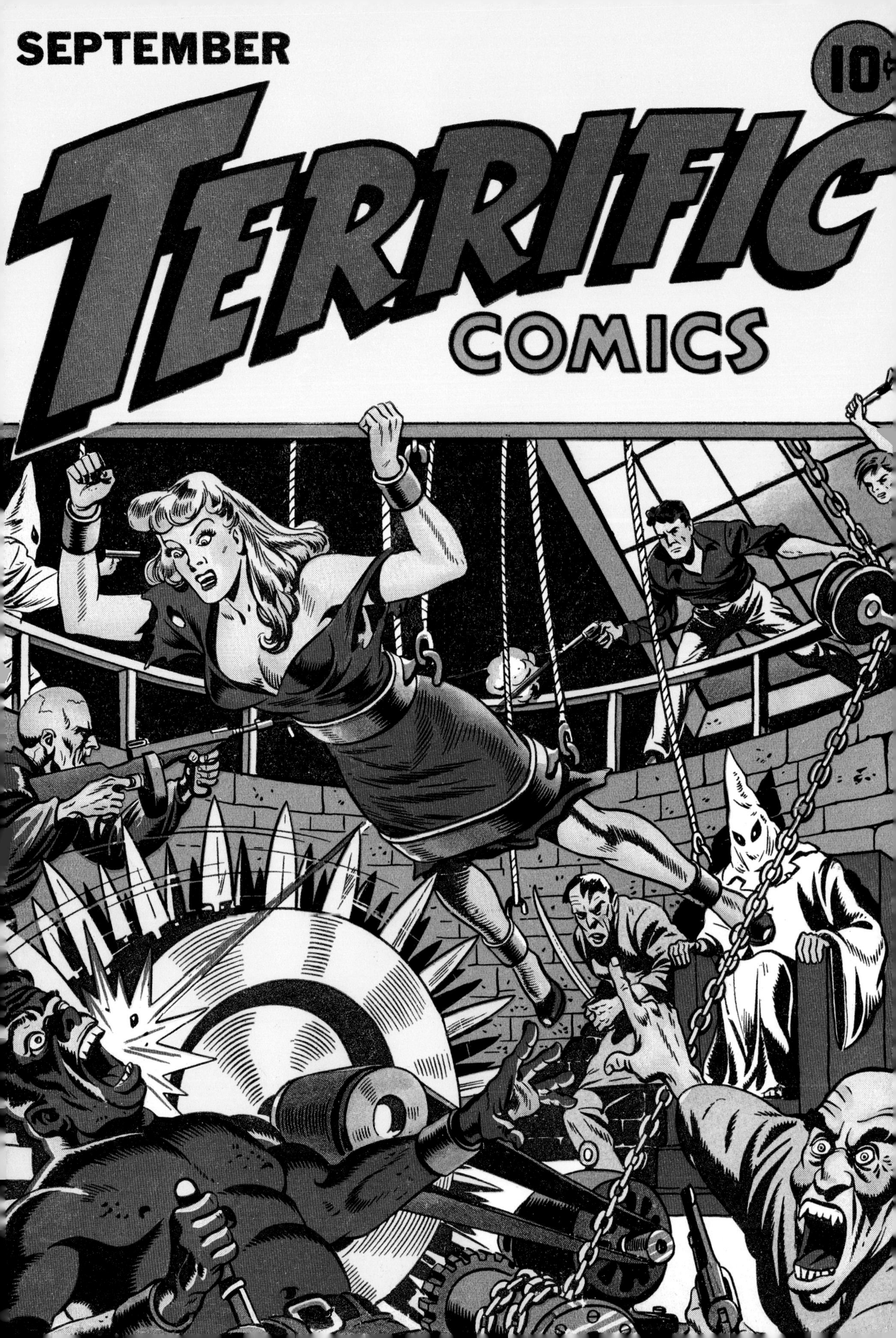
SEPTEMBER
10¢
TERRIFIC
COMICS

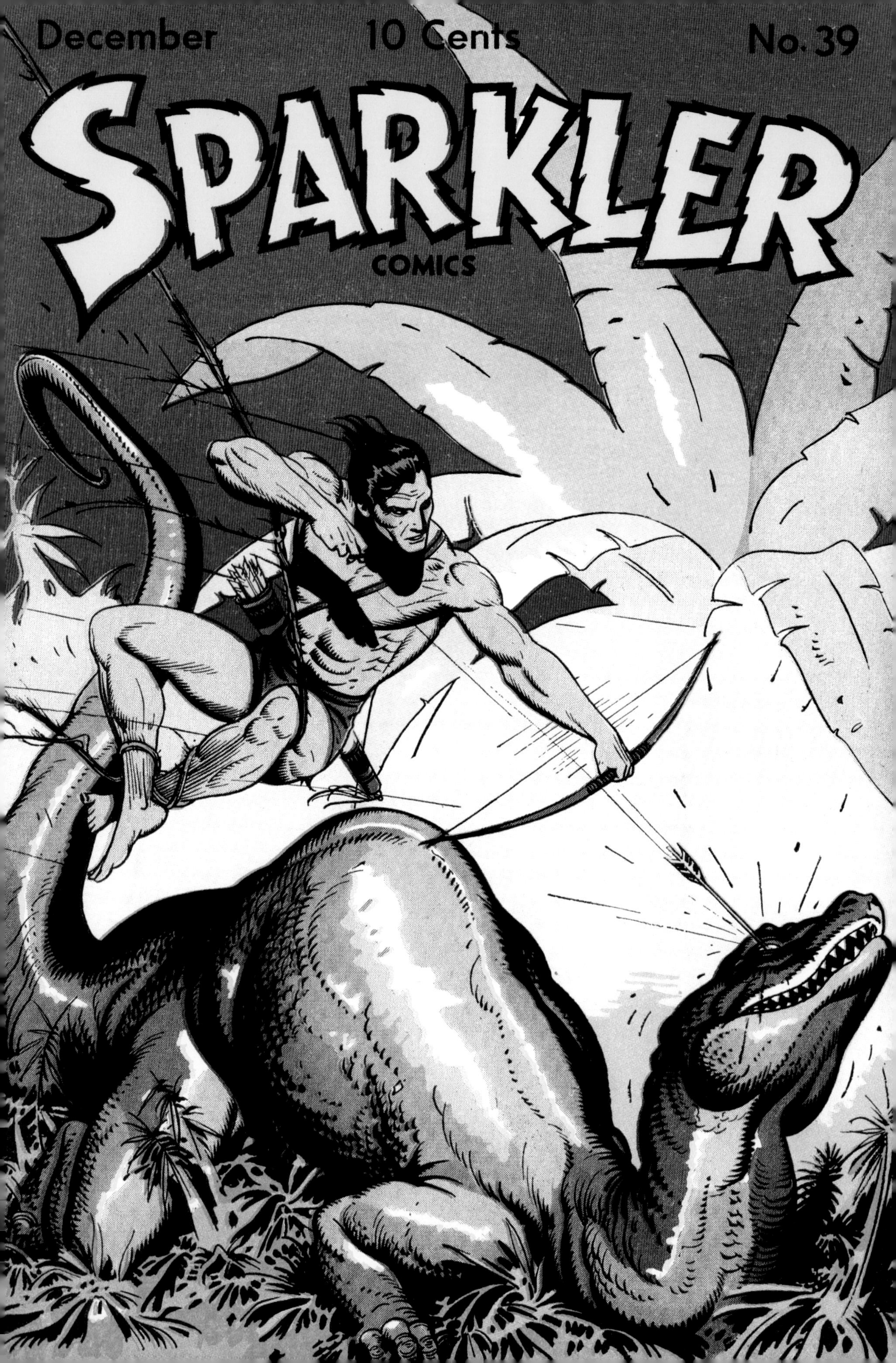
December
10 Cents
No. 39
SPARKLER
COMICS

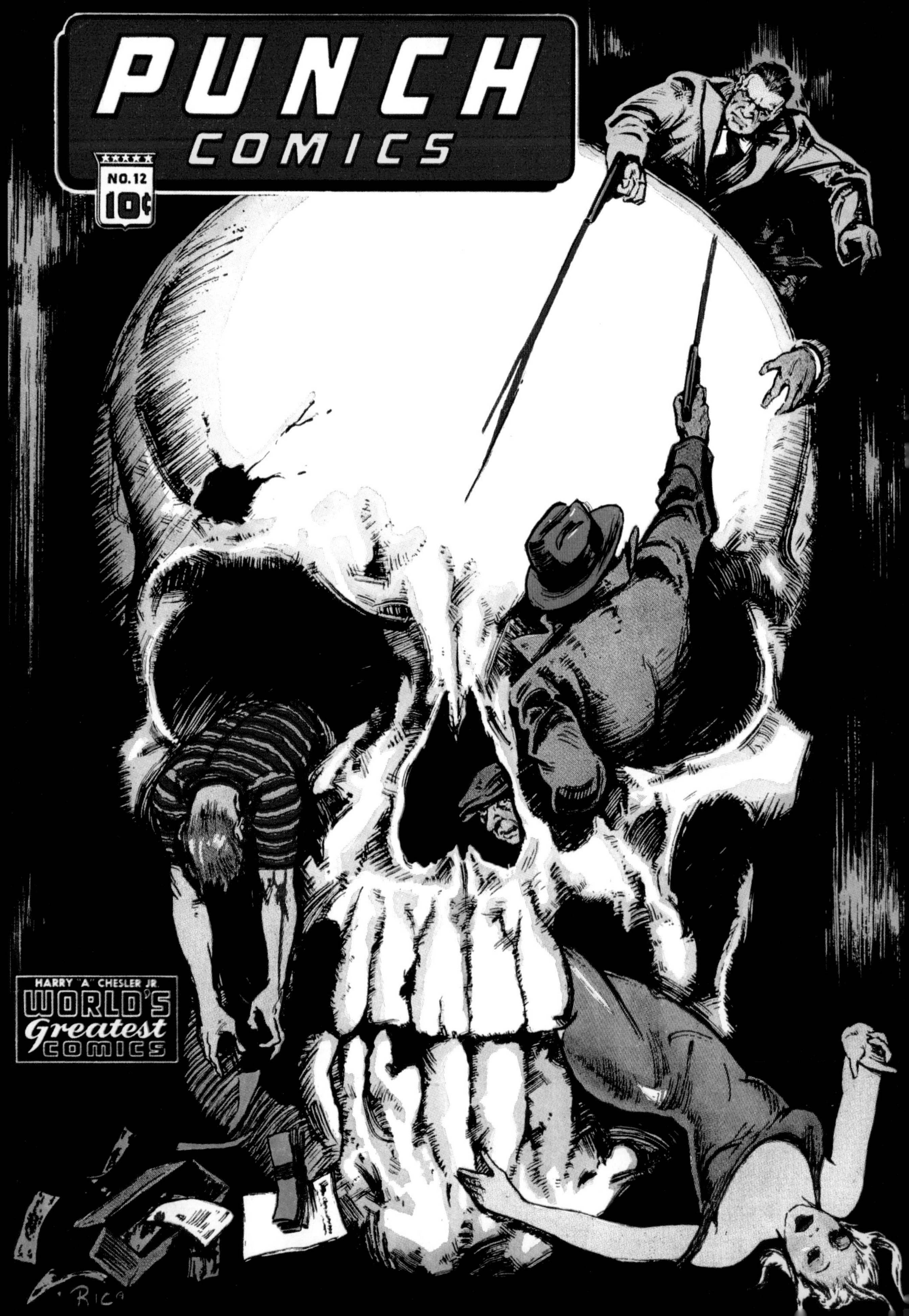
PUNCH COMICS
NO. 12
10¢
HARRY "A" CHESLER JR.
WORLD'S Greatest COMICS
RICO

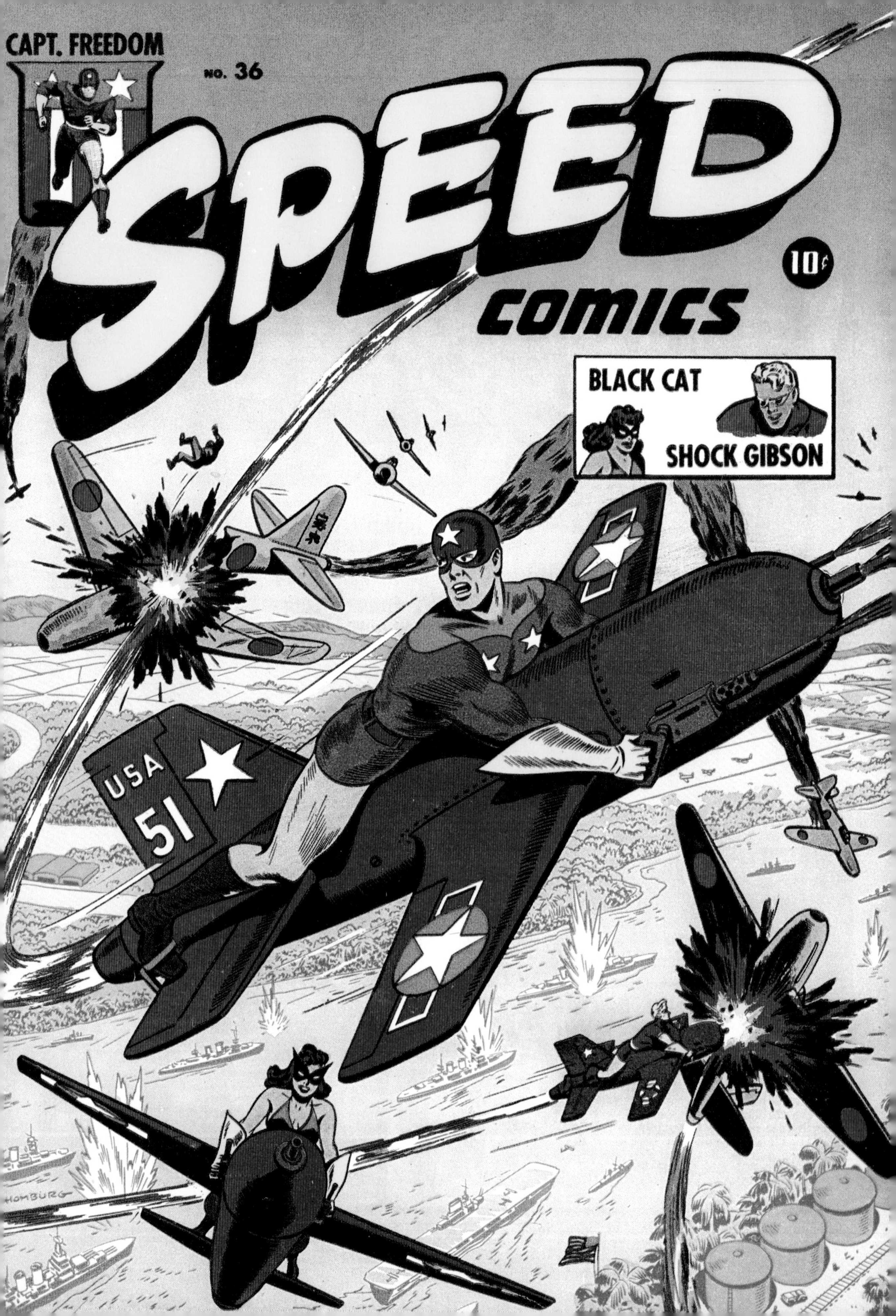
CAPT. FREEDOM
NO. 36
SPEED
10¢
COMICS
BLACK CAT
SHOCK GIBSON
USA
51
HOMBURG

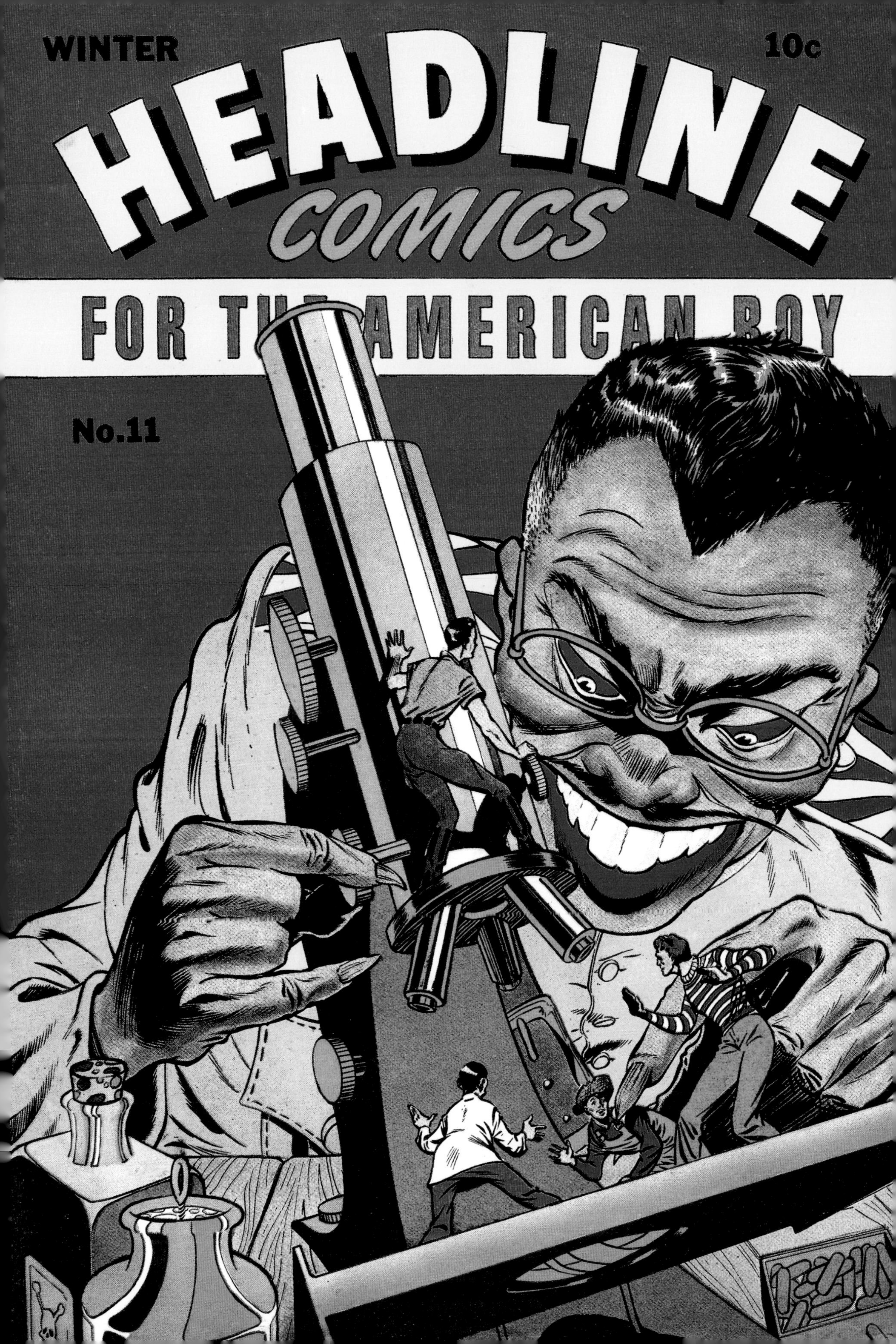
WINTER
10c
HEADLINE
COMICS
FOR TH AMERICAN BOY
No.11

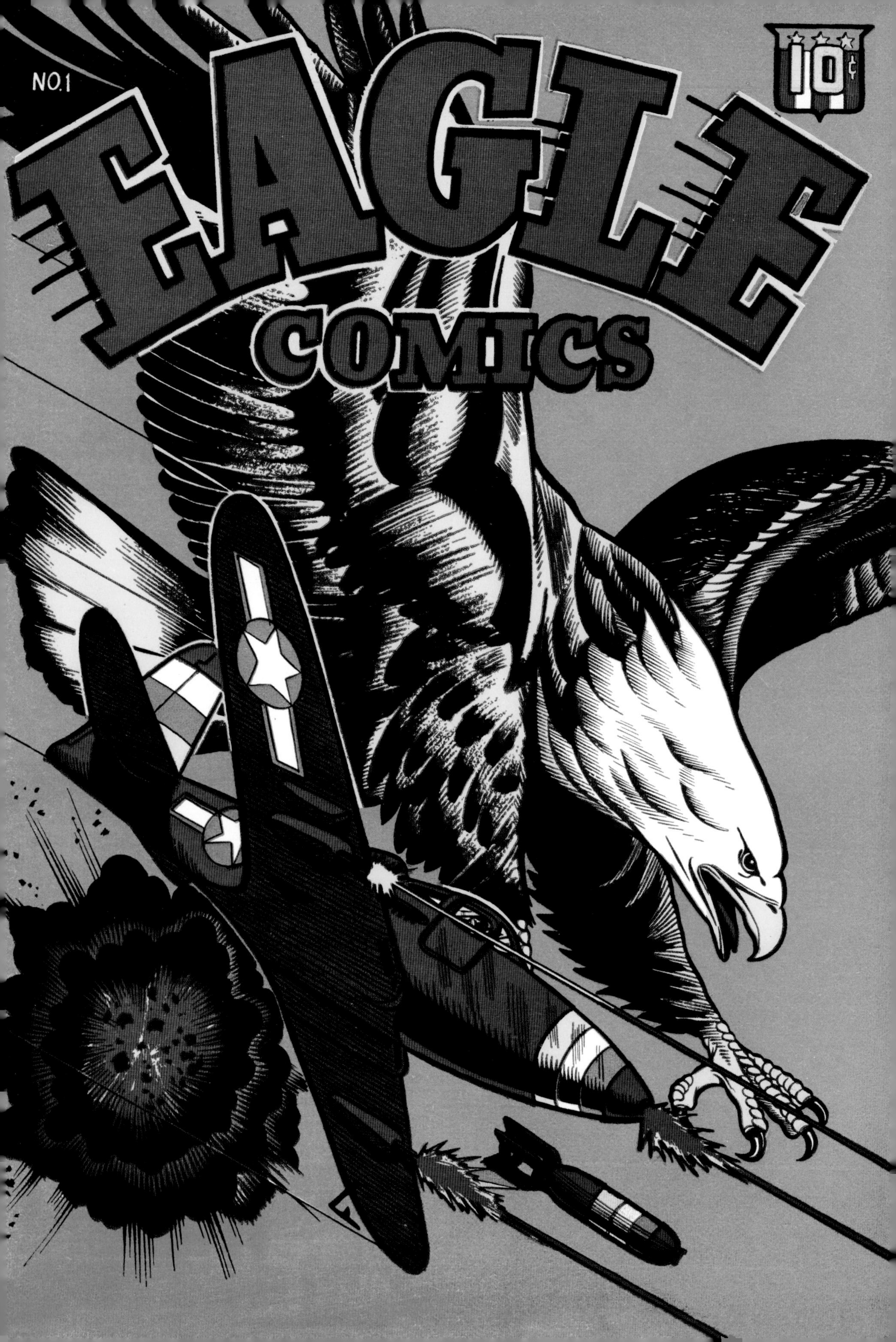
NO.1
EAGLE
COMICS
10¢

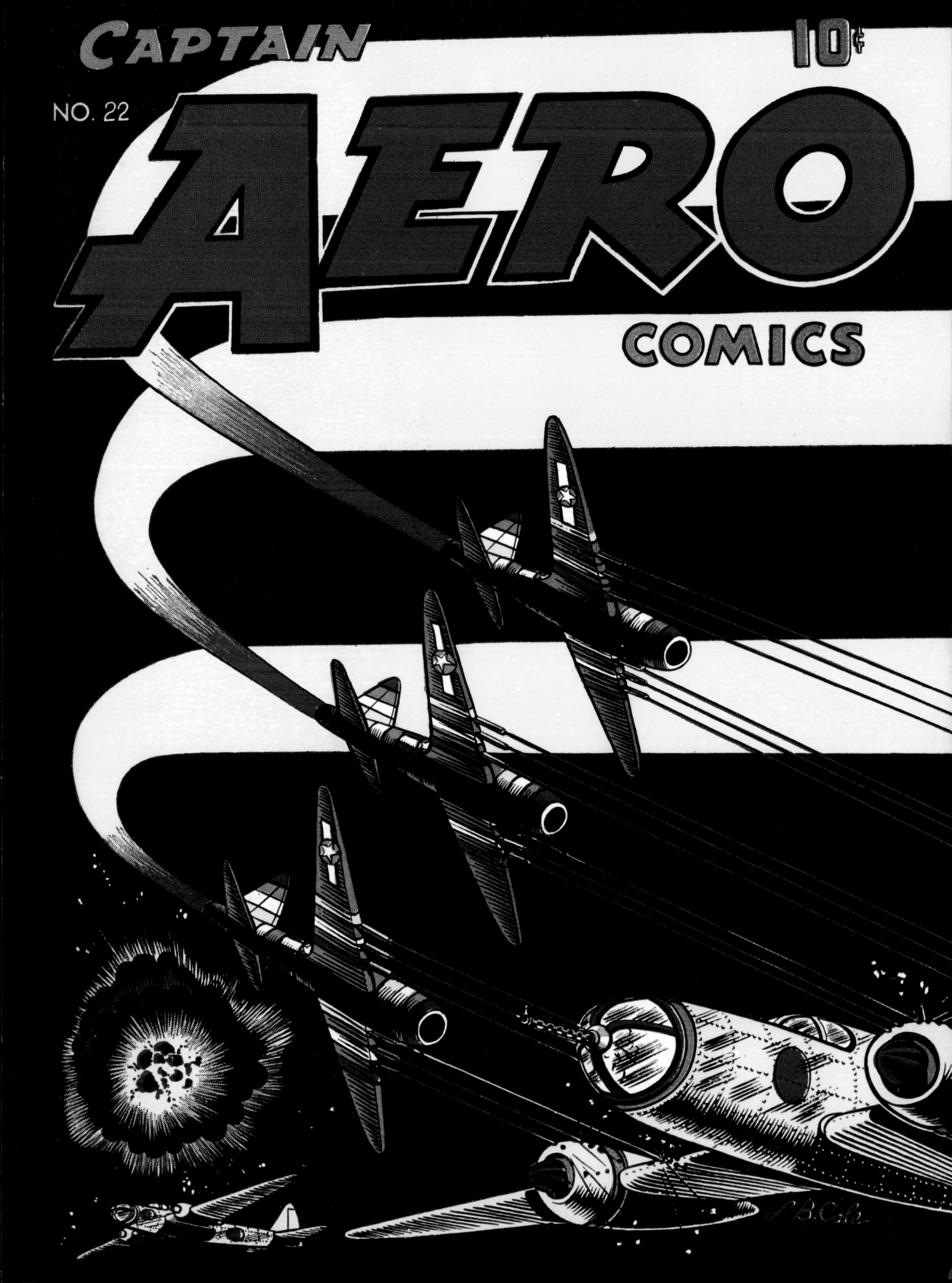
CAPTAIN
10¢
NO. 22
AERO
COMICS

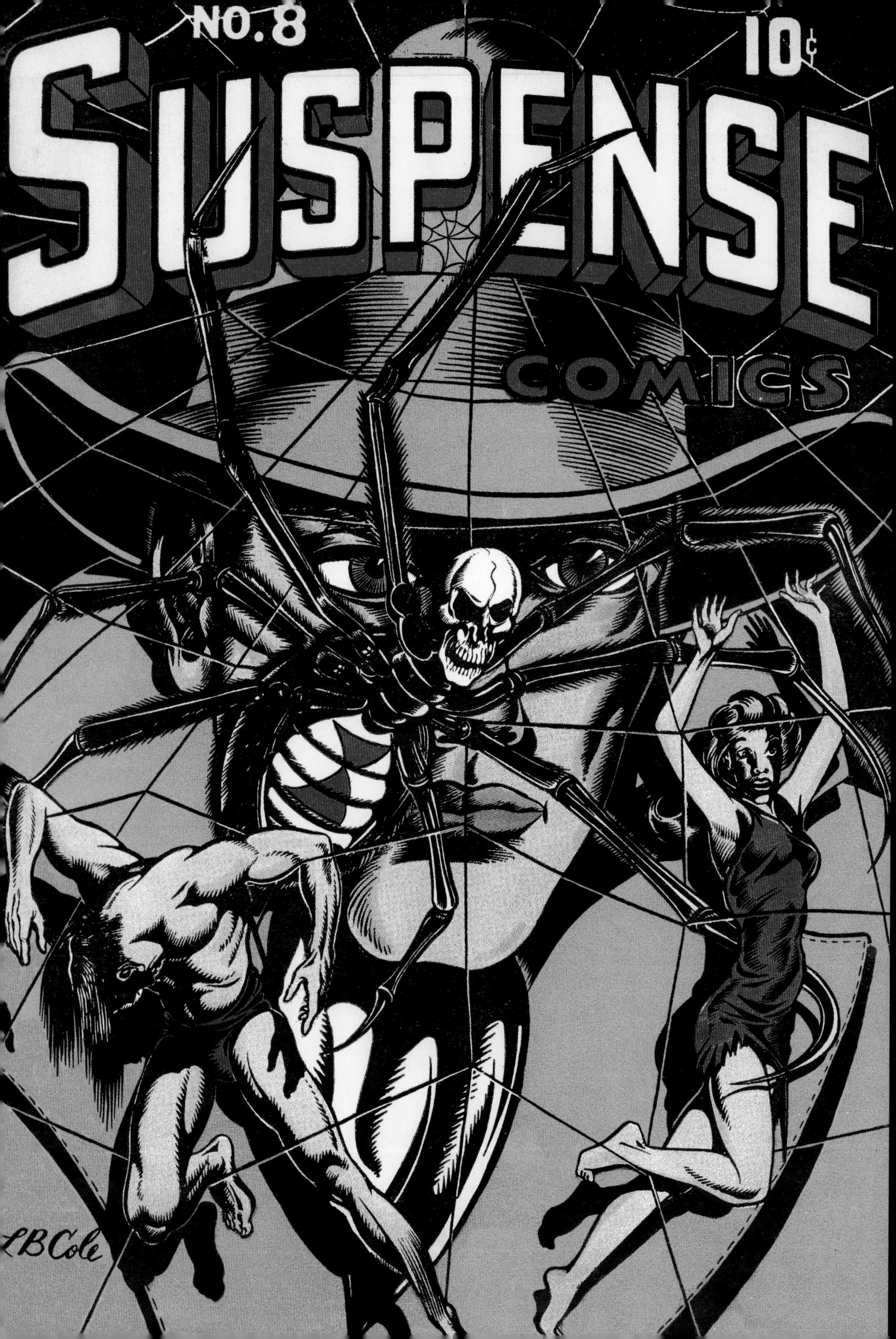
NO. 8
10¢
SUSPENSE
COMICS
L.B. Cole

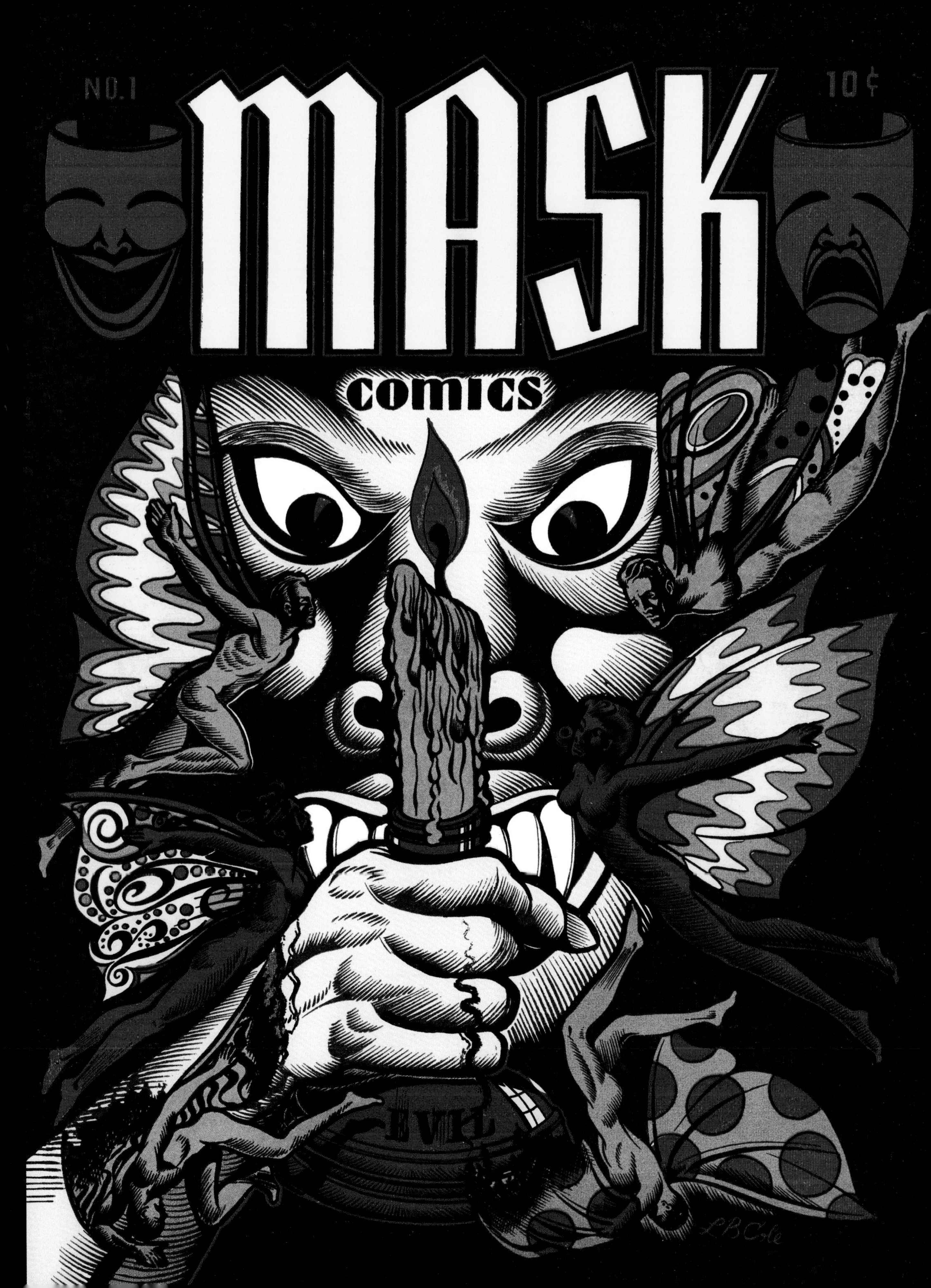
NO.1
10¢
MASK
comics
EVIL
L.B.Cole

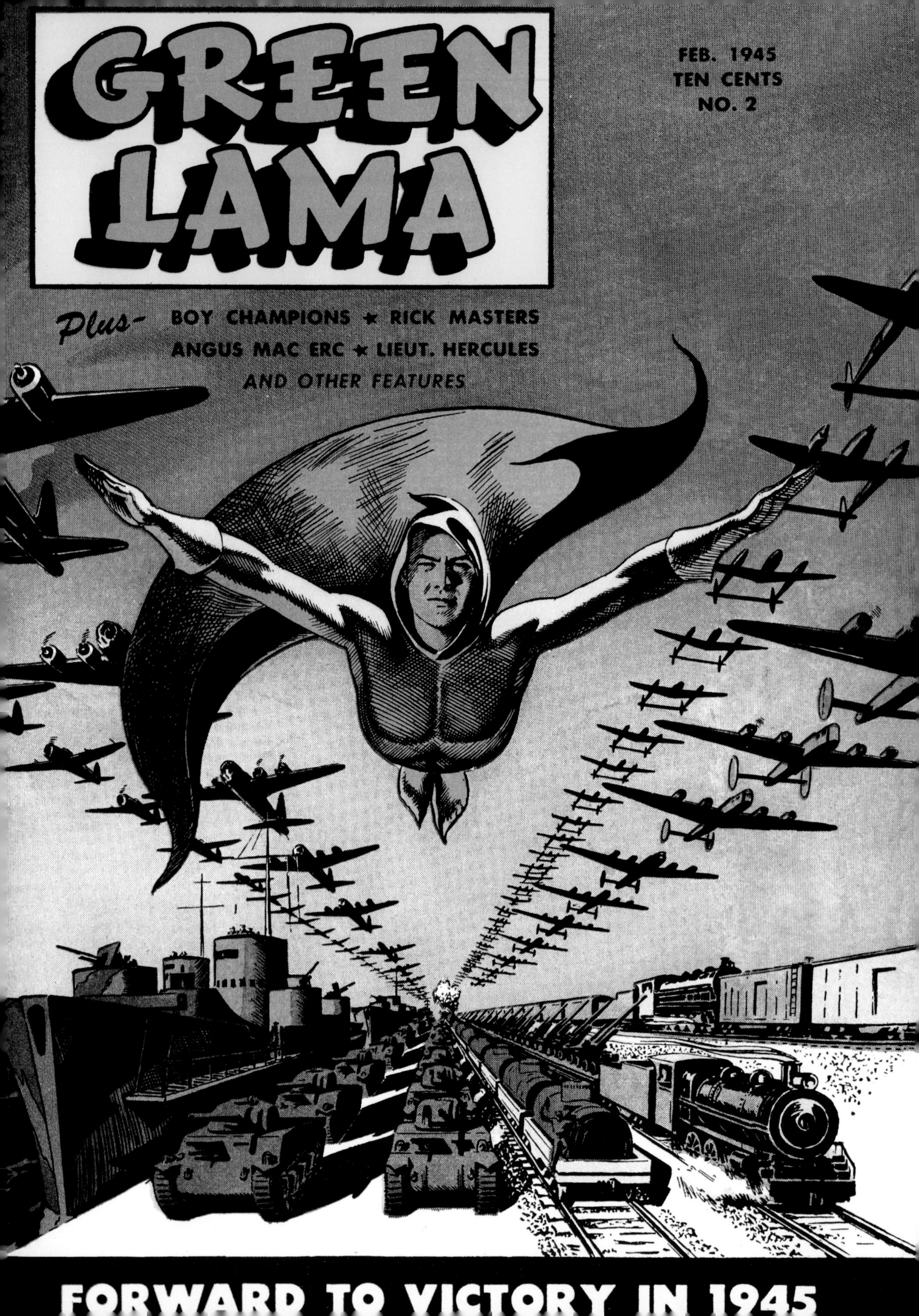
GREEN LAMA
FEB. 1945
TEN CENTS
NO. 2
Plus-
BOY CHAMPIONS ★ RICK MASTERS
ANGUS MAC ERC ★ LIEUT. HERCULES
AND OTHER FEATURES
FORWARD TO VICTORY IN 1945

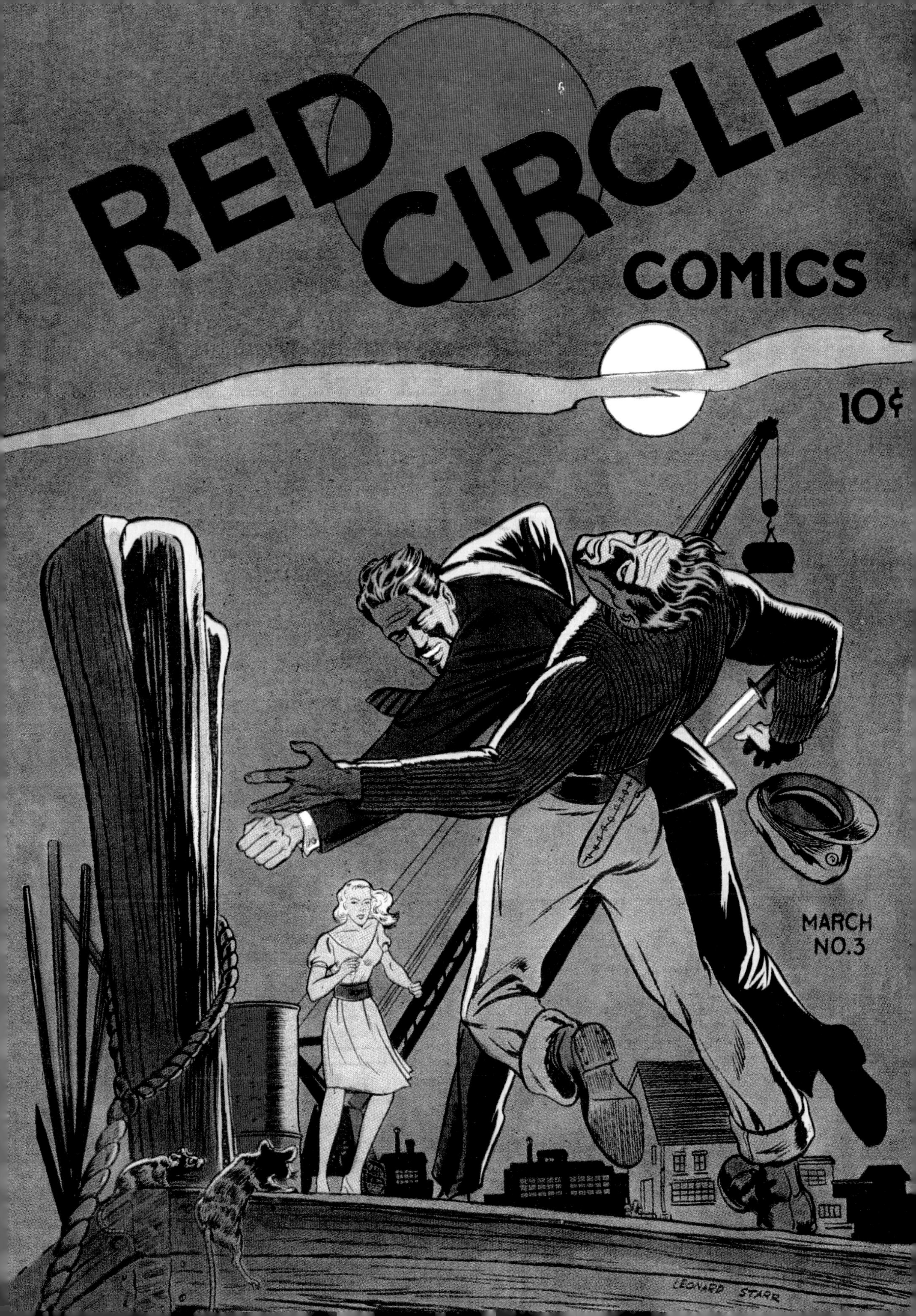
RED CIRCLE
COMICS
10¢
MARCH
NO.3
LEONARD STARR

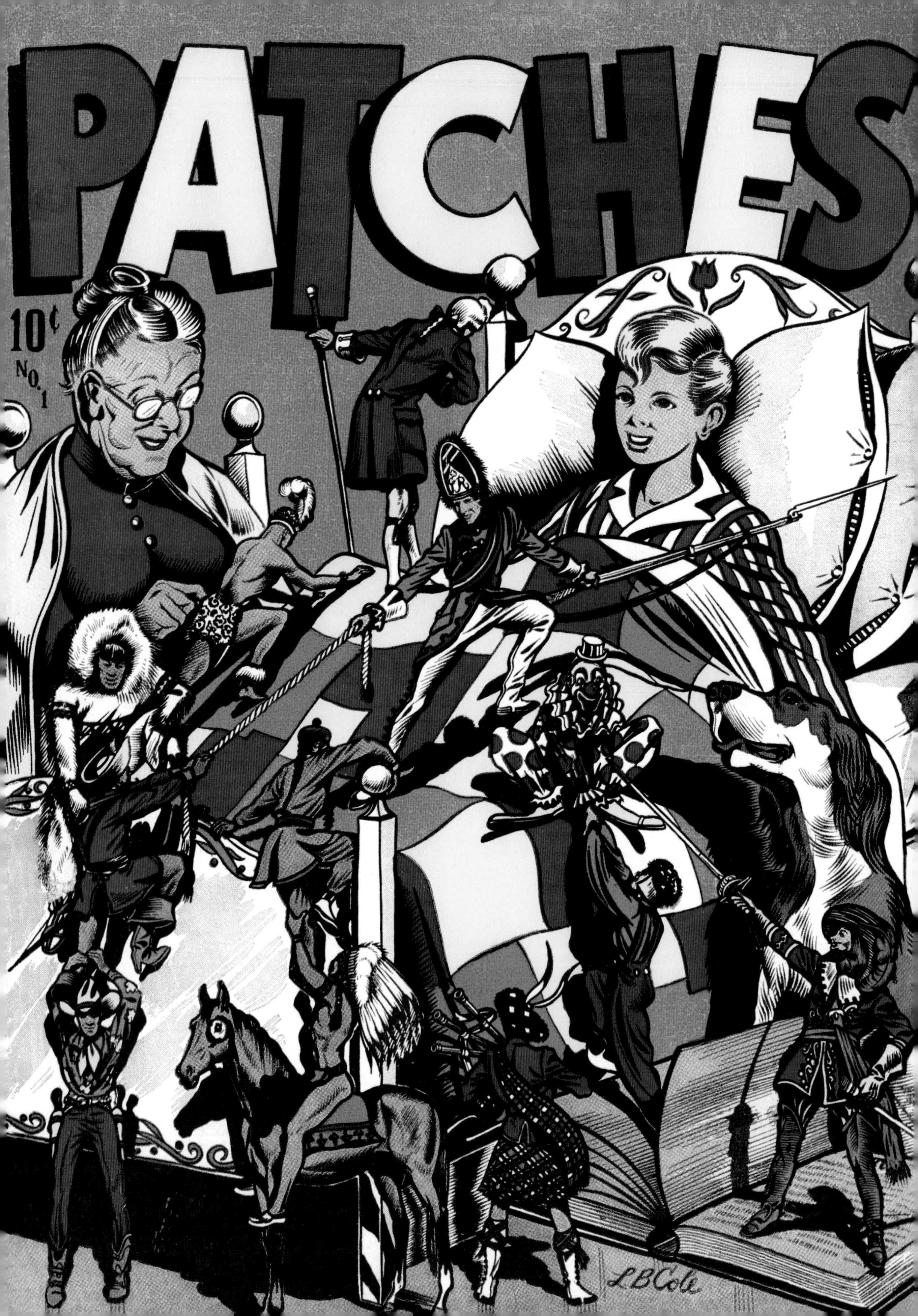
PATCHES
10¢
No. 1
L.B.Cole

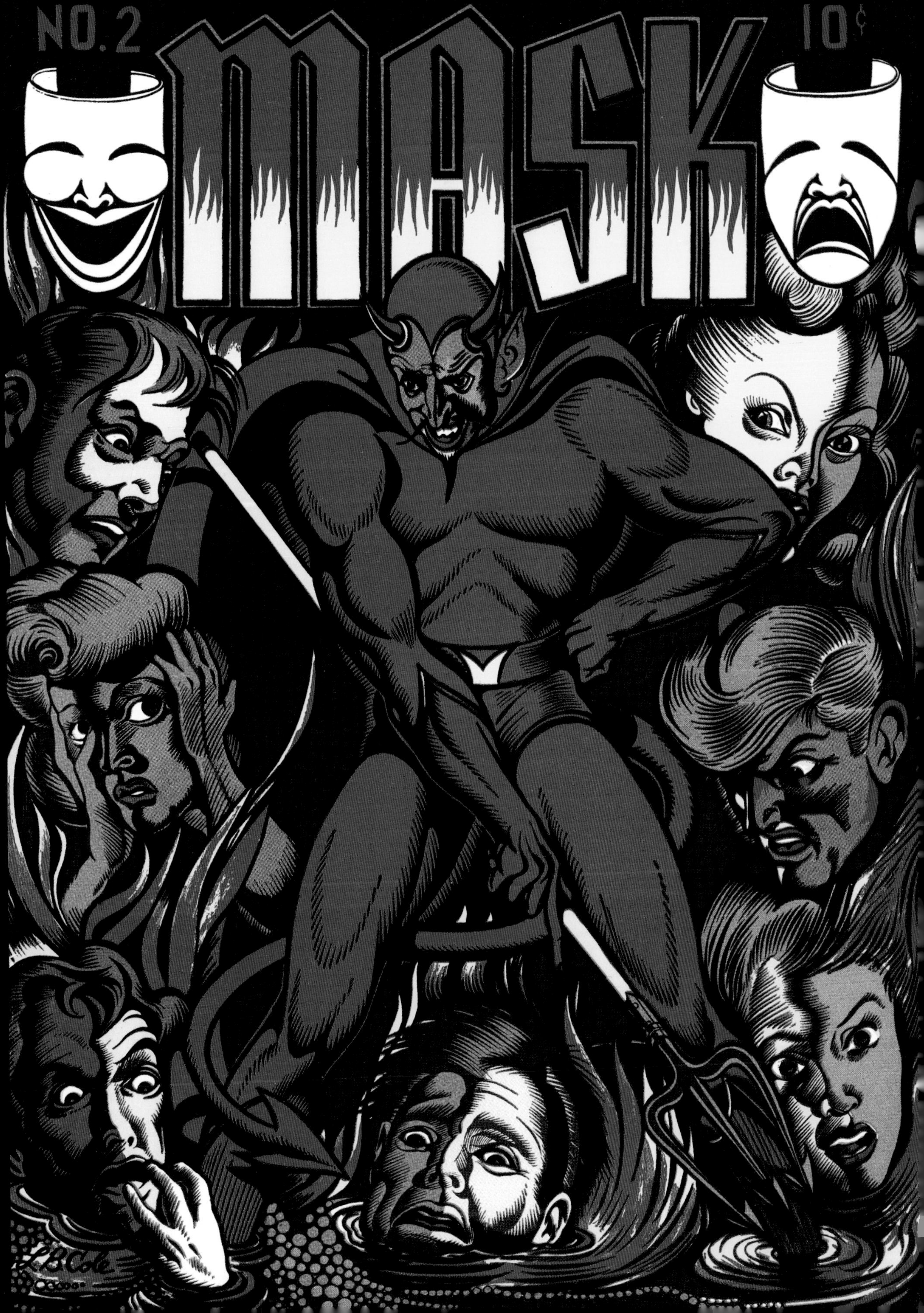

NO. 2
MASK
10¢
L.B. Cole

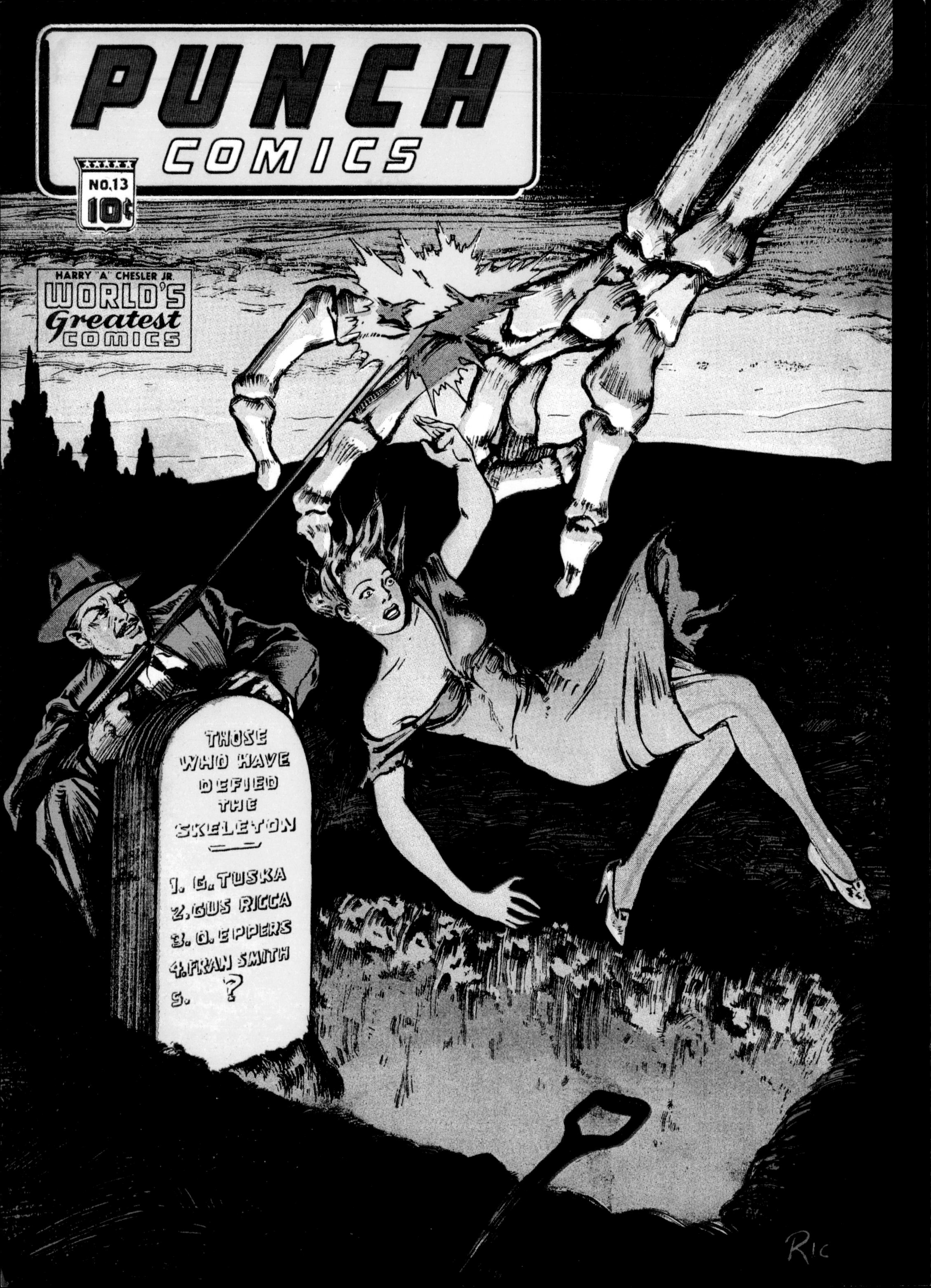

PUNCH
COMICS
NO. 13
10¢
HARRY 'A' CHESLER JR
WORLD'S
Greatest
COMICS
THOSE
WHO HAVE
DEFIED
THE
SKELETON
1. G. TUSKA
2. GUS RICCA
3. O. EPPERS
4. FRAN SMITH
5. ?
RIC

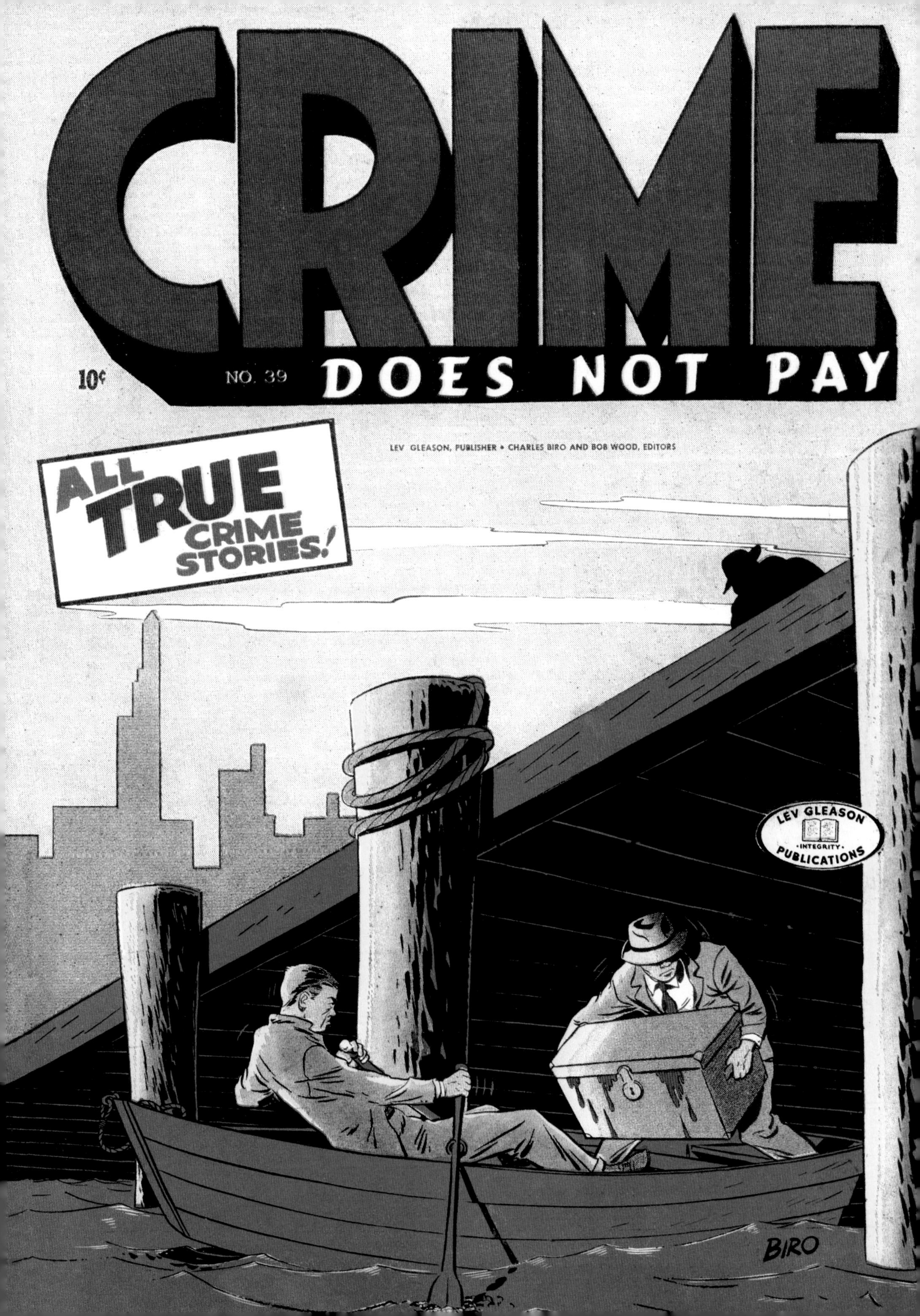
CRIME
10¢
NO. 39
DOES NOT PAY
LEV GLEASON, PUBLISHER • CHARLES BIRO AND BOB WOOD, EDITORS
ALL TRUE CRIME STORIES!
LEV GLEASON
INTEGRITY
PUBLICATIONS
BIRO

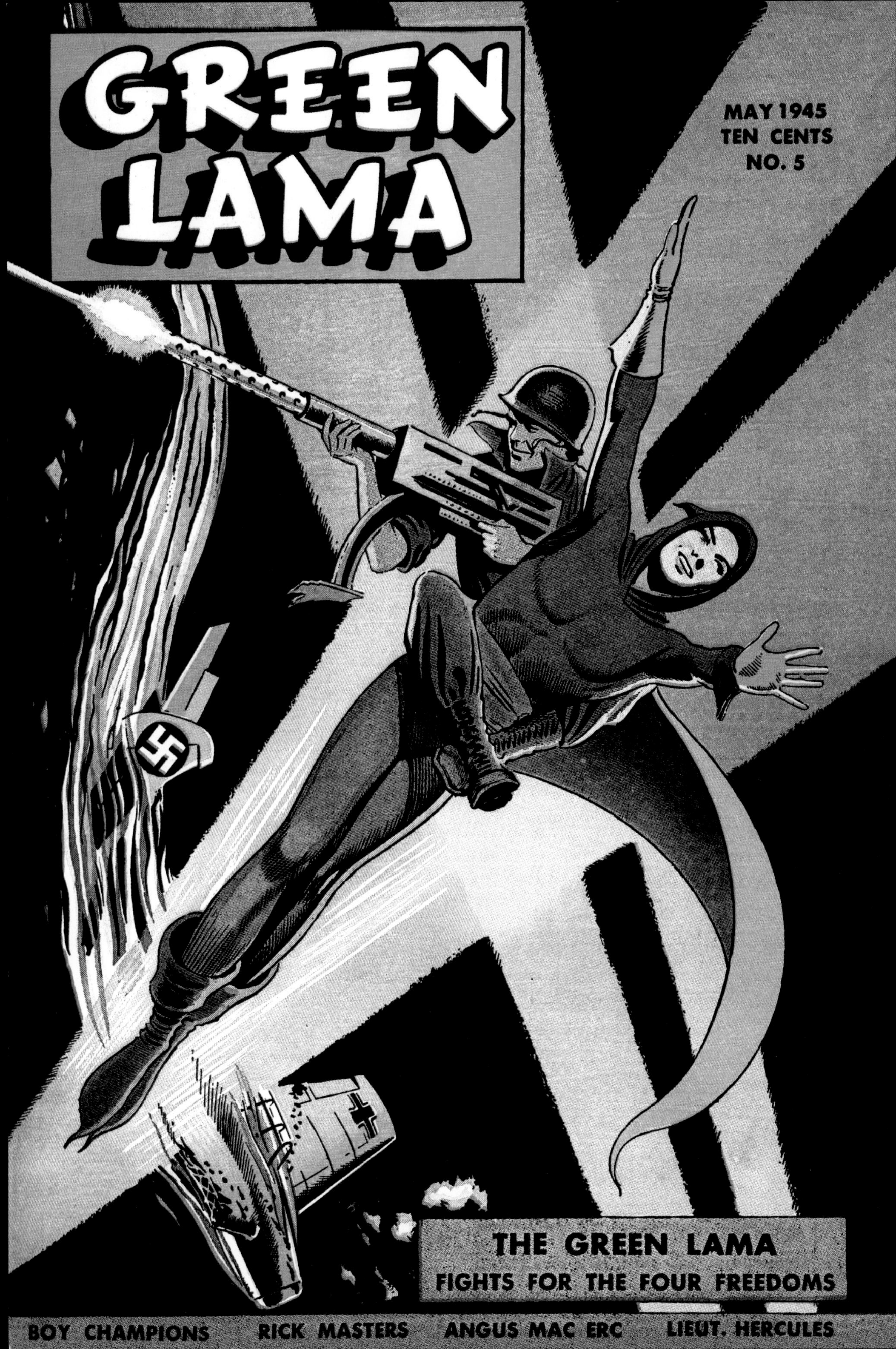

GREEN LAMA
MAY 1945
TEN CENTS
NO. 5
THE GREEN LAMA
FIGHTS FOR THE FOUR FREEDOMS
BOY CHAMPIONS
RICK MASTERS
ANGUS MAC ERC
LIEUT. HERCULES

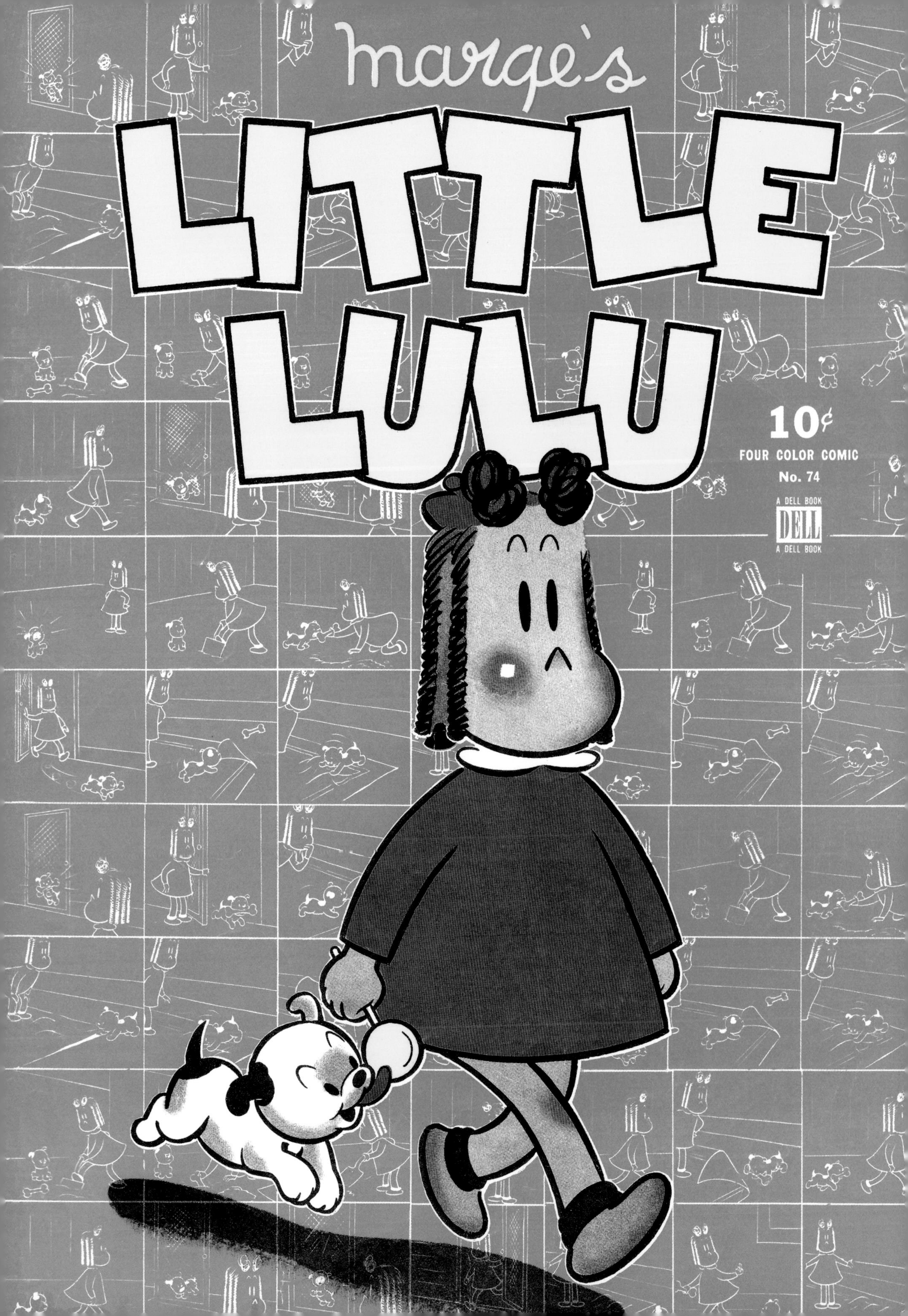
marge's
LITTLE LULU
10¢
FOUR COLOR COMIC
No. 74
A DELL BOOK
DELL
A DELL BOOK

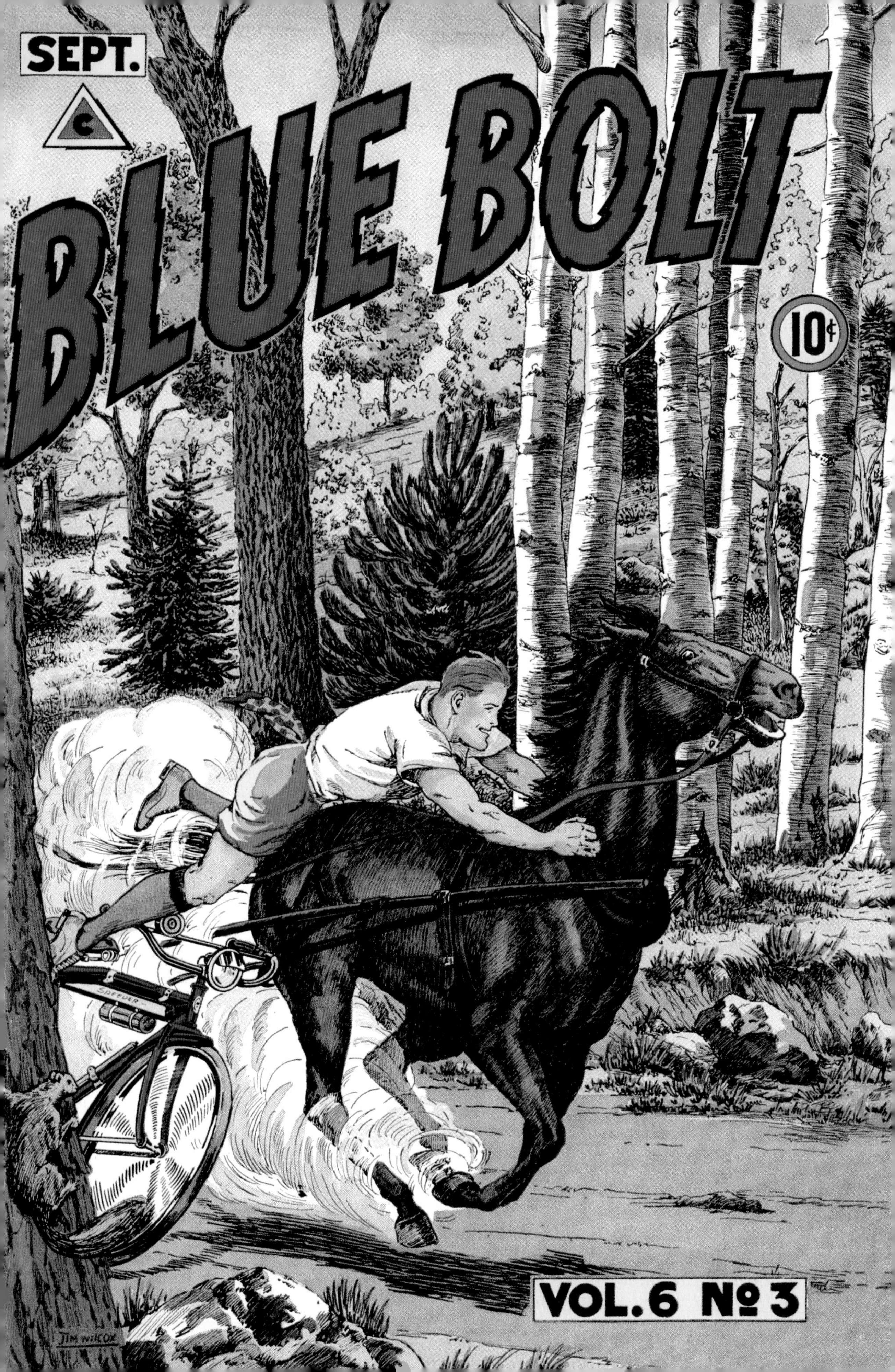
SEPT.
C
BLUE BOLT
10¢
VOL.6 No 3
JIM WILCOX

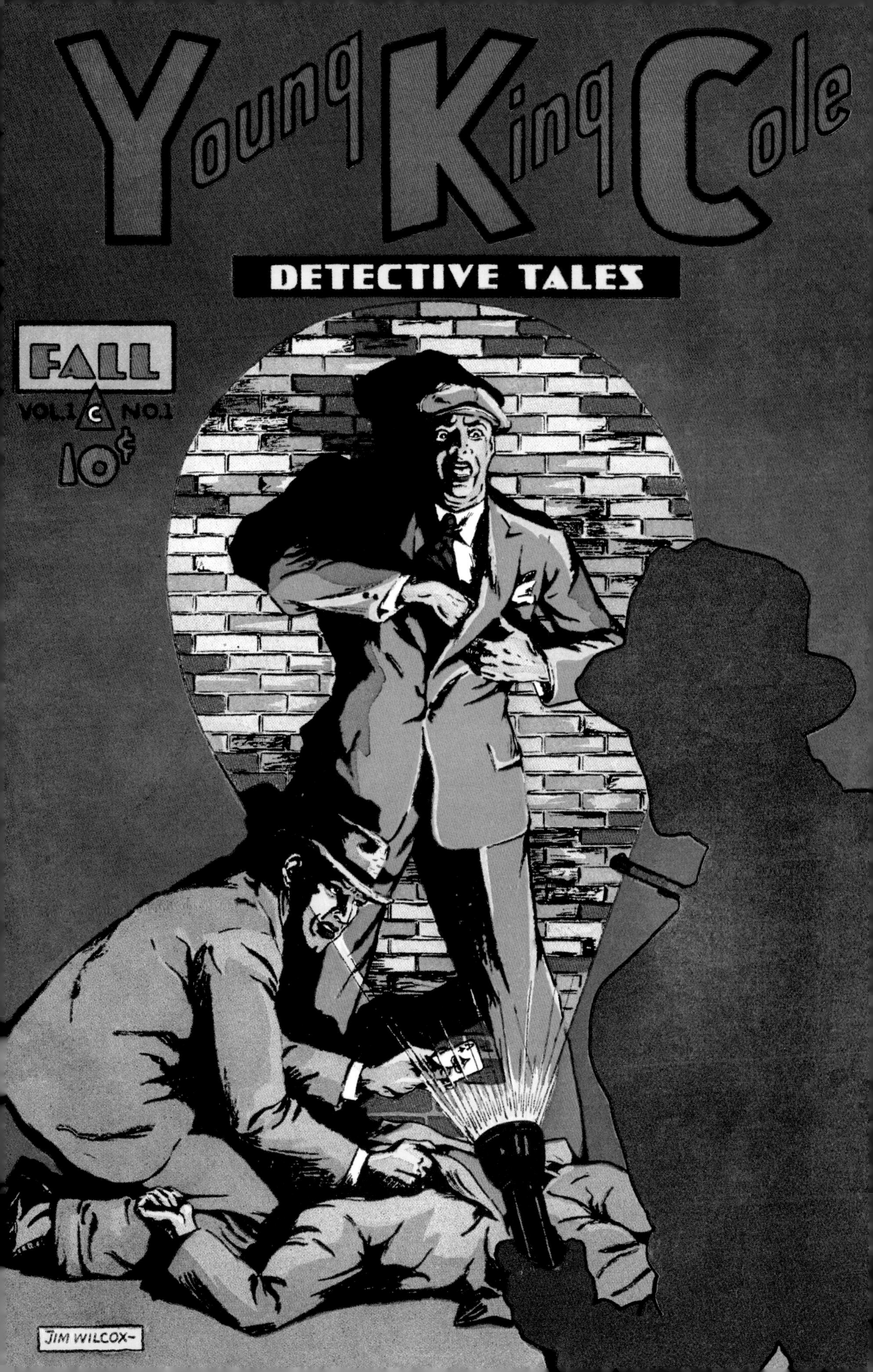
Young King Cole
DETECTIVE TALES
FALL
VOL.1 C NO.1
10¢
JIM WILCOX-

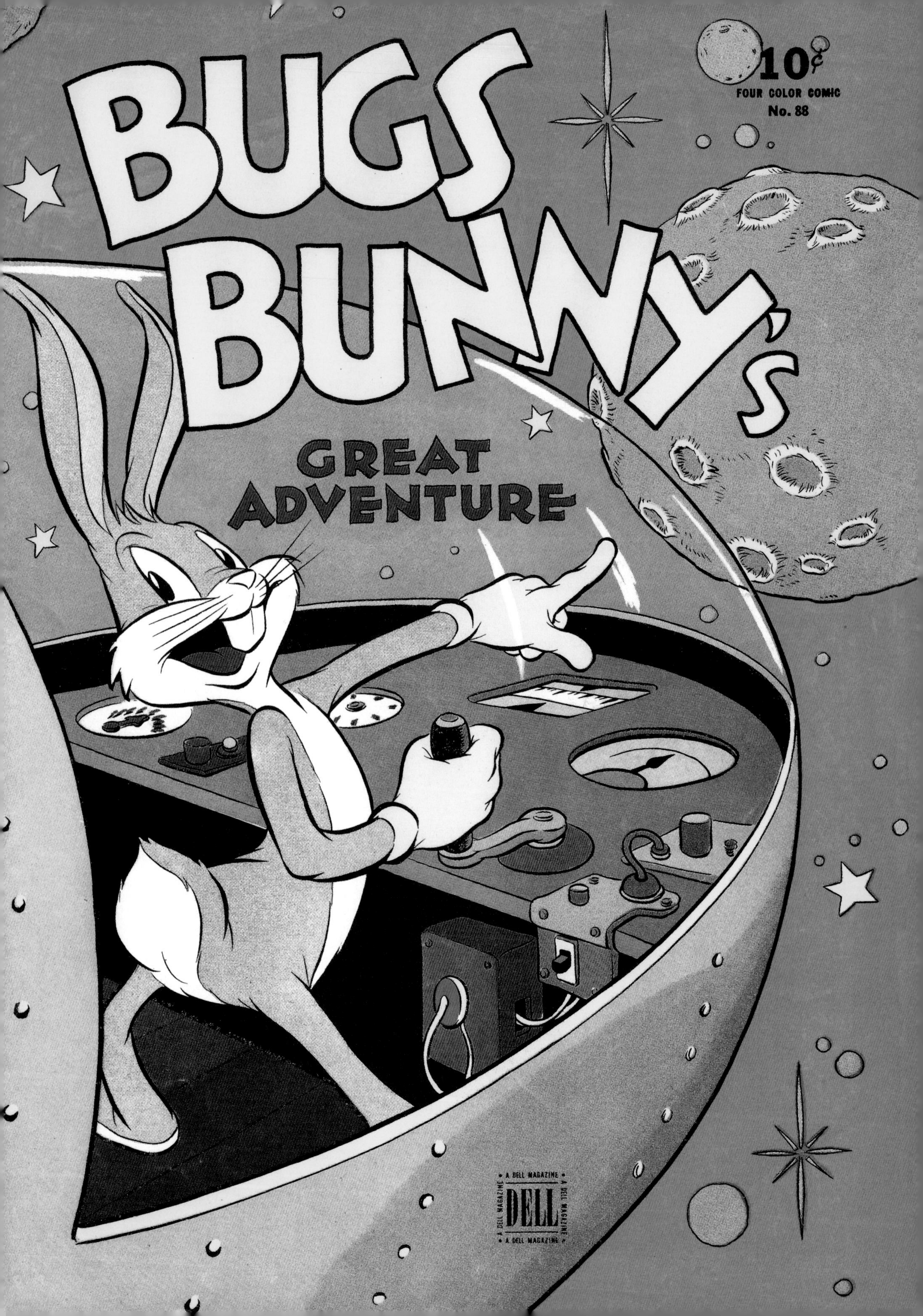

10¢
FOUR COLOR COMIC
No. 88
BUGS BUNNY'S
GREAT ADVENTURE
A DELL MAGAZINE
DELL

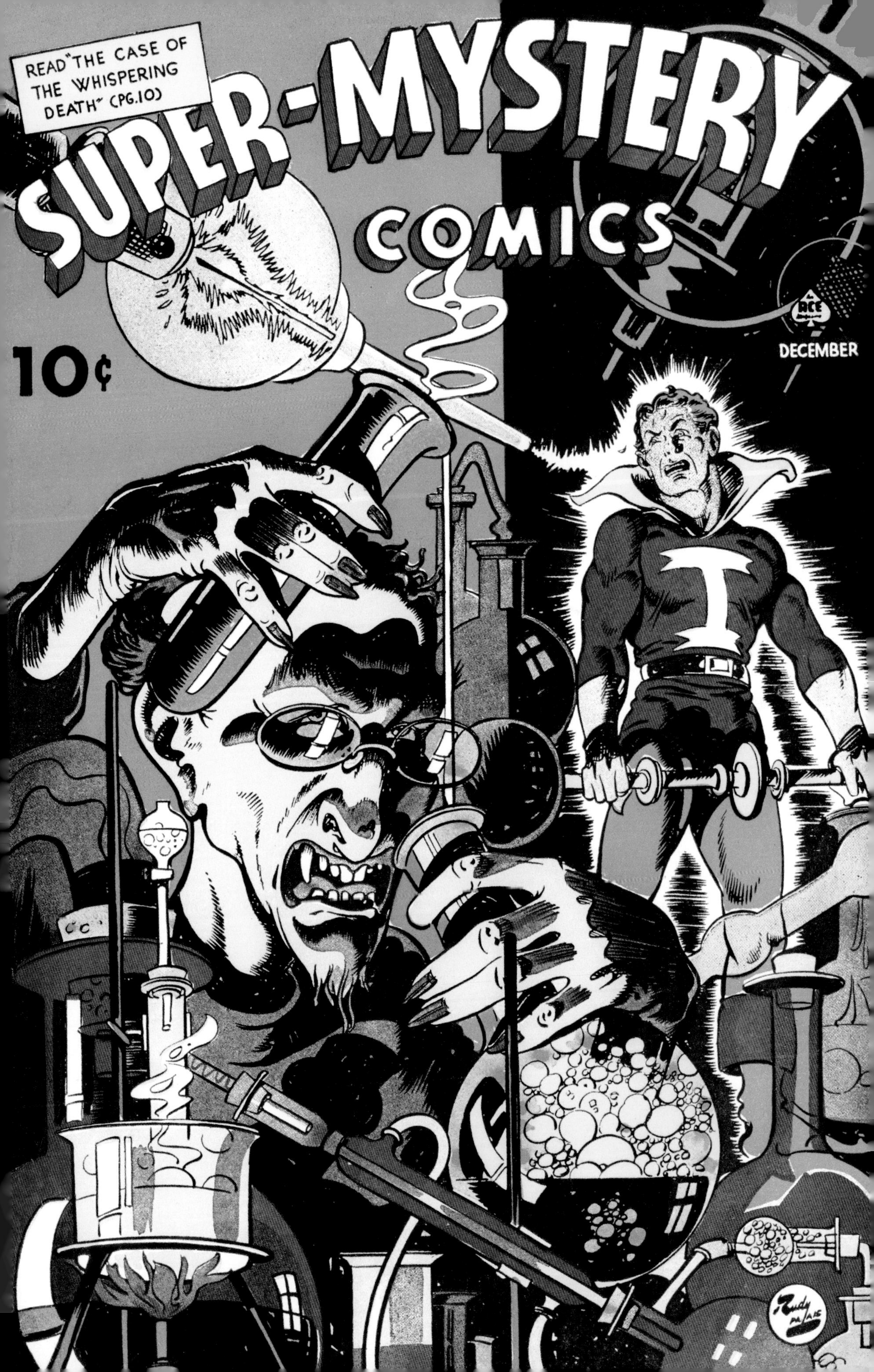

READ "THE CASE OF THE WHISPERING DEATH" (PG.10)
SUPER-MYSTERY COMICS
10¢
ACE
DECEMBER

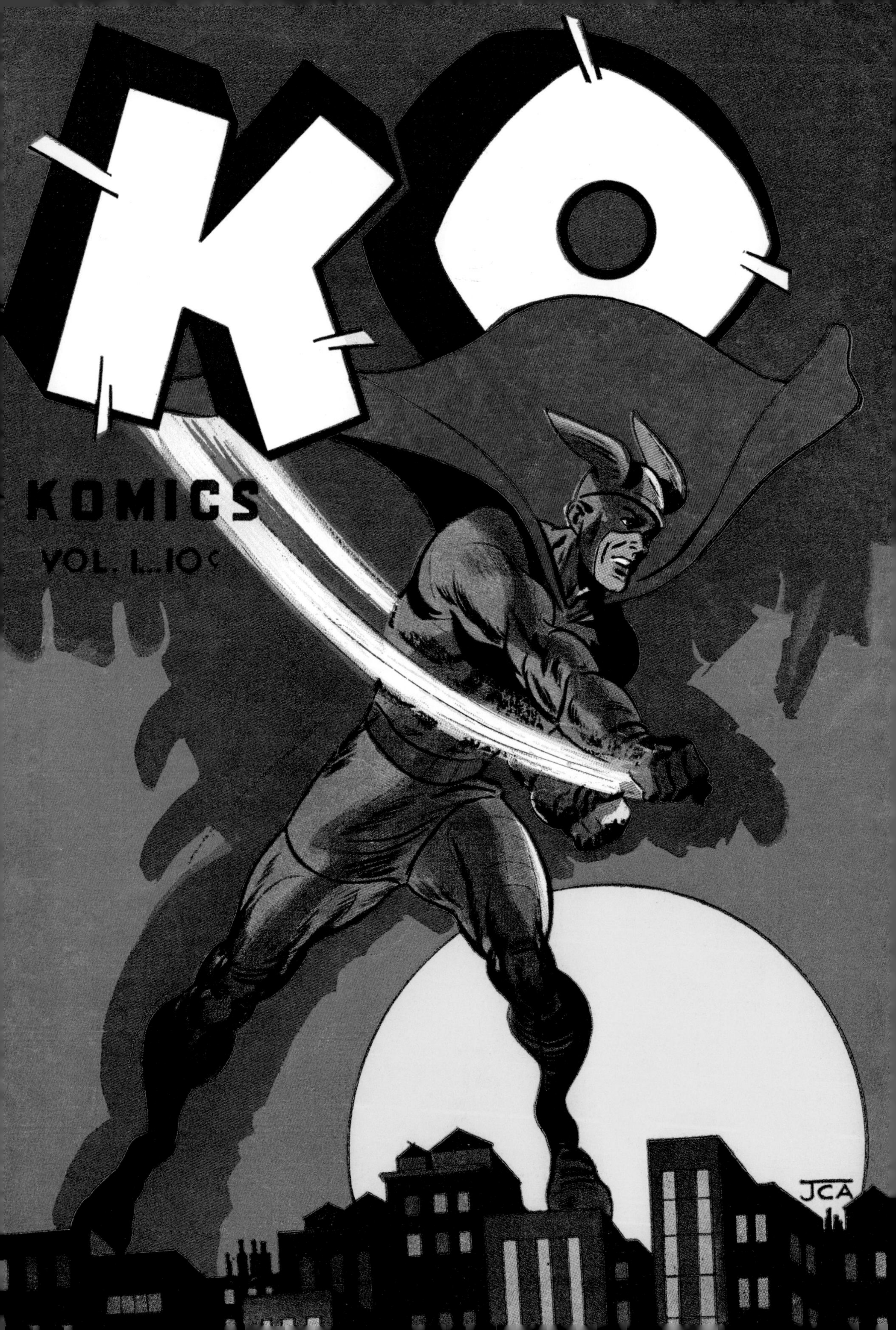
KO
KOMICS
VOL. 1...10¢
JCA

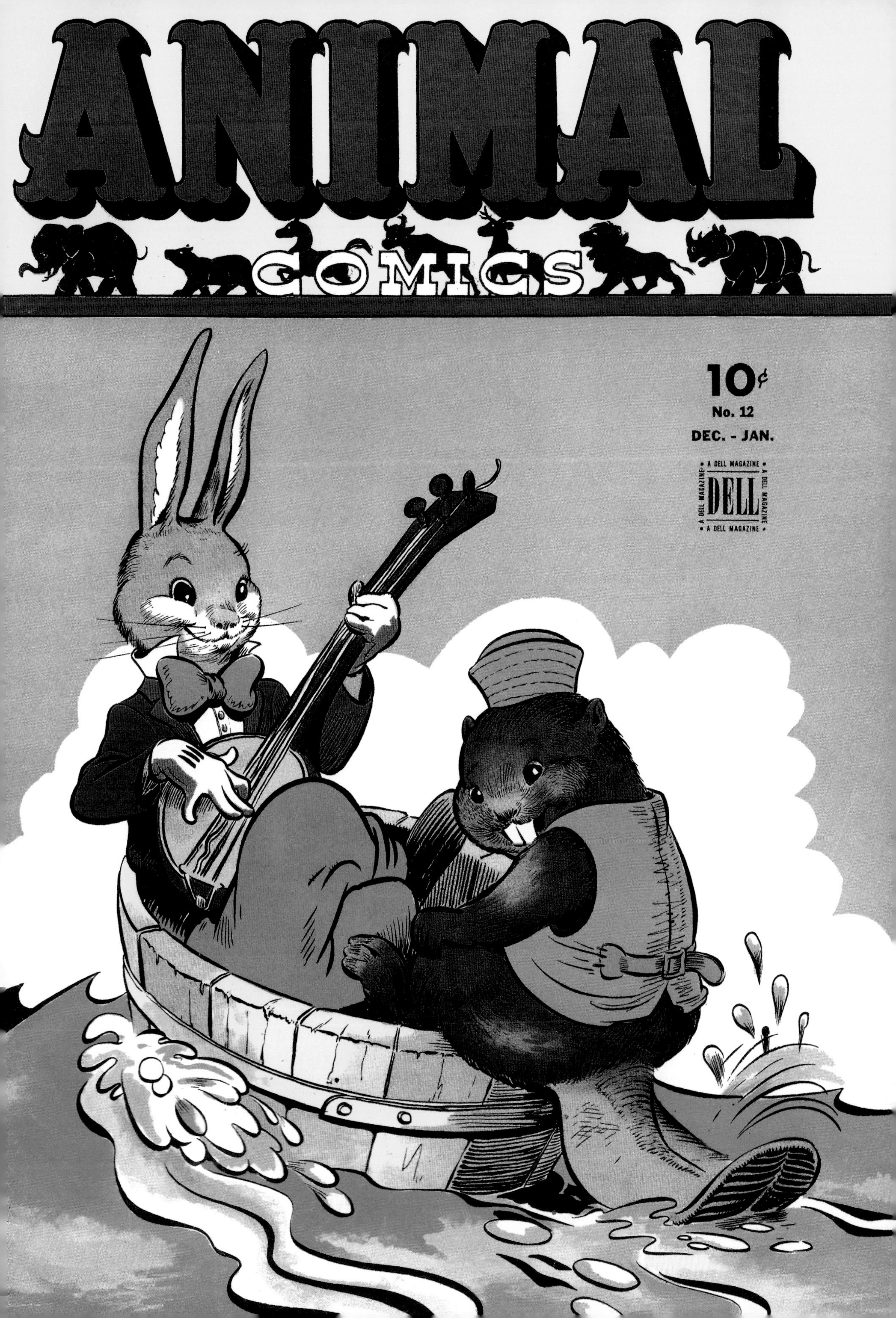
ANIMAL
COMICS
10¢
No. 12
DEC. - JAN.
A DELL MAGAZINE
DELL

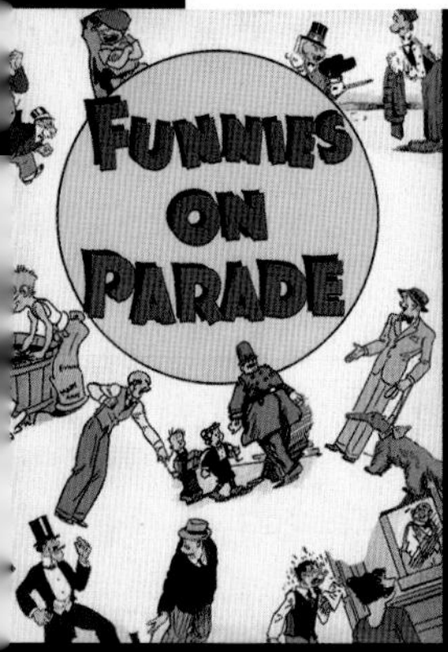
Funnies on Parade

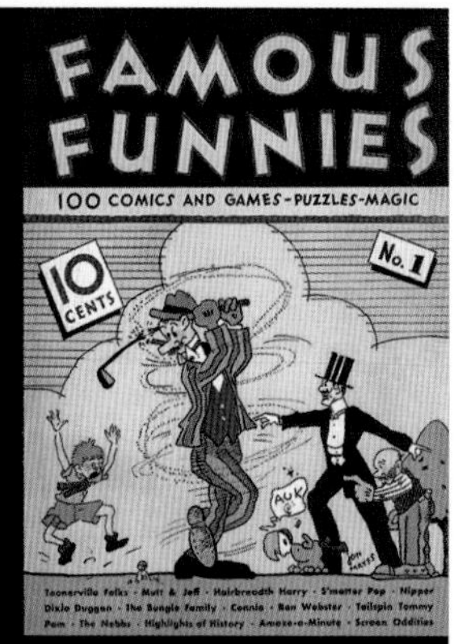
FAMOUS FUNNIES
100 COMICS AND GAMES-PUZZLES-MAGIC
10 CENTS
No. 1

FUNNIES ON PARADE, 1933
UNKNOWN ARTIST

FAMOUS FUNNIES no. 1, July 1934
JON MAYES

GENERALLY CONSIDERED to be the first comic book, the 32-page *Funnies on Parade* was created at Connecticut's Eastern Color Printing, a major printer of newspaper comics sections. It was marketed as a giveaway obtainable by sending in coupons from Procter and Gamble soap products, and it featured strips from the McClure and the McNaught syndicates.

ALSO PUBLISHED by Eastern, *Famous Funnies* 1 was the first 10-cent newsstand comic book. There had been a previous *Famous Funnies* 1 (Feb. 1934 cover date), but Eastern could not find a distributor willing to take a chance on the new periodical. After watching it completely sell out through other venues, American News agreed to distribute the monthly title.

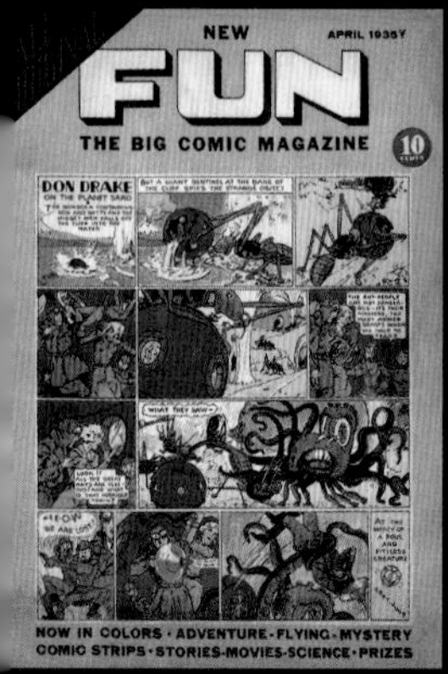
NEW
FUN
THE BIG COMIC MAGAZINE
10 CENTS
NOW IN COLORS · ADVENTURE-FLYING-MYSTERY
COMIC STRIPS·STORIES-MOVIES-SCIENCE·PRIZES

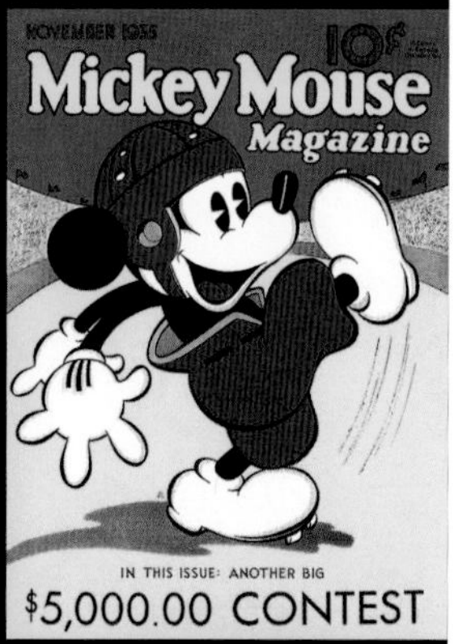
NOVEMBER 1935
10¢
Mickey Mouse
Magazine
IN THIS ISSUE: ANOTHER BIG
$5,000.00 CONTEST

NEW FUN no. 3, April 1935
CLEM GRETTER

MICKEY MOUSE MAGAZINE no. 3, November 1935
WALT DISNEY STUDIO

THE FIRST COMIC BOOK to contain entirely new material, publisher Malcolm Wheeler-Nicholson's *New Fun* hit the newsstands in early 1935. At 11 ½ × 15 ½ inches, it was designed to give the appearance of a newspaper tabloid, as Nicholson's main motivation in producing it was to market his one-page strips to syndicates. His editor, Lloyd Jacquet, would become a major force in the new medium.

ANOTHER OVERSIZED (8 ½ × 11 ½ inches) book to appear in 1935, *Mickey Mouse Magazine* sported simple yet beautifully drafted cover images. The new reprint comic books on the horizon (*Popular Comics, Tip Top Comics, King Comics*) at first crowded their covers with unwieldy groups of characters, but they came to realize the sound marketing strategy of designing covers around a single star.

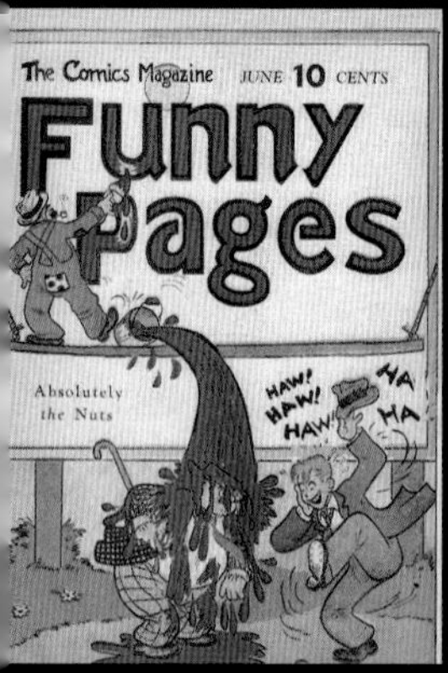
The Comics Magazine JUNE 10 CENTS
Funny Pages
Absolutely the Nuts
HAW! HAW! HAW!
HA HA

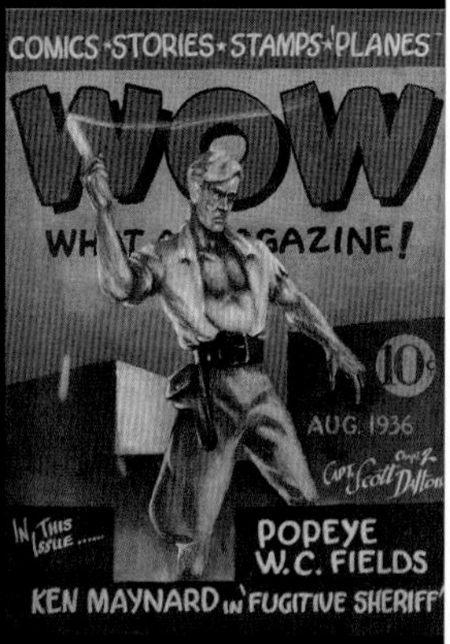
COMICS·STORIES·STAMPS·PLANES
WOW
MAGAZINE!
10¢
AUG. 1936
IN THIS ISSUE.....
POPEYE
W.C. FIELDS
KEN MAYNARD IN FUGITIVE SHERIFF

THE COMICS MAGAZINE no. 2, June 1936
SHELDON MAYER

WOW WHAT A MAGAZINE! no. 2, August 1936
WILL EISNER

WILLIAM COOK AND JOHN MAHON started at Wheeler-Nicholson's National Allied, but left in early 1936 (taking along Lloyd Jacquet) to form a new comic book company, Comics Magazine, Inc. Their first title, *The Comics Magazine,* made its debut in May 1936. By the second issue that appellation shrunk on the covers in deference to *Funny Pages,* which became the official title with the sixth issue.

DAVID MCKAY PUBLICATIONS began publishing comics in early 1936 with the sixth newsstand comic book, *King Comics,* followed in April 1937 by *Ace Comics* (both relied heavily on King Features newspaper reprints). In between, McKay released the four-issue *Wow What a Magazine!,* a part-reprint, part-original title that joined editor Samuel "Jerry" Iger with artist Will Eisner.

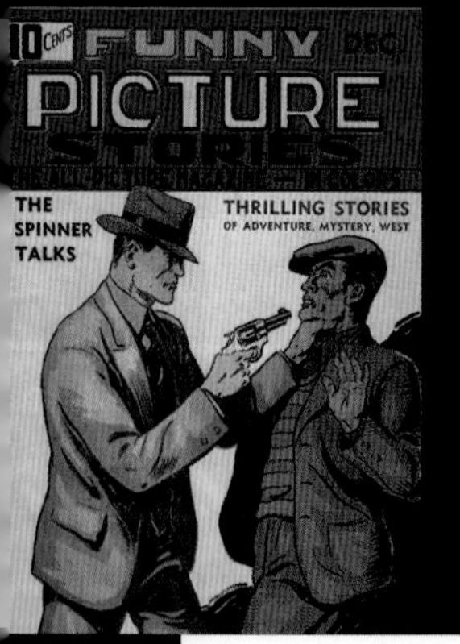
10 CENTS
FUNNY
DEC.
PICTURE
STORIES
THE SPINNER TALKS
THRILLING STORIES
OF ADVENTURE, MYSTERY, WEST

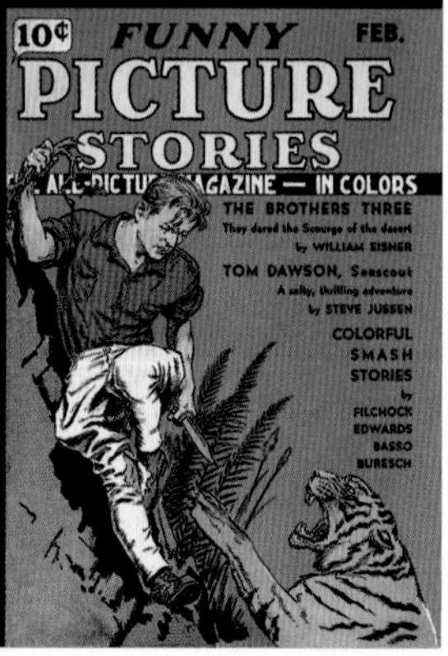
10¢
FUNNY
FEB.
PICTURE
STORIES
ALL-PICTURE MAGAZINE — IN COLORS
THE BROTHERS THREE
TOM DAWSON, Seascout
COLORFUL SMASH STORIES

FUNNY PICTURE STORIES no. 2, December 1936
WILLIAM ALLISON

FUNNY PICTURE STORIES no. 4, February 1937
RODNEY THOMPSON

YOU MAY HAVE noticed that the word "comics" has yet to appear prominently on any of the covers. At this time it was still up in the air what exactly to call the new periodical ("comics" eventually won out, with "funnies" losing steam by the early 1940s). For their three books following *The Comics Magazine (Funny Pages),* Cook and Mahon took a stab at using the more serious sounding "picture stories." The term never caught on, and two of the titles, *Detective Picture Stories* and *Western Picture Stories,* were canceled after short runs. *Funny Picture Stories,* the most successful of the three, updated its name to *Comic Pages* after its 23rd issue. It still went belly-up three issues later, in late 1939.

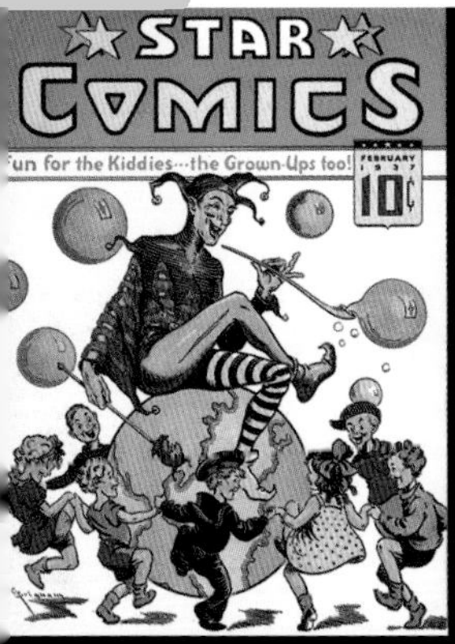
STAR
COMICS
Fun for the Kiddies---the Grown-Ups too!
FEBRUARY 1937
10¢

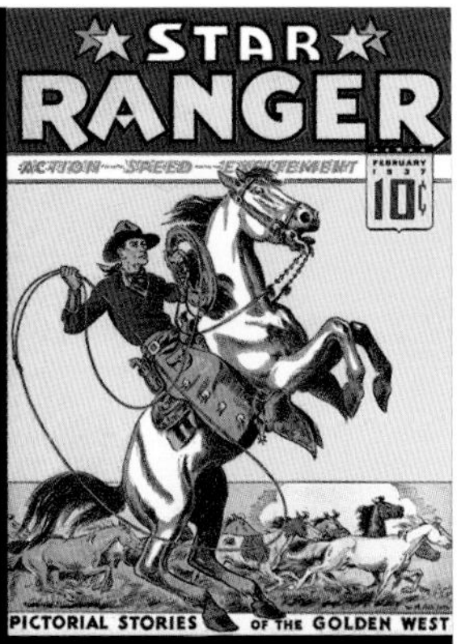
STAR
RANGER
ACTION—SPEED—ENTERTAINMENT
FEBRUARY 1937
10¢
PICTORIAL STORIES OF THE GOLDEN WEST

STAR COMICS no.1, February 1937
W.C. Brigham

STAR RANGER no.1, February 1937
William Allison

HARRY "A" CHESLER, JR. established the country's first comic book "sweatshop" in a Manahattan warehouse in early 1936, providing material for both National Allied and Comics Magazine, Inc. Late that year Chesler branched into publishing with the slightly oversized (8 ¼ × 11 inches) *Star Comics* and *Star Ranger*. After six issues he sold the titles to Frank Temerson and I.W. Ullman's Ultem Publications (who reduced them to standard size) though Chesler continued to package them. Before it closed in the late 1940s, Chesler's shop was the point of entry for scores of comic book artists. Another packaging service run by Will Eisner and Jerry Iger followed quickly on Chesler's heels, with other independent shops to come.

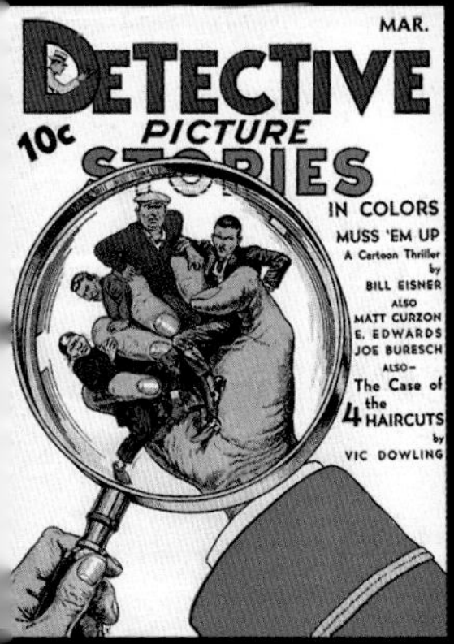
MAR.
DETECTIVE
10¢ PICTURE
STORIES
IN COLORS
MUSS 'EM UP
A Cartoon Thriller
by
BILL EISNER
ALSO
MATT CURZON
E. EDWARDS
JOE BURESCH
ALSO—
The Case of the 4 HAIRCUTS
by
VIC DOWLING

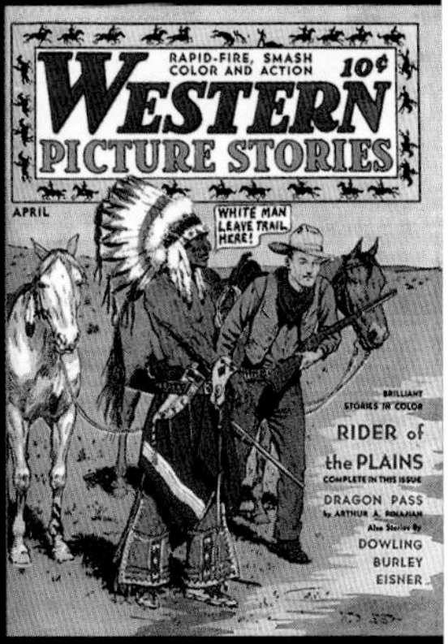
RAPID-FIRE, SMASH
COLOR AND ACTION
10¢
WESTERN
PICTURE STORIES
APRIL
WHITE MAN LEAVE TRAIL HERE!
RIDER of the PLAINS
DRAGON PASS
DOWLING
BURLEY
EISNER

DETECTIVE PICTURE STORIES no.4, March 1937
Rodney Thompson

WESTERN PICTURE STORIES no.3, April 1937
William Allison

THE FIRST COMIC BOOK devoted to a single theme, *Detective Picture Stories* arrived in late 1936. These early Cook and Mahon books routinely credited their artists and writers on the covers, a practice almost immediately dispensed with. Fearing its creators would use their names as bargaining chips, publishers and packagers sought to keep them as anonymous as possible, often retaining the same pen name on a feature no matter who had actually written or drawn it.

WITH A COVER DATE of February 1937, *Western Picture Stories* 1 tied Chesler's *Star Rangers* 1 in becoming the first western comic book. Both *Western Picture Stories* (four issues) and *Detective Picture Stories* (five issues) were on a monthly schedule, and both folded within six months of their respective debuts.

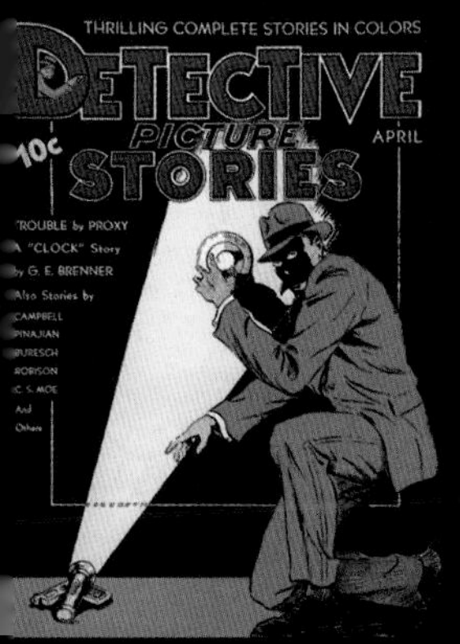
THRILLING COMPLETE STORIES IN COLORS
DETECTIVE
10¢ PICTURE APRIL
STORIES

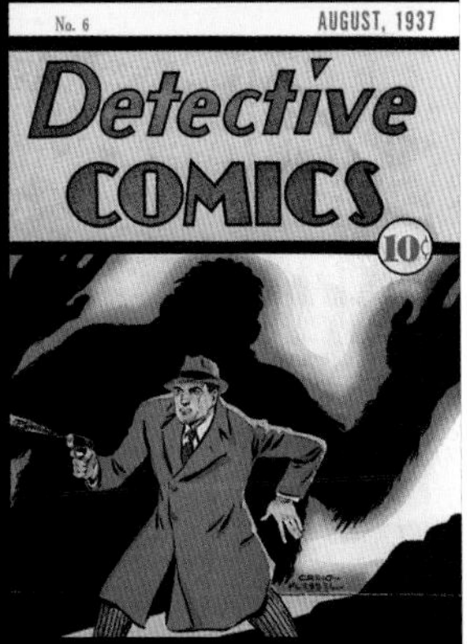
No. 6
AUGUST, 1937
Detective
COMICS
10¢

DETECTIVE PICTURE STORIES no.5, April 1937
George E. Brenner

DETECTIVE COMICS no.6, August 1937
Creig Flessel

THE FINAL ISSUE'S cover of *Detective Picture Stories* features the first masked comic book hero, the Clock, drawn by his creator, artist/writer George E. Brenner. In late 1937 Brenner moved to Everett A. "Busy" Arnold's Quality Comics and continued his signature character in *Feature Funnies*, a book that combined newspaper strip reprints with original material.

DETECTIVE COMICS 1 (March 1937) was the last National Allied title created during Malcolm Wheeler-Nicholson's reign. Advertised as "a high-stepping detective magazine in pictures," it was helmed by talented editor Vin Sullivan, who had the graphic sense to allow Creig Flessel's stirring cover images to stand on their own, often entirely free of blurbs.

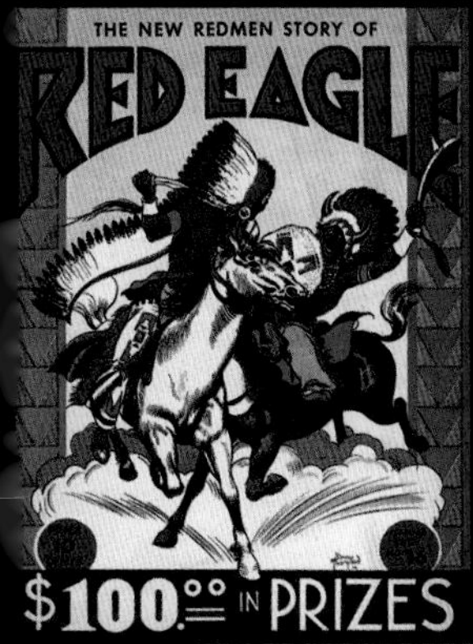
THE NEW REDMEN STORY OF
RED EAGLE
$100.00 IN PRIZES

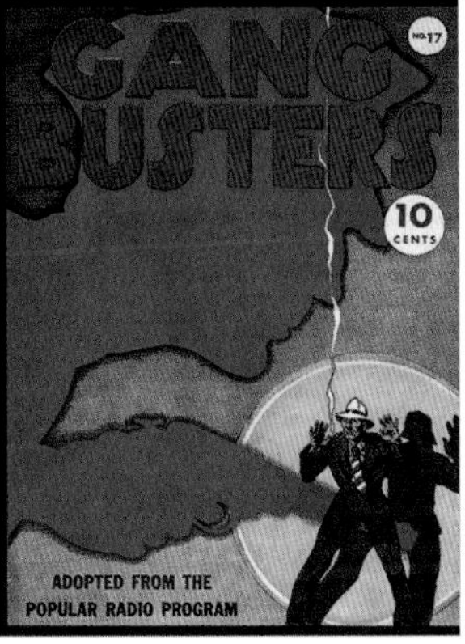
No. 17
GANG
BUSTERS
10 CENTS
ADOPTED FROM THE
POPULAR RADIO PROGRAM

FEATURE BOOK no.16, August 1938
Jimmy Thompson

FEATURE BOOK no.17, September 1938
Jimmy Thompson

PUBLISHER DAVID MCKAY'S *King Comics* consisted primarily of King Features strip reprints, but it also contained an ambitious new feature, *Redmen*, chronicling the adventures of a Mohawk warrior. Laid out across the centerfold in Sunday-newspaper-strip fashion, *Redmen* introduced the work of Jimmy Thompson, the first notable African-American artist/writer in comic books. His Indian tales were well researched, sensitively written, and displayed a high level of draftsmanship. After McKay started the *Feature Book* reprint series in 1937, he allowed Thompson to create two original one-shots, *Red Eagle* and *Gang Busters*. Best known for his 1940s work on DC's *Robotman*, Thompson remained in comics until the early 1950s.

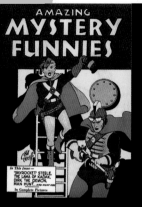

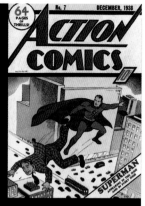

AMAZING
MYSTERY
FUNNIES
In This Issue—
"SKYROCKET" STEELE,
THE LAMA OF KADAK,
DIRK, THE DEMON,
In Complete Pictures

64 PAGES OF THRILLS!
No. 7
DECEMBER, 1938
ACTION
COMICS
SUPERMAN

AMAZING MYSTERY FUNNIES no.3, November 1938
BILL EVERETT

ACTION COMICS no.7, December 1938
JOE SHUSTER

COOK AND MAHON'S Comics Magazine, Inc. went out of business in mid-1937. Its remaining titles, *Funny Picture Stories* and *Funny Pages,* were sold to Ultem, who hired Harry Chesler to package them. About five months later the company was sold to pulp publisher Centaur Publications. With Lloyd Jacquet rehired as art director, a new group of titles were added, spearheaded by *Amazing Mystery Funnies,* showcasing the work of 21-year-old artist/writer Bill Everett. This cover presents Everett creations Skyrocket Steele and Dirk the Demon.

MALCOLM WHEELER-NICHOLSON lost control of his company – now called Detective Comics, Inc., or DC – just as *Action* 1 (June 1938) hit the stands, introducing Jerry Siegel and Joe Shuster's industry-transforming creation. This was Superman's second cover appearance.

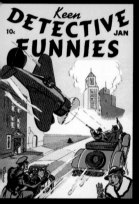

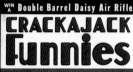

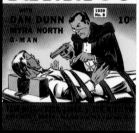

Keen
DETECTIVE
FUNNIES
10¢
JAN

WIN A Double Barrel Daisy Air Rifle
CRACKAJACK
Funnies
WITH
DAN DUNN
MYRA NORTH
G-MAN
1939 No. 8
10¢

KEEN DETECTIVE FUNNIES v.2 n.1, January 1939
TERRY GILKISON

CRACKAJACK FUNNIES no.8, January 1939
JAMES GARY

KEEN DETECTIVE FUNNIES was Centaur's revamp of Cook and Mahon's *Detective Picture Stories.* Calling himself "Uncle Joe," co-owner and editor Joe Hardie began each book with a personal message to the reader in an attempt to create a loyal fan base. Cover artist Terry Gilkison had been doing illustrations for Centaur's book division and he branched into comics along with the company.

DELL CONTINUED to create new titles in 1936 and 1937 with the newspaper-strip reprint anthologies *The Funnies* and *The Comics.* Starting in mid-1938, its fourth comic book, *Crackajack Funnies,* featured a mixture of original and reprinted material. This cover was based on a panel from interior feature *Tom Traylor G-Man.*

JAN
STAR
RANGER
FUNNIES
10¢
JACK COLE

JUMBO
COMICS
10 Bigger & Better Funnies 10
HEY! LEMME OFF THIS CONTRAPSHUN!
YIPPIE!
BIG PAGES–BIG PICTURES–BIG TYPE–EASY TO READ

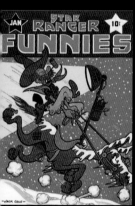

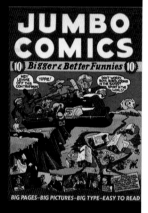

STAR RANGER FUNNIES v.2 n.1, January 1939
JACK COLE

JUMBO COMICS no.5, January 1939
WILL EISNER

BORN IN NEW CASTLE, Pennsylvania, Jack Cole learned how to cartoon via the Landon School of Illustration and Cartooning correspondence course. In 1936, he moved with his wife to Manhattan, and the following year he joined the Chesler staff. Cole's first comics work appeared in 1938-39 issues of *Funny Pages* and *Star Ranger Funnies,* including this, his first cover.

FICTION HOUSE'S *Jumbo Comics* was the first title completely packaged by the new partnership Eisner & Iger. True to its name, the first eight *Jumbos* were oversized – 10 ½ × 14 ½ inches, just shy of tabloid size (11 × 17 inches). With its ninth issue the title assumed standard Golden Age comic book dimensions (about 7 ½ × 10 ½ inches).

TiP ToP
COMICS
No. 34
10¢
FEBRUARY
FIVE pages of
TARZAN!

10¢
AMAZING
FEB
MYSTERY
FUNNIES

TIP TOP COMICS no.34, February 1939
PAUL BERDANIER

AMAZING MYSTERY FUNNIES v.2.n.2, February 1939
BILL EVERETT

HITTING THE NEWSSTANDS in early 1936, *Tip Top Comics* was the first title published by a newspaper syndicate, United Feature, filled with reprinted strips such as *Li'l Abner, Nancy,* and *Tarzan.* Its first editor was Lev Gleason, a former Eastern Printing salesman who would soon start his own comic book line. The Tarzan cover is by Paul Berdanier, an illustrator and fine artist who dabbled in comics.

THROUGHOUT ITS short history, Centaur was plagued with distribution problems. It attempted over 30 titles, but most folded after a handful of issues. *Amazing Mystery Funnies* held on with a respectable run of 23 issues, finally succumbing in the summer of 1940.

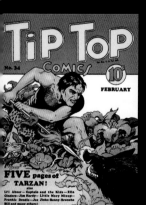

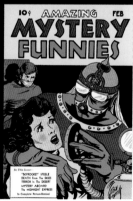

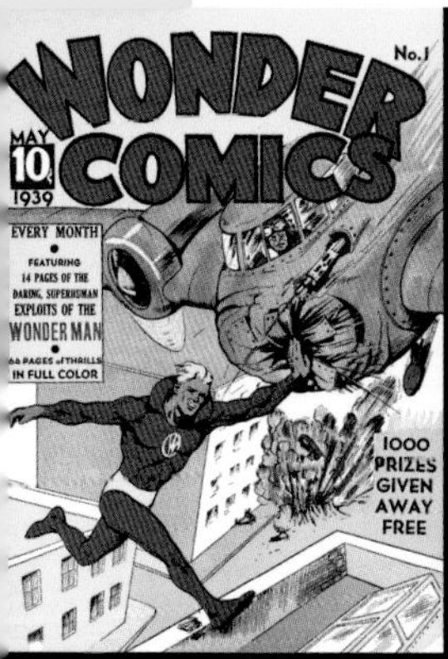
WONDER COMICS
No.1
MAY 10¢ 1939
EVERY MONTH
FEATURING 14 PAGES OF THE DARING, SUPERHUMAN EXPLOITS OF THE WONDER MAN
64 PAGES of THRILLS IN FULL COLOR
1000 PRIZES GIVEN AWAY FREE
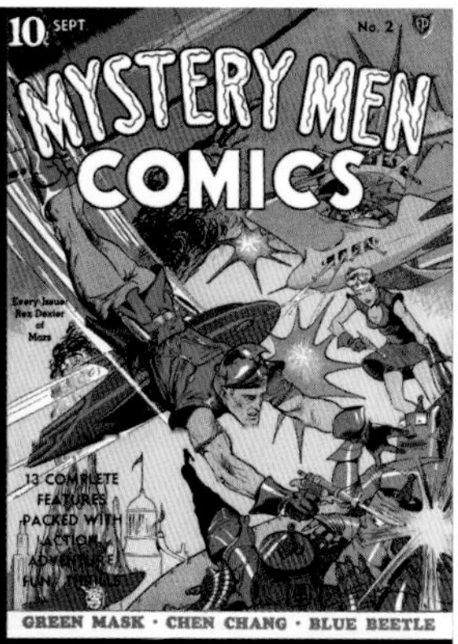
10¢ SEPT
No. 2
MYSTERY MEN COMICS
13 COMPLETE FEATURES PACKED WITH ACTION
GREEN MASK · CHEN CHANG · BLUE BEETLE

WONDER COMICS no.1, May 1939
Will Eisner

MYSTERY MEN COMICS no.2, September 1939
Will Eisner and Lou Fine

DC ACCOUNTANT Victor Fox had early first-hand knowledge of the vast sums Superman was shoveling into the company. Fox decided to become a comic book publisher himself, setting up shop in the same building that housed his former employer. He then hired Will Eisner to create another Superman. Somewhat half-heartedly, Eisner came up with Wonder Man, introduced in Fox's first title, *Wonder Comics*. DC immediately sued, and won (the most damaging piece of evidence may have been the similarity of the *Wonder* cover with *Action* 7's, shown earlier). Fox cancelled *Wonder*, but launched four new superhero titles, each conceived, edited, and art directed by Eisner. In the process he made great artistic strides; one need only compare *Wonder* 1's cover with that of *Mystery Men* 2.

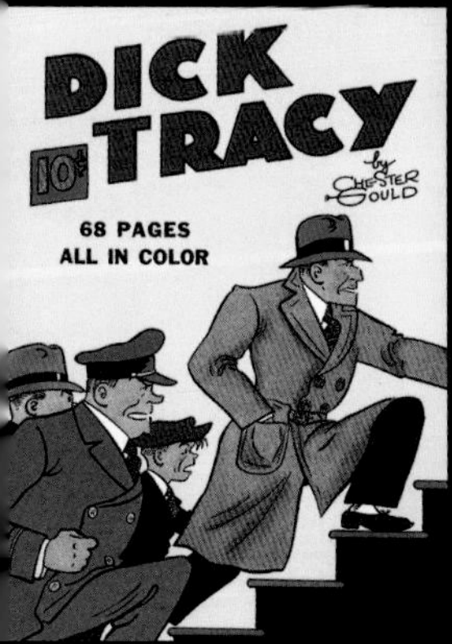
DICK TRACY
10¢
by CHESTER GOULD
68 PAGES
ALL IN COLOR
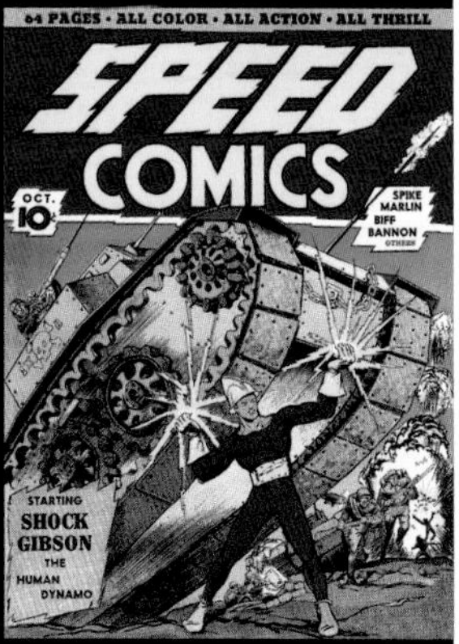
64 PAGES · ALL COLOR · ALL ACTION · ALL THRILL
SPEED COMICS
OCT. 10¢
SPIKE MARLIN
BIFF BANNON
OTHERS
STARTING SHOCK GIBSON THE HUMAN DYNAMO

FOUR COLOR no.1, September 1939
Attributed to Chester Gould

SPEED COMICS no.1, October 1939
Attributed to Bob Powell

FOUR COLOR was conceived by Dell as a tryout series for its various licensed properties – if a book sold well, the subject could be rewarded with its own separate title. While not certifiably the work of *Dick Tracy* creator Chester Gould, this cover certainly captures his breathless approach to graphics, with Tracy bounding the stairs four at a time.

SPEED COMICS was initially published by Frank Temerson's Brookwood Publishing until he sold the title in mid-1941 to former Fox employee turned publisher Alfred Harvey. Harvey enlisted his brothers Leon and Robert to respectively take charge of the editing and accounting. The three started the Harvey publishing empire that continues to this day, though it's no longer family owned.

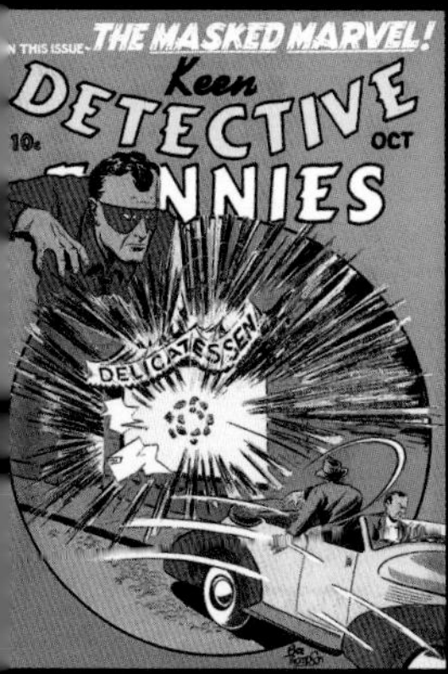
IN THIS ISSUE - THE MASKED MARVEL!
Keen DETECTIVE FUNNIES
10¢
OCT
DELICATESSEN
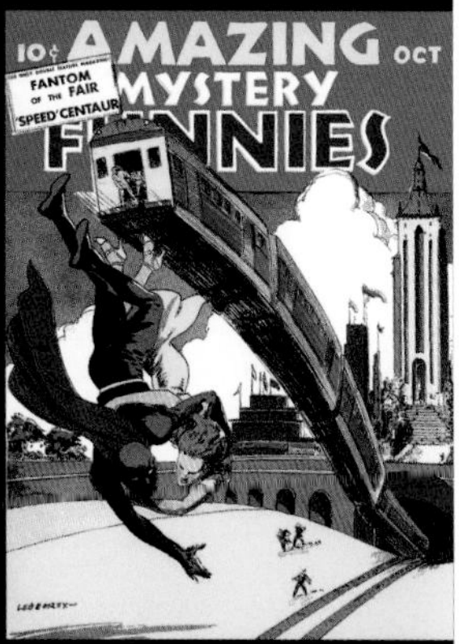
10¢ AMAZING MYSTERY FUNNIES OCT
FANTOM OF THE FAIR
SPEED CENTAUR

KEEN DETECTIVE FUNNIES v.2 n.10, October 1939
Ben Thompson

AMAZING MYSTERY FUNNIES v.2 n.10, October 1939
Leo Morey

SMELLING MONEY, Centaur entered the superhero fray pronto. Beginning with the July 1939 issue of *Keen Detective Funnies* and for the rest of its run, the blurb "In this issue – The Masked Marvel!" was prominently displayed above the title (though curiously with the hero only occasionally pictured). Artist/writer Ben Thompson came up with the reclusive antisocial hero, who would suddenly appear, correct some mischief, then just as quickly return to seclusion.

THAT SAME MONTH, The Fantom of the Fair and Speed Centaur alternated on *Amazing Mystery Funnies* covers, tossing Skyrocket Steele to the comic book junk heap. Paul Gustavson's Fantom was inspired by New York's 1939 World's Fair, the setting for his early adventures. Peruvian cover artist Leo Morey was a Lloyd Jacquet find.

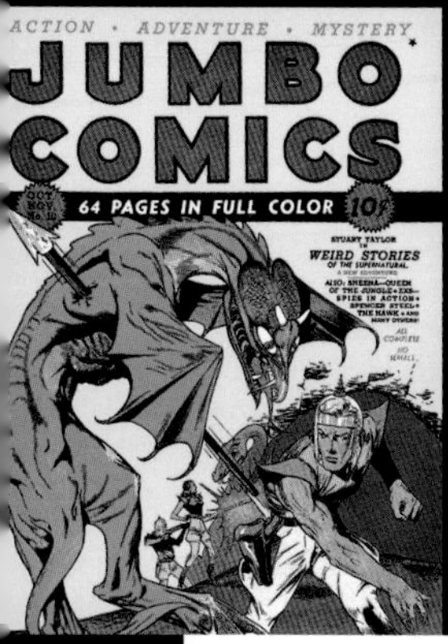
ACTION · ADVENTURE · MYSTERY
JUMBO COMICS
64 PAGES IN FULL COLOR 10¢
WEIRD STORIES
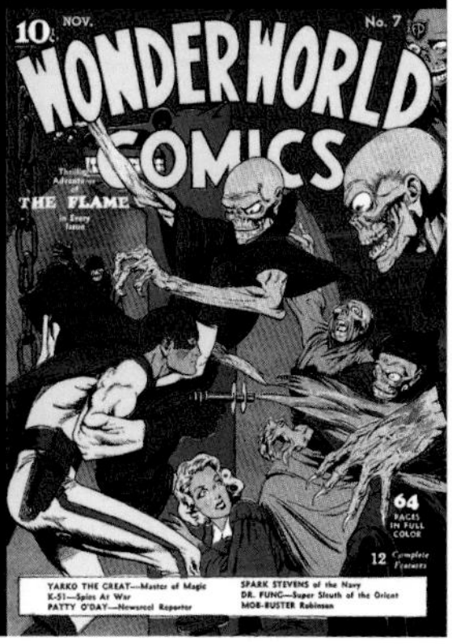
10¢ NOV.
No. 7
WONDERWORLD COMICS
THE FLAME
64 PAGES IN FULL COLOR
12 Complete Features

JUMBO COMICS no.10, October-November 1939
Will Eisner and Lou Fine

WONDERWORLD COMICS no.7, November 1939
Will Eisner and Lou Fine

WILL EISNER drew the early *Jumbo* covers through issue 12, two of which were inked by Lou Fine. Note the cover blurb "All Complete, No Serials," to further distinguish the comic book from its episodic newspaper-strip ancestry.

LOU FINE continued to ink Eisner's Fox covers as well, including this *Wonderworld* classic featuring the Flame. Fine also handled the Flame stories inside, many of which were laid out by Eisner. After the DC lawsuit, Fox heroes were endowed with substantially fewer powers – about all the Flame could do was shoot a gun that spat fire.

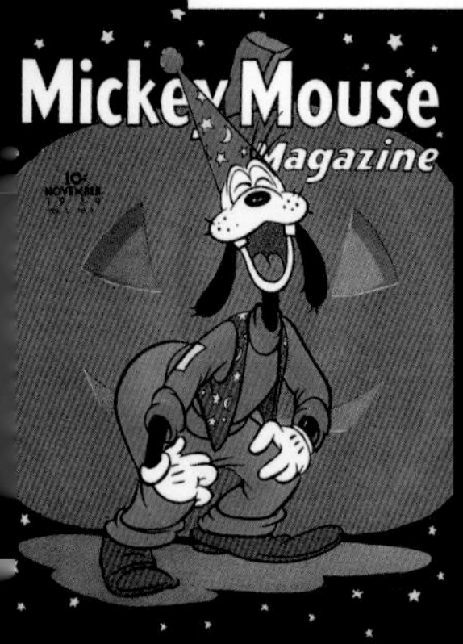
Mickey Mouse
Magazine
10¢
NOVEMBER
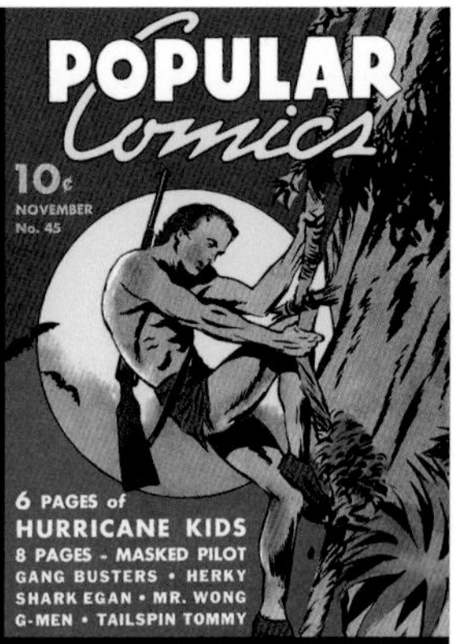
POPULAR
Comics
10¢
NOVEMBER
No. 45
6 PAGES of
HURRICANE KIDS
8 PAGES - MASKED PILOT
GANG BUSTERS • HERKY
SHARK EGAN • MR. WONG
G-MEN • TAILSPIN TOMMY

MICKEY MOUSE MAGAZINE v.5 n.2, November 1939
WALT DISNEY STUDIO

POPULAR COMICS no.45, November 1939
BILL ELY

ANOTHER LESSON in the power of bold graphic simplicity, this Halloween cover featuring Goofy appeared toward the end of *Mickey Mouse Magazine's* 60-issue run. The title continued on with great success for Dell as *Walt Disney's Comics and Stories.*

INTRODUCED WITH a February 1936 cover date, *Popular Comics* was Dell's first standard-sized comic book. (In 1929 founder George Delacorte and Eastern Printing had attempted what many consider the very first comic book series, *The Funnies*, a weekly tabloid of new material that failed after 36 issues.) *Popular* mixed reprints with original material such as the Hurricane Kids by artist Bill Ely, who worked prolifically in comic books into the 1960s.

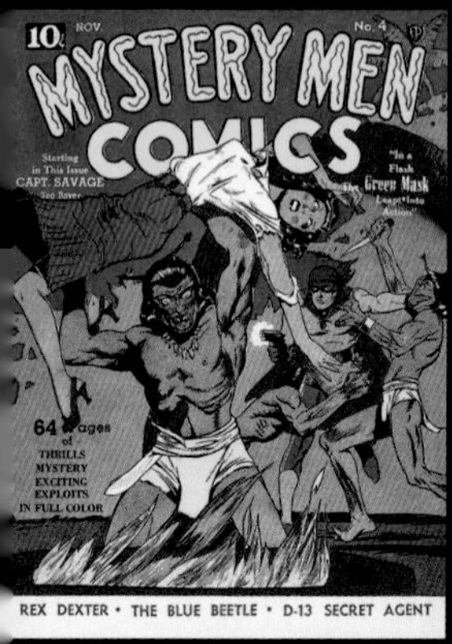
10¢
NOV.
No. 4
MYSTERY MEN
COMICS
64 Pages
REX DEXTER • THE BLUE BEETLE • D-13 SECRET AGENT
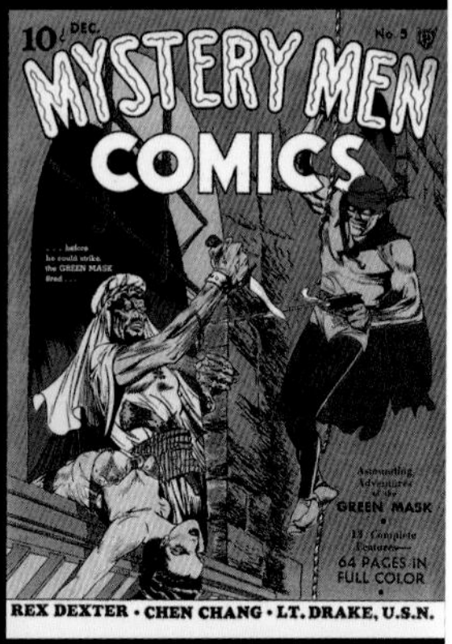
10¢
DEC.
No. 5
MYSTERY MEN
COMICS
GREEN MASK
64 PAGES IN
FULL COLOR
REX DEXTER • CHEN CHANG • LT. DRAKE, U.S.N.

MYSTERY MEN COMICS no.4, November 1939
WILL EISNER AND LOU FINE

MYSTERY MEN COMICS no.5, December 1939
WILL EISNER AND LOU FINE

WHILE SUPERMAN'S unprecedented success led most publishers to aim their material squarely at preteens, Will Eisner had a steadfast belief that graphic narrative could appeal to an older audience. To test his theory, by late 1939 his covers became more sexually charged – with distressed damsels wearing less and less each month.

MYSTERY MEN cover star the Green Mask began his career as another post-DC-lawsuit Fox hero with no powers apart from a costume, mask, and gun. By mid-1940, however, the tidal wave of Superman clones became too much for even DC to stop. With the coast now clear, Fox revamped the Green Mask, exposing him to "vita-rays" which left him invulnerable, incredibly strong, and able to fly. Sound familiar?

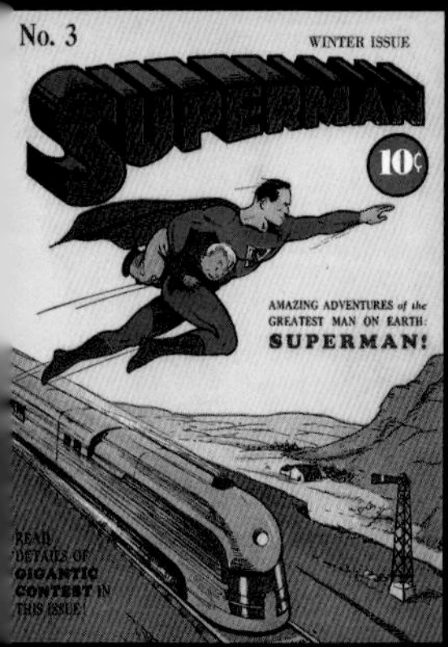
No. 3
WINTER ISSUE
SUPERMAN
10¢
AMAZING ADVENTURES of the
GREATEST MAN ON EARTH
SUPERMAN!
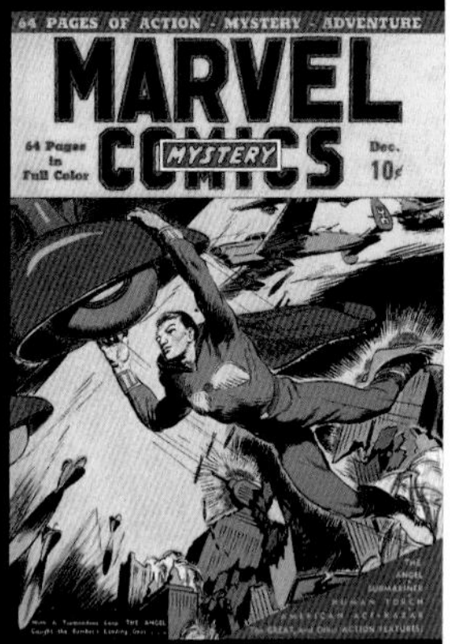
64 PAGES OF ACTION · MYSTERY · ADVENTURE
MARVEL
MYSTERY
COMICS
Dec.
10¢

SUPERMAN no. 3, Winter 1939
JOE SHUSTER

MARVEL MYSTERY COMICS no.2, December 1939
CHARLES J. MAZOUJIAN

IN ADDITION TO starring in *Action Comics*, by mid-1939 Superman had his own syndicated strip plus a new self-titled quarterly comic book; Joe Shuster had to start a studio of artists to keep up with demand. Here we find Supes giving a ride to a representative of that section of the demographic most coveted by comic book publishers.

WITH PARTNERS John Mahon and Frank Torpey, in 1939 Lloyd Jacquet started a new packaging service, Funnies, Inc., taking with him his best Centaur artists, including Bill Everett and Carl Burgos. Its first book, *Marvel Comics* 1 (for Timely publisher Martin Goodman), introduced Everett's Sub-Mariner and Burgos' Human Torch. The second cover (with the title changed to *Marvel Mystery*) featured the Angel, wearing a costume that looks vaguely familiar.

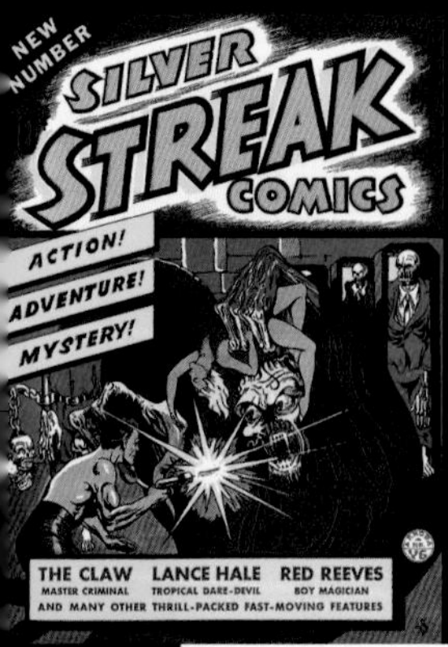
NEW NUMBER
SILVER
STREAK
COMICS
ACTION!
ADVENTURE!
MYSTERY!
THE CLAW LANCE HALE RED REEVES
AND MANY OTHER THRILL-PACKED FAST-MOVING FEATURES
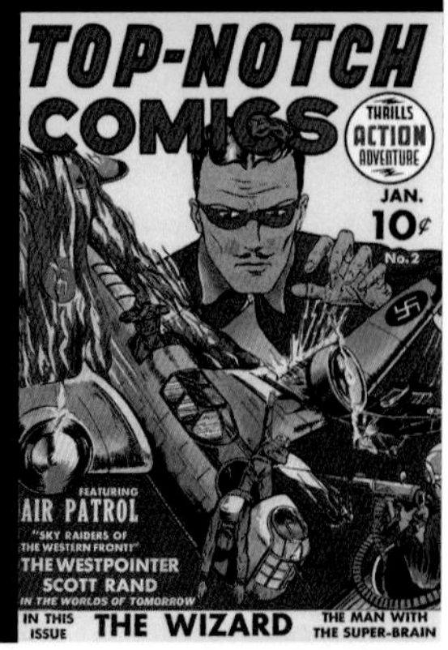
TOP-NOTCH
COMICS
THRILLS
ACTION
ADVENTURE
JAN.
10¢
No. 2
AIR PATROL
THE WESTPOINTER
SCOTT RAND
IN THIS ISSUE
THE WIZARD
THE MAN WITH THE SUPER-BRAIN

SILVER STREAK COMICS no.2, January 1940
JOE SIMON

TOP-NOTCH COMICS no.2, January 1940
EDD ASHE

THOUGH NOT ENDOWED with the art chops of his finest contemporaries, Joe Simon was smart, industrious, and had a knack for timing. He assumed the Fox editing after Eisner & Iger left, and supplemented his income with various freelance accounts, including Funnies, Inc. The packager's new title, *Silver Streak Comics* (for publishers Arthur Bernhard and Lev Gleason), commenced with consecutive Simon covers.

MLJ ENTERED the field with *Blue Ribbon Comics* (Nov. 1939), followed closely by *Top-Notch Comics* (Dec. 1939), *Pep Comics* (Jan. 1940), and *Zip Comics* (Feb. 1940). *Top-Notch* featured the Wizard, a tuxedo-clad hero with a "super-brain." Cover artist Edd Ashe also handled the interior stories.

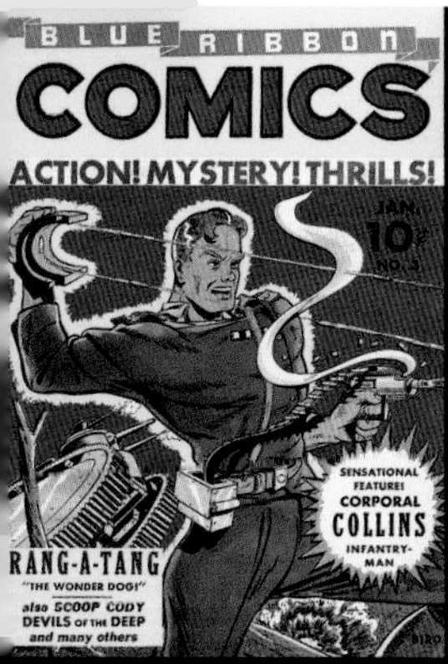
BLUE RIBBON
COMICS
ACTION! MYSTERY! THRILLS!
JAN.
10¢
SENSATIONAL FEATURE! CORPORAL COLLINS INFANTRY-MAN
RANG-A-TANG
"THE WONDER DOG!"
also SCOOP CODY
DEVILS OF THE DEEP
and many others
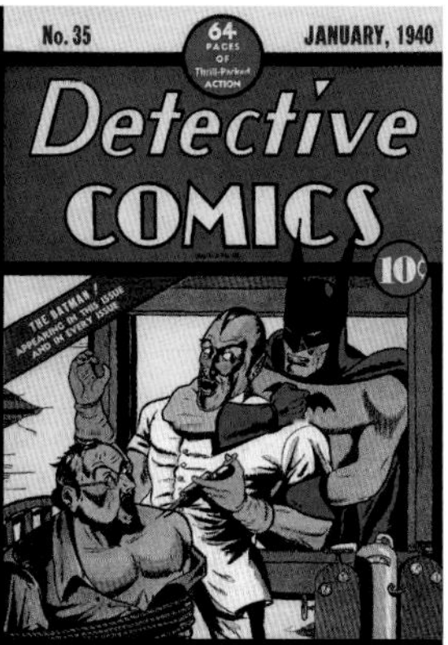
No. 35
64 PAGES OF Thrill-Packed ACTION
JANUARY, 1940
Detective
COMICS
10¢

BLUE RIBBON COMICS no.3, January 1940
CHARLES BIRO

DETECTIVE COMICS no.35, January 1940
BOB KANE AND SHELDON MOLDOFF

ISSUES 3 THROUGH 5 of *Blue Ribbon* sported robust covers by Charles Biro of his one-man army, Corporal Collins Infantryman. Here he returns fire with his "famous fabri-steel flexible repeller," which "magnetizes the bullets and returns them with added speed."

BOB KANE AND BILL FINGER'S caped crusader cemented DC's stature as the preeminent superhero company. This marks Batman's ninth appearance in *Detective,* when he was still a no-nonsense solo vigilante, killing criminals with gunfire or by nonchalantly tossing them off buildings. His increasing popularity compelled DC to soften his edge three issues later by pairing him with a young sidekick – which naturally led to an avalanche of young sidekicks throughout the industry.

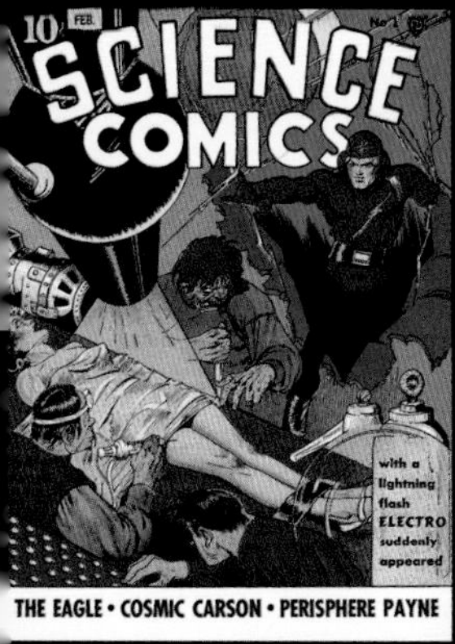
10¢ FEB.
SCIENCE
COMICS
with a lightning flash ELECTRO suddenly appeared
THE EAGLE • COSMIC CARSON • PERISPHERE PAYNE
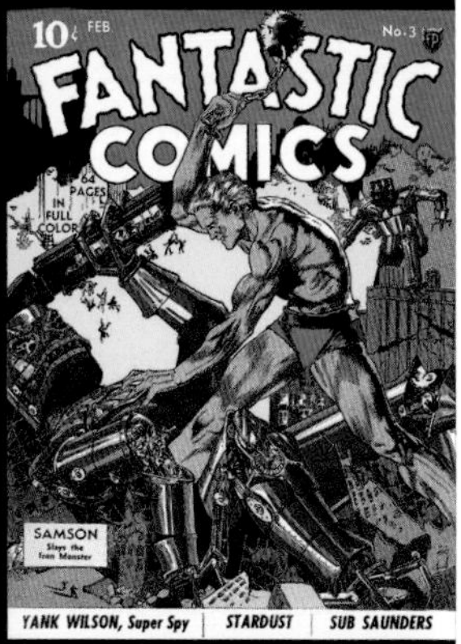
10¢ FEB
No. 3
FANTASTIC
COMICS
64 PAGES IN FULL COLOR
SAMSON
YANK WILSON, Super Spy
STARDUST
SUB SAUNDERS

SCIENCE COMICS no.1, February 1940
WILL EISNER AND LOU FINE

FANTASTIC COMICS no.3, February 1940
WILL EISNER AND LOU FINE

ANOTHER SPLENDID Eisner/Fine cover kicks off *Science Comics'* inaugural issue. It introduces Electro, an Eisner superhero with the ability to harness and transmit electricity (by the second issue his name was changed to Dynamo). *Science Comics* lasted eight issues, the shortest run of the Fox superhero titles.

ROBOT COVERS have always been a niche genre for collectors. This classic example features Samson, an Eisner creation based on the Biblical strongman (with interior stories drawn by staffer Alex Blum). The cover inspired the following issue's lead story, where Samson again battles giant robots. The ability to grow larger made for a great cover, but was not an actual power of Samson's – in the story he remained man-sized.

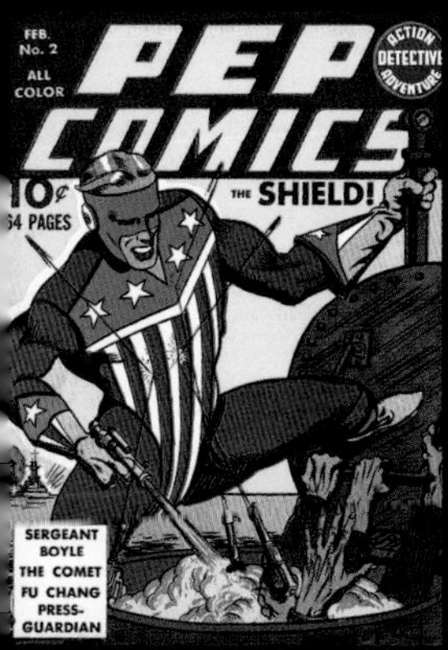
FEB. No. 2
ALL COLOR
PEP
COMICS
ACTION DETECTIVE ADVENTURE
10¢
64 PAGES
THE SHIELD!
SERGEANT BOYLE
THE COMET
FU CHANG
PRESS-GUARDIAN
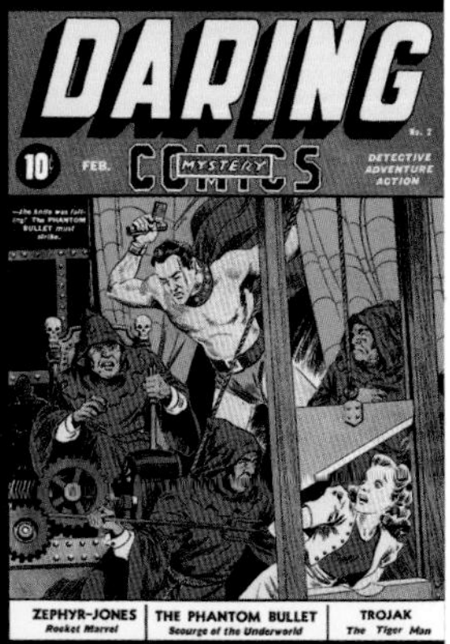
DARING
10¢ FEB.
MYSTERY
COMICS
DETECTIVE ADVENTURE ACTION
ZEPHYR-JONES
Rocket Marvel
THE PHANTOM BULLET
Scourge of the Underworld
TROJAK
The Tiger Man

PEP COMICS no.2, February 1940
IRV NOVICK

DARING MYSTERY COMICS no.2, February 1940
ALEX SCHOMBURG

POSSESSING SUPERMAN-LIKE powers, the ultra patriotic Shield "devotes his life to shielding the government from all enemies," a "G-Man Extraordinary" reporting directly to FBI chief J. Edgar Hoover. *Pep* cover artist Irv Novick, a Chesler alumnus, also drew the Shield stories inside, which he continued doing until the character was canceled in 1947. Novick then left comics for advertising but returned in 1954 to begin a long tenure at DC.

OUR FIRST of 14 covers by Alex Schomburg features items from his early stock in trade: cultist hooded figures, arcane mechanical devices, and imminent decapitation. The scantily clad dog-collared hero is the Phantom Bullet, a Joe Simon invention that came and went with this issue.

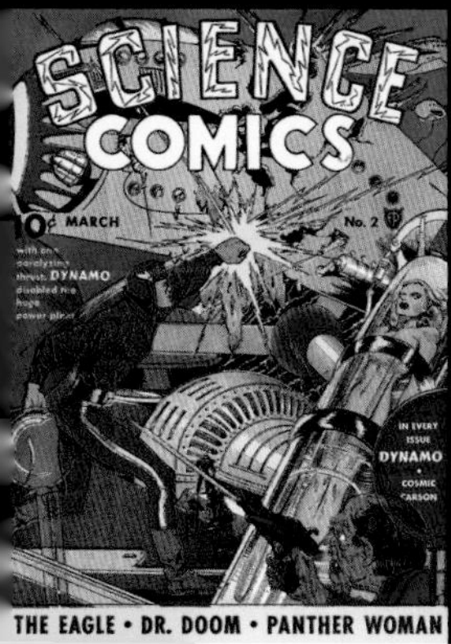
SCIENCE
COMICS
10¢ MARCH
No. 2
IN EVERY ISSUE
DYNAMO
THE EAGLE • DR. DOOM • PANTHER WOMAN
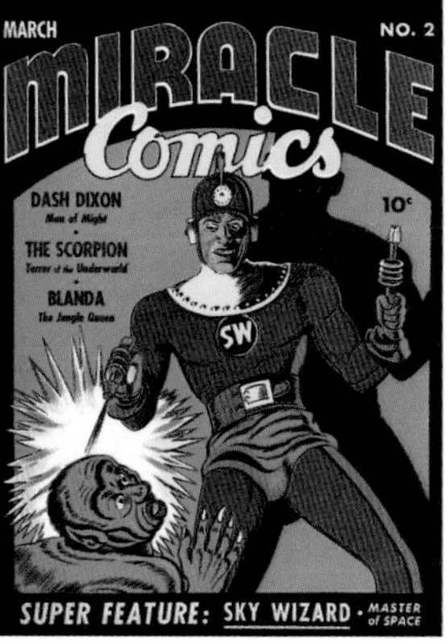
MARCH
NO. 2
MIRACLE
Comics
DASH DIXON
Man of Might
THE SCORPION
BLANDA
The Jungle Queen
10¢
SW
SUPER FEATURE: SKY WIZARD • MASTER of SPACE

SCIENCE COMICS no.2, March 1940
WILL EISNER AND LOU FINE

MIRACLE COMICS no.2, March 1940
EMILE SCHURMACHER

THE SECOND AND FINAL Eisner/Fine *Science* cover presents Dynamo rescuing a female who is about as naked as you can get on the cover of a 1940 comic book. This was one of Eisner's last covers before leaving Fox and he may have intentionally pushed the envelope, knowing there was little Fox could do to him in the face of public outcry – not that anybody complained.

MAGAZINE PUBLISHER Hillman Publications entered comics in 1940 with two superhero titles, *Rocket Comics* and *Miracle Comics,* neither of which lasted more than four issues. Switching gears, their next title, *Air Fighters Comics,* utilized war themes and airplane action, and fared much better.

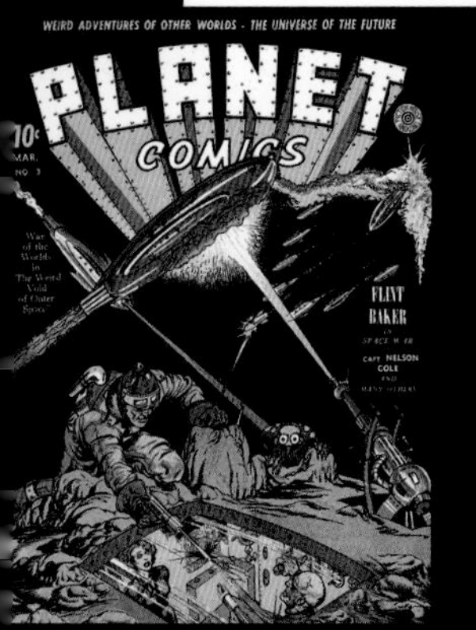
WEIRD ADVENTURES OF OTHER WORLDS - THE UNIVERSE OF THE FUTURE
PLANET
COMICS
10¢

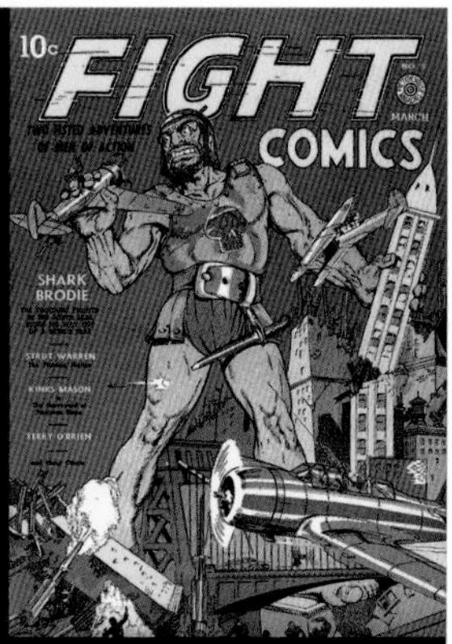
10¢
FIGHT
COMICS
SHARK BRODIE

PLANET COMICS no. 3, March 1940
WILL EISNER

FIGHT COMICS no.3, March 1940
WILL EISNER

NOW THAT comic books had proven their profitability, Fiction House added three new Eisner & Iger books to *Jumbo: Fight Comics, Jungle Comics,* and *Planet Comics,* all cover-dated January 1940. The titles were based on established Fiction House pulps *Fight Stories, Jungle Stories,* and *Planet Stories,* in the company's hopes of adapting the older stories and covers to the new medium. With Harry Chesler's shop and Lloyd Jacquet's Funnies, Inc. Eisner & Iger became one of the top three comic book packagers of the early Golden Age, helping start the careers of Dick Briefer, Lou Fine, Bob Kane, Jack Kirby, Mort Meskin, and Bob Powell.

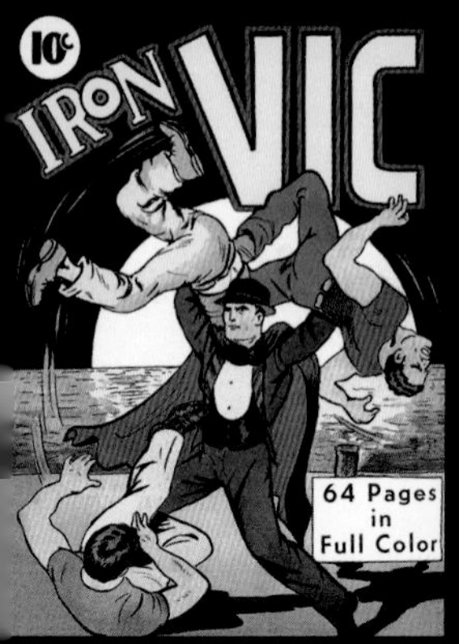
10¢
IRON
VIC
64 Pages in Full Color

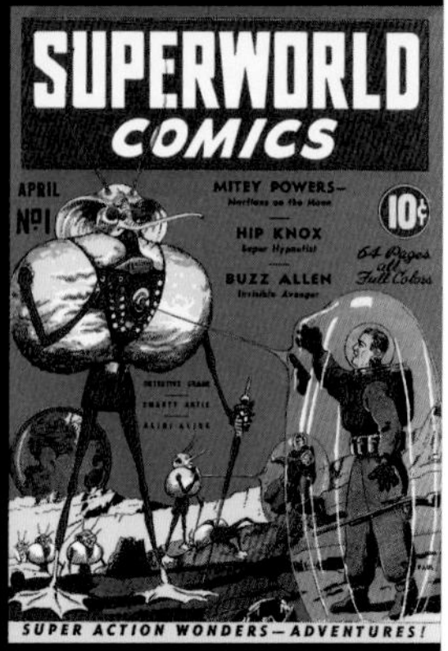
SUPERWORLD
COMICS
APRIL
No1
MITEY POWERS—
HIP KNOX
BUZZ ALLEN
10¢
SUPER ACTION WONDERS—ADVENTURES!

SINGLE SERIES no.22, 1940
BERNARD DIBBLE

SUPERWORLD COMICS no.1, April 1940
FRANK PAUL

TO FURTHER recycle its newspaper strips, in late 1938 United Feature Syndicate created its *Single Series* line of comic books. Bernard Dibble's original one-shot *Iron Vic* was an exception, created specifically for the red-hot superhero market. The plainclothes crime fighter took advantage of his super strength to become the world's greatest baseball player, attending to criminals part-time between games.

PULP PUBLISHERS struggled to get a handle on the new medium. *Amazing Stories* founder Hugo Gernsback took a misguided whack at it with his futuristic *Superworld Comics,* assuring readers in its first issue that "no superhuman feats impossible of accomplishment are printed." It died after three issues.

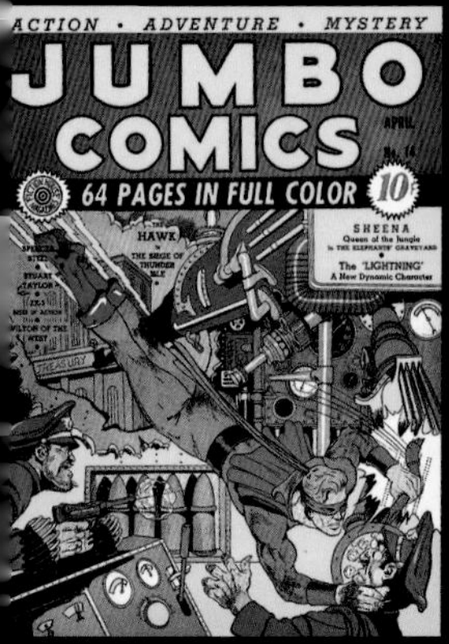
ACTION · ADVENTURE · MYSTERY
JUMBO
COMICS
64 PAGES IN FULL COLOR
10¢
SHEENA

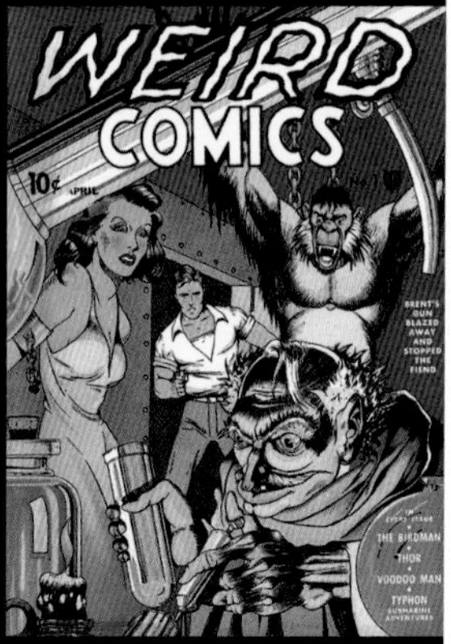
WEIRD
COMICS
10¢

JUMBO COMICS no.14, April 1940
BOB POWELL

WEIRD COMICS no.1, April 1940
GEORGE TUSKA

EISNER & IGER staff artist Bob Powell succeeded Will Eisner as *Jumbo Comics'* cover artist, doing a respectable job emulating his boss's approach. In 1940 Eisner sold his half of the partnership to Iger and started his own smaller studio, taking Powell and Lou Fine with him.

THE FIFTH Fox comic book, *Weird Comics,* was its final Eisner-created title. Its first cover, probably helped along by Eisner, is by Eisner &Iger staff artist George Tuska. After Eisner's departure, Fox hired Joe Simon to take over as editor and main cover artist. Iger continued to supply the Fox interiors but he closed the account after not getting paid in four months. He took Victor Fox to court and eventually received his money.

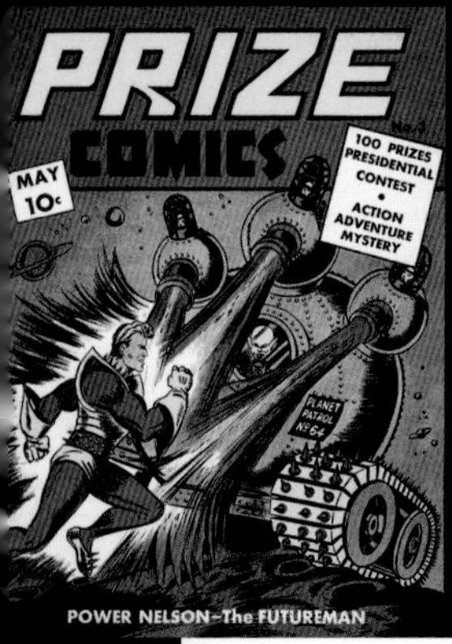
PRIZE
COMICS
MAY
10¢
100 PRIZES PRESIDENTIAL CONTEST
ACTION ADVENTURE MYSTERY
POWER NELSON–The FUTUREMAN

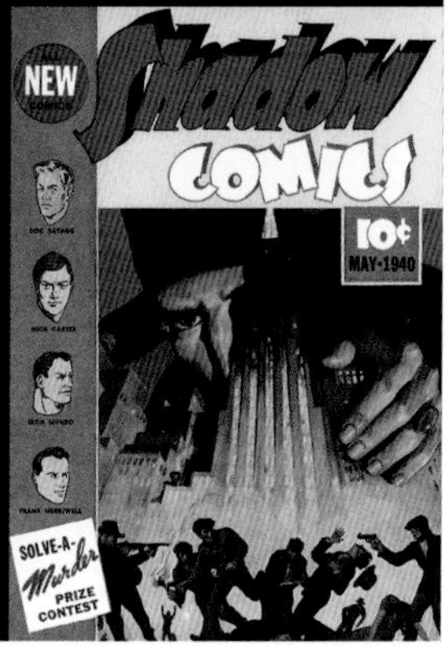
NEW
Shadow
COMICS
10¢
MAY-1940
SOLVE-A-Murder PRIZE CONTEST

PRIZE COMICS no. 3, May 1940
ATTRIBUTED TO DICK SPRANG

SHADOW COMICS no.3, May 1940
ATTRIBUTED TO GEORGE ROZEN

PRIZE COMICS was the first comic title of pulp magazine producer Prize Publications. It's unclear where Prize got its early material. It may have come from a small studio run by artists Ed Kressy, Norman Fallon, and attributed cover artist Dick Sprang, who drew the early *Power Nelson* stories. On the other hand, Tarpé Mills and William Rowland also contributed, and they worked through Funnies, Inc.

STREET AND SMITH PUBLICATIONS got into the act with two titles devoted to its star pulp characters, Doc Savage and the Shadow. The early *Shadow* issues recycled painted pulp covers – this one came from its January 1, 1933 issue. It's unsigned but appears to be the work of George Rozen, the main *Shadow* cover artist at the time.

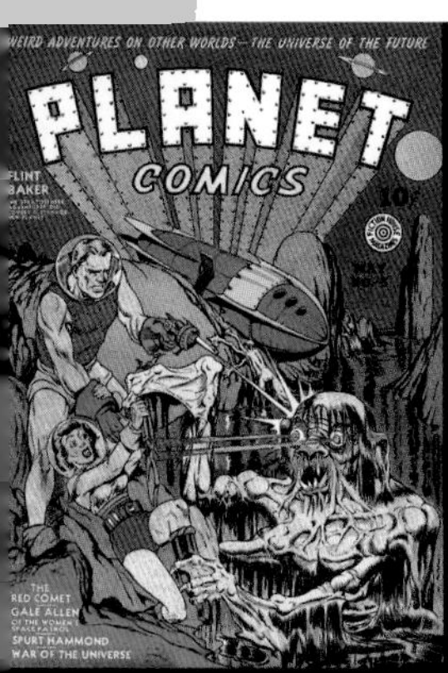
WEIRD ADVENTURES ON OTHER WORLDS – THE UNIVERSE OF THE FUTURE
PLANET
COMICS
10¢
RED COMET
GALE ALLEN
SPURT HAMMOND
WAR OF THE UNIVERSE
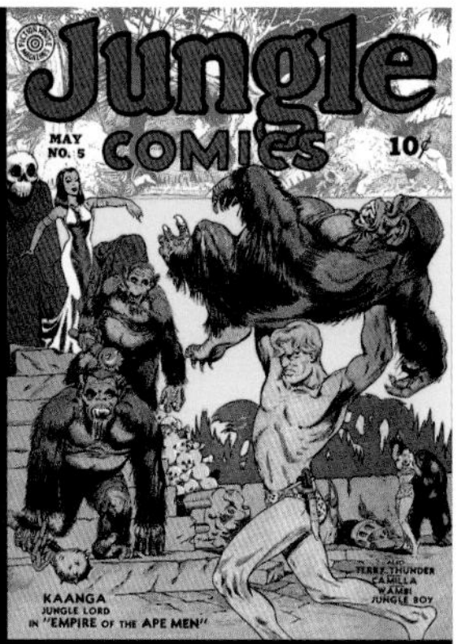
Jungle
COMICS
MAY
No. 5
10¢
KAANGA
JUNGLE LORD
IN "EMPIRE OF THE APE MEN"

PLANET COMICS no.5, May 1940
WILL EISNER

JUNGLE COMICS no.5, May 1940
WILL EISNER

TWO LATE EISNER Fiction House covers done shortly before the break-up of Eisner & Iger, both likely inked by Bob Powell. Eisner's new studio worked exclusively for Quality publisher Busy Arnold, providing art for several titles, including the Eisner-edited *Military Comics*, plus a new weekly syndicated 16-page comic-book-sized color newspaper section featuring Eisner's new creation, the Spirit. The renamed S.M. Iger Studio also contributed to Quality titles, though Arnold would eventually create an in-house staff of artists, writers, and letterers. Iger stayed busy, retaining the Fiction House account (until that company ended its comic book operations in late 1953), as well as packaging books for emerging publishers.

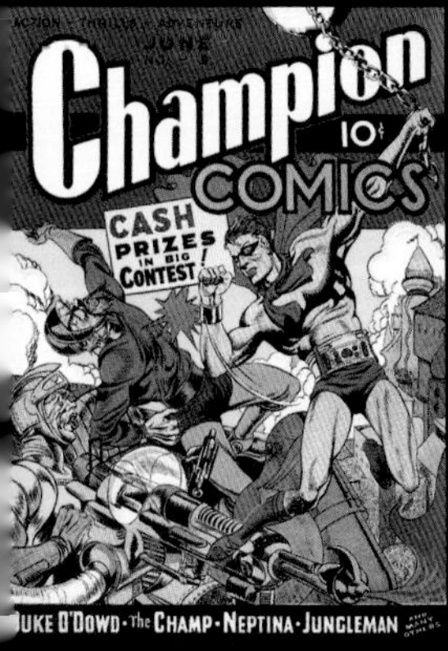
Champion
10¢
COMICS
CASH PRIZES IN BIG CONTEST!
DUKE O'DOWD · The CHAMP · NEPTINA · JUNGLEMAN
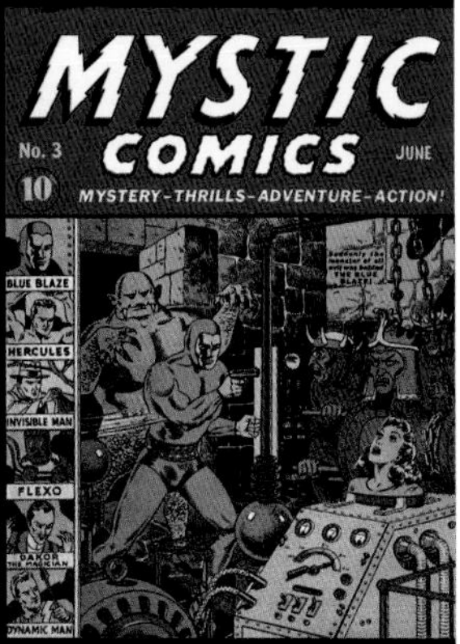
MYSTIC
COMICS
No. 3
JUNE
10¢
MYSTERY – THRILLS – ADVENTURE – ACTION!
BLUE BLAZE
HERCULES
INVISIBLE MAN
FLEXO
DAKOR
DYNAMIC MAN

CHAMPION COMICS no.8, June 1940
ATTRIBUTED TO JOE SIMON

MYSTIC COMICS no.3, June 1940
ALEX SCHOMBURG

ARTIST JACK KIRBY met Joe Simon during Simon's editing tenure at Fox. Impressed by Simon's profligate freelancing, Kirby suggested they work together, and Simon readily agreed. They began their partnership on the second issue of Novelty's *Blue Bolt* (July 1940), though their first collaboration in print arguably appeared a month earlier on the cover of *Champion Comics* 8. On separate occasions Simon has stated both that it was his work alone and a "Simon & Kirby studio" job.

LIKE THE COVER of *Daring Mystery* 2 shown earlier, this one, for the third issue of Timely's *Mystic Comics*, is prototypical Schomburg. Again we find cloaked villains, prominent machinery, and a woman about to have something horrible done to her head.

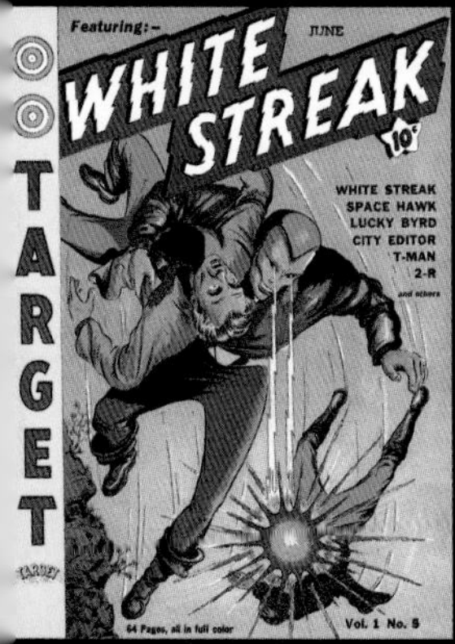
Featuring:–
JUNE
WHITE STREAK
10¢
WHITE STREAK
SPACE HAWK
LUCKY BYRD
CITY EDITOR
T-MAN
2-R
TARGET
Vol. 1 No. 5
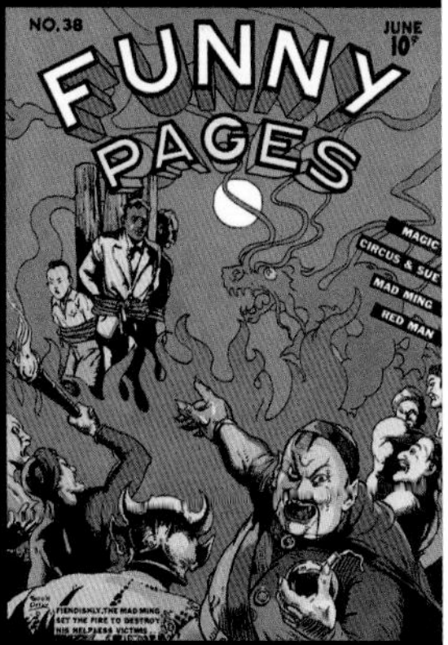
NO. 38
JUNE
10¢
FUNNY
PAGES
MAGIC
CIRCUS & SUE
MAD MING
RED MAN

TARGET COMICS v.1 n.5, June 1940
BILL EVERETT

FUNNY PAGES no.38, June 1940
HAROLD DELAY

CARL BURGOS' creation White Streak (also known as Manowar) routinely used his power of eye-shooting electronic rays to electrocute his adversaries. Burgos' style was a bit rough to merit a cover assignment, so Lloyd Jacquet chose wonder boy Bill Everett for this one.

BACK AT JOE HARDIE'S Centaur Publications, Cook and Mahon's original title *Funny Pages* was still chugging along. Jacquet continued to supply the art, only now through his Funnies, Inc. packaging service. Classically trained illustrators such as Harold DeLay – who created this cover starring his Mad Ming – helped retain the exotic flavor of those early Cook and Mahon "picture books." This may have been a deliberate decision on Jacquet's part, who after all was there at the start.

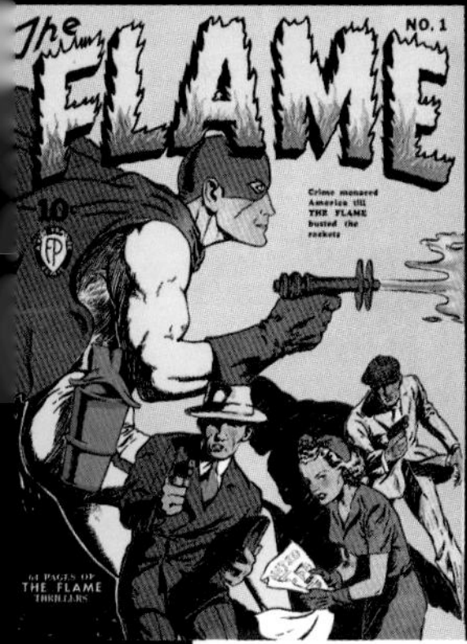
The
FLAME
NO. 1
10¢
64 PAGES OF
THE FLAME
THRILLERS
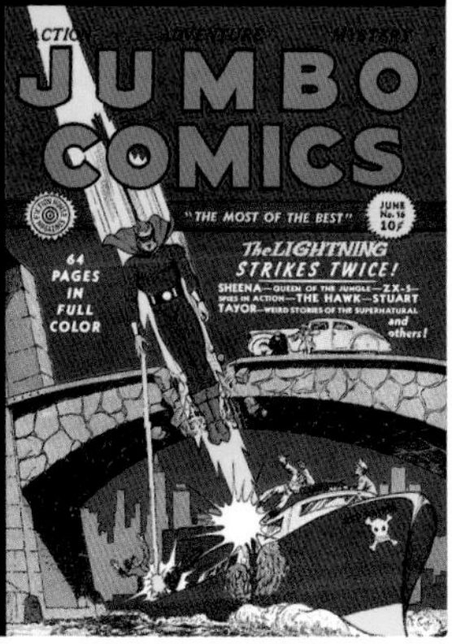
JUMBO
COMICS
"THE MOST OF THE BEST"
64 PAGES IN FULL COLOR
The LIGHTNING STRIKES TWICE!
and others!

THE FLAME no.2, Summer 1940
EDD ASHE

JUMBO COMICS no.16, June 1940
BOB POWELL

PUBLISHERS REALIZED they could repackage stories from their anthology books into quarterly titles devoted to a single character (though readers eventually caught on to this chicanery and insisted on brand new stories). *The Flame* contained *Wonderworld* and *Mystery Men* reprints.

FOR JUMBO COMICS 16, Bob Powell contributed his second and final Lightning cover, with the hero making another effective diagonal entrance. The electrically charged hero never reached higher than second-tier status before being permanently shelved. From here on in, every *Jumbo* cover featured Sheena Queen of the Jungle, a bankable property and Jerry Iger's favorite character.

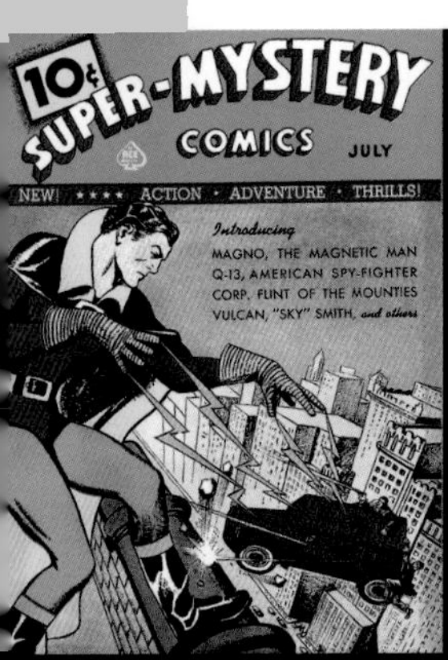
10¢
SUPER-MYSTERY
COMICS
JULY
NEW! ★★★★ ACTION · ADVENTURE · THRILLS!
Introducing
MAGNO, THE MAGNETIC MAN
Q-13, AMERICAN SPY-FIGHTER
CORP. FLINT OF THE MOUNTIES
VULCAN, "SKY" SMITH, and others

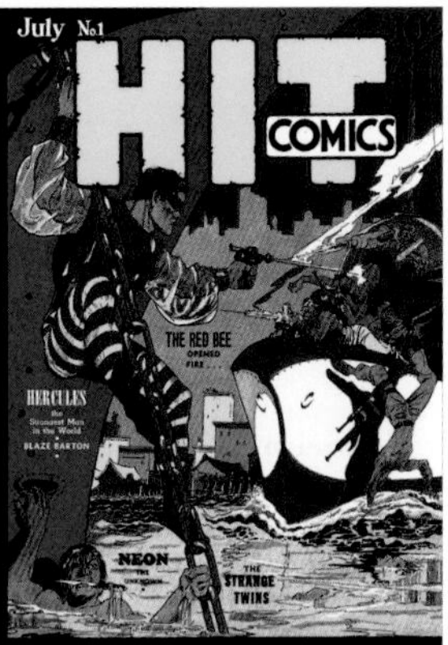
July No1
HIT
COMICS
THE RED BEE
HERCULES
NEON
THE STRANGE TWINS

SUPER-MYSTERY COMICS v.1 n.1, July 1940
ATTRIBUTED TO HARRY LUCEY

HIT COMICS no.1, July 1940
WILL EISNER AND LOU FINE

ACE MAGAZINES had over a dozen pulps on the newsstand when it tested the comic book waters with two 1940 titles, *Sure-Fire Comics* and *Super-Mystery Comics*. The star of the latter was Magno the Magnetic Man, who used his power of magnetism to hurl himself and metal objects though space. Harry Lucey, Magno's first artist, is best known today for his two decades of stylish and expressive work on the *Archie* comic book series.

THE FIRST ISSUE of Quality's *Hit Comics* commenced with the best of the late Eisner/Fine covers. The early *Hits* mixed Iger shop art with Eisner's studio, though gradually Iger took over – aside from Lou Fine's upcoming run of dazzling solo covers.

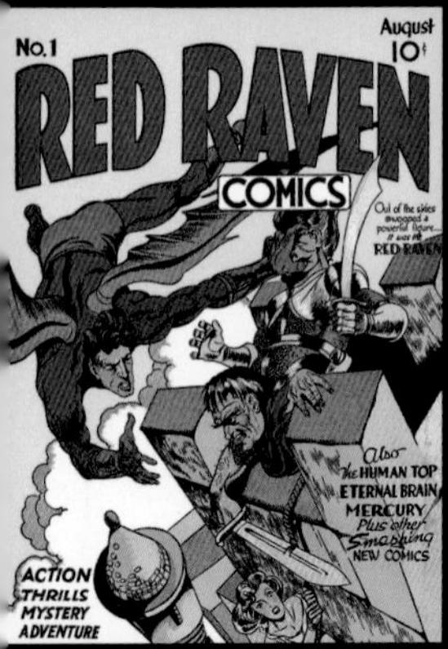
No.1
August
10¢
RED RAVEN
COMICS
Also
The HUMAN TOP
ETERNAL BRAIN
MERCURY
NEW COMICS
ACTION
THRILLS
MYSTERY
ADVENTURE

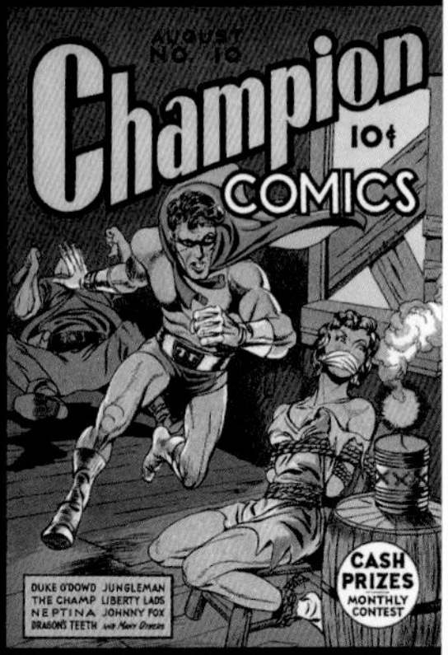
AUGUST
No. 10
Champion
10¢
COMICS
CASH
PRIZES
MONTHLY
CONTEST

RED RAVEN COMICS no.1, August 1940
JACK KIRBY AND JOE SIMON

CHAMPION COMICS no.10, August 1940
JACK KIRBY

RED RAVEN, the first Timely character to debut in his own title, never made it to a second issue. To showcase Carl Burgos' more provocative hero, the title continued as *The Human Torch*. Joe Simon began freelance editing at Timely with this book, as he concluded his short tenure at Fox. With Jack Kirby now at his side, there was no stopping him.

INITIALLY RELEASED by Worth Publishing, *Champion Comics* was renamed *Champ* with issue 11, then eventually sold off to Harvey, where it died after its 25th issue. Jack Kirby's first solo cover appeared on *Champion* 10, featuring the short-panted shirtless Duke O'Dowd. Compared with Simon's bold strokes, Kirby's inks were practically delicate, indicative of his great influence, Lou Fine.

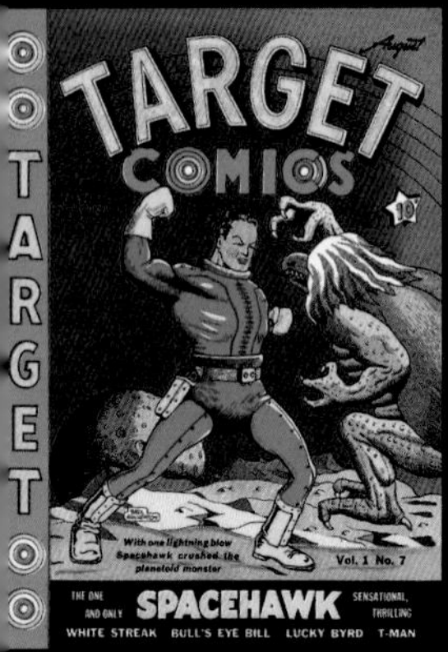
August
TARGET
COMICS
TARGET
Vol. 1 No. 7
SPACEHAWK
WHITE STREAK BULL'S EYE BILL LUCKY BYRD T-MAN

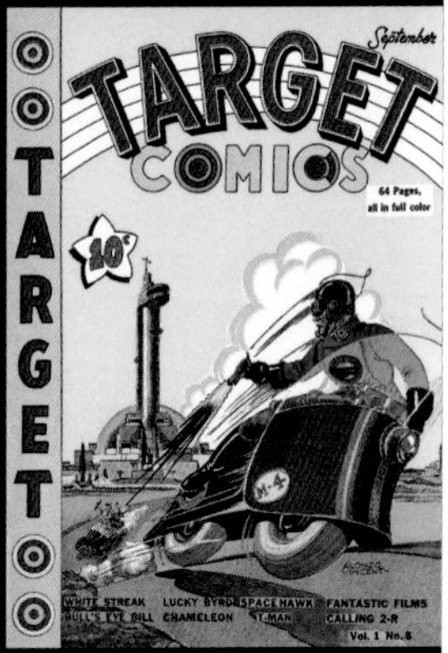
September
TARGET
COMICS
64 Pages,
all in full color
10¢
TARGET
Vol. 1 No. 8

TARGET COMICS v.1 n.7, August 1940
BASIL WOLVERTON

TARGET COMICS v.1 n.8, September 1940
ALONZO VINCENT

ANOTHER LLOYD JACQUET discovery, Basil Wolverton hailed from the Pacific Northwest. In 1938 he mailed art samples to Jacquet, who hired him to do science fiction stories for *Amazing Man Comics* and *Amazing Mystery Funnies*. After Funnies Inc. had won the Novelty account in 1940, Wolverton introduced his somber space hero Spacehawk in the fifth issue of *Target Comics*.

ALONZO VINCENT'S *Calling 2-R* was one of the more imaginative Golden Age features. It centered around the futuristic force-field-encased village of Boyville, inspired by the real-life center for homeless young males, Boys Town. Its leader is benevolent scientist the Skipper, shown here defending his "mecca" from infiltrators.

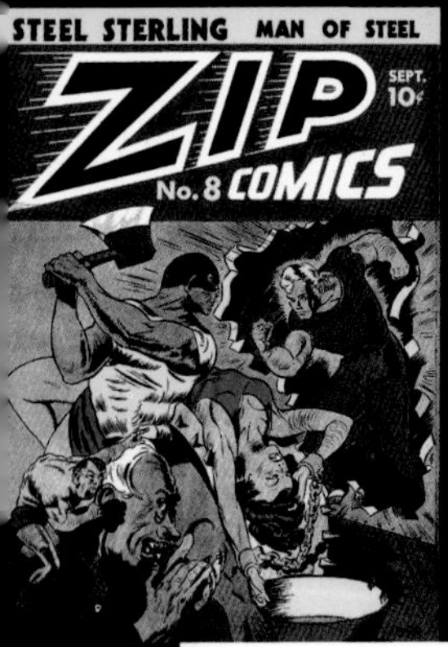
STEEL STERLING MAN OF STEEL
ZIP
SEPT.
10¢
No. 8 COMICS

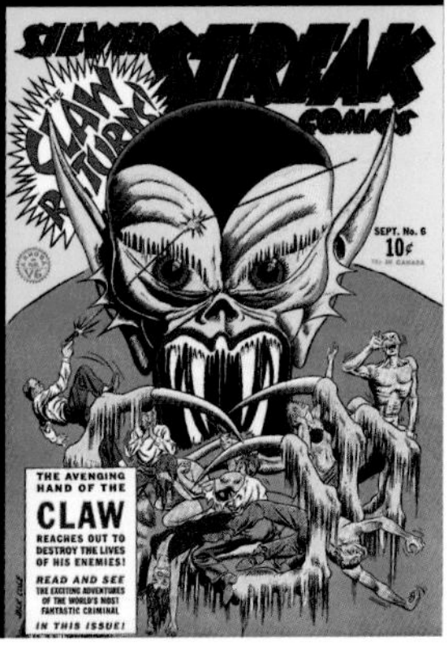
SILVER STREAK
COMICS
SEPT. No. 6
10¢
THE AVENGING
HAND OF THE
CLAW
REACHES OUT TO
DESTROY THE LIVES
OF HIS ENEMIES!
READ AND SEE
IN THIS ISSUE!

ZIP COMICS no.8, September 1940
CHARLES BIRO

SILVER STREAK COMICS no.6, September 1940
JACK COLE

ONE OF THE GREAT comic book raconteurs, Charles Biro got started in comic books in 1936 as a "big-foot" cartoonist for the Harry Chesler studio. Biro moved to superhero work at MLJ's *Zip Comics*, contributing covers and stories starring his "man of steel" Steel Sterling. Biro would soon settle in at Lev Gleason Publications, where he became a big fish in a small pond.

SILVER STREAK COMICS began slightly off kilter by featuring as its star Jack Cole's supernatural villain, the Claw. Cole was a major presence in the title's first year, regularly turning in at least two stories, with the rest of the book filled by Funnies, Inc. In issue 7 Cole is even listed as editor in the book's yearly Statement of Ownership.

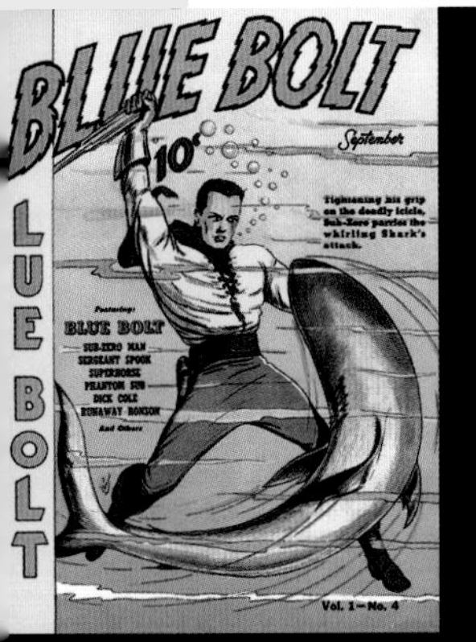
BLUE BOLT
September
10¢
BLUE BOLT
Vol. 1—No. 4
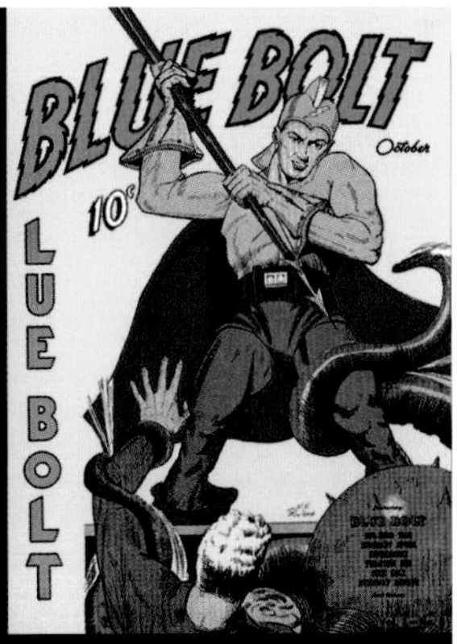
BLUE BOLT
October
10¢
BLUE BOLT

BLUE BOLT v.1 n.4, September 1940
Bill Everett

BLUE BOLT v.1 n.5, October 1940
W.E. Rowland

BILL EVERETT had an affinity for water. He often based his characters (most famously Sub-Mariner) in or around it, giving his art an evocative added texture. Water is also crucial to the plots of Venusian superhero Sub-Zero, endowed with the power of shooting a freezing ray from his hands. Sub-Zero was created by Eisner & Iger alumnus Larry Antonette (now at Funnies, Inc.), though Everett did one memorable story, as well as this cover.

ARTIST WILLIAM E. ROWLAND was a charter member of Funnies, Inc.; he worked primarily on Centaur, Novelty, and Prize titles. Although a capable draftsman, Rowland's story continuities were stilted and unimaginative, and he left the field in 1943.

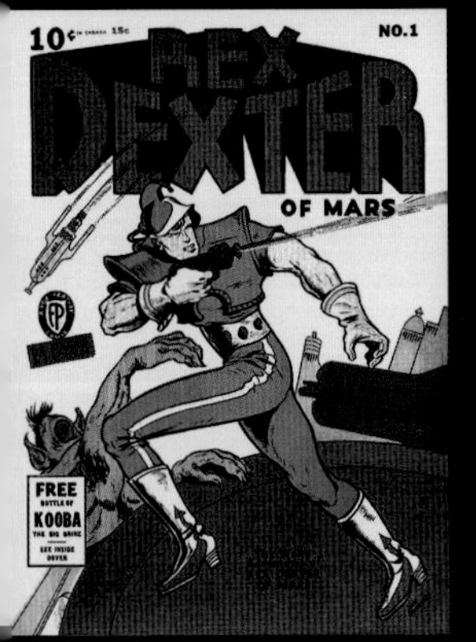
10¢
NO.1
REX DEXTER
OF MARS
FREE
KOOBA
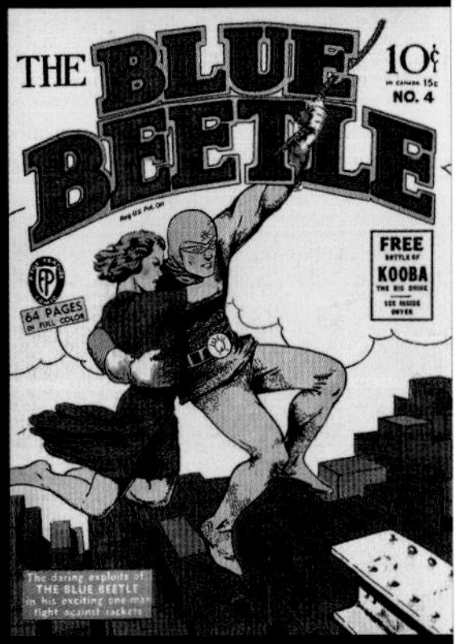
THE BLUE BEETLE
10¢
NO. 4
FREE
KOOBA
64 PAGES

REX DEXTER OF MARS no.1, Fall 1940
Dick Briefer

THE BLUE BEETLE no.4, Fall 1940
Edd Ashe

TWO CHARACTER-DRIVEN Fox reprint titles hit the stands in the Fall of 1940, one past its prime, the other a proven winner. Artist/writer Dick Briefer provided the cover for the book devoted to his creation, Rex Dexter Of Mars, though it wasn't successful enough to merit a second issue. Briefer would abandon superheroes altogether, move to Prize and concentrate on redefining Frankenstein.

THE BLUE BEETLE was hands down the most popular Fox title, lasting 60 issues until becoming a casualty to the public's preference for more believable themes as the 1940s drew to a close. One of Edd Ashe's most iconic covers graced its fourth issue.

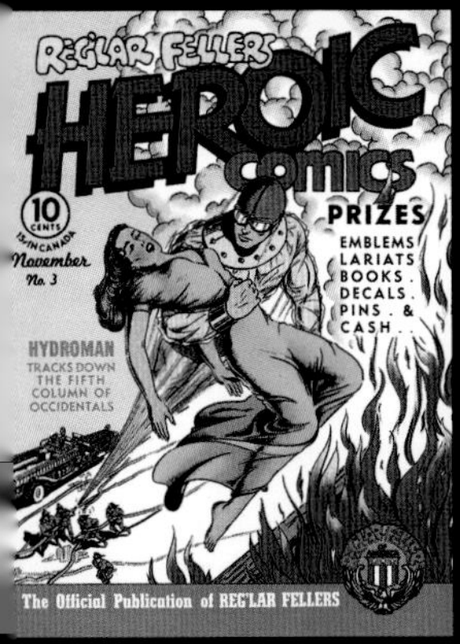
REG'LAR FELLERS
HEROIC
comics
10 CENTS
November
No. 3
PRIZES
EMBLEMS
LARIATS
BOOKS
DECALS
PINS &
CASH
HYDROMAN
TRACKS DOWN
THE FIFTH
COLUMN OF
OCCIDENTALS
The Official Publication of REG'LAR FELLERS
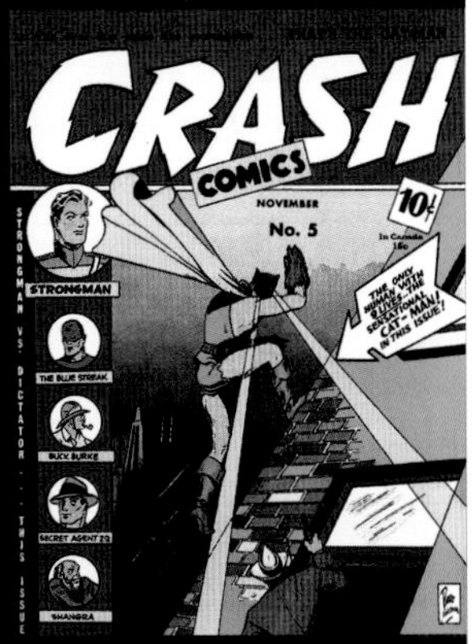
CRASH
COMICS
NOVEMBER
No. 5
10¢
STRONGMAN

REG'LAR FELLERS HEROIC COMICS no.3, Nov. 1940
Bill Everett

CRASH COMICS no.5, November 1940
Bert Whitman

ANOTHER WATER-BASED Bill Everett character, Hydroman made a splash in the first issue of Eastern's *Reg'lar Fellers Heroic Comics*. In his origin story, a chemist discovers a serum that gives his friend Bob Blake the power to turn into a geyser at will. The chemist also invents *translite*, a cellophane-like fabric impervious to bullets. Donning helmet, goggles, neck bracelet, boots, and a body wrapped in translite, Hydroman sported one of the era's more elaborate costumes.

PUBLISHED BY Frank Temerson's Tem Publications, *Crash Comics* lasted just five issues. It remains notable for running Jack Kirby's early science fiction series, *Solar Legion*, and for introducing the Cat-Man in its fourth issue.

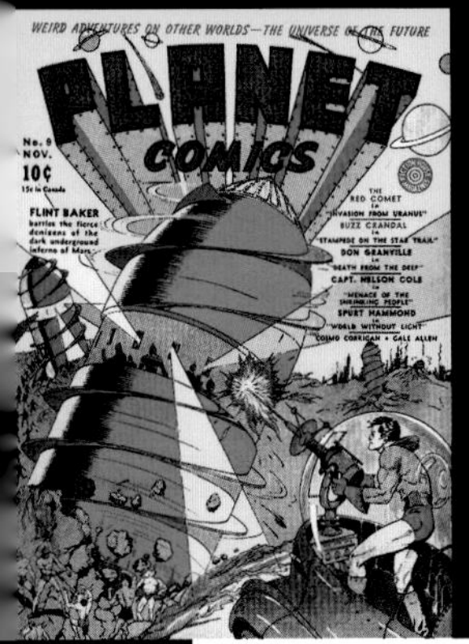
WEIRD ADVENTURES ON OTHER WORLDS—THE UNIVERSE OF THE FUTURE
PLANET
COMICS
No. 9
NOV.
10¢
FLINT BAKER
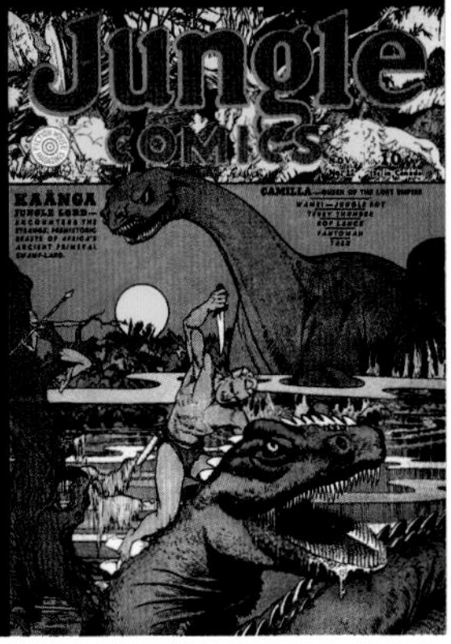
Jungle
COMICS
KAANGA

PLANET COMICS no. 9, November 1940
Nick Viscardi

JUNGLE COMICS no.11, November 1940
Dan Zolnerowich

FOLLOWING EISNER'S departure many of his protégés remained at the Iger studio, where they continued to work on Fiction House titles. Nick Viscardi (later shortened to Cardy) was eventually summoned by Eisner to draw the *Spirit* section back-up feature, *Lady Luck*, as well as contribute to the Quality line.

ANOTHER TALENTED Eisner disciple, Dan Zolnerowich became Fiction House's main cover artist from mid-1941 until mid-1943, staying faithful to the template set forth by Eisner: dramatic compositions, evocative settings, dynamic figure drawings, and sumptuous inking – with a little sex always welcome.

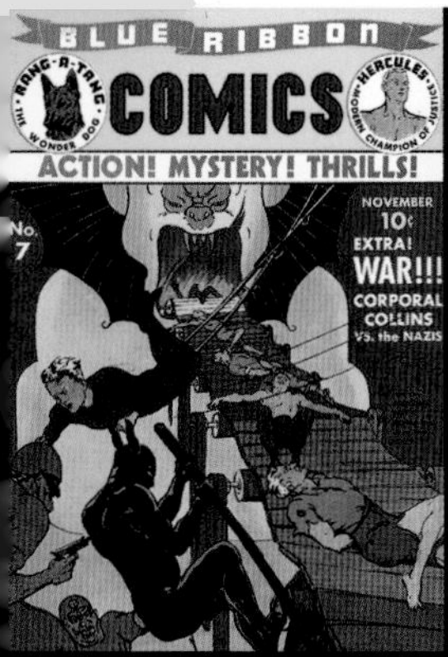
BLUE RIBBON
COMICS
RANG-A-TANG THE WONDER DOG
HERCULES MODERN CHAMPION OF JUSTICE
ACTION! MYSTERY! THRILLS!
No. 7
NOVEMBER
10¢
EXTRA!
WAR!!!
CORPORAL COLLINS Vs. the NAZIS

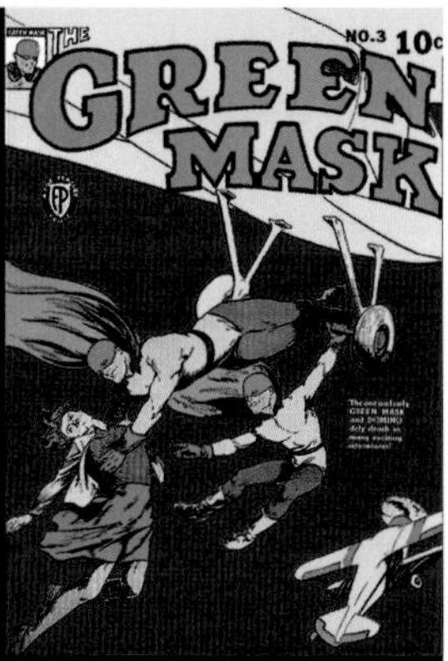
THE
GREEN MASK
NO.3 10¢

BLUE RIBBON COMICS no.7, November 1940
Ed Smalle

THE GREEN MASK no.3, Winter 1940
Edd Ashe

ARTIST ED SMALLE got started at the Chesler factory, submitting work for MLJ's *Top-Notch* and *Blue Ribbon Comics.* For the latter he drew Rang-a-Tang the Wonder Dog, who's pictured on two of Smalle's three *Blue Ribbon* covers. The third, the only cover featuring MLJ hero the Fox, presents this hellish situation.

IN EARLY 1940 Edd Ashe succeeded Joe Simon as principal Fox cover artist. The 32-year old son of realist painter Edmund Marion Ashe was well trained, with a sure grasp of anatomy and composition. He worked prolifically into the 1960s as a cartoonist and illustrator, and finished his career as a respected art instructor.

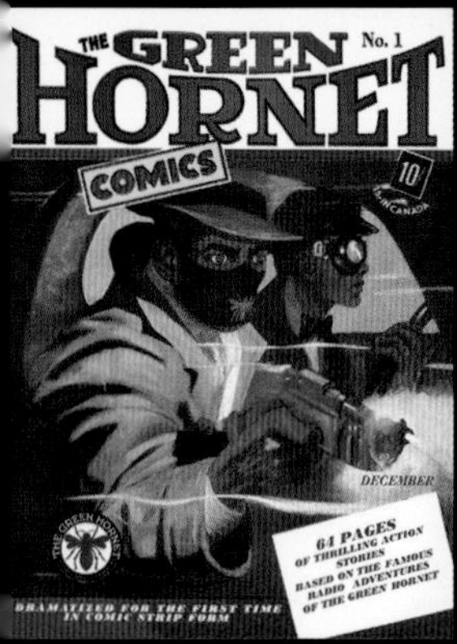
THE GREEN HORNET
No. 1
COMICS
10¢
DECEMBER
64 PAGES OF THRILLING ACTION STORIES BASED ON THE FAMOUS RADIO ADVENTURES OF THE GREEN HORNET
DRAMATIZED FOR THE FIRST TIME IN COMIC STRIP FORM

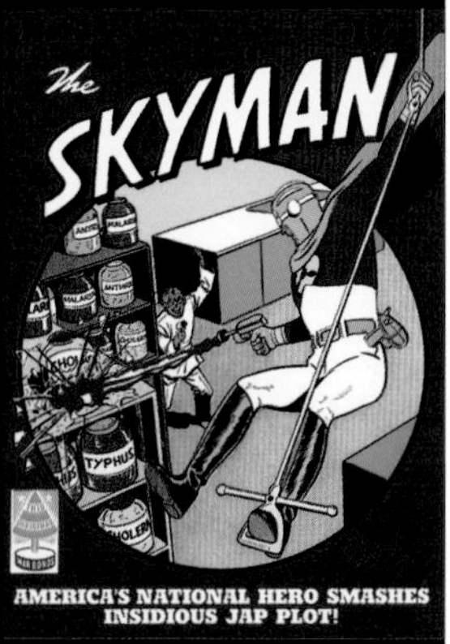
The
SKYMAN
TYPHUS
AMERICA'S NATIONAL HERO SMASHES INSIDIOUS JAP PLOT!

GREEN HORNET COMICS no. 1, December 1940
Unknown

SKYMAN no. 2, 1941
Ogden Whitney

THIS UNUSUAL PAINTED cover to the first issue of *Green Hornet Comics* leads one to suspect the title was initially conceived as a pulp magazine, then switched formats when it became obvious that comic books had overtaken pulps in popularity.

ARTIST OGDEN WHITNEY learned his craft at DC, his stories appearing in 1939-40 issues of *Adventure Comics.* When editor Vin Sullivan left DC to start his own publishing house, Columbia Comics Corporation, in partnership with the McNaught Syndicate, he assigned Whitney and writer Gardner Fox to do Skyman, the flagship hero of its single regular title, *Big Shot Comics.* The acrobatic aviator also appeared four times in his own title.

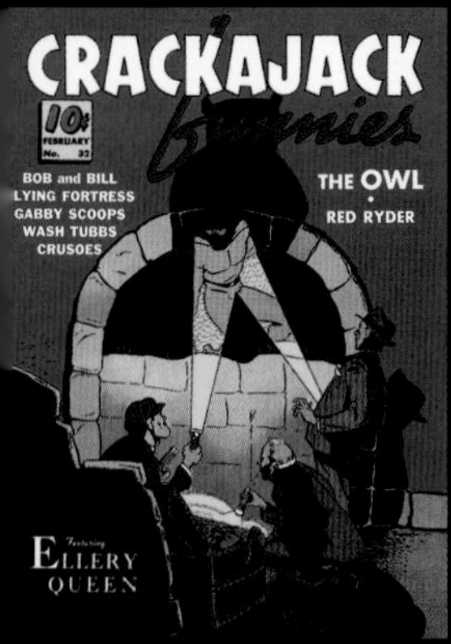
CRACKAJACK
funnies
10¢
FEBRUARY No. 32
BOB and BILL
FLYING FORTRESS
GABBY SCOOPS
WASH TUBBS
CRUSOES
THE OWL
RED RYDER
Featuring ELLERY QUEEN

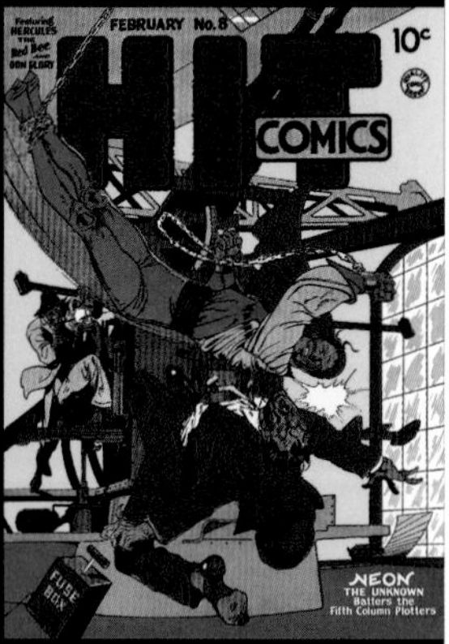
FEBRUARY No. 8
10¢
HIT
COMICS
FUSE BOX
NEON THE UNKNOWN Batters the Fifth Column Plotters

CRACKAJACK FUNNIES no.32, February 1941
Frank Thomas

HIT COMICS no.8, February 1941
Lou Fine

ARTIST/WRITER FRANK THOMAS began at Centaur in 1939. The Eye, his first notable creation, was a large floating eyeball that vexed criminals with incessant scoldings and various eyeball rays until they cracked and turned themselves in. Thomas created the Owl for issue 25 of Dell's *Crackajack Funnies* (July 1940) to update the reprint title's image with an original superhero.

WILL EISNER continued laying out *Hit* covers until Lou Fine assumed the entire job with the fifth issue. Fine took to the task with the enthusiasm of a caged bird set free, delivering a series of Golden Age covers unsurpassed for their combination of action, figure drawing, and draftsmanship.

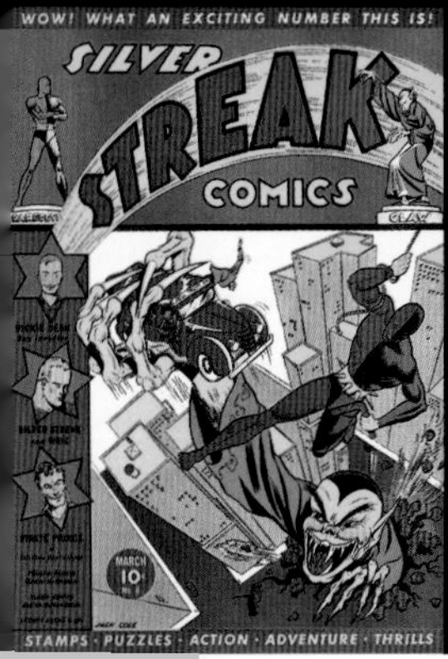
WOW! WHAT AN EXCITING NUMBER THIS IS!
SILVER STREAK
COMICS
MARCH 10¢
STAMPS · PUZZLES · ACTION · ADVENTURE · THRILLS

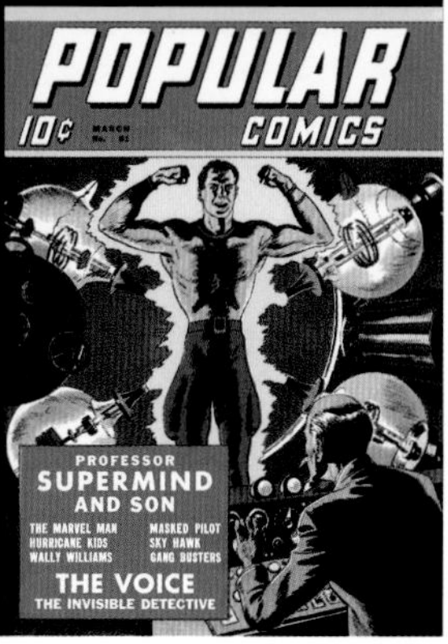
POPULAR
10¢
COMICS
PROFESSOR
SUPERMIND AND SON
THE MARVEL MAN
HURRICANE KIDS
WALLY WILLIAMS
MASKED PILOT
SKY HAWK
GANG BUSTERS
THE VOICE
THE INVISIBLE DETECTIVE

SILVER STREAK COMICS no. 8, March 1941
Jack Cole

POPULAR COMICS no.61, March 1941
Attributed to Maurice Kashuba

JACK COLE'S high-water mark at *Silver Streak* came with the seventh issue, where he contributed 40 pages. Issue 8's cover was his last, with his final story appearing in issue 10. Cole moved to Quality's *Smash Comics* to work on its *Spirit*-inspired feature, *Midnight.* Their generous page rates allowed him to turn in more accomplished work than his MLJ output, which often appeared rushed.

DELL REPRINT title *Popular Comics* introduced two original superheroes to remain competitive. First it presented Martan the Marvel Man in issue 47 (Dec. 1939), then Supermind and Son thirteen issues later (Feb. 1941). Supermind was a scientist whose "ultra frequency apparatus" imbued his son with Superman-like powers.

TWO-FISTED ADVENTURES OF MEN OF ACTION
FIGHT
COMICS
10¢
FEB. No. 11

Jungle
COMICS
10¢
MAY
KAANGA—
JUNGLE LORD
VALLEY OF THE KILLER-BIRDS

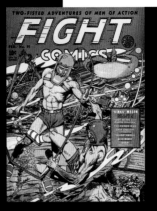

FIGHT COMICS no.11, February 1941
Dan Zolnerowich

JUNGLE COMICS no.17, May 1941
John Celardo

HERE'S ANOTHER PAIR of Fiction House covers that continue the Eisner tradition. Eisner was listed as art director into 1941, though he had moved to Quality a year earlier, at which time the Fiction House titles became solely an Iger Studios package. The offbeat underwater scene was Zolnerowich's second cover for *Fight Comics*.

ARTIST JOHN CELARDO turned in this dark ballet for *Jungle Comics* just before Zolnerowich took over and started his two-year cover string. At Eisner & Iger's since the late 1930s, Celardo stayed with Iger until the early 1950s. He then worked at Standard as one of Alex Toth's primary inkers, before landing the *Tarzan* syndicated daily strip in 1954, holding on to that plum assignment for a decade.

No. 5
SPRING ISSUE
BATMAN
10¢

ALL BRAND NEW FEATURES
THE HUMAN TORCH
10¢
also
THE SUB-MARINER
No. 3
40 ACTION-PACKED PAGES OF HUMAN TORCH and TORO

BATMAN no.5, Spring 1941
Bob Kane

THE HUMAN TORCH no.3, Spring 1941
Alex Schomburg

WHILE NEVER ACCUSED of being a great artist, Bob Kane did have some training under his belt and was capable of creating imaginative images, as this *Batman* 5 cover attests. Batman's missing chest emblem might strike some as a major slip-up, but things were looser in those days.

THE HUMAN TORCH was the most ubiquitous Timely hero of the Golden Age, appearing as cover hero on his own quarterly title as well as the monthly *Marvel Mystery Comics*, and sharing the stage with Captain America and Sub-Mariner on *All-Select* and *All-Winners*. Equally ubiquitous was Alex Schomburg, responsible for practically every cover.

No. 22
MAY
10¢
AMAZING-MAN
COMICS

TEN TERRIFIC BREATHTAKING STORIES!
SILVER STREAK
COMICS
JUNE No. 11
Featuring THE NEW SENSATION CAPTAIN BATTLE in "GREAT PERIL"
SILVER STREAK
DICKIE DEAN
PRESTO MARTIN
CLOUD CURTIS
Does Daredevil get The Claw at last?
HIGH ADVENTURE TO HOLD YOU SPELLBOUND

AMAZING-MAN COMICS no.22, May 1941
Paul Gustavson

SILVER STREAK COMICS no.11, June 1941
Don Rico

TWO CONCURRENT covers contrast Centaur's traditional illustrative approach with *Silver Streak*'s more modern use of graphic design. In the *Amazing Man* 22 cover, the logo is relegated to its own box, separated from the image; for *Silver Streak* 11, the logo and graphics are incorporated into a poster-like unified design, giving it added punch on the newsstand. Artist Don Rico began as a staff artist at the Jack Binder studio, which by this time was packaging the title.

DESPITE THEIR early innovations, Centaur never fully changed with the times and seemed like an anachronistic leftover from the 1930s. This coupled with weak distribution led to their demise in late 1941.

JUNE
No. 12
10¢
HIT
COMICS
ANOTHER SENSATIONAL ADVENTURE OF HERCULES
IN THIS ISSUE
THE RED BEE · DON GLORY

DAREDEVIL
BATTLES
HITLER

HIT COMICS no.12, June 1941
Lou Fine

DAREDEVIL BATTLES HITLER no.1, July 1941
Charles Biro and Bob Wood

LOU FINE again demonstrates his mastery of line, anatomy, and composition, using deft foreshortening to create a sophisticated depth of field. Though Fine's comic book career lasted barely five years (he left in 1944) his refined style and artistry set the Golden Age standard.

PUBLISHER LEV GLEASON hired Funnies, Inc. to assemble *Daredevil Battles Hitler*, which consisted of *Silver Streak* characters battling guest villains Adolf Hitler, Josef Goebbels and Hermann Goering. Cover artists Charles Biro and Bob Wood took over the editing with the second issue, and the title continued with great success as *Daredevil Comics*.

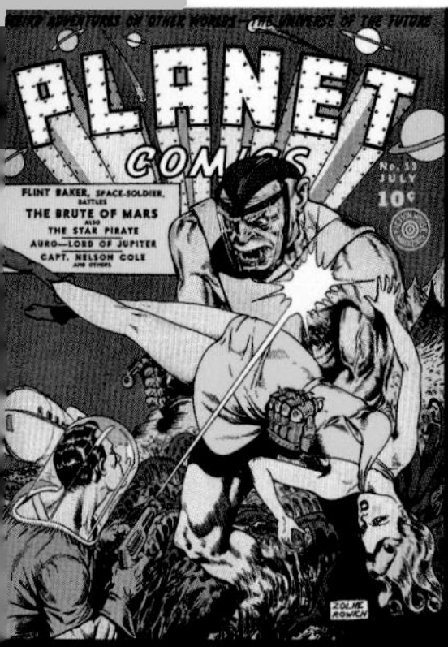
PLANET
COMICS
No. 13
JULY
10¢
FLINT BAKER, SPACE-SOLDIER, BATTLES
THE BRUTE OF MARS
THE STAR PIRATE
AURO—LORD OF JUPITER
CAPT. NELSON COLE

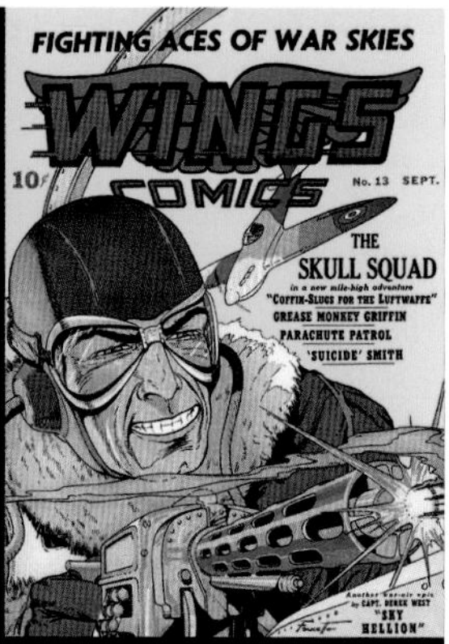
FIGHTING ACES OF WAR SKIES
WINGS
COMICS
10¢
No. 13 SEPT.
THE
SKULL SQUAD
GREASE MONKEY GRIFFIN
PARACHUTE PATROL
'SUICIDE' SMITH

PLANET COMICS no.13, July 1941

DAN ZOLNEROWICH

WINGS COMICS no.13, September 1941

GENE FAWCETTE

DAN ZOLNEROWICH streamlined his Fiction House cover compositions as time went on, simplifying his backgrounds and concentrating on two or three large figures, then drawing the hell out of them. Unusual color palettes also helped his covers stand out on the newsstand.

EISNER & IGER alumnus Gene Fawcette stuck with Jerry Iger after Will Eisner left in early 1940. He succeeded Eisner as art director on several Fiction House titles, while continuing to draw stories and a series of *Wings* covers. In the mid-1950s, Fawcette provided illustrations for the science fiction magazines *Amazing Stories* and *Famous Fantastic Mysteries*.

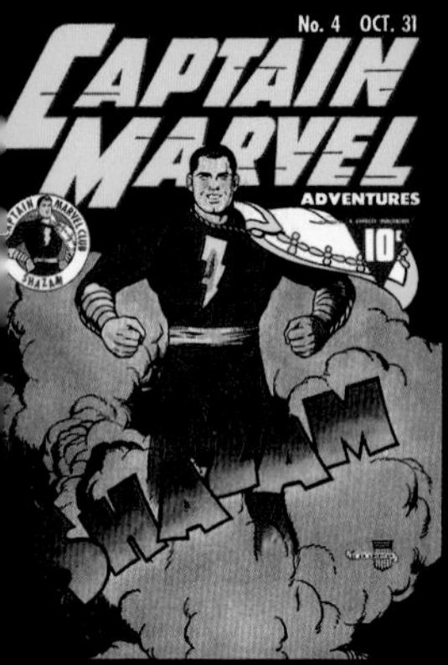
No. 4 OCT. 31
CAPTAIN
MARVEL
ADVENTURES
10¢

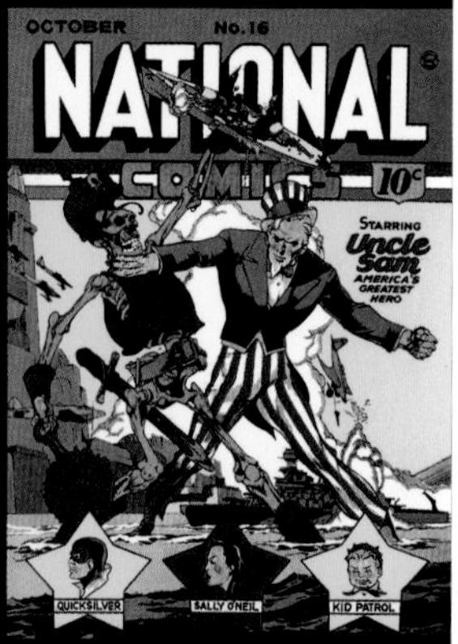
OCTOBER
No. 16
NATIONAL
COMICS
10¢
STARRING
Uncle
Sam
AMERICA'S
GREATEST
HERO
QUICKSILVER
SALLY O'NEIL
KID PATROL

CAPTAIN MARVEL ADVENTURES no.4, Oct. 1941

ATTRIBUTED TO C.C. BECK

NATIONAL COMICS no.16, October 1941

LOU FINE AND REED CRANDALL

OFTEN ATTRIBUTED to regular *Captain Marvel* artist C.C. Beck, this cover's realism, sense of drama, prominent smoke, and the character's looking directly at the reader lead one to suspect Mac Raboy, who had just started doing Fawcett covers.

ONE OF Lou Fine's most talented disciples, Reed Crandall entered comics via the Eisner & Iger studio. Working prolifically on Quality features Doll Man, the Ray, and Blackhawk, he quickly matured into one of the top draftsmen in the field, remaining in comics for over 30 years. After inking several of Fine's late covers, Crandall joined Al Bryant, Jack Cole, Gill Fox, and Alex Kotsky as the primary Quality cover artists.

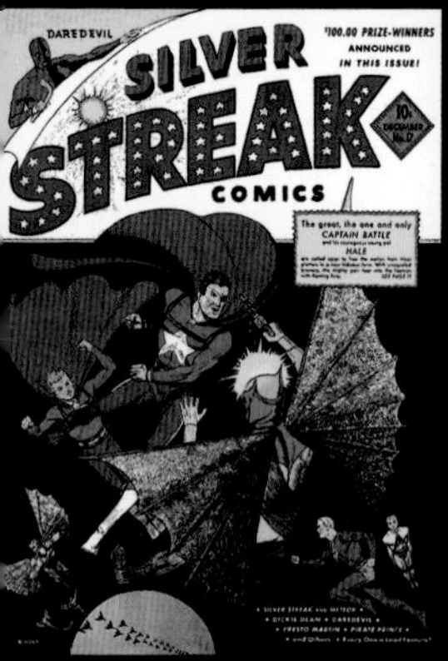
DAREDEVIL
$100.00 PRIZE-WINNERS
ANNOUNCED
IN THIS ISSUE!
SILVER
STREAK
COMICS
10¢

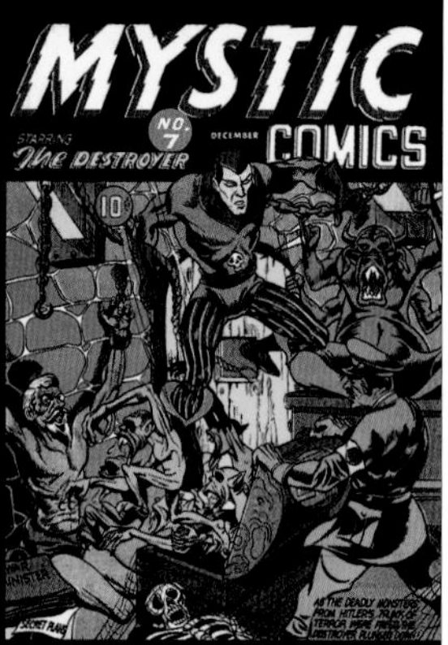
MYSTIC
No. 7
COMICS
The DESTROYER
10¢

SILVER STREAK COMICS no.17, December 1941

JACK BINDER

MYSTIC COMICS no.7, December 1941

JACK KIRBY AND JOE SIMON

BY THE ELEVENTH issue of *Silver Streak*, Jack Binder's patriotic hero Captain Battle (who showed up two months after Simon & Kirby's Captain America) had taken over as cover star. Binder was hired as Chesler art director in early 1937, and he started his own Manhattan shop in late 1940. His brother, writer Otto Binder, followed him into the field and wound up creating over 3,000 comic book scripts.

BY MID-1941 Joe Simon and Jack Kirby had become head honchos at Timely, promoted to editor and art director, respectively. Earlier in the year they hit pay dirt with the first issue of *Captain America* (March 1941), the most influential comic book franchise since Superman, securing Timely's position as a major player.

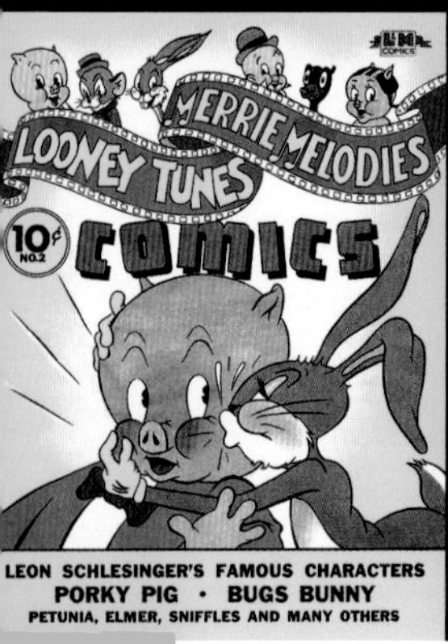
MERRIE MELODIES
LOONEY TUNES
10¢
No.2
COMICS
LEON SCHLESINGER'S FAMOUS CHARACTERS
PORKY PIG • BUGS BUNNY
PETUNIA, ELMER, SNIFFLES AND MANY OTHERS

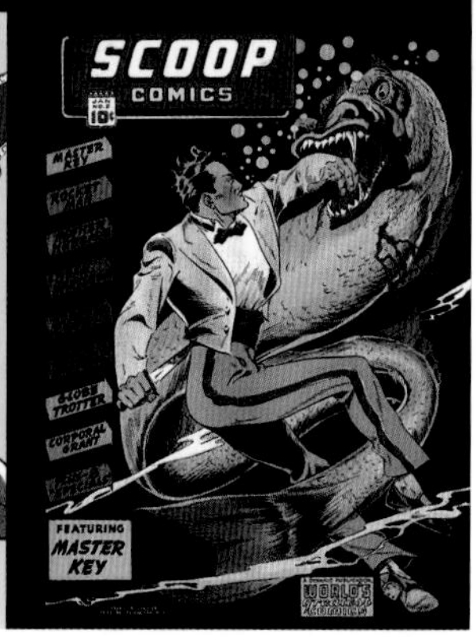
SCOOP
COMICS
10¢
FEATURING
MASTER
KEY

LOONEY TUNES & MERRIE MELODIES no.2, Dec. 1941

UNKNOWN

SCOOP COMICS no.2, January 1942

CHARLES SULTAN

AFTER DISNEY halted its animated shorts in 1939 to concentrate on feature films, producer Leon Schlesinger filled the void with his irreverent *Looney Tunes* and *Merrie Melodies*. As the cartoons reached peak popularity during the early 1940s, a comic book spin-off seemed like a sound investment. It was, lasting over 20 years for Dell.

CHARLES SULTAN started with Eisner & Iger in 1939, then moved a year later to Chesler, quickly rising to art director. Like many Chesler artists of the 1940s, his style was heavily influenced by Lou Fine, this cover being a prime example.

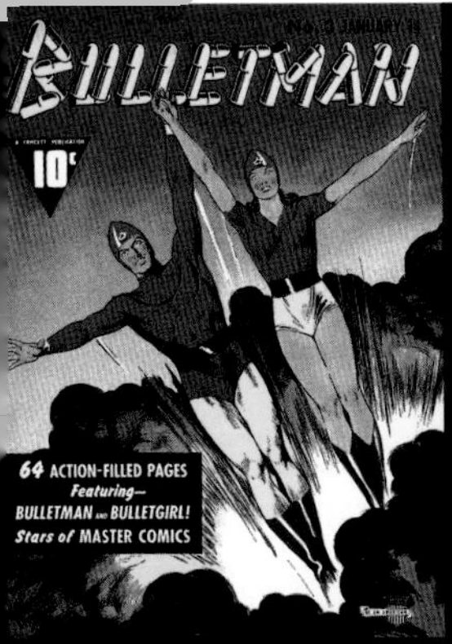
BULLETMAN
10¢
64 ACTION-FILLED PAGES
Featuring—
BULLETMAN AND BULLETGIRL!
Stars of MASTER COMICS
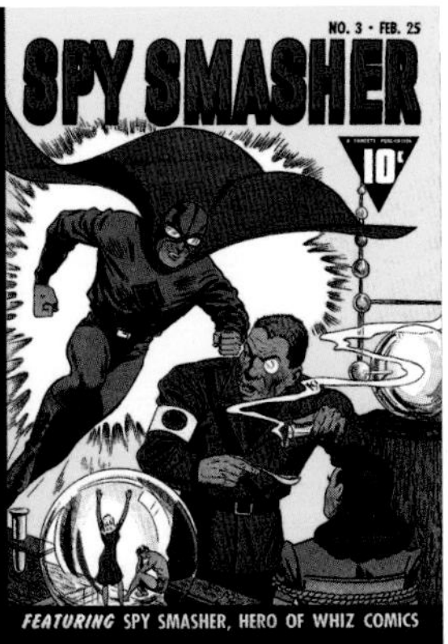
NO. 3 • FEB. 25
SPY SMASHER
10¢
FEATURING SPY SMASHER, HERO OF WHIZ COMICS

BULLETMAN no.3, January 1942
Mac Raboy

SPY SMASHER no.3, February 1942
Jack Binder studio

BULLETMAN MADE his debut in Fawcett's *Nickel Comics*, a 36-page five-cent biweekly that failed after eight issues. In mid-1941 the character was given its own full-length 64-page title, packaged by the Jack Binder studio (which also filled books for Lev Gleason, Prize, and Street and Smith). Mac Raboy managed to contribute one cover, the best remembered of the run.

ANOTHER JACK BINDER package for Fawcett, *Spy Smasher* tapped into the growing concern over foreign espionage infiltrating the U.S. government. Nazis had been regularly depicted as villains in comic books since the early 1940s, almost two years before America and Germany officially declared war.

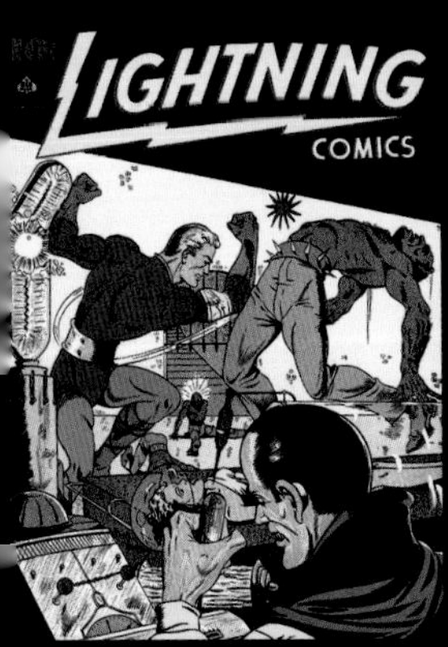
LIGHTNING
COMICS
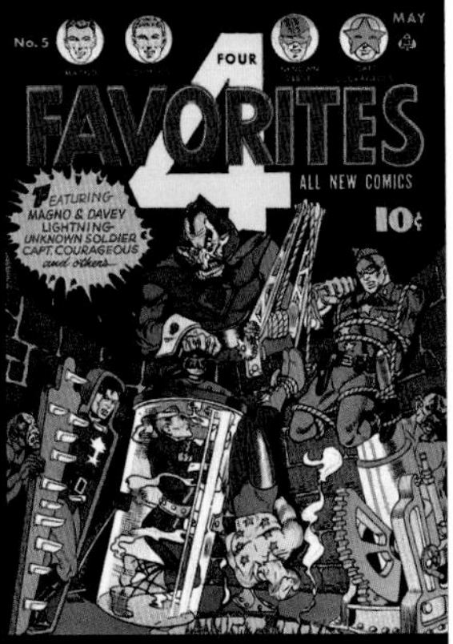
No. 5
MAY
FOUR
FAVORITES
ALL NEW COMICS
10¢
FEATURING MAGNO & DAVEY LIGHTNING UNKNOWN SOLDIER CAPT. COURAGEOUS and others

LIGHTNING COMICS no.11, February 1942
Jim Mooney

FOUR FAVORITES no.5, May 1942
Dave Berg

ACE SUPERHERO Lightning emerged in the first issue of *Sure-Fire Comics*, the title changing to *Lightning Comics* with issue 4 (Dec. 1940). Its peak period came three issues later with the arrival of artist Jim Mooney, whose clean unadorned style presaged the superhero work of the 1960s resurgence. After freelancing at Quality and Timely, Mooney moved to DC in 1946 and stayed for over 20 years.

TAKING ITS CUE from DC's *All-Star* and Timely's *All-Winners*, Ace combined four of its heroes (Captain Courageous, Lightning, Magno, and the Unknown Soldier) into a single title, *Four Favorites*. Artist Dave Berg, who did the classic torture-chamber cover, is best known for his four decades of humorous work on "The Lighter Side" series for *Mad*.

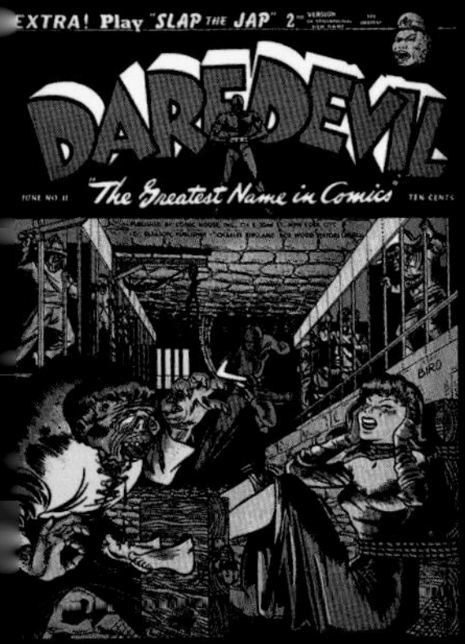
EXTRA! Play "SLAP THE JAP" 2
DAREDEVIL
The Greatest Name in Comics
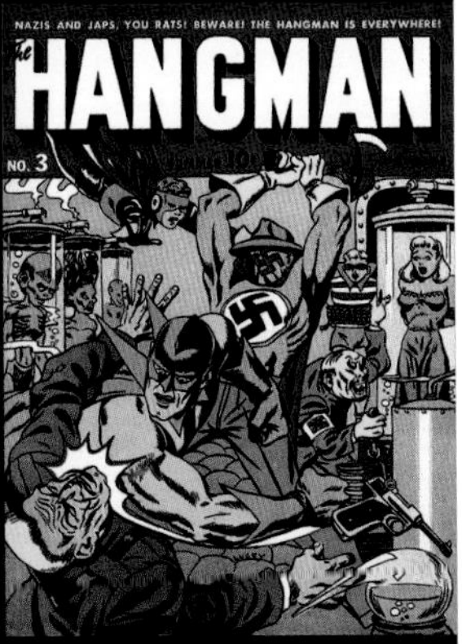
NAZIS AND JAPS, YOU RATS! BEWARE! THE HANGMAN IS EVERYWHERE!
the HANGMAN
NO. 3

DAREDEVIL no.11, June 1942
Charles Biro

HANGMAN COMICS no.3, Summer 1942
Harry Lucey

CHARLES BIRO had no problem dragging readers to a debased level if it resulted in sales. Here a hunchback attempts to tickle a woman to madness, presumably so he can then incarcerate her with the rest of his victims (a rat crawling up his eye socket ices the cake). Biro's antics turned out to be sound marketing – *Daredevil* was one of the few titles that weathered the superhero die-off in the late 1940s.

HARRY LUCEY kicks off our World War II propaganda covers with this raucous *Hangman* offering. Introduced in MLJ's *Pep Comics* 17 (July 1941), the Hangman chose to become a crime fighter after witnessing the death of his older brother, the Comet – the first time a company bumped off a failing superhero to make room for a new one.

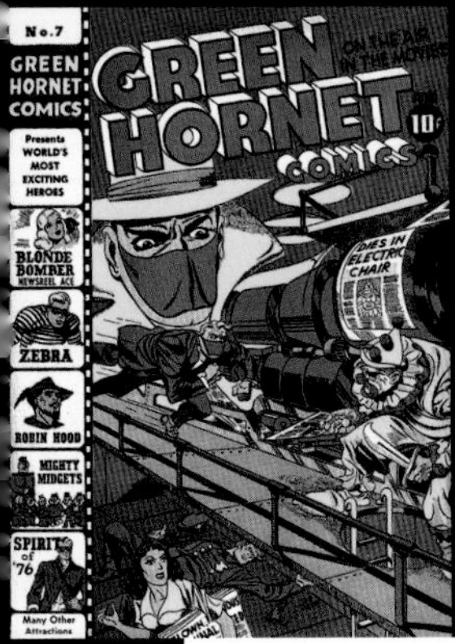
No. 7
GREEN HORNET COMICS
GREEN HORNET COMICS
10¢
Presents WORLD'S MOST EXCITING HEROES
BLONDE BOMBER
ZEBRA
ROBIN HOOD
MIGHTY MIDGETS
SPIRIT of '76
Many Other Attractions
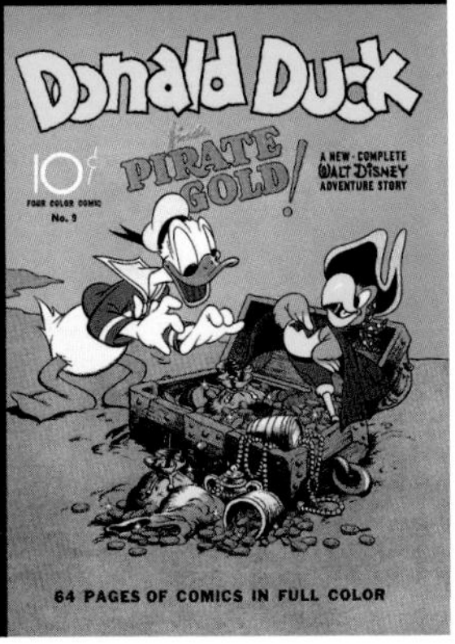
Donald Duck
10¢
FOUR COLOR COMIC No. 9
finds PIRATE GOLD!
A NEW • COMPLETE WALT DISNEY ADVENTURE STORY
64 PAGES OF COMICS IN FULL COLOR

GREEN HORNET COMICS no.7, June 1942
Jack Kirby and Joe Simon

FOUR COLOR no.9, August 1942
Hank Porter

SIMON & KIRBY had known Al Harvey since their days at Fox; when the publisher acquired the rights to three Temerson titles, *Champ*, *Green Hornet*, and *Speed*, S&K agreed to supply covers. But as the team had just negotiated a deal with DC to create new properties, they signed their Harvey covers with an alias, Jon Henri.

HANK PORTER worked from 1935 to 1950 as staff artist for the Walt Disney publicity department. In late 1937 he illustrated the 20-week run of the syndicated Sunday color strip *Snow White and the Seven Dwarfs* as well as *Pinocchio* two years later. This was the first time Donald Duck was featured in *Four Color*, and it introduced the work of the "good" Duck artist, Carl Barks.

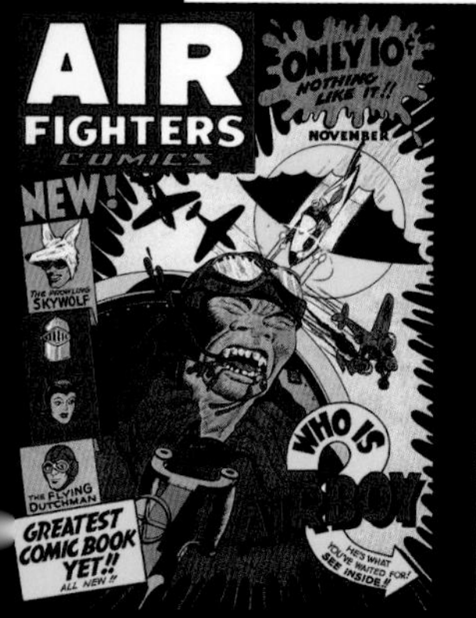
AIR FIGHTERS COMICS
ONLY 10¢ NOTHING LIKE IT!!
NOVEMBER
NEW!
WHO IS AIRBOY
GREATEST COMIC BOOK YET!!
ALL NEW!!
HE'S WHAT YOU'VE WAITED FOR! SEE INSIDE!

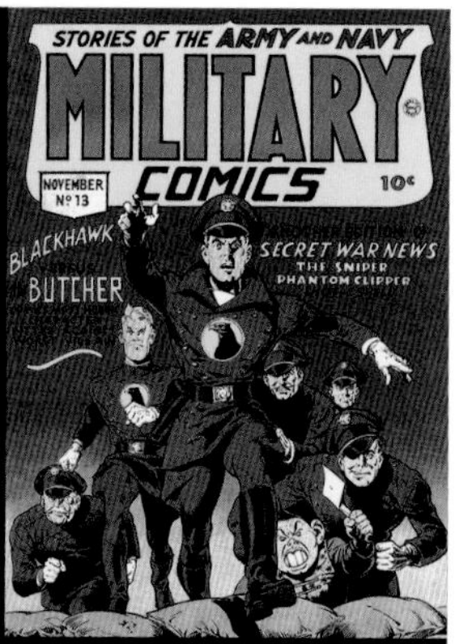
STORIES OF THE ARMY AND NAVY
MILITARY COMICS
NOVEMBER No 13
10¢
BLACKHAWK
BUTCHER
SECRET WAR NEWS
THE SNIPER
PHANTOM CLIPPER

AIR FIGHTERS COMICS v.1 n.2, November 1942
CHARLES BIRO

MILITARY COMICS no.13, November 1942
REED CRANDALL

PACKAGED BY FUNNIES, INC., the first issue of *Air Fighters* seemed like another destined-for-failure Hillman offering; it was in fact shelved after its first issue. But new Hillman editor Ed Cronin enlisted Charles Biro to help revamp the title. It reappeared a year later completely overhauled, modernized by Biro's splashy covers and his kid hero, Airboy, who became so popular that in 1945 the title was changed to *Airboy*. It became Hillman's most successful comic book, lasting over 100 issues.

A RIP-ROARING Reed Crandall cover displays the charging Blackhawk squad in full-chested glory. While Will Eisner was away in the Army producing posters and educational material, the title he created ranked among the best sellers of the war years.

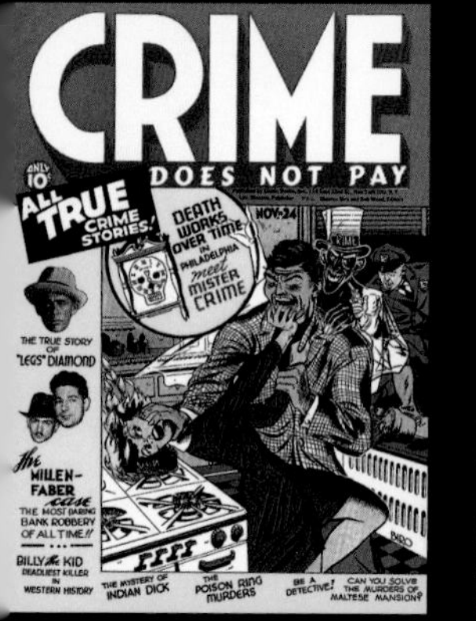
CRIME DOES NOT PAY
ONLY 10¢
ALL TRUE CRIME STORIES!
NOV.-24
DEATH WORKS OVERTIME IN PHILADELPHIA
MEET MISTER CRIME
THE TRUE STORY OF "LEGS" DIAMOND
THE MILLEN-FABER CASE
BILLY THE KID
THE MYSTERY OF INDIAN DICK
THE POISON RING MURDERS
BE A DETECTIVE!

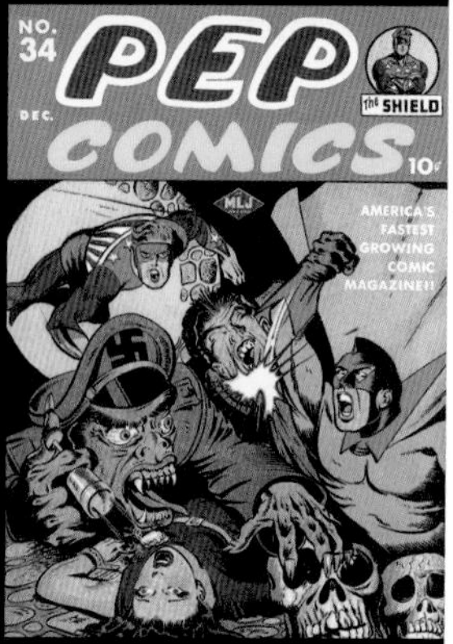
NO. 34
DEC.
PEP COMICS
THE SHIELD
10¢
MLJ
AMERICA'S FASTEST GROWING COMIC MAGAZINE!!

CRIME DOES NOT PAY no.24, November 1942
CHARLES BIRO

PEP COMICS no.34, December 1942
BOB FUJITANI

NEVER ONE to underestimate the power of sensationalism, Charles Biro built a perfect platform for it in *Silver Streak*'s replacement title *Crime Does Not Pay*. Biro's misogynistic cover for the third issue undoubtedly got the thumbs-up from coeditor Bob Wood, a chronic woman abuser convicted in 1958 of beating to death a female acquaintance.

THIS BIZARRE *Pep* cover by Bob Fujitani features the Hangman and arch enemy Swastika, as the Shield recedes into the background. All the MLJ superheroes were living on borrowed time by this point – Archie would capture the *Pep* cover nine issues later. The Shield remained a back-up feature until *Pep* 66 (March 1948), when the teen sensation and his ilk took over the entire MLJ line.

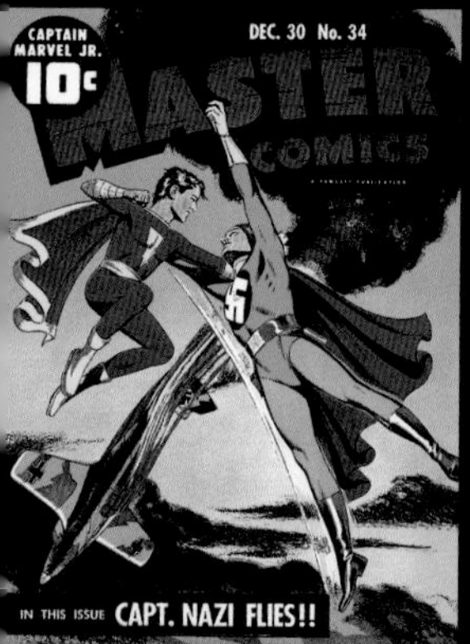
CAPTAIN MARVEL JR.
10¢
DEC. 30 No. 34
MASTER COMICS
IN THIS ISSUE CAPT. NAZI FLIES!!

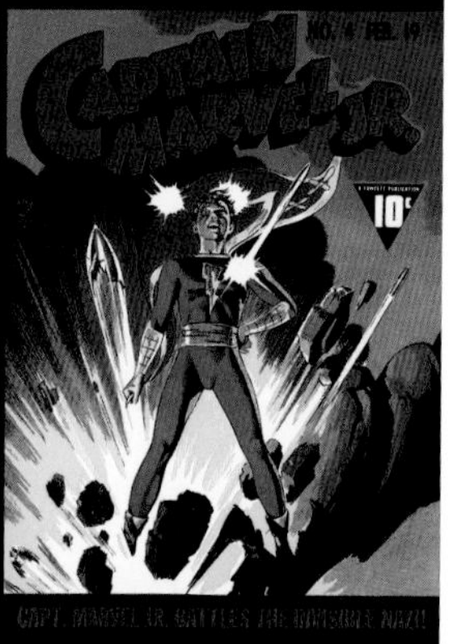
CAPTAIN MARVEL JR.
10¢

MASTER COMICS no. 34, December 1942
MAC RABOY

CAPTAIN MARVEL JR. no.4, February 1943
MAC RABOY

THE CAPTAIN MARVEL titles were the backbone of Fawcett's comics line. *Captain Marvel Adventures* regularly outsold *Superman*, which bugged DC to no end. Even though Captain Marvel was less a Superman clone than a host of other characters, in 1941 DC slapped Fawcett with a copyright infringement suit. After a decade of costly litigation, Fawcett decided to end its comic book operations in 1953.

MAC RABOY SPENT so much time refining his figure drawings that to help him meet deadlines he hired a background artist, Bob Rogers (born Rubin Zubovsky, at the time he went by the name of Ruby Zubof). A major talent in his own right, Rogers, who had earlier worked with Lou Fine, seamlessly adapted his style to Raboy's.

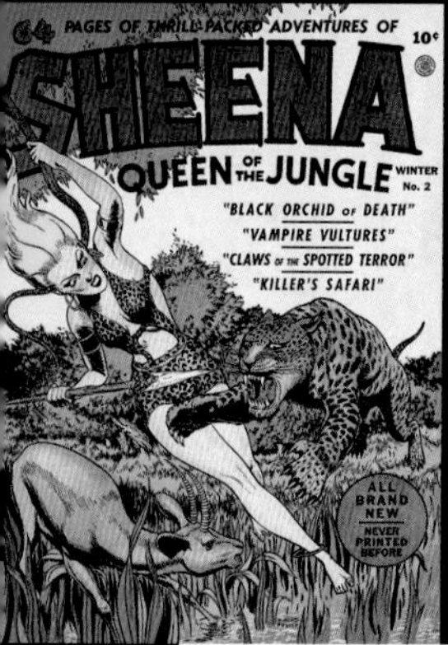
64 PAGES OF THRILL-PACKED ADVENTURES OF
10¢
SHEENA
QUEEN OF THE JUNGLE
WINTER No. 2
"BLACK ORCHID OF DEATH"
"VAMPIRE VULTURES"
"CLAWS OF THE SPOTTED TERROR"
"KILLER'S SAFARI"
ALL BRAND NEW
NEVER PRINTED BEFORE

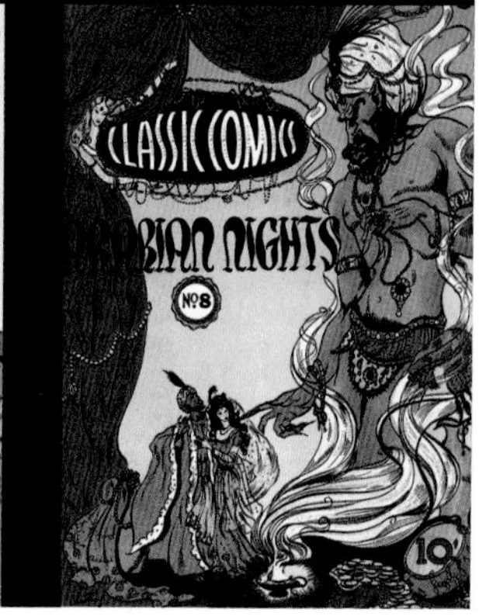
CLASSIC COMICS
ARABIAN NIGHTS
No 8
10¢

SHEENA QUEEN OF THE JUNGLE no.2, Winter 1942
DAN ZOLNEROWICH

CLASSIC COMICS no.8, February 1943
LILLIAN CHESTNEY

THE MOST VALUABLE Iger property, Sheena Queen of the Jungle was given her own quarterly title in early 1942 (she continued as star of *Jumbo Comics*). For the cover of its second issue, Dan Zolnerowich displays his ability to freeze a split second of action.

CLASSIC COMICS was fairly loose about its logo before standardizing it with their ninth issue (Mar. 1943). Here artist Lillian Chestney's logo and title are integral to her cover design. Chestney's entire comics output consisted of two notable *Classic* titles, *Arabian Nights* and *Gulliver's Travels*. She worked primarily as an illustrator, her decorative style gracing many children's books.

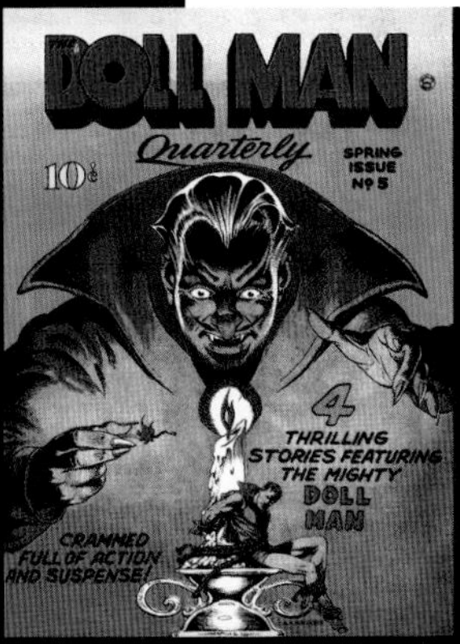
DOLL MAN
Quarterly
10¢
SPRING ISSUE No 5
4 THRILLING STORIES FEATURING THE MIGHTY DOLL MAN
CRAMMED FULL OF ACTION AND SUSPENSE!

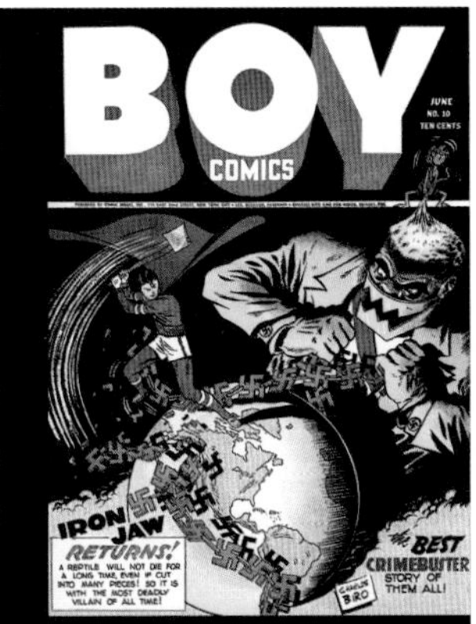
BOY
COMICS
JUNE
IRON JAW RETURNS!
THE BEST CRIMEBUSTER STORY OF THEM ALL!

DOLL MAN QUARTERLY no.5, Spring 1943

Al Bryant

BOY COMICS no.10, June 1943

Charles Biro

ARTIST AL BRYANT entered comic books as soon as he graduated from Brooklyn's Pratt Institute in 1940. He started at Iger's doing work for Fiction House but soon became part of the Quality art staff. Bryant was heavily influenced by Will Eisner, as this *Doll Man* cover shows. An Eisner creation, the hero had the power to shrink to doll size while attaining super strength.

BOY COMICS was another successful Lev Gleason title created and edited by Charles Biro and Bob Wood. Its early issues featured boy hero Crimebuster's travails against Iron Jaw, "executive director of Nazidom's spies and saboteurs in America." For his last appearance in issue 11, Biro did away with his iron jaw to reveal an exposed lower skull, which was disturbing but not nearly as menacing.

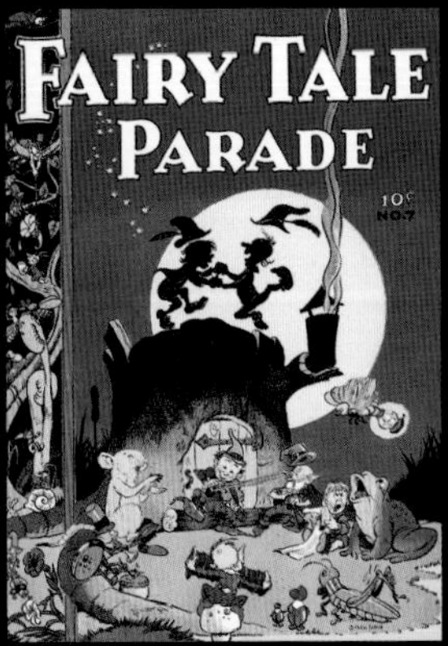
FAIRY TALE
PARADE
10¢
No 7

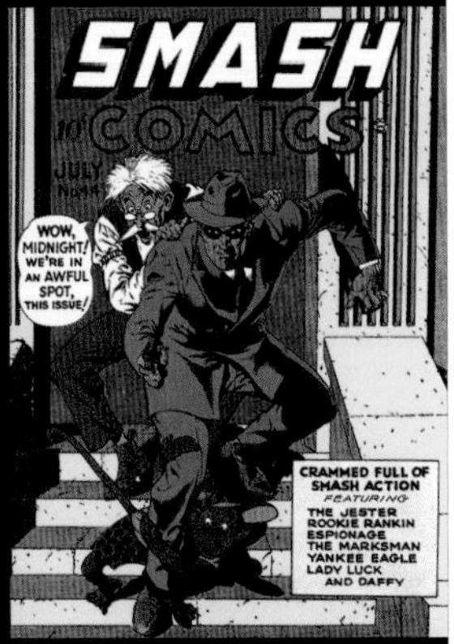
SMASH
COMICS
WOW, MIDNIGHT! WE'RE IN AN AWFUL SPOT, THIS ISSUE!
CRAMMED FULL OF SMASH ACTION FEATURING THE JESTER ROOKIE RANKIN ESPIONAGE THE MARKSMAN YANKEE EAGLE LADY LUCK AND DAFFY

FAIRY TALE PARADE no.7, June-July 1943

Walt Kelly

SMASH COMICS no.44, July 1943

Reed Crandall

IN 1938 WESTERN PUBLISHING, Dell's parent company, hired German expatriate and Broadway stage designer Oskar Lebeck to edit and art direct Dell's comic books. Lebeck's sense of style and culture left an indelible impression on the entire line, and the imprint became the class of the industry. Among Lebeck's discoveries was artist/writer Walt Kelly, for whom he created *Fairy Tale Parade*.

BY THIS TIME Jack Cole had become swamped by Plastic Man, both in *Police Comics* and in the hero's brand new solo title. Midnight remained as cover hero on *Smash Comics*, but Cole's interior art duties were assumed by Paul Gustavson, who considerably loosened up his style to fill the void left by his predecessor.

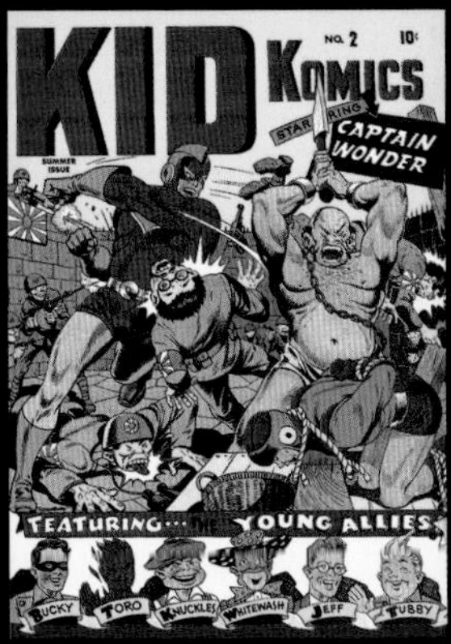
No. 2 10¢
KID KOMICS
CAPTAIN WONDER
TEATURING... YOUNG ALLIES
BUCKY
TORO
KNUCKLES
WHITEWASH
JEFF
TUBBY

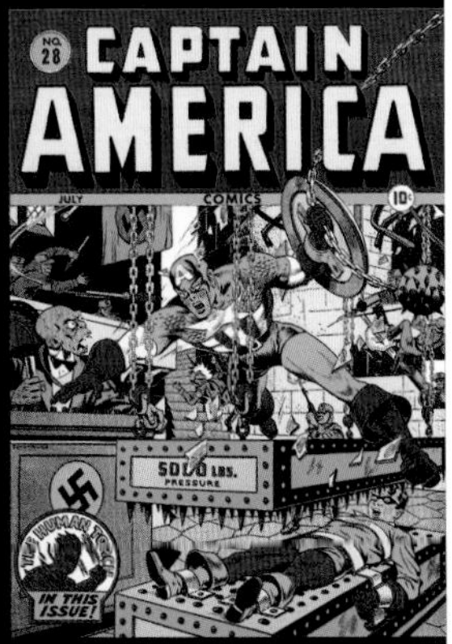
No. 28
CAPTAIN
AMERICA
JULY
COMICS
10¢
5000 LBS. PRESSURE
IN THIS ISSUE!

KID KOMICS no.2, Summer 1943

Alex Schomburg

CAPTAIN AMERICA no.28, July 1943

Alex Schomburg

KID KOMICS showcased a group of young civilian crime fighters occasionally aided by super sidekicks Bucky (Captain America) and Toro (the Human Torch). Simon & Kirby created the team as *Captain America* back-up feature the Sentinels of Liberty. They were renamed the Young Allies when given their own title in mid-1941, just as S&K were leaving Timely for DC, where they continued the concept with their Boy Commandos and Newsboy Legion.

FEELING CHEATED by Timely publisher Martin Goodman, who reneged on a profit-sharing deal, Simon & Kirby abandoned *Captain America* after its tenth issue and signed a contract with DC. Alex Schomburg began as *CA* cover artist with issue 26 (May 1943), doing the bulk of them for the next three years.

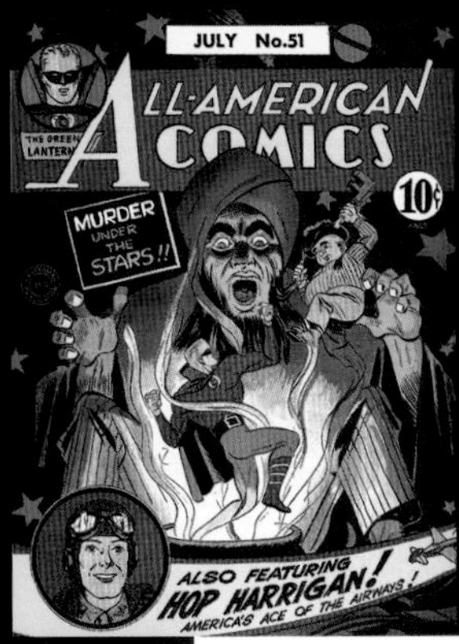
JULY No.51
ALL-AMERICAN
COMICS
10¢
THE GREEN LANTERN
MURDER UNDER THE STARS!!
ALSO FEATURING HOP HARRIGAN!
AMERICA'S ACE OF THE AIRWAYS!

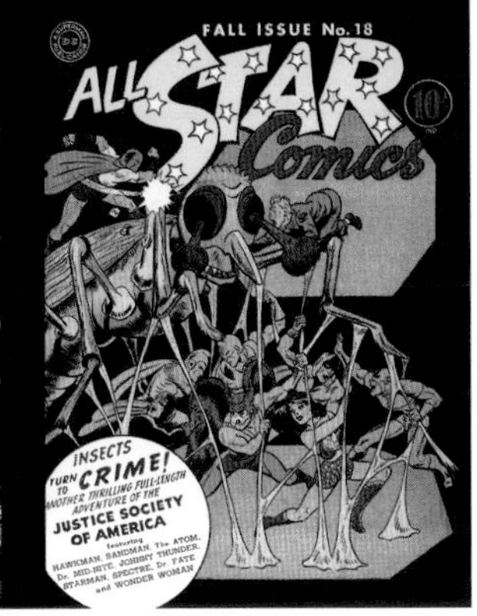
FALL ISSUE No. 18
ALL STAR Comics
10¢
INSECTS TURN TO CRIME!
JUSTICE SOCIETY OF AMERICA

ALL-AMERICAN COMICS no.51, July 1943

Irwin Hasen

ALL-STAR COMICS no.18, Fall 1943

Frank Harry

ALL-AMERICAN COMICS was a subsidiary of DC, run independently by co-owner M.C. Gaines (while working as a salesman at Eastern Printing, Gaines is credited with the idea of marketing the comic book as a ten-cent newsstand periodical instead of a giveaway premium). Many of DC's most popular titles fell under the All-American imprint, including *All-American Comics* (starring Green Lantern), *Flash Comics* (with the Flash and Hawkman), and *Wonder Woman*. *All-Star Comics* introduced the novel concept of combining all of AA's superheroes into a single unified group, the Justice Society of America. Editor Sheldon Mayer, Gaines' right-hand man, was a major force in the company's success.

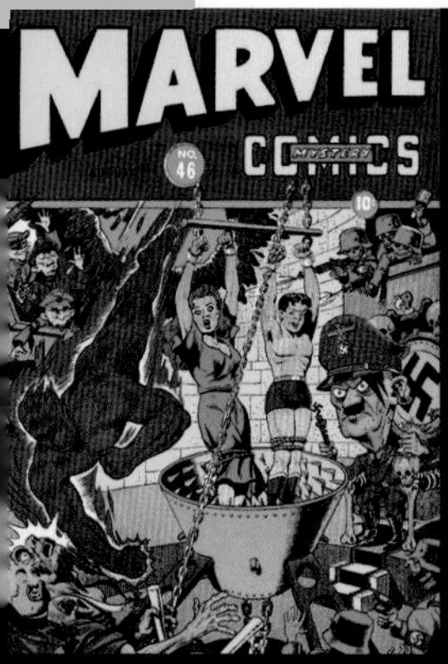
MARVEL
COMICS
NO. 46

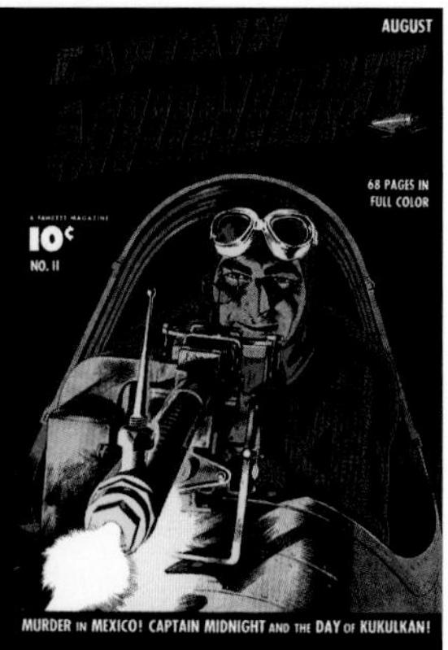
AUGUST
68 PAGES IN FULL COLOR
10¢
NO. 11
MURDER IN MEXICO! CAPTAIN MIDNIGHT AND THE DAY OF KUKULKAN!

MARVEL MYSTERY COMICS no.46, August 1943

Alex Schomburg

CAPTAIN MIDNIGHT no.11, August 1943

Mac Raboy

HERE SCHOMBURG'S caricatures of Germans attain a level of distortion usually reserved for the Japanese. In another of the artist's stock cover situations, torture is mere seconds away, with a uniformed dominant figure (in this case a bloated-headed green Hitler) and his lackeys on hand to observe the grim deed.

AVIATION HERO Captain Midnight began as a radio star in 1938. His first comic book appearance came in the July 1941 issue of Dell's *The Funnies*, continuing for a year until the title changed formats. A year later Fawcett updated the character, giving him his own title, a snazzy red costume, and a variety of gizmos. The book lasted for a solid five years, with Jack Binder's studio packaging the early issues.

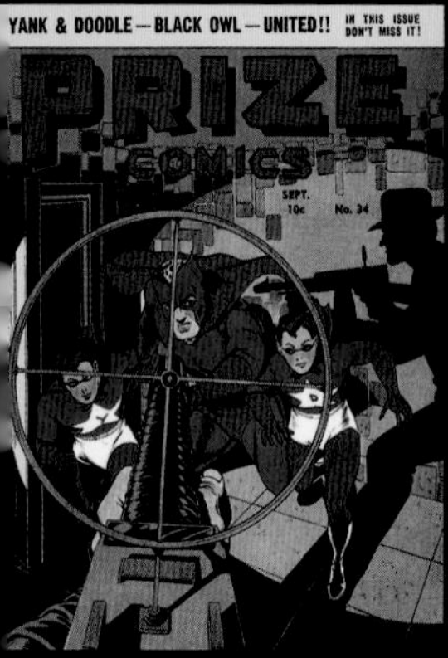
YANK & DOODLE—BLACK OWL—UNITED!! IN THIS ISSUE DON'T MISS IT!
PRIZE
COMICS
SEPT. 10c No. 34

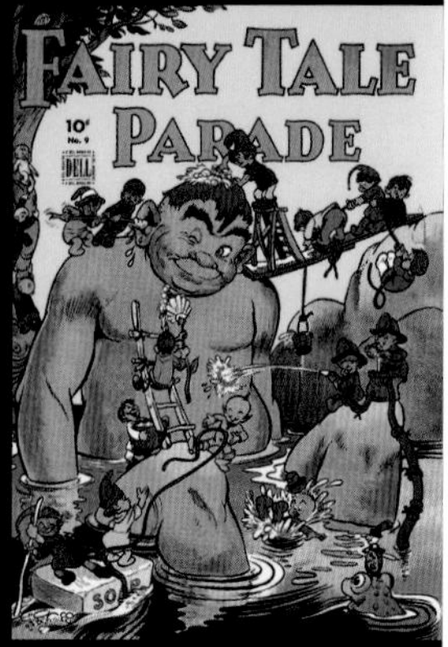
FAIRY TALE
PARADE
10¢
DELL

PRIZE COMICS no.34, September 1943

Jack Binder Studio

FAIRY TALE PARADE no.9, November 1943

Walt Kelly

BY THE SEVENTH issue of *Prize Comics*, Power Nelson was usurped as cover hero, first by Batman knock-off Black Owl, then by "America's Fighting Twins," Yank and Doodle. It seemed only a matter of time before the newer trio combined forces, which they did with this issue. *Prize's* packager Jack Binder had been steadily losing his art staff to the war, and he closed his shop in late 1943. Binder remained in comic books into the early 1950s as a Fawcett artist and as sales agent for the C.C. Beck-Pete Costanza studio.

WALT KELLY'S COVER for the last issue of *Fairy Tale Parade* loses the decorative border of its first eight issues to free up space for a giant, his cleaning crew, and several interested spectators.

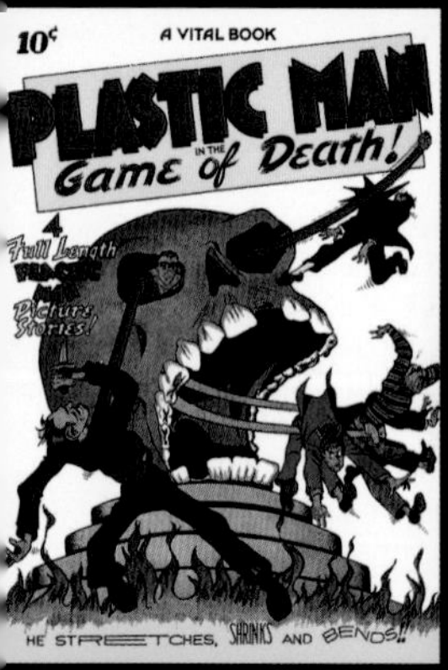
10¢
A VITAL BOOK
PLASTIC MAN
Game of Death!
HE STRETCHES, SHRINKS AND BENDS!

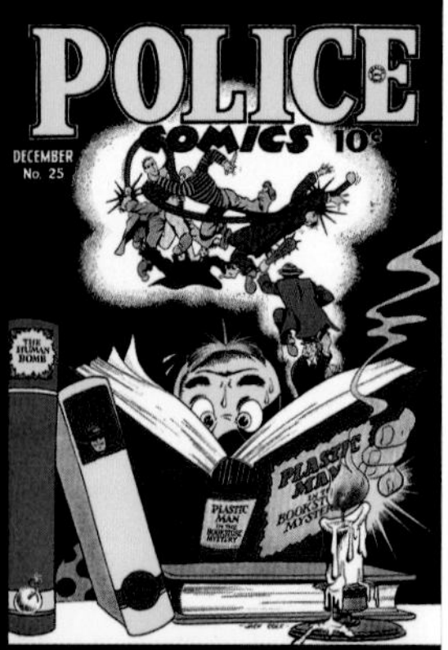
POLICE
COMICS
10¢
DECEMBER
No. 25

PLASTIC MAN no.1, Summer 1943

Jack Cole

POLICE COMICS no.25, December 1943

Jack Cole

IN THE PREMIERE issue of Quality's *Police Comics* (Aug. 1941), Jack Cole at last created a vehicle worthy of his prodigious imagination. He initially pitched his stretchable shape-changing hero to publisher Busy Arnold as the India Rubber Man, but Arnold, who had surer instincts about marketing, suggested Plastic Man. Cole was off and running, creating hundreds of inventive action-packed pages for well over a decade. In these two covers the artist makes respective cases for the graphic punch of simple black, and white, backgrounds. The feverish character immersed in the book on the *Police* cover is Plastic Man's comedic sidekick, Woozy Winks, with Cole giving Quality colleague Will Eisner and his Spirit a shout-out.

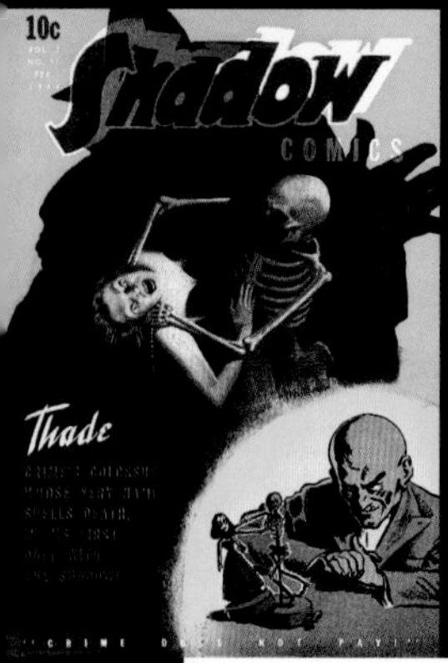
10c
Shadow
COMICS
Thade

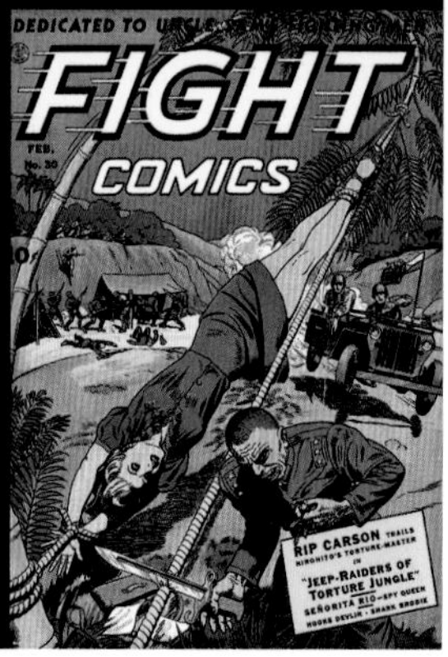
FIGHT
COMICS
FEB.
RIP CARSON
"JEEP-RAIDERS OF TORTURE JUNGLE"

SHADOW COMICS v.3 n.11, February 1944

Vernon Greene

FIGHT COMICS no.30, February 1944

Joe Doolin

THE SHADOW'S most prolific artist, Vernon Greene started illustrating for the pulp in 1940, then drew the syndicated strip until its cancellation in 1942. He had also been doing stories for *Shadow Comics* since its 1940 debut, later sharing covers with the Jack Binder studio. This example of Greene's work is an unnerving mix of cartooning and photographic realism.

ARTIST JOE DOOLIN had been doing covers and illustrations for pulps since 1925. He began drawing comics for Fiction House in 1941 with a fully developed technique at his command, and in 1943 began a five-year run as main cover artist. Here he uses a woman as a human slingshot to command newsstand attention.

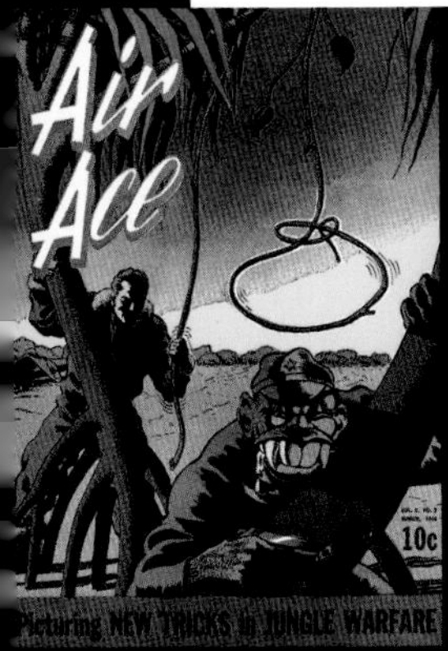
Air Ace
10¢
Picturing NEW TRICKS in JUNGLE WARFARE
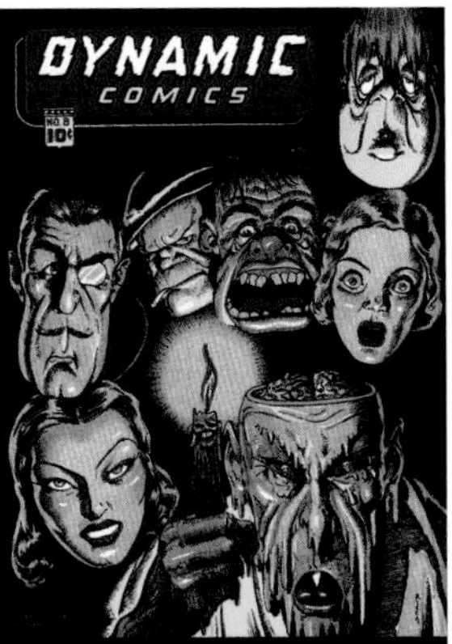
DYNAMIC
COMICS
10¢

AIR ACE v.2 n.2, March 1944
UNKNOWN

DYNAMIC COMICS no.8, March 1944
GUS RICCA

AS THE WAR dragged on, caricatures of the Axis enemies grew ever more hostile, particularly of the Japanese. Artists had an easier time depicting them as the "other" by exaggerating their stereotypical non-Caucasian features. An especially brutal portrayal appeared on this *Air Ace* cover by an uncredited artist.

ARTIST GUS RICCA began his career in the 1930s as an illustrator for magazines such as *Collier's* and *Esquire*. He started in comic books at Harry Chesler's studio circa 1940 and in 1944 was assigned to art direct *Dynamic Comics*. Though he drew stories for a number of companies, Ricca was at his most memorable in a series of strikingly quirky covers for *Dynamic* and *Punch Comics*.

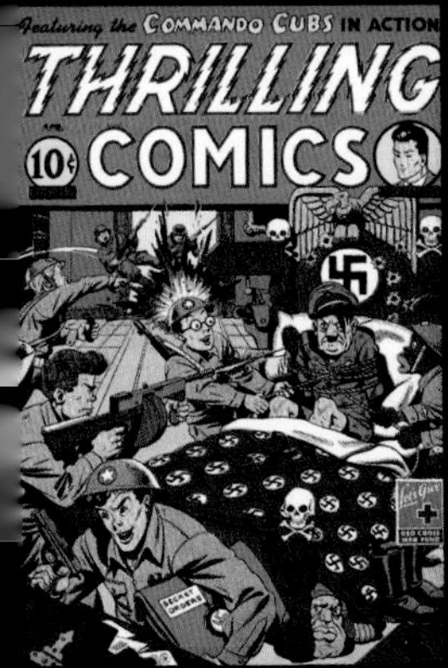
Featuring the COMMANDO CUBS IN ACTION
THRILLING
10¢ COMICS
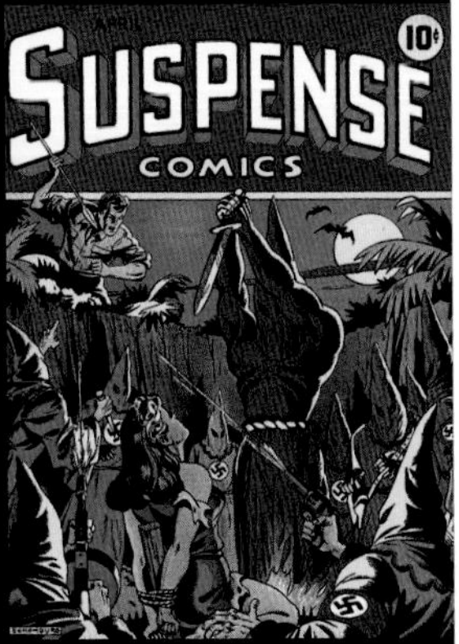
SUSPENSE
10¢
COMICS

THRILLING COMICS no.41, April 1944
ALEX SCHOMBURG

SUSPENSE COMICS no.3, April 1944
ALEX SCHOMBURG

TWO COVERS issued in the same month lay at opposite ends of the Schomburg spectrum. For Standard's *Thrilling Comics*, the Commando Cubs trap the hapless Hitler at his most asinine, on the phone in his pajamas and bed, both festooned with swastikas, as Italian dictator Benito Mussolini crouches under the mattress.

SWASTIKAS ALSO proliferate in the more disturbing situation kicking off *Suspense Comics* 3, the cover many consider the most coveted Schomburg of them all. Despite large print-runs, many books published by Continental Magazines have become scarce. Copies of this book even in rough condition command considerable sums on those rare occasions one surfaces.

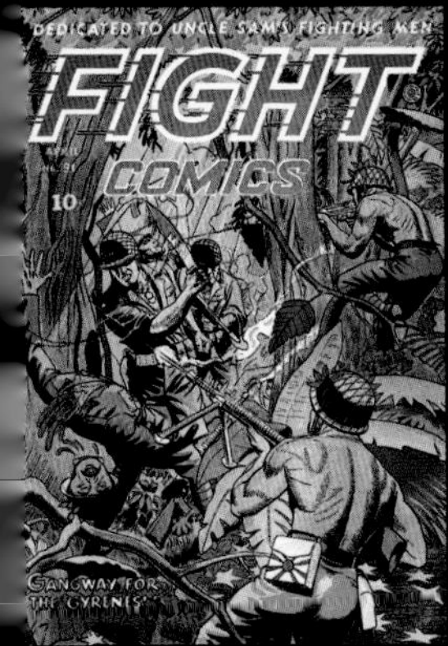
DEDICATED TO UNCLE SAM'S FIGHTING MEN
FIGHT
COMICS
10
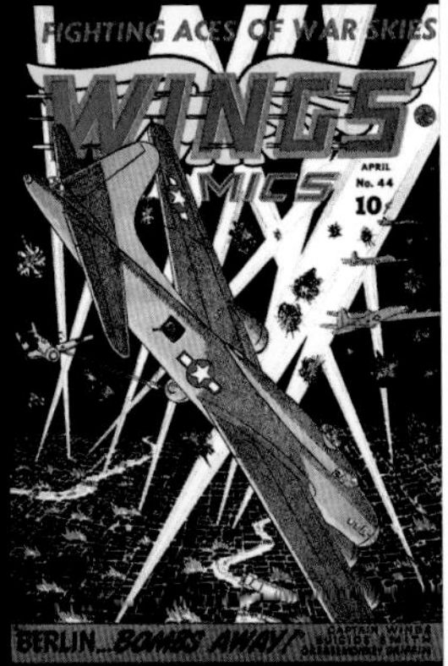
FIGHTING ACES OF WAR SKIES
WINGS
COMICS
APRIL
No. 44
10¢
BERLIN...BOMBS AWAY!

FIGHT COMICS no.31, April 1944
JOE DOOLIN

WINGS COMICS no.44, April 1944
ART SAAF

THE THREAT of decapitation was a fairly common Golden Age theme, with a few stories even going through with the grisly event. This, however, appears to be the only time it was actually pictured on a cover. That the victim is a Japanese soldier indicates how complete America's hatred had become in the light of atrocities such as the Bataan Death March, knowledge of which had been made public in January 1944 – about the time this cover was created.

A MAGAZINE ILLUSTRATOR since 1938, self-taught Art Saaf decided in the early 1940s to advance his skills, studying at New York's Art Students League, Pratt Institute, and the School of Arts and Mechanics. He entered comics via the Iger studio, working on Fiction House titles before moving to Standard in the late 1940s.

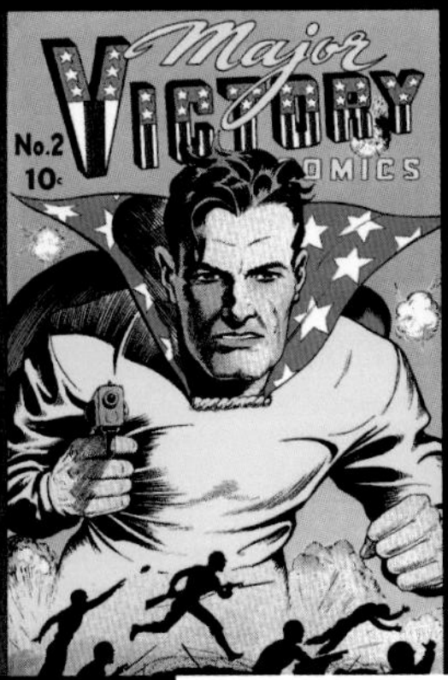
Major
VICTORY
COMICS
No.2
10¢
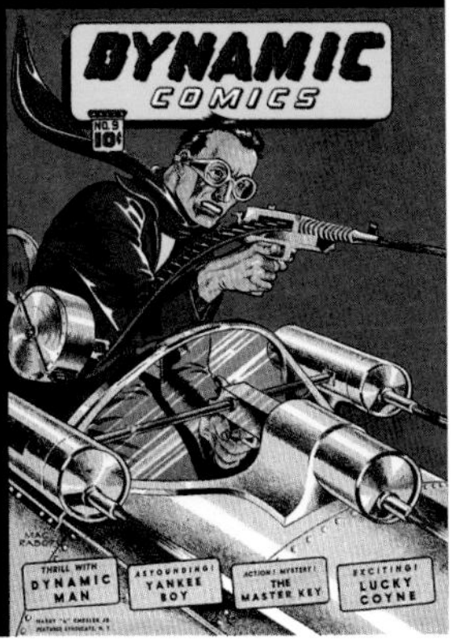
DYNAMIC
COMICS
10¢
THRILL WITH DYNAMIC MAN
ASTOUNDING! YANKEE BOY
ACTION! MYSTERY! THE MASTER KEY
EXCITING! LUCKY COYNE

MAJOR VICTORY no.2, 1944
CHARLES SULTAN

DYNAMIC COMICS no.9, May 1944
MAC RABOY

CHARLES SULTAN did the covers and art direction for the four 1941-42 issues of Chesler's *Yankee Comics*, as well as early issues of *Dynamic* and *Punch* before Gus Ricca took over. Sultan's Major Victory stories from *Dynamic* were repackaged in three quarterly 1944-45 issues of *Major Victory*, sprinkled with other Chesler reprints, some that stretched back to his earliest comic books. Like Centaur, Chesler made liberal use of old material to fill out his books.

ONE OF THE FEW covers signed by Mac Raboy, his only example for *Dynamic* is likely a leftover from Raboy's earlier Chesler period. The unusual use of charcoal shading gives the airplane a well-defined metallic texture.

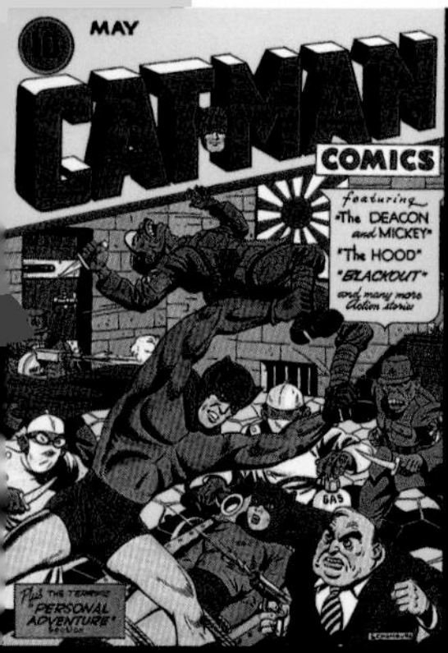
MAY
CATMAN
COMICS
featuring
The DEACON and MICKEY
The HOOD
BLACKOUT
and many more Action stories
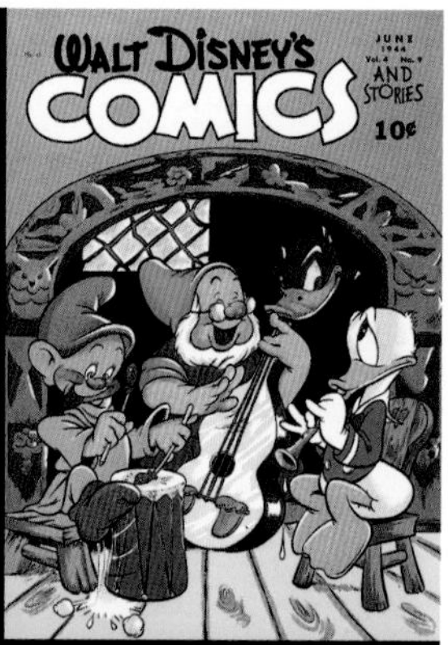
WALT DISNEY'S
COMICS
AND STORIES
10¢

CAT-MAN COMICS no.24, May 1944
ALEX SCHOMBURG

WALT DISNEY'S COMICS AND STORIES v.4 n.9, June 1944
WALT KELLY

FOLLOWING HIS first two appearances in *Crash Comics*, the Cat-Man was given his own title in early 1941 and a new orange short-pants costume by Charles M. Quinlan, the feature's primary artist. Alex Schomburg's single *Catman* cover presents the hero in a typically Schomburgian situation – vastly outnumbered, facing multiple knives and point-blank guns, yet somehow grabbing an adversary by his ankles to retaliate.

WALT KELLY elevates anthropomorphism to a sublime level in this cover for *Walt Disney's Comics and Stories*, as Dopey's drum sticks and Doc's string bass are brought to life, the latter also serving as Donald Duck's devilish *doppelgänger*.

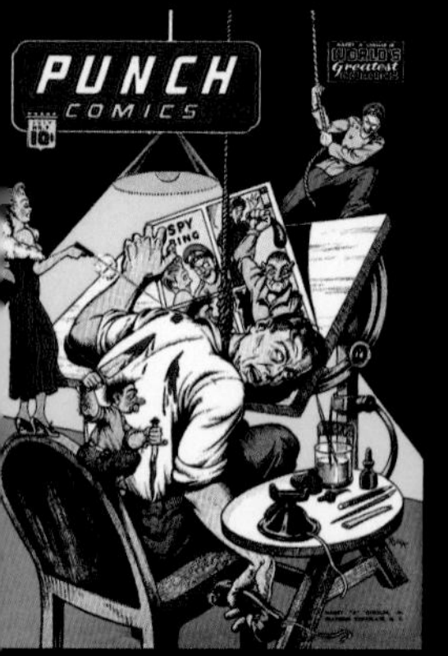
PUNCH
COMICS
10¢
SPY RING
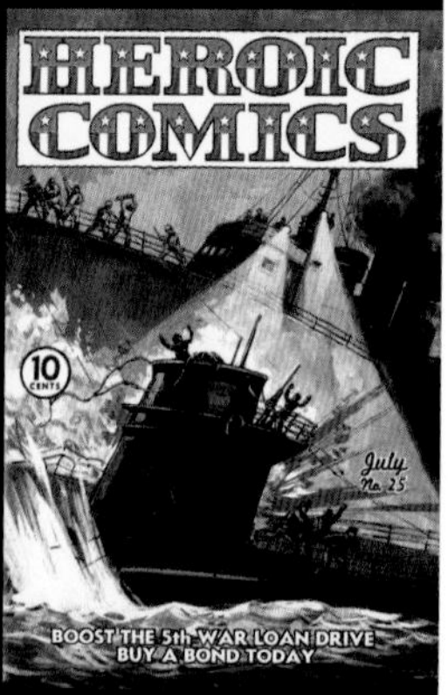
HEROIC
COMICS
10 CENTS
July No. 25
BOOST THE 5th WAR LOAN DRIVE
BUY A BOND TODAY

PUNCH COMICS no.9, July 1944
GUS RICCA

HEROIC COMICS no.25, July 1944
UNKNOWN

HERE'S AN IMAGE comic book artists of the time could relate to, as they faced relentless pressure to create imagery for dozens of panels with a looming deadline hanging over them. For this cover we find Gus Ricca at the end of his rope trying to come up with a cover, then finding the inspiration to channel his despair into the blank page in front of him.

HEROIC COMICS dropped the awkward *Reg'lar Fellers* from its title after its 15th issue, while revamping the format to focus on stories of wartime heroism (with a few superheroes hanging on temporarily as back-up features). *Heroic*'s new approach was signaled by its militaristic covers, now painted instead of inked for increased realism.

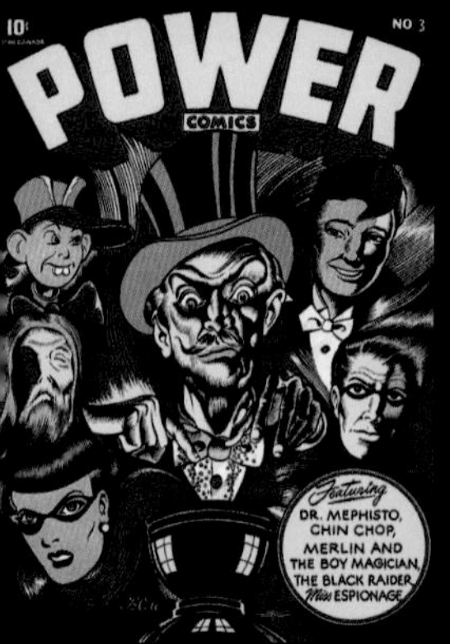
10¢
NO 3
POWER
COMICS
featuring
DR. MEPHISTO,
CHIN CHOP,
MERLIN AND
THE BOY MAGICIAN,
THE BLACK RAIDER,
Miss ESPIONAGE
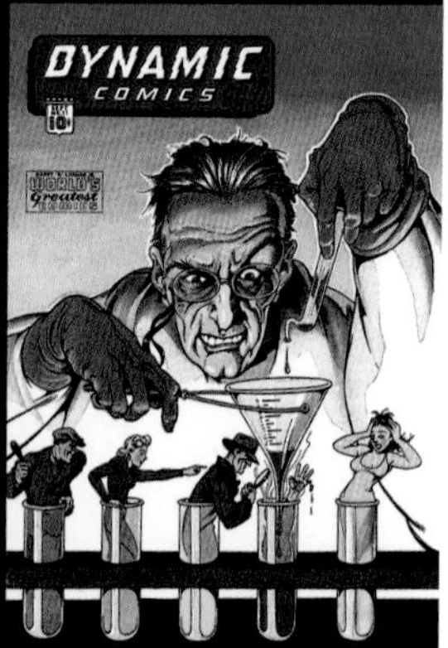
DYNAMIC
COMICS
10¢

POWER COMICS no.3, 1944
L.B. COLE

DYNAMIC COMICS no.11, September 1944
GUS RICCA

OUR FIRST OF seven entries by Leonard Brandt (L.B.) Cole, this cover for the third issue of *Power Comics* features the "evil genius of crime," Dr. Mephisto, surrounded by the rest of the title's lineup. The book was packaged by Frank Temerson's Continental Magazines (with Cole as art director) for Narrative Publishers, a possible Temerson subsidiary. The title was put to sleep after four issues.

ANOTHER STRIKING "large vs. small" image by Gus Ricca bejewels the second cover of Chesler's *Dynamic Comics*. Ricca's use of backlighting creates a radiant halo around his deftly inked mad scientist, with a luminous color scheme providing added luster.

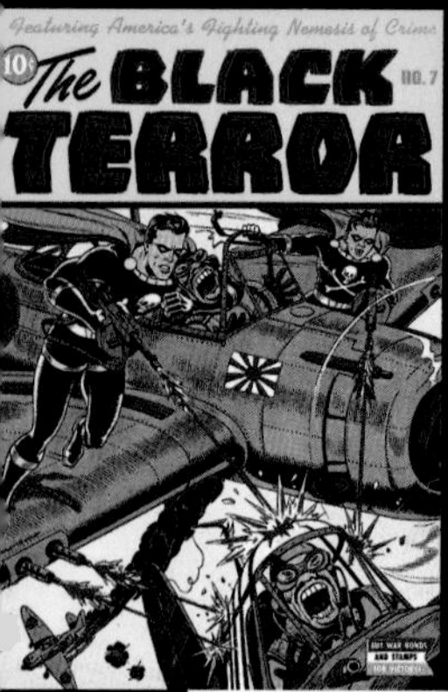
Featuring America's Fighting Nemesis of Crime
10¢
The BLACK
TERROR
NO. 7
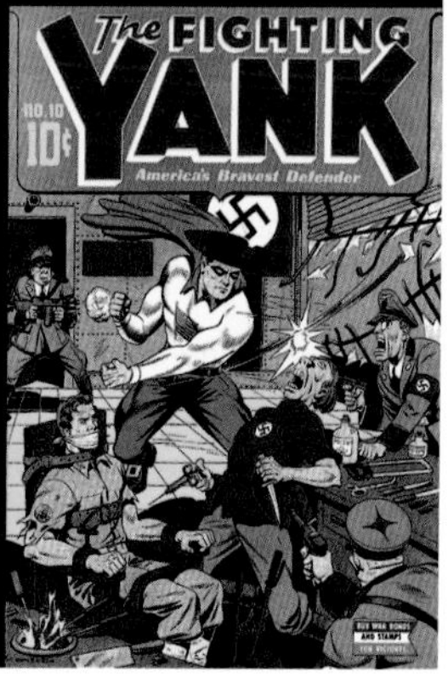
The FIGHTING
YANK
NO. 10
10¢
America's Bravest Defender

THE BLACK TERROR no.7, August 1944
ALEX SCHOMBURG

THE FIGHTING YANK no.10, December 1944
ALEX SCHOMBURG

ALEX SCHOMBURG'S history with Better/Standard/Nedor publisher Ned Pines stretched back to the early 1930s, when the artist contributed text illustrations to the publisher's pulp titles. He did his first cover for the September 1939 issue of *Startling Stories*. Over the first half of the 1940s, Schomburg provided practically every comic book cover for the bulk of the company's non-humorous line – *America's Best, The Black Terror, Exciting, The Fighting Yank, Real Life,* and *Startling* (with many covers for *Thrilling* as well). Schomburg's ability to keep his images intricate, exciting, and admirably non-repetitive is a testament to the Puerto Rican-born artist's tireless imagination and work ethic.

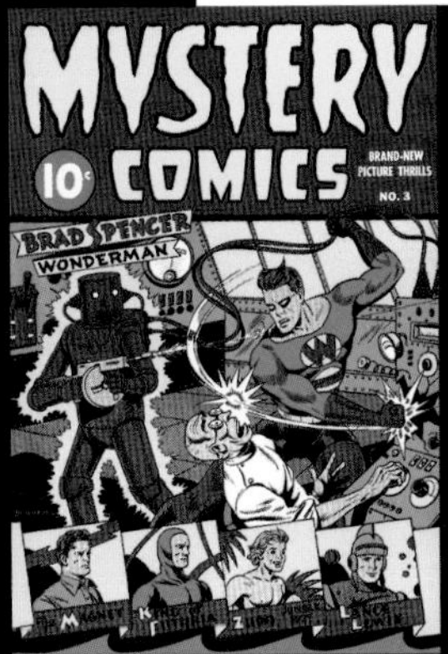
MYSTERY
10¢ COMICS
BRAD SPENCER
WONDERMAN
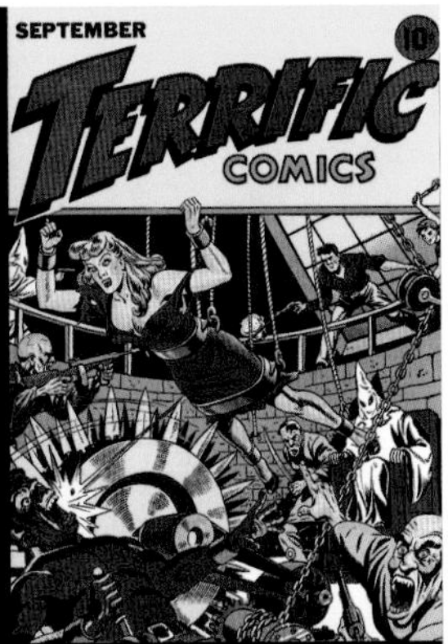
SEPTEMBER
10¢
TERRIFIC
COMICS

MYSTERY COMICS no.3, 1944
ALEX SCHOMBURG

TERRIFIC COMICS no.5, September 1944
ALEX SCHOMBURG

MYSTERY COMICS was a four-issue series packaged by Standard for book publisher Wm. H. Wise & Co., which released a small group of one-shot and short-run comic books, most with no month listed. A typical anthology offering superhero, science fiction, and jungle fare, *Mystery* could also boast above-average art, including Schomburg handling the Wonderman stories and Everett Raymond Kinstler penciling the first installment of the medieval *Silver Knight*.

WOMEN IN BONDAGE, a recurring theme in comic books, gets even kinkier here as Schomburg adds suspension to the mix. *Terrific Comics* 5 is another scarce book published by Frank Temerson's Continental Magazines.

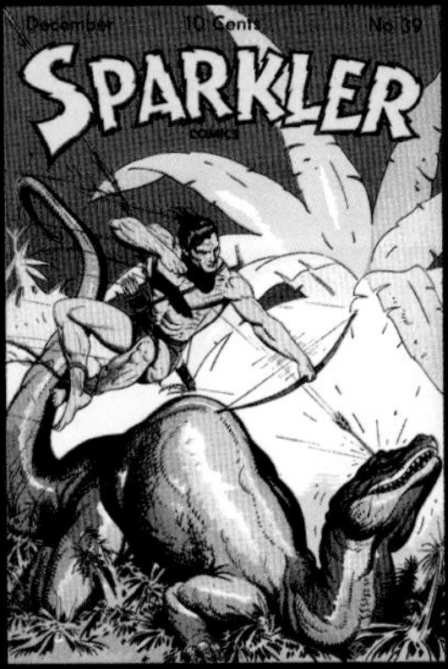
SPARKLER
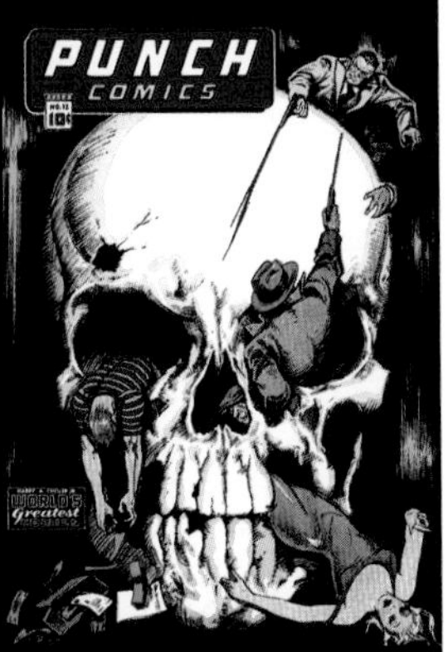
PUNCH
COMICS

SPARKLER COMICS no.39, December 1944
BURNE HOGARTH

PUNCH COMICS no.12, January 1945
GUS RICCA

SPARKLER COMICS was a United Feature Syndicate reprint title initially featuring on its covers an original superhero, Spark Man. After his power to self-generate static electricity failed to excite the masses, covers were then alternated among three UFS properties: *Nancy*, *The Captain and the Kids*, and *Tarzan*. The syndicate had the sense to commission the actual strip artists to do the artwork, with *Tarzan's* Burne Hogarth contributing a number of elegant designs.

GUS RICCA'S COVER for *Punch Comics* 12 certainly gets one's attention, making its point simply, stylishly, and chillingly. The image shows the strong connection between the crime genre and its evolutionary off-shoot, horror, still five years away from taking hold of the industry.

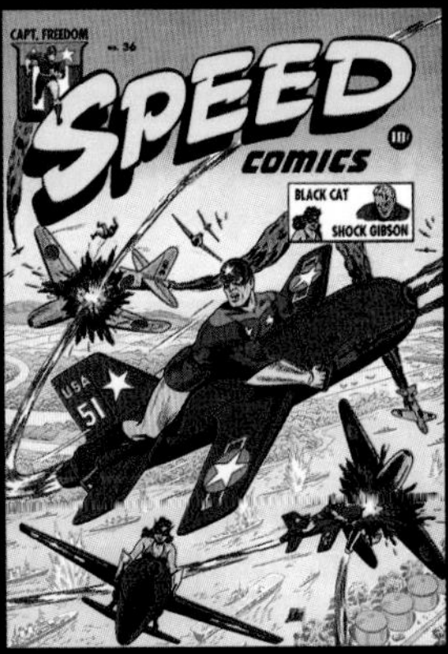
CAPT. FREEDOM
SPEED
comics
BLACK CAT
SHOCK GIBSON
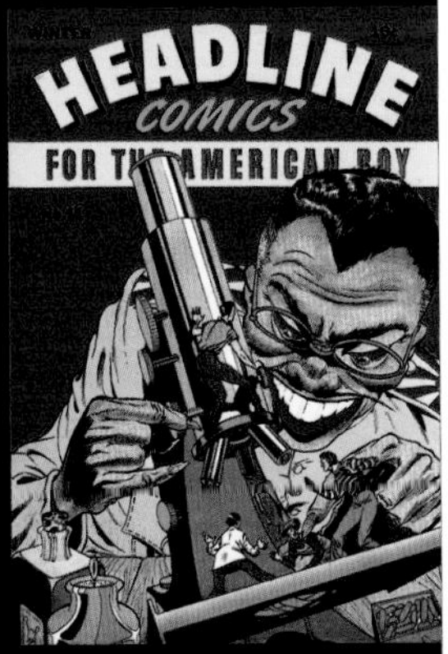
HEADLINE
COMICS

SPEED COMICS no.36, January 1945
ALEX SCHOMBURG

HEADLINE COMICS no.11, Winter 1945
ATTRIBUTED TO JACK BINDER STUDIO

ON OUR FINAL Schomburg cover (and his last for Harvey's *Speed Comics)* Black Cat, Captain Freedom, and Shock Gibson do their best to make a dent in the Japanese air force. The background is rendered in a limited two-color palette, causing the foreground group to pop in full four-color resplendence.

ONE LAST DIG at those diabolical Japanese (note the blood-red eyeballs and filed-to-a-point fingernails) in a classic "large vs. small" cover image. *Headline Comics* was a quarterly Prize anthology that featured the Junior Rangers until issue 23 (March 1947), when Simon & Kirby took it over and changed its format to "all true crime cases."

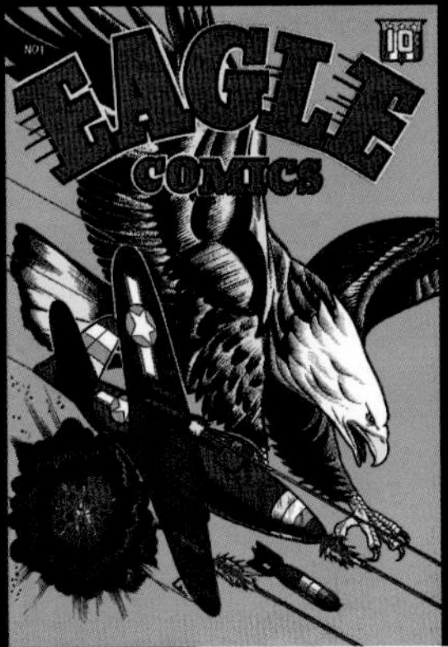
EAGLE
COMICS
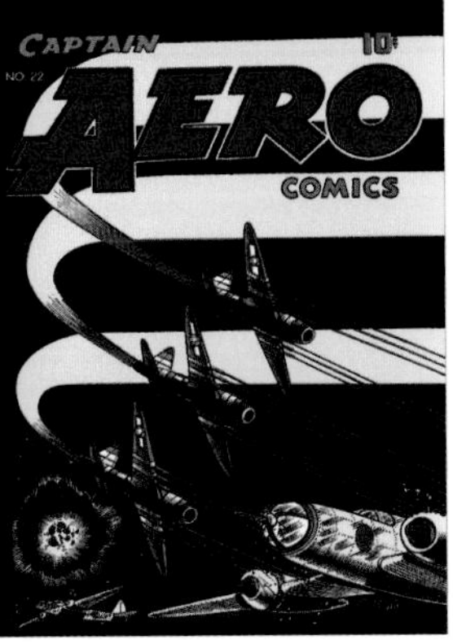
CAPTAIN
10¢
AERO
COMICS

EAGLE COMICS no.1, February-March 1945
L.B. COLE

CAPTAIN AERO COMICS no.22, February 1945
L.B. COLE

AVIATION AND MILITARY titles increased significantly during the war, reflecting the new audience of millions of servicemen. Each month thousands of comic books were purchased by the U.S. government and made available to G.I.s at commissaries and as part of their rations. This older demographic led publishers to pursue more adult themes, which continued after the war.

THESE TWO AVIATION covers by L.B. Cole appeared simultaneously on newsstands in late 1944. Rural Home Publishing's *Eagle Comics* lasted just two issues, while Holyoke's *Captain Aero* had a 26-issue run. The title was taken over by Continental toward the end, with Cole assuming the roles of art editor and cover artist.

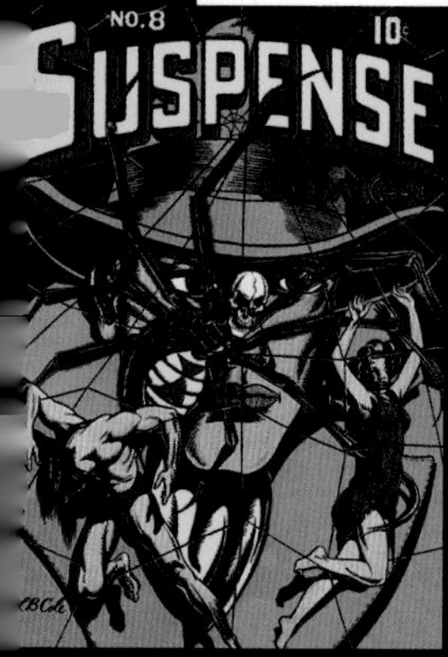
NO. 8
SUSPENSE
10

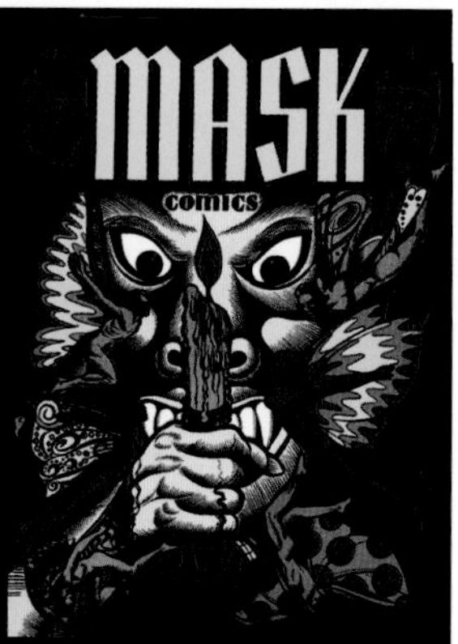
MASK
COMICS

SUSPENSE COMICS no.8, February 1945
L.B. Cole

MASK COMICS no.1, February-March 1945
L.B. Cole

ARRIVING THE SAME month as our previous two examples, this additional pair will give an idea of the amount of real estate L.B. Cole's covers were taking up on the newsstand, eventually surpassing even Alex Schomburg's considerable monthly output. Cole started his career as an art director at Consolidated Lithographing, helping design many of its cigar bands and liquor labels. It was instilled in him that brand names and images must communicate clearly and be instantly recognizable even at a distance. Cole applied these principles to his attention-grabbing comic book covers, which began appearing in 1944 on Rural Home and Frank Temerson titles.

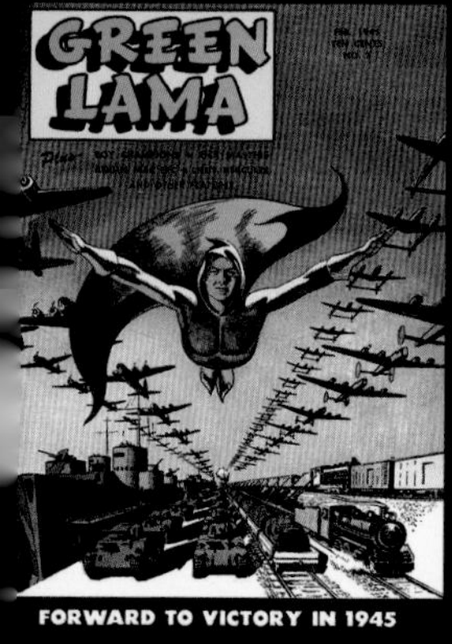
GREEN LAMA
FORWARD TO VICTORY IN 1945

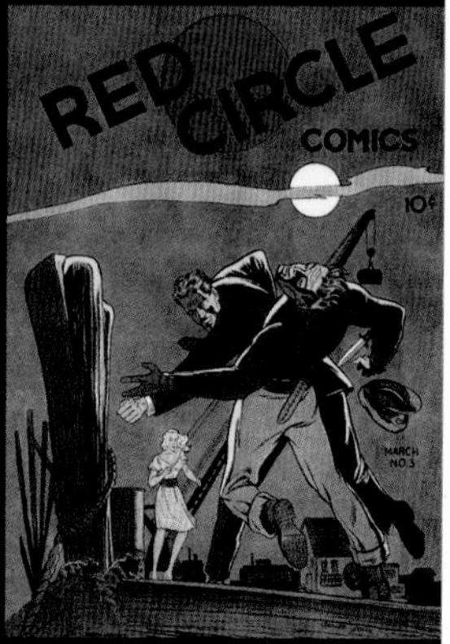
RED CIRCLE
COMICS
10¢

GREEN LAMA no. 2, February 1945
Mac Raboy

RED CIRCLE COMICS no.3, March 1945
Leonard Starr

WRITER KENDALL CROSSEN created the Green Lama in 1940 for the pulp *Double Detective Stories*; he later penned his early comic book adventures in 1941-43 issues of *Prize*. In 1944 Crossen started Spark Publications, devoting its flagship title to his hooded hero – though Mac Raboy gave him a much needed face and body lift.

RURAL HOME'S *Red Circle Comics* was a short-lived (four-issue) anthology series that showcased work by future syndicated artist Leonard Starr, whose strip *Mary Perkins on Stage* would begin in 1957 and last over two decades. His understated noirish cover of *Red Circle* 3 features undercover agent Anthony Cobat, hero of Starr and inker Frank Bolle's opening story.

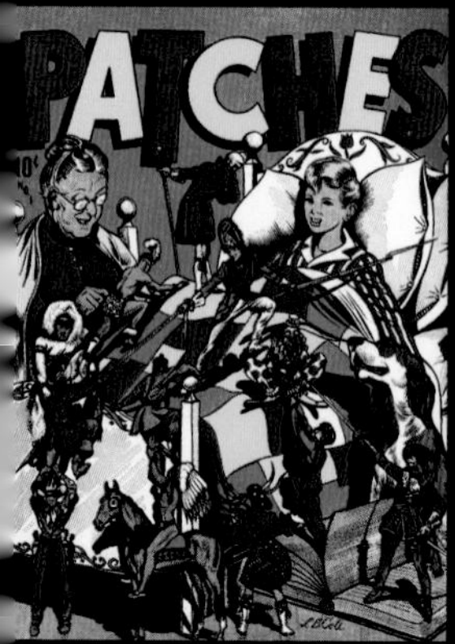
PATCHES

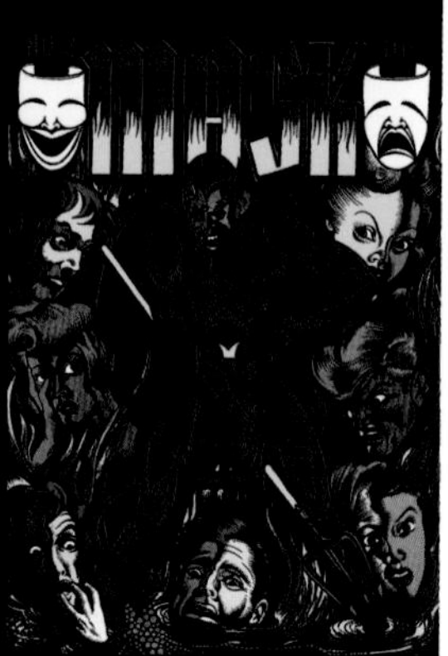

PATCHES no.1, March-April 1945
L.B. Cole

MASK COMICS no.2, April-May 1945
L.B. Cole

L.B. COLE INSISTED on complete freedom when designing covers, which publishers and editors were happy to grant, fully aware that his covers were the books' main selling point. As these two examples demonstrate, the artist was nothing if not adaptable. Here he moves from the innocent storybook fantasy of *Patches* 1, straight down to *Mask* 2's unvarnished depths of hell, with Satan himself taking glee in the suffering of sinners. Cole's personal preference was apparently with the darker side – he often experimented with lurid and hallucinogenic themes, and in 1995 he told interviewer Scotty Moore that the cover of *Mask* 2 was his all-time favorite.

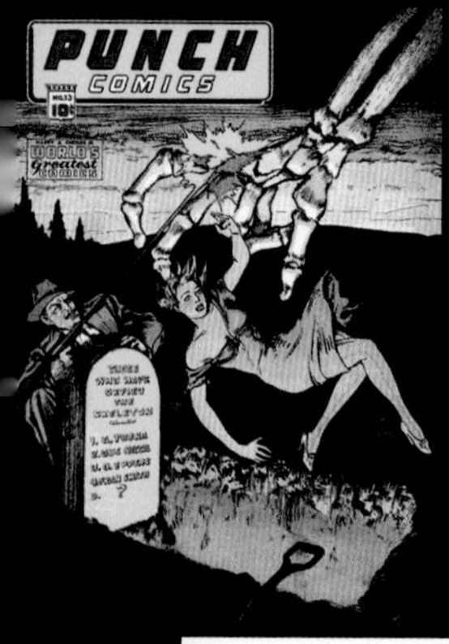
PUNCH
COMICS

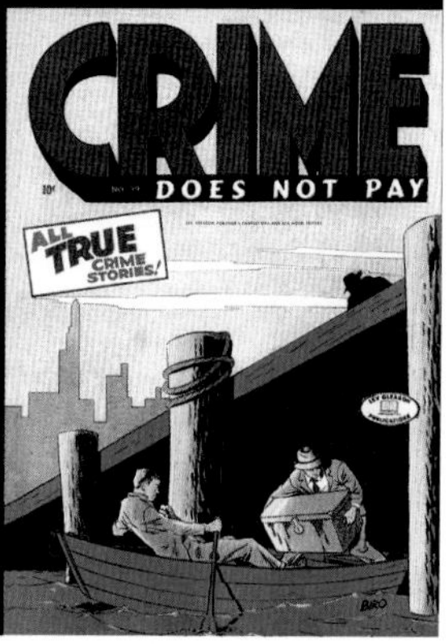
CRIME
DOES NOT PAY
ALL TRUE CRIME STORIES!

PUNCH COMICS no.13, April 1945
Gus Ricca

CRIME DOES NOT PAY no.39, May 1945
Charles Biro

GUS RICCA'S macabre sense of humor is again displayed on the cover of *Punch Comics* 13 as he inscribes his name on the open grave's tombstone, adding fellow Chesler artists George Tuska, Otto Eppers, and Fran Smith.

ONE OF THE few socially aware comic book publishers, Lev Gleason gave editors Charles Biro and Bob Wood a cut of the profits, presumably a tidy sum considering that combined circulation of their three titles (*Crime Does Not Pay, Daredevil*, and *Boy Comics*) routinely rose above four million copies. This cover of *Crime Does Not Pay*, with its subdued image and scarcity of blurbs, is remarkably restrained for Biro.

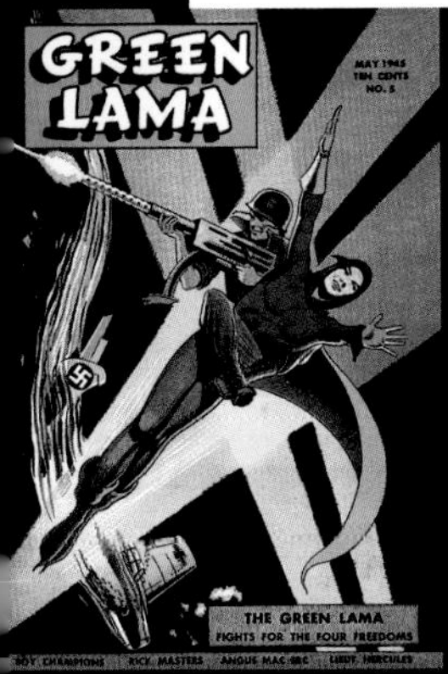
GREEN LAMA
MAY 1945 TEN CENTS NO. 5
THE GREEN LAMA FIGHTS FOR THE FOUR FREEDOMS

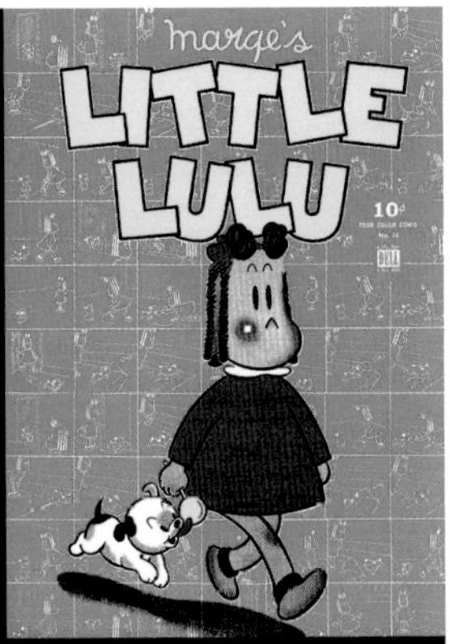
marge's
LITTLE LULU
10¢

GREEN LAMA no.5, May 1945
MAC RABOY

FOUR COLOR no.74, June 1945
JOHN STANLEY

SPARK PUBLICATIONS had the makings of a top-flight company. Mac Raboy contributed some of his finest stories and covers, and as art editor he assembled an accomplished staff that included Mort Lawrence, Mort Meskin, and Jerry Robinson. Nevertheless, after about 18 months the company declared bankruptcy.

JOHN STANLEY was handpicked by Dell's Oskar Lebeck to adapt Marjorie Henderson Buell's single-panel *Saturday Evening Post* strip *Little Lulu* for comic books, and as usual Lebeck's instincts were on the money. Stanley had a hilarious knack for capturing kids as they often behaved – vain, manipulative, conniving, obliviously self-centered. His simple graphic style served his ideas without fussiness, a fine example of which is this cover, *Lulu*'s first.

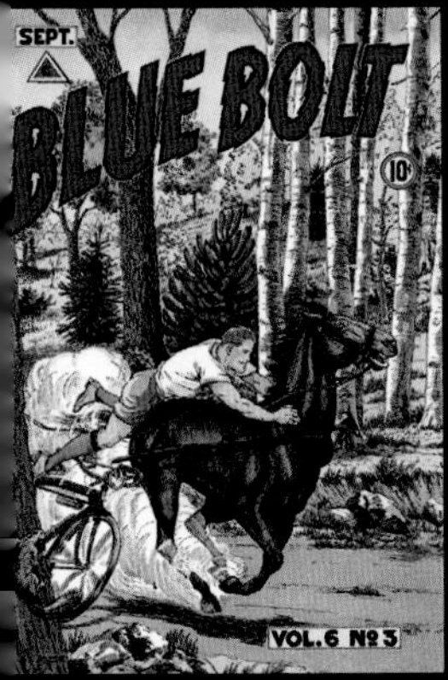
SEPT.
BLUE BOLT
10¢
VOL.6 No3

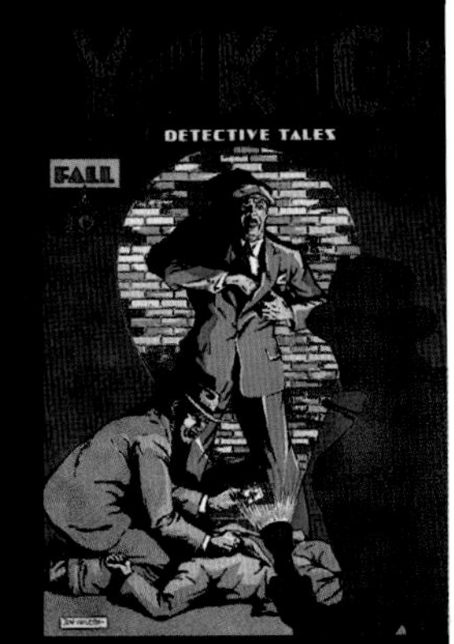
DETECTIVE TALES
FALL

BLUE BOLT v.6 n.3, September 1945
JIM WILCOX

YOUNG KING COLE v.1 n.1, Fall 1945
JIM WILCOX

ARTIST JIM WILCOX began his career in the late 1930s at Harry Chesler's studio. In 1942 he moved to Lloyd Jacquet's Funnies Inc., taking over Novelty's *Blue Bolt* feature Dick Cole following the sudden death of creator Bob Davis. Wilcox did the bulk of his work at Novelty for *Blue Bolt*, *4 Most*, and *Young King Cole*, while also contributing to Centaur, Dell, Fawcett, and Gilberton titles. Despite Wilcox's excellent drawing skills, he was more illustrator than storyteller, with his panel continuities somewhat stiff and repetitive. It was as a cover artist where he really came to life, as these two examples demonstrate.

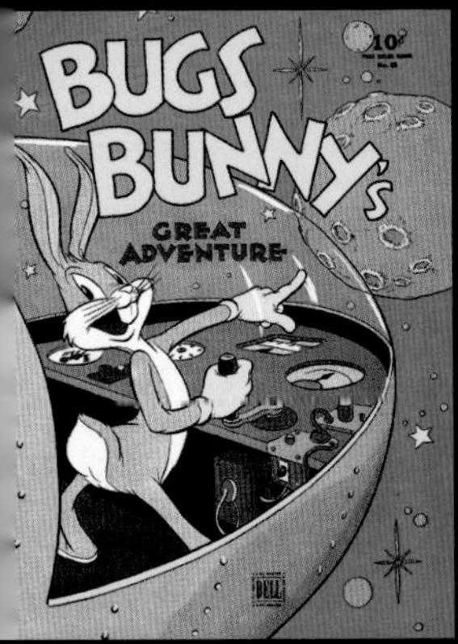
10¢
BUGS BUNNY'S
GREAT ADVENTURE

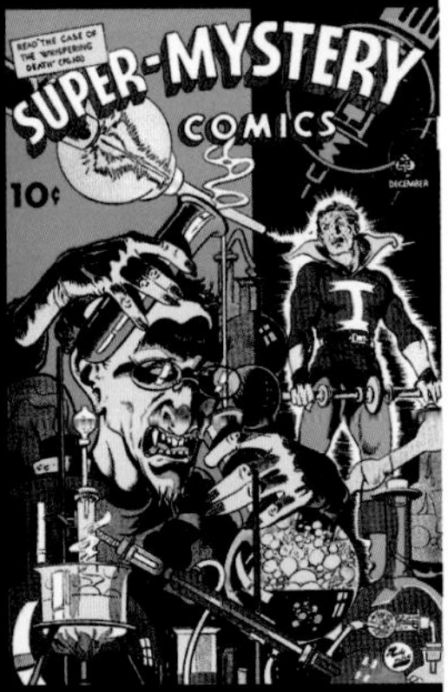
SUPER-MYSTERY
COMICS
10¢

FOUR COLOR no.88, September 1945
CARL BUETTNER

SUPER-MYSTERY COMICS no.27, December 1945
RUDY PALAIS

CARTOONIST CARL BUETTNER learned his craft as an animator for the Disney and the Harman-Ising studios. He arrived at Dell in the early 1940s, specializing in Disney and Warner Brothers cartoon titles, and he was soon promoted to art director.

ARTIST RUDY PALAIS grew up in the same New York City neighborhood as boyhood pal Charles Biro. Palais started at Iger's studio, moved to Quality, and then became a busy freelancer, working for a number of companies while doing exceptional work for *Crime Does Not Pay* and *Classics Illustrated*. He wrapped up his comic book career in the mid-1950s on Harvey titles, turning in some of the most skewed horror art of the era.

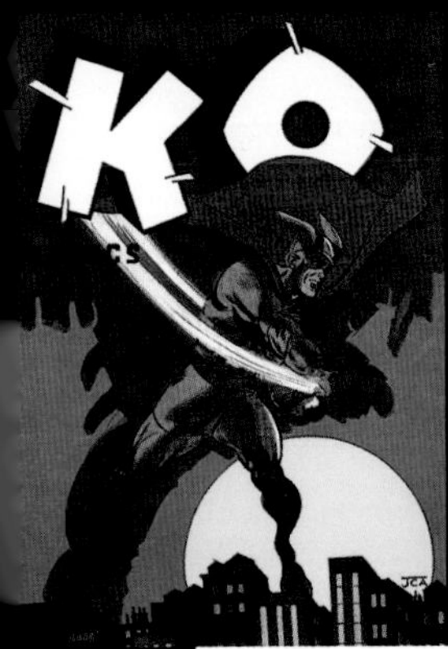
KO

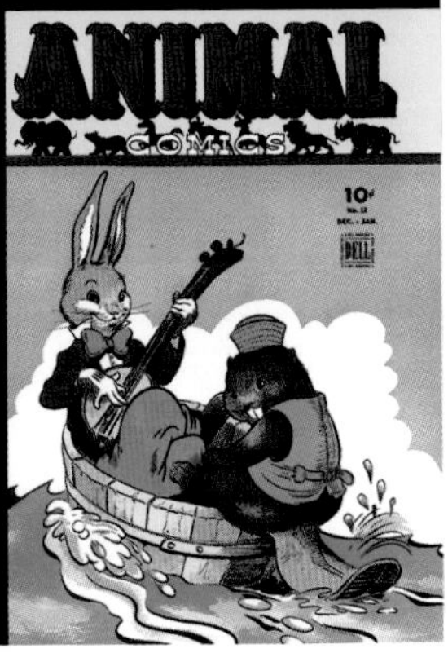
ANIMAL
COMICS
10¢

KO KOMICS 1945
JACK KIRBY AND UNKNOWN INKER

ANIMAL COMICS no.12, December 1945
WALT KELLY

PUBLISHED BY Gerona Publishing (a Rural Home imprint), this one-shot's cover displays a superhero who doesn't appear in the interior, apparently a minor detail when a Jack Kirby cover was available. It's signed "JCA," but the inker has never been identified.

WE SAIL OFF into the Atomic Age with this charming seafaring image by Walt Kelly. *Animal Comics* was another classic Dell book conceived by Oscar Lebeck to showcase Kelly's art, though it also contained fine work by Dan Noonan, John Stanley, and others. The title's first issue introduced Kelly's inhabitants of Okefenokee Swamp in late 1941, eight years before the *Pogo* newspaper strip was nationally syndicated.

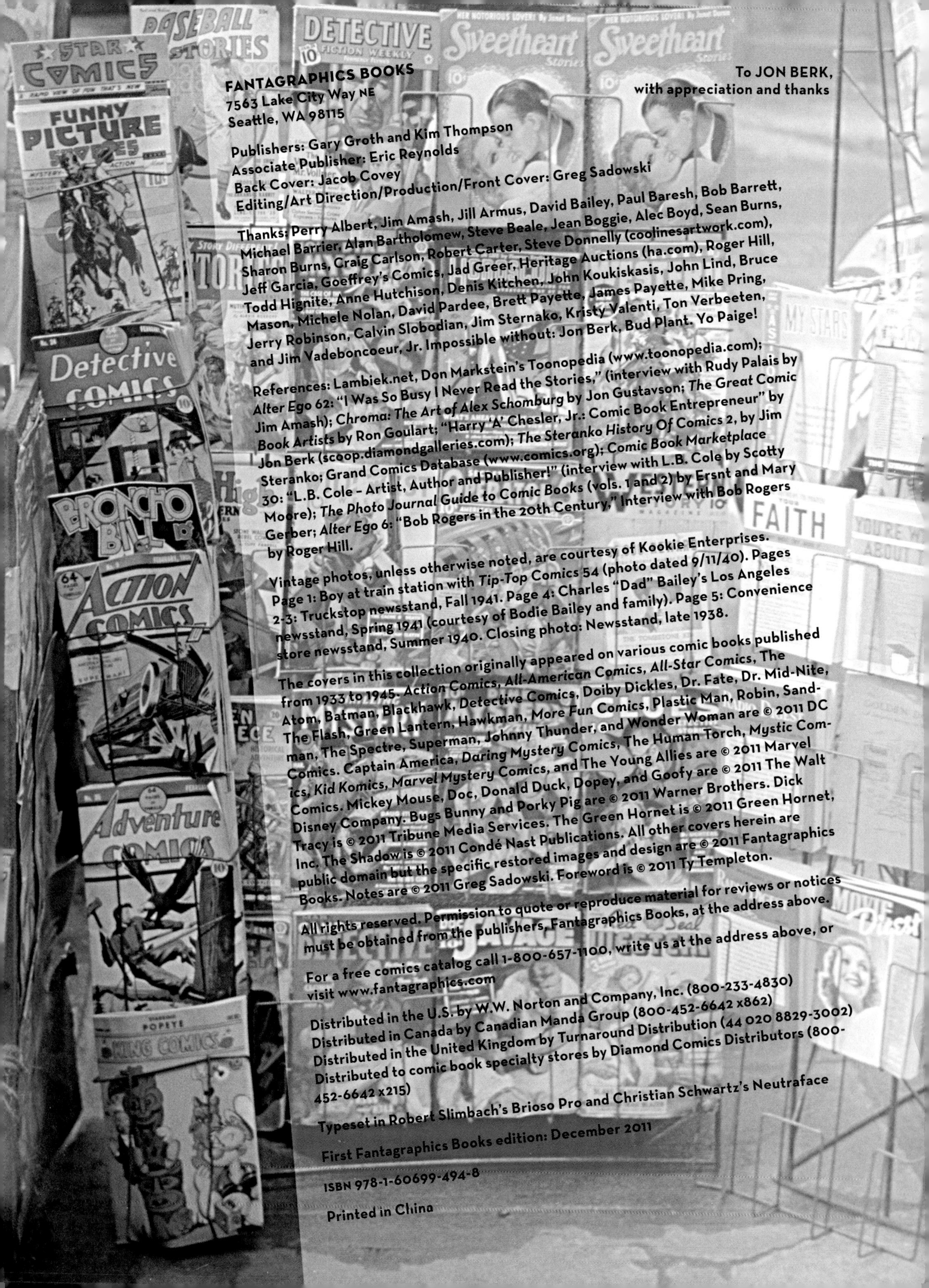
STAR COMICS
BASEBALL STORIES
DETECTIVE FICTION WEEKLY
Sweetheart Stories
Sweetheart Stories
FUNNY PICTURE STORIES
Detective Comics
BRONCHO BILL
ACTION COMICS
Adventure Comics
POPEYE
KING COMICS
MY STARS
FAITH

FANTAGRAPHICS BOOKS
7563 Lake City Way NE
Seattle, WA 98115

To JON BERK,
with appreciation and thanks

Publishers: Gary Groth and Kim Thompson
Associate Publisher: Eric Reynolds
Back Cover: Jacob Covey
Editing/Art Direction/Production/Front Cover: Greg Sadowski

Thanks: Perry Albert, Jim Amash, Jill Armus, David Bailey, Paul Baresh, Bob Barrett, Michael Barrier, Alan Bartholomew, Steve Beale, Jean Boggie, Alec Boyd, Sean Burns, Sharon Burns, Craig Carlson, Robert Carter, Steve Donnelly (coolinesartwork.com), Jeff Garcia, Goeffrey's Comics, Jad Greer, Heritage Auctions (ha.com), Roger Hill, Todd Hignite, Anne Hutchison, Denis Kitchen, John Koukiskasis, John Lind, Bruce Mason, Michele Nolan, David Pardee, Brett Payette, James Payette, Mike Pring, Jerry Robinson, Calvin Slobodian, Jim Sternako, Kristy Valenti, Ton Verbeeten, and Jim Vadeboncoeur, Jr. Impossible without: Jon Berk, Bud Plant. Yo Paige!

References: Lambiek.net, Don Markstein's Toonopedia (www.toonopedia.com); *Alter Ego* 62: "I Was So Busy I Never Read the Stories," (interview with Rudy Palais by Jim Amash); *Chroma: The Art of Alex Schomburg* by Jon Gustavson; *The Great Comic Book Artists* by Ron Goulart; "Harry 'A' Chesler, Jr.: Comic Book Entrepreneur" by Jon Berk (scoop.diamondgalleries.com); *The Steranko History Of Comics* 2, by Jim Steranko; Grand Comics Database (www.comics.org); *Comic Book Marketplace* 30: "L.B. Cole – Artist, Author and Publisher!" (interview with L.B. Cole by Scotty Moore); *The Photo Journal Guide to Comic Books* (vols. 1 and 2) by Ersnt and Mary Gerber; *Alter Ego* 6: "Bob Rogers in the 20th Century," Interview with Bob Rogers by Roger Hill.

Vintage photos, unless otherwise noted, are courtesy of Kookie Enterprises. Page 1: Boy at train station with *Tip-Top Comics* 54 (photo dated 9/11/40). Pages 2-3: Truckstop newsstand, Fall 1941. Page 4: Charles "Dad" Bailey's Los Angeles newsstand, Spring 1941 (courtesy of Bodie Bailey and family). Page 5: Convenience store newsstand, Summer 1940. Closing photo: Newsstand, late 1938.

For a free comics catalog call 1-800-657-1100, write us at the address above, or visit www.fantagraphics.com

Distributed in the U.S. by W.W. Norton and Company, Inc. (800-233-4830)
Distributed in Canada by Canadian Manda Group (800-452-6642 x862)
Distributed in the United Kingdom by Turnaround Distribution (44 020 8829-3002)
Distributed to comic book specialty stores by Diamond Comics Distributors (800-452-6642 x215)

Typeset in Robert Slimbach's Brioso Pro and Christian Schwartz's Neutraface

First Fantagraphics Books edition: December 2011

ISBN 978-1-60699-494-8

Printed in China